Selections from the Municipal Chronicles of the Borough of Abingdon from A.D. 1555 to A.D. 1897. Edited by B. Challenor.

Anonymous, Bromley Challenor

Selections from the Municipal Chronicles of the Borough of Abingdon from A.D. 1555 to A.D. 1897. Edited by B. Challenor.

Anonymous
British Library, Historical Print Editions
British Library
Challenor, Bromley
1898
vii. 396, lix. xxvi. p. ; 4°.
10352.dd.26.

GESELSCHAFT · MUSEUM · IN · MÜNCHEN

SELECTIONS

FROM THE

𝔐unicipal 𝔠hronicles

OF THE

BOROUGH OF ABINGDON,

𝔣rom 𝔄.𝔇. 1555 to 𝔄.𝔇. 1897.

EDITED BY

BROMLEY CHALLENOR,

Town Clerk.

ABINGDON :

Printed and Published by William H. Hooke, Market Place.

1898

EDITOR'S PREFACE.

CONSIDERABLE public attention has of late years been given to the rich collection of Records in the possession of the various Municipalities in this Country, and it occurred to the writer some years since, that it might be of interest to antiquarians and others who are interested in the past history of Abingdon if the Municipal Records of the Borough, or at least so much of them as are of general or local interest, were published in a concise form.

With that idea in view, the writer accordingly undertook the task of extracting from the Minute Books and other Records of the Corporation, from the year 1555 to the present time, what seemed to him to be the most interesting of the entries therein contained.

It is much to be regretted, as well as a matter of surprise, that the Municipal Records of the Town are so few in number. All that are of any value are now preserved in a small chest in the Council Chamber, and consist principally of the Minute Books from the Incorporation of the Borough in 1555 to the present time, the various Charters which were granted by the Crown to the Borough from time to time, and a few old account books, the latter being unfortunately few in number and of a comparatively modern period.

What has become of the Records which must have accumulated during the past three and a half centuries it is difficult to say; unless they disappeared when the Council unfortunately appointed a Committee, in the year 1865, to examine the papers and other documents which were then in existence, with instructions to destroy the useless (?) documents, and to take steps for preserving the others. It is recorded (p. 288) that this Committee spent several *hours* in looking through the Records, and therefore it must be assumed that the papers examined were either very few in number, or were only very hastily scrutinized, for those which were preserved by the Committee and which have accumulated since, have taken the writer several months to peruse, for the purpose of this work. It is however a lamentable fact, that many valuable papers were rejected by the Committee as of little or no value, and were actually sold for a few shillings to a marine store dealer as *waste* paper; fortunately a portion of the rejected Records fell

into good hands, for the valuable and most interesting Accounts of the
Chamberlains and Bailiffs of the Borough, from A.D. 1631 to A.D. 1834, were
purchased at the time by the late Mr. John Preston, the Father of the present
Borough Accountant, for a sovereign. The purchaser (who fully appreciated
the value of the papers) had the whole bound together in 20 volumes, and
the writer is not without hope that these valuable papers will one day (and
that at no distant date) find their way back to their proper place in the
Municipal Chest. It is to be hoped that when this desirable event shall have
happened, another hand will complete the work the writer has begun by
undertaking their publication, a work which will undoubtedly prove to be
of a most interesting character, and also throw considerable light on the
Municipal, Political, and Domestic history of the people of Abingdon in the
days that have gone bye, and thus completely finish the Municipal Chronicles
of the Borough.

In the present work it has been decided to publish, Firstly—The various
Charters (9 in number) under which the Town obtained the privileges which
the Inhabitants have for so many years enjoyed. The first, or Charter of
Incorporation, granted by Phillip and Mary, was procured in the year
1555, through the instrumentality of Sir John Mason, Knight, to whose
memory the people of Abingdon owe an everlasting debt of gratitude.
This Charter is written in the monkish Latin of the period, and the
translation reproduced herein is said to have been the work of Mr. Recorder
Holt, in or about the year 1665. As this Charter was the foundation of the
liberties of the people of Abingdon in past ages, it has been thought better
to publish the translation rather than the original, as being more likely to be
appreciated by the majority of the readers of this work rather than the difficult
abbreviated Latin of the original. Secondly—The most interesting Minutes
of the Corporation from A.D. 1556 to A.D. 1897, comprising a period of
nearly three and a half centuries. From the year 1556 to 1835 the selected
entries in the Minute Books have been extracted *verbatim et literatim*, while
those since that date have been summarized, care being taken in every case
to follow the phraseology of the recording scribe as far as possible.

In this work naturally the Corporation Diary stands foremost in point
of interest, as it is a continuous record of the life of the Town written by
those who were in a large measure responsible for its History; while in the
Appendix are contained the Rules and Regulations made from time to time
by the Council for the good government of the Town, and copies of other
interesting documents in the possession of the Corporation. The Appendix
also records the names of those men who have in times past well and
worthily served their Town, either as Mayors, Members of Parliament,
Members of the Council, or Officers of the Municipality.

DEDICATION.

1898.

TO THE

MAYOR, ALDERMEN AND BURGESSES

OF THE

BOROUGH OF ABINGDON,

IN THE

COUNTY OF BERKS,

THIS VOLUME IS INSCRIBED,

IN GRATEFUL ACKNOWLEDGEMENT OF THE UNVARYING KINDNESS

THE EDITOR HAS RECEIVED AT THEIR HANDS

DURING THE MANY YEARS

HE HAS HAD THE HONOUR

TO BE

THEIR CHIEF OFFICER.

It is to be feared that many errors will be found by the reader of this volume, and therefore the Editor humbly and respectfully asks pardon for the same, without waiting for them to be pointed out by the friendly critic.

The writer cannot conclude these remarks without acknowledging the great obligations he is under to those who have assisted him in his task of preparing this work for publication. His thanks are therefore especially due to Mr. F. Morland, for the assistance he rendered during the preparation of the MSS. of the earlier part of Part II. for publication; to the late Mayor (Mr. Councillor Pryce), for the able and valuable assistance he rendered in examining and correcting the proofs as the work was passing through the press; and to Mr. A. Welch, for the care and labour he devoted to the preparation of the Index of the work, without which it would have been shorn of much of its utility.

THE EDITOR.

The Firs,
        Abingdon.
August, 1898.

CONTENTS.

PART I.

PART II.

APPENDIX.

Records of the Borough of Abingdon.

PART I.

*THE CHARTER OF INCORPORATION

GRANTED BY

PHILLIP & MARY, A.D. 1555.

Charter of
Philip & Mary
A.D. 1555.

Phillip and Mary, by the Grace of God King and Queen of England, Spain, France, of both Sicilyes, Jerusalem, and Ireland, Defenders of the Faith, Arch Dukes of Austria, Dukes of Burgundy, Milan and Brabant, Earls of Haspurge, Flanders and Tirol. Whereas our Town of Abingdon, in our County of Berks, is an ancient and populous Town, and Inhabited by many poor people, and which Town is the Capital Town in our said County of Berks, and is in so great ruine and decay for want of repairing of the Houses and Buildings within the same, that it is very likely to come to extream calamity (as we are credible informed) if remedy thereof be not by us provided. And whereas our beloved subjects, the Inhabitants of the same Town, have most humbly besought us that we would graciously and liberally show and extend to them our royall favour and munificence, and that for the bettering of the same Town we would vouchsafe to incorporate the same Town and the Inhabitants thereof, and to make, ordain, and create a body corporate of a Mayor, Bailiffs, and Burgesses. **Know yee** therefore, that we, to the request and desire of our aforesaid Subjects, graciously condescending of our special grace and of our certain knowledge and mere motion will ordain, constitute, decree, declare and grant, and by these

* This translation of the Charter is said to have been made by Mr. Recorder Holt, about A.D. 1658. [Ed.]

A

presents for us the Heires and Successors of us the aforesaid Queen, do will, ordain, constitute, decree, declare and grant to the aforesaid Inhabitants and Men of Abingdon, that the said Town of Abingdon, in our said County of Berks, from henceforth be and shall be a free Borough of itselfe and by itselfe, exempt from all hundreds, Counties and Shires, incorporate in deed, fact and name, for ever of the Men in the Borough aforesaid, being of a Mayor, Bailiffs and Burgesses, by the name of the Mayor, Bailiffs and Burgesses, of the Borough of Abingdon, in the County of Berks, and that the said Mayor, Bailiffs and Burgesses, of the said Borough, from henceforth be and shall be a Body Corporate and Politick, and a perpetuall Commonalty of itselfe, in deed, fact and name, for ever.

Abingdon constituted a Free Borough.

And that the same Mayor, Bailiffs and Burgesses, of the same Borough for the time being, and their Successors from henceforth for ever shall be a Body Corporate, and a perpetuall Commonalty in deed, fact and name, at all times to endure, and shall have perpetuall succession, and by these Presents for us the Heires and Successors of us the aforesaid Queen, the same Mayor, Bailiffs and Burgesses, we do really and fully erect, make, create, ordain, constitute, declare and incorporate a Commonalty and Body Corporate and Politick of itselfe and by itselfe for ever.

The Mayor, Bailiffs, and Burgesses, to be a Body Corporate.

And we will and comand by these Presents that from henceforth they be called and named the Mayor, Bailiffs and Burgesses, of the Borough of Abingdon aforesaid, in the County of Berks. And also we will and by these Presents for us the Heirs and Successors of us the aforesaid Queen, we do grant, constitute, ordain and declare, that the said Borough of Abingdon aforesaid, and the circuits and precincts thereof, and the Jurisdiction and liberty of the same from henceforth shall extend and stretch, and may and shall be able and ought to extend and stretch as well in length as breadth as in circuit, unto, by and through the bounds, metes and limits following (that is to say): from the little Bridge called the Abbey Locks, built upon and over the River of Thames on the East part of the Borough aforesaid, unto the Bridge of the Ock called the Ock Bridge on the West part of the same Borough, and from the Stone Crosse situate upon a new Bridge commonly called a New Bridge on the South part, unto the Boundary and Meer Stone marked with the leaden Letter A, situate near unto a little Hill called Barrow Hill, without the barrs of the publick Street of Barrow Street called the Bore Street Barrs, in the meeting

The Title of the Corporation.

The limits of the Borough.

together of two public Ways leading towards the aforesaid Borough of Abingdon on the North part, and from the Boundary and Meer Stone situate upon the little Bridge of St. Helene called St. Helen's Bridge, dividing and parting the said Borough of Abingdon from the hundred of Ock where the little Stream of the Ock falls into the River of Thames on the South West part, unto another certain Boundary marked with the Leaden Letter A, situate without the Barres of the publick Street of the Wyneyard called the Wyneyard Barres, in the meeting together of two publick Ways leading towards the said Borough of Abingdon on the North East part, so that is to say, that the compasse and circuit of the Borough aforesaid shall extend and stretch itselfe from the Locks aforesaid, called the Abbey Locks, through the whole River Thames, including the same River unto the Bridge called the New Bridge built upon and over the said River of Thames, and from the aforesaid Bridge called the New Bridge including the whole River of Thames unto the aforesaid little Bridge of St. Helene called St. Helen's Bridge, where the said little Stream of the Ock falls unto the Thames as aforesaid, and from thence by and through the aforesaid little Stream of the Ock including the same little Stream unto the aforesaid Bridge of the Ock called the Ock Bridge, and from the said Bridge called the Ock Bridge directly by and through the publick way leading from the same Bridge to a little Close called the Trynitie Closes, and from thence by and through the Common way leading by the aforesaid little Hill called Barrow Hill unto the aforesaid Boundary and Meer Stone without the aforesaid Barres of the Bore Street, situate in the meeting together of the aforesaid two publick ways leading towards the aforesaid Borough, and from thence by and through another publick way a little turning towards the North untill you come to a certain Crooked little Ditch inclining towards the East, which said little Ditch together with the aforesaid publick way includes on the right hand Fitzharris Farm and a certain piece of Arable Land called Fitzharris piece, and the Fields, Meadows and Pastures called Fitzharris Closes to the same Farm belonging and apperteyning, and from thence by another Ditch on the right hand also including a certain Close called Pykes Close unto the aforesaid Boundary and Meer Stone without the Barres of the Publick Street of the Weyneyard aforesaid, situate in the meeting together of two publick ways leading towards the Borough of Abingdon aforesaid, and from

The limits of
the Borough.

the same Meer Stone by and through another publick way turning towards the East towards the River of Thames, and including a certain Conventuall Close called the Covent-Close, being wholly ditched, and partly hedged, and partly paled, and one other little Close called the Pytenry, and from the corner of the same Close called the Pytenry through the said River of Thames including the same River unto the Locks aforesaid; and that the Soile and Land, with all Lanes, Streets, Ways, Places, Closes and Corners whatsoever, lying and being within the aforesaid Boundaries, Meers and Limitts, shall be and shall be reputed and taken to be within the Borough aforesaid and the Liberties thereof, and all and singular Messuages, Houses, Buildings, Lands, Tenements, Grounds and Soils whatsoever within the aforesaid Meers, Boundarys, Limitts and Precints from henceforth be and shall be reputed to be parts and parcells of the said Borough of Abingdon, now by these Presents into a Body Corporate and Politick, erected and incorporated, and that it shall

The Mayor, &c.,
to make
perambulation.

and may be lawful for the aforesaid Mayor, Bailiffs and Burgesses of the Borough of Abingdon aforesaid for the time being, and for their Successors to make perambulation or perambulations thereof for the true and better knowledge thereof to be had as often as it shall please them, or to them shall seem convenient, and this without any Writ or Warrant therefore of us, the Heires or Successors of us the aforesaid Queen in this behalfe, in any manner to be had or prosecuted.

𝕬𝖓𝖉 𝖜𝖊𝖊 will, and by these presents for us the Heires and Successors of us the aforesaid Queen, we do grant to the aforesaid Mayor, Bailiffs and Burgesses, and Men of Abingdon aforesaid, that they and their Successors, by the name of the Mayor, Bailiffs and Burgesses of the Borough of Abingdon, in the County of Berks, may and shall be

Authority
to sue.

able to plead and be impleaded, sue and be sued, and defend and be defended, answer and be answered unto in all Courts and places of us, the Heirs and Successors of us the aforesaid Queen, and in other Courts and places whatsoever, as well within this our Kingdom of England as elsewhere within any other our Dominions whatsoever, and before whatsoever Judges or Justices or other Persons whatsoever, as well in all and singular other causes, matters and things whatsoever, of what kind or nature soever they be in the same manner and form as other our liege People inabled or in the Law capable, may or can plead and be impleaded, answer and be

answered unto, defend and be defended. And that the said Mayor, To have a Common Seal.
Bailiffs and Burgesses of the Borough aforesaid, and their Successors
may have and shall have, and may and shall be able to have a Comon
Seale to serve for all and singular their causes and Businesse to be
done and transacted, and that it shall and may be lawful for them
and their Successors, the same Seale att their pleasure to break,
change, and to make a new. And that the same Mayor, Bailiffs and Power to hold Land.
Burgesses, by the name of the Mayor, Bailiffs and Burgesses of the
Borough of Abingdon, in the County of Berks, be and shall be
persons able and in the Law capable to purchase, have, receive, take
and possesse, to them and their Successors in fee and perpetuity or
otherwise, Lordshipps, Mannors, Lands, Tenements, Rents, Reversons,
Services, Possessions and Hereditaments which are not held
immediately of us by Knights' Service, nor by any other Service in
Capite, nor of any other person or persons by Knights' Service,
so that the same Lordshipps, Mannors, Lands, Tenements, Rents,
Revertions and Hereditaments do not exceed the clear yearly value
of One Hundred Marks. And also we will and by these presents for Council to consist of 12 Principal Burgesses.
us and the Heires and Successors of us the aforesaid Queen, we do
grant to the aforesaid Mayor, Bailiffs and Burgesses and their
Successors, that all waies from henceforth there be and shall be in
the Borough aforesaid twelve Men of the better and more honest and
discretest Men, Inhabitants of the said Borough of Abingdon, who
shall be called and shall be the principall Burgesses of that Borough,
which said Mayor, Bailiffs, and Capitall Burgesses may and shall be
able to elect, take, and associate to themselves sixteen others or more And 16 Secondary Burgesses.
according to their sound discretions, of the better, honester and
discreeter Men, Inhabitants of the Borough aforesaid, which shall be
called the secondary Burgesses of the same Borough, and which said
Mayor, Bailiffs, principal Burgesses, and the said other sixteen or
more called secondary Burgesses, shall make and shall be called the
Comon Council of that Borough, for all things, causes, matters, acts,
Ordinances and Businesse touching or concerning the Borough
aforesaid, and the rule and government thereof, and the publick
utility and profitt of the same Borough and the Inhabitants thereof
for the time being, from time to time, by them or the greater part of
them, to be made and done for the better goverment and rule of the
Men, Inhabitants, and the causes, things, and businesse of the said
Borough for the time being. And further, wee will and for us the

Heires and Successors of us the aforesaid Queen, by these presents we do grant to the aforesaid Mayor, Bailiffs and Burgesses, and their Successors, that they and their Successors, by their Comon Council or by the greater part thereof, may have authority, power and

Power to make Bye Laws. lycence to make, constitute, ordain and establish, good, wholesome, honest and reasonable institutions, ordinances, Laws and constitutions, as well for the better Rule and Governance of the Mayor, Bailiffs and Burgesses, and other Officers, Artificers and Inhabitants of the Borough aforesaid for the time being, how and in what manner they shall behave themselves in their Offices and Business, and for the victualling of the same Borough for the publick good and comon profitt of the Borough aforesaid, and of the Country adjoining, as also for the better preservation of the Lands, Tenements, Possessions and Revenues, by these our Letters Patents to the Mayor, Bailiffs and Burgesses of the Borough aforesaid, gave, granted or assigned, and for other causes and Businesse touching or concerning the Borough aforesaid, which said institutions, ordinances and constitutions, being good, honest and reasonable, we will and comand by these Presents, to be kept and preserved, so that the Laws, Institutions and Ordinances by the same Mayor, Bailiffs and Burgesses to be made, be not nor shall be repugnant or contrary to the Laws and Statutes of our Realm of England, or the Prerogative of us the Heirs and Successors of us the aforesaid Queen.

Appointment of Officers. We will alsoe, and for us the Heirs and Successors of us the aforesaid Queen, by these Presents, we do grant that in the said Borough of Abingdon, from henceforth there be and shall be from time to time an Officer who shall be called and shall be the Town

Town Clerk. Clerk of the same Borough, to do and execute all and singular the Matters and Things which to the Office of Town Clerk do belong and apperteyne, or shall hereafter belong or apperteyne, or ought to apperteyne. And that there be and shall be in the said Borough of Abingdon, from time to time for ever, an Officer who shall be called

Chamberlain. the Chamberlain of the said Borough of Abingdon, to do and execute such necessarie Business which by such an Officer may be and shall be done and performed; and that there be and shall be in the said

Serjeants-at-Mace. Borough from time to time for ever, two Officers called Serjeants att Mace, for the executing of Precepts, Commands, Attachments, and other Processes in the same Borough to them directed by the Mayor, Bailiffs and other Officers of the same Borough, as the case shall happen, require and be necessary or needfull, which said Sergeants att Mace from time to time into their Offices shall be chosen, elected, admitted and preserved by the aforesaid Mayor, Bailiffs and principall Burgesses of the Borough aforesaid, and their Successors for the time being, or by the greater part of them, and that there be and shall be from time to time for ever, an Officer who shall be Clerk of the Markett, within the said Borough of Abingdon, to do, execute, performe and exercise all and singular the Matters and Things within the Borough aforesaid, which from time to time to the Office of Clerk of the Markett belongs and apperteynes, or which ought to belong and apperteyne to be done and performed.

Clerk of the Market.

And also we will, and for us the Heirs and Successors of us the aforesaid Queen, by these presents, we do grant to the aforesaid Mayor, Bailiffs and Burgesses, and their Successors, and also do ordain that there be and shall be in the said Borough one Burgesse of a Parliament, and the Heires of us the aforesaid Queen, and that the aforesaid Mayor, Bailiffs and Burgesses, in the said Borough of Abingdon, and their Successors, as often as and whensoever our Parliament of us our Heires and Successors of us the aforesaid Queen shall happen to be summoned, begin, or to be called by virtue of our Writt, and the Heires of us the aforesaid Queen for Election for Burgesses of Parliament to them directed or to be directed or otherwise by their Election they may and shall have power, authority and lycense to chose, elect and nominate a discreet and honest Man of the said Borough to be a Burgesse of our Parliament, and the Heires of us the aforesaid Queen for the same Borough, and the same Burgesse so elected at the expence and Costs of the said Borough and Comonalty of the same, shall send to our Parliament our Heires and Successors of us the aforesaid Queen, wheresoever it shall be holden, in the same manner and form as in other Boroughs of our Realme of England hath been and shall be used and accustomed, which said Burgesse, so elected and nominated, we will, shall be present, and to stay and tarry at our Parliament, our Heires and the Successors of us the aforesaid Queen, at the Expences and Charges of the said Borough of Abingdon and the Comonalty of the same during the time which the same Parliament shall happen to be holden, in like manner and forme as other Burgesses of Parliament for whatsoever Borough or Boroughs within our said Realme of England, to and ought and are accustomed and used to do, and

The Council to Elect a Member of Parliament.

which said Burgesse, in the said Parliament, shall have his voice as well affirmative as negative, and all and singular other matters and things shall do and execute, and may and shall be able to have, do and execute, by reason and means whatsoever as other Burgess or Burgesses of any other Borough within this Realm of England may and shall be able to do.

And ſo the end that all and singular the Premises may have and take, do and more full effect, **Know yee** that wee, of our more ample, larger and more abundant grace, and of our certain knowledge and meer motion have assigned, nominated, made and ordained, and by these presents for us the Heires and Successors of us the aforesaid Queen, do assign, nominate, make and ordain our beloved Richard Mayott, being a good and honest Man, and an Inhabitant of the said Borough of Abingdon, to be the first and for the time that now is Mayor of the Borough of Abingdon aforesaid, the Office of Mayor of the same Borough, faithfully upon his Oath to execute and in the same Office to stay and continue untill the Feast of Saint Michael the Archangel next coming, and from the same Feast untill one other fitt Person shall be elected and chosen and duly sworn, preserved and admitted, the same Office faithfully to execute, and by these Presents we do make, create, constitute and declare the said Richard Mayott to be the Mayor of the Borough aforesaid, during the time and term above said.

Richard Mayott to be first Mayor.

And alsoe wee have assigned, nominated, made and ordained, and by these Presents do assigne, nominate, make and ordain, our beloved Richard Ely and William Blacknall, being Inhabitants of the said Borough of Abingdon, to be the first and for the time that now is, Bailiffs of the same Borough, the said Office of Bailiffs of the said Borough shall faithfully upon their Oaths to execute until the said Feast of St. Michael the Archangel next coming, and from the same Feast until two other Persons shall be elected and duly sworn and admitted faithfully to execute the same Office, and we do make, create, constitute and declare by these Presents the said Richard Ely and William Blacknall Bailiffs of the Borough aforesaid, during the time and term above said. **And also wee** have assigned, nominated, made and ordained, and by these Presents do assign, nominate, make and ordain the said Richard Mayott, Richard Ely and William Blacknall, and our beloved William Mathew, Thomas Toules, James Fisher, Humphry Bostock, Thomas Orpwood, Ralph Bostock, Thomas Jenyns, John Chaunterell, and William Whytington, being good and

Richard Ely and William Blacknall first Bailiffs.

honest Men, Inhabitants of the said Borough of Abingdon, upon
their Corporall Oaths taken before the aforesaid Richard Mayott, the
now Mayor, to be the twelve first and for the time that now is
principall Burgesses of the same Borough, which said Burgesses and
every of them shall continue and endure as long they and every of
them shall well behave him and themselves in their Offices aforesaid.

Furthermore, we have assigned, nominated, made, ordained
and constituted and for us the Heires and Successors of us the aforesaid
Queen, by these presents we do assigne, nominate, make, ordain and
constitute our beloved Thomas Medowes, an Inhabitant of the said
Borough, on his Corporall Oath before the present Mayor, Bailiffs and
Burgesses, or the greater part of them, taken and to be taken, to be
the first and for the time that now is Chamberlain of the said Borough
of Abingdon, and well and faithfully to execute all and singular the
matters and things which to that Office do belong or apperteyne, or
ought to belong or apperteyne, untill the Feast of St. Michael the
Archangell next coming, and from thence untill another fit and proper
person into the said Office shall be elected, shall be duly pr'served,
admitted and sworn faithfully to execute the same, and by these
presents we do make, create, constitute and declare the said Thomas
Medowes, Chamberlain of the Borough aforesaid, during the time and
term abovesaid, which said Chamberlain that now is and his
Successors yearly on his going out of and departure from his Office,
shall yield, give up and render his just, true and reasonable accompt
unto the aforesaid Mayor, Bailiffs and Burgesses, or some Auditors by
them the said Mayor, Bailiffs and Burgesses or the greater part of
them already assigned, or to be assigned, all well Issues and Profitts
of his said Office, as of all Payments and Expences by him made,
laid out and expended, so that if it shall by chance happen the said
Chamberlain or any other of his Successors shall be found behind in
arreares, that then it shall be lawfull to and for the said Mayor,
Bailiffs and Burgesses, or the Auditors, the aforesaid Chamberlain so
being behind in arreares, to committ and send to Prison, and there in
the said Prison to continue and abide, nor thence be acquitted or
discharged untill he shall have paid and discharged to the said Mayor,
Bailiffs and Burgesses the arreares so being behind, or otherwise
shall compound with them to make satisfaction for the same.

And we have assigned, nominated, made, ordained and constituted, and for us the Heires and Successors of us the aforesaid

B

First Principal Burgesses.
First Chamberlain.
First Common Clerk.

First Common
Clerk.

Queen, by these pr'sents do assigne, nominate, make, ordain
and constitute our beloved Wm. Sympson, Gentleman, upon his
Corporall Oath, before the aforesaid Mayor, Bailiffs and principall
Burgesses that now are, or before the greater part of them, taken or
to be taken to be the first and for the time that now is Com'on Clerk
of the said Borough of Abingdon, and well and faithfully to do and
execute all and singular the matters and things which to the said
Office do belong or apperteyne or ought to belong or apperteyne
during the natural life of him the said Wm. Sympson. And we
do by these presents make, ordain and constitute the said Wm.
Sympson, Com'on Clerk of the Borough aforesaid, for and during his
life aforesaid. **And further** we will, and for us the Heires and
Successors of us the aforesaid Queen, by these presents, Do grant to

The Mayor
Clerk of the
Market.

the aforesaid Mayor, Bailiffs and Burgesses of Abingdon aforesaid
and their Successors, that the Mayor of the same Borough for the
time being from henceforth from time to time to be and shall be Clerk
of our Markett, our Heires and Successors of us the aforesaid Queen,
withinn the Borough aforesaid, and that he may and shall do, exercise,
perform and execute all and singular the matters and things which to
the Office of Clerk of the Markett belong and apperteyne there to be
done and performed, in like manner as the Clerk of the Markett of our
Household, and the Heires of us the aforesaid Queen may do or ought
to do by reason and colour of his Office aforesaid, and that no other
Clerk of our Markett, our Heires and Successors of us the aforesaid
Queen, within the Borough of Abingdon aforesaid, shall in anyways
enter or come in or intermeddle himselfe there any thing that
belongs to the Office of the Clerk of the Markett there to do or
perform.

We will, moreover, and for us and the Heires and
Successors of us the aforesaid Queen, we do ordain and grant that
the Mayor of the said Borough of Abingdon, for the time being

The Mayor
a Justice of the
Peace within the
Borough.

from henceforth be and shall be a Justice of our Peace within the
said Borough and the pr'cincts and liberty's of the same Borough of
and for all and singular the Matters and things which to a Justice of
our Peace our Heires and Successors of us the aforesaid Queen
belong, to be inquired into, heard and determined within the same
Borough, and the pr'cincts, metes, limitts and bounds and perambulations of the same Borough happening or arising in as large and
ample manner and form as any Justices of the Peace in any Cities,

Boroughs, or Countys of our Realm of England may do and have been accustomed to do or ought to do, and that no other Justice of our Peace, our Heires or Successors of us the aforesaid Queen from henceforth shall intermeddle himselfe or enter or come in to do any thing which to a Justice of Peace there belongs, Except our Justices,　　.　　.　　.
our Heires and Successors of us the aforesaid Queen, and other our Justices the Heires and Successors of us the aforesaid Queen, by Comision or Comissions of us the Heires and Successors of the aforesaid Queen, from time to time to be assigned, nominated and authorized within the said Borough of Abingdon and p'cincts thereof.

Moreover, we will, and for us and the Heires and Successors of us the aforesaid Queen, by these presents we do grant that the Mayor of the said Borough of Abingdon, for the time being, as soon as he shall be so elected to be Mayor, be and shall be Coroner of us and the Heires of us the aforesaid Queen, and all and singular the Matters and Things which to the Office of Coroner belongs, shall do and execute within the Borough aforesaid, and that before he takes upon himselfe the Office of Coroner aforesaid, he shall take an Oath before the old Mayor and Bailiffs and some other of the principal Burgesses or before the greater part of them, well and faithfully by himself to do and execute the said Office of Coroner. And that no other Coroner of us the Heires and Successors of us the aforesaid Queen, shall in anyways intermeddle in the said Borough or the pr'cincts thereof.

The Mayor Coroner.

And further, of our more abundant grace we will, and of our certain knowledge and mere motion for us and the Heires and Successors of us the aforesaid Queen, by these presents we do grant to the aforesaid Mayor, Bailiffs and Burgesses of the said Borough of Abingdon, and to the Inhabitants in the said Borough and their Successors, that they shall have and shall be able to have within the same Borough a certain House or Com'on Hall which shall be called the Council house of the said Mayor, Bailiffs and Burgesses, and the rest of the inhabitants and their Successors for ever, as well for their Meetings, Assemblies and Congregations in the same to be made, as also all and all manner of Courts, Pleas, Causes, Matters, Councills and other their businesse whatsoever there from time to time to be held, celebrated, handled and to be done as to them shall seem necessary and convenient. **And also** of our more ample grace we will, and of our certain knowledge and mere motion for us the Heires

The Council House.

and Successors of us the aforesaid Queen, by these pr'sents we do
grant to the aforesaid Mayor, Bailiffs and Burgesses, and to the rest
of the Inhabitants of the Borough aforesaid for the time being and
their Successors for ever, that from henceforth they and their
Successors yearly from time time, every year on the first day of the
Month of September, between the hours of nine and twelve before
noon of the same Day, shall meet together and may and shall be able
to meet together in the aforesaid house or Com'on hall called the
Councill house, or in any other convenient place within the said
Borough of Abingdon, and that then and there it shall and may be
lawfull for the Secondary Burgesses and other the Burgesses and
Men of the Inferior sort in the said Borough, Inhabitants, to nominate
and assigne two men of the more grave and discreet men then being
principall Burgesses of that Borough, to that end, intent and purpose
that the aforesaid Mayor, Bailiffs and the rest of the principall
Burgesses of the same Borough or the Major part of them shall choose

Election of Mayor.

and elect and may and shall be able to choose and elect one of those
two Burgesses so by the aforesaid Inhabitants and inferior Burgesses
nominated and assigned and to be nominated and assigned the
Office of Mayor within the Borough aforesaid, and the liberties thereof
to execute, perform and exercise for one whole year, from the feast
of St. Michael the Archangel then next following, which said Man so
to the Office of Mayor elected upon and after his Corporall Oath
taken, shall bear the Office of Mayor of the said Borough of Abingdon
for one whole year then next following, vizt.: from the Feast of St.
Michaell the Archangell inclusively, untill the same Feast of St.
Michaell the Archangel exclusively, one whole entire year to be
compleated; and from the same Feast of St. Michael the Archangell
exclusive, untill another sufficient and fit person the said Office
faithfully to execute shall be duly elected, pr'served, admitted and
sworn, and if any one so hereafter elected to be Mayor of the
Borough aforesaid after that Election shall be notified to him shall
refuse the Office of Mayoralty aforesaid upon him to accept and take
without a reasonable cause, that then it shall be lawfull for the Mayor,
Bailiffs and Capitall Burgesses of the said Borough for the time being

Penalty for refusing the Office of Mayor.

or the greater part of them, such man or Person so refusing to com'itt
and send to prison, there to be kept and remain safe, nor thence to be
freed and discharged untill he will take upon him and exercise the
said Office, or shall pay, render and satisfye to the said Mayor, Bailiffs

and Burgesses a competent sume of Money according to their sound discretions for his fine and ransome in this behalfe, to be made done and paid, or shall otherwise compound with them for satisfaction thereof. **And further,** we will, and by these pr'sents we do grant to the aforesaid Mayor, Bailiffs and Burgesses, and their Successors, that every Person to the Office of Mayor of the Borough of Abingdon aforesaid, elected and hereafter to be elected, shall take and shall be able to take his Corporall Oath before his last pr'decessor in the same Office, if the said predecessor shall be living and then pr'sent, and if the said predecessor shall be then dead and absent, that then he shall take and shall be able to take the Oath before the Bailiffs and Capitall Burgesses of the same Borough for the time being or the greater part of them then there present, and if by chance it shall happen that the Mayor of the said Borough of Abingdon for the time being during the time in which he should be Mayor of the same Borough, and within and before the time appointed and determined for his Office aforesaid be compleated shall die or be removed from his Office aforesaid, that then it shall and may be lawfull for the aforesaid Bailiffs and Burgesses as well Capitall as the other and for the rest of the Men in the said Borough for the time being or the greater part of them to assemble and meet together anew in the said house or any other convenient place within the Borough aforesaid, within eight Days next following the Death or removall of the said Mayor of the Borough aforesaid, and that they shall and may be able there to nominate, assigne and elect any fit Man of the member of the Capitall Burgesses to be Mayor of the aforesaid Borough of Abingdon, in the place and stead of the aforesaid late Mayor being dead or removed in manner and form abovesaid, which said Man so anew elected upon and after his Corporall Oath before the aforesaid Bailiffs and Burgesses and the rest of the said Men in the said Borough, being Inhabitants or the greater part of them then there pr'sent imediately and solemnly to be made and taken, shall faithfully bear and exercise the Office of Mayor of the same Borough untill the Feast of St. Michaell the Archangell then next following, and from the same Feast untill another sufficient and fit person the said Office faithfully to execute shall be duly elected, pr'ferred, sworn and admitted, in manner and form abovesaid.

And moreover, of our more ample grace we will, and of our certain knowledge and mere motion for us the Heires and Successors

Mayor to take an Oath.

Election on casual vacancy in Office of Mayor.

of us the aforesaid Queen, by these presents we do grant to the aforesaid Mayor of our said Borough of Abingdon, that from henceforth He and his Successors, Mayors of the Borough aforesaid for the time being, yearly from time to time every year, wheresoever and whensoever to him according to his sound direction it shall seem

The Mayor to elect one Bailiff.

convenient, shall nominate, elect and assigne and may and shall be able to nominate, elect and assigne one fit and discreet Man of the Inhabitants of the Borough aforesaid, whether he be Capitall or Secondary Burgesse of the Borough aforesaid, to be one of the Bailiffs of the same Borough from the Feast of St. Michaell the Archangell then next following, such Election, Assignamt and Nomination for one whole year and fully to be compleat. We will also, and for us our Heires and Successors of us the aforesaid Queen, we do grant to the aforesaid Mayor, Bailiffs and Burgesses of our aforesaid Borough of Abingdon, and to the rest of the Men in the said Borough being Inhabitants and their Successors for the time being for ever, that from henceforth they and their Successors yearly from time to time, every year on the said first Day of the Month of September, between the hours of nine and twelve before the forenoon of the same Day, or any other Days and Months whensoever to them or the greater part of them it shall seem convenient and necessary, shall and may assemble and meet together in the aforesaid House called the Councill House, or in any other convenient place within the Borough aforesaid, and there it shall and may be lawfull for the aforesaid Secondary Burgesses and the other Burgesses and the Men of the Inferior sort in the said Borough being Inhabitants to ratifye and confirm, cause to be ratified and confirmed, and to admit the Election, Nomination and Assignement of the Bayliffe for the year then following by the Mayor of the same Borough, made or to be made (as is aforesaid) so as the same Election be made and shall be made upon a fit, meet and sufficient man to bear and exercise the said

The Inhabitants to elect the second Bailiff.

Office. And that it shall and may be lawfull to the said Inhabitants then there present another good, honest and able man being an Inhabitant of the same Borough and one of the Secondary Burgesses of the Borough aforesaid, to nominate, assigne and elect to be another of the Bayliffs of the Borough aforesaid, and to be associate with the aforesaid Bayliff by the Mayor nominated, elected and assigned, from the Feast of St. Michaell th' Archangell then next following, for one whole year to be compleated, which said Men so to the Office of

Bayliffs elected upon and after their Corporall Oaths in form following solemnly and duly done and taken and to be done and taken, shall together bear the Office of Bailiffs of the Borough aforesaid for one whole year next coming, vizt.: from the Feast of St. Michaell the Archangell inexclusively, untill the same Feast of St. Michaell the Archangell exclusively one whole year to be compleated, and from the same Feast of St. Michaell the Archangell untill two other able and sufficient Men shall be duly elected, preferred, admitted and sworn, the same Office faithfully to execute, and if any person or persons be hereafter elected unto the Office of Bailiffs of the aforesaid Borough of Abingdon after the same Election shall be notified to him or them, shall refuse to take upon himselfe the Office of Bailiffe aforesaid without a reasonable cause, It shall and may be lawfull for the aforesaid Mayor, Bailiffs and Capitall Burgesses of the same Borough for the time being or the greater part of them, such Person or Persons so refusing to com'it and send to Prison, there safely to be kept and to remain and continue, nor thence to be freed or discharged untill he or they will take upon themselves the said Office, and shall take the Oath the same Office to bear and execute, or shall pay, render and satisfye to the said Mayor or Capitall Burgesses a competent Sum of Money to and for the use of the Commonalty of the same Borough for their fine and ransome in this behalf to be made, done and paid, or shall otherwise Compound with the said Mayor and Burgesses for satisfaction thereof, and so upon any such refusal to execute the Offices aforesaid or either of them, the Mayor, Bayliffs and Burgesses of the said Borough of Abingdon, and the rest of the Men in the said Borough being Inhabitants, shall go and proceed to a new Election in manner and form abovesaid.

Penalty on Bailiffs refusing to serve.

𝕬𝖓𝖉 𝖋𝖚𝖗𝖙𝖍𝖊𝖗 we will, and by these presents we do grant to the aforesaid Mayor, Bailiffs and Burgesses, and their Successors, that the Bailiffs of the same Borough elected and hereafter to be elected shall take their Corporall Oath before the Mayor and Capitall Burgesses for the time being if the same Mayor shall be living and then pr'sent, and if the aforesaid Mayor shall be then dead or absent, that then the same Bayliffs shall take their Corporall Oath before the late Bayliffes their Predecessors and the Capitall Burgesses or the greater part of them then there being pr'sent to exercise the Office aforesaid, and well and faithfully to do and performe all things which to the said Office belong, and if by chance it shall happen the aforesaid Bayliffs

Bailiffs to take an Oath.

of the said Borough of Abingdon for the time being or either of them during the time in which they should be Bailiffs of the same Borough, and within and before the time determined and appointed for their Office aforesaid be compleat and ended and shall dye or be removed from their Office aforesaid, that then it shall and may be lawfull for the aforesaid Mayor and Burgesses as well Capitall as Burgesses of the inferior sort and the rest of the Men in the same Borough then being Inhabitants or the greater part of them to assemble and meet together anew in the said house or in any other convenient place within the said Borough aforesaid, within the space of Eight Days then next following the death or removall of the said Bayliffs or either of them, unless some urgent cause do obstruct or let the same, and there shall and may be able to nominate, assigne and elect one other or others, meet, able and fit Men to be Bayliffe or Bayliffes of the aforesaid Borough of Abingdon, in the place and Head of the aforesaid Bayliffs or Bayliffe so dead or removed in manner and form abovesaid, which said Bayliffe or Bayliffes so anew elected and chosen upon and after their Corporall Oath in form above the said Office well and faithfully to execute imediately and solemnly taken and to be taken shall bear and exercise the Office aforesaid untill the Feast of St. Michaell the Archangell then next following, and from the same Feast untill other meet and sufficient Men the said Office duly to execute shall be duly in form aforesaid elected, preferred, admitted and sworn.

Election on casual vacancy in Office of Bailiff.

And further we will, and for us and the Heires and Successors of us the aforesaid Queen, we do grant to the aforesaid Mayor, Bayliffs and Burgesses of our aforesaid Borough of Abingdon and their Successors, that as often as and whensoever it shall happen any Burgesse of the Borough aforesaid for the time being shall dye or be removed from his place and Office, that then and so often it shall and may be lawfull for the aforesaid Mayor, Bailiffs and Capitall Burgesses then surviving, or the greater part of them, one of the better and honester men being Inhabitants of the Borough aforesaid to be a Burgesse and unto the Office of Burgesse of the same Borough to elect, nominate, substitue, make and appoint in the place of him so being dead or removed, and so from time to time, as often as the case shall happen, and every person so nominated and elected to be nominated and elected unto the Office of Burgesse of the Borough aforesaid, shall take his Corporall Oath before the aforesaid Mayor,

Election on vacancy in Office of Burgess.

Bayliffs and Burgesses for the time being or the greater part of them, his said Office well and faithfully to exercise and execute.

And further we will, and for us the Heires and Successors of us the aforesaid ·Queen, by these pr'sents we do grant to the aforesaid Mayor, Bayliffs and Burgesses of our said Borough of Abingdon and their Successors, that the Clerk of the Markett of the same Borough shall take his Corporall Oath before the aforesaid Bayliffs and Burgesses of the same Borough for the time being or before the greater part of them, his Office well and faithfully without any fear, gift, reward or favour to exercise and execute.

The Clerk of the Market to take an Oath.

We will, moreover, and for us the Heires and Successors of us the aforesaid Queen, we do grant to the aforesaid Mayor, Bayliffs and Burgesses of the Borough of Abingdon aforesaid, for the time being, that they and their Successors for the time being, from time to time whensoever it shall please them, after the death and decease of the aforesaid William Sympson, shall nominate, elect, choose and appoint one fit person to be the Com'on Clerk, called a Town Clerk of the Borough aforesaid. And that it shall and may be lawful for the aforesaid Mayor, Bayliffs and Burgesses and their Successors for the time being and the greater part of them from time to time, on any reasonable cause, their said Com'on Clerk to remove and expell from his Office, and the same or any other in his place to substitute and admit, as to the aforesaid Mayor, Bayliffs and Capitall Burgesses or the greater part of them for the time being shall seem expedient and necessary, which said Com'on Clerk shall take his Corporall Oath before the aforesaid Mayor, Bayliffs and Burgesses, or before the greater part of them his Office aforesaid well and faithfully to exercise and execute. **And we will,** and by these Presents for us the Heires and Successors of us the aforesaid Queen, we do grant to the aforesaid Mayor, Bailiffs and Burgesses, that they and their Successors from time to time, whensoev'r it shall please them, shall nominate, elect and constitute two or more Officers according to their sound discretions, which shall be called Serjeants at Mace, for the execution of processes and Commands and other Businesse which to the same Office belong or shall belong in the said Borough from time to time to execute and perform in manner and form as the Serjeants at Mace in our City of London do and execute, which said Serjeants at Mace so nominated, constituted and elected, and to be nominated, constituted and elected, shall take their Corporall Oath before the

The Mayor, &c., to appoint the Town Clerk.

And Two Serjeants-at-Mace.

c

aforesaid Mayor, Bayliffs and Burgesses for the time being, or the greater part of them, their said Office aforesaid well and faithfully to execute and exercise. [Here followed a Grant of a Court of Record to be held before the Bayliffes every Tuesday. But the same is rated out of the Record, being surrendered in Chancery 18th March, 7 Eliz., by James Fisher, one of the principall Burgesses, who was authorized to make such surrender by vertue of a writing from the Mayor, Bailiffs and Burgesses, under the Common Seal of the Corporation.]

And moreover, we will, and for us the Heires and Successors of us the aforesaid Queen, by these presents we do grant to the aforesaid Mayor, Bayliffs and Burgesses of the said Borough of

The Mayor, &c., to have the Assize of Bread, Ale, &c.

Abingdon and their Successors, that they may and shall have within the same Borough and the Bounds and Liberties thereof, the assize and assay of Bread, Wine, Ale and Beer, and of all other Victuals

Also of Weights and Measures.

w'tsoever. And also of all Measures and Weights whatsoever, and the correcting and amending of the same, and of all other things which to the Office of Clerk of the Markett of our Household or the Heires of us the aforesaid Queen do belong or apperteyne, together with the Corrections and Punishments of the same, and w'tsoever to the same Office belongs to do or execute as often as and when it shall be expedient and necessary. And that they have and shall have all Fines, Amercements and all other profitts thereof arising to the use and profitt of the Commonalty of the same Borough of Abingdon.

And further, know Yee, that wee of our more ample and abundant grace and of our certain knowledge and meer motion, have

Grant of a Court Leet.

given and granted and by these pr'sents for us and the Heires and Successors of us the aforesaid Queen ·Do give and grant to the aforesaid Mayor, Bayliffs and Burgesses of Abingdon aforesaid, and their Successors, a Leet and View of Frankpledge of all and singular the Inhabitants and Resiants as well being wholly as not wholly Resiants within the said Borough of Abingdon and within the said Limitts and Bounds thereof for the time being and from time to time for ever, and all things apperteyning or belonging and which shall apperteyne and belong and ought to apperteyne and belong to the View of Frankpledge within the said Borough twice by the Year, that is to say, one turne or time within one Month next after the Feast of St. Michaell th' Archangell, and one other turne or time within one Month next after the Feast of Easter before the Mayor of the same Borough only for the time being every year to be holden.

And that the Sheriffe and other our Officers, our Heires or the Successors of us the aforesaid Queen of the said County of Berks, shall not in anyways intermeddle themselves to have or keep Leet or View of Frankpledge or Court of View of Frankpledge of Laws within the Borough aforesaid, the Limitts or Liberties thereof.

And wee will, and by these presents for us the Heires and Successors of us the aforesaid Queen, we do grant to the aforesaid Mayor, Bayliffs and Burgesses of the said Borough of Abingdon and their Successors, that from henceforth for ever they may have and hold and may and shall be able to have and hold one Markett in every Monday in every Week in the said Borough of Abingdon, all that Day to be holden and kept. And five fairs there yearly to be kept and holden, one of the same fairs there to be kept and holden Yearly on the feast of the Translacon of St. Edmund the Bisshopp, and on the Eve and the Morrow of the same feast. And one other fair there Yearly to be kept and holden on the feast of St. Margarett the Virgin, and on the Eve and the Morrow of the same feast; the third fair there in the said Borough Yearly to be kept and holden on the feast of the Nativity of the blessed Mary the Virgin, and on the Eve and the Morrow of the same feast. The fourth fair in the Borough aforesaid Yearly to be kept and holden on the feast of St. Andrew the Appostle, on the Eve and the Morrow of the same feast. The fifth fair there Yearly to be kept and holden on the first Monday in Lent, from year to year every year for ever to continue, together with a Court of pye powder to the same Markett and fairs aforesaid belonging during the time of the same Market and fairs, together with Stallage, Piecage, Tolle, Fines, Amer'em'ts and all other profitts, Com'odities and Emolum'ts w'tsoever to such like sort of Marketts and Fairs with Court of pye powder belonging, apperteyning and happening, and from and out of the same Markett, Fairs, w'th Court of pye powder arising or issuing. And w'th all other Liberties and free Customs unto us to such like Marketts and Fairs belonging or apperteyning to the profitt, use, behoof and utility of the Comonalty of the same Borough for the time being, and to be taken and converted unlesse the Marketts and Fairs aforesaid be to the Nusanc of Neighbouring Marketts and Fairs.

And we will of our more ample and abundant grace and favour and of our certain knowledge and meer motion for us the Heires and Successors of us the aforesaid Queen, by these presents

Grant of a
Market on
Mondays.

And of five
Fairs yearly.

With a Court of
Pye powder and
Tolls, &c.

To have return of all Writs, &c.

we do grant to the aforesaid Mayor, Bailiffs and Burgesses of the aforesaid Borough of Abingdon and their Successors, that they and their Successors for the time being from henceforth may have and shall have from time to time retorns as well of Assizes as of all and all manner of precepts, Writts, Bills, Commands and Warrants of us our Heires and Successors of us the aforesaid Queen, and also of Summonses, Estreats and precepts out of our Exchequer, our Heires and Successors of us the aforesaid Queen, and of the Estreats and precepts of our Justices, our Heires and Successors of us the aforesaid Queen, in their Circuits as well for the pleas as the Common pleas, or of any other Justices w'tsoever, and also of Attachm'ts as well of pleas of the Crown as of others in the said Borough, Precincts and Liberties thereof, and full Execution there of the same, so that no Sheriffe, Bayliffe, or other our Minister, our Heires or Successors of us the aforesaid Queen, the said Borough, Suburbs, Liberties or precincts thereof, shall enter or come into for any Office or anything his Office there touching or concerning to be done or performed, so neverthelesse that it shall be lawfull for the Sheriffe of our said County of Berks in the aforesaid Borough to proclaim his Writs of exigent or outlawry, and to be proclaimed and there to keep and hold his Court called the County Court. And that the said Mayor, Bayliffs and Burgesses of the said Borough of Abingdon and their Successors from henceforth have and shall have and may and shall be able to have and enjoy for the use of the Comonaltye of the same Borough, Goods and Catells, Wayfes and Estrayes w'tsoever within the said Borough of Abingdon, and within the said Lymitts and Bounds of the same from time to time arising, happening, chancing or coming.

And we will, and by these presents for us the Heires and Successors of us the aforesaid Queen, We do grant to the aforesaid Mayor, Bayliffs and Burgesses of the Borough of Abingdon

Grant of a Gaol.

and their Successors, that they may have and shall have within the same Borough a certain Goal. All Felons w'tsoever within the same Borough and liberties of the same taken or to be taken in the same Goal, safely and securely to be kept and looked unto by the space of three Days and three nights and not any longer more or above unlesse necessity doth urgently require or otherwise to the contrary, and for the Correction and Punishment of other trespasses and Malefactors w'tsoever untill y^t they shall be lawfully delivered from the said Goale, according to the Law and Custom of our Realm of England.

𝔄nd further, know yee, that we in considerac'on that the said Mayor, Bayliffs and Burgesses of the Borough of Abingdon aforesaid and their Successors, may and shall be able from time to time the better to susteyne and support the charges in the Borough aforesaid of our speciall grace and of our certain knowledge and meer motion have granted and given lycense and by these pr'sents for us the Heires and Successors of us the aforesaid Queen, as much as in us is, Do grant and give especiall lycense, free and lawfull faculty, power and authority to the aforesaid Mayor, Bayliffs and Burgesses of the Borough aforesaid and their Successors to have, take, receive and purchase to them and their Successors for ever as well of us and the Heires and Successors of us the aforesaid Queen, as of any of our Subjects and Liege People, or any other person w'tsoever, Mannors, Messuages, Lands, Tenem'ts, Rectorys, Tythes, Rents, Revertions and Profitts and other Possessions, Revenues and Hereditam'ts whatsoever which are not held of us the Heires or Successors of us the aforesaid Queen in Capite by Knights' Service, nor of us or any other person or persons by Knights' Service without our speciall lycense, our Heires or Successor of us the aforesaid Queen, or without the lycense of the Lord or Lords of whom the aforesaid Lands and Hereditam'ts are holden, so as the same Mannors, Messuages, Lands, Tenem'ts, Rectoryes, Rents, Revertions and Services, or other possessions, Revenues and Hereditaments do not exceed the clear yearly value of Forty Pounds by the Year, the statute of Lands and premises not to be put into Mortmain or any other statute as Ordinance or restraint to the contrary heretofore made, enacted, ordained or provided, or any other thing, cause or matter in anywise notwithstanding.

Licence to purchase and hold lands, &c., in Mortmain.

𝔄nd whereas our Most Dear and Loving Brother, Edward the Sixth, late King of England, by his Letters Patents under his great Seale of the late Court of Augmentations and Revenues of his Crown, made bearing date at Westminster the fourteenth Day of July, in the third Year of his Reign, hath granted, delivered and to farm letten and demised to William Blacknall, all the Scite of the Fulling Mill, then being wholly in ruin and decay in Abingdon, in his County of Berks, near unto three other Water Mills there, And all the Land, Soyle and Ground where the same Fulling Mill was scituate and built, and all the Water and the Course of the Water to the same Fulling Mill, running, belonging or apperteyning, and all the house called the

Recital of Lease of the Fulling Mill and Coseners' Inn, &c., to William Blacknall.

Coscner's house, otherwise called the Coscner's Inne, and all his parcell of Land called Cosener's Close, conteyning by estimation halfe-an-acre, situate and being near unto and hard by the Mill aforesaid, in Abingdon aforesaid, which said premises then lately did belong and apperteyne to the late Monastery of Abingdon, in the County aforesaid. **And whereas** also our aforesaid late Brother of us the aforesaid Queen, by the same his Letters Patents, hath granted, delivered, and to farm letten and demised to the aforesaid William Blacknall, all and all manner of Tythes of w'tsoever sort coming, arising and issuing out of and in the Fulling Mill aforesaid and the rest of the p'mises, and out of and in the Fulling Mill there anew to be built and erected To have and to hold the aforesaid Scyte of the said Fulling Mill and the Land, Soyle and Ground where the same Mill was scituate and built, and the aforesaid Water and course of Water to the same Mill running, belonging or apperteyning, and the aforesaid house called the Coscner's Close, and the said parcell of Land called the Cosener's Close, and the Tythes aforesaid, and all and singular other the p'misses with the appurtenances to the afores'd William Blacknall, his Exc'rs and Assignes, from the Feast of St. Michaell the Archangell then last past unto the end of the term, and by the Term of Forty Years then next following and fully to be compleat Paying therefore Yearly unto our said Brother of us the aforesaid Queen, his Heires and Successors, during the first Ten Years of the said Term of forty years, Forty-six Shillings and Eight pence of lawfull Money of England, and during all the residue of the said Term of Forty Years after the end and expiration of the said first ten yeares of the said Term, Four pounds Six shillings and Eight pence of lawfull Money of England yearly, at the Feasts of the Annunciation of the Blessed Virgin Mary and St. Michaell the Archangell, unto the hands of the Baylliffs or Receivers of the pr'mises for the time being, by equall portions to be paid.

Recital of Lease of the Tythes of the said Mill to William Blacknall.

Recital of Lease of three Water Mills and Fishery to John Wellisbourne.

And whereas also by the same Letters Patents it is recited that whereas our Dear Father, Henry the Eighth, late King of England, by his Indenture under his great Scale of the late Court of Augmentations of the Revenues of his Crown, bearing date at Westminster the twenty-ninth day of March, in the thirtieth year of his reigne, among other things hath granted, delivered, and to farm letten and demised to John Wellisbourne, Esquire, three Water Mills under one Roffe, together with the Ponds and Pools and the whole

course of Water to the same belonging and running, with the
Appurtunces in Abingdon aforesaid, in the said County of Berks,
belonging and apperteyning to the said late Monastery of Abingdon,
in the same County then dissolved, together w'th the Tythe of the
same Mills and the whole Fishery of the Waters in Abingdon
aforesaid, to the said late Monastry in like manner belonging and
apperteyning, together with the Tythe of the same To have and
to hold all the aforesaid Mills and Fishery with the Appurtunces to
the aforesaid John Wellisbourne and his Assigns, from the Feast of
St. Michaell the Archangell then last past, unto the end of the term
and by the terme of one and twenty Years then next following and
fully to be compleated Yielding then yearly to our said Father of
us the aforesaid Queen, his Heires and Successors for the aforesaid
Mills and Tythe of the same Six pounds Thirteen shillings and Four
pence, and for the aforesaid Fishery Six pounds Thirteen shillings
and Four pence, at the Feasts of the Annunciation of the Blessed
Virgin Mary and St. Michaell the Archangell, or within one Month
after either of the said Feasts by equall portions to be paid as by
the same Indenture among other things it doth fully appear.

𝔄𝔫𝔡 𝔴𝔥𝔢𝔯𝔢𝔞𝔰, Further, our aforesaid Brother of us the
aforesaid Queen, by his aforesaid Letters Patents hath delivered,
granted, and to farm demised and letten to the aforesaid William
Blacknall, All those three Water Mills under one Roffe in Abingdon
aforesaid, together with the Ponds and Pools and the whole course of
Water to the same belonging and running, with the Appurtunc's in
Abingdon aforesaid, in the said County of Berks, to the said late
Monastry of Abingdon in the said County of Berks then belonging
and apperteyning, together w'th the Tythes of the same Mills and
the said whole Fishery of the Waters in Abingdon aforesaid to the
said late Monastrey in like manner belonging and apperteyning,
together with the Tythe of the same, together with the Houses,
Edifices and Buildings, Sewers, Wears, Locks and other Comodities
and proffitts w'tsoever in Abingdon aforesaid or elsewhere, to the
p'mises or either of them, or any parcell of them belonging or
apperteyning, or with them, or by reason, colour or meanes of them,
occupied or used To have and to hold the aforesaid three Mills and
Fishery and Tithe of the same and other the p'rmises to the said
John Wellisbourne as aforesaid demised or with the same or by
reason, meanes or colour of the same being occupied and used with

Recital of Lease
of three Mills
and Fishery,&c.,
to William
Blacknall.

the appurtunc's to the aforesaid William Blackuall, his Executors and Assignes, from the Feast of St. Michaell the Archangell, which shall be in the year of our Lord one thousand five hundred fifty and nine unto the end of the Term, and by the Term of thirty years then next following and fully to be compleated, Yielding then yearly to our said Brother of us the aforesaid Queen, his Heires and Assignes, for the aforesaid three Mills and Tithe thereof, Six pounds Thirteen shillings and Four pence, and for the aforesaid Fishery and Tythe thereof and other the pr'mises to the same belonging and apperteyning, Six pounds Thirteen shillings and Four pence of lawfull Money of England, at the Feasts of the Annunciation of the Blessed Virgin Mary and St. Michaell the Archangell, or within one Month after either of the said Feasts unto the hands of the Bayliffs or Receivers of the Pr'misses for the time being by equal portions to be paid during the term aforesaid As by the same Letters Patents amongst other things more fully it appeareth The Revertion and Revertions of all and singular the pr'misses in the aforesaid Letters Patents expressed and specified, to us and the Heires and Successors of us the aforesaid Queen by full right belonging and apperteyning.

And whereas also our said Dear Brother of us the aforesaid Queen, Edward the Sixth, late King of England, by his Letters Patents under his Great Seale of the late Court of Augmentations and Revenues of his Crown, made bearing date at Westminster the thirteenth day of May, in the fifth Year of his reigne, hath delivered,

Recital of Lease of Fitzharris Farm to Thomas Tesdale.

granted and to farm demised and letten unto Thomas Tesdale, All that his Farm called Fitzharris, and all Houses and Barnes and Arrable Lands, Fields, Meadows and Pastures and Appurtunc's, and all and all manner of Tythes of the same, in Abingdon, in the County of Berks, formerly in the tenure of Ralph Cradock, Yeoman, as fully   .   .   . and wholly, and in as full large and ample manner and form as the said Ralph Cradock and Elizabeth his Wife or one William Danield the same pr'misses heretofore had held and occupied; Except neverthelesse allways to our said Brother, his Heires and Successors all-together reserved all Woods and Underwoods of, in and upon the same Premises growing and being To have and to hold all and singular the same pr'misses with the Appurtunc's, except before excepted, to the aforesaid Thomas Tesdale his Executors and Assignes, unto the Term and for the Term of one and twenty years then next following and fully to be compleated;

Yielding therefore yearly to our said Brother his Heires and Successors, Eighteen pounds and Eight pence of lawfull Money of England, at the Feasts of Saint Michaell the Archangell and the Annunciation of the Blessed Virgin Mary or within one Month after either of the said Feasts, unto the hands of the Bayliffs or Receivers of the premises for the time being by equall portions to be paid during the term aforesaid As by the same Letters Patents amongst other things more fully it doth appear. The Revertion thereof to us and the Heires and Successors of us the aforesaid Queen by full right belonging and apperteyning.

Know yee that wee, of our more ample grace and of our certain knowledge and mere motion in considerac'on that the Mayor, Bayliffs and Burgesses of the Borough of Abingdon may and shall be able from henceforth the better to support and susteyne the charges of the same Borough, have given and granted and by these presents for us and the Heires and Successors of us the aforesaid Queen Do give and grant to the aforesaid Mayor, Bayliffs and Burgesses the aforesaid Revertion and Revertions of the aforesaid scy'e of the aforesaid Fulling Mill, being in ruin and decay, and of all and singular other the premises in the aforesaid Letters Patents bearing date the said fourteenth day of July, in the said third year of the Reign of our said Brother of us the aforesaid Queen expressed and specified, and the aforesaid yearly rent of Forty six Shillings and Eight pence, and the aforesaid yearly rent of Four pounds Six shillings and Eight pence, and the aforesaid yearly rent of Six pounds Thirteen shillings and Four pence, and also the aforesaid yearly rent of Six pounds Thirteen shillings and Four pence in the same Letters Patents as is aforesaid reserved and the aforesaid Revertion of the aforesaid Farme called Fitzharris, and of all and sing'ar other the p'misses in the aforesaid Letters Patents bearing date the said thirteenth Day of May, in the fifth year of our said Brother of us the aforesaid Queen expressed and specified, and all the aforesaid yearly rent of Eighteen pounds and Eight pence by the same Letters Patents reserved as is aforesaid. **And wee Do give** and for the Considerac'ons aforesaid by these pr'sents for us and the Heires and Successors of us the aforesaid Queen, we do grant to the aforesaid Mayor, Bayliffs and Burgesses of our said Borough of Abingdon All those Messuages, Tofts, Cottages, Lands, Tenem'ts, Burgages, Shops, Cellars, Solars, Curtelages, Gardens, Rents,

Grant of the Reversion of the Fulling Mill, Fitzharris Farm, &c.

D

Grant of certain
Properties of the
late Monastery. Revertions and Services, and other our hereditam'ts w'tsoever, with the appurtunc's now or lately in the severall tenures or occupations of Joan Wyks widow, Thomas Bisley, John Denton Esq're, William Johnson, Robert Hewlett, Thomas Davy, Richard Smith, John Duckett, Hugh Blount, Elizabeth Fisher, Helen Hampson, Leonard Collins, William Hanby, Richard Toye, Richard Parker, John Lock, William White, Robert Hewlett, and William Pinfolde, scituate, lying and being in Burford Street, otherwise called Butcher row, in Abingdon, in our County of Berks, to the late Monastery of our Blessed Virgin Mary of Abingdon, in the said County of Berks, heretofore belonging and apperteyning and being parcell of the possessions thereof. And also all those Messuages, Tofts, Cottages, Lands, Tenements, Burgages, Shops, Cellars and Solars, Curtelages, Gardens, Rents, Revertions and Services and other our hereditam'ts, with the appurtunc's now or lately in the severall tenures or Occupations of John Hurst, Henry Barker, John Hobbins, William Kisby, John Fraynoke, John Bryans, Anthony Lancaster, Richard Thornebury, Miles Gerrard, Thomas Hathorne, John Bentham, Roger Wells, Thomas Mylam, Ralph Batts, Thomas Whitacres, Adam Payne, Richard Arnall, John Hudd, Margaret Clarke, William White, Thomas Warner Dryng, Thomas Wyther, Thomas Read, Thomas Milles, Eleanor Patson Widow, Edmund Gardiner, Richard Armster, Richard Tysdale, Christopher Taylor, Robert Waltham, Eleno Noke Widow, Robert Carter, Thomas Bisley and Thomas Jennings, scituate, lying and being in Sterte Street, in Abingdon aforesaid, in the said County of Berks, to the said late Monastery there heretofore belonging and apperteyning and being parcell of the possessions of the same. And all those Messuages, Tofts, Cottages, Lands, Tenem'ts, Burgages, Shops, Cellars, Solars, Curtelages, Gardens, Rents, Revertions, Services and other our Hereditaments w'tsoever, with the Appurtunc's now or lately in the severall Tenures of Richard Ballard, Richard Large, Thomas Golde, Thomas Bisley, John Blissett, John Johns, John Stoker, Thomas Robins, James Braybrook, Hugh Hopkins, James son and heir of Thomas Braybrook, William Sympson, Robert Bisley, Thomas Phillips, Oliver Hyde Esq're, Thomas Lambert, Robert Bisley, Anthony Hungerford, Richard Beast, Richard Large, and William Yate, scituate, lying and being in West St. Hellen's Street in Abingdon aforesaid, in the said County of Berks, To the said late Monastery heretofore belonging

and apperteyning and being parcell of the Possessions of the same. And also all those Messuages, Tofts, Cottages, Lands, Tenem'ts, Burgages, Shopps, Cellars, Solars, Curtelages, Gardens, Rents, Revenues and Services, and other our Hereditam'ts w'tsoever, with the Appurtunc's now or late in the severall Tenures of James Watter, Richard Smith, William Mathon, James Braybrooke, Robert Aldworth, John Langley, William Mathew, William Keyling, Gilbert Freeman, Jno. Sympson, Agnes Grove, Rich'd Wright and Wm. Smith, Gilbert Freeman, Richard Smith, Henry Harper, Elizabeth Hyde and Elizabeth Branch, scituate, lying and being in East St. Hellen's Street in Abingdon aforesaid, in the aforesaid County of Berks, to the said late Monastery of the Blessed Virgin Mary, of Abingdon aforesaid, heretofore belonging and apperteyning, and being parcell of the possessions of the same. And also all those our two Messuages or Tenem'ts with the Appurtunc's now or late in the severall Tenures of Thomas Read and Thomas Woodward, scituate and being in Lumbard Street in Abingdon aforesaid, in the said County of Berks, to the said late Monastery heretofore belonging and apperteyning and being parcell of the Possessions of the same. And allso all those Messuages, Tofts, Cottages, Lands, Tenements, Burgages, Shops, Cellars, Solars, Curtelages, Gardens, Rents, Revenues, Services and other our Hereditam'ts w'tsoever, with the Appurtunc's now or late in the severall tenures of Robert Foreman, Michael Fisher, John Langley, John Edwards, Humphry Bostock, Roger Coke, John Hyde, John Tuscote, John Bolks, Ralph Hans, John Cole, Anne Bonde, John Tuckey, John Carey and John Shene, scituate, lying and being in little bury Street in Abingdon aforesaid, in the said County of Berks, to the aforesaid late Monastery heretofore belonging and apperteyning, and being parcell of the possessions of the same. And also all those Messuages, Tofts, Cottages, Lands, Tenements, Burgages, Shops, Cellars, Solars, Curtilages, Gardens, Rents, Revertions and Services and other our Hereditam'ts whats'r, with the Appurtunc's now or late in the severall tenures of Thomas Eyres, Wm. Blackhouse Churchwarden of St. Elene, William Backhouse, Robert Ling, Robert Sayer, Thomas Bisley, Thomas Golde, John Hutt, Thomas Bisley, Thomas Drink, Robert Reasen, Joan   . John Chaunterell, Wardens of the Parish Church of Sonningwell, William Sympkins, Henry Goodchild, John Ayre and Jno. Chaunterell, scituate, lying and being in Boar Street in Abingdon aforesaid, in the said County of Berks, to the aforesaid late

Monastery heretofore belonging and apperteyning, and being parcell
of the poss'ions of the same. And also all those Messuages, Tofts,
Lands, Tenem'ts, Burgages, Shops, Cellars, Solars, Curtilages, Gardens,
Rents, Revertions and Services and other our Hereditam'ts w'tsoever,
with the Appurunc's now or late in the severall tenures of Philip
Swift, Garret Stanber, Thomas Atkinson, John Borne, George Furrett,
Thomas Bisley, Thomas Rowland, Richard Elye, Thomas Gold, James
Braybroke, Thomas Golde, Robert Overthrowe, Richard Beverley,
Elizabeth Hyde, Richard Smith, Roger Allen, William Alderley the
younger, James Strainge, Richard Cowper, Thomas Payne, Thomas
Orpwood, John Addams, Richard Elye, Thomas Rowland, Joan
Amerlowe, Thomas Bisley, William Bakhouse, Thomas Consers,
Richard Elye and the heires of Nicholas Hewitt, scituate, lying and
being in Ock Street in Abingdon aforesaid, in the said County
of Berks, to the said late Monastrey heretofore belonging and
apperteyning, and being parcell of the poss'ions of the same. And
also all those Messuages, Tofts, Cottages, Lands, Tenem'ts, Burgages,
Shopps, Cellars, Solars, Curtilages, Gardens, Rents, Revertions,
Services and other our Hereditam'ts w'tsoever, with the Appurtenances
now or late in the severall tenures of John Hyde, George Tuckwell,
Richard Chester, William Barker, John Whitwell, John Langley,
Thomas Woodward, Thomas Milles, Thomas Rode, Stephen
Whitington, Thomas Reade, Ralph Bostock, John Mitchell, John Hutt,
Thomas Bisley, Thomas Golde, Thomas Reade, John Willmott, James
Braybroke and Robert Forman, situate, lying and being in a Street
called the Bury in Abingdon aforesaid, and to the said late Monastrey
heretofore belonging and apperteyning. And also all those Messuages,
Cottages, Lands, Tenem'ts, Burgages, Shops, Cellars, Sollars,
Curtilages, Gardens, Rents, Revertions and Services, and other our
Hereditam'ts w'tsoever, with the Appurtunc's now or late in the
several tenures of James Braybroke, William Smith, John Bonge,
Nicholas Rixon, John Taylor, Warden of the Parish Church of
Sonningwell, Thomas Golde, William Yate, Thomas Meadowe,
Robert Ashely, Thomas Barnade, Thomas Bisley, scituate, lying and
being in the Brode Street in our said Town of Abingdon aforesaid,
and to the said late Monastery heretofore belonging and apperteyning.
And also all those Messuages, Cottages, Lands, Tenements, Burgages,
Shops, Cellars, Solars, Curtilages, Gardens, Rents, Revertions and
Services, and other our Heredit's w'tsoever, with the Appurtunc's now

or late in the severall tenures of Edward Alexander or Oliver Hyde, John Smith, Joan Poynter, Oliver Hyde, Thomas Read, John Tyndall, Nicholas Harris, John Tindall, John Pyers, Robert Pyke, and Roger Bright, scituate, lying and being in the Wineyard in Abingdon aforesaid, and to the said late Monastery heretofore belonging and apperteyning. And also all those Messuages, Cottages, Lands, Tenem'ts, Burgages, Shops, Cellars, Solars, Curtilages, Gardens, Rents, Revertions and Services, and other our Hereditam'ts w'tsoever, with the Appurtunc's now or late in the severall tenures of John Smith, Oliver Wellbourne, Robert Welling, William Welling and Thomas Medowe, situate, lying and being in Otwell Lane in Abingdon aforesaid, and to the said late Monastery heretofore belonging and apperteyning, and also all those our two Gardens and our one Tenement and our one Garden with the Appurtenances now or late in the severall tenures of Steven Whytington, James Braybroke and Elizabeth Tasker, scituate, lying and being in St. Edmund's Lane in Abingdon aforesaid and to the said late Monastery heretofore belonging and apperteyning. And allso all that scite of the Fulling Mill in Abingdon aforesaid, near unto the three Water Mills there, and the whole Land, Ground and Soyle whereon the same Fulling Mill was scituate and built, and all Waters and courses of Water to the same Fulling Mill running, belong or apperteyning, and all and all manner of Tythes of w'tsoever kind or sort out of and in the Fulling Mill aforesaid coming, growing, arising or issuing, with their and every of their Appurtunc's now or late in the Tenure or occupation of William Blacknall, and to the said late Monastery heretofore belonging and apperteyning. And also all those our three Water Mills built and erected under one Roffe in Abingdon aforesaid, and all Pools and Ponds and the whole course of Water to the same Mills belonging and running, with the Appurtnc's in Abingdon aforesaid. And also all and all manner of Tythes and Tenths of the said three Mills and each and every of them. And all our Fishery and Liberty of Fishing in the Waters of Abingdon aforesaid, and the tenths and tythes of the same Fishery. And also all and all manner of Tenths and Tythes Yearly and from time to time coming, growing, issuing or renewing out of the Buildings, Edifices, Sewers, Wears, the Locks and all other Comodities and proffiitts whatsoever in Abingdon aforesaid or elsewhere to the aforesaid three Water Mills to either of them or any parcell of them belonging or with them or either of them by reason, means or colour of the same being occupied or used, heretofore in the tenure or occupation of John Wellisbourne or his Assignes, and now or late in the tenure or occupation of the said William Blacknall, and to the said late Monastery heretofore belonging and apperteyning. And also all that severall Bushey or Thorne Close with the Appurtunc's conteyning by estimation one acre lying and being in Bagley, in our said County of Berks, now or late in the tenure or occupation of Oliver Wellisbourne, and to the said late Monastery heretofore belonging and apperteyning. And also all that house or Goale with the Appurtenances scituate and being in the Middle of the Markett in Abingdon aforesaid, in which said House as well the view of Frankpledge as the Court of Portrive and pye powder have been used and accustomed to be holden and to the said late Monastery heretofore belonging and apperteyning. And also all that our little Close of Land called the Trinitie Close, with the Appurtenuc's conteyning by estimation one rod or perch lying and being in Abingdon aforesaid, now or late in the Tenure or Occupation of William Wise and to the said late Monastery heretofore belonging and apperteyning. And all that our Messuage and Tenem't with the Appurtunc's scituate and being in Bore Street in Abingdon aforesaid, and all our Lands, Fields, Meadowes, Pastures, Com'ons and hereditaments whatsoever, as well within the Town of Abingdon aforesaid as in the fields there to the said Messuage and Tenement in anyways belonging or apperteyning or with the same being heretofore demised, lett, used or enjoyed, with their and every of their Appurtunc's now or late in the Tenure or Occupation of Robert Kepe or his Assignes, and to the said late Monastery heretofore belonging and apperteyning. And all that our farm and our heredit's with the Appurtunc's called Fitzharris, and all our houses, Arrable Lands, Fields, Meadows, Pastures and heredit's whats'r with the Appurtunc's scituate, lying and being in the Town and fields of Abingdon aforesaid, and all and all manner of Tenths and Tythes in Abingdon aforesaid, with their and every of their Appurtunc's lately in the tenure or occupation of Ralph .   . and now or late in the tenure or occupation of Thomas Tesdale or his Assignes, and to the said late

Grant of Profits, &c., of Fairs and Office of Clerk of Market and Courts, &c.

Monastery heretofore belonging and apperteyning. And also all Issues, Com'odities, Proffitts and Emolum'ts whats'r of out of and in the Fairs in Abingdon aforesaid to be held. And of and out of the

Office of Clerk of the Markett there, and all issues and proffitts of, out of and in the view of ffrankpledge, pye powder and Court of Portrive from time to time chancing, happening, coming, arising or growing. And also all that our yearly rent of Six pence and Service to us belonging and apperteyning, issuing out of our Tenem't now or late in the Tenure or Occupation of William Powell, scituate and being in Burford Street in Abingdon aforesaid, to the late Chauntry of the Blessed Virgin Mary, in Abingdon aforesaid, heretofore belonging and apperteyning and being parcell of the possessions and revenues of the same. And also all our Lands, Tenements and heredit's whats'r now or late in the Tenure or Occupations of James Fisher, William Applebye, John Bargeman and Robert Overthrowe, situate, lying and being in East St. Helene's Street aforesaid, and to the said late Chauntry heretofore belonging and apperteyning. And also all that our yearly rent of one penny and Service to us belonging and apperteyning, issuing out of one Tenement now or lately in the Tenure of Richard Forde in Abingdon aforesaid, and to the said late Chantrey sometime since belonging and apperteyning. And all that our yearly rent of one penny and Service to us belonging and apperteyning, heretofore parcell of the Possessions and Revenues of the said late Chantery, and issuing out of a Tenem't in the Tenure of John Sharpe, in the Bore Street aforesaid. And also all those our nine Messuages or Tenem'ts and our five Gardens and our Orchard with the Appurtunc's now or late in the severall Tenures of Alice Watson, William Bray, John Broke, the aforesaid Alice Watson, Henry Atkins, Robert Whitton, Thomas Bastly, Joan Aurlowee, and John Francys, situate, lying and being in Ock Street aforesaid, and to the said late Chantrey some time since belonging and apperteyning. And also all that our Messuage and Tenement with the Appurtenc's now or late in the Tenure or Occupation of Thomas Bisley, in the Bury in Abingdon aforesaid, and to the said late Chantery some time since belonging and apperteyning. And also all that our Messuage and Tenm't with the Appurtunc's now late in the tenure or occupation of Thomas Bisley, in the Bury in Abingdon aforesaid, and to the said late Chantery some time since belonging and apperteyning. And also all those our three Messuages and Tenem'ts with the Appurtunc's now or late in the severall tenures or occupations of William Crouche and John Coxe, scituate and being in the Wineyard aforesaid. And also all those our eight

Grant of certain Properties of the late Chauntry of S. Mary, the Virgin, in Abingdon.

Grant of certain
Property of late
Chauntry called
St. Totte's
Chauntry,
Oxford.
Messuages or Tenm'ts and our three Gardens with their and every of
their Appurtunc's now or lately in the several tenures of John Shreeve,
John Collins, William Harris, Henry Bande, Thomas Chipman,
Edmund Thyndall and Elizabeth Miller, or their Assignes, scituate,
lying and being in Abingdon aforesaid, being lately parcell of the
Lands, Possessions, and Revenues of the late Chantery vulgarly
called St. Tottes Chauntry, founded within our City of Oxford.
And also all that our Barne with the Appurtunc's scituate in the South
side of the Ock Street aforesaid, and our Close of Land to the same
Barne adjoining conteyning by estimation Three acres. And all
And of certain
Properties of
Fraternity of
The Holy Cross.
Lands, Meadowes and Pastures in Wick field in Abingdon aforesaid,
with their and every of their Appurtunc's now or lately in the tenure
or occupation of William Keling and his Assignes, and to the late
fraternity of the Holy Cross in Abingdon aforesaid, some time since
belonging and apperteyning, and being lately parcell of the Poss'ons
of the same.   And all that our Back house and Close of Land to the
same house adjoining on the East side of the Bore Street aforesaid.
And of
Properties
formerly given
for Obytes.
And our three Acres of Land with the Appurtunc's now or late in the
Tenure or Occupc'on of Thomas Thesdale or his Assignes, scituate
and being in the Town and Fields of Abingdon aforesaid and
heretofore being gave, granted, assigned and apointed for the
perpetuall sustentation of our Yearly Obyte in the Parish of
St. Nicholas in Abingdon aforesaid. And allso all those our two
Tenem'ts and one Garden with the Appurtunc's, scituate and being
in the South and North sides of the Bore Street aforesaid, and being
heretofore gave, granted, assigned and appointed for the perpetual
sustentation of the aforesaid Yearly Obyte, and our Tenem't with
the Appurtunc's scituate in the Corner of the North side of the Ock
Street aforesaid, and one Garden with the Appurtunc's now or late
in the Tenure or Occupation of John Meadowe or his Assignes, and
being heretofore gave, granted, assigned and appointed for the
perpetuall sustentation of a Yearly Obyte in the Church of St. Hellene
in Abingdon aforesaid, and one other Cottage of ours and one Garden
of ours with the Appurtun'es, scituate and being on the West side of
East St. Helen's Street aforesaid, and being heretofore gave, granted,
assigned and appointed for the perpetual sustentation of the said
yearly Obyte in the aforesaid Church of St. Helene.

We give alsoe, and for the considerations aforesaid by these
presents for us and the Heires and Successors of us the aforesaid

Queen, We do grant to the aforesaid Mayor, Bayliffs and Burgesses of our said Borough of Abingdon aforesaid All and all manner of our Woods, Underwoods and Trees whatsoever, out of, in and upon the premises growing or being, and the Revertion and Revertions whatsoever of all and singular the Pr'misses and every part and parcell thereof, and also the Rents and yearly Proffitts whatsoever reserved upon any demises, leases and grants whatsoever in anyways made of the pr'mises in any part or parcell thereof. 𝕎𝕖 𝕘𝕚𝕧𝕖 𝕒𝕝𝕤𝕠𝕖, and by these pr'sents for the Considerations aforesaid for us and the Heires and Successors of us the aforesaid Queen, We do grant to the aforesaid Mayor, Bayliffs and Burgesses of our said Borough of Abingdon, All and singular the aforesaid Messuages, Mills, Cottages, Lands, Tenemt's, Gardens, Cellars, Solars, Tythes, Tenths, Woods, Underwoods, Rents, Revertions, Services, and all and singular other the premises above expressed and specified, as fully, freely and wholly, and in as large and ample manner and form as any Abbot of our said late Monastery or any Chanters, Chaplains, Priests, Governors, Masters or Incumbents of the said late Chantrys and Fraternity or any or either of them or any other person or persons heretofore having, possessing or being seized thereof, have at any time had, held or enjoyed, or ought to have had, held or enjoyed, the premises or any part or parcell thereof, and as fully, freely and wholly, and in as large and ample manner and forme as all and singular the premises by reason, meanes, colour or pretence of the dissolution of the said late Monastery, or by reason, means, colour or pretence of any Act or Acts of Parliament, or by any other lawfull meane, right or title now are in our hands or ought to be in our hands, or came or ought to come into our hands, or unto the hands of our most dear and loving Father of us the aforesaid Queen, Henry the Eighth, late King of England, or unto the hands of our most dear and loving Brother of us the aforesaid Queen, Edward the sixth, late King of England, which said Messuages, Lands, Tenem'ts, Rents, Revertions and Services, and all other the pr'misses are now extended to the clear yearly value of One hundred and two pounds sixteen Shillings and seven pence. 𝕋𝕠 𝕙𝕒𝕧𝕖, 𝕙𝕠𝕝𝕕 and enjoy the aforesaid Revertion and Revertions and the aforesaid yearly Rents, and also the aforesaid Messuages, Tofts, Cottages, Lands, Tenements, Burgages, Shops, Cellars, Solars, Curtilages, Gardens, Rents, Revertions and Services, and all and singular other the pr'misses above expressed and specified to the aforesaid Mayor,

Grant to the Corporation of the before mentioned Properties.

E

Bayliffs and Burgages of the Borough of Abingdon and their Successors for ever, To the proper use and behoofe of them the said Mayor, Bayliffs and Burgages and their Successors for ever, **To hold** of us and the Heires and Successors of us the aforesaid Queen as of our Mannor of Grenewyche in our County of Kent, by Fealty only in free socage and not in capite. **And yielding and Paying** therefore yearly unto us the Heires and Successors of us the aforesaid Queen, One hundred and two pounds Sixteen Shillings and Seven-pence of lawfull Money of England att the Feasts of the Annunciation of the Blessed Virgin Mary and St. Michaell the Archangell, at the receipt of our Exchequer, our Heires and Successors every Year by equal portions to be paid for and in lieu of all other rents, Services and Demands whatsoever to us our Heires or Successors in any manner or by any meanes to be therefore yielded, paid or done.

At Quit-Rent reserved to the Crown.

And further, of our more ample and abundant grace and favour we do give and for the considerations afores'd for us our Heires and Successors We do grant to the aforesaid Mayor, Bayliffs and Burgesses of the said Borough of Abingdon, all Issues, Rents, Revertions and Proffitts of all and singular the aforesaid Messuages, Lands, Tenem'ts and all and singular other the Premisses above expressed and specified with the Appurtun'ces from the Feast of St. Michaell the Archangell last past coming or growing, **To have** to them the said Mayor, Bailiffs and Burgesses of our gift without accompt or any other thing therefore to us our Heires or Successors by any means to be yielded, paid or done. **And moreover** of our more ample grace and favour We do give and by these presents for the Considerac'ons afores'd for us our Heires and Successors, We do grant to the aforesaid Mayor, Bayliffs and Burgesses of the said Borough of Abingdon and their Successors, that wee and the Heires and Successors of us the aforesaid Queen, yearly and from time to time will exonerate, discharge, acquitt, save and keep harmlesse and indempnified as well them the said Mayor, Bailiffs and Burgesses as the aforesaid Messuage, Lands, Tenem'ts and all and singular other the pr'misses with their and every of their Appurtunc's and every parcell thereof against us our Heires and Successors of us the aforesaid Queen and against all and every other Person and Persons whatsoever, of and from all and all manner of Corrydes, Rents, Pentions, Portions, Fees, Annuities, and all other charges and

Grant of the Reversions, &c., to the Corporation.

sumes of Money whatsoever out of the aforesaid Messuages, Lands, Tenements and other the Premisses with the Appurtenances, or out of any part or parcell thereof by any meanes, issuing, going or to be paid or thereupon charged or to be charged, except the rent and Service above by these pr'sents reserved, and except the demises and grants of the Premisses or any part or parcell thereof by any meanes made upon which the old rent or more shall be reserved, and except the Covenants being in such demises and grants, and except Five Shillings issuing out of part of the Premisses and yearly to be paid to the Vicar of the Parish Church in Abingdon aforesaid for the time being, And except Fifteen Pounds and Twelve Shillings issuing out of part of the Premisses and yearly to be paid unto six Poor People in the Almshouse called the Hospitall of St. John, within the precincts of the said late Monastery as of an ancient custome hath been used to be allowed. **Moreover**, we will, and by these present we do firmly injoyne and comand as well the Treasurer, Chancellour and Barons of our Exchequer, our Heires and Successors as all our Receivers, Auditors and other Offices and Ministers whatsoever of us our Heires and Successors of us the aforesaid Queen for the time being that they and every of them upon the only sight or Demonstration of these our Letters Patents, or upon the Enrollement of the same without any other Writt or Warrant by us the Heires or Successors of us the aforesaid Queen to be sued forth or prosecuted, shall make and from time to time caused to be made a full, whole and due allowance and manifest discharge of all and all manner of such rents, fees, annuity's and sumes of Money charges whatsoever issuing or to be paid out of the premisses or thereupon charged or to be charged (Except before excepted) unto the aforesaid Mayor, Bailiffs and Burgesses, their Heires and Assignes. And these our Letters Patents or the Inrollm't thereof shall be yearly and from time to time a sufficient warrant and discharge in this behalfe as well to the said Treasurer, Chancellour and Barons of our Exchequer, our Heires and Successors of us the aforesaid Queen as unto all Receivers, Auditors and other Officers and Ministers whatsoever of us the Heires and Successors of us the aforesaid Queen for the time being. **We will also**, and by these presents We do grant to the aforesaid Mayor, Bayliffes and Burgesses of the said Borough of Abingdon that may have and shall have these our Letters Patents under our great Seale of England duly made and sealed without fine or fee, great or small

Charter to issue without fee in the Hanaper.

to us in our Hanaper or elsewhere to our use by any meanes for the same to be yielded, paid or done, because that expresse mention of the yearly value or of the certainty of the Premisses or either of them or of other gifts or grants by us or by any of the Progenitors of us the said Queen to the aforesaid Mayor, Bayliffs and Burgesses of the said Borough of Abingdon before this time made in these presents is not made or any Statute, Act, Ordinance, Provisoe or restraint thereof to the contrary made, enacted, ordained or provided, or any other thing, cause or matter whatsoever in any wise notwithstanding.

In Witnesse whereof, we have caused these our Letters to be made Patents.

Witnesse ourselves at Westminster, the Twenty fourth day of November, in the third and fourth Yeares of our Reignes.

THE CHARTER

GRANTED BY

ELIZABETH, A.D. 1565.

Elizabeth, by the Grace of God of England, France, and Ireland, Queen, Defender of the Faith, &c., **To all to whom** these present Letters shall come Greeting, **Whereas** Lord Phillip and our most dear and loving Sister Mary, late King and Queen of England, by their Letters Patents under their Great Seal of England made bearing date at Westminster the twenty fourth day of November, in the third and fourth years of their reigns, amongst other things did will and grant unto the Mayor, Bayliffs and Burgesses of their Borough of Abingdon, in the County of Berks, and their Successors, that they and their Successors then and from thenceforth for ever should have and hold and might and should be able to have power to have and hold one Court of Record before the Bayliffs of the same Borough for the time being, or his or their sufficient Deputy or Deputies in the Common Hall within the Borough aforesaid or in any other more convenient place within the said Borough from Week to Week, on every Tuesday Weekly (Except in the Weeks of Whitsuntide, Christmasse and Easter), to be holden, kept and celebrated of all and all manner of Pleas, Plaints and Actions, personal or mixed, and of Debts, Accounts, Trespasses, Covenants, Contracts, Detinues, Withholdings, Contempts and Offences within the said Borough of Abingdon, and the Suburbs, Liberties and precincts of the same made, moved, had, committed or chancing, happening or arising, or to chance, happen or arise, so as the same did not exceed five pounds in one entire Sum, and of all and all manner of Debts, Accompts, Covenants, Detinues, Detainings and withholdings of Deeds, Charters, Writings, Escripts, Evidences and Minuments, and of the taking and detaining of Cattle and Beasts and of other Contracts whatsoever and of whatsoever causes or

Recital of grant of Court of Record by Charter of Philip & Mary, to be held before the Bayliffs.

things within the Borough aforesaid, the suburbs, liberties or precincts of the same or any parcel thereof arising, happening or chancing. And that the same Bayliffs and their Successors upon the same Plaints, Pleas, Quarrels and Actions, should have authority, power and licence, the persons, Defendants against whom the same Plaints, Pleas, Quarrells and Actions in the aforesaid Covenant should chaunce or happen to be raised, levied or moved, to bring unto Pleas by Summonses, Attachments and Distresses, according to the usage and Custome of their City of London, to the Serjeants at Mace of the said Borough for the time being or either of them to be directed, and for default of Chattels and Lands of the same Defendants within the Borough aforesaid and the Limits, Bounds and Liberties and thereof, where or by which they might be Summoned, attached or distreined by attachment or taking of their Bodies according to the Custome in the said City of London used. And that all and singular the same and like sort of Pleas, Plaints, Quarrels and Actions abovesaid shall be severally heard and determined, and should be derayned, deduced, drawn and ended by like processes, Considerations, Judgments and Executions of Judgments as and by which the like Pleas, Plaints and Complaints in the said City of London were derayned, deduced, drawn and ended, and that the executions of Processes and those Judgments should be had and made by the aforesaid Sergeants at Mace, or either of them according to the Law and Custome of their Realm of England, or according to the Liberties, Privileges and Customs of the said City of London. And that the Bayliffs of the aforesaid Borough of Abingdon for the time being and their Successors should and might have, take and levy to the use and profit of the Commonalty of the same Borough from time to time all Fines, Amerciaments, Forfeitures and other profits whatsoever of, out of, and in, the Court aforesaid lawfully coming, issuing, arising, chancing or happening, as such, and the like Fines, Amerciaments and Profits in the said City of London are taken and levied, as by the said Letters Patents amongst other things more fully it appeareth.

And reciting the inconvenience of holding the Court before the Bayliffs. And because the aforesaid Court is to be holden before the Bayliffs of the aforesaid Borough and not before the Mayor thereof, great inconvenience, damage and disadvantage hath befallen and happened, and seems very likely daily to befall and happen, unto the same Borough, as we are informed, by reason that whosoever hath once born the Office of Mayor of the said Borough, by the Orders and the Statutes

of the same Borough is disabled and incapacitated to exercise the
Office of Bailiff in the same, whence it happens, as we are likewise informed, that our beloved subjects the Inhabitants of the Borough
aforesaid have been oftentimes compelled to elect and chuse such
persons unto the Office of Bayliff as were very unfit to decide and
determine the Causes, Complaints and Quarrells in the Court aforesaid,
to be ended and determined to the great scandal and disgrace of the
same Court, and to the greatest prejudice of all our Subjects who
either pleaded or were impleaded in the same Court.   And therefore
the Mayor, Bayliffs and Burgesses of the Borough aforesaid have
most humbly besought us that we would now give our aid and
assistance and relieve them in this behalf.   And that they and their
Successors may have and hold from henceforth for ever of our gift
and grant our other Court of Record within the Borough aforesaid,
before the Mayor of the same Borough for the time being in the form
in these our Letters Patents under written.   And to the same intent *And surrender by Corporation of Court under prior Charter.*
and purpose the said Mayor, Bayliffs and Burgesses for themselves
and their Successors, their aforesaid liberty of holding a Court of
Record before the Bayliffs of the aforesaid Borough for the time
being, in manner and form above written, and to them by the
aforesaid recited Letters Patents gave and granted and all and
singular the Matters and Things in the same Letters Patents
concerning the same Court of Record to be holden before the Bayliffs
have surrendered unto us our Heires and Successors, Which said *Grant of a New Court of Record.*
Surrender we do accept by these Presents.   Know therefore
that we graciously and affectionately condescending to the petition
and request of our aforesaid Subjects, and in Consideration of the
Surrender aforesaid, and also for the bettering and improving of the
whole Borough aforesaid of our especial grace and of our certain
knowledge and meer motion, Will and by these presents for us our
Heires and Successors, We do grant to the aforesaid Mayor, Bayliffs
and Burgesses of the said Borough of Abingdon and their Successors
that they and their Successors from henceforth for ever may have,
and hold, and may and shall be able and have power to have and
hold one Court of Record before the Mayor of the same Borough for *To be held before the Mayor.*
the time being, or his sufficient Deputy or Deputies in the aforesaid
Common Hall, within the Borough aforesaid, or in any other more
convenient place within the said Borough, from Week to Week, every
Tuesday Weekly (Except the Weeks of Whitsuntide, Christmas and

Easter), 𝕿𝖔 𝖇𝖊 𝖍𝖔𝖑𝖉𝖊𝖓, celebrated and kept, of all and all manner of Pleas, Plaints, and Actions, personal or mixed, and of Debts, Accompts, Trespasses, Covenants, Contracts, Detinues, Withholdings, Contempts and Offences within the said Borough of Abingdon, the Suburbs, Liberties and Precincts of the same, made, moved, had, committed or chancing, happening or arising, or to chance, happen or arise, so as the same do not exceed five pounds in one entire Sum and of all and all manner of Debts, Accounts, Covenants, Detinues, Detainings and Withholdings of Deeds, Charters, Writings, Escripts, Evidences and Miniments, and of the taking and detaining of Cattle and Beasts, and of other Contracts whatsoever, causes or things within the Borough aforesaid, the Suburbs, Liberties and Precincts of the same, or any parcel thereof arising, chancing or happening. And that the same Mayor and his Successors, upon the same Plaints, Pleas, Quarrels and Actions, shall have authority, power and Licence the Persons, Defendants, against whom the same Plaints, Pleas, Quarrels and Actions in the aforesaid Court shall chance or happen to be raised, levied or moved, to bring unto Pleas by Summons's, Attachments and Distresses, according to the Custome of our City of London used, to the Serjeants at Mace of the said Borough for the time being or either of them to be directed, and for default of Chattels and Lands of the same Defendants within the Borough aforesaid and the Limits, Bounds and Libertyes thereof, where or by which they may be Summoned, attached or distrained by Attachment on taking of their Bodies, according to the Custome in the said City of London used, and that all and singular the same and like sort of Pleas, Plaints, Quarrels and Actions abovesaid, shall be severally heard and determined, and shall be derayned, deduced, drawn, brought and ended, by like Processes, Considerations, Judgments and executions of Judgments, as and by which the like Pleas, Plaints and Complaints in the said City of London are derayned, deduced, drawn, brought and ended, and that the executions of Processes and those Judgments shall be had and made by the aforesaid Serjeants at Mace or either of them according to the Law and Custom of our Realm of England, or according to the Liberties, Privileges and Customs of our said City of London, and that the said Mayor of the aforesaid Borough of Abingdon for the time being and his Successors, shall and may have, take and levy to the use and profit of the Commonalty of the same Borough from time to time, All Fines, Amerciaments, Forfeitures and other Profits whatsoever of, out of, and in the Court aforesaid, lawfully coming, issuing, arising, chancing or happening as such and the like Fines, Amerciaments and Profits in the said City of London are taken and levied, And that without Accompt or any other thing for that cause in anywise to be yielded, paid or done to us our Heires or Successors.

𝕎𝕖 𝕨𝕚𝕝𝕝 𝕒𝕝𝕤𝕠, and by these Presents We do grant to the aforesaid Mayor, Bayliffs and Burgesses of the said Borough of Abingdon, that they may and shall have these our Letters Patents under our Great Seal of England duly made and sealed without Fine or Fee to us in our Hanaper or elsewhere to our use, for the same to be yielded, paid or made, 𝔅𝔢𝔠𝔞𝔲𝔰𝔢 that express mention of the true yearly value or certainty of the premises or either of them, or of any Gifts or Grants by us or by any of our Progenitors to the aforesaid Mayor, Bayliffs and Burgesses of the Borough of Abingdon aforesaid heretofore made in these Presents is not made, any Statute, Ordinance, proviso or restraint thereof to the contrary made, enacted, ordained, proclaimed or provided, or any other thing, cause or matter whatsoever in anywise notwithstanding.

Charter to ... without fee ... the Hanaper

𝕴𝕟 𝖂𝖎𝖙𝖓𝖊𝖘𝖘 whereof, we have caused these our Letters to be made Patents.

𝖂𝖎𝖙𝖓𝖊𝖘𝖘 ourselves at Westminster, the nineteenth day of March, in the seventh year of our Reign.

THE CHARTER

GRANTED BY

JAMES I., 16TH FEB., A.D. 1609.

𝕵𝖆𝖒𝖊𝖘, by the Grace of God of England, Scotland, France and Ireland, King, Defender of the Faith, &c., 𝕿𝖔 𝖆𝖑𝖑 𝖙𝖔 𝖜𝖍𝖔𝖒 these present Letters shall come, Greeting, know yee, that wee, as well for and in consideration of the Sume of Fifty pounds nine Shillings and four pence of good and lawful Money of England, at the receipt of our Exchequer at Westminster, unto the Hands of our Beloved Servant William Bowyer, Knight, one of the Tellers of the same our Exchequer unto our use by our beloved Subjects The Mayor, Bayliffs and Burgesses of the Borough of Abingdon, in our County of Berks, in hand, well and truly paid, whereof we acknowledge ourself to be fully satisfyed, and the same Mayor, Bayliffs and Burgesses of the Borough aforesaid and their Successors to be thereof acquitted and discharged for ever by these presents as for divers other good causes and considerations us to these presents especially moving of our especial grace and of our certain knowledge and mere motion, We have given, granted and confirmed, and by these presents for us our Heires and Successors Do give, grant and confirm unto the aforesaid Mayor, Bayliffs and Burgesses of the Borough aforesaid and their Successors, All that our Tenement, and all that our Backhouse lying and being in a certain Street called Bore Street, on the East side of the same Street, and one Close to the same House adjoining, and three acres of our Land in the Fields of Abingdon aforesaid, which said Premisses were formerly given to the use of an Obyte in the Church of St. Nicholas, in Abingdon aforesaid, in our said County of Berks, to be solemnized, and lately were or were reputed to have been in the tenure or occupation of Thomas Thesdale or his Assignes, and by a Particular thereof are extended or are menc'oned to be extended unto the yearly value of

Grant to the Corporation of divers Properties described.

Fifteen Shillings. And all that our Tenement lying and being in a certain Street called Brode Street, in Abingdon aforesaid, in the said County of Berks, on the South side of the same Street, which said Tenement or House was formerly gave and limited To the use of an Obyte in the aforesaid Church of St. Nicholas, to be solemnized, and lately was or was reputed to have been in the Tenure or Occupc'on of Thomas Hovell or his Assigns, and by a Particular is extended or is menc'oned to be extended to the yearly value of Thirteen Shillings and four pence. And also all that our Tenement or House and Garden or piece of Land to the same Tenement adjoining, with all Houses, Tenements and Buildings upon the same piece of Land lately built and erected, lying and being in the Bore Street aforesaid, in the said Borough of Abingdon, on the South side of the same Street, Which said last menc'oned Tenement, Garden or piece of Land and Buildings aforesaid lately were or were reputed to have been in the tenure or occupc'on of William Keling or his Assignes, and to the use of an Obyte in the Church of St. Nicholas aforesaid to be solemnized, lately gave and limited, and by a Particular thereof are extended or are menc'oned to be extended to the yearly value of Five Shillings. And also all that our Tenement or Stable lying and being in a certain Street called East St. Hellen's Street, on the West side of the same Street, in ye aforesaid Town of Abingdon, in our said County of Berks, which said Tenement or Stable lately was or was reputed to have been in the tenure or occupation of Richard Smithe or his Assignes, and by a Particular thereof is extended or is menc'oned to be extended to the yearly value of Six Shillings and eight pence. And also all that Messuage or Tenement lying and being in Bore Street aforesaid, within the aforesaid Town of Abingdon, lately in the Tenure or Occupac'on of John Keep or his Assigns. And all that our Lane, Entrance or Passage to the said Messuage or Tenement belonging or appertaining called Irish Lane, extending and leading towards Brode Street aforesaid, with the Brode Gate there, And all Lands, Meadows, Pastures, Commons, Dove Cotes, Pidgeon Houses, Gardens, Ditches, Watercourses, the Daums with the Stream called the Sterte, and one part of one Croft or little Close, and all those trees in the same Croft or little Close planted and growing, lying and being near unto the Watercourse called the Sterte, with all their Appurtunc's within the Town and Fields of Abingdon aforesaid, and all Meadows, Pastures

and Com'ons in Drayton Wike and Sutton Wike, with the Appurtune's
to the said Messuage or Tenement in anywise belonging or
appertaining. And also all that our Close in Abingdon aforesaid to
the late Office called St. Edmond's Office belonging or appertaining,
with all Houses, Edifices and Buildings upon the same Close lately
built, abutting or bordering upon Bore Street, on the West side and
the Backside of the same Messuage on the East side, And also all
that our small Garden in Abingdon aforesaid lately to the Office
called the Hampuers Office belonging or appertaining, lying and
being on the North part of the said late Tenement lately in the
Tenure or Occupation of the said John Keep. And also all those
two Hydes of Meadow with the signe of the four Pools or Pits, lying
and being in Abingdon aforesaid, in the Meads called Abingdon
Meads; And all those Lands in Abingdon Fields, formerly parcell of
the demesne Land of the Manour of Norecotte and lately belonging
to the Monk called the Monk of the Works, containing by estimac'on
Ninety two acres of Land; And also all that half of an Hyde of
Meadow with the signe of the two Ribbs lying and being in
Abingdon aforesaid in the aforesaid Meads; And all those our Lands
lying and being in the Field or Furlong called Larkehill in Abingdon
aforesaid, lately belonging to the Office of Chamberlain of the said
late Monastery of Abingdon, containing by Estimac'on Twelve acres,
and all that fourth part of an Hyde of Meadow lying and being in
Abingdon Mead aforesaid, formerly in the Tenure or Occupc'on of
the aforesaid Jno. Keep or his Assigns; And all that parcell of our
Pasture or the Leyes in Abingdon aforesaid, containing by estimation
Six acres, abutting and shooting upon Abingdon Mead aforesaid,
which said Messuage, Lane, Lands, Meadows, Pastures and other the
last menc'oned and recited Premises by a Particular thereof are
extended or are menc'oned to be extended to the yearly value of
Five Pounds nine Shillings and eight pence; And all our Tythes and
Tenths growing, issuing, renewing, chancing, happening or arising
within the Town and Fields of Abingdon aforesaid, in our said County
of Berks, or within any or either of them to the aforesaid late
Monastery of Abingdon lately belonging, which said Tythes and
Tenths aforesaid are or lately were or were reputed to have been in
the tenure or occupc'on of William Bostock, Gentleman, or his
Assigns, or by a Particular thereof are extended or are menc'oned to
be extended to the yearly value of Three pounds thirteen Shillings

and four pence; And also all that piece of our Waste land lying and being in Abingdon aforesaid in a certain Street there called Burford Street, and five small Tenements thereupon, lately built and erected with the Gardens or Backsides to the same belonging near unto a Bridge there com'only called the Harte Bridge or the New Bridge, on the South side, between a Tenement called the Harte on the West side and the Malthouse to the late Monastery of Abingdon belonging on the East side, which said piece of Waste Land and houses thereupon built and erected, by a Particular thereof are extended or are menc'oned to be extended to the yearly value of Five Shillings; And all that small house in Abingdon aforesaid lately built and erected upon a certain piece of Land lying on the North side of a certain Street called Ock Street, near unto the Crosse called Riddle Crosse, which said house is or lately was reputed to have been in the tenure or Occupc'on of John Athoe or his Assigns, and by a Particular thereof is extended or is menc'oned to be extended to the yearly value of Three Shillings and four pence; And also all those several parcels of our Land lying and being in the Fields of Abingdon aforesaid, in our said County of Berks, containing by estimac'on Six acres and an half, which said six acres and an half were heretofore occupyed with the aforesaid Tenement called the Backhouse and lately were or were reputed to have been in the tenure or occupation of John Arnolde, or his Assignes, and now are or are reputed to be in the tenure or occupation of James Hyde, Gentleman, or his Assigns, and by a Particular thereof are extended or are menc'oned to be extended to the yearly value of Sixteen Shillings; And also all that parcell of Land containing Two acres of Land with the Appurtenances in Wekefield, in the Parish of Sutton Courtney, in our said County of Berks, heretofore occupied with the aforesaid Tenement in East Saint Hellen's Street, which said parcell of Land formerly was or was reputed to have been in the tenure or Occupac'on of Richard Smithe, and now are or are reputed to be in the tenure or Occupe'on of Thomas Mayott, Gent., or his Assigns, and by a Particular thereof are extended to the yearly value of Five Shillings. 𝔚𝔢 𝔤𝔦𝔳𝔢 also, and by these presents for us our Heires and Successors for the considerations aforesaid, We do grant to the aforesaid Mayor, Bayliffs and Burgesses of the Borough of Abingdon aforesaid and their Successors, all and singular our Messuages, Mills, Houses, Edifices, Buildings, Structures, Barns, Stables, Dove Cotes,

Pidgeon Houses, Orchards, Gardens, Lands, Tenements, Meadows,
Feedings, Pastures, Com'ons, Demesne Lands, Wastes, Rushes,
Heaths, Moors, Marshes, Woods, Underwoods, Woody Lands and
Trees whatsoever, and all the Land, Ground and Soylo of the same
Woods and Trees, the Profitts, Com'odityes, Waters, Watercourses,
Fisheryes, Fishings, Rents, Penc'ons, Porc'ons, Revenues, Free folds
or Foldages, Com'ons, Customes, Tythes of Sheafes or Shocks of
Corn or Grain and Hay, Wool, Flax, Hemp and Lambs, and all other
Tythes and Tenths whatsoever, as well great as small, free Warrens,
and all other our Rights, Jurisdic'ons, Franchesceyes, Libertyes,
Priviledges, Profitts, Com'odityes, Advantages, Emoluments and
Hereditaments whatsoever, with their and every of their appurtenances of w'tsoever kind, sort, nature or species they be, and by
whatsoever names they are known, named or called, scituate, lying
and being, coming, growing, renewing, chancing, happening, or
arising within the Town, Fields, Parishes, Places or Hamletts of
Abingdon, Sutton Courtney, Sutton Week and Drayton Weeke
aforesaid, or elsewhere whatsoever in our aforesaid County of Berks,
to the aforesaid Messuages, Lands, Tenements, Meadows, Feedings,
Pastures and other the premises by these presents above granted or
menc'oned to be granted or to any or either of them anyways
belonging, appertaining, incident or appendant, or being over,
heretofore had, known, accepted, taken, occupyed, used or reputed,
as members, parts or parcells of the same Messuages, Lands,
Tenements and other the premises above by these presents granted
or menc'oned to be granted, or to any or either of them; And also
our Reverson and Reversons, remainder and remainders whatsoever
of all and singular the said Premisses and every of them above by
these presents granted or menc'oned to be granted, and of every
part and parcell thereof. **And further**, of our more abundant,
especial grace, and of our certain knowledge and meer motion for
us our Heires and Successors, We have given and granted, and by
these presents Do give and grant to the aforesaid Mayor, Bayliffs
and Burgesses and their Successors, that they the aforesaid Mayor,
Bayliffs and Burgesses of the Borough aforesaid and their Successors,
from henceforth for ever, shall have, hold and enjoy, and may and
shall be able and have power to have, hold, use and enjoy, within
the premises above by these presents granted or mentioned to be
granted, and within every part and parcell thereof from henceforth

With Liberties
and Franchises
of the late
Monastery
thereto
belonging.

for ever so many so greate such the like and the same Libertyes, Franchesyes, Customes, Free Warrens, Goods and Chattels of Felons and Fugitives of Felons de se, and of Persons outlawed, deodands and all other our Rights, Jurisdicons, Francheseys, Libertyes, Priviledges, Profitts, Commodityes, Advantages, Emoluments and Hereditaments whatsoever, as and which and as fully, freely and wholly and in as large and ample manner, form, as any Abbot or Prior of the aforesaid late Monastery of Abingdon or any other person or persons the aforesaid Messuages, Lands, Tenements, Meadows, Feedings, Pastures and other the Premisses or any part or parcell thereof heretofore having, Possessing, or being seized thereof, have ever had, held or enjoyed, or ought to have, hold or enjoy in the premisses above by these presents before granted or in any part or parcell thereof by reason, means, colour or pretence of any Charter, gift, grant or confirmation or of any Letters Patents by us or by any of our Progenitors or Predecessors heretofore had, made or granted or confirmed, or by reason, means, colour or pretence of any lawfull prescription, usage or custome heretofore had or used, or otherwise by any lawfull meanes, right or title whatsoever, and as fully, freely and wholly and in as large and ample manner and form as all and singular the premisses above by these presents granted or menc'oned to be granted or any part or parcell thereof unto our hands or unto the hands of any of our Progenitors or Predecessors by reason, means or pretence of the Dissolution or Surrender of any late Monastery or Priory, or by reason, means or pretence of any Exchange or Purchase, or of any Gift or Grant, or of any attainder or forfeiture, or by reason, means or pretence of any Act or Acts of Parliament, or by reason of Escheat, or by any other lawfull means, right or title came or ought to come, and now are or ought to be in our hands. 𝕿𝖔 𝖍𝖆𝖛𝖊, 𝖍𝖔𝖑𝖉 𝖆𝖓𝖉 𝖊𝖓𝖏𝖔𝖞 all and singular our aforesaid Messuages, Lands, Tenements, Tenths, Tythes, Meadows, Feedings, Pastures, Commons, Demesne Lands, Wastes, Rushes, Heaths, Moors, Marshes, Woods, Underwoods, Woody Lands and Trees whatsoever, Fruits, Proffitts, Com'odityes, Advantages, Emoluments, Possessions and Hereditaments whatsoever, and all and singular other the Premisses above by these presents before granted or mentioned to be granted with their and every of their Appurtenances. And our Reverc'on and Reverc'ons, Remainder and Remainders whatsoever of all and singular the said Premisses and every of them to the aforesaid Mayor, Bayliffs and Burgesses of the Borough of Abingdon aforesaid and their Successors, To the only proper use and behoof of the aforesaid Mayor, Bayliffs and Burgesses of the Borough aforesaid and their Successors for ever. **To hold** of us, our Heires and Successors, as of our Manor of East Greenwyche, in our County of Kent, by fealty only in free and Com'on Socage and not in Capite or by Knights Service; **And yielding** therefore yearly unto us our Heires and Successors, Twelve Pounds twelve Shillings and four pence of lawfull Money of England, at the Receipt of our Exchequer, at Westminster, at the Feasts of Saint Michaell the Archangell and the Annunciation of the Blessed Virgin Mary, by equal porc'ons to be paid every year for ever, for all Rents, Services, Exacc'ons and Demands whatsoever to be therefore unto us our Heires and Successors in anywise yielded, paid, done or made. **Wee will**, nevertheless, and by these presents for us our Heires and Successors, We declare and Ordain, and the aforesaid Mayor, Bayliffs and Burgesses of the Borough aforesaid for themselves and their Successors, doe covenant and grant to and with us our Heires and Successors by these presents, That they, the aforesaid Mayor, Bayliffs and Burgesses of the Borough aforesaid and their Successors from to time, shall submit themselves, and absorve, perform and fulfill all and singular such Orders and Decrees as by our Court of Exchequer Chamber our Heires and Successors from time to time hereafter shall be made or appointed for or concerning any controversies which at any time hereafter shall grow, arise or be moved of or concerning the Premisses, or any of them, between the aforesaid Mayor, Bayliffs and Burgesses of the Town of Abingdon aforesaid and their Successors and any persons that now have or are reputed to have the Estate, Title or Interest in or to the same premisses or any parcell thereof by or under a title prior or before the time of the making of these presents in Esse or so pretended, their Assignes, Executors or Administrators.

And further, of our more abundant especial grace, and of our certain knowledge and mere motion for the Considerac'ons aforesaid Wee have given, granted, pardoned, remitted, released, discharged and confirmed, and by these presents for us our Heires and Successors Do give, grant, pardon, remitte, release, discharge and confirme to the aforesaid Mayor, Bailiffs and Burgesses of the

Borough of Abingdon aforesaid and their Successors, All and singular Intrusions and Entryes of and in the aforesaid premisses above by these presents before granted or menc'oned to be granted, or of, in, and upon any part or parcell thereof heretofore by the aforesaid Mayor, Bayliffs and Burgesses of the Borough aforesaid or their Predecessors, or by any other person or persons at any time heretofore had or made, without lawfull meanes, right or title, and all and singular the Issues, Fines, Rents, Revenues, Yearly Proffitts, Arrearages, whatsoever of all and singular the Premisses above expressed and specified, and by these presents before granted or menc'oned to be granted, and of every part and parcell thereof anyways before the Date of these our Letters Patents hitherto coming, growing, happening, chancing, incurred or payable, and all arrearages thereof, Except the Rent and Service before the making of these presents to us coming or issueing, or menc'oned to be coming or issuing out of the premisses or any part or parcell thereof, and unto us due and to be paid, and before any of our Auditors being in charge, and all arrearages thereof, and Except all and all manner of Fines, Issues, Sumes of Money, Forfeitures and Arrearages whatsoever to us due, incurred, forfeited or payable, for or in respect of Conveyance or Alienac'on of the premisses or any part or parcell thereof heretofore had, made, permitted or suffered, without the Licence of us or any of our Progenitors in that behalf not being first obtained. **And further,** Wee will, and by these presents for us our Heires and Successors We do signifye and declare our good pleasure and Intent to be, and likewise the same Mayor, Bayliffs and Burgesses of the Borough aforesaid, for themselves and their Successors are willing and do assent that these our Letters Patents or any thing in them contained shall not anyways extend to discharge, remitt or release any Debts or Sumes of Money to us before the making of these our Letters Patents due, incurred or payable, otherwise than of Fines, Issues, Rents, Revenues and Yearly Proffitts, above by these presents to the same Mayor, Bayliffs and Burgesses gave, before granted, pardoned, remitted, released, discharged or confirmed or menc'oned, or intended, to be given, granted, pardoned, remitted, released or discharged, Nor other means, methods, Courts or rights which we before the making of these presents had or might or ought to have to levy, receive and recover the same Debts or Sumes of Money or either of them, out of,

Charter not to release existing Debts to the Crown.

G

in or upon the aforesaid Lands, Tenements and other the Premisses above by these presents before granted or menc'oned to be granted, or out of, in or upon any part or parcell thereof.

Rent reserved
not to be in
addition to rent
reserved by
earlier Charter.
𝔓rovided always, and by these presents of our more ample especiall grace, and of our certain knowledge and meer motion we will, and for the Considerac'ons aforesaid for us our Heires and Successors, We do grant unto the aforesaid Mayor, Bayliffs and Burgesses of the Borough of Abingdon aforesaid for the time being and their Successors, That 𝔚hereas, by certain Letters Patents of our late Sovereign Lord and Lady, Philip and Mary, late King and Queen of England, under the great Seal of England, sealed, bearing date the twenty fourth day of November, in the third and fourth yeares of their reigns, to the same Mayor, Bayliffs and Burgesses of the Borough aforesaid made and granted, a certain yearly rent of One hundred and two pounds Sixteen Shillings and Seven-pence is reserved for divers Lands, Tenements and Hereditaments in the same Letters Patents to the aforesaid Mayor, Bailiffs and Burgesses granted or menc'oned to be granted unto them the aforesaid King and Queen, and to the Heires and Successors of the aforesaid Queen for ever payable, these our Letters Patents, or any thing in the same contained or the aforesaid Letters Patents of the aforesaid Lord and Lady, Philip and Mary, or any thing in them contained shall not anyways extend to charge the aforesaid Mayor, Bayliffs and Burgesses of the Borough aforesaid or their Successors, or the aforesaid Messuages, Lands, Tenements, Houses or other the Premises by the said Letters Patents of the said Lord and Lady, Philip and Mary, above by these presents before granted or menc'oned to be granted, or either of them or any part or parcell thereof, with any payment of any double rent or double tenure, or with the payment of any greater or other Sume of Money, or greater or other Sume of Money than only with the payment of the aforesaid Sume of One hundred and two pounds Sixteen shillings and Seven-pence, by the year in the whole, yielding as well for the rent aforesaid by these our Letters Patents as for the rent aforesaid by the aforesaid Letters Patents of the aforesaid Lord and Lady, Philip and Mary, reserved But that the aforesaid rent of Twelve pounds Sixteen shillings and Four-pence by these our Letters Patents reserved shall be only as parcell of the aforesaid yearly rent of One hundred and Two pounds Sixteen shillings and Seven-pence, by the aforesaid

Letters Patents of the aforesaid Lord and Lady, Philip and Mary, reserved, hereafter yearly payable to us our Heires and Successors out of and for the aforesaid Premises above by these presents before granted or menc'oned to be granted, and that no other Services shall hereafter be due or to be done to us our Heires or Successors by reason or pretence of the aforesaid Letters Patents by the aforesaid King and Queen menc'oned to be granted, or by reason of these our Letters Patents for or in respect of the premises or any part or parcell thereof than the Services which belong to our Mannour of Greenwyche, by fealty only in free and com'on Socage and not in Capite, nor by Knight's Service; and that yearly so often as the aforesaid Mayor, Bayliffs and Burgesses and their Successors shall pay or cause to be paid to us our Heires and Successors the aforesaid Sume of One hundred and Two pounds Sixteen shillings and Seven-pence in the aforesaid Letters Patents of the aforesaid late King and Queen, Philip and Mary, to them and the Heires and Successors of the aforesaid Queen reserved as aforesaid, and to us our Heires and Successors now due and payable, That then and so often the aforesaid Mayor, Bayliffs and Burgesses of the Borough of Abingdon aforesaid shall be from time to time discharged and acquitted of and from the payment of the aforesaid rent or Sume of Twelve pounds Twelve shillings and Four-pence above in these presents to us our Heires and Successors for the premisses above by these presents before granted or menc'oned to be granted, and of every part and parcell thereof reserved And that we, our Heires and Successors, the Mayor, Bayliffs and Burgesses of the Borough of Abingdon aforesaid and their Successors, will thereof discharge and acquitt by these presents, any thing in these presents to the contrary thereof in any wise not-withstanding. **And further,** of our more ample especiall grace, Indemnity against Charges. and of our certain knowledge and meer motion, We will, and by these presents Do grant unto the aforesaid Mayor, Bayliffs and Burgesses and their Successors, That we, our Heires and Successors for ever yearly, and from time to time, will discharge, acquitt and keep indemnifyed as well the aforesaid Mayor, Bayliffs and Burgesses and their Successors as the aforesaid Lands, Tenements, Meadows, Feedings, Pastures and all and singular the Premisses above by these presents before granted or menc'oned to be granted, and every part and parcell thereof, with their and every of their Appurtenances against us our Heires and Successors according to the true intent and meaning of these our Letters Patents, of and from all and all manner of Corrodyes, Rents, Fees, Annuityes, Penc'ons, Porc'ons and Sumes of Money, and charges whatsoever out of the premisses above by these presents before granted or menc'oned to be granted, or out of any part or parcell thereof unto us our Heires or Successors any ways issueing or to be paid, or thereupon towards us our Heires or Successors charged or to be charged, Except the Services, Tenures, Rents, Fines, Forfeitures and other the premisses in these presents to us our Heires or Successors above by these presents excepted and reserved, and except the demises and grants for term of life, lives or years, and the Covenants and Condc'ons in the same, and the covenants and charges which any farmer or farmers of the premisses by reason of any of their Indentures, Leases or Demises is or are bound or obliged to do and discharge. **We willing,** also, and by these presents for us our Heires and Successors firmly enjoining, charging and commanding as well the Treasurer, Chancellour and Barons of our Exchequer aforesaid, our Heires and Successors, as all and singular Auditors and other our Officers and Ministers, our Heires and Successors whatsoever, for the time being, that they and every of them upon the only demonstration of these our Letters Patents or the Inrollment thereof without any other writt or warrant of and from us our Heires or Successors in any wise to be had, obtained or prosecuted, shall doe and make, and from time to time shall cause to be made and done unto the aforesaid Mayor, Bayliffs and Burgesses and their Successors, full, whole, entire and due allowance and manifest discharge of and from all and singular such Corrodyes, Rents, Fees, Annuityes, Penc'ons, Porc'ons and Sumes of Money and charges whatsoever, Except the aforesaid Services, Dues, Sumes of Money and tenures afore reserved as aforesaid, and by the aforesaid Mayor, Bayliffs and Burgesses and their Successors, according to the true intent and meaning of these our Letters Patents, payable, to be done or performed out of the premisses or any of them, unto us our Heires or Successors any ways issueing or to be paid, or thereupon towards us our Heires or Successors charged or to be charged, and these our Letters Patents or the Inrollment of the same shall be yearly and from time to time a sufficient Warrant and Discharge in that behalfe, as well to the said Treasurer, Chancellour and Barons of our Exchequer aforesaid, our Heires and Successors, as to all and singular Receivers, Auditors and other Officers and

Ministers of us our Heires and Successors whatsoever for the time being. **Provided always, nevertheless,** that if the Premises above by these presents before granted or menc'oned to be granted, or any part or parcell thereof was or were heretofore granted unto any person or persons in fee tail, or for any lesser, smaller or more inferiour estate or estates, and that the same Estates in fee tail, or the lesser and more inferiour Estates thereof before the date of these our Letters Patents have been altogether consumed, accomplished, extinguished, expired, ended and determined, and that by reason only thereof the same or any of them before the making of these presents have reverted or devolved unto us or at least ought to revert, remain, descend, revolve, or come back, and Wee, thereupon, have been in possession of the same at the time of the making of these presents or ought to be; That then as to such of the premisses only above by these presents before granted or menc'oned to be granted, whereof such Estate tail, or any less Estate was heretofore granted and is now ended and determined, by reason whereof wee are thereof seized and ought to be seized, These our Letters Patents shall be altogether void and of none effect in the Law, and notwithstanding for the rest and residue shall stand and be good and sufficient in the Law any thing in these presents to the contrary thereof notwithstanding. **And further,** of our more ample especial grace, and of our certain knowledge and meer motion, for the Considerac'ons aforesaid, Wee have covenanted and granted for us our Heires and Successors to and with the aforesaid Mayor, Bayliffs and Burgesses and their Successors, that at the next Parliament or at the next Session of Parliament within this our Realm of England, to be holden, Wee, our Heires or Successors, will give and grant, and well vouchsafe to give and grant our Royall and free assent and consent to any Act, Bill or Petition by the same Mayor, Bayliffs and Burgesses and their Successors, or any of them in the same Parliament or Sessions of Parliament to be exhibited, brought or referred for the better Corfirmac'on, establishment and assurance and secure grant of all and singular the Premisses above by these presents before granted or menc'oned to be granted, and of every parcell thereof unto the aforesaid Mayor, Bayliffs and Burgesses of the Borough aforesaid, and their Successors according to the true intent, meaning and effect of these our Letters Patents, and of our Proclamation in that behalf lately published.

And further, of our more ample especiall grace, and of our certain knowledge and meer motion, Wee will, and by these presents for us our Heires and Successors Wee grant unto the aforesaid Mayor, Bayliffs and Burgesses of the Borough of Abingdon aforesaid and their Successors, That these our Letters Patents or the Inrollment of the same shall be in all things and by all things firm, valid, good, sufficient and effectual in the Law towards and against us our Heires and Successors, as well in all our Courts as elsewhere within our Realm of England, without any Confirmac'ons, Licences or Tolerac'on of us our Heires or Successors hereafter by the aforesaid Mayor, Bayliffs and Burgesses and their Successors to be procured or obtained, notwithstanding the misnaming or misreciting or not naming or not reciting the aforesaid Messuages, Lands, Tenements, Meadows, Feedings, Pastures and other the premisses above by these presents before granted or menc'oned to be granted, or any part or parcell thereof, And notwithstanding the not finding of Office or Offices, Inquisic'on or Inquisic'ons of the premisses above by these presents before granted or menc'oned to be granted, or any part or parcell thereof by which our title ought to be found before the grant of these our Letters Patents, And notwithstanding the misreciting, misnaming or not reciting any Hamlett, Parish, Place or County in which the Premisses or any part or parcell thereof is or are, And notwithstanding any true, full or certain mention is not made of the names of the Tenants, Farmers or Occupyers of the Messuages, Lands, Tenements and Heredits aforesaid, or any of the Premisses, or of any part or parcell thereof, And notwithstanding any mistakes or defects of the certainty or computac'on or of the declaration of the true yearly value of the premisses or any part or parcell thereof, or of the yearly rent reserved out of, in and upon the Premisses, or out of, in and upon any parcell thereof in these our Letters Patents expressed and contained, And notwithstanding the statute made and published in the Parliament of our late Soverign Lord, King Henry the Sixth, late King of England, our Progenitor, in the Eighteenth year of his reign, And notwithstanding any other Defects in naming or in not naming or in misnaming the nature, kinds, sorts, species, quantitys or qualitys of the premisses or any parcell thereof. *We will*, also, and by these presents wee do grant unto the aforesaid Mayor, Bayliffs and Burgesses of the Borough of Abingdon aforesaid, that they may and shall have these our Letters Patents under our

Charter to issue
without fee in
the Hanaper.

Great Seal of England in due manner made and sealed, without fine or fee, great or small, to us in our Hanaper or elsewhere to our use to be therefore any ways yielded, paid, done or made. Because express mention of the true yearly value or of the certainty of the Premisses or any of them, or of other gifts or grants by us or by any of our Progenitors or Predecessors unto the aforesaid Mayor, Bayliffs and Burgesses of the Borough aforesaid, heretofore made, is not made in the premisses or any statute, act, ordinance, provisoe, proclamac'on or restraint to the contrary thereof heretofore had made, published, ordained or provided, or any other thing, cause or matter whatsoever in anywise notwithstanding.

In Witness whereof, we have caused these our Letters to be made Patents.

Witness ourselves at Westminster, the sixteenth Day of February, in the seventh year of our Reign over England, France and Ireland, and over Scotland the Forty third.

THE CHARTER

GRANTED BY ·

JAMES I., 3RD MARCH, A.D. 1609.

𝕵𝖆𝖒𝖊𝖘, by the Grace of God of England, Scotland, France and Ireland, King, Defender of the Faith, &c. 𝕿𝖔 𝖆𝖑𝖑 𝖙𝖔 𝖜𝖍𝖔𝖒 these present Letters shall come, Greeting, 𝖂𝖍𝖊𝖗𝖊𝖆𝖘 our Borough of Abingdon, in our County of Berks, is a very populous Borough and the Chief Town of our County of Berks aforesaid, and the Inhabitants of the same Borough by the name of the Mayor, Bayliffs and Burgesses of the Borough aforesaid, or by other names, divers liberties, Franchises, Customs, Immunities and prehemenences, have, and have used and enjoyed by reason or colour, means or pretence of divers Charters and Letters Patents by divers of our Progenitors or Predecessors, late Kings and Queens of this our Realm of England, heretofore made, granted or confirmed, or by reason, colour, means or pretence of divers prescriptions, usages and Customs in the same Borough of old used and accustomed. 𝕬𝖓𝖉 𝖜𝖍𝖊𝖗𝖊𝖆𝖘 our well beloved and trusty Counseller, William Lord Knollis and our well beloved and trusty Counseller, John Parry, Knight, Chaunceller of our Duchy of Lancaster, and our beloved David Williams, Knight, one of our Justices of our Court of Common Pleas, and also our beloved Subjects the Mayor, Bayliffs and Burgesses of the aforesaid Borough of Abingdon, most humbly besought us that for the better rule, governance, improvement and bettering of the same Borough, we would graciously shew and extend our Royal grace and Munificence and that we would grant, confirm and ratify to the said Mayor, Bayliffs and Burgesses of the Borough aforesaid and their Successors, the Liberties, Franchises, Customs, Immunities and preheminences heretofore by them or their Predecessors by Colour and pretence of any Charters and Letters Patents by any of our Progenitors or Predecessors late Kings and Queens of this Realm of England, heretofore made, granted or confirmed, or by reason, colour or pretence of any prescriptions, usages or Customs in the same Borough used, had or enjoyed And also that we would vouchsafe to grant to the same Mayor, Bayliffs and Burgesses, some other new liberties, Jurisdictions as to such it shall seem meet. We therefore, willing that from henceforth for ever in the same Borough continually there be had one certain and undoubted manner and way of and for the keeping of our Peace and for the Rule and Governance of the same Borough and our People there inhabiting and others thereto resorting And that the Borough aforesaid from henceforth for ever be and remain a Borough of the Peace, and quiet to the fear, dread and terror of evil delinquents, and to the reward of good Men, and hoping that if by our grant they may enjoy more ample and larger honours, liberties and privileges, then they will think themselves more specially and strongly obliged to employ and shew their Services hereafter to the utmost of their power to us our Heirs and Successors Of our more especial grace and of our certain knowledge and meer motion we will and grant, and by these presents for us our Heirs and Successors we do grant to the aforesaid Mayor, Bayliffs and Burgesses of the Borough aforesaid and their Successors, that they and their Successors from henceforth for ever may and shall have, in the Borough aforesaid, one discreet Man, learned in the Laws of England, in the form lower in these presents mentioned, to be elected and chosen, who shall be and shall be called, the Recorder of the Borough aforesaid, and for the better executing our will and grant in this behalf we have assigned, nominated, constituted and made, and by these presents for us our Heirs and Successors We do assign, nominate, constitute and make our beloved Walter Dayrell, Esquire, learned in the Laws of England, to be the first and for the time that now is Recorder of the Borough aforesaid, to continue in the same Office during the good pleasure of the Mayor and principal Burgesses of the Borough aforesaid for the time being, or the greater part of them, (of which the Mayor for the time being we will to be one) and that from time to time and at all times after the death or removal of the aforesaid Walter Dayrell, the Mayor and principal Burgesses of the Borough aforesaid for the time being or the greater part of them (of which the Mayor of the same Borough for the time being we will to be one) shall and may have power and be able to nominate, elect and chuse one other discreet Man, and learned in the

Margin notes:

Borough to be a Borough of the Peace.

With a Recorder.

First Recorder.

Election of Recorder.

H

Laws of England, to be Recorder of the Borough aforesaid. And

that the aforesaid Walter Dayrell and every other who so as aforesaid
from time to time shall be elected, chosen, preferred and nominated
to be Recorder of the Borough aforesaid before he or they shall be
admitted to execute the same Office, shall take a Corporal Oath before
the Mayor of the Borough aforesaid for the time being, to do and
execute all and singular the matters and things which to the Office
of Recorder of the Borough aforesaid do belong, and that after such
Oath so as aforesaid taken, he and they shall have and execute the
same Office of Recorder of the Borough aforesaid during the good
pleasure of the Mayor and principal Burgesses of the Borough
aforesaid for the time being or the greater part of them (of which
the Mayor for the time being we will to be one), and so as often as
the case shall happen. **And further**, we will, and by these

presents for us our Heirs and Successors We do grant to the aforesaid
Mayor, Bayliffs and Burgesses of the Borough aforesaid and their
Successors, that the aforesaid William Lord Knollis, Thomas Parry,
Knight, and David Williams, Knight, during their natural lives, and
also the Mayor of the Borough aforesaid now being, and every Mayor
of the Borough aforesaid hereafter for the time being, for one year
next following after that he hath quitted and gone out of the Office
of Mayoralty, and the Recorder of the Borough aforesaid for the
time being, at all times hereafter be and shall be the Justices of us
our Heirs and Successors, and every one of them shall be our
Justice our Heirs and Successors, within the Borough aforesaid and
the Liberties and Precincts of the same, and to keep and cause to be
kept all Ordinances and Statutes made and published for the good of
our Peace, and for the preservation and maintenance of the same,
and for the quiet Rule and Governance of our People and of our
Heirs and Successors in all their Articles in the Borough aforesaid,
according to the meaning, form and effect of the same, and to punish
all offending against the form of those Ordinances or Statutes or
either of them in the Borough aforesaid, as according to the form and
Ordinance of those Statutes shall be to be done And all those who
shall threaten any of our People, our Heirs and Successors, of and
concerning their Bodies or of the burning of their Houses, to find
sufficient Security of the Peace for their good behaviour towards us
our Heirs and Successors, and our People, our Heirs and Successors,
and if they shall refuse to find such Security then to cause them to

be kept safe in our Prison, our Heirs and Successors, until they shall find such Security, and that the said William Lord Knollys, Thomas Parry, Knight, and David Williams, Knight, during their natural lives, and the Mayor of the Borough aforesaid for the time being, and also the last Predecessor of every Mayor during one whole year next following after that he hath quitted and gone out of the Office of Mayoralty And also the Recorder of the Borough aforesaid, for the time being, or any two or more of them (of which the Mayor and Recorder of the Borough aforesaid we will to be two) be our Justices and our Heirs and Successors to enquire by the Oath of good Men and true of the Borough aforesaid, by whom the truth of the matter may be better known, of all and all manner of Felonies, Witchcrafts, Inchantments, Sorceries, Arts, Magic, Trespasses, Forestallings, Regratings, Ingrossings and Extortions whatsoever, and of all and singular other Misdemeanours and offences whatsoever of which our Justices, our Heirs or Successors may lawfully or ought to enquire into by whomsoever and howsoever within the Borough aforesaid, the Liberties or precincts of the same, heretofore done or committed, or which hereafter shall chance or happen there to be done, committed or attempted, and also of all those who in the Borough aforesaid either walk or ride, or shall hereafter presume to walk or ride with armed force in riotous Meetings and Assemblies against our Peace, our Heirs and Successors, to the disturbance of our People, our Heirs or Successors. And also of all those who have laid in wait, or shall hereafter presume to lay in wait, to mayhem or kill our People, our Heirs or Successors And also of Hosts and Hostelers and all and singular other persons who in abuse of Weights and Measures or in selling of Victuals against the form of the Ordinances or Statutes or either of them thereupon for the Common Profit of our Realm of England and our people our Heirs and Successors thereof made and published, have offended or attempted, or shall hereafter presume to offend or attempt in the Borough aforesaid, and also of all Constables, Goalers and other Officers who in the execution of their Offices concerning the premises or any of them have misbehaved themselves, or shall hereafter presume to misbehave themselves, or have been or shall hereafter chaunce or happen to be slack, remiss or negligent in the Borough aforesaid, and of all and singular Articles and Circumstances and other things whatsoever by whomsoever and howsoever within the Borough aforesaid or the Liberties or Precincts

thereof done or committed, or which hereafter shall there happen to
be done, committed or attempted howsoever, concerning the premises
or any of them, and the Indictments whatsoever heretofore before
the Mayor of the Borough aforesaid taken, or which before the
aforesaid William Lord Knollis, Thomas Parry, Knight, and David
Williams, Knight, and the Mayor of the Borough aforesaid for the
time being, and every one that was Mayor of the Borough aforesaid
within one year next following after that he hath quitted or gone out
of his Office of Mayoralty, and the Recorder of the Borough aforesaid
for the time being, or any two or more of them (of which the Mayor
and Recorder of the Borough aforesaid we will to be two) shall
hereafter chance or happen to be taken to inspect and consider and
to continue processes thereupon against all and singular the persons
so indicted, or which hereafter shall happen to be so indicted, until
they are taken, render themselves or are outlawed, and to hear and
determine all and singular the Felonies, Witchcrafts, Inchantments,
Sorceries, Arts, Magic, Trespasses, Forestallings, Regratings,
Ingrossings, Extortions, Riotous Meetings and Assemblies, and
Indictments aforesaid, and all and singular other the premises,
according to the Laws and Statutes of our Realm of England, as in
such and the like case hath been accustomed or ought to have been
done, and to correct and punish the same Offenders and every of
them for their Offences by Fines, Ransoms, Amerciaments, Forfeitures
and other ways, as according to the Law and Custom of our Realm
of England, or the Form of the Ordinances or Statutes aforesaid, hath
been used and accustomed to be done, so nevertheless that they do
not proceed to the determination of any Treason Felony or other
Offence whatsoever touching the loss of life or members within the
Borough aforesaid, the liberties and Precincts thereof, without our

Justices to take
Oaths.

Special Licence, our Heirs or Successors And that the aforesaid
William Lord Knollis, Thomas Parry, Knight, and David Williams,
Knight, and every Mayor of the Borough aforesaid, for one whole
year following after that he hath quitted or gone out of his Office of
Mayoralty And also the Recorder of the Borough aforesaid for the
time being, and every of them, shall take a Corporal Oath before the
Mayor of the Borough aforesaid for the time being, the Office of
Justice of Peace rightly and faithfully to execute, and the Oaths in
that behalf by the Laws and Statutes of this our Realm of England
provided by the Justices of Peace required to be taken, and that the

Mayor of the Borough aforesaid for the time being, shall and may have, power, Licence and Authority to give and administer such Oath as is aforesaid, as well to such aforesaid Recorder as to such Justice of Peace, by virtue of these Presents without any Warrant or Commission of us our Heirs or Successors to be had, obtained or prosecuted. **And further,** we will, and by these Presents for us our Heirs and Successors as much as in us lyes, We do grant unto the aforesaid Mayor, Bayliffs and Burgesses of the Borough aforesaid and their Successors, that the Mayor of the Borough aforesaid, for the time being, and his Successors, so long as he shall happen to be in the Office of Mayor of the same Borough, and also the Bayliffs of the same Borough for the time being and their Successors so long as they shall happen to be in the Office of Bayliffs of the same Borough, and also the principal Burgesses of the same Borough for the time being not being above the number of twelve, so long as they shall happen to be in the Office of principal Burgesses of the same Borough, shall not be put or impannelled to appear before our Justices, our Heirs or Successors, at Assizes and Nisi prius, within the County of Berks, to be taken without the liberties and Precincts of the same Borough, in any Juries, Assizes, Recognizances or Inquisitions whatsoever, neither shall they or any of them in any manner forfeit any Issues or Amerciaments on that account to us our Heirs or Successors, unless they or either of them have Lands and Tenements without the Borough aforesaid, the Limits and Precincts thereof for which he or they ought to be charged, but they and every of them be and shall be therefore quit and discharged from time to time for ever.

Mayor, Bailiffs and Twelve Principal Burgesses exempt from serving on Juries without the Borough.

And further, we will, and by these presents for us our Heirs and Successors, we do grant unto the aforesaid Mayor, Bayliffs and Burgesses of the Borough aforesaid and their Successors, that they and their Successors henceforth for ever shall and may have, hold and keep within the Borough aforesaid a Court of Record before the Mayor of the same Borough for the time being, or his sufficient Deputy, in the Common Hall within the Borough aforesaid, or in some other more convenient place within the same Borough, every Tuesday Weekly (Except in the Weeks of Whitsuntide, Christmas and Easter), of all and all manner of Pleas, Plaints and Actions, personal or mixed, and of Debts, Accounts, Trespasses, Covenants, Contracts, Detinues, Detainings, Withholdings, Contempts and

Grant of a Court of Record to be held before the Mayor.

Offences, within the said Borough of Abingdon, and the suburbs, Liberties and Precincts thereof, moved, had, committed or arising, or to arise, so as they do not exceed the Sum of Ten pounds in one entire Sum.   And that the same Mayor and his Successors on such and the like Pleas, Plaints, Complaints and Actions, may and shall have Power, Authority, Liberty and Licence, the Persons, Defendants against whom such and the like Pleas, Plaints or Actions in the aforesaid Court shall happen to be levied or moved, to bring to Pleas by such and the like taking and arresting of the Bodies, Summonses, Attachments and Distresses according to the Custom in the same Borough used, to the Serjeants at Mace of the said Borough for the time being, or either of them, to be directed.   And that all and singular such and the like Pleas, Plaints and Actions shall be severally heard and determined, and shall be derayned, deduced, drawn, brought and ended by such and the like Processes, Considerations, Judgments and executions of Judgments, by which such and the like Pleas have been used and accustomed to have been brought and determined in the same Borough, and the Executions of those Processes and Judgments by the aforesaid Serjeants at Mace, or either of them, shall be done, made and had, according to the Law and Custom of this our Realm of England, and according to the liberties, privileges and Customs of the said Borough of Abingdon.   And that the said Mayor of the said Borough of Abingdon and his Successors for the time being, shall and may, from time to time, have, take and levy to the use and profit of the Commonalty of the same Borough, all and all manner of Fines, Amerciaments, Forfeitures and other Profits whatsoever, out of and in the Court aforesaid lawfully issuing, arising, happening, chancing or befalling, as in the same Borough heretofore was used and accustomed, and that without any Account or any other thing for that cause to us our Heirs or Successors in anywise to be yielded, paid, done or made.

Grant of Two Annual Fairs.

And further, we will, and by these presents for us our Heirs and Successors, we do grant unto the aforesaid Mayor, Bayliffs and Burgesses of the Borough aforesaid and their Successors, that they and their Successors shall and may, and shall and may be able and have power to have, keep, hold and enjoy, within the Borough aforesaid and the Precincts and Liberties thereof, every year for ever, two Fairs or Marts, one of the same Fairs or Marts on the

Feast of St. Mark the Evangelist, and on the Eve and the Morrow of the same Feast, and the other on the Feast of St. James the Apostle, and on the Eve and the Morrow of the same Feast, there, every year for ever, to be held and kept and continued during all those days every year for ever, together with a Court of Pye powder there in the time of the same Fairs or Marts to be held, and with all Liberties and free Customs, Tolls, Stallage, Pickage, Fines, Amerciaments and all other Profits, Commodities, Advantages and Emoluments whatsoever to such Fairs and Marts, and Court of Pye powder belonging, happening, chancing, arising or issuing, so nevertheless that the aforesaid Fairs or Marts, or either of them be not to the damage or nuisance of other Neighbouring Fairs or Marts near adjacent.

With a Court of Pye Powder.

And further, we will, and by these Presents for us our Heirs and Successors, we do grant unto the aforesaid Mayor, Bayliffs and Burgesses of the Borough aforesaid and their Successors, that they and their Successors shall and may, and shall and may be able and have power to have, hold and keep within the Borough aforesaid, one Market every Friday, in every Week throughout the year for ever, to be holden and kept, and that all and singular the Persons to the same Market coming and resorting shall and may from henceforth for ever, sell and buy and expose to sale as well Corn, Grain, as Victuals as other things whatsoever, according to the Laws, Customs and Statutes of our Realm of England.

And of a Market every Friday for Corn, Grain, Victuals, &c.

And further, as well for the better Relief, support and maintenance of the poor and infirm Inhabitants dwelling within the aforesaid Borough of Abingdon as for the public benefit and profit of the same Borough, of our especial grace, certain knowledge and mere motion, we will, and by these presents for us our Heirs and Successors we do grant unto the aforesaid Mayor, Bayliffs and Burgesses of the Borough aforesaid and their Successors for ever, that they and their Successors shall and may have, hold and keep, and shall and may be able and have power to have, hold and keep for ever a Wool Market in the said Borough of Abingdon, for the selling and buying of Woollen Thread and Yarn every Week, yearly, and every year on Mondays, to be holden and kept in manner and form in these presents before expressed and specified, together with all Profits, Commodities, Emoluments and free Customs to such Wool Markets happening, arising, befalling, belonging or appertaining,

And of a Wool Market every Monday.

unless the same Market be to the nuisance of the Neighbouring Markets or either of them (to wit), that it shall and may be lawful as well to the aforesaid Mayor, Bayliffs and Burgesses of the Borough aforesaid, and to their Successors, as to every Freeman inhabiting in the Borough aforesaid for the time being, from time to time, at their will and pleasure, to buy at any Market within the said Borough of Abingdon at all times hereafter perpetually to be holden, any Sheeps Wools, Woollen Thread and Yarn, brought and to be brought into the said Borough of Abingdon on the days and times appointed and determined on, and in which the same Market shall be holden and kept, and so much of the same Sheeps Wools, Woollen threads and Yarn so bought, and to be bought, as is sufficient from time to time, and at all times hereafter the Men, Women, Boys and Girls in the same Borough from time to time dwelling, and to put and commit to the Working thereof as it shall seem best to the same Mayor, Bayliffs and Burgesses of the Borough aforesaid and to their Successors, and to every Freeman being a subject of us our Heirs and Successors, and being an Inhabitant of the Borough aforesaid, from time to time, who shall buy the same Wools, Woollen Threads and Yarn, or either of them so as aforesaid within any such Wool Market, within the Borough aforesaid, at any time hereafter by virtue of these Patents to be holden, to cause to be wrought or employed, or by Labour and Industry to be converted to any use within the said Borough of Abingdon, to-make and erect a Stock thereof, as well the poor Inhabitants of the said Borough for the time being to exercise and employ in, with and by their Manual Labour, and to avoid Sloth and Idleness (the beginning and cause of all evils especially amongst the poor Inhabitants of the same Borough), as to relieve the poor Inhabitants of the same Borough with their Industry and honest labour of their hands. And because Wools, Woollen Threads and Yarns so as aforesaid into the Borough aforesaid, from time to time, on the days on which the aforesaid Wool Market shall be holden, brought and to be brought, may increase to a greater quantity than will be necessary and convenient, the poor aforesaid within the Borough aforesaid to set to working thereof We will and by these Presents of our more abundant especial grace, and of our certain knowledge and mere motion, We do grant to the aforesaid Mayor, Bayliffs and Burgesses of the Borough aforesaid and their Successors, that it shall and may be lawful to and for the aforesaid Mayor,

Bayliffs and Burgesses of the Borough aforesaid and their Successors, and every Freeman being a Subject of us our Heirs or Successors, being an Inhabitant within the Borough aforesaid, the rest and residue of the same Wools, Woollen Threads and Yarns from time to time bought or to be bought within the Borough aforesaid at their will and pleasure to sell within any City, Town or Borough within this our Realm of England, so as the aforesaid Wools, Woollen Threads and Yarns so as aforesaid to be sold without the Borough aforesaid do not exceed in the whole, in any one year, above or beyond one thousand Tods of Wool, Woollen Threads and Yarn, the statute of the fifth year of our late Sovereign Lord Edward the sixth, late King of England, made and ordained, concerning the limitation of the times of buying and selling of Wools, or any other statute, act, ordinance, prescription, custom, usage or any other thing, cause or matter whatsoever to the contrary thereof in anywise notwithstanding. **And moreover**, we will, and by these presents for us our Heirs and Successors we do command that all and singular Tolls, Stallages, Pickages, Fines and Amerciaments, and all and singular Profits, Commodities, free Customs and Emoluments whatsoever, coming, issuing, arising, happening or chancing, belonging or appertaining to the said Market, and the Profits, Commodities and Emoluments from time to time coming, issuing, arising, happening or chancing for the selling of the aforesaid residue of the Wool, Woollen Thread and Yarn, without the Borough aforesaid, so as aforesaid every year to be sold, shall be taken, disposed and converted, as well to discharge, maintain and support the public Charges and Expences of the same Borough, and for the public good and the common utility and profit of the same Borough as for and towards the relief, support and maintenance of the poor and infirm Men and Women, Boys and Girls within the said Borough inhabiting and from time to time dwelling and abiding. **And also**, we will, and by these presents for us our Heirs and Successors we do grant unto the aforesaid Mayor, Bayliffs and Burgesses of the Borough aforesaid and their Successors, that they and their Successors shall have, use and enjoy, and may and shall be able and have power to have, use and enjoy, in, for and about the weighing of Thread and Wool in the aforesaid Market, to be sold and weighed, such and the like weights that are used and have been used in, for and about the weighing of Thread and Wool in the Market or Fair held

Tolls, &c., to be to discharge the Public Expenses of the Borough, and for relief of Poor.

Grant of Weights as in Borough of New Woodstock.

I

within the Borough of New Woodstock, in our County of Oxon.
And further, of our more ample and abundant especial grace,
and of our certain knowledge and mere motion we will, and by these
presents for us our Heirs and Successors we do give, grant, confirm,
ratify and approve to the aforesaid Mayor, Bayliffs and Burgesses of
the Borough aforesaid and their Successors, all and all manner the
Messuages, Mills, Lands, Tenements, Fields, Meadows, Pastures,
Commons and so many, so great, such the same and the like Liberties,
Franchises, Immuniments, Exemptions, Privileges, Discharges,
Jurisdictions, Wastes, Void Places, Soils, Commodities, Profits,
Emoluments and Hereditaments whatsoever as and which by Letters
Patents of our late Sovereign Lord and Lady, Philip and Mary, late
King and Queen of England, our Progenitors, to the same Mayor,
Bayliffs and Burgesses made, bearing date at Westminster, the
twenty fourth day of November, in the third and fourth years of
their Reigns, or by Letters Patents of our late Sovereign Lady
Elizabeth, late Queen of England, to the same Mayor, Bayliffs and
Burgesses made, bearing date at Westminster, the nineteenth day of
March, in the seventh year of her Reign, granted or mentioned to be
granted, or which the Mayor, Bayliffs and Burgesses of the Borough
aforesaid or their Predecessors, by whatsoever name or names, or by
whatsoever Incorporation, or by pretence, color or means of whatsoever name or Incorporation, have heretofore had, held, used, enjoyed
or occupied, or ought to have held, used or enjoyed, or do now have,
hold, use and enjoy or occupy to them and their Successors, by
reason, pretence, color or means of any of the aforesaid Letters
Patents of the aforesaid Lord and Lady, Philip and Mary, and the
aforesaid Lady, Elizabeth, or any Charters, Grants or Letters Patents
by any of our Progenitors or Predecessors, late Kings or Queens of
England, in any manner heretofore made, granted or confirmed, or
by whatsoever other lawful means, manner, right or Title, Custom,
usage or prescription heretofore lawfully used, had or accustomed,
although the same or either of them have been lost or forfeited, or
although the same or either of them have been misused or disused,
abused or discontinued **To have, hold, and enjoy**, to the
aforesaid Mayor, Bayliffs and Burgesses of the Borough aforesaid and
their Successors for ever, and yielding and paying therefore yearly
to us our Heirs and Successors, so many, so great, such like and the
same Fee Farm Rents, Services, Sums of Money and Demands

whatsoever as and which have been accustomed heretofore to be yielded and paid, or ought to be yielded and paid, unto us for the same. *Wherefore*, we will, and by these presents for us our Heirs and Successors firmly enjoyning we command that the aforesaid Mayor, Bayliffs and Burgesses of the Borough aforesaid and their Successors shall have, hold, use and enjoy, and shall and may be able and have power to have, hold, use and enjoy for ever, all the Liberties, Authorities, Jurisdictions, Franchises, Exemptions, Immunities, and Discharges aforesaid, according to the tenor and effect of these our Letters Patents, and the aforesaid other Letters Patents in these Presents above mentioned, without the occasion, let, hindrance or impediment of us our Heirs or Successors, the Justices, Sheriffs, Escheators or other Bayliffs, Officers or Ministers whatsoever of us our Heirs or Successors, we being unwilling that the same Mayor, Bayliffs and Burgesses of the Borough aforesaid or any or either of them, by reason of the Premises or either of them, by us or by our Heirs or Successors, our Justices, Sheriffs or other our Bayliffs or Ministers whatsoever our Heirs or Successors, shall be therefore molested, aggrieved or anywise distressed or troubled We willing, and by these Presents charging and commanding as well the Treasurer, Chancellor and Barons of our Exchequer at Westminster, and other our Justices, our Heirs and Successors, as our Attorney and Solicitor General for the time being and every of them, and all other Officers and Ministers of us our Heirs and Successors whatsoever, that neither they nor either or any of them shall prosecute or continue, or cause to be prosecuted or continued, any Writ or Summons of Quo Warranto or any other our Writ or Writs or Processes whatsoever against the aforesaid Mayor, Bayliffs and Burgesses of the Borough aforesaid, or any or either of them, for any Causes, Matters, Things or Offences, claim or usurpation, or either of them duly claimed, used, attempted, had or usurped, before the day of the making of these Presents We willing, also, that the Mayor, Bayliffs and Burgesses of the Borough aforesaid, or any or either of them, shall not be molested, disturbed or hindered by any or either the Justices, Officers or Ministers aforesaid, in or for the due use, claim or usurpation of any other Liberties, Franchises or Jurisdictions within the Borough aforesaid, the Liberties, Limits and Precincts thereof, before the making of these our Letters Patents, or shall be forced to make Answer unto them or either or any of them.

Because that express mention is not made in these Presents of the true yearly value of, or any other value or certainty of the premises or either of them, or of any Gifts or Grants heretofore made by us or by any of our Predecessors or Progenitors to the aforesaid Mayor, Bayliffs and Burgesses of the Borough of Abingdon aforesaid, any Statute, Act, Ordinance, Proviso, Proclamation or restraint to the contrary thereof heretofore had, made, enacted, ordained or provided, or any other thing, cause or matter whatsoever in anywise notwithstanding.

In Witness whereof, we have caused these our Letters to be made Patents.

Witness ourself at Westminster, the third Day of March, in the year of our Reign over England and France and Ireland, the seventh, and over Scotland the Forty third.

THE CHARTER

GRANTED BY

JAMES I., 21st JUNE, A.D. 1620.

𝕵𝖆𝖒𝖊𝖘, by the Grace of God, of England, Scotland, France, and Ireland, King, Defender of the Faith, &c., 𝕿𝖔 𝖆𝖑𝖑 𝖎𝖔 𝖜𝖍𝖔𝖒 these present Letters Patents shall come, Greeting, 𝖂𝖍𝖊𝖗𝖊𝖆𝖘 our late Sovereign Lord and Lady, Philip and Mary, late King and Queen of England, by their Letters Patents, made bearing date at Westminster, in the County of Middlesex, the twenty fourth day of November, in the third and fourth years of their reigns, for the Considerations in the same Letters Patents expressed, for themselves, the Heirs and Successors of the aforesaid Queen did grant unto the Mayor, Bayliffs and Burgesses of the Borough of Abingdon, in the County of Berks, and their Successors, amongst other things, that from henceforth for ever they shall have and hold, and shall be able and have power to have and hold, One Market every Monday, in every Week, in the said Borough of Abingdon, by and through that whole day, to be holden from year to year, every year for ever, together with Stallage, Piecage, Toll and all other Profits, Commodities and Emoluments whatsoever to such Market belonging, appertaining and happening, and out of the same Market coming, issuing, arising or chancing, and with all other Libertys and free Customs unto the same Lord and Lady, Philip and Mary, to the same Market belonging and appertaining, to the use and behoofe and utility of the Commonalty of the same Borough, for the time being, to be taken and converted as by the Letters Patents aforesaid more fully it is manifest and doth appear. 𝕬𝖓𝖉 𝖜𝖍𝖊𝖗𝖊𝖆𝖘, also, we by our Letters Patents under our Great Seal of England sealed, bearing date at Westminster, the third day of March, in the year of our Reign over England, France and Ireland the seventh, and over Scotland the forty third, All the Liberties, Privileges and Franchises

[marginal note:] Recital of Grant of Markets under Charter of Philip and Mary.

[marginal note:] And under prior Charter of James I.

aforesaid amongst other things unto the same Mayor, Bayliffs and Burgesses of the Borough aforesaid and their Successors, have ratified and confirmed, although the same or any or either were forfeited or lost, and although the same or either of them were misused or disused, abused or discontinued.

And moreover, whereas, we by the same our Letters Patents have granted unto the aforesaid Mayor, Bayliffs and Burgesses of the Borough aforesaid and their Successors amongst other things, that they and their Successors shall have, hold and keep, and shall be able and have power to have, hold and keep, within the Borough aforesaid, one Market every Friday in every Week through the year, to be holden and kept, and that all and singular Persons to that Market coming or resorting shall have power and be able from henceforth for ever to buy and sell, and expose to Sale, as well Corn as Victuals, as other things whatsoever **And further,** by the same Letters Patents, We have granted to the same Mayor, Bayliffs and Burgesses and their Successors, that they and their Successors shall have, hold and keep, and shall be able and have power to have, hold and keep for ever a Wooll Market, in the said Borough of Abingdon, for the selling and buying of Wooll, Woollen Thread and Yarn, every Week, yearly, and every year on Mondays, to be holden and kept in manner and form in the said Letters Patents expressed and specified, together with all Profits, Commodities, Emoluments and free Customs to the said Wooll Market chancing, arising, happening, belonging and appertaining, unless the said Market should be to the nuisance of the Neighbouring Markets or either of them, as by the same our Letters Patents more fully it appeareth.

Know yee, We therefore willing and intending that the aforesaid Mayor, Bayliffs and Burgesses of the Borough aforesaid and their Successors for ever, shall quietly and peaceably have and hold, and shall be able and have power to have and hold the aforesaid Markets, Stallage, Piecage, Toll and other Commodities, Profits and Commodities above mentioned **And further,** willing unto the same Mayor, Bayliffs and Burgesses of the Borough aforesaid, that now are, to show and perform further and more lasting favor, by these our Letters Patents, of our Special Grace and of our certain knowledge and meer motion by these Patents have ratified, approved and confirmed unto the same Mayor, Bayliffs and Burgesses and their

Successors, the aforesaid Markets, Stallage, Piecage, Toll and all
other Profits, Commodities and Emoluments whatsoever, to the same
Markets belonging, appertaining or happening, or out of the same
Markets coming, issuing, arising or chancing. 𝕬𝖓𝖉 𝖆𝖑𝖘𝖔 for the
better security and assurance of the Premises unto the aforesaid
Mayor, Bayliffs and Burgesses of the Borough and their Successors,
𝖂𝖊 𝖌𝖎𝖛𝖊 and by these Presents grant to the same Mayor, Bayliffs
and Burgesses of the Borough aforesaid, The aforesaid Markets,
Stallage, Piecage, Toll and all other Profits, Commodities and
Emoluments whatsoever aforesaid 𝕬𝖓𝖉 𝖋𝖚𝖗𝖙𝖍𝖊𝖗, that the same
Mayor, Bayliffs and Burgesses of the Borough aforesaid and their
Successors for ever, shall have and hold, and shall be able and have
Power to have and hold, the aforesaid Market, every Monday in
every Week, every year in the same Borough, by that whole day to
be holden, And the aforesaid other Market, every Friday in every
Week, every year in the same Borough to be holden, And all
Commodities to the same Markets or either of them belonging or
appertaining, To the use, behoofe and utility of the Commonalty of
the same Borough for the time being, to be taken and converted, as
by the aforesaid several Letters Patents are severally granted or
mentioned to be granted, And also the aforesaid Wooll Market for
the buying and selling of Wool, Woollen Thread and Yarn, every
Week in the Borough aforesaid, yearly on Mondays, to be holden
and kept, with all Profits, Commodities and free Customs to the
aforesaid Wooll Market happening, arising, belonging or appertaining.
𝕬𝖓𝖉 𝖋𝖚𝖗𝖙𝖍𝖊𝖗, of our more abundant grace, certain knowledge   Grant of Tolls
and mere motion, by these Presents we give, grant and confirm unto   of Grain, Corn
the Mayor, Bayliffs and Burgesses of the Borough aforesaid and their   and Malt.
Successors, that the same Mayor, Bayliffs and Burgesses of the
Borough aforesaid and their Successors from henceforth for ever
hereafter, from time to time, shall have and take by themselves, their
Ministers or Servants, as well upon the aforesaid days of the Markets
aforesaid, and either of them, as upon every other day in the Week
yearly, of all kind and sort of Grain, Corn and Malt, which from time
to time shall be sold or exposed to sale within the Borough aforesaid,
or which shall be brought into the Borough aforesaid to be sold
within the Borough aforesaid, of every person so selling or exposing
to sale, or bringing to be sold, any Grain, Corn or Malt, the Toll
following (to wit): for every quarter of the same Grain, Corn and

Malt so as aforesaid sold or exposed to sale, or brought unto the Borough aforesaid to be sold within the same Borough as aforesaid, one measure called a quart, and so according to that Rate for a greater or lesser quantity.   And also that the aforesaid Mayor, Bayliffs and Burgesses of the Borough aforesaid and their Successors from henceforth for ever, shall have, enjoy and take out of the Market aforesaid Piccage, Sums of Money for the shewing of the Wares called Shew Money, Stallage, Tollage, Toll, Custom, Profits, Rights and Jurisdictions of whatsoever kind or sort, unto any of the Markets in anywise belonging or appertaining, or in the same Markets or either of them in anywise lawfully received, had or used, although they are not above particularly or by certain names declared or named in these Letters Patents or in the aforesaid Letters Patents of King Philip and Queen Mary, or in our aforesaid Letters Patents, and that from time to time, it shall be lawful to and for the same Mayor, Bayliffs and Burgesses and their Successors, by virtue of our Grant in these our Letters Patents contained, to take and receive to the use and utility of the Commonalty of the same Borough to the same Markets, All reasonable Sums of Money as they or their Predecessors have heretofore had or taken, or might have had or taken, or as in any other Markets by virtue of any Letters Patents, usage, Prescription or other lawful means whatsoever are due, taken, received or payable, or have been used or ought to be had, used, taken or received.

And also of our more abundant especial grace, certain knowledge and mere motion, for us our Heirs and Successors, by these Presents **We do grant** unto the same Mayor, Bayliffs and Burgesses of the Borough aforesaid and their Successors, for aid, help and assistance to pave the Borough aforesaid, and to repair and mend the Bridges and Ways of the Borough aforesaid, that they by themselves, their Ministers or Servants may from henceforth for ever, from time to time, have and take out of the Wares and things brought or carried, or to be brought or carried unto or through the Borough of Abingdon aforesaid, or in the Markets aforesaid or Fairs in the same Borough to be holden, or otherwise in the Week to be sold, these Sums of Money and Customs under written (to wit): of every Hogshead of Wine, Oil or Vinegar, one penny; of every Cart loaded with Combustible Wood, Iron, Coals of both sorts, wrought Stones or other such like Things to be sold, or Wares, one penny; and

(marginal note:) And of Tolls of other Wares.

of every greater or lesser quantity according to that Rate; and of every Weigh of Cheese, Butter and Salt and other Wares, one penny, and according to that rate for every greater or lesser weight; of every Broad Cloth one penny; and of every Kersey one halfpenny, and so according to that rate; and of every hundred of Sea Fish brought or carried unto or through the Borough of Abingdon aforesaid to be sold one penny, and so according to that rate for every greater or lesser quantity; of every Ox, Bull, Cow, Heifer, Horse, Mare, Colt and Beast to be sold, one penny; of six Sheep to be sold one penny, and so according to that rate for any greater or lesser number; of every Calf and Hog to be sold one halfpenny; of every Trussell, Stall or parcel of Ware, of the value of Twenty Shillings or more, one penny; and of every Merchandize and thing to be sold not here specified exceeding the value of five shillings, one halfpenny. **To have, hold and enjoy** the aforesaid Marketts, Toll and other the Premises with the appurtenances, unto the aforesaid Mayor, Bayliffs and Burgesses of the Borough aforesaid and their Successors for ever, **And yielding and paying** therefore yearly unto us our Heirs and Successors, so many, so great, such like and the same Fee Farm Rents, Services, Sums of Money, and Demands whatsoever as and which have heretofore been accustomed to be yielded and paid, or ought to be yielded to us for the same. **Wherefore**, we will, and by these Presents for us our Heirs and Successors, we firmly charge and command that the aforesaid Mayor, Bayliffs and Burgesses of the Borough aforesaid and their Successors shall have, hold, use and enjoy, and shall be able and have power to have, hold, use and enjoy all the aforesaid Markets, Tolls, Piecage, Stallage and other the Premises above granted or mentioned to be granted, according to the tenour and effect of these our Letters Patents, and the aforesaid other Letters Patents above in these Presents mentioned, without occasion, let, hindrance or impediment of us our Heirs or Successors, or of the Justices, Sheriffs, Escheators or other Bayliffs, Officers or Ministers of us our Heirs or Successors whatsoever, we being unwilling that the same Mayor, Bayliffs and Burgesses of the Borough aforesaid, or any or either of them, by reason of the Premises or either of them shall be therefore molested, grieved or troubled, or in anywise disturbed by us or by our Heirs or Successors, the Justices, Sheriffs or other Bayliffs or Ministers of us our Heirs or Successors whatsoever.

J

We willing, and by these Presents charging and commanding as well the Treasurer, Chancellour and Barons of our Exchequer, at Westminster, and other the Justices of us our Heirs or Successors, as our Attorney and Solicitor General for the time being, and every of them, and all other Officers and Ministers of us our Heirs and Successors whatsoever, that neither they nor any or either of them shall prosecute or continue or cause to be prosecuted and continued any Writ or Summons of Quo Warranto or any other our Writ or Writs or Process whatsoever against the aforesaid Mayor, Bayliffs and Burgesses of the Borough aforesaid, or any or either of them for any Causes, Things, Matters, Offences, Claim or Usurpation, or any of them duly claimed, used, attempted, had or usurped, before the day of the making of these Presents **Because** express mention of the true yearly value or of any other value or certainty of the Premises or any of them, or of other Gifts or Grants by us or by any of our Ancestors or Progenitors unto the aforesaid Mayor, Bayliffs and Burgesses of the Borough heretofore made, is not made in the Premises, or any Statute, Act, Ordinance, Proviso, Proclamation or restraint to the contrary thereof heretofore had, made, published, ordained or provided, or any other thing, cause or matter whatsoever in anywise notwithstanding.

In Witness whereof, we have caused these our Letters to be made Patents.

Witness ourself at Westminster, the twenty first Day of June, in the year of our Reign over England, France and Ireland, the seventeenth, and over Scotland the Fifty second.

THE CHARTER
GRANTED BY
JAMES II., 26TH FEB., A.D. 1686.

James the second, by the Grace of God, of England, Scotland, France and Ireland, King, Defender of the Faith, etc, **To all to whome** these present Letters shall come, Greeting. **Whereas** our Bourrough of Abingdon, in our County of Berks, is a very populous Burrough, and the Cheife Towne of our County of Berks aforesaid, and the Inhabitants of the said Bourrough by the name of the Maior, Bayliffes and Burgesses of the Bourrough aforesaid, or by some other names, have had, used and enjoyed diverse libertyes, Franchises, Immunities and preheminences, as well by reason or pr'tence of divers Charters and Letters Patent by some of our progenitors or Ancestors, late Kings or Queens of this Realme of England, heretofore made granted or confirmed, as by reason or pretence of some prescriptions, usages or customs in the Said Bourrough used, had or enjoyed, and wee willing that From henceforth For Ever in the Said Bourrough be Continualy had one Certaine and undoubted measure of and For the Keeping of our peace And for the better rule and goverment of the said Bourrough and of our people there Inhabiteing and others thither resorting And that the Bourrough aforesaid from henceforth for Ever be and remaine a Bourrough of peace and quiett, To the Dread and Terror of evill offenders And For the reward of good men, And hopeing that if they shall enjoy more ample Honours, libertyes and priviledges by our grant, they will think Themselves oblidged most Specially and Strongly hereafter to doe us our Heires and Successors all the Services they can, of our Speciall grace Certaine knowledge and meere motion **Wee** have willed, ordained, constituted, declared and Granted, and by these p'sents for us our Heires and Successors **Doe will**, Ordaine, constitute, Declare and Grant to the said Maior, Bayliffes and Burgesses of the Bourrough aforesaid and their Successors, that the said Bourrough of Abingdon, in the said County of Berks, from henceforth for ever

Borough to be a Free Borough.

be and shall be a Free Bourrough of it Selfe and by it Selfe, exempt from all hundredes, Countyes and shires, Corporate in Deed, fact and name, by the name of Maior, Aldermen and Burgesses of the Bourrough of Abingdon, in the County of Berks, And that the said Maior, Aldermen and Burgesses of the said Bourrough and their Successors from henceforth for ever shall be one body Corporate and one Comnualty, perpetuall in deed, fact and name, for ever hereafter, and shall have A perpetuall Succession. And the Said Maior, Aldermen and Burgesses one Comnualty and one Body Corporate and Politique of and by themselves, really and fully wee doe erect, make, Create, ordaine, constitute, declare and Incorporate for us our Heires and Successors for ever by these p'sents. And wee will and Command that from henceforth for ever they shall be called and named Maior, Aldermen and Burgesses of the Bourrough of Abingdon, in the County of Berks. And we will and by these p'sents for us our Heires and Successors doe Grant to the Said Maior, Aldermen and Burgesses and men of Abingdon aforesaid, that they and their Successors by the name of Maior, Aldermen and Burgesses of the Bourrough of Abingdon, in the County of Berks, shall and may plead and be Impleaded, sue and p'secute, and defend and be defended. answere and be answered in all Courts and places of us our Heires and Successors, And in all other Courts and places whatsoever as well being within this our Realme of England as else where within our Dominions whatsoever, and before whatsoever Judges or Justices or other persons whatsoever, As well in all and singular other Causes, businesses and matters of whatsoever kind or Nature they be, in the same manner and Forme as our other Leige people, persons able and capable in Law, may or can pleade and be impleaded, answere and be answered, defend and be defended, and That the said Maior, Aldermen and Burgesses of the said Bourrough and their Successors have, and shall and may have a Common Seale to Serve for the doeing and treating of all and singular their Causes and businesses, and that it will, may and shall be Lawfull to and for them and their Successors the s'd Seale att their pleasure to break, Change, and new make. And that the Said Maior, Aldermen and Burgesses, by the name of Maior, Aldermen and Burgesses of Abingdon, in the County of Berks, bee and shall bee p'sons able and Capable in Law to purchase, have and receive, take and possesse to them and their Successors, in fee and perpetuity or otherwise, any

By name of Mayor, Aldermen and Burgesses of the Borough of Abingdon.

With a Common Seal.

Power to hold Lands not exceeding 1(?) marks yearly value.

Lordships, Mannours, Lands, Tenements, rents, revenues, Services, possessions and Hereditaments whatsoever, Soe as the Said Lordships, Mannoures, lands, Tenements, rents, revenues And Hereditaments doe not Exceed the Cleare yearly value of a hundred Marks, and Further, wee will, and by these presents for us our Heires and Successors, doe Grant to the Said Maior, Aldermen and Burgesses To have a
Mayor. of the Bourrough aforesaid and their Successors, that they and their Successors from henceforth for ever have and shall have in the Bourrough aforesaid one honest and Discreet man in manner and Forme in these p'sents hereafter Mentioned to be Chosen, which shall be and shall be named Maior of the Bourrough aforesaid, And alsoe a discreet man And learned in the Lawes of England In manner and Forme hereinafter in these p'sents mentioned to be Chosen, which shall be and shall be named Recorder of the Bourrough A Recorder. aforesaid, and Twelve of the better, more honest and discreet men, Inhabitants of the Bourrough aforesaid, which shall be And shall be called Aldermen of the Said Bourrough, and Twelve other honest Twelve
Aldermen. and discreet men, Inhabitants of the Bourrough aforesaid, which shall be and shall be called Burgesses of the Said Bourrough, And one other honest and Discreet man which shall be and shall be called c'mmon Clarke of the Said Bourrough, to doe and Execute all and A Common
Clerk. Singular things which to the office of common Clarke doe appertaine or ought to appertaine, And two other honest and Discreet men Two Bailiffs. which shall be and shall be called Bayliffes of the bourrough of Abingdon aforesaid. We will, alsoe, and for us our Heires and Successors doe grant that there be and shall be in the Said Bourrough of Abingdon, from time to time for ever, one officer which shall be called Chamberlaine of the Said Borough of Abingdon, to doe and A Chamberlain. Execute such necessary businesses which by such like officer are and shall bee to be done and performed. And that there be and shall be in the said Bourrough, from time to time for ever, Three Three Serjeants
at Mace. officers Called Serjeants att the Mace, For the Executeing the p'cepts, Mandates. And other p'cesse within the said Bourrough to them to be directed by the Maior, Aldermen, and other officers of the said Bourrough, as the Case shall happen, exact, required and be necessary, which Serjeants att the Mace, from time to time, shall be chosen, admitted and p'moted to their offices by the said Maior, Aldermen and Common Councell of the Borough aforesaid by these pr'sents constituted, and Their Successors For the time being, or by the

A Clerk of the Market.

Greater part of them.   And that there be and shall be, from time to time for Ever, one officer which shall be Clarke of the Markett, within the Said Bourrough of Abingdon, to doe, exercise and Execute all and Singular Such things within the Bourrough aforesaid which from time to time to the office of Clarke of the Markett belonge and Appertaine or ought to belong and Appertaine to be don.

And alsoe, we will, and for us our Heires and Successors by these presents, grant to the said Maior, Aldermen, Burgesses and their Successors, And likewise we have ordained that there be and

A Burgess of Parliament.

shall be in the said Bourrough one Burgesse of the Parliament of us our Heires and Successors, And that the said Maior, Aldermen and Common Councill for the time being in the said Bourrough of Abingdon, and their Successors, as often and whensoever a Parliam't of us our Heires and Successors shall happen to be Sum'oned, Incoate or called by virtue of the writt of us our Heires and Successors, For Election of Burgesses of Parliament to them directed, or to be directed or otherwise, by their Election, have and shall have power, Authority and Licence of Electing, Nominating, one Discreet and honest man, of the said Burrough, to be Burgesse of ye Parliament of us our Heires and Successors for the said Burrough,

To be sent at the Costs and Charges of the Borough.

And the same Burgesse soe elected at the Costs and Charges of the said Burrough and Com'nnalty thereof, shall send to the Parliam't of us our Heires and Successors, wheresoever it shall be then held, in the same manner and forme as in other Burroughs of our Realme of England it hath bin or shall be used and accustomed, which Burgesse soe chosen and nominated we will shall be pr'sent and abide att the Parliament of us our Heires and Successors, at the Costs and Charges of the said Burrough of Abingdon and Com'nnalty thereof, during the time that such Parliam't shall happen to be held, in such like manner and forme as any other Burgesses of Parliament for any other Burrough or Burroughs whatsoever within our said Realme of England doe or ought and use to doe, which said Burgesse, in such Parliament, shall have his vote as well Affirmative as Negative, and shall and may doe, Execute all and singulare other things there, by any way or meanes whatsoever as any other Burgesse or Burgesses of any other Burrough within this Realme of England may or can doe. And that all and Singular the pr'misses may obtain more due and full effect.

Know yee, that wee of our more Ample and Speciall Grace,

And of our certaine knowledge and meere motion, have assigned, nominated, made and ordained, and by these presents for us our Heires and Successors doe Assigne, nominate, make and ordaine our well beloved John Sanders, the Elder, Esqre., of the Bore Street, an honest man and Inhabitant of the said Burrough of Abingdon, to be our First and pr'sent Maior of the Burrough of Abingdon The first Mayor under this Charter. aforesaid, to Execute faithfully the Office of Maior of the said Burrough, by his Oath, And in the said office to abide untill the Feast of St Michael the Arch Angell, which shall be in the yeare of Our Lord God One thousand Six hundred Eightie and Seven, and from the said Feast untill another fitt person be elected and duely p'moted, admitted and sworn, to execute the said Office Truely, And him the said John Sanders wee make, Create, constitute and declare by these p'r'sents, Maior of the said Burrough dureing the Terme aforesaid. **And moreover** we have Assigned, nominated and ordained, and by these pr'sents for us our Heires and Successors doe assigne, nominate, make and ordaine our welbeloved William Finmore, Esqre., learned in ye laws of England to be our First and The first Recorder. pr'sent Recorder of the Burrough aforesaid, To Continue in the said Office during his naturall life, And that From time to time, and att all times after the death or removeall of the said William Finmore, the Maior and Aldermen of the Said Burrough, for the time being, or the Greater part of them, whereof the Maior of the said Burrough for the time being wee will to be one, shall and may nominate and Elect one other discreet man, and learned in the lawes of England, to be Recorder of the said Burrough; And that the said William Finmore and every other person w'ch soe as Aforesaid from time to time shall be elected, a Corporall oath before the Maior of the said Burrough for the time being to doe and Execute all and singular those things which to the Office of Recorder of the Burrough aforesaid appertaine, and that then and from thence forth he and they shall and may have and exercise the said office of Recorder of the Burrough aforesaid, And soe as often as the Case shall happen or req're. And we have Assigned, nominated and made our well The firs Bayliffs. beloved William Rawlins, and W'll. Cheney, the younger, to be the First and pr'sent Bayliffes of the said Burrough, first taking their respective Oaths before the said John Sanders, the pr'sent Maior, for the due execution of the office of Bayliffes for the said Burrough untill the feast of St. Michael the Arch Angell next coming, and From the Said feast untill two other persons shall be Chosen and in due manner admitted and sworne Faithfully to Execute the Said office: And the said William Rawlins, and W'll. Cheney, Bayliffes of the Burrough aforesaid during the Terme Aforesaid.

Wee make create, constitute and declare by these presents,

The first Aldermen.

𝕸𝖔𝖗𝖊𝖔𝖛𝖊𝖗 we have assigned, nominated, made and ordained, and by these presents doe Assigne, nominate, make and ordaine the said John Sanders, Richard Pusey, gent, James Curteen, the elder, Jonathan Haws, George Winchurch, for the pr'sent Appointed to be Chamberlaine of the said Burrough, John Payne, John Claxon, W'll. Cheyney, the Elder, Robert Sellwood, Robert Blackeller, James Corderoy, and Thomas Sanders, honest men, Inhabitants of the said Burrough of Abingdon, upon their Corporall Oathes, taken before the said John Sanders the pr'sent Maior, to be the first and p'sent Aldermen of the said Burrough during their respective naturall lives; 𝖀𝖓𝖑𝖊𝖘𝖘𝖊 in the meanetime, they or any of them For any reasonable Cause be or shall be amoved From their said Offices,

The first Burgesses.

𝕬𝖓𝖉 wee have Assigned, Nominated, Constituted and made, and by these pr'sents For us our Heires and Successors doe Assigne, nominate, Constitute and make our well beloved the said William Rawlins, William Cheney, the younger, and alsoe our beloved James Curteen, the younger, Edward Allam, John Mayott, the younger, John Tanner, Michael Rowlins, Richard Ely, Thomas King, Thomas Baylis, Thomas Blissett, and Thomas Piccard, to be the First and p'sent Burgesses of the said Burrough dureing their respective naturall lives, unlesse in the meantime, for any reasonable cause, they or any of them be or shall be Amoved From their Said offices.

𝕸𝖔𝖗𝖊𝖔𝖛𝖊𝖗, wee have Assigned, Nominated, made, Ordained and Constituted and For us our Heires and Successors by these p'sents doe assigne, nominate, make, ordaine and Constitute our beloved George

The first Chamberlain.

Winchurch, Inhabitant of the Said Burrough, upon his Corporall Oath, to be taken before the said Maior, Aldermen and Common Councell, or the greater part of them, to be the First and p'sent Chamberlain of the said Burrough of Abingdon, and well and truly to Execute all and Singular those matters w'ch to the Said office belong or Appertaine, or ought to belong and Appertaine, untill another fitt and able person shall be Elected, promoted, admitted and Sworne to the due Execution of the Said office by and before the Maior, Aldermen and Common Councell of the Burrough aforesaid,

For the Time being, or the Greater part of them, and him The said George Winchurch, Chamberlin of the Burrough aforesaid during the Terme Aforesaid **Wee** make, Create, Constitute and declare by these pr'sents, w'h pr'sent Chamberlaine and his Successors shall yearly Give a Just, True and reasonable Account to the Said Maior, Aldermen and Common Councell, or Certaine Audito's by them the said Maior, Aldermen and Common Councell, or the greater part of them, for this purpose Assigned or to be assigned, as well of the yssues and p'fitts of his office aforesaid, as of the payments and Expences by him layd out, soe as if it happen the said Chamberlaine or any other his Success' to be found behind or in Arreares, That then it shall be well Lawfull for the Said Maior, Aldermen and Common Councell, or the Greater part of them, or to the Audito's aforesaid, the Chamberlaine Soe being behind and in Arreares, to Committ and Send to prisson, And there In prisson Aforesaid to remaine, and not to depart out thence untill he shall have Satisfied the Said Maior, Aldermen and Common Councell of the Arrearages Soe being behind, or otherwise doe or shall Compound with them for the satisfection of the Said Arreares. **And** wee have Assigned, nominated, made, Ordained and Constituted, and for us our heirs and Successo's by these p'sents, doe assigne, nominate, make, ordain And Constitute our beloved Richard Hart, Gent., upon his Corporall Oath before the Said p'sent Maior, Aldermen and Common Councell, or the greater part of them, Taken or to be Taken to be our First and p'sent Towne Clarke of the Said Burrough of Abingdon, And well and truly to Execute all and Singular those things which to that Office belong and Appertaine, or ought to belong and Appertaine During his naturall Life. And him the Said Richard Hart, Towne Clarke of the Burrough aforesaid, During his said Life, wee make, ordain and Constitute by these p'sents. **And we have** Assigned, nominated and made, and be these p'sents for us our Heires and Successo's, doe assigne, nominate, constitute and make our beloved Francis Carter, Andrew Etty, and John Woodley, to be the first and p'sent Serjeants att the Mace of the Burrough aforesaid, during the good pleasure of the Maior, Aldermen and Common Councell, or the Greater part of them. **Moreover, wee will,** and for us our Heires and Successo's, doe ordaine and grant that John Stonehouse, Barronett, Edmund Warcupp, Knt., Humphry Hide, Esqre., Charles Perrott, Doctor in Law, James Stonehouse, Esqre., Paul Calton, Esqre., Robert Mayott, Esqre.,

Marginal notes:
First Chamberlain.
First Town Clerk.
First Serjeants at Mace.
First Justices of the Peace for the Borough.

K

Edm'd. Wiseman, Junr., Esqre., and Thomas Read, Esqre., during
their respective naturall lives, And also the Maior of the Said
Burrough for the time being, during the time of his Maioralty and
for one whole year next Ensuing after he shall depart out of the Said
Office of Maior, And the Recorder of the Said Burrough for the
time being and every one of them be and shall be Justices of the
Peace within the Said Burrough, and p'cincts and Libertyes thereof
of us Our heires and Successo's, to Inquire, hear and Determine of
and Concerning all and Singular matters which to the Justices of the
Peace of us our heires and Success's doe belong, within the Said
Burrough and the p'cincts, moots, Limits, bonds, and p'ambulacons
of the Said Burrough happening in as large manner and forme as any
other Justices of the Peace in any Citties, Burroughs or Counties of
our Realme of England may use or ought to doe, and to keep and
Cause to be kept within the Burrough aforesaid all Ordinances and
Statutes made for the Good of our Peace and for the Conservac'on
thereof, and for the quiett rule and goverm't of the people of us our
heires and Successo's in all their Articles According to the force,
forme and Effect of the Same; And to punish all Offenders within
the Said Burrough against the forme of the said Ordinances and
Statutes or any of them as According to the forme of the said
Ordinances and Statutes is to be done, and to Cause all those which
shall threaten any of the people of us our heires and Successo's of
Bodylie hurt, or of Burning of their houses, to finde Sufficient Securytie
for the peace or good behaviour towards us our heires and Successo's,
and the people of us our heires and Success's, and if they shall
refuse to find Such Securytie then to Cause them to be Safe kept in
the prison of us our heires and Success's untill they shall finde Such

Justices to hold Quarter Sessions. Securytie. And that the Said John Stonehouse, Bart., Edin'd.
Warcupp, Knt., Humphry Hide, Charles Perrott, James Stonehouse,
Paul Calton, Robert Mayott, Edm'd. Wiseman, the younger, Thomas
Read, and the Maior of the said Burrough for the time being, and
also the Last p'decessor of every Maior During one year next Ensueing
after he shall depart out of the Office of Maior, And also the
Record'r of the Said Burrough for the time being, or any two or more
of them, whereof the Maior and Record'r of the Burrough aforesaid
wee will to be two, have and hold, and may have and hold within the
Burrough aforesaid, Sessions of the Peace, to be held Four times in
the year, that is to say, within the space of one week before or after

the Sessions of the Peace for the Said County of Berks, as to the Maior of the Burrough aforesaid for the time being shall Seeme to be most fit and convenient, and be Justices of us our heires and Success's, to Enq'e by the Oath of honest and lawfull men of Burrough aforesaid, by whome the truth of the matter may be best knowne, of all and all manner Felonyes, poysonings, Inchantm'ts, Sorceries, Magick arts, Trespasses, forestalings, regratings, ingrossings and Extorc'ous whatso'r, and of all and Singular other misdeeds and offences of which Justices of Peace of us our heires and Successo's Lawfully may and ought to Enquire, by whomsoe'r or howsoever heretofore made or done, or which hereafter shall happen to be made or Attempted within the Said Burrough, liberties or p'cincts thereof, 𝔄𝔫𝔡 alsoe of all those who within the Burrough aforesaid have gon or Ridden or hereafter shall p'sume to goe or Ride in Companyes or with force and Armes against the peace of us our heires and Success's to the disturbance of the people of us our Heires and Successo's, and alsoe of all those who have layen in waite, or hereafter shall p'sume to lye in waite there to maime or kill, and alsoe of Inkeepe's, And of all and Singular other persons which have offended or Attempted or hereafter shall p'sume to offend or Attempt in Abuse of weights and measures or in Sale of victuals Contrary to the Forme of the Ordinances and Statutes or any of them thereupon made for the Common p'fitt of our Realme of England, And the people of us our Heires and Successo's of the same. And also of all Constables, Keepers of Prissons and other Officers which in the Execution of their offices have behaved themselves or hereafter shall p'sume to behave themselves unduely, or have bin or hereafter shall happen to be Cold, remisse or negligent within the Burrough aforesaid, in or About the p'misses or any of them, And of all and Singular Articles and Circumstances and other things whatsoever, by whomesoever and howsoever within the Burrough aforesaid or Liberties and p'cincts thereof made or done, or which hereafter shall happen to be made or Attempted in any manner concerning the p'misses or any of them, And to inspect all Indictm'ts heretofore before the Maior of the said Burrough taken, or any other person which hath bin Maior of the said Burrough, or any other person which shall be Maior of the Burrough aforesaid, within one Year next After he shall depart out of the Said Maioralty, or before the Recorder of the Said Burrough hereafter to be taken, And to make out and Continue p'cesse thereupon against all and Singular persons Soe Indicted, or who hereafter shall happen to be Soe Indicted untill they be taken, render Themselves or be outlawed, and to hear and determine all and singular the Felonies, Incantac'ons, Sorceries, arts, Magick, Trespasses, fore Stallings, regrateings, Ingrossings, extorc'ons, assemblies, Indictments Aforesaid, and all and singular other the p'misses According to the Lawes and Statutes of this our Realme of England, and as in Such like case used or ought to be done, and to Chastize and punish the Said offenders and every of them for their offences by Fines, Ransomes, amercem'ts, forfietures, or in any other manner as According to the Law and Custome of this our Realme or the Forme of the ordinances or Statutes aforesaid is Accustomed to be done Soe as never the lesse they doe not p'ceed to the Determinac'on of any Treason felonie or other offence whatsoever touching losse of life or member within the Burrough aforesaid, Liberties and p'cincts thereof, without the Spiciall License of us our heires or Successo's.

And to take Oaths.

And that the Said John Stonehouse, Bart., Edmund Warcupp, Knt., Humphry Hide, Charles Perrott, James Stonehouse, Paul Calton, Robert Mayott, Edmund Wiseman, Jun., Thomas Read, and every Maior of the Burrough Aforesaid for one whole year next after he shall depart out of his Office of Maioralty, and alsoe the Record'r for the Same Burrough for the time being and every of them, shall take a Corporall Oath Truly and Faithfully to Execute the office of Justice of the Peace, and the oathes in that behalfe by the Lawes and Statutes of our Realme of England Provided, required to be taken by Justices of the Peace before the Maior and Record'r of the Burrough aforesaid, for the time being, or one of them, And that the Maior and Record'r of the Burrough aforesaid, for the time being, and Either of them, have and shall have full power, Licence and Authority to give and Minester Such Oath as aforesaid to such like Justices of the Peace by force of these p'sents, without any Warrant or Commission from us our heires and Successo's to be obtained or p'secuted, And that the Maior of the Burrough aforesaid shall take Such oath before the said Justices or any two or more of them to whome wee give the same power and Authority by these P'sents to

The Common Council.

Administer to the said Maior Such Oaths as aforesaid **And also, wee will,** for us our heires and Successo's by these P'sents doe Grant to the Said Maior, Aldermen and Burgesses and their Successo's, That ye Maior, Record'r, Aldermen, Towne Clark, Bayliffes, and

Burgesses of the Burrough aforesaid, for the time being, together
with the Justices of the Peace within the Burrough afores'd, Liberties
and p'cincts thereof by these p'sents Constituted and Appointed shall
make and be and shall be called the Common Councell of the Said
Burrough, for all things, Causes, matters, Acts, ordinances and
Businesses touching or Concerning the Burrough Aforesaid, And the
rule and governm't thereof, And the Publick p'fitt and com'odity of
the Said Burrough And Inhabitants thereof for the time being, from
time to time, by them or the greater part of them to be made or
done for the better rule and Goverment of the Inhabitants and
Causes, things and Businesses of the Said Burrough for the time
being.

   And further, wee will, and by these p'sents for us our heires Grant of a
Court of Record.
and Successo's doe grant to the s'd Maior, Aldermen and Burgesses
of the Burrough Aforesaid And their Successo's, that they and their
Successo's from henceforth for ever have and hold and may have
and hold within the Burrough afores'd a Court of record before
the Maior of the Said Burrough, for the time being, or his Sufficient
deputy, in the Common hall, within the Burrough aforesaid or any
other Convenient place within the Said Burrough, From week to
week every Tuesday in the week, Except the weeks of Pentecost,
the Nativytie of our Lord, and Easter, of all and all manner of
Plaints, Quarrels and Actions, p'sonall or mixt, and of Debt,
account, Trespass, Covenant, Contract, detinue, contempt and
offence within the Said Burrough of Abingdon, and Surburbs,
Liberties and P'cincts thereof, made, moved, had, Committed, ariseing,
or to Arise, soe as they Doe not Exceed the summe of Twenty pounds
in one intire Sume; And that the Said Maior and his Successo's,
upon such like Complaints, Pleas, Quarrels and Actions, have and
shall have power, Authority and Licence the persons Defe'ts Against
whome such like plaints, Quarrels or Actions in the Said Court shall
happen to be Levyed or moved, to bring into plea by such and such
like arrests of their bodyes, sum; Attachm'ts and Distresses, and
According to Custome in the Said Burrough used to be directed to
the Serjeants att the Mace of the Said Burrough, for the time being,
or any of them, And that Such like plaints, Quarrels and Actions
aforesaid to be Severally heard and determined, and by such like
p'cesses, Considerations, Judgments and Executions of Judgm'ts be
brought on and Determined by which such like Plaints in the said

Burrough use to be brought on and determined, and that the
execuc'ons of the Said pr'cesses and Judgments be made and done by
the said Serjeants att the Mace, or one of them, according to the
Lawes and Customes of this our Realme of England, and according
to the Liberties, priviledges and Customes of the Said Burrough of
Abingdon.   And that the Mayor of the Said Bourrough of Abingdon
and his Success's, for the time being, have, take and Levy, and
from time to time shall and may have, take and Levy to the use and
profitt of the Commonalty of the Said Burrough, all and all manner
of Fines, amerciam'ts, Forfeitures and other p'fitts whatsoever of
and in the Said Court lawfully comeing, ariseing, accreiving or
happening, as in the Said Burrough hath bin heretofore used and
accustomed, And that without any Account or any other thing therefore to us or heires or Successo's in any manner to be yeilded,
paid or made. **And alsoe** of our further grace, wee will, and of
our certaine knowledge and merre moc'on for us our heires and
Successo's by these p'sents, doe grant to the Said Maior, Aldermen
and Burgesses and other Inhabitants of the Burrough aforesaid, for
the time being and their Successo's for ever, that from henceforth
they and their Successo's yearly, from time to time, every yeare the
first day of September, between the houres of nine and Twelve in
the fore noone of the said day, shall and may meet and Assemble in
the said house or Common Hall called the Councell house, or any
other Convenient place within the Said Burrough of Abingdon, And
that then and there it shall and may be Lawfull to the Burgesses and
men of Inferior Sort, Inhabiting in the Said Burrough, to Nominate
and Assigne two of the most grave and Discreet men then being
Aldermen of the Said Burrough to the intent and purpose that the
Said Maior and Aldermen of the Said Burrough, or the greater part
of them, shall and may choose one of the Said two Aldermen Soe by
the said Inhabitants and Burgesses Nominated and Assigned, and to
be nominated and Assigned to the office of Maior within the Said
Burrough and Libertyes thereof, to have and Execute for one whole
year From the feast of St. Michael the Arch Angell then next
Ensuing, which said Man Soe to the office of Maior Elected, after his
Corporall oath taken, shall have the office of Maior of the Said
Burrough of Abingdon for one whole year then next Following,
that is to say, from the Feast of St. Michael the Arch Angell Inclusively, unto the Feast of St. Michael the Arch Angell exclusively,

Election of Mayor.

one whole yeare Compleat, and from the said Feast of St. Michael the Arch Angell exclusively, untill another Fit and Sufficient person be duely elected, p'moted, admitted and Sworne faithfully to Execute the Said office. And if any one Soe hereafter elected Maior of the Said Burrough after the Said Election shall be made knowne to him, shall, without any reasonable cause refuse to take the office of Maioralty upon him, That then it shall be Lawfull for the Maior and Aldermen of the Said Burrough, for the time being, or the greater part of them, to Committ Such p'son soe refuseing to prison, there to be Safe kept and remaine, And not to be delivered From thence untill he shall be willing to take upon him and Exercise the Said office, or shall pay unto the said Maior, Aldermen and Burgesses such Competent Summe of money for a Fine and Ransome in that behalfe, or otherwise doe or shall compound with them For the Same. 𝕬𝖓𝖉 𝖋𝖚𝖗𝖙𝖍𝖊𝖗, wee will, and by these p'sents doe Grant to the said Maior, Aldermen and Burgesses and their Successo's, that Every person chosen or hereafter to be Chosen Maior of the Burrough of Abingdon Aforesaid, shall and may take his Corporall Oath before his last p'decessor in the Said office, if the Said p'decessor be alive and then p'sent, And if his Said p'decessor be dead or Absent, then before the Aldermen of the Said Burrough, for the time being, or the greater part of them then there p'sent; And if it happen the Maior of the Said Burrough of Abingdon for the time being to Dye or be removed from his office aforesaid before the p'fixed time for the Determination thereof be expired, That then it shall and may be lawfull to the Said Aldermen and Burgesses and other men in the said Burrough, for the time being, or the greater part of them, to Assemble a new in the said house or any other Convenient place within the Burrough Aforesaid, within Eight dayes next after the death or removeall of the Said Maior of the Burrough Aforesaid, And there to nominate, Assigne and Elect any other fitt man of the Aldermen to be Maior of the said Burrough of Abingdon in the place and stead of the Maior late dead or removed in Manner and forme afores'd, which man soe newly Elected, Immediately after he has taken his Corporall oath before the Said Aldermen, Burgesses and other men In the Said Burrough Inhabiting, or the Greater part of them then there p'sent, Shall hold and Exercise the office of Maior of the said Burrough untill the Feast of St. Michael the Arch Angell then next ensueing, And from the said Feast untill another Fitt and Sufficient

Mayor to take an Oath.

Election in Vacancy in the Office of Mayor.

person be duely Chose, Sworne and Admitted Faithfully to Execute the

The Mayor to nominate one of the Bayliffs.

Said office, **And more over**, of our Further Grace, **wee will**, and of our Certaine knowledge and meere motion for us our heires and Successo's doe Grant to the said Maior of the said Burrough of Abingdon, That from henceforth he and his Successo's, Maiors of the Burrough of Abingdon For the time being, yearly from time to time, Every yeare wheresoever and whensoever it shall Seeme meet to him, According to his discretion, shall and may Nominate, elect and Assigne a fitt and discreet p'son of the Twelve Burgesses of the Burrough aforesaid or their Successo's, to be one of the Bailliffes of the Said Burrough from the Feast of St. Michael the Arch Angell then next ensueing, such Assignem't, Election and nominacon for one whole year Fully to be Compleat. **Wee will**, alsoe, and for us our heires and Successo's, doe grant to the said Maior, Aldermen and Burgesses

The Council and other Inhabitants to nominate the other Bayliff.

of our Said Burrough of Abingdon and other men Inhabiteing in the Said Burrough and their Successo's, for the time being for ever, that henceforth they and their Successo's yearly, from time to time and every yeare, the Said first day of Septr., between the houres of Nine and twelve in the Forenoon, or any other dayes and month whensoever to them or the greater part of them it shall seeme fitt and necessary, shall and may Assemble in the Said house called the Councell house or any other Convenient place within the Said Burrough, And that it shall and may be Lawfull for the said Inhabitants then there p'sent to nominate, Assigne and elect another good honest and able man of the Burgesses in the Burrough aforesaid, to be the other Bayliffe of the Said Burrough, And to Associate with the said Bayliffe, nom-inated, elected and Assigned by the Maior from the Feast of St. Michael the Arch Angell then next Following, For one whole yeare Compleat, which man so to the office of Bayliffes elected, after their

Bailiffs to take an Oath.

Corporall Oath in Form following Solemly and duly taken and to be taken, shall together leave the Office of Baylliffes for the Said Burrough for one whole year then next Coming, That is to Say, From ye Feast of St. Michael the Arch Angell Inclusively, until the Said Feast of St. Michael the Arch Angell exclusively, one whole year Compleat, And from the Said Feast of St. Michael the Arch Angell until Two other persons fitt and able be duely Elected, Admitted and Sworne to Execute the Said office. If any person or persons Soe hereafter to be Elected to the Office of Bayliffes of the Said Burrough of Abingdon, after the said Election shall be made

knowne to him or them, doe or shall refuse to take upon him or them
the Said office of Bayliffe without any reasonable Cause, That then
it shall and may be Lawfull to the Said Maior and Aldermen of the
Said Burrough for the time being, or the greater part of them, to
Committ p'son or p'sons soe refuseing to prison, to be Safely there kept
and remaine, and not to be thence delivered untill they shall be
willing to take upon them and Exercise the Said Office and take the
oath for the Execution thereof, or shall yeild and pay a Competent
Summe of money unto the Said Maior, Aldermen And Burgesses to
the use of the Com'unalty of the Said Burrough for their Fine and
Ransome in that behalfe, or otherwise Compound and agree with the
Said Maior and Burgesses for the Same, and Soe upon any Such
refusall to Execute the offices aforesaid or any of them The Said
Maior, Aldermen and Burgesses and other Inhabitants of the Said
Burrough of Abingdon, may p'ceed to a new Election in manner
and Forme aforesaid. **And further**, wee will, and by these   The Bailiffs to take an Oath.
p'sents doe grant to ye Said Maior, Aldermen and Burgesses and
their Successo's, that the Bayliffes of the S'd Burrough Chosen and
hereafter to be Chosen shall take their Corporall oath before the
Maior and Aldermen for the time being, if the Said Maior be alive
and then p'sent, and if the Said Maior be Dead or Absent, Then the
Said Bayliffes shall take their oathes before his pr'decessor's, the Late
Maior and Aldermen or the greater part of them Then there pr'sent,
to Exercise the office Aforesaid, And all and Singular things which to
the Said office doe appertaine; And if it happen the Said Bayliffes
of the Said Burrough of Abingdon for the time being, or Either of
them to dye or be removed From their Said office within the time
pr'fixed From the Expiration thereof, then it shall and may be Lawfull
to and for the Said Maior, Aldermen and Burgesses and other
Inhabitants in the Said Burrough, or the Greater part of them, to
Assemble a new in the said house or any other Convenient place
within the Said Burrough within the Space of Eight dayes next after
the death or removuall of the Said Bayliffes, or Either of them, And
there to nominate, Assigne and Choose Some other Fitt and able person
or persons to be Bayliffe or Bayliffes of the Said Burrough, in the
place and Stead of the Bayliffe or Bayliffes Soe removed or dead, in
manner and Forme aforesaid; Which Said Bayliffe or Bayliffes Soe new
Elected, after his Corporall oath in Forme Aforesaid Taken Duely and
truly to Execute the Said office untill the Feast of Saint Michael the

L

Arch Angell Then next Following, And from the Said Feast untill other sufficient p'son be duely in Forme aforesaid elected, Admitted and Sworne truely to Execute the Said office. **And further,** wee will, and for us our heires and Successo's Doe Grant to the Said Maior, Aldermen and Burgesses and their Successo's, That as often and whensoever it shall happen any of the Aldermen of the Said Burrough, for the time being to Dye or be removed from his office, That then and Soe often it shall and may be Lawfull for the Maior and other Aldermen for the time being, or the greater part of them, to Choose one of the Burgesses or of the better Inhabitants of the Said Burrough into the office of Alderman of the Said Burrough in the place of him soe dead and removed, And soe as often as the Case shall require, And every person Soe nominated And Elected or to be nominated and Elected into the office of Alderman of the Burrough Aforesaid, Shall take his Corporall oath before the Maior of the Said Burrough for the time being, well and truely to Exercise and Execute his Said office. **And further,** wee will, and for us our heires and Successo's, doe Grant to the Said Maior, Aldermen and Burgesses of our Said Burrough of Abingdon and their Successo's, that as often and whensoever it shall happen any Burgesse of the Said Burrough for the time being, to Dye or be removed from his place and office, That then and soe offten it shall and may be Lawfull to and for the said Maior, Aldermen and Bayliffes Then Surviveing, or the greater part of them, to Choose, nominate and pr'ferr one of the best and most honest Inhabitant of the Said Burrough to the office of Burgesse in the place of him soe dead or removed, and soe from time to time, as often as the Case shall happen, and every p'son soe nominated And Elected, or to be nominated and Elected to the office of Burgesse of the Said Burrough, shall Take his Corporall oath before the Said Maior, Aldermen and Burgesses, for the time being, or the greater part of them, well and truely to Exercise and Execute his said office. **Moreover, wee will,** and For us our heires and Successo's doe grant to the Said Maior and Aldermen of the Burrough of Abingdon aforesaid, for the time being, that they and their Successo's for the time being, from time to time, whensoever it shall please them after the death or removeall of the Said Richard Hart, shall and may nominate, Elect and Constitute a Fitt p'son to be Towne Clark of the said Burrough, which Town Clarke shall take his Corporall oath before the Said Maior, Aldermen

Election of an Alderman on a Casual vacancy.

And of a Burgess.

And of a Town Clerk.

and Burgesses, or the greater part of them, well and Truely to Exercise
and Execute his Said office.   **And wee** will, and by these pr'sents
for us our heires and Successo's doe grant to the Said Maior, Aldermen
and Burgesses and their Successo's, that the Common Councill of
the Burrough aforesaid, for the time being, from time to time,
whensoever it shall please them, or the greater part of them, whereof
the Maior of the Said Bourrough **Wee** will alwayes to be one, shall
and may nominate, elect and Constitute three or more officers
According to their discretion, who shall be Called Serjeants att the mace,
for the Executeing p'cesse, and p'cepts and other Businesse which
to the Said office belong and Appertaine within the Said Burrough,
from time to time to be Executed and p'formed, in Such Like manner
and Forme as the Serjeants att mace of our City of London doe and
Execute, which Serjeants att the mace Soe nominated, constituted and
Elected, or to be nominated, Constituted and Elected, shall take their
Corporall oathes before the Said Maior, Aldermen and Burgesses for
the time being, or the greater part of them, well and truly to Execute
and Exercise their Said office, And from time to time shall be
removeable From their Said offices att the pleasure of the Said
Common Councell, or the greater part of them, whereof the Maior of
the Said Burrough for the time being wee will to be one, And Soe of
the other Inferior officers of the Said Burrough; **Provided
alwayes** and wee doe by these p'sents reserve to us our heires and
Successo's full power and Authority att the will and pleasure of us
our heires and Successo's in privy Councell made, and under the
Seale of the Said privy Councell to them Respectively Signified to
remove and Declare to be removed, The Maior, Recorder, Towne
Clarke, And any of the Justices of the peace, Aldermen, Bayliffes or
Burgesses of the Burrough aforesaid, in these p'sents nominated and
Appointed, or hereafter to be Chosen, nominated or Appointed, And
as often as we our heires and Successo's by any such order in Privy
Councell Made shall declare Such and Such like persons or officers for
the time being, or any of them, to be removed from their respective
offices as Aforesaid, **That then** and soe often all and Every Such
p'son and persons soe removed, or declared or to be declared to be
removed from their respective offices, be and shall be Ip'o facto and
without any Further pr'cesse really and to all intents and purposes
Amoved and removed, And soe as often as the Case shall happen
anything to the Contrary thereof in anywise not withstanding.

And moreover, of our Further Grace and meere motion, wee doe by these p'sents grant and Confirme to the Said Maior, Aldermen and Burgesses of the Said Burrough and their Successo's, That the Said Maior, Aldermen and Burgesses of the Burrough aforesaid And their Successo's hence forth for Ever hereafter, from time to time, shall and may have and receive by themselves, their Ministers or Servants, as well upon the Market dayes and Either of them as upon every other day in the weeke yearly of all Sorts of graine, wheat and malt, which within the Burrough Aforesaid, from time to time shall be Sold or Exposed to Sale, or which shall be brought to the Burrough aforesaid to be sold within the said Burrough, of Every person Soe Selling or Exposing To sale or bringing to be sold any Graine, wheat or Malt, ye Toll Following, That is to say; For Every quarter of Such like Graine, wheat or Malt soe as aforesaid Sold or Exposed to be Sold, or brought to the Burrough aforesaid to be sold within ye Said Burrough as is aforesaid, one measure Called a quart, and Soe according to that rate for a Greater or Lesser quantity; **And alsoe** that the Said Maior, Aldermen and Burgesses of the Burrough Aforesaid, and Their Successo's From hence forth for ever hereafter, shall and may have, enjoy and receive of the market Aforesaid, picage, Sums of money for shewing of Wares Called shew money, Stallage, Tollage, Tolls, Customes, profitts, rights and Jurisdictions of what kind or nature so ever to any Markets in any manner belonging or Appertaining, or in the Said markets or any of them in any manner lawfully received, had or used, altho they be not p'ticularly in these letters patents or in any other Letters patents of any of our p'genit's or Ancestors, Kings and Queens of England, named or Expressed, and that From time to time, it shall and may be Lawfull for the Said Maior, Aldermen and Burgesses and their Successo's, by force of this our Grant in these our letters patents Contained, to take and receive to the use and behoofe of the Cominalty of the Said Burrough in the Said Markets, all reasonable Summs of money as they or their p'decesso's have had or received, or Could or might receive, and as in any other Markets by force of any other Letters patents, usage, prescription, or any other lawfull way or means whatsoever have bin Due, received, taken or payable, or have bin accustomed or ought to have bin had, received or taken. **And** of our further grace, Certaine knowledge and meere motion, **Wee will,** and for

Grant of Tolls on Grain sold in the Borough.

And of Picage and Stallage.

us our heires and Successo's by these p'sents Doe grant to the Said
Maior, Aldermen and Burgesses of the Burrough of Abingdon Aforesaid and their Successo's, That they and their Successo's for the
time being, from hence forth, shall and may have, from time to time, Of Assizes, &c.
returne as well of Assises as of all manner of precepts, writs, bills,
mandates and warrants, as of Summons, Estreats and precepts out
of the Excheq'r of us our heires and Success'rs the Estreâtes and
precepts of the Justices in Eire of us our heires and Successo's, as
well Concerning pleas of the Crowne as Common pleas, or of any
other Justices whatsoever, **And alsoe** the attachm'ts as well of
pleas of the Crowne as of other pleas within the Said Burrough, the
precincts and Libertyes thereof, And the full Execution of the Same,
Soe that no Sheriffe, Bailiffe or any other officer of us our heires or
Successo's shall or may Enter the Said Burrough or the Suburbs,
precincts or liberties thereof to doe or Execute any thing in his
office or in any manner touching or Concerning the Same, soe as
neverthelesse it shall and may be lawfull to the Sheriffe of our
Said County of Berks, within the Said Burrough to proclaime his
writts of Exigen' and proclimations, And there to hold his Court
Called the County Court; And that the Said Maior, Áldermen and
Burgesses of the Burrough of Abingdon aforesaid and their
Successo's from henceforth, shall and may have and enjoy to the
use of the Cominalty of the Said Burrough, all goods and Chattles
waived, and Extreats whatsoever within the Said Burrough of
Abingdon or the limits or bounds thereof from time to time hapen-
ing, Ariseing or Accrewing. **And wee will**, and by these p'sents And of a Gaol.
for us our heires and Successo's, doe Grant to the Said Maior,
Aldermen and Burgesses of the Burrough aforesaid and Their
Successors, that they shall and may have within the Said Burrough
a certaine Goal, Safely and Securely to keep and preserve in the
Said Goal all manner of 'Fellons within the Said Burrough and
Liberties thereof Taken, and to be Taken, by the Space of three
dayes and three nights And no longer, unlesse necessity urgeth to
the Contrary or otherwise requireth, And for the Correction And
punishment of other Trespassers and Offenders whatsoever untill
they shall be from thence Lawfully delivered According to the
Lawes and Customes of this our Realme. **And further**, wee
will, and by these p'sents for us our heires and Successo's, doe will
and Command the Said Maior, Aldermen and Burgesses and their

Grant to the
Vicar out of the
Rents, &c., of
the Rectory.

Successo's that yearly and Every year out of the rents and profits from time to time issuing out of the rectory or p'sonage Impropriate of the Said Burrough, they pay or Cause to be paid unto the vicar of the p'ish Church of the Burrough aforesaid, for the time being, The full and intire Summe of Twenty pounds of lawfull money of England, the said Payment to be made Every halfe yeare, at the Feasts of the Anuntiac'on of the Blessed virgin Mary And St Michael the Arch Angell, by Even portions, The first payment to begin at Such of the Said Feasts next Ensueing the date of these our Letters patents. And further, of our more Free grace,

Confirmation of
prior Charters.

Certaine Knowledge and meere motion, wee doe grant and Confirme, for us our heires and Successo's, to the said Maior, Aldermen and Burgesses of the Burrough aforesaid and their Successo's, All and all manner Mannors, Lops, messuages, mills, Suits to mills, lands, Tenem'ts, meadows, pastures, Commons, Barnes, heath and Furze, mores, marishes, woods, underwoods, Tofts, Cottages, and rents. Tithes, issues, Commodityes and Services, And also the revertion and revertions of the Same debts, Markets, Faires, Tolles, Stallages, Courts and Soe many, Soe Great, Such the same and Such like, Libertyes, powers, Francheses, imunityes, Exemptions, priviledges, Quittances, Jurisdictions, wasts, voyd Grounds, Commodities, profitts, Emolum'ts, and hereditam'ts whatsoever, which in and by these pr'sents are not Changed or Altered, as and w'ch by the Letters patents of our Ancest's, Phillip and Mary, Late King and Queen of England, To the Maior, Baylifles and Burgesses made, bearing date at Westmi'ster, The 24th day of November, in the Third and Fourth year of their raigne, or by the Letters patents of the Lady Elizabeth, late Queen of England, to the Maior, Bayliffes and Burgesses made, bearing date at Westmi'ster, the 19th day of March in the Seventh yeare of her raigne, or by the Letters patents of our most dear Grandfather, James, Late King of England, to ye Maior, Bayliffes and Burgesses made, bearing date at Westmi'ster, ye 16th day of February, in the yeare of his raigne, That is to say of England, France and Ireland ye Seventh, and of Scotland the 43d, or by the Letters patents of our Said Grandfather, James, late King of England, to the Maior, Bayliffes and Burgesses made, bearing date at westmi'ster, The third day of March, in the yeare of his raigne of England, France and Ireland ye 7th, and of Scotland ye 43d, granted or mentioned to be granted, or w'ch the said Maior,

Aldermen and Burgesses, or ye Maior, Bayliffes and Burgesses of the Borough aforesaid or their Predecessors, by whatsoever name or names, or by whatsoever incorporation or by pretence of any name or incorporation whatsoever heretofore had, held, used or Enjoyed, or ought to have, hold or Enjoy, or now have, hold, use, occupy or enjoy, to them and their Successo's by reason or Colour of any Letters patents of ye Said Lord and Lady, philip and Mary, the Said Lady Elizabeth, our Said Grandfather, King James, or any other Charters, grants or letters patents by any of our Progenit'rs or Ancest'rs, late Kings or Queens of England, in any manner heretofore made, granted or Confirmed, or by any other Lawfull meanes, right, title, Custome, usage or prescription heretofore lawfully used, had or accustomed, altho' the same or any of them were Forfeited or lost, or altho' the same or any of them were ill used, not used, abused or discontinued; **To have, hold and Enjoy,** to the Said Maior, Aldermen and Burgesses of the Burrough aforesaid and their Successo's for ever, yeilding and Paying therefore yearly to us our heires and Successo's Such and Soe many and Such like Fee Farmes, rents, Services, Summs of money and demands whatsoever, as to us for the Same heretofore they used or ought to yeild and pay. **Wherefore,** wee will, and by these p'sents for us our heires and Successo's, Firmely Command and Enjoine that the Said Maior, Aldermen and Burgesses of the Burrough aforesaid and their Successo's, have, hold, use and Enjoy, and shall and may have, hold, use and Enjoy for ever all powers, Libertyes, Authorityes, Jurisdictions, Francheses, Exemptions, Imunityes and Freedoms afores'd, and all other the p'misses, According to the Tenour and Effect of these our Letters patents, And of the said other Letters patents above in these p'sents mentioned, without any let or Impedim't by us our heires or Successo's, or of the Justices, Sheriffes, Escheat'rs, or other Bayliffes, officers or ministers whatsoever, of us our heires or Successo's, not willing that the said Maior, Aldermen and Burgesses of the Burrough aforesaid or any of them by reason of the pr'misses or any of them by us our heires or Successo's our Justices, sheriffes or other Bayliffes or ministers whatsoever of us our heires or Successo's be Letted, molested, hindred, greived, or in any manner disturbed or vexed. **And moreover,** of our further speciall grace, Certaine Knowledge and meere motion, **Wee will,** and by these p'sents for us our heires and Successo's, doe grant to the said

Reservation of the Fee Farm Rents, &c.

Maior, Aldermen and Burgesses of the said Burrough of Abingdon, and their Successo's, That these our Letters patents or the Inrolem't thereof shall be in and by all things firme, Valid, Good, Sufficient, and Effectuall in Law against us our heires and Successo's, as well in all our Courts as else where within our Realme of England without any Confirmations, Lycences or Tolerations from us our heires or Successo's hereafter by the Said Maior, Aldermen and Burgesses and their Successo's to be procured or obtained, notwithstanding the ill naming, ill reciting, or not nameing or not reciteing the Said messuages, Lands, Tenements, meadowes, pastures, feedings, and other the pr'misses above by these p'sents granted or mentioned to be granted, or of any part or p'cel thereof, And not withstanding the not finding of office or offices, inquisition or inquisitions of the pr'misses above by these p'sents granted or mentioned to be granted, or of any part or p'cell thereof by which our Title ought to be found before the makeing of these our Letters patents, And not withstanding the ill reciting, ill nameing, or not reciteing any Lease or Grant of the pr'misses or of any part or p'cel thereof being of record or not of record or otherwise howsoever heretofore made, And not withstanding the ill nameing, or not naming any Towne, hamlett, p'ish, place or County, in which the p'misses or any part or p'cel thereof are or be, and not withstanding there be not herein any true, full and Certaine mention of the names of the Tenants, Farmers or occupiers of the messuages, lands, Tenements and hereditaments aforesaid, or any of the pr'misses or any p'te or p'cell thereof, and not withstanding the Statute made and ordained in the p'liament of the late Lord, King Henry the Sixth, our Ancest'r, in the 18th year of his Raigne, for that Expresse mention is not made of the true annuall value or of the Certainty of ye p'misses or any of them, or of any gifts or Grants by us or by any of our Ancest's or Predecesso's to the Said Maior, Aldermen and Burgesses of the Burrough Aforesaid or their predecesso's before these times made, or any Statute, ordinance, provision, proclamation or restriction to the Contrary hereof heretofore had, made, provided or ordained, or any other thing, Cause or matter whatsoever in any wise notwithstanding.

𝕴𝖓 𝖂𝖎𝖙𝖓𝖊𝖘𝖘𝖊 whereof wee have Caused these our Letters to be made patent.

𝕎𝕚𝕥𝕟𝕖𝕤𝕤𝕖 our Selfe at Westmi'ster, the 26th day of February, in the Second year of our Raigne.

By writ under the privy Seale.

PIGOTT.

For the Fine in the hanaper, £6 : 13 : 4

THE CHARTER

GRANTED BY

GEORGE II., 20TH MAR., A.D. 1739.

George the second, by the Grace of God, of Great Britain, France and Ireland, King, Defender of the Faith, &c., **To all to whom** these Presents shall come, Greeting, **Whereas** by an Inquisic'on taken at Abyngdon, in Our County of Berks, the Tenth day of June, in the Tenth Year of Our Reign, before Mathew Wymondesold, Esquire, Sheriffe of the County aforesaid, by Virtue of Our Writt of Ad quod Dampnum to him directed, and to the said Inquisic'on annexed, by the Oaths of good and lawfull men of the said County, it was found, That it would not be to the prejudice of Us or any other or to the Injury of the Neighbouring Markets if We should Grant to the Mayor, Bayliffes and Burgesses of the Borough of Abyngdon, in the said County, A Licence that they might have and Hold at the Borough of Abyngdon aforesaid, One Market upon Tuesday, Wednesday, Thursday, and Saturday, in every Week Perpetually, for the Buying and Selling only of All manner of Corn and Grain usually Sold in Markets, and All Tolls and other Profits belonging and Appertaining to Markets for Corn and Grain, over and above the Markets which the said Mayor, Bayliffs and Burgesses were then Intituled unto, on Monday and Fryday in every Week, Provided the said Grant be made to the said Mayor, Bayliffs and Burgesses and their Successors Condic'onally that they do not take or Demand any Toll for Corn and Grain Sold in the said Markets held in the said Borough, on Monday and Fryday in every Week, or brought into the said Borough on Monday and Fryday in every Week, or so as they the said Mayor, Bayliffs and Burgesses do Release and Discharge their Right and Title of Toll of All Corn and Grain that should be brought to or Sold in the said Borough on Monday and Fryday, and that the time of Sale of All such Corn and Grain as should be so

Reciting Inquisition under Writ of Ad quod damnum.

brought to be sold on Monday and Fryday, should begin to be sold by Ten of the Clock in the forenoon of the same days, As by the said Writt and Inquisic'on on the Files of our Court of Chancery remaining of Record (relac'on being thereunto had) may more fully and at large appear. **And whereas** the said Mayor, Bayliffs and Burgesses have by their Petic'on humbly represented unto Us that they are Willing and Desirous and do Consent and Agree not to take or demand any Toll for Corn and Grain Sold in the said Markets, held in our said Borough, on Monday and Fryday in every Week, or brought into Our said Borough on Monday and Fryday in every Week, and that the time of Sale of All such Corn and Grain as shall be so brought to be Sold on Monday and Fryday shall begin to be sold by Ten of the Clock in the forenoon of the same Days. **Now know ye** that Wee of our especial Grace, certain knowledge and meer moc'on, **have** Given and Granted, And by these presents for Us Our Heirs and Successors **Do** Give and Grant unto the said Mayor, Bayliffs and Burgesses of Abyngdon aforesaid and their Successors, Our especial Licence that they shall and may Have and Hold One Market upon Tuesday, Wednesday, Thursday and Saturday, in every Week throughout the Year, at our Borough of Abyngdon aforesaid, for the Buying and Selling All manner of Corn and Grain only usually sold in Markets, together with All Tolls and other Profits belonging and Appertaining to Markets for Corn and Grain, over and above the Markets which the said Mayor, Bayliffs and Burgesses are now Intituled unto, on Monday and Fryday in every Week, Pursuant to the said Inquisic'on, **Provided** that the said Mayor, Bayliffs and Burgesses and their Successors do not take or demand any Toll for Corn and Grain Sold in the said Markets held in the said Borough on Monday and Fryday in every Week, or brought into the said Borough on Monday and Fryday in every Week, Or So as they the said Mayor, Bailiffs and Burgesses do Release and Discharge their Right and Title of Toll of All Corn and Grain that shall be brought to or Sold in the said Borough on Monday and Fryday in every Week, And So as that the time of Sale of All such Corn and Grain as shall be so brought to be sold on Monday and Fryday in every Week, shall begin by Ten of the Clock in the forenoon of the same days. **Provided** also, that if the said Mayor, Bayliffs and Burgesses and their Successors do at any time hereafter take or demand any Toll for Corn and Grain Sold in the said Markets held in the said Borough on Monday and

And Petition of Mayor, Bailiffs, and Burgesses.

Grant of a Corn Market on Tuesdays, Wednesdays, Thursdays and Saturdays, in addition to Monday and Friday Markets.

No Tolls to be taken on Corn.

And to begin by 10 o'clock.

Fryday in every Week, or brought into the said Borough on Monday and Fryday in every Week, That then these Our Letters Patent and all Liberties and Privileges hereby Granted shall Cease, determine and become utterly null and void to all Intents, Construcc'ons and purposes whatsoever, Any thing herein before contained to the contrary Notwithstanding. **To have**, hold and Enjoy the said Markets and the Tolls and Profits above by these Presents Granted, or menc'oned to be Granted, to the said Mayor, Bayliffs and Burgesses and their Successors for ever, And this without any Account or any other thing to be therefore rendered, paid or made, to Us Our Heirs or Successors for the same. **Wherefore**, We Will, and do by these Presents for Us Our Heirs and Successors Strictly Charge and Command that the said Mayor, Bayliffs and Burgesses and their Successors, by virtue of these Presents, shall and may freely, Lawfully and Quietly Have, Hold and Keep the said Markets for ever, together with the said Tolls and Profits, according to the tenure and true intent of these Our Letters Patent, without Molestac'on, Trouble, Grievance or Contradicc'on of Us Our Heirs or Successors, Or of any Sheriffs, Escheators, Bailiffs, Officers or Ministers of Us Our Heirs or Successors whatsoever, And this without any other Warrant, Writt or Process hereafter to be procured or obtained in that behalf. **Lastly**, Wee Will, and do by these Presents for Us Our Heirs and Successors Grant to the said Mayor, Bayliffs and Burgesses and their Successors, that these our Letters Patent or the Inrollment or Exemplificac'on thereof shall be in and by all things good, firm, valid, sufficient and Effectual in the Law, according to the true intent and meaning thereof.

In Witness whereof Wee have caused these Our Letters to be made Patent.

Witness Our Self, at Westminster, the twentieth day of March, in the Twelfth Year of our Reign.

By Writt of Privy Seal.

COCKS.

THE CHARTER

GRANTED BY

GEORGE III., 23RD AUG., A.D. 1774.

George the third, by the Grace of God, of Great Britain, France and Ireland, King, Defender of the Faith, and so forth, **To all to whom** these Presents shall come, Sends Greeting, **Whereas** our late Noble Progenitors the Lord and Lady, King Philip and Queen Mary, late King and Queen of England, by their Letters Patent Sealed with the Great Seal of England, and bearing date at Westminster, the twenty second day of November, in the fourth year of their Reign, granted (amongst other things) for themselves their Heirs and Successors, to the Inhabitants and Men of the Town of Abingdon, in our County of Berkshire, That the said Town should from thenceforth be a free Borough of itself and by itself, Exempt from all Hundreds, Counties and Shires, and the Inhabitants thereof, and of the Limits and Precincts in the said Letters Patent described and set forth, were thereby incorporated in Deed and fact by the Name of the Mayor, Bailiffs and Burgesses of the Borough of Abingdon, in the County of Berks, with such Capacities, Powers, Privileges and Franchises as are therein more at large set forth. And it was by the said Letters Patent further Granted that there should be always from thenceforth within the said Borough, twelve Men of the better and more honest and discretest Men, Inhabitants of the said Borough of Abingdon, who should be called and should be the Principal Burgesses of that Borough, Which said Mayor, Bailiffs and Capital Burgesses might and should be able to Elect, take and associate to themselves sixteen others or more according to their sound discretion of the better, honester and discreeter Men, Inhabitants of the Borough aforesaid, who should be called the Secondary Burgesses of the same Borough, and which said Mayor, Bayliffs, principal Burgesses and the said other sixteen or more

(margin note: Recitals of Charter of Philip and Mary.)

called Secondary Burgesses, should make and should be, and should be called the Common Council of the said Borough, for the purposes therein mentioned.   And the said King and Queen did assign, create and nominate Richard Mayott, in the said Charter named, to be the first and modern Mayor of the said Borough of Abingdon, the Office of Mayor of the same Borough faithfully upon his Oath to Execute, and in the same Office to stay and continue until the Feast of Saint Michael the Archangel then next coming, and from the same Feast until one other fit Person should be elected and chosen and duly sworn, preferred and admitted, the same Office faithfully to execute. And the said King and Queen did further Grant to the said Mayor, Bailiffs and Burgesses, and to the rest of the Inhabitants of the Borough aforesaid for the time being and their Successors for ever, That they and their Successors should yearly on the first day of the Month of September, between the Hours of Nine and twelve in the Forenoon of the same day, assemble in the Common Hall of the said Borough, or other convenient Place therein, and that it should be lawful then and there for the said Secondary Burgesses and other the Burgesses and Men of the Inferior Sort in the said Borough, Inhabitants, to nominate and assign two Men of the more Grave and discreet Men then being principal Burgesses of that Borough To the end, intent and purpose that the aforesaid Mayor, Bailiffs and the rest of the Principal Burgesses of the same Borough or the Major part of them should choose and elect one of those two Burgesses so by the aforesaid Inhabitants and inferior Burgesses nominated and assigned, the Office of Mayor, within the Borough aforesaid and the Liberties thereof, to Execute, perform and exercise, for one whole year, from the Feast of Saint Michael the Archangel then next following, Which said Man so to the Office of Mayor elected, upon and after his Corporal Oath taken should bear the Office of Mayor of the said Borough of Abingdon, for one whole year then next following that is to say, from the Feast of Saint Michael the Archangel inclusively, until the same Feast of Saint Michael the Archangel exclusively, one whole and entire year to be compleated, and from the same Feast of Saint Michael the Archangel exclusive, until another sufficient and fit Person the said Office faithfully to Execute should be duly elected, preferred, admitted and sworn.   And the said King and Queen did further Grant to the aforesaid Mayor, Bailiffs and Burgesses and their Successors, that every Person to the Office of Mayor of the Borough of Abingdon aforesaid elected and thereafter to be elected should take and should be able to take his Corporal Oath before his late Predecessor in the same Office, if the said Predecessor should be living and then present, and if his said Predecessor should be then dead or absent, that then he should take and should be able to take the Oath before the Bailiffs and capital Burgesses of the same Borough for the time being or the greater part of them then there present. **And** the said King and Queen did assign, nominate, make and ordain Richard Ely and William Blacknall, being Inhabitants of the said Borough of Abingdon, to be the first and modern Bailiffs of the same Borough, the said Office of Bailiffs of the said Borough faithfully upon their Oaths to execute until the said Feast of Saint Michael the Archangel next coming, and from the same Feast until two other Persons should be elected and duly sworn and admitted faithfully to execute the same Office. **And** the said King and Queen did further Grant to the aforesaid Mayor of the said Borough of Abingdon, that from thenceforth he and his Successors, Mayors of the said Borough for the time being, should yearly from time to time, every year wheresoever and whensoever to him according to his sound discretion it should seem convenient, nominate, elect and assign one fit and discreet Man of the Inhabitants of the said Borough, whether he be Capital or Secondary Burgesses of the Borough aforesaid, to be one of the Bailiffs of the said Borough from the Feast of Saint Michael the Archangel then next following such Election, Assignment and Nomination, for one whole year to be compleat and ended. **And** the said King and Queen did further Grant to the said Mayor, Bailiffs and Burgesses of the said Borough of Abingdon, and to the rest of the Men in the said Borough being Inhabitants and their Successors, that from thenceforth they and their Successors yearly, from time to time, every year on the said first day of the Month of September, between the Hours of Nine and Twelve in the Forenoon of the same Day, or any other days and Months whensoever to them or the greater part of them it should seem convenient and necessary, should and might assemble and meet together in the aforesaid House called the Councel House, or in any other convenient Place within the Borough aforesaid, and there it should and might be lawful for the aforesaid Secondary Burgesses and the other Burgesses and the Men of the inferior Sort in the said Borough being Inhabitants, to ratify and confirm and to admit the

Election, Nomination and Assignment of the Bailiff for the year then following by the Mayor of the same Borough made or to be made as aforesaid, so as such Election should be made upon a fit, meet and sufficient Man to bear and exercise the said Office. And that it should and might be lawful to the said Inhabitants then and there present, another good, Honest and able Man, being an Inhabitant of the same Borough and one of the Secondary Burgessses of the Borough aforesaid, to nominate, assign and elect, to be another of the Bailiffs of the Borough aforesaid, and to be associate with the aforesaid Bailiff by the Mayor nominated elected and assigned, from the Feast of Saint Michael the Archangel then next following, for one whole year to be completed, Which said Men so to the Office of Bailiffs elected, upon and after their Corporal Oaths in form therein mentioned solemnly and duly done and taken, and to be done and taken, should together bear the Office of Bailiffs of the Borough aforesaid for one whole year next coming, Vizt., from the Feast of Saint Michael the Archangel inclusively, until the same Feast of Saint Michael the Archangel exclusively, one whole year to be compleated, and from the same Feast of Saint Michael the Archangel until two other able and sufficient Men should be duly elected, preferred, admitted and sworn the same Office faithfully to execute. And the said King and Queen did further Grant to the aforesaid Mayor, Baliffs and Burgesses, and their Successors, that the Bailiffs of the same Borough elected and thereafter to be elected should take their Corporal Oath before the Mayor and Capital Burgesses for the time being, if the same Mayor should be living and then present, and if the aforesaid Mayor should be then dead or absent, that then the same Bailiffs should take their Corporal Oath before the late Bailiffs, their Predecessors, and the Capital Burgesses or the greater part of them then there being present, to exercise the Office aforesaid, and well and faithfully to do and perform all things which to the said Office belong. And the said King and Queen did assign, nominate, make and ordain the said Richard Mayott, Richard Ely, and William Blacknall, and also William Mathew, Thomas Tonks, James Fisher, Humphry Bostock, Thomas Orpwood, Ralph Bostock, Thomas Jenyns, John Chaunterell, and William Whytington, being good and honest Men, Inhabitants of the said Borough of Abingdon, upon their Corporal Oaths taken before the aforesaid Richard Mayott, the then Mayor, to be the twelve first and modern Principal Burgesses of the same Borough, which said Burgesses and every of them should continue and endure as long as they and every of them should well behave him and themselves in their Offices aforesaid. And the said King and Queen did further Grant to the aforesaid Mayor, Bayliffs and Burgesses of the aforesaid Borough of Abingdon and their Successors, that as often as and whensoever it should happen any Burgess of the Borough aforesaid, for the time being, should die or be removed from his Place and Office, that then and so often it should and might be lawful for the said aforesaid Mayor, Bayliffs and Capital Burgesses then surviving, or the greater part of them, one of the better and honester Men, being Inhabitants of the Borough aforesaid, to be a Burgess and unto the Office of Burgess of the same Borough to elect, nominate, substitute, make and appoint, in the place of him so being dead or removed, and so from time to time, as often as the Case should happen, and every Person so nominated and elected or to be nominated and elected into the Office of Burgess of the Borough aforesaid should take his Corporal Oath before the aforesaid Mayor, Bayliffs and Burgesses for the time being, or the greater part of them, his said Office well and faithfully to exercise and Execute. And the said King and Queen by the said Letters Patent did further Ordain and Grant that the Mayor of the said Borough of Abingdon, for the time being from thenceforth, should be a Justice of the Peace, within the said Borough, and the Precincts and Liberties of the same Borough, of and for all and singular the Matters and Things which to a Justice of their said Majesties' Peace and of the Heirs and Successors of the aforesaid Queen belonged, to be enquired into, heard and determined within the same Borough and the Precincts, Metes, Limits and Bounds and Perambulations of the same Borough happening or arising, in as large and ample manner and form as any Justices of the Peace in any Cases, Boroughs or Counties of the Realm of England might do and had been accustomed to do or ought to do, and that no other Justice of the Peace should intermeddle himself or come in to do anything which to a Justice of Peace there belonged, except the Justices Itinerant of their said Majesties or of the Heirs and Successors of the aforesaid Queen and other the Justices of the said King and Queen or of their Heirs and Successors by Commission or Commissions of their said Majesties or of the Heirs and Successors of the aforesaid Queen from time to time to be assigned, nominated and authorized

N

Reciting also
Charter of 7th
Jac. I.

within the said Borough of Abingdon, and the Precincts thereof.

And whereas Our Royal Predecessor, Lord James the First, King of England, by his Letters Patent sealed with the Great Seal of England, bearing date at Westminster, the third day of March, in the seventh year of his Reign, of his special Grace, certain knowlege and meer motion, for himself, his Heirs and Successors, granted to the Mayor, Bayliffs and Burgesses of the Borough aforesaid and their Successors, that they and their Successors from thenceforth for ever might and should have in the Borough aforesaid one discreet Man, learned in the Laws of England, in the form therein mentioned to be elected and chosen, who should be the Recorder of the Borough aforesaid. **And** the said King James, for the better Execution of his Will and Grant in that behalf, did for himself his Heirs and Successors, Assign, Nominate, Constitute and make his beloved Walter Dayrell, Esquire, learned in the Laws of England, to be the first and modern Recorder of the Borough aforesaid, to continue in the same Office during the good pleasure of the Mayor and principal Burgesses of the Borough aforesaid for the time being, or the Major part of them (of whom the Mayor for the time being should be one), And that from time to time, and at all times after the death or removal of the aforesaid Walter Dayrell, the Mayor and principal Burgesses of the Borough aforesaid, for the time being, or the major part of them, of whom the Mayor of the same Borough for the time being should be one, should and might have power and be able to nominate, elect and chuse one other discreet Man, learned in the Laws of England, to be Recorder of the Borough aforesaid. And that the aforesaid Walter Dayrell and every other who so as aforesaid from time to time should be elected, chosen, preferred and nominated to be Recorder of the Borough aforesaid, before he or they should be admitted to Execute the same Office, should take a Corporal Oath before the Mayor of the Borough aforesaid for the time being, to do and Execute all and singular the Matters and Things which to the Office of Recorder of the Borough aforesaid did belong, and that after such Oath so as aforesaid taken, he and they should have and Execute the same Office of Recorder of the Borough aforesaid during the good pleasure of the Mayor and principal Burgesses of the Borough aforesaid for the time being, or the greater part of them (of which the Mayor for the time being should be one), and so often as the case should happen. **And** the said

late King James Willed, and by his said Letters Patent for himself
his Heirs and Successors granted to the said Mayor, Bayliffs and
Burgesses of the said Borough and their Successors, That William
Lord Knolles, Thomas Parry, Knight, and David Williams, Knight,
during their natural lives, and also the Mayor of the Borough
aforesaid then being, and every Mayor of the said Borough thereafter
for the time being, for one year next following after that he had
quitted and gone out of the Office of Mayoralty, and the Recorder of
the Borough aforesaid for the time being, at all times thereafter be
and should be Justices of the said late King James, his Heirs and
Successors, and every one of them, to keep, preserve and maintain
the Peace of the said late King James, his Heirs and Successors,
within the Borough aforesaid, and the Liberties and Precincts of the
same.   And also to keep and cause to be kept all Ordinances and
Statutes made and published for the good of the Peace of the said
King James, and for the preservation and maintenance of the same.
And also for the quiet Rule and Governance of the People of his
said Majesty and his Heirs and Successors in all their Articles in the
Borough aforesaid, according to the meaning, form and effect of the
same, and to punish all offending against the form of those Ordinances and Statutes, or either of them, in the Borough aforesaid, as
according to form and Ordinance of those Statutes should be to be
done.   And all those who should threaten any of the People of him
his Heirs and Successors of and concerning their Bodies, or of the
Burning of their Houses, to find sufficient Security of the Peace for
their good Behaviour towards him his Heirs and Successors, and the
People of him his Heirs and Successors.   And if they should refuse
to find such Security, then to cause them to be kept safe in the
Prison of the said King his Heirs and Successors until they should
find such Security.   And that the said William Lord Knolles,
Thomas Parry, Knight, and David Williams, Knight, during their
natural Lives, and the Mayor of the Borough aforesaid for the time
being, and also the last Predecessor of every Mayor during one whole
year next following after that he had quitted and gone out of the
Office of Mayoraalty, and also the Recorder of the Borough aforesaid
for the time being, or any two or more of them (of which the Mayor
and Recorder of the Borough aforesaid should be two) should be
Justices of the said late King his Heirs and Successors, to enquire by
the Oath of good Men and true of the Borough aforesaid by whom

the truth of the Matter might be better known, of all and all manner
of Felonies, Witchcrafts, Inchantments, Sorceries, Arts Magic,
Trespasses, Forestallings, Regratings, Ingrossings and Extortions
whatsoever, and of all and singular other Misdemeanors and Offences
whatsoever of which the said King's Justices, his Heirs or Successors,
might lawfully or ought to enquire into, by whomsoever or howsoever,
within the Borough aforesaid, the Liberties or Precincts of the same,
thentofore done or committed, or which thereafter should chance or
happen there to be done, committed or attempted, and also of all
those who in the Borough aforesaid either walked or rode, or thereafter should presume to walk or ride, with armed force in riotous
Meetings and Assemblies against the Peace of the said King, his
Heirs and Successors, to the disturbance of the People of the said
King, his Heirs and Successors, And also of all those who had lain in
wait, or should thereafter presume to lie in wait, to mayhem or Kill
the People of the said King, his Heirs or Successors.   And also of
Hosts and Hostelers and all and singular other Persons who in abuse
of Weights and Measures or in the selling of Victuals, against the
form of the Ordinances or Statutes or either of them thereupon for
the Common Profit of the Realm of England and the People of the
said King, his Heirs and Successors, thereof made and published, had
offended or attempted, or should thereafter presume to offend or
attempt in the Borough aforesaid.   And also of all Constables,
Goalers or other Officers who in the Execution of their Offices concerning the Premises or any of them had misbehaved themselves, or
should thereafter presume to misbehave themselves or had been or
should thereafter chance or happen to be slack, remiss or negligent
in the Borough aforesaid, and of all and singular Articles and Circumstances and other things whatsoever by whomsoever and howsoever
within the Borough aforesaid or the Liberties and Precincts thereof
done or committed, or which thereafter should there happen to be
done, committed, or attempted howsoever concerning the Premises
or any of them.   And the Indictments whatsoever theretofore before
the Mayor of the Borough aforesaid taken, or which before the
aforesaid William Lord Knollis, Thomas Parry, Knight, and David
Williams, Knight, and the Mayor of the Borough aforesaid for the
time being, and every one that was Mayor of the said Borough,
within one year next following after that he had quitted or gone out
of his Office of Mayoralty, And the Recorder of the Borough

aforesaid for the time being, or any two or more of them (of which the said late King James willed that the Mayor and Recorder aforesaid should be two) should thereafter chance or happen to be taken, to inspect and consider and to continue Processes thereupon against all and singular the Persons so Indicted, or which thereafter should happen to be so Indicted, until they should be taken, render themselves or be outlawed, and to hear and determine all and singular the Felonies, Witchcrafts, Inchantments, Sorceries, Arts Magic, Trespasses, Forestallings, Regratings, Ingrossings, Extortions, riotous Meetings and Assemblies, and Indictments aforesaid, and all and singular other the Premises, according to the Laws and Statutes of the Realm of England as in such and the like case had been accustomed or ought to have been done, or to correct and punish the same Offenders and every of them for their Offences by Fines, Ransoms, Amerciaments, Forfeitures and other ways as according to the Law and Custom of the Realm of England or the Form of the Ordinances or Statutes aforesaid had been used and accustomed to be done, so nevertheless that they did not proceed to the determination of any Treason Felony or other Offence whatsoever touching the loss of Life or Members within the Borough aforesaid, the Liberties and Precincts thereof, without the special Licence of the said late King James, his Heirs or Successors. And that the aforesaid William Lord Knollis, Thomas Parry, Knight, and David Williams, Knight, and every Mayor of the Borough aforesaid, for one whole year following after that he hath quitted or gone out of his Office of Mayoralty, And also the Recorder of the Borough aforesaid, for the time being, and every of them, should take a Corporal Oath before the Mayor of the Borough aforesaid, for the time being, the Office of Justice of the Peace rightly and faithfully to Execute, and the Oaths in that behalf by the Laws and Statutes of his said Majesty's Realm of England provided, by the Justices of Peace required to be taken. And that the Mayor of the Borough aforesaid, for the time being, should and might have Power, Licence and Authority to give and administer such Oath as aforesaid as well to such aforesaid Recorder as to such Justice of Peace by Virtue of the said Letters Patent without any Warrant or Commission of his said Majesty, his Heirs or Successors, to be had, obtained or prosecuted, as by the said recited Letters Patent (amongst other things) more fully appears. And whereas, although it appeared necessary by the said last mentioned Charter to create five Justices of the Peace in addition to the one appointed by the former Charter, Yet Provision was therein made for the continuance of no more than two of them. **And whereas** the Mayor, Bayliffs and Burgesses of our said Borough of Abingdon, have by their Petition, humbly represented to us that by reason of there being only three Justices of the Peace within the said Borough, great Inconveniences arise by means of Sickness, Infirmity or other Causes whereby two of the said Justices are often prevented from Meeting, and by means whereof several Acts, Matters and Things which by the Laws of this Realm cannot be done but in the presence of two Justices, often remain unfinished and neglected, And that by one or more modern Acts of Parliament common Brewers of Ale or Beer, Innkeepers or Distillers, or other Sellers of or Dealers in Ale or any Kind of spirituous Liquors, or interested in any of the said Trades or Businesses, or being a Victualler or Malster, are rendered incapable of Executing the Office of a Justice of the Peace for the Granting any Licence for Selling Ale, Beer or any Liquors by Retail, by means whereof a greater Number of Justices are now necessary than might have been in former times. **And whereas** the said Mayor, Bayliffs and Burgesses of the said Borough of Abingdon have therefore humbly besought Us to extend the said Charter, by Granting an Increase of Justices of the Peace for the said Borough of Abingdon, by enabling and empowering the said Mayor, Bayliffs and Capital Burgesses of the said Borough, together with the Secondary or Assistant Burgesses of the Borough aforesaid, Annually to elect and chuse two more fit and discreet Persons out of the Body of the said Capital Burgesses, (not then being Mayor or Mayor elect, or Justice of Peace for the said Borough, for the time being, as the last Mayor after his Office ended), And that such Election might be had on the same day in every year that the Election of a Mayor is had, and immediately after the Mayor is Elected by and in pursuance of the present Charter of the said Borough of Abingdon. **Now know ye**, that **wee**, being willing to remedy the said Inconvenience, and of Our special Grace, certain knowledge and meer motion, **Have** Given and Granted, And by these Presents for Ourself, our Heirs and Successors, **Do** Give and Grant to the said Mayor, Bayliffs and Burgesses of our said Borough of Abingdon, in the County of Berks, and their Successors, That the said Mayor,

And reciting Petition by Mayor, &c., representing inconvenience of having three Justices only.

And praying powers to elect two Justices annually.

Bayliffs and Capital Burgesses, together with the Secondary or Assistant Burgesses of the Borough aforesaid, for the time being, and their Successors for ever from henceforth, yearly on the first day of the Month of September, immediately after the Mayor of the said Borough shall be elected by and in pursuance of the said Charter granted to the said Borough by the said King Philip and Queen Mary, shall meet together and may and shall be able to meet together in the Common Hall called the Council House or in any other convenient Place within the said Borough of Abingdon, and that then and there it shall and may be lawful for the said Mayor, Bayliffs and Capital Burgesses, together with the Secondary or Assistant Burgesses of the said Borough for the time being, to nominate, elect and choose and shall and may be able to Nominate, Elect and choose two Men of the more grave and discreet Men out of the Body of the said Capital Burgesses of the said Borough, Provided that such two Men so to be chosen nor either of them shall be the then Mayor of the said Borough, nor the Mayor then elected for the year ensuing, nor the then Justice by virtue of the said Charter of King James the first as having been the Mayor for the year then preceding. And the said two Capital Burgesses so elected, shall be and be called Justices of our Peace, and the Office of Justices of the Peace of and within the Borough aforesaid, and the Precincts and Liberties thereof, shall respectively execute, perform and exercise for one whole year, from the said first day of September in each and every year, in as full large and ample manner to all Intents and purposes as Our other Justices of the Peace in and for the said Borough are empowered and enabled to do by force and Virtue of the said Charters or Letters Patent hereinbefore mentioned or either of them, Which said two Men so to the Office of Justices of the Peace elected and each of them shall take a Corporal Oath before the Mayor of the Borough aforesaid, for the time being, at and immediately after such their Election, the Office of Justice of the Peace in and for the said Borough rightly and faithfully to Execute, and such other Oaths as other Justices of our Peace are by the Laws and Statutes of this Our Realm of England required to take, and that the Mayor of the Borough aforesaid, for the time being, shall and is hereby authorized and empowered to administer such Oaths as aforesaid to such Justices of the Peace by Virtue of these Presents without any other Warrant or Commission of us Our Heirs or Successors to be had or prosecuted .

Grant of powers to elect two Justices of the Peace annually for one year.

Elected Justices to take Oaths.

To hold Office for one year from 1st Sept. and until Election of Successors.

in that behalf. **And** from and immediately after such Corporal Oath respectively taken, they and each of the said Persons so as aforesaid nominated and elected shall bear the Office of Justice of Our Peace of, for and within the said Borough of Abingdon, for one whole year next following, that is to say, from the First day of September inclusive, until the First day of September exclusively, one whole and entire year to be compleated, And from the said first day of September exclusive, until two others sufficient and fit Persons, the said Office of Justices of the Peace faithfully to Execute shall be duly elected, admitted and sworn, and if by chance it shall happen that the two Capital Burgesses so to be elected and admitted to the Office of Justices of the Peace of and within the said Borough, or either of them, shall die or be removed from his or their Office or Offices of Capital Burgess during the period herein before mentioned of and for their said Offices of Justices of the Peace, Then it shall and may be lawful for the said Mayor, Bayliffs and Capital Burgesses,

Powers to Mayor, &c., to elect in case of Death or Removal.

together with the Secondary and Assistant Burgesses of the said Borough for the time being, or the greater part of them, to assemble and meet together a new in the said House or any other convenient place within the said Borough aforesaid, within eight days next following the Death of the said Justices of the said Borough of Abingdon, or of either of them, or the Removal of them or either of them from the said Office of Capital Burgesses. And that they shall and may be able then and there to nominate, elect and choose two other fit Men of the Number of Capital Burgesses qualified in manner above mentioned, to be Justice or Justices of the Peace for the said Borough of Abingdon, in the place and stead of the said Justices or Justice being dead or removed, in manner and form abovesaid, Which said two Men or Man (as the case shall happen) upon and after taking the several Oaths above mentioned before the Mayor of the said Borough, whom Wee hereby Authorize and Impower to Administer the same, shall bear and exercise the Office of Justices or Justice of the Peace of and within the same Borough until the first day of September then next following, And from the same first day of September until two other fit and discreet Persons the said Office faithfully to Execute shall be duly Nominated, elected, chosen, sworn and Admitted, in manner and form abovesaid.

In Witness whereof Wee have caused these Our Letters to be made Patent.

𝔚𝔦𝔱𝔫𝔢𝔰𝔰 ourself, at Westminster, the twenty third day of August, in the Fourteenth year of our Reign.

By Writ of Privy Seal.

COCKS.

THE CHARTER

GRANTED BY

WILLIAM IV., 3RD JUNE, A.D. 1836.

William the Fourth, by the Grace of God, of the United Kingdom of Great Britain and Ireland, King, Defender of the Faith, **To** our trusty and well beloved The Mayor, Aldermen and Burgesses of the Borough of **Abingdon,** and to the Inhabitants of the said Borough and to all Others whom it may concern, Greeting, **Whereas** the Council of the said Borough has, pursuant to the Provisions of an Act passed in the sixth year of our Reign, intituled " An Act to provide for the regulation of Municipal Corporations in England and Wales," signified by Petition to Us in our Council the desire of the Council of the said Borough that a Separate Court of Quarter Sessions of the Peace shall continue to be holden in and for the said Borough. **Now, know ye,** that We, having taken the matter of the said Petition into our consideration and being above all things anxious to promote the due administration of Justice. have thought fit to comply with the said Petition, And We therefore do hereby grant unto the said Borough that a Separate Court of Quarter Sessions of the Peace shall henceforward continue to be holden in and for such Borough according to the Provisions of the said Act. **And further,** Know Ye, that We do assign the Recorder, for the time being, of the said Borough, one Justice to enquire the Truth more fully by the Oath of good and lawful Men of the aforesaid Borough by whom the Truth of the matter shall be better known, of all and all manner of Felonies and misdemeanors, and of all and singular other Crimes and Offences of which Justices of our Peace may or ought lawfully to inquire, by whomsoever or after what manner soever in the said Borough done or perpetrated or which shall happen to be there done or attempted,

Grant of a Court of Quarter Session.

And of all and singular Articles and Circumstances and all other things whatsoever that concern the Premises or any of them by whomsoever and after what manner soever in our aforesaid Borough done or perpetrated, or which hereafter shall there happen to be done or attempted in what manner soever. And to inspect all Indictments whatsoever so before him the said Recorder taken or to be taken, or before Others late our Justices of the Peace in the aforesaid Borough made or taken and not yet determined, and to make and continue Processes thereupon against all and singular the persons so Indicted, or who before the said Recorder hereafter shall happen to be Indicted, until they can be taken, surrender themselves or be Outlawed. And to hear and determine all and singular the Felonies, Misdemeanors and Offences aforesaid, and all and singular other the Premises according to the Laws and Statutes of England as in the like case it has been accustomed or ought to be done before and by our Courts of Quarter Sessions, in England. And the same Offenders and every of them for their Offences by fines, ransoms, amerciaments, forfeitures and other means, as according to the Law and Custom of England or form of the Ordinances and Statutes aforesaid it has been accustomed or ought to be done to chastise and punish. **Provided always**, that if a case of difficulty upon the determination of any of the Premises shall happen to arise before the said Recorder, for the time being, then Judgment shall in nowise be given thereon before him, unless in the presence of one of our Justices of the one or other Bench or of one of our Justices appointed to hold the Assizes in the County of Berks. **And**, therefore, We Command the said Recorder, for the time being, that to keeping the Peace, Ordinances, Statutes and all and singular other the Premises he diligently apply himself; And that at certain days and places which he shall appoint for these purposes, into the Premises he make enquiry and all and singular the Premises hear and determine and perform and fulfil them in the aforesaid form, doing therein what to Justice appertains according to the Law and Custom of England, Saving Unto us the Amerciaments and other things to us therefrom belonging. **And** We Command, by the tenor of these presents, the proper Officers of the aforesaid Borough, that at certain days and places which the said Recorder shall make known to them, they cause to come before him, the said Recorder so many and such good and lawful Men of the said Borough by whom the Truth in the matter in the Premises shall be the better known and inquired into.

In Witness whereof, We have caused these Our Letters to be made Patent.

Witness Ourself at Westminster, the third day of June, in the Sixth Year of our Reign.

By Writ of Privy Seal.

EDMUNDS.

Records of the Borough of Abingdon.

PART II.

SELECTIONS FROM THE CHRONICLES

OF THE

UNREFORMED CORPORATION

(A.D. 1555 TO A.D. 1835).

The Orders whiche haithe Bene made within the Borowghe of Abingdone by the Maior, Head Burgesses and Secondarye Burgesses, as co'cernenge the good rule of the said Borowghe by all there Comon assent, as hereafter followithe :—

An Ordre for the Avoyd-enge of the Butchers' stalles, and that all the Shoppes shalbe from henceforthe furnished.

An ordre taken for and concernenge the Stalles or standings of Butchers, Strangers in the Butcher Rowe, viz. :—

23rd April, A.D. 1556, 3rd and 4th Philip & Mary. Richard Mayott, *Mayor.*

Imprimis. Yt is ordred and decreed by the Comon Counselle that all the shoppes standinge on the Easte syde of the said Rowe beinge not at this p'nte occupied with Butchers, from the north end of the said East syde, unto the ten'te in the tenure of Leonard Collens shalbe ymedyatlye voyded and made cleare of all other ten'nts, And that done, the said shoppes shalbe furnished and prepaired for Butchers, and that the said shoppes so furnished and prepared shalbe demysed to Butchers, strangers and other, by the yeare for certen yerelye rente, or elles for ij*d.* everye markette and Faire ; And that none other shall sette fourthe anye standings for Forrein Butchers or butchers

Inhabytinge within this Borowghe before all the said shoppes shalbe furnished with butchers which be occupiers; and suche as be nowe ten'nts and notte butchers shalbe warned by ye serjaunts to avoid there shopps before Michelmas.

An Order made for Butchers Stalles. } **First** yt is ordeyned and decreed by the comon councell that all suche shoppes as stand on the east syde of the said Rowe or Shambille from the north ende thereof unto Leonard Collyns house, beinge at this p'nte ordred, made and occupied as butchers shoppes, shalbe ymedyatlye avoyded of all suche persones as nowe do inhabite within the same, And shalbe furthwith at the costs and chargs of the Chamber of the said Borowghe p'paired and made redye for butchers' shoppes, and so to be used for butchers eyther by the yeare for a certen rent, or ells for ij*d.* every markette and Faire, and that none other of the inhabiturs shall sette furth anye standings untill the said shoppes be furnished, upon payne of forfeyte for everye tyme doinge to the contrarye ij*d.*

For butchers. } **Also**, yt ys ordeyned, that none of the said inhabitors after warnenge to them geven, shall kepe anye open standinge for anye butchef, at anye tyme, so longe as anye of the said Shoppes be unfurnished, or vacante of a ten'nte, upon the lyke payne.

St. Margrets Fayre. } **Itm.** yt is ordred and agreid that Sainte Margretts Faire shalbe kepte on places comonlye used, savnge that the horse markette shalbe kepte in Bore Strete and the Brode Strete.

For nighte walkers to be redde of the Lawe daye. } **Itm.** if anye nighte walker be taken within this Borowghe after the houres of tenne in the somer, that is to saye, from the Feaste of Phillippe and Jacobe, otherwyse called Maye Daye, untill the feast of St. Mychell th'archangell, or after the hower of ix. in the wynter, that is to saye, from the said feast of St. Mychell untill the said first daye of Maye, the same shalbe comytted to ward for yt night at the comaundmente of Mr. Maior, for the tyme beinge, untill the next morenge, and to be amercyed at the discrecion of Mr. Maior for his late walkinge at xij*d.*, th'one half whereof to the use of the chamber of this Borowgh, and the other half thereof to the constables that shall so aprehende the same night walker. Provided alwayes A lawefull cause to be accepted and allowed.

An Ordre that no Inholder or others shall lodge anye Stranger above thre dayes and thre nyghts. **Item.** that from hencefurthe no Inholder or other inhabytante within this Borowghe shall Lodge or mayntene within his house anye gests, artificer or stranger above the space of thre dayes and thre nights, but he shall gyve knowlege to Mr. Maior thereof, for the tyme beinge, that he maye be examyned of the cause of his abode within the said Borowghe, And everye Inholder and other Inhabytante so offendinge shall forfeyte to the Chamber of this Borowghe iijs. iiijd., and farther suffre ymprisonement at the pleasure of Mr. Maior of the said Borowghe.

An Ordre for the Comyttinge of any freman to warde upon his othe. **Item.** whatsoever Freman beinge upon his othe, and commytted by Mr. Maior, for the tyme beinge, to ward for enie cause, doe not ymedyatlye comytte himself to warde and there remayne untill he shalbe lawfullie discharged, the same Freman for his disobedyence shalbe disfranchised.

The name of the prysone. **Item.** the name of the common Prysone of this Borowghe shalbe called and knowne by the name of gate howse.

An Ordre for the Avoydenge of undre ten'nts by a daye to be redde at the Lawe Daye. **Item.** for dyvers good consideracons yt is agreid that all the underten'nts nowe dwellinge or inhabyting within this Borowghe, shalbe removed and avoyded on this side the feast of the natyvitie of o'r Ladie next comeinge, And that after the said Feaste no Inhabytante to receive into his howse anye underten'nte without lycence of Mr. Maior, upon payne to lose xs., and his fredome, if he be a Freman, and be disfranchised, and if he be no Freeman, to suffre ymprisonment at Mr. Maior's pleasure, and to make Fyne at his discrecion and his bretherne the principall burgesses for the tyme beinge.

An Ordre for clubbes to be had in everye Fremans howse. **Item.** for the more tranquillitie of this borowghe, and the better avoydenge of Barrators and P'turbars of the Quenes M'ties peace, as also certen other inconveniences that might ensue, yt is established and ordred that everye inhabytante within this Borowghe shall forthwith and with all speid convenyent, p'pare and have in redynes a good and sufficiente Clubbe for the cons'vacion of the said peace, the same alwayes to remayne in the shoppes of everye Inhabytante or some other convenyent place next adjoinenge to the strete, and whatsoever Inhabytante shalbe founde negligente in this behalf, after the feast of the Natyvytie of our Ladye next comenge, the same shall paye for everye mouthe he shalbe so founde without his said clubbe xij*d.*, the one half whereof to the use of the Chamber, and the other half to the taker of everye such offendour.

An Ordre for byenge and } **Itm.** yt is lykewise ordeyned and
selling of Rawe hydes. established, that no man'r of persone or persones that shall bye anye hides, skynnes or Felles, shall not bye the same before theye shalbe brought and openlye laid w'thin the p'cincte of the Burye, that is to saye the corners of the good wyf goldsmythe's, and Thomas Davis, the gate at Thomas Jennen's Dore, and Ric'd. Hille's corner, and Mr. Mathewe his corner, and Caries corner, under payne to forfyte the stuf sold out of the said p'cinte, Except Saynte Edmondes faire, and the sergiantes of the same Borowghe to foresee the said ordre.

An Ordre for Butchers, } **And further,** yt is also estab-
beinge strangers. lished, that when and after the said Shoppes shalbe furnished and placed w'th Butchers, then every of the strange Butchers that shalbe repaire to the markette with victualles, shall have Lyb'te to take standynges or Stalles on the other syde of the rowe, So that the said Stalles or standinges be not sette above the uppermoste shoppe of the Butchers' Strangers, and to paye every m'kett day j*d.* for every the said Stalles to the use of the Towne.

(The above orders were confirmed by the Common Council during the Mayoralty of Thomas Smythe, in the year 1584.)

30th Decr., A.D. 1557. 4th and 5th Philip & Mary. Humphrey Bostock, *Mayor.*
An ordre that no burgesse } **Also,** yt is agreid, that no Burgesse
shall speake in the defence of shall speake for anye man that shalbe
anye offendo'r upon a payne. offendo'r before his face, and after be brought before Mr. Maior and the other Burgesses in the councell howse, at anye tyme upon payne to forfeyte for everye offence vj*s.* viij*d.* Provided that this ordre shalbe redde foure tymes a yeare.

An ordre for openenge shoppe windowes upon Soundayes. } **Jtm.** that no occupiers, victulers, or other, w'thin this Borowghe, shall upon the Soundaye, after service belle be ronge, Selle there victualles or wayres in the s'vice tyme upon the Sabothe daye, upon payne of everye man that shall so offende to forfeyte for everye tyme vj*s.* viij*d.* Provided alwayes that Inholders shalbe clerelye exempted out of this ordre for travelengé men, and for none other.

An ordre for the eleccon of secondary burgeses to be head burgesses. } **Jtm.** yt is decreid by Mr. Maior and the princypall burgeses of this Borowghe, that from and after the daye above wrytten, everye Secondarye Burgesse that hereafter shall be chosen or elected one of the princypall Burgesses, shall paye to the Chamber of this Borowghe, at everye tyme he or theye shall be so elected or chosen, the somme of fortye shillinges,

12th January, A.D. 1557. 4th and 5th Philip & Mary. Richard Mayott, *Mayor.*

An ordre that every burgesse upon eney acc'on comenced againste him shalbe Somoned at the first tyme. } **Jtm.** yt is lykewyse agreid by the said maior and burgeses, that from and after the daye nextabovesaid, all and everye burgesse that shall have anye acc'on com'enced againste him Shall not be arrested, but the sergiante shall goe to him and Somone him to Appeare at the next courte to be holden to answere the said acc'on, and the sergiant shall have of the pl' for so somonenge hym, ij*d.* And yf he or theye doe not come to answere the acc'on, at the said courte, Then the sergiante to arreste him and bringe him to the towne clerke, theyre to put yn bayle accordinge to the ordre and dewe course of the lawe.*

12th March, A.D. 1557. 4th and 5th Philip & Mary. Richard Mayott, *Mayor.*

An ordre that iiij of the secondarye Burgesses shall appere upon everye acc'on above the some of xls. } **Jtm.** yt ys lykwyse agreid and stablished by the said maior and burgesses of the said Borowghe, that no Secondarye burgesse shalbe Somoned to appeare upon anye Jurye undre the some of xls., And above the somme of xls., yt is agreid that Six of the Secondarye burgesses shalbe Somoned, whereof foure to be appoynted wth the residewe of the Comons when tyme and nede shall require. And in weightie matters w'ch excede and amounte unto the Some of Fyve pounds, Then twelf of the said Secondarye Burgesses shall appeare when tyme requirithe. *

* These Orders were cancelled 27th March, A.D. 1584, 26th Elizabeth, at a Common Council.

P

An ordre towching the Jaylo'r. | ℑℳ. yt ys Lykewyse agreid by the said Maior and Burgesses that the

Jayler for the tyme beinge shall have for hys Fee of everye forryner, p'soner, at hys discharge, iiij*d.* And of everye freman, p'soner, at hys discharge, ij*d.*

MARKETTS ANDE FAYRES.

𝔉irste of everye Lynnen Draper and wolen drape' havinge a tylte stalle, or w'thoute Tylte, of tenne or twelf foote longe } iiij*d.*

ℑℳ. of everye tanner for his stall, for ev'y m'ket   ... j*d.*

ℑℳ. everye Fayre, oneles he doe agree for the hole yeare ... ij*d.*

ℑℳ. Yron mongers and smythes, every m'ket daye   ... j*d.*

ℑℳ. Every Fayre daye   ...   . ij*d.*

ℑℳ. Ropers and Collemakers, of every shewe day   ... ij*d.*

ℑℳ. for all oth'r stalles, excepte butchers, every daye   ... j*d.*

20th October,
A.D. 1559.
1st Elizabeth
Thomas Tonck,
Mayor.

𝔒rders made in the tyme of Thomas Tonkes, Maior, the xx*th* daye of Octrobre, Anno Regni Elizabethe, etc., Primo.

An Ordre that the Maior shall not doe anye acte wch maye be p'iudiciall to this Corporacon [under a penalty of £40].   *   *   *

An Ordre that the Maior shall not breake anye ordre made by comone Councell [without the whole assent of the Council, under a penalty of £40].   *   *   *   *   *

An ordre that the Maior for the tyme beinge shall not absent himself above the space of xij dayes. | ℑℳ. we doe ordeyne and decree, that the Maior for the tyme beinge of this Borowgbe, after his othe taken, shall not absente him self furthe of the

saime towne Duringe the tyme of his office, at anye tyme above the space of xij. Dayes, w'thout Lawfull Deputye Admytted by the hole councelle of the headburgesses or the more p'te of them, upon payne of forfature to the Chambre of this borowgbe x.*li.*, to be levyed of his goodes, And if he absente him self undre the noumbre of those dayes, then to make a deputye suche as he shall thinke mete. And that he shall not dep'te out of this Borowghe and dwelle in anye other Forreyne place Duringe the tyme of his office, upon payn of 40.*li.* Provided that if the said Maior doe not agree w'th his said bretherne to forfayte the payne above p'scribed.

An ordre that no p'sone, after he haithe borne the office of Meyraltye, shall dep'te out of the towne upon payne of tenne poundes   .   .   . **Jfm.** we doe ordeyne, constitute and decree, that if anye p'sone after he haithe bene once Maior Dep'te out of this Borowghe, and Dwelle in anye other Forreyne place, then to paye to th' use of the chamber of this Borowghe X.*li.*, to be levyed of his goodes and cattalles, before his gooddes Dep'te from thence, Excepte yt be upon agremente by the Maior and princypall burgesses of this Borowghe.

An ordre concernenge the p'ambulacons to be made betwixt Easter and mychelmas upon a payne. **Jfm.** yt is decreed and stablished by the common Councell of this Borowghe, that from hencefurthe the p'ambulacons shalbe holden from thre yeares to thre yeares, or soner if nede shall require upon urgente causes, Betwene Easter and mychelmas, at suche tyme as the Maior shall thinke good, calling there unto all the Burgesses and Free men of the Borowghe. And that everye pryncypalle Burgesse that shalbe absente w'thout lycence or Lawfull excuse to forfeyte to the chamber iij*s*. iiij*d*. And everye Secondarye Burgesse xx*d*. And everye howsholder, beinge a Freman and an artificer, to forfeyte xij*d*. And it is further orderyd that the Maior not p'formynge this order shall Forfeyte xl*s*., and so shall evry Maior w'ch Follow'th and dothe nott Doe the said P'ambulacon.

An ordre that ye inhabytantes of this Borowghe shalbe devided into sevrall companyes. **Jfm.** we doe ordeyne, constitute and Decree that the inhabytantes of this Borowghe shalbe Devided into Severall companyes, for the better utylytie and good ordre of them selfes and theyre famylyes; And that yt shalbe Lawfull for the maior for the time beinge and his bretherne the pryncypalle Burgesses, or the more p'te of them, at there Discrecons, to devide the same, and to Devide so manye mysteryes or facultyes into evry companye as theye shall thinke good.

An ordre that no forryner shall have his fredome under V.li.

An ordre that no forryner shall bye or selle w'th an other forryner anye thinge within this lib'te upon payne [of forfeiture, except on fair and market days].   *   *   *   *   *   *

An ordre that no Free man shall exempte him self out of this borowghe above a yeare and a Day and not paye scotte and lotte upon a payne [of losing his freedom].   *   *   *   *   *

An ordre for the collectinge of money ["for the furnishing of harnesse" and rendering and preserving the collector's accounts].
*   *   *   *   *   *

And concernenge the head burgesses and Secondarye burgesses wearinge their gownes. **Jtm.** yt is concluded, condiscended and agreid, that everye headburges shall not come to Comon councell without his gown, undre payne of vjs. viijd. And everye secondarye Burges for makenge the lyke default iijs. iiijd., or anye other asemble appointed by the Maior shall forfeyte for everye tyme that he or theye shall so offend, the payne above said.

19th Sept., A.D. 1561. 3rd Elizabeth. Oliver Hide, Mayor.

For spekinge unsemely wordes in ye Counsell howse. **Jmprimis.** yt ys condiscended, concluded and agreeid by comone Councelle, that there shalbe no man'r of unseamelye wordes styrred, raysed or multiplied w'thin the comon Councelle to the Disquietinge of the reaste; But that in all matters beinge put in question in the same howse shalbe reasoned and answered reasonablie and charytablie. And what so ever he be that shall offend therein shalbe comytted for his offence to warde, Or suche fyne to be sessed upon his head as by the dis'recon of the Maior and his bretherne, the princypall burgesses, shalbe thought mete, or by the more p'te of them.

For nott dep'tinge after the comon Counselle are assembled. **Jtm.** it ys condiscended and agreeid that after the Comon councell be once Sette and anye matters there put in question, That then none of the comon councell shall Dep'te out of the howse w'thout Lycence of the Maior, or Some other Reasonable Cause for the tyme beinge, upon payne of iijs. iiijd. or to be Comytted to ward.

That no freman shall take no prentice under [the term of] *seven yeares* ["and that he be free borne, that is to saye, that he be an englyshe man borne"]   *   *   *   *

No Man shalbe Maior before he haithe bene bayllie.   *   *   *

No freman shall serve as a souldior w'thout lycence to be redd of the Lawe daye. **Jtm.** for as muche as at Dyvers tymes heare tofore the freemen of this Borowghe have used to serve other foreyn townes in the Quene's Ma'ties affaires and her p'genitors, Leavinge the towne Destitute to the great slaunder thereof, And besides that Leavinge his famylie, that is to saye, his wife and children behinde him, wherebye the towne is charged at findinge of her or them so lefte behinde. For Reformac'on whereof yt is condiscended and agreeid by the hole assent and consent of the comon Councell of the Borowghe, That if anye free of this Borowghe doe at anye tyme hereaft'r serve anye forrein towne w'thout Lycence of the Maior of this Borowghe for the tyme Beinge, shalbe from thence-furthe taken as a forryner, And lose his fredome and lib'tie of this borowghe for ever.

Prentices that weare bounde before the Corporac'on [entitled to be enrolled as freemen on payment of 2/6 by the Master]. *   *   *

Everye Freeman shall inrolle his apprentice w'thin a certen space lymyted upon a payne. *   *   *   *.

The comon Councell holden at Abyngdone the xj*th* Daye of Decembre, Anno Regni Eliza. Regine, &c., Quinto, before Thomas Orpwoode, Maior of the same boroughe.

11th December A.D. 1562. 5th Elizabeth. Thomas Orpwood, *Mayor.*

Inprimis. yt is agreid by Thomas Orpwood, Maior, the Princypall burgesses and comon Councell of this Borowghe, that if anye p'sone or p'sones doe make anye evell reporte upon Mr. Maior or anye the burgesses in the hearinge of anye the said burgesses, or anye other Freman, that then the same burges that shall heare anye suche reporte to make relacon of yt ymedyatlye or w'thin xxiiij howres after unto the Maior or his Deputye for the tyme beinge, undre the payn of vj*s.* viij*d.*

Itm. yt is decreid by the said Maior, pryncipall burgesses and comon Councell, that if anye of the Comon councell shall reveale, declare or saye anye wordes beinge Spoken in the councelle howse, Excepte againste the crowne, w'ch god Defende, out of the councell howse, then suche p'sone so founde faultye shall forfeyte to the chambre of this borowghe vj*s.* viij*d.*

It ys ordeynede and agreid by Mr. Maior, the pryncipall Burgesses and Comon Councelle of this Borowghe, that everye Freman that shall absente himself from the walke of the p'ambulacon at a Daye appointed shall forfeyte iij*s.* and iiij*d.*

21st July. A.D. 1563. 5th Elizabeth. Thomas Orpwood, *Mayor.*

𝔘𝔱 is orderyd that no Inkep', vintener, Alehowse Kep', nor other vittailer, shall make to Sell in his Howse by retayle or to his Gestes eny qr. bred or jd. ijd. iijd. or iiijd. bred beinge in losse [*under a penalty*].

𝔘𝔱 ys also Further Orderyd That no p'son or p'sons inhabitinge w'hin this Towne, beinge an Inkep', Alehowse kep', vintener, or vittayler, shall brue in his Howse anye Beere or Ale to be sold, offerid or drunke in his Howse, either by the pinte potte, quarte pottell or gallon potte, under the payne to Lose for evry potte so sould xs.

𝔘𝔱 is further ordereid That no p'son or p'sons inhabitinge w'thin this Towne shall suffer his or there hogges or pigges to wander in the Co'on Streates, or w'thin the Churche yarde of S. Ellyn's, w'thout havinge a keper or Follower, or yf eny p'son or p'sons Do Feade eny there Hogges in the streates or nere unto Burforde, yf eny mans Hogges or Hogge be taken contrary to this ordre, yt shall be Lawfull for the Baylyffes for the tyme beinge to take the Hogges or Hogge so offendinge, and to put them in the pownd untill xd. be pade for evry hogg, and the money taken therefor shalbe paid half to the Baylyffes and half to the use of the Towne.

20th July,
A.D. 1580.
22nd Elizabeth.
Humphrey
Hyde,
Mayor.

An order providing that any burgess elected a Principal Burgess, and refusing to serve when elected, shall "*be comited to warde and* "*prison,* * * * * *there to remayne without bayle or* "*maynepryse untill suche tyme as he do paye such fyne and Some of* "*money as shalbe taxed or sett downe by the Maior, Baylyffes and* "*Principalle Burgesses,* * * * *or take ye othe of a* "*principall Burges.*" * * * * * *

The Maior's Allowance. } 𝔘𝔱 is agreed that evry Maior from henceforthe servinge one Hole yere in the office of the Maior, shall uppon his Juste accompte made and all arrerage by hym dewe to the said Towne uppon the said Accompte paide, have Allowed hym For his yeres paynes and chardges Twentie powndes, And yf he dye w'thin the yere then Xl.

1st September,
A.D. 1583.
25th Elizabeth.
William
Braunche,
Mayor.

𝔄t this daye Cam' Humfrey Hyde, gent, and deliv'd to the said Maior, to the Use of the Towne, one Silver Goblett, weyinge xviijoz, or thereaboutes, for th'arrerage heretofore Dewe out of All the Land of Oliver Hyde, gent, Decessed, beinge in Abendon, Shipton and Sonnyngwell, of the yerely Rent of xvjs. * * * * *

Jt is Ordered that theire shalbe no shepe pennes sett above th' ende of the Layne cauled St. Edmondes lane, on th'on side, and Robarte Connes al's Conwayes howse on th'other syde of the streate, and evry one w'ch haithe eny sheppe pennes before theire dores shall, for evry three pennes, paye weekly towardes the mendinge of the Streate j*d*.   *   *   *   *   *   *

27th November, A.D. 1583. 26th Elizabeth. Thomas Smythe, *Mayor.*

Jt is ordered that all forreyners w'h are Farmers, or w'h doe bye eny Rawe hydes within the m'kett of this Bourowghe, shall for evry two Rawe hydes w'h he byethe, bring and sell one tanned hyde of good leather, uppon payne to forfeyte for evry hyde ij*s.* vj*d.*, and so after the Rate for a greater Quantitie.

Whereas there is a care had by the Mayor, &c.,   *   *   * to avoid the daunger of fyer and mysdemeners and for the good govenement of The Boroughe, Yt is ordered by the Mayor, &c.,   * *   *   * that yerelie from the feaste of Sainte Michael Th'archangell, unto the feaste of Th'assension, That two howseholders dwelling together next adioynyng, shall either in theire owne p'sons or els finde two sufficient howsholders to watche for them, w'ch shalbe allowed by Mr. Mayor nightlie by order, And there to watche from eighte of the clock in th'afternoone, untill fyve of the clock in the mornynge, pena qmlibt v.*s*, and those w'ch watche shall geve there next nieghbor warnyng to watche the next nyght following, and then to shewe themselves to the Mayor or his Deputie at the Crosse by eighte of the clock as aforsaide, w'th sufficyent weapon for watchemen.

25th October, A.D. 1584. 26th Elizabeth. Thomas Mayott, *Mayor.*

Jt is ordered that from hensfurthe owte of evrye howse w'ch shall have iiij p'sons Dwelling therin, that one at leaste shalbe at the S'rmon on Thu'sdaies, yf more than iiij then two being of discresstion, pena vj*d*.

27th October, A.D. 1585. 27th Elizabeth. Paul Orpwood, *Mayor.*

Jtm. it is ordered that noe p'son or p'sons shall buye anye Corne or grayne on the Markett daye but in the open Markett place, and pyched there after the comon Bell is runge, on forfayture of the Corne to the poore, th'one half at the charges of the byer, and th'other of the seller. *

   * A similar order was made prohibiting the sale of wool before "the Markett bell be rung."

Jt is ordered that from hencefurth yerelie upon Alsaintes, the princes hollyday, Christmas day, Easter daie, and Whitsundaye, all

18th November, A.D. 1585. 28th Elizabeth. Paul Orpwood. *Mayor.*

the principall and secondary burgesses shall geve attendance upon the Mayor for the tyme being, unto the Churche and so home againe, upon paine evry one making defaulte for every tyme iij*s*. iiij*d*., unlesse a Reasonable excuse be showed to the contrarye.

Item. it is ordered that evrye one of the principall and secondarye Burgesses shall attend upon the Mayor for the tyme being, upon sufficient warnying to them geven, at evrye Comon Counsell, upon payne of evry one making defaulte iij*s*. iiij*d*. unless a reasonable excuse be shewed of his absence and allowed by the Mayor.

Item. It is ordered that from hencefurthe, Mr. Will'm Braunche, Mr. Lyonell Bostocke, Mr. John Fyssher, Mr. Rysbye, Mr. Anthonye Teysdall, Mr. Anthony Bostocke, Mr. Blacknoll, of banbury curte, Will'm Welling, and Richard Bolte, and evrye of them, shall bring into the Marckett everye Marckett daye, thre busshelles of maulte, and all other p'sons Inhabiting w'thin this Borowghe, using the trade of maulting, shall likewise bring into the Marckett evrye Marckett daye, two Bushelles of maulte, upon paine of evry one making defaulte for evrye tyme iij*s*. iiij*d*. *

28th Sept.,
A.D. 1586.
29th Elizabeth.
Paul Orpwood,
Mayor.

The Causes that Thomas Teysdall, gent., Dothe alledge to the Mayor, Baylyffes and Burgesses to be Reasonable causes, whic he shoulde not take upon hym to be Mayor for this yere next following, to w'ch he was elected unto, the first of September last, and desirethe theie maye be allowed accordinglie.

First. this I saie, that a foure yeres agon, being elected to the said Office, I fulfilled the said Charter & to my Charge paide the fine, also that my dwelling and mansion howse is nyne or Tenne myles hence at Kydlington, where my busynes is so greate at this tyme, that my absence from thence maye torne me to suche losses that it is hard to Recover again. Also that I have in this Borowghe neither howse, furnyture for a howse, p'vision or any thing towards the same acordinglie. • • • • • •

(An order allowing these causes " with others secretly known," and discharging the fine, is signed by the Mayor, Paul Orpwood, and others.)

12th January,
A.D. 1588.
30th Elizabeth.
William Kysbie,
Mayor.

Item. is also further ordered by the Comen Councell of the said Boroughe, That yf Richard Quelche and Thomas Teysdall, gents, do not come to the Mayor for the tyme being before the Firste daye of Maye next comyng, or shewe a lawfull cause whic theie or either of

* This order was revoked at a Council held on the 4th August, A.D. 1587.

them do exempte themselves owte of the Towne or not Companyng w'th the Mayor for to geve theire good advises for the Govnement of the said Boroughe, That then he w'ch shall not come and shewe cause, and the cause allowed lawfull by the Mayor, Baylyffes and principall Burgesses or the more p'te of them, That then he or theie not Comyng as aforsaid shalbe disfranchised of his principall burgessheppe, and one or two others Chosen in his or theire Roomes.

𝕴𝖙𝖒 is ordered that from hensforth there shall noe p'son or p'sons caule any of the Principall Burgesses or Secondary Burgesses knave or other name of reproche, upon payne to forfayte v.s, or els be comytted to prison for fyve Daies w'thoute bayle or mayneprise, this order to be redd at the Lawe daie.

For Malte measurers. } 𝕴𝖙 is ordered that from hensforthe there shalbe twoe mesurers for all the maulte whiche shalbe soulde within the Corporacon, or delivered oute of the Markett, and to take for everie flore iiij*d.*, and after that rate for a lesser Some, the buyer to paie the one ij*d.* The Seller th'other ij*d.* And that everie resiaunte sellinge Maulte, or delyveringe of Maulte, whiche shall Sell and delyver anye Maulte without the mesures or one of them shall measure the same, shall forfeyte for everie Quarter delyvered j*d.* yf the said mesures be to be founde or Attendinge uppon Warninge geven.   And the Seller shall paye the whole to the mesures uppon the Bargayne. And yf the mesures cannott be founde, or doe not Come & mesures uppon Warninge geven, (yf there shalbe suffered) then the saide mesures shall lose there Fee.

A decree that the bayleiffes } 𝕴𝖙 is ordered and decreede   *   *
shall enter with bond to paie }   *   for the better saffetie and dis-
the Fee Farme. }   charge of the pay'mt of the Fee Farme of the saide Borrowghe,   *   *   *   that the said nowe Baylieffes and all others w'ch shalbe heareafter elected Baylieffes, shall become and enter into bonde in obligacion of the Some of Twoe hundred Powndes,   *   *   *   w'th Condicion for the true paymente of the said Fee Farme into the queenes Ma'ties receipte of Exschequor.   *   *   *   *

12th November, A.D. 1590. 32nd Elizabeth. William Lee, *Mayor.*

21st May, A.D. 1591. 33rd Elizabeth. William Lee, *Mayor.*

15th October, A.D. 1591. 33rd Elizabeth. William Hart, *Mayor.*

Q

A decree that the baylieffes and Constables shall attend on the Mayor to accompanie him to the churche.

𝕴𝖙𝖒. It is also ordered and decreede that from hensforthe the Baylieffes and Constables for the tyme beinge shall, on everie Sabothe Daye and other Festifall Daies and publike Sarmons or lector Daies, attende on the Mayor for the tyme beinge, at his dwellinge howse, to th'entente to accompanye the said mayor to the churche, havinge noe lawfull excuse to the Contrarie, uppon paine of everye one w'ch shall make defaulte herof to forfeite unto the Chamber the some of xijd. Provided alwaies and the meaninge ys that yf the said Baylieffes and Constables have lawfull excuse and busines, that then the said Baylieffes and Constables shall thereof geve notice unto the said Mayor for the tyme beinge, or otherwise appointe one other his Deputie to supplie his place, otherwyse to paye the said penaltie w'thout contradixon therof.

𝕴𝖙𝖒. it is further ordered that wheare heeretofore there were divers orders and lawes made for the repressinge of bakinge and brewinge, it is nowe thought good by consent that the Mayor shall not be charged by not putinge in execucion the saide severall Statuts or orders * * * untill suche tyme as there shalbe further order made for the appointment of Common Brewers within the said Borrowghe of Abingdon * * * * *

20th January,
A.D. 1592.
34th Elizabeth.
William Hart,
Mayor.

A decree that the Comon Counsell shall quietlie behave them selfes, and not use any loude speches.

𝕴𝖙𝖒. it is ordered at this Comon Counsell, for the better quietnes in making of orders and lawes h'rafter to be made towching the Benyfytt and Comon Weale of the same, that from hensforthe aswell principall as secondary Burgeses shall in decent and quiett manner (according to theire antiquitie in choyse of theire Burgesshippes) kepe theire place, And also shall likewise quietlie behave them selves w'thoute speaking or using any manner of open or loude speaches, the one to the other, but shall directelie, according to theire best skill, geve theire good counsell and Judgement (being therunto moved by the Mayor for the tyme being) upon payne of ev'ye one using hym self to the contrary to forfayte and paie unto the Chamber of this Boroughe the some of ijs. vjd. to be presentlie paide before he dep'te forthe of the said Counsell, other Wise to comytt hym self to prison, and there to remayne untill he shall willinglie do the same.

A decree that hanson shall not occupie w'thin this Boroughe. **Itm.** it is ordered at this Comon Counsell, that John Hanson, for some speciall abuse hertofore comytted by hym, And for that it is thoughte that there are sufficient occupiers of the trade w'ch he usethe, that the said John Hanson shall not be suffred to occupie or use his trade w'thin this Boroughe but onelie upon Fayers or Marckette daies and not otherwise.

[Anthony Appletre, B.A., was this day appointed Master of the Free School, in the place of Richard Humfrey, resigned.]

6th July, A.D. 1697.

It is aggreed that the Chamb'lyn shall paie unto Alexand'r Raynoldes, xvjs. viijd. for Ringing the bell to the Mornyng and Evenyng prayer, for two yeres and a half ended at o'r lady daie last, to be deducted oute of his arrerage of Rente.

5th April, A.D. 1599. 41st Elizabeth. Francis Little, Mayor.

Whereas, Will'm Blacknall, gent., among others, is rated and taxed by Mr. Mayor that nowe is, to pay a weekly contribucon for the supplye of the releif of the poore of the parish of St. hellyns * w'thin the said Borough, according to the statue in that case provided. And whereas the said Will'm Blacknall doth refuse to pay such somes of money as he is taxed to pay, and therefore is to be destreyned for the same by the Churchwardens and Overseers of the said p'ishe of St. Nicholas. Itt is therfore agreed that the said Churchwardens and Overseers shalbe from hensforth defended and saved harmles by the Mayor, Bayliffes and Burgesses, in the performing of there said office against the said Will'm Blacknall, concerning the p'misses.

19th April, A.D. 1599. 41st Elizabeth. Francis Little, Mayor.

* ? St. Nicholas.

John Wynsmore, confessed that he did sett his hand to a late peticon exhibited to the Lordes of the Counsell against the Mayor, Bayliffes and principall Burgesses, and against the Master and Gov'nors of the hospitall.

20th July, A.D. 1599. 41st Elizabeth. Francis Little, Mayor

Alsoe, that one part of that peticon was to p'vent the obteyninge of a newe charter, whereby he feareth would be obteyned authoritie to restrayne Foreyners and to doe other thinges hurtfull to the Corporacon, and he further confessed that there was inserted into that peticon that the Mayor and Masters of the towne doe putt the revenues and proffitts of the Corporacon into there owne purses, And that the nowe Mayor and his associates have greatly oppressed the Inhabitantes of the Towne by racking of rentes and other taxacons. And to these thinges he said that he would sette his hand agayne.

Whereas the above named John Wynsmore was accused before this Comon Counsell, here assembled, for settinge his hand unto the peticon before menconed, and for joyninge him self (being a sworne member of this incorporacon) w'th dyv's factious and troublesome p'sons whoe have malitiously and slaunderously exhibited the said peticon to the privy Counsell, wherein are conteyned the Articles above remembered and dyv's other false and unhonest accusations against the Mayor, Bayliffes and principall Burgesses of this Borough, and against the Master and Gov'nors of Christ's hospitall, w'thin the said Boroughe. Itt is therefore ordered by the Comon Counsell nowe assembled and by the authority of the same, that from hensforth the said John Wynsmore shall stand and be suspended from the place and office of a Secondary Burgesse of this Borough untill the aforesaid peticon and the contentes thereof shalbe duly proved.

25th September,
A D. 1599.
41st Elizabeth.
Frauncis Brooke
alias Little,
Mayor.

It is agreed that Mr. Chamblen shall pay for the great mace and the twoe little maces, w'ch were lately bought, and that the money w'ch he shall pay for the same shalbe allowed unto him upon his accompt, And alsoe that he shall accompt for the old mace w'ch was lately sould.

28th September,
A.D. 1599.
41st Elizabeth.
Francis Little,
Mayor.

Whereas Anthony Teisdall, gent., the 1st of this instant September, was lawfully elected to be Mayor of this Borough for the yere next ensueing, and hath byn required by a p'cept to him lately directed from Mr. Mayor that nowe is, according to former usuage in this behalf, to appeare before him this p'nte day, to take a corporall othe for th'execucon of his said office   *   *   *
And the said Mr. Anthony Teisdall, appearing here this p'nte day before the Mayor   *   .*   *   refuseth to take upon him the said office of Mayraltie, and to take an othe for th' execucon of the same office, alleaging to excuse him self in this behalf that he was Mayor of the said Borough the last yere, And that th' execucon of his said office was then very chargeable unto him. And therefore, the said Mr. Teisdall desireth the Mayor   *   *   .*   to admytt and allowe of theis reasons by him alleaged, and to p'ceed

to elect some other man to the said office of Mayor for the yere next ensueing, according to the Charter of this Borough. Nowe the said Mayor   *   *   *   maturely considering of the said Mr. Teisdall his reasons formerly alleaged, doe well allowe of the same, and doe by this p'nte order discharge the said Mr. Anthony Teisdall of his said eleccon to the said office of Mayor of this Boroughe for the yere next ensueinge.

Itt is nowe agreed & ordered that the Chamblen of this Borough for the tyme being shall pay yerely out of the Chamber unto Mr. John Byrd, nowe schoolem'r of this Borough, for the Augmentacon of his wages and for maynteyning of an usher for the better keeping of the said Schoole, the some of V.*li.*   *   *   *   *

19th December, A.D. 1600. 43rd Elizabeth. Humphrey Hyde, Mayor.

Itt is ordered by the Mayor, Bayliffes & principall Burgesses that from hensforth neither the Bayliffes nor the Chamberlen of this Borough for the tyme being shall expend nor lay out any money of the treasure or stock belonging to the Chamber of this Borough w'thout the consent of the Mayor, Bayliffes and principall Burgesses, or the most part of them, declared in wrighting under there handes, and the same subscribed in the Counsell howse when they shalbe there assembled.   *   *   *   *   *   *   *   *   *

3rd January, A.D. 1601. 43rd Elizabeth. Humphrey Hyde, Mayor.

Itt is agreed that Mr. Chamblen shall p'vide, att the charges of the Chamber, ij great hookes, & xxtie leather buckettes, for p'venting the daunger that may happen by fyer (this to be p'ntlie done); alsoe itt is likewise agreed that he shall buy for the purpose aforesaid ij verie longe & strong ladders of Fyrr woodd.

4th March, A.D. 1602. 44th Elizabeth. William Lee, Mayor.

At this day Frauncis Little, Robte Payne, & Anthony Teisdall, gents., were no'iated & elected to be veiwers of moundes & boundes w'thin this Borough (together w'th John Fyssher, sen., gent., formerlie chosen), according to an auncient custome here used.

13th December, A.D. 1603. 1st James I. John Blacknall, Mayor.

Md. that this daie Willm Carter, an Inhabitant of this Boroughe, was called before the Mayor, Baylliffes and Burgesses of the said Boroughe, and being in the Counsell howse was required for the some of fortie shillinges to be a freeman of the same, who utterlie refused the same.

10th May, A.D. 1604. 2nd James I. John Blacknall, Mayor.

Md. that this p'nte day Mr. Maior, being assisted and associated w'th Mr. Robte Kysbey, minister, John Fyscher, senr., Willm Lee, Frauncys Little, Robte Payne, Anthony Teisdall, Chr'ofer Teisdall,

10th December, A.D. 1604. 2nd James I. Thomas Orpwood, Mayor.

Thomas Maiott, John Frauncys, gents., principall Burgesses, Thomas Read & Robert Ayres, Bayliffes of this Borough, did repaire unto the freschoole, And called before them the Schoolem'r & Schollers of the said schoole, And did cause the orders made and appointed by Mr. John Roice, deceassed, for the gov'ment of the said schoole to be publiklie read. And did examyn the Schollers howe they did p'flitt in there learning, And did alsoe admonishe the Schoolem'r to be carefull & diligent in the teaching & instruccon of the Children comitted unto him.

4th January, A.D. 1605. 2nd James I. Thomas Orpwood, *Mayor.*

Itt is likewise ordered that the Chambelen shall yerely pay unto Walter Dayrell, Esquire, whoe is this p'nte day elected to be of Counsell w'th this Corporacon, Fortie shillinges for his fee. * * *

6th August, A.D. 1605. 3rd James I. Thomas Orpwood, *Mayor.*

Whereas by the Charter of this Borough, Itt is graunted unto the Mayor, Bayliffes & Burgesses that they shall and may have a comon seale to serve for all there causes and busynes to be done and ordered. And whereas atthis tyme and longe heretofore they have used a comon seale, made of brasse, w'th a Scutchen Wreathed & the Armes of this Borough therein engraven. And whereas, alsoe, the said maior, Bayliffes & Burgesses have latelie caused a newe seale of sylver to be made, wherein is likewise engraven a Scutchen, not wreathed, w'th the Armes of the Towne. And upon the back thereof the p'ente yere of o'r lord, 1605, w'th the p'ticuler names of all the said maior, Bayliffes & Burgesses. Itt is nowe ordered that the said seale of brasse shalbe p'ntlie broken and defaced; And that from hensforth the said seale of silver & noe other shalbe the Comon seale of the s'd Boroughe.*

* This Seal is still in the possession of the Corporation.

6th March, A.D. 1606. 3rd James I. Thomas Mayott, *Mayor.*

Md. that the vjth day of March, Anno D'ni 1605 [old reckoning] the Mayor, Bayliffes & Burgesses received a l're from Mr. Richard Smythe, a principall Burgesse of this Borough, all written w'th his owne hand, the tenor & effect thereof followeth, vizt.:—

"Mr. Maior, and you the rest of my brethern, the great love and "number of kindly partes w'ch I have received both gen'ally from "you all & p'ticulerly (almost) from evry of you, doe in true estimacon "of yo'r desertes, exact more thanckfullnes from me then ever I was "able to p'forme in the execucon of that office of Burgesshipp w'ch I "hold amongst you: yett if my abode hadd contynued w'th you, my

" desire would have byn to have made corespondencye to yo'r good
" willes, And (if I knowe you well) you would have accepted of my
" endevors, But seeing it hath soe pleased god to w'thdrawe me that I
" cannot by p'sonall attendance satisfie the place I hold, I am to
" intreat you to add this to the rest of yo'r favoures towardes me, that
" I may rather seem to have departed from you by honest surrender
" then violent deprivation, To w'ch end I pray you that itt may be
" registred that I have, and by theis p'ntes doe voluntarily yeeld and
" resigne into yo'r handes all right, title, estate, and interest, w'ch I
" have unto the office of a Principall Burgesse of yo'r Borough. And
" I doe desire that of such my cession & resignacon this my l're may
" be sufficient testymonye, In the Acomplishing wherof you shall
" bothe make way for the dignifieing of some well worthy of such a
" place, and very thoroughly gratifie me, whoe would be lothe to lye
" as a block in any man's passage towardes due preferment, For my
" owne part, howsoev'r, I shall seeme to have byn taken from you
" either as plucked by the hand or fallen like an autume leafe, yet my
" heartes wishe for the bodye of yo'r state shalbe that itt may growe
" & flourishe ev'more in wealth, unitie & dignitie, And I shall alwaies
" reckon itt amongst the best of my fortunes, that I have byn some-
" tymes thought a fitt member of soe honest a Corporation, In which
" earnest desire of yo'r welfare and thanckfull remembrance of yo'r
" love, very hartiely comending me to you all, I comitt you to godes
" holy proteccon, And soe take my leave.

Jan. 12, 1605,

Yo'r loving brother & freind,

Rich. Smythe."

Whereupon the said Mayor, Bayliffes & Burgesses, the said vj*th*
of March, did accept the resignacon of the said Mr. Smythe, of his
said office of a Principall Burgesse.   *   *   *   *   *   *

2Itd. that itt is agreed that an office shalbe buylt on hardings *31st October, A.D. 1606.* shopp, & th'entry attb'end of the Guildhall, And to th'end the same *4th James I. Fraucis Little,* be done w'th all conveniences and to the least charges of the *Mayor.* Chamber, Mr. Maior, that nowe is, Mr. Robte Payne, Mr John Blacknall & Mr. Lawrence Stevenson, are to be entreated & appointed to conferre w'th workmen of skyll, both concerning the plott of the buylding and the charges thereof, & to make relac'n unto the Company w'th all convenient speed.

20th October,
A.D. 1609.
7th James I.
John Mayott,
Mayor.

It is ordered by the Maior, bayliffes & principall Burgesses, that the Inhabitantes of this Boroughe usinge the Craft & mysterie of Shoomakers & Cordwayners w'thin the said Boroughe, shalbe from hensforth a Company or Fellowshipp of them selves, and be called by the name of Master & Wardens of the said Fellowshipp. And the said Maior, Bayliffes & Burgesses, doe create and make the said Inhabitantes usinge the said Craft or mysterie w'thin this Boroughe, a Company or fellowshipp of master & Wardens of the fellowshipp of the Craft & mysterie of shoemakers & Cordwayners, w'thin the said Boroughe.

13th December,
A.D. 1609.
7th James I.
John Mayott,
Mayor.

It is ordered   •   •   •   that Walter Dayrell, Esquier, shalbe created Recorder for the said Boroughe by the new Charter.

9th July,
A.D. 1613.
11th James I.
Richard Curtyn,
Mayor.

This Daie, it is aggreed, that Mr. Willm Hartt shall have wekelie, owte of the Chamber, xij*d.* towardes his maynetennce in regard he hath borne the office of Mayor w'thin this Boroughe to his greate charge, And likewise he is to have bestowed upon hym a sute of Apparell.

15th August,
A.D. 1613.
11th James I.
Richard Curtyn,
Mayor.

This daie, it is aggreed,   •   •   •   •   that from hensfurth the Judges and Mr. Fowler shall have allowed them owte of the Chamber of this boroughe, at ev'y Assises, this allowance following and no more, that is to saie, one hogeshedd & one barrell of strong beare, and one barrell of myeld beare, yf lesse will not serve, for Mr. Fowlers horsemeat fouretene shillinges, and ten shillinges in wyne to the Judges ev'y assises.

Also, it is aggreed, that from hensefurth the Chamber shalbe at no more Charges in setting upp a boothe for the Judges at the Assises, by reason the sherif of the Sheare ought to be at the charges therof.

7th December,
A.D. 1614.
12th James I.
Christopher
Teesdale,
Mayor.

Whereas John Fyssher, sen., gen., on the first daie of September last, was elected and chosen Mayor for the yere following. The said John Fyssher being Required to take upon the said office, dothe for certenne causes to hym knowen, refuse to be sworne, and therefore to be fyned, w'ch he hathe paid and satisfied accordinglie, being iijs. iiij*d.*, And so he is therof discharged.

7th December,
A.D. 1614.

[On this day Thomas Read resigned his office of Secondary Burgess on his being appointed Town Clerk.]

𝔉or as muche as John Fyssher, sen., hatho bene an auncient Burgesse of this Towne, and is nowe growen into suche decaie of his estate as that he is not able to maynetcine hym self in suche sorte as is fitt for a principall Burgesse of this Boroughe, and as may stand w'th the Creditt and Reputac'on of this Corporac'on. It is therefore ordered that the said John Fyssher shall have yerelie, during his naturall lyfe, allowed unto hym forthe of the Chamber twentie nobles p' ann. forthe better maynetynyng of hym self as a principall Burgesse, to be paid unto hym quarterlie by equall porcons. Provided alwaies, that yf the said John Fyssher shall at any tyme herafter Carrie hym self unquietlie or dissorderlie, or shall by any evill speches or otherwise slaunder or Scandoll any of the principall burgesses, or shall at any tyme herafter take upon hym to be Mayor of this boroughe, that then the said yerely allowance shall cease and determyne.

𝔑𝔡. That this Daie it is ordered and aggreed by the Mayor, Baylliffes and burgesses, that from hensfurthe the Baylliffes of the said Boroughe, for the tyme beinge, shall quarterlie, yeerlie paie owte of the benyfitt w'ch they receave for pickedge and Stallage of the faiers and M'ckettes of this Boroughe, the some of Foure Poundes towardes the maynetenance of mornyng & evenyng pr'ers in St. Nicholas Churche, to be paid unto such p'sons as the mayor, Baylliffes and burgesses or the most p'te of them shall appointe, the first payment therof to begin at Christmas next.

25th August, A.D. 1618. 16th James I. Francis Little, Mayor.

𝔗𝔥𝔦𝔰 Daie it is ordered and aggreed, * * * * that Thomas Goddard shall from hensfurth weekelie, on Twesdaie mornyng, swepe and make cleane the marckctt place and the Channells Round Aboute, and also the m'ckett place where the sho-makers staules do nowe use to stand, and before Mr. Thomas Mayott's howse to the m'ckett howse, and to the highe waie there; For the w'ch the Mayor, for the tyme beinge, shall paie unto hym owte of his allowance xxxs. yerelie, and also is to have the toll of all the bessnes.

6th September, A.D. 1618. Francis Little, Mayor.

𝔄lso it is ordered that the Mayor, for the tyme being, shall yerelie, from hensfurth, paie owte of the toll of the Corne m'ckett, the some of foure poundes towardes the maynetenin' of mornyng and evenyng prayer in St. Nicholas Churche, to be paid unto suche p'sons as the Mayor, Baylliffes and burgesses, or the must p'te of

R

them, shall appointe, to be paid quarterly, the first payment therof to begy'n at Christmas next.

This Daie it is aggreed by the Mayor • • • • that the Pickadge and Stallage of the faiers and wekelie m'ckettes shalbe lett and graunted unto any sufficient p'son that will have the same by lease for yers, at suche yerely rente as can be gotten for the same, and that the Baylliffes, for the tyme being, shall have allowed them towardes the charges of theire Baylliffes Dynner yerely, and for theire charges in paying of the fee Farme and all man'r of charges in p'curing the quietus est, the some of VI*li.* xiij*s.* iiij*d.* to be paid them yerely by the Chamberlyn by a Tickett.

No. that this Daie it is ordered by the Mayor, Baylliffes and Burgesses, that the Mayor, for the tyme being, shall from hensfurtho yerelie paie owte of his allowance of XX*li.*, towardes the maynetenance of Mornying and Evenyng praier in St Nicholas Churche, the some of Foure poundes, to be paid Quarterlye, the first payment to begyn nowe at Christmas last, And to be paid yerelie, unto suche p'son and p'sons as the Mayor, Baylliffes and burgesses or the moste p'te of them shall appoint; And in Considerac'on therof it is also aggreed and ordered by the said Mayor, Baylliffes and burgesses, that the Mayor, for the tyme being, shall have from hensfurthe to his owne use all suche • • • • , some and somes of money forfayted at the leete and Lawe Daies holden for the said Boroughe, in the tyme of his mayraltie, So that the same be gathered w'thin the tyme of his said mayraltie.

No. That this daie it is aggreed by the Mayor • • • that from hensfurth it shalbe lawfull to the Mayor, for the tyme being, to electe and choose an officer, called the Overseer of the Hogges, wandering in the streates and lanes of this borough, to ympounde them according to an order hertofore made.

This Daie Mr. Chr'ofer Capper is elected to be Reader at Sainte Nicholas Churche, and to have the allowance form'ly graunted.

Whereas the Mayor, Baylliffes and burgesses hath heretofore bene at greate charges in Repairing and amending the glasse windowes, benches and pavements of the guildhall, by reason of playes there suffered to be plaied, For the avoyding wherof it is this day ordered that no mayor of this Borough from hensfurthe shall geve any leave or license nor p'mytt or suffer any players whatsoev'r to play in the said Guildhall w'thoute consent of eight of the principall burgesses, graunted at theire meting in the Counsell howse of the said Boroughe, upon paine to forfaite and lose fortie shillinges for ev'y tyme, to be abated of his allowance.

This Daie it is ordered by the Mayor, Baylliffes and Burgesses, that from hensfurthe the preacher w'ch shall yerely preache a sermon on Good Frydaye, shall geve thanckes to god for the benefit conferred upon this Towne by the Benefactors following, viz. :—

22nd March, A.D. 1625. 22nd James I. Thomas Clempson, *Mayor*.

Kinge Phillipp and Quene Marye,	Founders of this Corporacon.
Sr. John Mason, Knight,	P'curer therof.
Quene Elizabethe and Kinge James,	Of Famous memory, for graunting more p'vileges and liberties to this Borough.

And for all other benefactors to the same, as were :

Richard Mayott, gent.,	the first mayor of this Towne.
Olyver Hyde, esquier, and James Fyssher, gent.,	sometymes also Mayors therof.
John Royse, Esquier,	founder of the Freschole and other worckes of pyetie and charitie.
Thomas Teisdall, esquier, Will'm Benet, gent, and John Kente,	especiall benefactors of the said Schole.

Sr. Thomas Smythe,
    Knighte,
Mrs. Katheryne Hide,
    Widowe.
John Barnes, Esquier,
Phillipp Marryner, gent.,
Will'm Dunche, Esquier,
    and
Mary his Wief,
Richard Bisley,
John Goddier,
Gabriell Barber, gent.,

    especiall benefactors to the poore Inhabitantes and trades men of this Towne.

17th January, A.D. 1628. John Mayott, Mayor.

[James Heron, appointed Town Clerk in the place of Thomas Reade, resigned.]

2nd August, A.D. 1628.

[Charles Holloway, Esq., appointed Recorder in the place of Walter Dayrell, Esq., deceased.]

2nd October, A.D. 1628. 4th Charles I. John Bradford, Mayor.

𝕱orasmuch as the eleccon of Mr. Hollowaie to be recorder of this Boroughe was disorderlie and surrepticiouslie made, and therefore merelie voyd, as wee are advised by learned counsell, for that itt was made w'thout any lawfull warning given to the company being electors, And that the Major parte of the company when Mr. Hollowaie came to be sworne, protested against it and did testifie theire dislike therof by goeing awaie from the place, And yett the said Mr. Hollowaie did then wilfullie take his othe. Therefore wee, the Mayor and the Major parte of the principall Burgesses, doe nowe declare that wee thinck him not fitt to hold the said place any longer, And to that purpose doe nowe determin our Will that the said Mr. Hollowaie shall be noe longer Recorder of this Boroughe.

[Thomas Tesdale, Esq., was the same day elected Recorder.]

21st January, A.D. 1629. 4th Charles I. John Bradford, Mayor.

𝖂hereas it hath bene heretofore aggreed by the Mayor, Bayliffes and Burgesses of this Boroughe, that the some of Fower poundes should be yerely paied by the Mayor, for the tyme being, for and towardes the maynetenaunce of Morning and Evening prayer, as by Two sev'all orders maye appere. And whereas likewise for the increase of the said maynetenaunce the Mayor, Bayliffes and Burgesses have bene sithence contented to allowe yerely foure poundes more towardes the reading the said prayers, Sithence w'ch tyme ytt hath bene decreed by Commissioners for charitable uses That the Bishopp of Sar' for the tyme being, shall from henceforth nominate suche parson as he shall thinck fitt to Reade morning and Evening prayer in the parishe Churche of St. Nicholas, Soe that the Mayor, Bayliffes and Burgesses have nowe nothing to doe in the Choice of the said Reader, nor in the placing or displacing of him, Therefore leaste that theire said voluntary allowaunce should in tyme be claymed as a dutie by some Reader w'ch the Mayor, Bayliffes and Burgesses shall not like of as being unfitt for the said place, Itt is nowe and hath bene longe since agreed by the Mayor, Bayliffes & Burgesses, That the said former gen'all grauntes and agreem'tes shall ceasse and be noe longer continewed; But yet nevertheles because Mr. John Stone, the nowe reader, was chosen by the Mayor, Bayliffes and Burgesses, And doth acknowledge the same to be but a voluntary allowaunce, from tyme to tyme, as they see occasion, Therefore it is nowe aggreed by the Mayor, Bayliffes and Burgesses, that the like some of Eighte poundes a yere shalbe from henceforth paied to the said Mr. Stone soe longe as he shall continue Reader, as was formerlie paied him, uppon this condic'on, that he shall well and duly execute & p'forme his dutie there, and shall not absent himselfe above Sixe weekes in one yere from his said Charge of Reading prayers, w'thout the speciall leave & licence of the Mayor for the tyme beinge.

[The Rt. Hon. Henry, Earl of Holland, elected High Steward of the place of the Rt. Hon. William, Earl of Banbury, resigned.]   *19th July, A.D. 1630.*

[Bolstrode Whitelocke, Esq., appointed Recorder in the place of Thomas Tesdale, resigned.]   *14th April, A.D. 1632.*

It is likewise ordered that the Chamblen for this Borough shall laye forth Five poundes, & noe more, towardes the making of a place fitt to kepe the prisoners in, at the workehouse, to be ymployde in such manner as Mr. Tesdale, Mr. Barton, & Mr. Banckes shall thincke fitt.   *27th March, A.D. 1633. 9th Charles .I. John Teasdale, Mayor.*

It is this daie agreed that Mr Mayor of this Boroughe, for the tyme being, shall weekelie meete, uppon the fridaie, about two of the clocke in the afternoone, for the better putting in execu'con of the orders of the house of Correc'cons, w'th Two of his Company in seignioritie everie moneth, uppon notice to them given.   *5th July, A.D. 1634. 10th Charles I. John Hawe, Mayor.*

13th August,
A.D. 1634.
10th Charles I.
John Hawe,
Mayor.

𝕿𝖍𝖎𝖘 daie it is agreed that the Two old houses betweene the poore mens' houses and Atherton's Backside, be forthw'th pulled downe, & the tymber solde & the monie therof bestowed towardes the rep'acons of some of the same houses in such manner as Mr. Tesdale, Mr. Barton, Mr. Bradford, & Mr. Chamberlen shall thinck fitt, & everie house have some backside allowed unto them equallie.

15th August,
A.D. 1635.
11th Charles I.
Benjamin
Teasdale,
Mayor.

𝕿𝖍𝖎𝖘 daie it is Agreed that Fortie shillinges be sent to Kingston towardes the repayring of the Highewaies at Kingston Hill, at the request of Mr. Lenthall, of Beselslighe.

𝕬𝖓𝖉 it is Agred that Mr. Maior be allowed xxs. w'ch he paied for A lecturer's licence at Salisburie.

20th January,
A.D. 1636.
11th Charles I.
Richard Barton,
Mayor.

𝕴𝖙 is this Daie Agreed that the house in the Abbie, nowe in the occupac'on of Will'm Kent, shalbe purchased for the use of the Boroughe, to make A workehouse if it maye be.

15th November,
A.D. 1636.
12th Charles I.
Edward
Franklyn,
Mayor.

𝕱𝖔𝖗 the better keeping the Fast appointed by his Ma'tie, everie Weeke uppon the Wednesdaye, according to his Ma'ties p'clamacon, It is ordered that St. Andrewes Faire be not held uppon the Wednesdaie, but shall be kepte uppon the Thursdaie after, and p'clamacon for that purpose is to be made w'thin this Borowe, To th' end the Countrie may take notice therof.

𝕱𝖔𝖗𝖆𝖘𝖒𝖚𝖈𝖍 as it appeared unto the Mayor　*　*　*　* that the late Ringing of the Markett Bell is p'judiciall to the Markett, and dothe much hinder the cominge in of Corne into the Markett w'thin this Boroughe. Itt is ordered that the m'kett Bell shall from Henceforth, during the tyme of Winter Ringe at Eleven of the Clocke, and during the tyme of Somer at xij of the Clock, And notice herof is likewise to be given to the Countrey, That they may bring in theire Corne accordinglie.

8th June,
A.D. 1637.
13th Charles I.
Edward
Franklyn,
Mayor.

𝕴𝖙 is this daie ordered by the maior　*　*　*　*. that if either of the S'jeauntes of this boroughe shall at any tyme hereafter keepe in his howse, or in any other place, any p'son or p'sons w'ch he or they shall arrest uppon any precept, warrant or p'ces to him or them directed, above sixe houres in the daye tyme, or above one houre after sonne setting, and shall not bring them to the gatehouse then he & they shall loose theire places.

𝔍𝔱 is this day further agreed by the Company that Twoe Barrells of Gunn Powder, nowe sent to this Towne by S'r Robert Pye, Knight, shalbe payed for by the Chamberlen of this Borough, to be kept for the use of this Borough.

28th September, A.D. 1640. 16th Charles I. John Mayott, Mayor.

[Mr. John Mayott fined one hundred marks for refusing to take office as Mayor, and committed] " *to the prison of this Boroughe, " there to remayne untill he shall Take uppon him the said office, or paie " the said fine.*"

3rd October, A.D. 1643.

[Mr. John Mayott accepted the Office of Mayor and afterwards died.]

10th October, A.D. 1643.

[Mr. Edmund Franklyn elected Mayor in the place of Mr. John Mayott, deceased.]

27th October, A.D. 1643.

[Mr. Edmund Franklyn fined one hundred marks and committed to prison for refusing to take Office as Mayor.]

28th October, A.D. 1643.

[Mr. Edmund Franklyn accepted the Office of Mayor.]

6th November, A.D. 1643.

[Mr. Richard Barton fined £40 for refusing to accept the office of Mayor and take the oath, and ordered to be committed to prison until he should take the oath, or pay the said fine.]

29th September, A.D. 1644.

[Mr. Richard Barton accepted the office of Mayor and took the oath.]

2nd October, A.D. 1644.

𝔉𝔬𝔯𝔞𝔰𝔪𝔲𝔠𝔥 as William Castell, heretofore one of the principall Burgesses of this boroughe, hath bene removed from his place of principall Burgesse and disfranchised att a Comon Councell held the eight Daie of November, 1643, by vertue of a order from the p'tended lord Cheiffe Justice, residing att oxford, Which proceedinges are declared by A councell of Warre, helde the 7th of this instant Marche, to be most illegall; Therefore the said Mr. Castell is this daye by the comon Councell of this Boroughe Restored to his former place of principall Burgesse, and all the Priviledges and Franchises of this Boroughe belonging to the place of A principall Burgesse of this boroughe, And doe order the Record of his Removall to be Razed and Blotted out.

8th March, A.D. 1645. 20th Charles I.

[The erased entry appears three pages earlier in the Records.]

[The said William Castell was at the same Council elected Mayor in the place of Mr. Richard Barton, deceased.]

𝔍𝔱 is Agreed that Mr. Langlie and Mr. Paine doe give upp uppon Thursdaye next, theire accomptes concerning the monies collected w'thin this boroughe for the use of the Garrison   *   *

1st April, A.D. 1647. 23rd Charles I. James Curten, Mayor.

29th September, A.D. 1647.

[Mr. Edmund Francklyn fined £40 for refusing to accept the office of Mayor, and ordered to be committed to prison until he should take the oath or pay the said fine.]

4th October, A.D. 1647.

[The said Edmund Francklyn compounded for the said fine, by paying the sum of 5/-.]

9th October, A.D. 1647.

[Mr. Richard Cheyney fined £40 for refusing to accept office of Mayor, and was ordered to be committed to prison until he took the oath or paid the fine.]

11th October, A.D. 1647.

[The said Richard Cheyney accepted office and took the oath.]

16th October, A.D. 1647. 23rd Charles, I. Richard Cheney, *Mayor.*

This Daie itt is Agreed that Humfrie Will'ms shall holde the Stalles of the m'kett & Fayres, & the Sceller under the m'kett howse for one yere from Mich'as last, payeing Tenne poundes for the same halfe yerelie * * * * And the said Humfrie Will'ms is to make cleane all the m'kett place & hill aboute the Round howse w'thin the Gutters, and soe from tyme to tyme kepe the same cleane, receveing xxs. of the Maior Towardes the same. * * * *

29th September, A.D. 1649.

[Mr. James Curten fined 5/- for refusing to accept the office of Mayor, and was committed to prison until he should take the oath or pay the fine.]

6th October, A.D. 1649.

[Mr. William Weeks elected Mayor.]

29th December, A.D. 1649.

[Bartholomewe Hall, Esq., "*Attornie Generall of the Dutchie*" elected Recorder.]

29th September, A.D. 1650.

[Mr. Francis Payne fined £40 for refusing to accept the office of Mayor, but afterwards, on the same day, he accepted office and took the oath.]

16th April, A.D. 1652. The Commonwealth, John Mayott, *Mayor.*

It is this day ordered that John Tesdale, gent., William Haynes, gent., and Will'm Dyer, shall forthwith pay unto Robert Payne, Chamberlen, towards the paym't for the Mace the sume of XXX*li.* * * * the same money to be paid out of the rents to be collected by the Bayliffes, and that Robert Payne shall pay the residue of the money due for the Mace out of the rents to be collected by him.

8th January, A.D. 1653. The Commonwealth, John Boulter, *Mayor.*

This Daie itt is Agreed That Twentie poundes p'cell of the monies given by Mr. Packer to be ymployed to sett the poore on worke, be delivered to Mr. John Mayott, woollen Draper, uppon his owne bond, to be ymployed to sett the poore to work.

𝔍𝔱𝔱 is ordered that from henceforth the m'kett Bell shall Ring at Tenne of the Clocke in the morninge, & in case the Bell Doe not Ring by Tenne of the Clocke, Then itt shalbe lawfull to sell corne att that howre w'thout Ringing the Bell, & p'clamacon to be made in the markett accordinglie.

3rd August, A.D. 1653. The Commonwealth. John Boulter, *Mayor.*

𝔍𝔱 is this day voted   *   *   *   * that the elecc'on of William Wells, Edward Bond, William Willmott, and William Cheyney, elected to be Secondary Burgesses of this Borough by the power of the late King, in December, 1643, was illegall.

11th December, A.D. 1655. The Commonwealth. John Hanson, *Mayor.*

𝔍𝔱𝔱 is ordered by the Comon Counceill, That One le'ccicon, One Cooper's Dictionarie, and one Rider's Dictionarie, be paid for by the Chamber, and chayned in the schoole, where is most convenient.

13th July, A.D. 1656. The Commonwealth. John Hanson, *Mayor.*

𝔍𝔱𝔱 is ordered by the Comon Councell, that for the better Clensing of the Streates w'thin this borough, A Scavenger be p'vided, and that he be paied Tenne poundes a yere.   *   *   *   *   *

31st July, A.D. 1656. The Commonwealth. John Hanson, *Mayor.*

𝔍𝔬𝔯𝔞𝔰𝔪𝔲𝔠𝔥𝔞𝔰 Bartholomew Hall, Esq'e, Recorder of this Borough, liveth farr remote or distant, and by reason of his greate ymploym'ts the Mayor, Bayliffs & principall Burgesses have beene & are destitute of his assistance & co'ncell; Itt is therefore Ordered   *   *   *   * that the said Bartholomew Hall be removed from the place of Recordershipp of this Borough.

24th September, A.D. 1656. The Commonwealth. John Boulter, *Mayor.*

John Boulter sworn "Mayor, Justice of the Peace, Clerke of the Markett and Coroner," for the year ensuing.

29th September, A.D. 1656.

Thomas Holt, Esq., elected Recorder.

17th October, A.D. 1656.

𝔗𝔥𝔦𝔰 Daie Sr. John Lenthall, Knight and Barouett, is elected & chosen Burgesse for this Corporac'on of Abingdon, for the p'liam't sumoned to be held att Westm'r, the xxvij*th* Daie of January next.

30th December, A.D. 1658. The Commonwealth. Francis Payne, *Mayor.*

𝔍𝔬𝔯𝔞𝔰𝔪𝔲𝔠𝔥 as very great and dangerous Fires have latly happened in many places neere onto this Borough, in this tyme of drought, and w'ch is greatly feared may happen within this Borough if diligent and watchfull care be not speedily taken for preventing thereof; It is ordered by Mr. Mayor and the Comon Counsell of this Borough that eight howsholders of the said Borough shall nightly watch from henceforth, ontill Ascenc'on day next comeing, and that one Constable or Tythingman be assisting those eight howsholders

9th April, A.D. 1659. The Commonwealth, Francis Payne, *Mayor.*

L S,

in their. said watchinges; And it is further ordered that the said Watch shalbe sett and beginne at tenne of the Clocke in the afternoone, and continue ontill Fower of the Clocke in the morning of every day.

30th March, A.D. 1660. The Commonwealth. John Mayott, *Mayor.*

This daie Sr. John Lenthall is elected & chosen Burgesse for this Corporac'on of Abingdon, for the p'liament summoned to be held att Westm'r, the xxv*th* daie of Aprill next.

23rd June, A.D. 1660. 12th Charles II. John Mayott, *Mayor.*

It is this day agreed by us, the Mayor & Comon Councell, that Mr. John Mayott, Mr. Edmond Francklyn, Mr. James Curten, Mr. Thomas Payne, Mr. Edward Bond and Mr. Jonathan Hawe, are appointed to tender unto his Ma'tie the graunt and surrender of the yearely Fee Farme rent of CIII*li.* xvj*s.* vij*d.,* & all o'r estate & interest therein, and they are alsoe appointed to advise w'th S'r George Stonhowse, Mr. Holt and Mr. Heron, concerning C*li.* to be tendered to his Ma'tie, and in case they shall advise them soe to doe, that then the said Mr. Mayott, Mr. Francklyn, Mr. Curten, Mr. Payne, Mr. Bond, & Mr. Hawe, doe borrowe the said C*li.* upon their securitie, for sixe monthes or more, of w'ch C*li.* & the paym't and security thereof wee doe hereby p'mise to save harmel's & indempnified the said persons; and it is alsoe agreed that their reasonable charges & expenses in their Journey shalbe repaid unto them out of the Chamber.

19th December, A.D. 1660. 12th Charles II. Thomas Payne, *Mayor.*

It is likewise ordered that Dr. Langley & Mr. Cornish, the nowe pretended Lecturers, be from henceforth dismissed from preaching the Lecture w'thin this Borough, and that their exhibic'on forth of the Chamber doe cease upon St. Thomas day next.

It is likewise ordered that the Chamberlen doe pay to John Richardson xx*s.* for the expenses of Souldiers at the Gatehowse.

29th March, A.D. 1661. 13th Charles II. Thomas Payne, *Mayor.*

This Daie Sr. George Stonhowse, Baronett, is elected and Chosen Burgesse for the Boroughe of Abingdon, for the p'liam't to be holden att Westm'r, the eighth Daie of Maye next.

31st July, A.D. 1661. 13th Charles II. Thomas Payne, *Mayor.*

This day the office of High Steward of this Borough is graunted unto Edward, Earle of Clarendon, Lord Chauncello'r of England, and likewise the exhibic'on of VI*li.* xiij*s.* iiij*d.,* to be paid unto him yearely, at Midsomer, To hold to him from Midsomer last.

𝔍𝔣 is ordered   *   *   *   * That from henceforth noe Lease be made or graunted to any tenaunt of any tenem't within the said Borough belonging to the Mayor, Bayliffes and Burgesses of the said Borough, in which tenem't Flues are made with Wood & Watles, and shalbe then standing, Until such tyme as the same. Flues shalbe first demolished, and Stone Chimneys shalbe sufficiently erected in the places of the same Flues

𝔍𝔣 is this day ordered   *   *   * that Seaven Pounds, five shillinges, sixe pence, disbursed by Mr. Francklyn & Mr. Weston in enterteyning the Judges at Maydenhead, the last Assizes, be paid unto them by the Chamblen.

𝔍𝔱𝔱 is this day Ordered   *   *   * that Fiftie poundes shalbe given to his Ma'tie, on the First day of May next, as a volontary p'sent.

𝔍 Edmond Francklyn, gent., Mayor of the Borough of Abingdon, and I James Curten, gent., Thomas Payne, gent., Edward Bond, gent., Jonathan Hawe, gent., William Willmott, gent., Will'm Weston, gent., being principall Burgesses of the said Borough and I   *   *   * being secondary Burgesses of the said Borough, doe (according to an Act of P'liam't entituled "An Act for the well Gov'ning & regulating of Corporac'ons,") declare that I hold that there lyes noe obligac'on upon me or any other p'son from the oath comonly called The solemne Leage & Coven't, and that the same was in it selfe an unlawfull oath and imposed upon the Subjects of this Realme against the knowne Lawes and Liberties of the Kingdome.

In the p'sence of the right Ho'ble. John, Lord Lovelace, S'r George Stonhowse, Barrt., & the rest of the Commissioners, whose names are subscribed.

    Lovelace,
    Geo. Stonhouse,
    H. Hyde,
    Geo. Purefoy,
    Fra. Pigott,
    H. Hyde, Jr.

(Signed)
Edmond Francklin, Maior,
James Curtaine,
Thomas Payne,
Edward Bond,
Jonathan Hawe,
Will Willmot,
William Weston.

26th May,
A.D. 1662.
14th Charles II.
Edmond
Franklyn,
Mayor.

Burgus Abingdon, ⎱ 𝕭𝖞 virtue of His Ma'ties Comission under
in Com Berk.   ⎰ the great Seale of England, bearing Teste
the Twentieth day of February last past, and by virtue of
and according to the ten'or forme and effect of a certaine
Act of P'liam't, Intituled An act for the well governing and
regulating of Corporac'ons, and for the better execuc'on of the
same, and the power and authority in the same Act menc'oned,
Wee, whose names are subscribed, Doe (by virtue of the said
Comission and in pursuance of the said Act) by this o'r Order under
o'r handes and Seales, Displace and remove Bedford Stacie, of the
Borough of Abingdon aforesaid, glover, from his Offices or pretended
Offices of principall Burgesse and Secondary Burgesse within the
said Borough. Dated the *xxvjth* of May, Anno D'ni 1662. Lovelace,
Geo. Stonhowse, H. Hyde, Geo. Purefoy, H. Hyde, Jr., Fra. Pigott.

17th July,
A.D. 1662.
14th Charles II.
Edmond
Franklyn,
Mayor.

𝕴𝖙 is likewise ordered & agreed that xls. be given to Mr.
Jennens, to be by him layd out towards the makeing of shelves for
a Library in the Freeschole, & towardes the p'viding of Chaines for
the Bookes in the same Library.

𝕴𝖙 is this day ordered that the weekly Lecture nowe preached in
St. Hellen's Church, shalbe preached from henceforth untill o'r
Lady day next at St. Nicholas Church, and from o'r Lady day next
untill Mich'as then following at St. Hellen's Church, and soe to
continue untill further Order.

𝕴𝖙 is likewise ordered that the Highway in the Boare Street,
neere the Whitehorse, be filled upp with Stones & gravell   *   *

𝕴𝖙 is this day ordered that new Gownes be speedily bought for
the Towne S'jeants, and Mr. Frauncis Payne, Mr. John Mayott,
Mr. Thomas Payne, Mr. Jonathan Hawe, Mr. Wm. Weston, Mr.
William Foster & Mr. S'lvanus Carter are desired to buy the Cloth
& Trimming for the same Gownes.

𝕴𝖙 is this day likewise ordered that aswell the principall as the
Secondary Burgesses & Bayliffs of this Borough doe p'vide for
each of themselves Gownes, after the fashion of Gownes used &
accustomed to be worne principall & Secondary Burgesses w'thin
this Borough, before the Last day of February next, upon the
penaltie following scil't:—For each principall Burgesse failing to
performe this Order, xs., and for each Secondary Burgesse, vs.;

and that they and each & ev'y of them doe attend on Mr. Mayor, in their Gownes, upon Easter day next, and soe yearely on Easter day from thence after, upon paine to forfeite xx*s*. a peece, unles reasonable excuse shalbe made to Mr. Mayor & the Comon Councell; and that from & after the said Last day of February each member of the Comon Councell (being sumoned to appeare in the Comon Councell) shall then and there appeare in his Gowne, upon the paine of xij*d*., all w'ch forfeitures are to be levyed by distresse & sale of the goodes of the sev'all p'sons offending.

This day one Silver Bowle, belonging to the Mayor, Bayliffes & Burgesses, w'th this inscription (Burgus de Abingdon) and w'ch remayned in the handes of Mr. Edmond Franckyn, was delivered by the same Mr. Franckyn to the p'per handes of Edward Bond, gent., Mayor, &c., for the use of this Corporac'on.

21st January, A.D. 1663. 14th Charles II. Edward Bond, Mayor.

[On this day 11 more of the Principal and Secondary Burgesses subscribed to the declaration mentioned on Page 147 before Lord Lovelace and three other Commissioners, And on the same day 16 other Principal and Secondary Burgesses were displaced and removed from their several offices of Principal and Secondary Burgesses, apparently for having refused to make the said declaration.

23rd January, A.D. 1663.

By another order of the same date, John Mayott and Francis Payne, two of the Principal Burgesses, were "removed & displaced" from office, for also refusing to subscribe the same declaration.]

[An Order was made on this day that no Lease should be granted to any person who should not "first take the Oathes of "Supremaucie and Obedience, according to the Statutes in that case "p'vided."]

5th August, A.D. 1663.

Likewise ordered that Mr. Curten, Mr. Hawe, Mr. Weston, Mr. Winch & Mr. Hullcotts, or any three of them, are appointed to order and dispose of the Mayor's Feast in such manner as they shall thinke fitt, and the sume of XXI*li*. is allowed for the expense thereof out of the Mayor's allowance, & the rest out of the Chamber, scil't, xx*s*.

5th August, A.D. 1663. 15th Charles II. Edward Bond, Mayor.

The fine of X*li*. is sett upon John Finmore, one of the principall Burgesses of this Borough, for refusing to joyne w'th the rest of his

13th August, A.D. 1663.

fellowe Burgesses in ordering the affaires of this Corporac'on, being thereunto somoned.

(This fine appears from a marginal note to have been remitted.)

The fine of V*li.* is sett upon Thomas Mayott, one of the Secondary Burgesses of this Borough, for the like.

3rd October,
A.D. 1663.
15th Charles II.
William
Cheyney,
  Mayor.

If is this day ordered that Mr. Curten, Mr. Hawe & Mr. Weston, doe direct and advise the Chamberlen in erecting Seates in St. Hellen's Church for the Scholers of the Free Schole, and alsoe in erecting of boxes at the Councell Howse for the p'servacon of the Towne evidences.

21st October,
A.D. 1663.
15th Charles II.
William
Cheyney,
  Mayor.

In consideracon that John King hath p'mised weekly to sweepe upp in heapes and carry away all the durte lying in and throughout soe much of the Markett place as is paved at the charges of the Corporac'on, he shall receive from the Corporac'on for his paines therein, over and above his yearely allowance, the sum of xxx*s.*

1st October,
A.D. 1664.
16th Charles II.
Jonathan Hawe,
  Mayor.

Ordered that Mr. Mayor doe entertaine at his Table on ev'y Sunday in every weeke, for the yeare ensueing, both the Towne S'jeantes, and upon ev'y tuesday in ev'y weeke, for this yeare ensueing, the Lecturer, on the same day the Minister & his wife & the two S'jeantes   *   *   *   *

6th January,
A.D. 1665.
16th Charles II.
Jonathan Hawe,
  Mayor.

If is this day ordered that a sette of brasse Weights of Averdupoise, from the weight of a quarter of a hundred downwardes to the smallest weight of that sorte, and alsoe a Beame necessary for those weightes & fitt for the weighing of a half a hundred weight, and alsoe a yarde and an Elle, be bought & p'vided by the Chamberlen for the use of this Corporac'on.

21st March,
A.D. 1665.
17th Charles II.
Jonathan Hawe,
  Mayor.

If is this day ordered that the Chamberlen doe pay unto Elias Ashmole, esqr., Windsor Herauld, Deputie to S'r Edward Bligh, Clairenseux King at Armes, the Sume of Fiftie shillinges for allowing the Comon Seale of the Corporac'on and Registring the names of the now Mayor, Bayliffes & Burgesses.

28th June,
A.D. 1665.
17th Charles II.
Jonathan Hawe,
  Mayor.

Forasmuch as divers persons inhabiting or residing in places infected w'th the Plague, or other pestilentiall disease, doe take upon them to travill w'th their Horses, Coaches, Waggons, Cartes and Carriages, from those infected places unto this Borough, whereby it is greatly feared that the Inhabitantes of this Borough through want of watchfullnes may in short tyme be infected w'th those contagious diseases (which God forbidde);   For remedy whereof It is Ordered * * * * that from henceforth two able Watchmen shall from day to day watch and attende at the Harte Bridge, within this Borough, from the discharge of the Nightwatch untill the charging of the same Watch, and that those Watchmen doe use such diligence that noe Inholder, Alehowsekeep', or Victualler, or other Person within this Borough doe receive into his or their Howses any person or persons whatsoever, or his or their servauntes, horses, coaches, waggons, cartes, or carriages, other than such person and persons as shall bring with them a sufficient Certificate in writing that the place from whence they came is free from the Infection of the Plague, or any other infectious disease; And it is further ordered that the Chamberlen of this Borough doe pay to each of the said Watchmen for such their attendance, Twelve pence by the day.

It is this day ordered * * * that (for the better p'servac'on of the inh'itantes of the said Borough from the infection of the Plague nowe dispersed in many places of this Kingdome) strict watch & ward be kept w'thin the said Borough, both by day & by night, by the Householders therein inh'iting after this mammer, videl't:—Twelve householders to be appointed by the Constables & Tythingmen of the said Borough to watch and warde each day from henceforth, from sixe of the Clock in the morning, untill sixe of the Clock in the afternoone, and Twelve other Householders to be like-wise appointed to watch each night from henceforth, from sixe of the Clock in the afternoone, untill sixe of the Clock in the morning, in such places as are hereafter menc'oned, videl't:—At the Hart-bridge, three watchmen; At St. Hellen's Bridge, two Watchmen; at the Ockbridge, two watchmen; at the upper ende of the Boare Street, two watchmen; at the upper ende of the Wineyard, two watchmen; and at the Abbey, one watchman; Upon paine that every such householder soe makeing default shall forfeite for every such defaulte ijs., to be levyed by distresse and sale of the goodes & chattells of the p'son soe offending; and the monies soe levyed to be imployed for the better support of the same Watch; And the Mayor, Bayliffes & Burgesses of this Borough, & every of them, are appointed to oversee the said Constables & Tythingmen in the execuc'on of this Order.   And in case the said Constables &

13th July, A.D. 1665. 17th Charles II. Jonathan Hawe, *Mayor.*

Tythingmen or any of them shalbe remisse or negligent in the execuc'on of this Order, that then upon Informac'on thereof made to the Mayor or some other Justice of the peace w'thin the said Borough, such course may be taken against them as the Lawe hath p'vided. And it is further ordered that noe householder inhabiting within the said Borough shall enterteine into his or their howse any man, woman or childe, or any goodes, wares or merchandizes w'ch come from any places suspected to be infected w'th the Plague, upon paine of such punishm't to be inflicted upon them as the Lawe hath p'vided. And it is further ordered that for the better p'serving of the Streetes w'thin the said Borough, from nuisances w'th Hogges & Pigges, the S'jeantes at Mace doe impound all such Hogges & Pigges as shallbe found in the same Streetes, and Deteyne them in Pound until they shalbe delivered by due course of Lawe.

19th July, A.D. 1665.

This day the Feast usually kept upon the First of September yearely, is left to the considerac'on of Mr. Mayor wheather he will thinke it fitt to keepe the same Feast or not. * * * * *

23rd August, A.D. 1665. 17th Charles II. Jonathan Hawe, Mayor.

If is this day ordered * * * that the now Chamberlen of the said Borough doe forthwith erect howses fitt and convenient for the enterteyning of such p'sons inhabiting within this Borough as shall happen to be visited w'th the Plague, The same howses to be erected at or neere the place called the royall Fort, in Box well neere the said Borough.

21th September, A.D. 1665. 17th Charles II. Jonathan Hawe, Mayor.

Whereas the Mayor, Bayliffes and Burgesses are determined to present to the Kinges Ma'tie of England, Sixtie poundes, and have borrowed of Will'm Sherwood the same sume, And whereas Will'm Cheyney, gent., Will'm Weston, gent., and Robert Blackaller, at the instance & request of the said Mayor, Bayliffes & Burgesses, have undertaken to become bound unto the said William Sherwood in the sume of 120*li.*, with condic'on for the paym't for the same 60*li.* w'th interest, at a day to come; It is this day ordered * * * that the yearely rent of 50*li.* reserved upon the Lease of the Tythes lately demised to Frauncis Payne, gent., be assigned by the said Mayor, Bayliffes and Burgesses to the said Will'm Cheyney, Will'm Weston & Robert Blackaller, for the indempnifieing of them from the paym't of the said 60*li.*, w'th intrest & damages if any be.

Ordered that an acc'on at Lawe be brought ag't Avery Hobbes 6th October, A.D. 1665. 17th Charles II. James Curten, Mayor. and John Clark, at the suite of the Corporac'on, for breach of their Articles for not finishing the buildinges at the Guildhall.

Fees of Homage paid to his Ma'tie Servauntes when his Ma'tie 16th October, A.D. 1665. passed through this Corporac'on, the   day of October, Anno D'ni 1665 videl't :—

	li.	s.	d.
To the Gentemen Ushers Dayley Weyters ...	05.	00.	0
To the Gent Ushers of the Privy Chamber ...	05.	00.	0
To the Gent Ushers Quarter Wayters ...	0 j.	00.	0
To the S'jeantes at Armes ...	03.	06.	8
To the Knight Harbinger ...	03.	06.	8
To the Knight Marshall ...	0 j.	00.	0
To the Sewers of the Chamber ...	0 j.	00.	0
To the Yeoman of the Wardrobe · ...	00.	16.	8
To the Grome and Pages of the Wardrobe ...	0 j.	00.	0
To the S'jeante Trumpett and Officers ...	03.	16.	0
To the Yeomen Harbingers, &c. ...	0 j.	00.	0
To the Fower Yeomen of the Month ...	02.	00.	0
To the Pages of the Presence ...	00.	10.	0
To the Yeomen Ushers ...	0 j.	00.	0
To the Gromes of the Chamber ...	0 j.	00.	0
To the Footmen ...	02.	00.	0
To the Coachmen ...	00.	10.	0
To the Surveyo'r of the Kinges Wayes ...	0 j.	00.	0
To the Porters at Gate ...	0 j.	00.	0
To the Kinges Jester ...	00.	10.	0
To the Yeoman of the Feild ...	00.	10.	0
Summe totall	36.	06.	0

[Signed,] Thomas Duppa, Gent. Usher.

There was alsoe given to Yeoman Usher White, who carryed the Kinges Sword, w'ch other Corporac'ons had done   00. 06. 8

Forasmuch as the Highwayes, Streetes and Lanes w'thin this 26th January, A.D. 1666. 17th Charles II. James Curten, Mayor. Borough are in great decay for want of scowring and clensing, and divers heapes of Dung & Soyle are there placed & erected to the comon nusance of his Ma'ties subjectes passing that way, For remedy whereof it is this day enacted and ordeyned by the Mayor, Bayliffes

T

and Burgesses of this Borough, that every Howscholder within this Borough doe from henceforth weekly sweepe into Heapes all the Dung and Soyle and Dust w'ch shall lye in the Streetes before, along and against his and their dwelling howses to the midle of the Street or Channell there, and the same (being soe swept upp) shall carry away before th'ende of the same weeke, upon paine to forfeite for every one makeing default xiid., w'ch said severall sumes soe forfeited, the Mayor, for the tyme being, is appointed to levye by Distresse and Sale of the goodes of the severall persons soe makeing default, and the severall somes soe levyed as aforesaid to imploy for and towardes the scowring, clensing and reforming thereof; And whatsoever the Mayor, for the tyme being, shall doe in pursuance of this Order, wee doe hereby ratifie; And doe hereby authorise & appoint the p'sons undernamed weekly to viewe wheather the Streetes be scowred, clensed and reformed, as they ought to be or not. If not, then to inquire through whose default the same is, and to certifie the Mayor, for the tyme being, thereof, that he may p'ceed therein according to this Order.

Mr. James Curten,
Mr. Thomas Hulcottes,   } for east St. Hellen's Street.

Mr. John Rusden,
Robert Morrice
and
Richard West,   } for west St. Hellen's Street.

John Slatter
and
Mr. John Whichelowe,   } for the Ockstreet.

Mr. Frauncis Payne,
Antoney Combe
&
Thomas Barfoot,   } for the Borestreet.

Wm. Hawkins
&
Thos. Barfoot,   } for the Broadstreet.

Mr. Porter,
Mr. John West,
Mr. Jos Claxon,   } for the Steart & Wineyard.

Mr. Wm. Cheyney,
Wm. Wells, Jun.,
Ambr. Deacon,
} for the Butcherow to the Gatehowse.

Wm. Wells, Senr.,
Mr. Blackaller,
Robt. Sellwood,
} for the Bury & Lanes adjoyning.

Mr. Sim. Hawkins,   for litle Bury Lane.

Mr. Geo. Winchcroft,
Mr. John Payne,
Mr. Wm. Foster,
Mr. Hawe,
} from the Lambe to the Market & for Lombard Lane.

Forasmuch as it hath beene made to appeare to us, the Mayor, Bayliffes & Burgesses, that Wm. Hopkins, one of the S'jeantes at Mace w'thin this Borough, hath extorsively received of Gill, gent., the summe of Five Shillinges, by colour or p'text of his office, It is this day ordered that the said Wm. Hopkins for the same & other misdemeano'rs by him comitted in the execuc'on of his office, be from henceforth, & is, removed from his said office of S'jeant at Mace. *1st March, A.D. 1666. 17th Charles II. James Curten, Mayor.*

This day William Hopkins is chosen one of the S'jeantes at Mace within this Borough. *2nd March, A.D. 1666. 17th Charles II. James Curten, Mayor.*

Ordered that the Chamberlen doe pay to Anthoney Combe, John Hobbes, Paull Coles, Thomas Rutter, John Wells, Thomas Hutchens & John Snowe, seaven of the Foote Souldiers for this Borough, for two dayes service by them done in conveying Men impressed into his Ma'tie's service, to Henley, twentie eight shillinges, and that he likewise pay to the two Drumers, for their service done upon the day of p'clayming Warre ag't the French Nation, [the sum is not mentioned]. *31st March, A.D. 1666. 17th Charles II. James Curten, Mayor.*

Whereas the Mayor, Bayliffes and Burgesses are determined to borrowe at interest of Robert Jones, Clerke, & Francis Fettiplace, Esq., the sume of two hundred poundes, for the use of his Ma'tie, upon the securitie of an Act of P'liam't, intituled, An Act for graunting the sume of Twelve hundred and Fiftie thousand poundes to the Kinges Ma'tie, for his present further supplie, to be paid to the Receivers Gen'all of this County; And whereas James *31st March, A.D. 1666. 17th Charles II. James Curten, Mayor.*

Curten, gent., Frauncis Payne, gent., Thomas Hulcottes, and John Whichelowe, at the instance and request of the said Mayor, Bayliffes and Burgesses, have undertaken to become bound unto the said Rob't Jones & Francis Fettiplace, in the sev'all sumes of two Hundred poundes, w'th condic'on for the paym't of one hundred poundes with interest at a day to come, It is this day ordered by the Mayor, Bayliffes & Comon Councell of this Borough, that the Farme called F'tz Harris Farme, in the occupac'on of Joane Badcock, widow, and the Farme called Steedes Farme, in the occupac'on of Wm. Foster, and alsoe the sev'all yearely rentes thereupon reserved, and the Leases thereof, be assigned & demised unto the said Mr. Curten, Mr. Payne, Mr. Hulcottes and Mr. Whichelowe, for the indempnifieing them & ev'y of them from the paym't of the said 200*li.* w'th interest & alsoe damages, if any be.

4th May,
A.D. 1666.
17th Charles II.
James Curten,
Mayor.

Ordered that the Chamberlen to pay to Mr. Yateman xxs. and to his man ijs. vj*d.*, for paines taken in p'curing money for this Corporac'on; and to Edm. Sherwood for makeing the security to save Mr. Curten, Mr. Fr. Payne, Mr. Hulcottes & Mr. Whichelow harmeles, in respect of their undertaking for monies for the use of the Corporac'on, xxs.

29th June,
A.D. 1666.
17th Charles II.
James Curten,
Mayor.

In respect Ambrose Deacon, one of the Bayliffes of this Borough, (to whose care & custody one of the keyes of the Comon Chest was comitted) hath absented himselfe from the Comon Councell & deteyned the same Key, for want of w'ch the busines of the Comon Councell was hindered, to the great p'judice of the Corporac'on, therefore he is amerced in ijs. vj*d.*, and alsoe to such further punishm't as shalbe thought fitt, in case he doe not, at his owne charges, repaire the Lock, w'ch the Comon Councell were enforced to breake open for dispatch of their busines.

5th October,
A.D. 1666.
18th Charles II.
William Cheyney,
Mayor.

It is ordered that Willm. Cheyney, gent., Mayor of this Borough for this yeare ensueing, doe enterteyne at his Table on every Sonday in every weeke, for this yeare ensueing, both the Towne S'jeantes, and upon every tuesday in every weeke, for this yeare ensueing, the Lecturer, the Minister and his wife, and the two S'jeantes, and that he pay to John King xxs. for sweeping the Markett place. In considerac'on whereof, wee doe allowe the said Mr. Cheyney 56*li.*, to be paid him quarterly by the Chamberlen, the first paym't to be made at St. Thomas' Day next, scil't, the Chamberlen to pay 54*li.* and the 40*s.* is for Tickettes.

Whereas at the last Court Leet holden for this Borough, the fine of 40*s.* was sett upon Henry Jerom (then chosen one of the Tythingmen of this Borough) for refusing to take his oath for the due execuc'on of his office, w'ch fine of 40*s.* was levyed & paid accordingly to Frauncis Carter & Wm. Hopkins, S'jeantes at Mace w'thin the said Borough; It is this day ordered (upon the petic'on of the said Henry Jerom) that the said fine be reduced to tenne shillinges & that the residue thereof, being xxx*s.*, be paid to him by the said S'jeantes.

28th November, A.D. 1666. 18th Charles II. William Cheyney, Mayor.

Ordered that if any of the principall or Secondary Burgesses shall, at any tyme from henceforth, reveale, disclose or make knowe, the actings or secrettes of the Comon Councell to any p'son or p'sons, being noe member of the Comon Councell, shall from thenceforth be amoved from his office of principall or Secondary Burgesse.

15th February, A.D. 1667. 18th Charles II. William Cheyney, Mayor.

Ordered that the Chamberlen doe pay to Edmond Sherwood xxvj*s.*, for monies by him paid to Mr. Babington for discharging an Indictm'nt ag't the Inh'itantes of the p'ish of St. Hellen's for not repairing the Highway betweene the Ockmill and Knightsham, and that he likewise pay xx*s.* for discharging an am'cem't sett att the Assizes upon that occasion.

29th March, A.D. 1667. 18th Charles II. William Cheyney, Mayor.

This day ordered that the Chamberlen doe pay to John Clarke and Avery Hobbes, in full discharge of all monies by them claymed, for building the Storehowse over the Towne Hall, the sume of Sixe poundes.

12th April, A.D. 1667. 18th Charles II. William Cheyney, Mayor.

[A further loan of £300 is made to the King, the money being borrowed at interest of Edward Weston of Shippon, on the Bond of William Cheyney, Mayor, & five others, who are indemnified by the Corporation.]

21st July, A.D. 1667. 18th Charles II. William Cheyney, Mayor.

This Day xx*s.* is ordered to be paid to Mr. Bayley for monies by him layd out in paying the money advanced to the Kinge's Ma'ty, and alsoe xx*s.* for his paines, in all xl*s.*

19th September, A.D. 1667. 18th Charles II. William Cheyney, Mayor.

Ordered that 5*li.* 8*s.* 6*d.* be paid by the Chamberlen to Mr. Wm. Foster, for monies by him layd out in enterteinem't of the Judges, over and above the monies by him received for that purpose.

26th December,
A.D. 1668.
19th Charles II.
John
Whichelowe,
Mayor.

Whereas John West, one of the Secondary Burgesses of this Borough, was nom'ated, elected & chosen Chamberlen of this Borough for the yeare ensueing, according to the Charter of the said Borough, and appeared this day before the Mayor, Bayliffes and principall Burgesses of the said Borough, and being then required to take his oath for the due execuc'on of his said office of Chamberlen, doth refuse to take the same oath; The said Mayor, Bayliffes and principall Burgesses doe assesse the fine of Five poundes upon the said John West, for refusing to take his oath for the due execuc'on of his said office of Chamberlen, and doe comitt the said John West to the Prison of the said Borough, there to remaine untill he shall take his oath for the due execuc'on of his said office of Chamberlen, or pay his said fine, or make his composic'on for the same, according to the Charter of the said Borough, w'ch said sume of 5*li.* was afterwardes remitted.

3rd June,
A.D. 1668.
20th Charles II.
John
Whichelowe,
Mayor.

Ordered that Mr. Hawe, Mr. Wells, sen., Mr. Blackaller and Mr. West doe buy cloth for the S'jeantes' Cloakes, and for John Kinges Coate, and alsoe triming for the same, in such manner as they or the major part of them shall thinke fitt.

[John King appears to have been Crier & Bellman.]

22nd July,
A.D. 1668.

[This Day a lease is granted to " John Lindsay, Citizen & gold-smyth of London," of certain premises in Birchin Lane, London, which " were lately demolished by reason of the late Fire w'ch " happened in London," at a rent of £20 per annum, " with coven'ts " to new build & other ordinary coven'ts."]

1st October,
A.D. 1668.
20th Charles II.
Thomas
Hulcottes,
Mayor.

This day Richard Mayott, M'r of Artes, is chosen by the Mayor, Bayliffes and Comon Councell of this Borough, to preach the Lecture w'thin this Borough in the place of Mr. Marten.

30th December,
A.D. 1668.
20th Charles II.
Thomas
Hulcottes,
Mayor.

It is ordered that Mr. Mayor for the tyme being, Mr. Will'm Weston & Mr. John Rutter, doe from henceforth, from tyme to tyme, for the yeare ensueing, view the decayes and wantes of reparac'ons within this Borough, and where reparac'ons are necessary, doe give notice thereof to the Chamberlen and require him to imploy Laborers and workemen about the repaireing thereof, Which Laborers and Workemen shalbe paid by the Chamberlen, for such their labo'r & worke, when the Bills of the Chamberlen of such repa'c'ons shalbe approved by Mr. Mayor, Mr. Weston and Mr. Rutter, or any two of them, and not otherwise.

𝕴𝖋 is this Day ordered that the Chamberlen Doe pay to such p'son as Mr. Mayor, for the tyme being, shall appoint, Three poundes, to be imployed towardes the p'curing of the next Assizes to be holden at Abingdon, for the County of Berks.

20th January, A.D. 1669. 20th Charles II. Thomas Hulcottes, *Mayor.*

[A Similar Order is again made, with the addition of a further payment of "xxs., for monies by Mr. Slade expended at Maydenhead, "on the Judges Servantes."

10th June, A.D. 1669. 21st Charles II. Thomas Hulcottes, *Mayor.*

𝕬𝖈𝖙𝖊𝖘 𝖆𝖓𝖉 𝕺𝖗𝖉𝖊𝖗𝖘 made at the Comon Councell, holden for the said Borough of Abingdon, the Thirtieth day of June, in the one and Twentieth yeare of the Raigne of our Soveraigne Lord, Charles the second, by the grace of God, King of England, Scotland, Fraunce and Ireland, Defendo'r of the faith, &c., Annoque D'ni 1669.

30th June, A.D. 1669. 21st Charles II. Thomas Hulcottes, *Mayor.*

𝕴𝖋 is this p'sent day, upon the humble suite and request of the Freemen of this Borough of Abingdon, by the Mayor, and Bayliffes, and the rest of the Comon Councell of the said Borough, for the better service to be had of all the Freemen of the said Borough, and for the better, exact and more civill governem't of the same, and the Comonalty thereof, Ordered, ordeyned and established that all the Freemen of the said Borough shalbe severed and devided, by the order and discretion of the Mayor, Bayliffes and Burgesses of the said Borough, or the more part of them, into three Companies, to be and continue, and to be named and reputed, three principall Companies of the said Borough; And that the first Company shalbe called by the name of the Company of Grocers of the Borough of Abingdon, and their Fellowes; The second Company shalbe called by the name of Butchers of the said Borough, and their Fellowes; and the third Company shalbe called by the name of the Company of Skynners of the said Borough, and their Fellowes; And it is further ordered, ordeyned and established, that all such Freemen of the said Borough as shall use or exercise the trade, mistery or occupac'on of Grocers, Mercers, Woollendrap's, Lynnendrap's, Haberdashers of Hattes, Feltmakers, Dyers, Hosyers, Apothecaryes, maulters, Iremongers, Spurryers, Scholemasters, Scriveners, Barbers, Upholsterers, Clothworkers & Sheremen, within the said Borough, shalbe sorted and severed to make upp the Company of Grocers, and shalbe called the Company of Grocers and their Fellowes, and be one and the same Company; And alsoe that all such Freemen of the said Borough as shall use or exercise any the trades of Butchers,

Vintners, Brewers, Bakers, Inholders, Victuallers, Tallowchandlers, Millers, Brasiers, Freemasons, Roughmasons, Coopers, Carpenters, Bricklayers, Slatters, Joyners and Trunckmakers, shalbe sorted and severed to make upp the Company of Butchers and their Fellowes, and shalbe and shalbe called the Company of Butchers and their Fellowes, and be one and the same Company; 'And alsoe that all such Freemen of the said Borough as shall use or exercise any the trades of Tanners, Cordwayners, Corryers, Glovers, P'chm'tmakers, Leather-sellers, Collermakers, Cutlers, Sadlers and Ropemakers, shalbe sorted and severed to make upp the Company of Skynners, and shalbe, and shalbe called, the Company of Skynners and their Fellowes, and be one and the same Company. **Neverthelcs**, it is ordered and established that if any other p'son or p'sons, Freeman or Freemen of the said Borough, shall use, occupy or exercise, any other lawfull trade, art, mistery or occupac'on, within the said Borough or the liberties thereof, It shalbe then lawfull to and for the Mayor, Bayliffes and Burgesses of the said Borough, or the more part of them, to allott such p'son or p'sons to be of such one Company of the said Three Companies as to them shall seeme meet and convenient. **Item**, it is ordered, established and decreed that it shall not be lawfull for any p'son or p'sons whatsoever, inhabiting or resiant within the said Borough or the liberties thereof, exercising, occupicing or useing any of the trades, craftes, misteries, or occupac'ons above rehersed, at any tyme or tymes hereafter, to open or sett upp, or procure to be opened or sett upp, for his private comodity, within the said Borough or the liberties thereof, to the hinderance of any other being a Freeman of the Comonalty, any more Shopps then one onely, or any more Stalls in the Markett of the said Borough or in any other place within the Liberties thereof, then one onely; **And** it is further ordered, established and decreed, that every person and p'sons doeing the contrary shall forfeite and pay for every such offence the sume of Five poundes of lawfull English money, unto the Mayor, Bayliffes and Burgesses of the said Borough, to be imployed and disposed to the use and benefitt of the Comonalty, whereunto his trade, mistery or occupac'on shalbe p'ticularly belonging or app'teyning. **And** it is further ordered by this p'sent Ordinance, that every p'son and p'sons whatsoever, of any of the said Companies or Borough, at the first opening of their Shopp or Shopps w'thin the said Borough, or the liberties thereof, shall, for

and in respect of such opening, pay and satisfie to the Mayor,
Bayliffes and Burgesses of the said Borough, to be imployed and
disposed to the use and benefitt of the Comonalty of such Company
whereunto his trade, mistery or occupac'on shalbe p'ticularly
belonging and apperteyning, the sume of Three shillings, fower
pence, of lawfull English money, Upon paine that every one soe
refuseing soe to doe, and doeing the contrary, shall forfeite and pay
to the said Mayor, Bayliffes and Burgesses the sume of Thirteene
shillings, fower pence, to the use and benefitt of the Comonalty of
such Company whereunto his trade, mistery or occupac'on shalbe
p'ticularly belonging or apperteyning. 𝕴𝖙𝖊𝖒, it is ordered,
ordeyned and established that there shalbe forever one Master and
two Wardens of each of the said Companies, to be annually chosen,
and that the p'sent Mayor of the said Borough shall have the nomin-
ao'on and choice of all and every the first Masters and Wardens of the
said Companies, who are to continue for one yeare, and afterwardes
till a newe elecc'on be made of others in their places, and forever
after the said first nominac'on and choyce, the Master & Wardens
for the tyme being of every of the said Companies shalbe nominated
and chosen annually by the Freemen of the said Companies, each
Company by and for itselfe, within the space of Twenty dayes next
after such day as the Mayor of the said Borough, for the tyme being,
shall have taken his oath for the due execuc'on of his office; Which
Master and Wardens, before they medle or deale in their office, shall
take their oath before the said Mayor for the tyme being, well and
truly to execute their office, and they shall have full power once
every month, from tyme to tyme, to searche, finde out, correct, and
punish, according to their discretions, otherwise then by imprisonm't,
all contemptes, offences, trespasses and misdemeano's, com'itted by
any of the Companies within the said Borough, contrary to any of
the Lawes abovementioned, and shall make certificate to the Mayor
for the tyme being, who shall award lawfull punishm't, according to
the offences com'itted; And if any of the Masters or Wardens shall
not well and truly execute their office, according to their oath and
according to this Ordinance, in searching, finding out, correcting,
punishing, or makeing Certificate of the said contemptes, offences,
trespasses and misdemeano's, then every Master and Warden of the
Companies aforesaid, for default thereof, shall loose and forfeite
Twenty shillings to the said Mayor, Bayliffes and Burgesses of the

U

said Borough, to be imployed and disposed of to the use and benefitt of the Comonalty of such of the said Company whereunto his mistery or occupac'on shalbe p'ticularly belonging or apperteyning. Item, it is ordered and agreed that if any person or p'sons doe, or shall, at any tyme or tymes hereafter, oppose themselves against or contrary to the said orders and constitutions, that then the said Mayor, Bayliffes and Burgesses, shall and will, asmuch as in them lyeth, and as farre forth as by the graunt of the Charter of the said Borough, to them graunted by the late King Philipp and Queene Mary, doth p'mitt, ayde and assist them the said Companies and either of them and their Successo's, against any such oppositions as shalbe soe made against them; And alsoe shall p'mitt and suffer them, the said severall Companies and their Successo's, at any tyme or tymes hereafter, to sue, prosecute or comence any suite or acc'on at the Lawe, in the name of the Mayor, Bayliffes and Burgesses, against any such p'son or p'sons, as shall make any such oppositions as aforesaid. Provided allwaies, that all such suite or suites, acc'on or acc'ons, soe to be comenced, shalbe at the costes and charges of the said severall Companies and their Successo's. And it is further ordeyned, that all forfeitures and penalties before appointed, for any cause touching the said Companies, shalbe levyed by distresse of the goodes of every offendo'r against any of the said Ordinances, by warr't under the hande of the Mayor of the said Borough, for the tyme being, by any officer or other p'son, of or within the said Borough, to whom such warr't shalbe directed.

15th February, A.D. 1670. 22nd Charles II. Simon Hawkins, *Mayor*.

Ordered that Mr. Recorder (togeither w'th Mr. Hawe) be desired to goe to the M'r of Pembrooke Colledge in Oxon, and treate with him concerning the not p'forming of the Will of Thomas Tesdale, Esqre., as to soe much of the same Will as doth concerne the Scholars of Mr. Tesdale's foundac'on, and that the Chamberlen Doe waite on Mr. Recorder w'th his fee of xxs., and it is further ordered that, in case the said M'r doe not give them an answere to their satisfacc'on, That then (for redresse therein) they waite on the Visito's appointed by the same will.

23rd September, A.D. 1670. 22nd Charles II. Simon Hawkins, *Mayor*.

This day Mr. Bevin is elected one of the Lecturers w'thin this Borough, in the place of Mr. Beeby.

8th December, A.D. 1670. 22nd Charles II. William Cheyney, *Mayor*.

It is ordered that the Floore of the Towne Hall, now fallen downe, be built upp & repaired w'th what convenient speed may be, and in such manner as Mr. Hawe, Mr. Frauncis Payne, Mr. Which-elowe, Mr. John Payne, Mr. Blackaller & Mr. Richard West, shall thinke fitt, who are desired to imploy workemen and labore's in that busines, w'ch workemen & laborers are to be, from tyme to tyme, satisfied their wages and materialls in repaireng paid by the now Chamberlen upon sight of Bills to be signed for that purpose.

The Chamber doth graunt that Three poundes be paid by the Chamb'len towardes the enterteinem't of the Judges at Maidenhead.

8th February, A.D. 1671. 23rd Charles II. William Cheyney, *Mayor.*

Ordered that six Ladders and six Buckettes of Leather to each Ladder be p'vided for the use of this Corporac'on, and placed in six severall places most convenient w'thin this Borough.

10th February, A.D. 1671. 23rd Charles II. William Cheyney, *Mayor.*

No. that this day Jonathan Hawe, gent., did pay to the Chamberlen 1js. to the use of the Chamber, being the remaining sume of 328li. by him received out of the Exchequ'r to the use of this Corporaco'n, Mr. Hawe haveing formerly accompted for and paid by the Order of the Chamber 325li. 9s., Which said remay'ing sume of 1js. soe paid by Mr. Hawe is in full of the said sum of 328li. Ordered that the Chamberlen doe pay to Mr. Hawe 10s. for paines by him taken in the busines of this Corporac'on.

31st March, A.D. 1671. 23rd Charles II. William Cheyney, *Mayor.*

Whereas the Mayor, Bayliffes and comon Councell are deter-mined to pave and pitch the Boarestreet w'th Stones and Peebles, and to that ende have appointed Mr. Frauncis Payne, Mr. Jonathan Hawe   *   *   *   all members of the Comon Councell, and alsoe Thomas Barfoot, Will'm Dickenson & Frauncis Badcock, or any five of the said members of the Comon Councell, to buy stones, peebles and other materialls for the doeing thereof, and to sett laborers and workemen about the same worke, And the moneyes w'ch, from tyme to tyme, will become due in respect of the same worke, shalbe paid by the Chamberlen when the Bills thereof shalbe signed by the said eight p'sons of the Comon Councell, or any five of them.

20th April, A.D. 1671. 23rd Charles II. William Cheyney, *Mayor.*

Whereas the Mayor, Bayliffes and Comon Councell of this Borough (haveing notice of the great decayes of the King's Highway in the Boarestreet within the said Borough), and considering the inability of the Inhabitantes of the said Borough to repaire the same (although by Lawe they ought soe to doe), have, at their owne costes and charges, sufficiently repaired the same, by

28th June, A.D 1671. 23rd Charles II. William Cheyney, *Mayor.*

pitching and paveing, and have thought it meet and convenient that a way and passage, for the King's leige people on foote, may be severed on each side of the said Street, from th'other way and passage lying in the midle of the same Street, for his Ma'ties leige people to passe, goe & travill, with their horses, cartes, wagons, and carriages, and that the said Footwayes, lyeing on both sides of the said Street, shalbe severed from the said Highway by Postes of Oake to be sett and placed there, at the costes & charges of the tenauntes, owners and occupiers of the respective Mesuages, landes and tenem'tes adjoyning, in such places of the said Street and in such manner, as Frauncis Payne, Jonathan Hawe,   *   *   *   or the more part of them, shall appoint; The said Mayor, Bayliffes and Comon Councell doe therefore order, and it is hereby by them ordered, that the tenantes, owners and occupiers of the Mesuages, lands and tenem'tes adjoyning to soe much of the said Street as lyeth before, along or against their respective tenem'tes, and every of them, for him and herselfe respectively, doe w'thin one month next ensueing, at their and every of their respective costes & charges, erect, sett up and place, in such places of the same Street, and in such manner, as is appointed by the said Frauncis Payne, Jonathan Hawe   *   *   *   good and sufficient Poastes of Oake, Upon paine to forfeite for every Poaste, w'ch shall not be, by him, her or them, soe erected, placed, & sett upp, respectively, Five shillings, to be levyed by distresse & sale of their respective goodes & chattells, Rendering the overplus (if any be).

6th September, A.D. 1671. 23rd Charles II. William Cheyney, *Mayor.*

Whereas, by the last Will of John Royce, Esqre., Founder of the Freeschole w'thin this Borough, the Mayor and principall Burgesses of the said Borough are authorized Visito's of the same Schole, and are thereby impowred to correct and reforme the mis- demeano's and abuses of Scholers there, and to eject and expell (if they shall finde cause) the Scholers offending; And whereas, by the Lawes and Ordinances of the said Schole, it is (amongst other things) ordeyned that the Scholers of the said Schole shall goe to Church and there heare Divine Service and Sermon; And Forasmuch as Wee, the said Mayor and principall Burgesses (being Visito's as aforesaid), haveing visited the said Freeschole, doe finde that Samuell Herne, John Hall, John Lockton, Will'm Turrold, Joseph Hall, Benjamin Greene, Joshua Garbrand, Richard Tesdale,   Tesdale, and Jaspell Tesdale, now Scholers in the said Freeschole, have absented themselves from their p'ish Church and have refused to come thither there to heare divine Service and Sermon (although admonished soe to doe by us, together with the Comon Councell of the said Borough), It is therefore ordered, and wee doe hereby order, that the said Samuell Herne, John Hall, John Lockton, W'm Tirrold, Joseph Hall, Benjamin Greene, Joshua Garbrand, Richard Tesdale,   Tesdale, and Jasper Tesdale, and every of them, be from henceforth ejected and expelled, and they and every of them are hereby, from henceforth, ejected and expelled the said Freeschole.

𝕱orasmuch as wee were this day informed by Dr. Hall, M'r of Pembrooke Colledge in Oxon, that a great p'te of the Revenewes of the Fellowes & Scholers of the said Colledge, (of the gift of Mr. Thomas Tesdale), is w'thheld by the Deane & Prebendes of Windsor, to the great impoverishing of the said Fellowes and Scholers, who have desired o'r assistance in their just defence of the said Suite; Wee, therefore, conceiveing o'rselves obliged, as Trustees of the said Mr. Tesdale's Will, doe order that the sume of Twenty poundes be paid to the handes of the said Dr. Hall, to be by him layd out towardes the p'secuc'on of the said suite for recovery of the same revenewes (soe w'thheld, as aforesaid), before the first day of the next Hillary Terme.

23rd November, A.D. 1671. 23rd Charles II. James Curten, Mayor.

[A lease granted to "Robert Payne, gent., of the Colonie of "Virginia" of a messuage in Broad Street late in the occupation of Thomas Payne, gent., his late father.]

2nd August, A.D. 1672.

𝕴t is this day ordered by us the Mayor, Bayliffes & Comon Councell of the said Borough, and soe agreed, that Seaven pounds by the yeare, yssueing out of parte of the rents, yssues and profitts of the howses, tenem'ts and Lands, purchased with the monies of Mr. Richard Wrigglysworth, (that is to say), Covent Close and the lands and howses called the George, in Abingdon, and the lands in Harwell, shall forever hereafter be imployed for the use of the Poore of Marcham, in the said County. And that the residue of the rents, yssues and profitts of the same howses, tenem'ts and lands, shalbe forever hereafter imployed for the binding of the children of such poore persons, in Abingdon aforesaid, apprentices every yeare as the Mayor, Bayliffes, and comon Councell of the said Borough, or the major parte of them, shall direct or appoint.

23rd January, A.D. 1673. 24th Charles II. John Claxon, Mayor.

7th February,
A.D. 1673.
25th Charles II.
John Claxon,
Mayor.

𝔚𝔥𝔢𝔯𝔢𝔞𝔰 the Mayor, Bayliffs and common Councell of this Borough are determined to pave and pitch with Stones and Peebles the common Streete leadeing from the Howse of Mr. Jonathan Hawe, towards Rudle Crosse, within this Borough, and have authorized the said Mr. Hawe, togeither with Mr. John Whichelowe * * * or any three of them to be Overseers of the same Worke, and to buy Stones, Peebles & other Materialls for that purpose, and to imploye Workemen & Laborers about Pitching and Paveing of the same Streete [here follows an Order for payment by the Chamberlain of the cost of the Materials & Labour for such work.]

𝔄𝔫𝔡 the said Mayor, Bayliffs and common Councell, conceiveing it necessary that West St. Helen's Streete be repaired as soone as conveniently may be, Doe desire Mr. Willian Foster & Mr. Richard West to take care that such Peebles as shalbe brought to Abingdon by Boates, or by the free gifte of any person, be layed upp & placed in convenient places at their discretion, to remaine there in ready-nesse till opportunitie be offered for repaireing the same Streete.

15th April,
A.D. 1673.
25th Charles II.
John Claxon,
Mayor.

𝔗𝔥𝔦𝔰 day ordered that Mr. Jonathan Hawe be, and is, appointed, by this Corporac'on, to attende his Grace the Duke of Ormond, Visito'r of Pembrooke Colledge in Oxon, and exhibite a Complaint ag't Dr. Hall, Master of the same Colledge, for refuseing to admitt into the same Colledge Richard Mayott, M'r of Arts, into the Fellow-shipp of William Barnes, Clarke, nowe vacant, and that the said Mr. Hawe doe then use his endeavo'r to obteyne from his Grace a Comission for Visiting the said Colledge.

11th July,
A.D. 1673.
25th Charles II.
John Claxon,
Mayor.

𝔒𝔯𝔡𝔢𝔯𝔢𝔡 that xxjs. vjd. be paid by the Chamberlen to Mr. Hawe, for monies by him given to his highnes the Duke of Ormond's Secretary in the busines of Pembrooke College, in Oxon, and that xxxs. more be likewise paid to him by the said Chamberlen, for monies by him, the said Mr. Hawe, expended in the prosecuc'on of the same busines.

26th September,
A.D. 1673.
25th Charles II.
John Claxon,
Mayor.

𝔗𝔬 th'ende the common Streets w'thin this Borough may, from henceforth, be kept in good repaire and be scowred and clensed from Dirte, Soyle and other publique Annoyaunces, the Mayor, Bayliffes and common Councell of this Borough, have enacted, and ordeyned * * * that from henceforth forever hereafter all Housholders within this Borough doe weekly, upon the Tuesdayes and Wednes-dayes in every weeke, sweepe upp and lay and place into heapes, ready and fitt to be carryed away in Carts, all the Dust, Dirte, Dung and Soyle, which shalbe lying in the comon Streets within this Borough, before, along and against their respective howses, unto the Midle of the respective Streets there, Upon paine to forfeite for every default, respectively, xij*d*., To be levyed by the Bayliffs of the said Borough, for the tyme being, To the use of the saide Mayor, Bayliffs and common Councell, by distresse and sale of the goods of the severall persons soe offending, Rendring the overplus (if any be). And it is hereby further enacted and ordeyned by the said Mayor, Bayliffs and common Councell, that from henceforth forever hereafter noe person shall p'sume to cast forth of his, her, or their, howse, any Buckashes, Dust, Durte, Soyle, or other Annoyance, upon paine to forfeite for every one soe offending the like summe of xij*d*., to be likewise levyed by the said Bayliffs for the tyme being, To the uses as abovesaid, in manner as abovesaid. **And** whereas William Cheyney, gent., for Tenne pounds by the yeare, to him agreed to be paid by the said Mayor, Bayliffs and common Councell, hath promised and undertaken that he the said William, with his Servaunts, Carts and Horses will weekly, upon the wednesdayes and thursdayes in every weeke, yearely hereafter, carry away from out of this Borough all the Dust, Durte, Dung and Soyle, which shalbe soe swept upp and layed and placed into heapes, upon paine to forfeite for every default v*s*., to be abated and discounted out of the said yearely summe of tenne pounds.

This day ordered that Mr. Jonathan Hawe and Mr. John Payne doe attende Mr. Recordo'r, and state the manner of Richard Pearton' elecc'on out of the Freeschole into Pembrooke Colledge, and take his advice therein and reporte the same to the common Councell, And it is further ordered that the Chamberlen doe deliver to them xx*s*. for Mr. Recorder's fee therein. 27th November, A.D. 1673. 25th Charles II. Simon Hawkins, *Mayor.*

If is this day ordered that XX*li*. be layd out in buying of Corne for releife of poore people within this Borough, and Mr. Frauncis Payne and Mr. Richard West are desired to buy the same Corne, and the Chamberlen is hereby appointed to pay unto them the same XX*li*. 7th February, A.D. 1674. 26th Charles II. Simon Hawkins, *Mayor.*

Ordered that Mr. James Curten, th'elder, and Mr. Hawe doe goe to London the next Terme in the busines of Pembrooke Colledge and Mr. Wrigglysworth his gifte. 22nd April, A.D. 1674. 26th Charles II. Simon Hawkins, *Mayor.*

19th May,
A.D. 1674.
26th Charles II.
Simon Hawkins,
Mayor.

Ordered that Mr. Jonathan Hawe, Mr. John Payne, Mr. Robert Blackaller, and Mr. Richard West, or any three or two of them, doe attende the Commissioners who are authorized by his grace the Duke of Ormond to visite Pembrooke College, in Oxon, and that Five pounds be delivered by the Chamberlen to Mr. John Payne, to be by him layd out in the prosecuc'on of this matter at the discretion of the persons abovenamed.

30th June,
A.D. 1674.
26th Charles II.
Simon Hawkins,
Mayor.

Whereas the Mayor, Bayliffs & common Councell of this Borough are determined to pave & pitch with Stones & Peebles the common Streete called west St. Helen's Streete within this Borough, & have authorized Jonathan Hawe, gent., John Payne, gent.,   * * *   or any three of them to be Overseers of the same worke . *   *   *

26th November,
A.D. 1674.
26th Charles II.
William
Cheyney,
Mayor.

Ordered that the Chamberlen doe provide a newe Gowne for the Lecturers.

20th April,
A.D. 1675.
27th Charles II.
William
Cheyney,
Mayor.

This day, Henry, Earle of Clarenden, is chosen high Steward of the Borough of Abingdon, to whom is graunted the yearely exhibition of 3*li.* 6*s.* 8*d.*

Whereas the Mayor, Bayliffs and common Councell of this Borough are determined to pave and pitch with stones and peebles the common Streete called East St. Helen's Streete, within the said Borough, and have authorized James Curten, gent., Thomas Hulcotts, gent.,   * * *   or any three of them to be Overseers of the same Worke *   *   *

15th July,
A.D. 1675.
27th Charles II.
William
Cheyney,
Mayor.

It is ordered that xx*s.* given by this Chamber to Captn. Henry Commerford whose service and loyaltie is certified by his Ma'tie under the Seale manuall, be paid to him by the Chamberlen.

31st July,
A.D. 1675.
27th Charles II.
William
Cheyney,
Mayor.

Forasmuch as Thomas Holt, Esqr., (who hath and exerciseth the office of Recordo'r of the Borough of Abingdon durcing the good pleasure of the Mayor & principall Burgesses of the said Borough) hath for a long tyme past removed his habitation and dwelling from Abingdon aforesaid, to Reading, a place twenty miles distant from Abingdon aforesaid, & from that time hitherto, hath & still doth inhabite at Reading aforesaid, Soe that by such his absence & the distance of the place of his habitac'on, the Mayor & comon Councell of the said Borough are altogetther destitute of the Councell & advice of the said Thomas Holt, in matters concerning the Weale of this Corporation, For w'ch & other causes Wee, the Mayor & principall Burgesses of the said Borough (whereof the said Mayor is one) Doe hereby declare that o'r will & pleasure is to amove the said Thomas Holt from his said office of Recordo'r of the said Borough; And the said Thomas Holt is hereby by us the said Mayor & principall Burgesses from henceforth utterly amoved from his said office of Recordo'r, to all intents and purposes whatsoever.

[Thomas Medlicott, Esq., is appointed Recorder.]

26th August, A.D. 1675.

Ordered that three sufficient Ladders be provided for the use of the Chamber, each Ladder to confeyne in bredth at the bottome two foote and a halfe, and at the topp thereof two foote, And alsoe Six other shorte Ladders, by Mr. Claxon & Mr. John Smyth, and that the charge thereof be paid by the Chamberlen upon sight of a Bill, signed by the said Mr. Claxon & Mr. Smyth.

23rd September, A.D. 1675. 27th Charles II. William Cheyney, Mayor.

Ordered that the Chamberlen doe pay to Frauncis Carter, for meate, drinke and tobacco provided for the common Councell on the day of the last Accompt, xxiijs. vjd., as appears by his Bill of the 28th of December, 1675.

6th January, A.D. 1676. 27th Charles II. John Payne, Mayor.

Forasmuch as the M'r & Wardens of the Company of taylor's have presumptiously, by their owne authoritie, and without the admission or allowance of the Mayor, Bayliffes and common Councell of this Borough, received into their said Company Wm. King, Wm. Midleton, John Butler, Thomas Hopkins, Wm. Cox, Thomas Hobbs, and divers other persons, and have administered unto each of them an oath of the freedom of their Company, before they or any of them were made freemen of this Borough, contrary to an Act of the comon Councell of this Borough, And have taken excessive summes of money of severall persons for their freedom of the said Company, to the great impoverishm't of the said persons & their families, and doe molest and trouble others of the same trade who can not buy their freedomes at soe greate a price, Therefore they are in mercie Vli.

Ordered that the Chamberlen doe pay to John Clarke xvs. in full discharge of his Bill for making the Duckingstoole.

17th March, A.D. 1676. 28th Charles II. John Payne, Mayor.

It is this day ordered that the Overseers for Inmates within their respective Watches doe from henceforth, from tyme to tyme, togeither with any one of the Tythingmen, make diligent inquiry after such Inmates, strangers, servaunts & others, comeing to inhabite

21st April, A.D. 1676. 28th Charles II. John Payne, Mayor.

v

there, and w'ch are likely to become chargeable to the parish, And doe make presentm't thereof monthly to Mr. Mayor, To th'ende such course may be taken against them as the Lawe hath provided.

𝔚𝔥𝔢𝔯𝔢𝔞𝔰 the Mayor, Bayliffes & comon Councell of this Borough, are determined to pave and pitch w'th Stones and Peebles the comon Street called the Broadstreete within this Borough, and have authorized John Claxon, gent., Robert Sellwood, gent., John Smyth, William Wells, Ambrose Deacon, or any three of them, to be Overseers of the same Worke   *   *   *

7th December, A.D. 1676. 28th Charles II. William Cheyney, *Mayor.*

𝔚𝔥𝔢𝔯𝔢𝔞𝔰, Thomas Holt, Esqr. (who was lately amoved from the office of Recordo'r of this Borough) Did enter a Caveat, before the Lords of his Ma'tie's privie Councell, that Thomas Medlicott, Esqr., (who was by the then Mayor and principall Burgesses duely chosen and sworne Recorder into the roome and place of the said Thomas Holt) should not be approved by his said Ma'tie and Councell, untill the said Thomas Holt were first heard therein, By w'ch the said Thomas Holt did endeavor to hinder the said Thomas Medlicott from the execuc'on of his said office, who (notwithstanding such the practice of the said Thomas Holt) was approved by his Ma'tie in Councell; And whereas alsoe the said Thomas Holt afterwards brought his Ma'ties writt of Mandamus, directed to the Mayor and principall Burgesses of the said Borough, commanding them to restore the said Thomas Holt to his said office, or shewe cause to the contrary; And whereas the said Mayor and principall Burgesses did directe and appoint the said Thomas Medlicott to make retorne of the said Mandamus, and by Councell to defend the same Retorne, which the said Thomas Medlicott hath done accordingly, and hath expended in defence of the same Cause, Twentie nyne pounds, nyneteene shillings, fower pence; All w'ch doeings of the said Mayor and principall Burgesses and of the said Thomas Medlicott, Wee, the Mayor, Bayliffes and common Councell of the said Borough, doe well approve of and doe thinke it fitt and reasonable that the said Thomas Medlicott be reimbused the said Twenty nyne pounds, nyneteene shillings, fower pence; And therefore it is ordered that the Chamberlen of the said Borough doe pay to the said Thomas Medlicott, the said Twentie nyne pounds, nyneteene shillings, fower pence, soe by him expended as aforesaid.

Jt is this day ordered by the Mayor, Bayliffes & comon Councell of the said Borough, that for the better clensing of the comou Streets w'thin the said Borough, from Dung, Dirte, & other annoyances, all the tenants, owners & occupiers of howses in east St. Helens Street, west St. Helens Street, Ockstreet, Boarestreet, Broadstreet, Bury Streets, Steart, & Buicherowe, doe from henceforth, weekly & every weeke, upon every tuesday & fryday in the same weekes, before eight of the clock in the afternoons of the same dayes, in decent & cleanely manner, sweep upp & lay & place in heapes all the Dust, Dirte, Dung, & Soyle, w'ch shalbe then in the same Streets, before, along, & against their respective howses, to th'ende the same may be carryed away by the comon Scavenger appointed for that service, Upon paine to forfeite for every one makeing defalt, xij*d*., To be levyed by James Clarke, by distresse & sale of the goods & chattells of every p'son soe offending, & the same to be taken to his owne use, Soe as the said James Clarke doe, at his owne charges, where default shalbe made, sweepe upp & lay & place in heapes the dirte, dung & soyle, in manner aforesaid. And in case he shall make default thereof, he, the said James Clarke, shall forfeite ij*s*. for every default, to be levyed of his goods & chattells, by distresse & sale thereof, as aforesaid.

Wee, the Mayor, Bayliffes and common Councell of the said Borough, takeing into our considerac'on the want of a convenient Howse wherein his Ma'ties Justices, assigned to take the Assizes for this County, may here sitt, And conceiving that upon the ground where the Market howse now standeth and next thereunto a Howse for that purpose may be most fitly erected, Doe order, and it is this day ordered, that the said Markett howse be demolished, and that a Howse for his Ma'ties Justices to take the Assizes in be there, and next thereunto erected and built. And Wee, the said Mayor, Bayliffes and common Councell doe hereby authorize and appoint John Paine, gent., Robert Blackaller, gent., James Curten, Vintner, Richard West, William Cheyney, mercer, George Drewe, and Thomas Sparks, or any Five of them, within a tyme convenient, to demolish, and to that purpose to employ and sett on worke Laborers and Artificers to take downe and demolish the same Markett howse, and to erect and cause to be erected there and next thereunto a Howse for his Ma'ties Justices to take the Assizes in   *   *   *

I, Jonathan Hawe, doe protest against this order.

27th April, A.D. 1677. 29th Charles II. William Cheyney, *Mayor.*

29th September, A.D. 1677. 29th Charles II. Robert Sellwood, *Mayor.*

**13th June,
A.D. 1678.
26th Charles II.
Robert Sellwood,**
Mayor.

𝕿𝖍𝖎𝖘 day it is ordered that the tymber trees now growing & standing in Bagley Close, be viewed by Mr. Payne, Mr. Blackaller, Mr. Winchurst, Mr. James Curten, the younger, & Mr. Richard West, or any two of them, and that soe many of those trees shalbe cutt downe and carryed to the new building in Abingdon, there to be imployed towards the building thereof as they shall thinke fitt, and that the same persons, or any two of them, doe make inquiry what tymber trees have beene cutt from off the same close, to th'ende such course may be taken ag't them as the Lawe hath provided.

**10th September,
A.D. 1678.
30th Charles II.
Robert Sellwood,**
Mayor.

𝕴𝖙 is this day ordered that the Stayres leading into the Sessions howse now in building shalbe erected on the outhowse of the same howse, at the discretion of the Overseers of the same work.

**13th December,
A.D. 1678.
30th Charles II.
John Payne,**
Mayor.

𝕱𝖔𝖗 the better preservac'on of this Borough in this tyme of danger iminent, It is ordered that from henceforth nightly, Eighteene able men doe watch from nyne of the Clock after noone day untill five of the clock in the morning, Which men shalbe householders, whereof one to be of the comon Councell, upon paine to forfeite for every one makeing default, iij*s.* iiij*d.*   *   *   *

**13th June,
A.D. 1679.
31st Charles II.
John Payne,**
Mayor.

𝕱𝖔𝖗 preventing the danger of fire w'ch may happen in this tyme of drought, It is ordered that each and every Inh'itant of any tenem't within this Borough, shall from henceforth dayly and every day sett and place a Cowle, filled with water, next his dwelling house, that the same water may be made use of for quenching of fire, if hapning, upon paine to forfeite for every one makeing default, for every day, xij*d.*

**27th April,
A.D. 1680.
32nd Charles II.
Robert
Blackaller,**
Mayor.

𝕿𝖍𝖎𝖘 day Order'd that Mr. Recorder receive twenty shillings of the Chamberlain for his paines in drawing an answere to his Ma'ties Letter.

**13th August,
A.D. 1680.
32nd Charles II.
Robert
Blackaller,**
Mayor.

𝕺𝖗𝖉𝖊𝖗'𝖉 that a New Coat be bought for John Coxhead, ye Belman, and yt ye Cloth, triming & making thereof, be left to the direcc'on of ye Mayor & Chamberlain & ye Overseers of ye reparac'ons.

**25th January,
A.D. 1681.
32nd Charles II.
Robert Sellwood,**
Mayor.

𝕺𝖗𝖉𝖊𝖗'𝖉 that no expences, either in meate or drinke, be expended on the day that the Chamberlen's feast is kept, after dinner is over.

It is this day order'd that no sealing money at the sealing of any Leases be paid to any principall or Secondary Burgesses of this Borough, but that the same be payd at the time of the grant of such Lease to such p'sons yt shalbe at such grant & no otherwise.

1st March,
A.D. 1682.
34th Charles II.
George
Winchurst,
Mayor.

It is this day order'd that in case any acc'on att Law shall be brought ag't Mr. Mayor, the Town clerke, or any other p'son, by Mr. Sherwood, Mr. Dickinson, Mr. Gearing, or any other Comoners or Inh'itants of Shippon, touching distresses lately deliv'd by this Corporac'on fro' a pound known by ye name of a pound for ye hundred of Hormer, within the Jurisdicc'on of this Borough, at ye suites of ye said Charles Sherwood, Mr. Dickinson & Gearing ag't Mr. John Jennings, that the same be defended at ye Charges of this Corporac'on.

6th November,
A.D. 1682.
34th Charles II.
William Foster,
Mayor.

Whereas by a former order and agreem't of ye Comon Councell of this Borough, the sume of Eleaven poundes, thirteen shillinges, & fower pence p' Ann. was allowed to Rob't Jenninges, the Scholem'r of the Free Schole, to be had and taken during the pleasure of the Mayor, Bayliffes & Burgesses of this Borough, It is hereby this p'sent day order'd & Declared that, fro' the feast of Th'annunciac'on of ye blessed virgin Mary last past, ye s'd yearely sume of Eleaven poundes, thirteen shillinges, fower pence, be no more payd to the said Rob't Jenninges, as afores'd, but shalthenceforth be & remain for ev'r to the only use of this Corporac'on.

24th April,
A.D. 1683.
35th Charles II.
William Foster,
Mayor.

This day a Lease is granted to Richard Greenwood, of the Citty of London, cheesmonger, of the use of the old Guildhall in Abingdon ev'y Monday & Fryday, being m'kett dayes, for the laying & placing of cheese for the Cheesm'kett, & ye use of ye Town Scales & weightes for ye weighing of cheese in the said Hall, fro' Lady-day last for 21 yres, at ye old rent of fifty two shillinges & ordnary Coven'ntes.

15th May,
A.D. 1683.
35th Charles II.
William Foster,
Mayor.

It is this day order'd that the Chamberlen for the time being doe pay unto Mr. Richd. Knight, Minister of this Borough the yearly sume of Twenty poundes p' Annum at Lady day & Mich'as by equall porc'ons the first paym't to begin at Lady day next And to continue untill ord'r made to the Contrary.

14th December,
A.D. 1683.
36th Charles II.
William
Hawkins,
Mayor.

It is this Day ordered That the Charter of the Taylers is made voide for the reasons here underwritten (That is to say), For that they have, contrary to an order of ye Comon Councell, made James

8th February,
A.D. 1684.
36th Charles II.
William
Hawkins,
Mayor.

Howes Free of their Company, before he was made free of ye Corporac'on, For w'ch act we doe declare All those that are free of ye whole Corporac'on of that Company be disfranchized, unlesse they give satisfacc'on to this Comon Councell within 14 daies next after the date hereof, or at our next Meeting.   Not appearing to be dealt with according to Law.   The Townclarke is ordered not to deliver any Coppie of this order to any p'son.

29th May,
A.D. 1684.
36th Charles II.
William
Hawkins,
Mayor.

It is this day ordered that Mr. Foster, Mr. Payn, Mr. Hawkins & Mr. Cheyney, jun., doe advise of all lawfull waies & meanes touching the Recovering of all such rentes & arrearages of Rentes, as shall be due & behind for the White Hart & Abbey Milles, with th' appurt'unces & putt the same in execuc'on   *   *   *   *

3rd June,
A.D. 1684.
36th Charles II.
William
Hawkins,
Mayor.

It is this day ordered that Richard Pleydall, Master of Artes of St. Mary's Hall in Oxon, by the Consent of the Mayor & principall Burgesses of this Borough, is elected & Chosen the Schoolemaster for the Freeschoole of the s'd Borough & Sworne into the s'd office in the place of Mr. Robert Jennings.

2nd July,
A.D. 1684.
36th Charles II.
William
Hawkins,
Mayor.

Order'd that Mr. Foster, Mr. Payn & Mr. Blackaller attend the L'd Clarendon touching the affairs of this Corporac'on.

19th May,
A.D. 1685.
1st James II.
Thomas
Hulcottes,
Mayor.

It is this day order'd that the Chamberlain pay to Fra' Carter yearly the sume of five shillinges by halfe yearly paym'tes, for his discharging the Corporac'on fro' all charges in ye repaires of ye Gatehouse the first paym't to begin on Mich'as day next.

9th November,
A.D. 1685.
1st James II.
William Foster,
Mayor.

This day a Surrender is made to his most Sacred Ma'tie King James the second, of all Charters & priviledges w'ch were heretofore granted to this Borough, and Mr. Mayor, Mr. Winchhurst, Mr. Payn, & Mr. Blackaller are desired to attend the Lord High Steward of this Borough touching the p'misses.

19th November,
A.D. 1685.
1st James II.
William Foster,
Mayor.

Wee doe hereby order and appoint Mr. Rich'd Hart to Sollicite his Ma'tie in our Names & behalfes for a New Charter.

2nd March,
A.D. 1686.
2nd James II.
William Foster,
Mayor.

Ordered y't ye Chamberlain pay Mr. Hawkins & Mr. King 25s. a peice for wine dranke when his Ma'tie was p'claym'd.

9th March,
A.D. 1686.
2nd James II.

Memorandum, that his Ma'ties writt of Quo warranto, being lately brought against this Borough, and thereupon a Surrender made by the said Borough, under their Comon Seale, to his Ma'tie, his Ma'tie hath been most gratiously pleased to gr't to this Borough a

New Charter, w'ch being this day p'duced and read, In p'suance of ye said Charter, John Saunders, gent., nominated in the said Charter to be Mayor, Alderman, Justice of the Peace, Clerke of the Markett, & Coroner, fro' ye date of ye s'd Charter, for & untill the Feast of St. Mich' th'archangell, w'ch shalbe in the year of Our Lord 1687, tooke the oathes & subscribed the declarac'on in the Act of Parliam't menc'on'd for regulating Corporac'ons, & the oath to execute his offices of Mayor, Alderman, Justice of the Peace, Clerke of the Markett, & Coroner, before S'r John Stonhouse, Barr't, Paul Calton, Esq., & Rob't Mayott, Esq., Com'rs for y't purpose in ye Charter afores'd named. And Wm. Finmore, Esq., in the s'd Charter nominated Recorder, & S'r John Stonhouse, Barr't, Paul Calton, Esq., & Rob't Mayott, Esq., therein named Justices of the peace for their lives for ye s'd Borough, tooke y'r oathes and subscribed the s'd Declarac'on, & the s'd Wm. Finmore tooke the oath of Recorder & Justice of peace before the Mayor in the Charter menc'oned, & ye s'd S'r John Stonhouse, Paul Calton, & Rob't Mayott, tooke the oath of a Justice of ye peace for ye s'd Borough before ye s'd John Saunders, gent., Mayor, & Wm. Finmore, Esq., Recorder, Com'rs in the s'd Charter for that purpose appointed. And Charles Perrott, D'r in Law, & James Stonhouse, Esq., did likewise take the oathes & subscribe the Declarac'on, as afores'd, & tooke their oathes as Justices of the peace for the s'd Borough, before John Saunders, gent., Mayor, & Wm. Finmore, Esq., Recorder, Com'rs named in the s'd Charter for that purpose, as afores'd.

𝕿𝖍𝖎𝖘 day the Comon Councell of this Burrough being mett, itt is ordered that Mr. William Forster, late Mayor of the Burrough aforesaid, doe forthwith, on notice hereof, deliver unto the new Mayor, John Saunders, Esq., all plate, bookes & other thinges relateing to the office of Mayor & now in Custody of the said Will' Forster.

12th March, A.D. 1686. 2nd James II. John Saunders, Mayor.

𝕿𝖍𝖎𝖘 day ordered that the Aldermen & Burgesses doe respectively appeare in their gownes on Whitsunday next, upon payne of each man makeing default to forfeite fourty shillings.

22nd April, A.D. 1686. 2nd James II. John Saunders, Mayor.

𝕺𝖗𝖉𝖊𝖗𝖊𝖉 the Seates in the Church where the Aldermen sett to bee newe lined, as formerly, & that the Chamberlayn take care for itt.

𝕺𝖗𝖉𝖊𝖗𝖊𝖉 y't the Chamberlyn pay Mr. Pickard for the new Mace foure poundes forthwith.

12th May, A.D. 1686. 2nd James II. John Saunders, Mayor.

[John Alder, of Pembroke College, in the University of Oxford, is elected Lecturer of the Borough, in the place of Marmaduke Hawe, deceased.]

𝕺𝖗𝖉𝖊𝖗𝖊𝖉 yt that the Charter bee translated into English by Mr. Record'r & Towne Clerke, and the coppy to bee kept in the Comon Chest, and this to bee done in foure moneths.

𝕺𝖗𝖉𝖊𝖗𝖊𝖉 this day that the doores and windowes made out of the butchers' Shopps into the Schoollhouse yard, bee imediatly stopped upp on notice given by the Serjeant att Mace.

𝕿𝖍𝖎𝖘 day itt was ordered by the Comon Councell that the bayliffes for the tyme being, and their successors doe and shall, from tyme to tyme, soe often as they come to church, sett in the seate that the Towne Clerke & Chamberlyn alwaies used to sett in, upon payne that each Bayliffe that att any tyme shall p'sume to sett in any of the Aldermen's Seates, p'ticulerly the Junior Aldermen's Seate, shall for each default forfeite twelve pence.

𝕴𝖙 is this day ordered that Mr. Curteene and Mr. William Cheyney shall be allowed and paid Thirty shillings by the Chamberline for their Charges in Carrying S'r Ralph Varney's Deed home, and for his man for looking out the Deed.

𝕿𝖍𝖎𝖘 day the p'sons hereafter named by the order of the King & Councell were removed from their respective places & offices in this Corporac'on, that is to say, James Corderoy, gent., from being Mayor & Alderman; John Saunders, Jonathan Hawe, Richard Pusey, Thomas Saunders, James Curtein, jun., from being Aldermen; Thomas King & Robert Cheney, from being Bayliffes and Burgesses; Simon Harcourt, Esq., fro' being Record'r; and Richard Hart, gent., from being Town clerke of this Corporac'on. And ye same day Wm. Foster, gent., was appointed & chosen Alderman & Mayor of the s'd Corporac'on; John Tompkins, Arthur Hern, Phillipp Lockton, Wm. Weston, & Wm. Hawkins, gent., were chosen Aldermen of ye s'd Corporac'on; John Jennings & George Drew, Burgesses & Bayliffs of ye same; Thomas Medlycott, Esqr., Record'r, & Henry Knapp, gent., Towne clerke of the said Corporac'on.

𝕿𝖍𝖎𝖘 day ye s'd Wm. Foster, John Tompkins, Arthur Hern, Wm. Hawkins, John Jenninges, Thomas Medlycott & Henry Knapp appeared & tooke the sev'all oathes appointed for the dew execuc'on of their respective offices & places; & the s'd Wm. Foster & Thomas Medlycott the Oathe menc'oned in the Act intitled "An act for the regulating Corporac'ons," and subscribed the declarac'on [against the Solemn league and covenant.]

𝕿𝖍𝖎𝖘 day the said George Drew appeared here and refused to accept the offices & places of Burgesse or Bayliffe of this Corporac'on, or to take the oathe for the due execuc'on thereof.

𝕿𝖍𝖎𝖘 day the aboves'd Wm. Weston & Phillipp Lockton appeared and tooke the oathe appointed for the due execution of their offices & places.

7th December, A.D. 1687. 3rd James II. William Foster, *Mayor.*

𝕿𝖍𝖎𝖘 day the p'sons hereafter named, by the Order of the King and Councell, were removed from their respective offices in this Corporac'on, that is to say: George Winchhurst, John Claxton, Robt. Sellwood, John Payn & Robt. Blackaller, from being Aldermen; George Drew, from being Bayliffe & Comon Councell man; Rich'd Ely, from being Chamberlain & Comon Councell man; Michaell Rawlins, Thomas Pickett, Thomas Bayly, Edward Allome, Rich'd Rose, John Ainger & John Whichelowe, from being Comon Councell men; & John Woodly, from being Serjeant at Mace of the s'd Borough.

26th December, A.D. 1687. 3rd James II. William Foster, *Mayor.*

𝕬𝖓𝖉 the same day Thomas Hulcottes, Charles Hughes, sen., & Robt. Payn, were appointed & chosen Aldermen of ye s'd Borough; Richard Smith, Richard Playdell, Charles Hughes, jun., John Hern & John Tull, were appointed & Chosen Comon Councell men of ye s'd Borough; & Edward Strainge was appointed & Chosen Serjant at Mace of ye s'd Borough. And ye same day ye s'd Thomas Hulcottes, Charles Hughes, sen., Rob't Payn, Richard Smith, Richard Playdell, Charles Hughes, jun., John Hern, & John Tull, & Edward Strainge, then appeared & sev'ally tooke the sev'all oathes for ye due execuc'on of their respective offices.

𝕿𝖍𝖎𝖘 day John Stevenson was appointed & chosen Alderman of ye s'd Borough, & the same day the s'd John Stevenson appeared & tooke the oathe for ye due execuc'on of his office.

30th December, A.D. 1687. 3rd James II. William Foster, *Mayor.*

𝕿𝖍𝖎𝖘 day likewise Mr. John Fountain was appointed & chosen Alderman of ye said Borough, & tooke the oathe for ye due execuc'on of his office.

w

$\mathfrak{This}$ day Mr. Marke Hawkins was elected and chosen a Comon Councell man & one of the Bayliffes of this Borough, and tooke the oathes for ye due execuc'on of his office.

3rd January,
A.D. 1688.
3rd James II. ,
William Foster,
Mayor.

$\mathfrak{This}$ day Marke Hawkins came in p'son & surrendred into the hands of the Mayor, Aldermen & Burgesses his office of Bayliffe & Comon Councell man of this Borough, together w'th all p'fitts & p'quisites thereunto belonging.

$\mathfrak{This}$ day Wm. Farmer, Edward Ricketts, Isaack Beckett & Francis Hyde, were elected and chosen Comon councell men of this Borough, & the s'd Wm. Farmer, Edward Ricketts & Francis Hyde tooke the oathes for the due execuc'on of their respective offices.

6th January,
A.D. 1688.
3rd James II.
William Foster,
Mayor.

$\mathfrak{This}$ day Isaack Beckett appeared & tooke the oathe for ye due execuc'on of his office whereunto he is elected.

13th January,
A.D. 1688.
3rd James II.
William Foster,
Mayor.

Mr. John Hern this day elected and sworn Chamb'lain.

15th February,
A.D. 1688.
4th James II.
William Foster,
Mayor.

$\mathfrak{This}$ day Mr. James Cord'roy, late Mayor, is allowed for his expences in his Mayoralty twelve pounds.

6th March,
A.D. 1688.
4th James II.
William Foster,
Mayor.

$\mathfrak{Order'd}$ yt ye Chamberlain pay to Mr. Simon Hawkins, for ye fire grates of ye Chamber, Sixe shillinges.

$\mathfrak{It}$ is this day ordered that ye Chamberlain pay to Mr. Knapp, the Town clerke, the sume of fifty guinneys and ten shillinges upon his giving a bond of 100*li*. penalty to ye Corporac'on to return the same to the Corporac'on if he does not p'duce p'sidentes from other Corporac'ons of ye paym't of moneys for charges & gratuityes to 20*li*. or upwards upon ye late Regulac'on of Corporac'ons before July next.

12th April,
A.D. 1688.
4th James II.
William Foster,
Mayor.

$\mathfrak{Ordered}$ yt Mr. Foster, ye p'sent Mayor, be allowed for his housekeeping 20*s*. a weeke, fro' ye time he came to his s'd office of Mayor untill Midsomer next, besides 40*s*. for tickett money for a year.

17th May,
A.D. 1688.
4th James II.
William Foster,
Mayor.

$\mathfrak{This}$ day is ordered in full Councell yt fifty guinneys & ten shillings be p'd Mr. Knapp, ye p'sent Townclerke, by Mr. Jenninges the p'sent Bayliffe, for his charges in getting ye mandates on the late Regulac'on.

9th July,
A.D. 1688.
4th James II.
William Foster,
Mayor.

$\mathfrak{This}$ day the Granary over the Guildhall is Leased to the Recorder of this Borough for one whole year under the rent of three poundes p' Ann., to be payd halfe yearly.

Order'd that upon Debating any matter in Comon Councell after a Question proposed in the house, noe person spake to it above once without Leave of the Mayor asked and granted.

19th July, A.D. 1688. 4th James II. William Foster, Mayor.

Order'd y't the Chamberlain pay to Wm. Prince, Super'sor of the high wayes, five poundes towardes repairing the Ockstreet.

This day it is order'd y't gownes be bought for the sixe Almsmen of St. John's Hospitall at the discretion of the Overseers of Reparations, this Charity to [continue during pleasure*].

26th August, A.D. 1688. 4th James II. William Foster, Mayor.

* These words are struck through and the following inserted :—"pro hac vice, tantum."

Order'd y't Mr. Mayor be allowed by the Chamber Sixteen pounds for making a Feast the first of September next.

This day the Company of Taylors disfranchised Feb. the 8th, 1683, are againe restored with all their priviledges thereunto belonging.

19th October, A.D. 1688. 4th James II. William Hawkins, Mayor.

This day the overseers of reparac'ons are appointed to make a Convenient place below ye New Hall for one of ye Judges of Assizes to sett in.

6th July, A.D. 1689. 1st William & Mary. William Hawkins, Mayor.

This day the house of Madam Saunders, in the Ockstreet, is appointed for entertayning the Judges & the New Inne for their horses.

Forasmuch as Thomas Medlycott, Esqr., (who hath & exerciseth the office of Record'r of the Borough of Abingdon during the good pleasure of the Mayor & Principall Burgesses of the s'd Borough) is by the s'd Mayor & Principall Burgesses removeable at pleasure, Wee, therefore, the Mayor & Principall Burgesses of the s'd Borough (whereof the s'd Mayor is one) Doe hereby declare that our will and pleasure is to amove the s'd Thomas Medlycott fro' his s'd office of Record'r of the s'd Borough, and the s'd Thomas Medlycott is hereby by us, the s'd Mayor & Principall Burgesses, fro' henceforth utterly amoved fro' his s'd office of Record'r To all intents and purposes w'tsoever.

1st October, A.D. 1689. 1st William & Mary. James Corderoy, Mayor.

This day Symon Harcourt, Esqr., is elected and Chosen Record'r of this Borough in the Room of Thomas Medlycott, Esqr., Removed fro' the s'd office, and tooke the oathes for the due execuc'on of his office of Record'r & Justice of the Peace, And alsoe tooke the oathes of Allegiance and Sup'macy   *   *   *

[*Signed*] Sim. Harcourt.

11th December,
A.D. 1689.
1st William &
Mary.
James Corderoy,
Mayor.

This day order'd y't ev'y p'son who after ye 18th day of this month shall lay any Raw hides on the New m'kett house paved floar or round ab't the same, or shall bring any horse or horses upon the s'd paved floar, shall, for ev'y offence, forfeit & pay to this Corporac'on 3s. 4d., proclamac'on being first made of this ord'r.

28th August,
A.D. 1691.
3rd William &
Mary.
RobertSellwood,
Mayor.

This day order'd that no Assize Bills for Bread & Beer shall bo allowed.

13th January.
A.D. 1692.
3rd William &
Mary.
William
Hawkins,
Mayor.

This day order'd in full & open Comon Councell that no Wine, Ale, Cakes, pipes, or tobacco, shalbe spent or eat or drunke at the charges of the Corporac'on, unles by a p'ticuler order for the same. And further order'd that noe Comon councell man of this Borough in the time of the Comon Councell holden, shall smoake any tobacco upon pain each p'son to forfeit ev'y time offending herein twelve pence,   *   *   *   And further order'd that ye last order for p'viding gownes for the principall & Secondary Burgesses bo put in execuc'on, & that Distinction be made between the Principall Burgesses & Secondary Burgesses gownes as form'ly.

10th August,
A.D. 1692.
4th William &
Mary.
William
Hawkins,
Mayor.

This day order'd that ye horse fair called Conduit faire bo removed into the Broad & bore Streets.

13th August,
A.D. 1692.
4th William &
Mary.
William
Hawkins,
Mayor.

Whereas, James Curteen, gent., One of the Principall Burgesses of this Borough, upon the Complaint of Robert Selwood, gent., John Payn, gent., & others, Comissioners within the s'd Borough, appointed by Act of Parliam't for levying the poll taxe this year for their Ma'ties' use, Setting forth that ye s'd James Curteen has indeavoured to obstruct the s'd Comissioners in levying and appointing the gathering the money due by the s'd Act, & publishing openly & frequently amongste their Ma'ties' subjectes that the s'd Comissioners are knaves, and acted knavishly in their taxac'ons by virtue of the s'd Act to the hinderance of the levying of their Ma'ties revenue due by the same Act, And the incouraging their Ma'ties Subjects to with-hold their paym'tes according to the s'd taxac'ons, Was on the Ninth day of this instant August, Sumoned before Wm. Hawkins, gent., Mayor of the s'd Borough, to Answere the s'd Complaint, who thereupon the same day appear'd, and being then by the s'd Mayor desired to stay in his p'sence in order for his giving security by recognizance to Answer the p'misses refused soe to doo and went away from the p'sence of ye Mayor without his leave, and refused to obey him w'thout being Conven'd before him with a warr't, upon w'ch the s'd Mayor hath ye same day issued out his warr't to app'hend the s'd James Curteen to Answer the p'misses directed to ye Constables & tythingmen of ye s'd Borough, who by virtue of ye s'd warr't did app'hend ye said James Curteen, who got himselfe discharged fro' ye s'd Constables by his p'missing them p'sently to appear according to ye tenour of ye s'd war't, but hath hitherto refused to doe ye same, against the duty of his office of principall Burgesse and a freeman of this Borough, It is therefore ordered this p'nt day by the Mayor and Comon Councell of this Borough that the said James Curteen be disfranchised and amoved from his office of principall Burgesse, And he is hereby amoved and discharged from the said office.

This day ordered y't the Mandamus brought for the restoreing Mr. James Curteen to the Office of principall Burgesse be returned and defended, and that Mr. Mayor, Mr. Sellwood, and Mr. Corderoy, be desired to manage and defend ye same   *   *   *

1st November, A.D. 1692. 4th William & Mary. Robert Blackaller, *Mayor.*

It is this day ordered by the Comon Councell That Mr. Henry Knapp doe mannage the busines against Mr. Curteene concerning his Mandamas, And the Comon Councell Did this day signe a Letter of Attorney for him to defend the busines.

24th November, A.D. 1692. 4th William & Mary. Robert Blackaller, *Mayor.*

It is this day ordered That every Comon Councell man that doth not appeare in his Gowne and attend the Mayor to Church on Christmas Day next, shall pay Tenn Shillings, without a reasonable Cause be shewne and approved of by the Comon Councell, And every Comon Councell man that Doth not Attend the Mayor to the Church in his Gowne on the First Sunday in every Month shall pay Five shillings, without a reasonable cause be shewn to the Comon Councell and approved of by them, And that a Warrant be made to Distraine every person that shall make default.

This day ordered y't a beam & Scales & what weightes & mesures shall be necessary for the Clarke of the M'ket for this Borough be p'vided at ye Corp' charges by Mr. Blackaller, Mayor.

20th July A.D. 1693. 5th William & Mary. Robert Blackaller, *Mayor.*

This day Mr. James Curteen lately removed from the office of Principall Burgesse of ye s'd Borough, was again restored to ye s'd office & tooke his place accordingly.

11th November, A.D. 1693. 5th William & Mary. George Drew, *Mayor.*

15th November, A.D. 1691. 6th William & Mary. James Curten, *Mayor.*

This day order'd y't a booke be provided at ye Charges of this Corporac'on for entring of Bylawes, & y't all Bylaws made for ten yeares past be entred in such book.

26th March, A.D. 1695. 7th William III. James Curten, *Mayor.*

This day the Bayliffes are allowed 40s. besides the taxes & allowance form'ly made, towards keeping the Bayliffes feast. And it is this day ordered that noe Mayors, Bayliffes or Chamb'lens feastes be henceforth made untill further order in full Councell be made for the same.

5th June, A.D. 1695. 7th William III. James Curten, *Mayor.*

It is this day ordered in Comon Councell that no Forraigner w'tsoever shall use any manner of trade within the Borough of Abingdon without first paying a fine of fifty poundes for his freedom.

23rd August, A.D. 1695. 7th William III. James Curten, *Mayor.*

This day, notwithstanding a former order, it is order'd that Mr. Mayor be allowed the Sume of Sixteen poundes towardes keeping a feast some short time after the elecc'on of the New Mayor.

27th November, A.D. 1695. 7th William III. John Payn, *Mayor.*

This day Thomas Fletcher hath undertaken to keep the Comon Pumps w'thin this Borough in repair, for w'ch he is to have the yearly salary of three pounds to be payd Quarterly   *   *.   * and the undertaker for his incouragem't is to be allowed timber sufficient for the making of two New pumps

4th August, A.D. 1696. 8th William III. John Payn, *Mayor.*

For the better Supplying the Inhabitantes of the said borough w'th water, a lease is granted to Tho' Piccard, of Abingdon, Gold Smith, of All that peice or plot of wast ground now used for a dunghill, in the Stert, in Abingdon, conteyning in length next the Street fifteen foot, & in breadth backward 16 foot, for the erecting a Cestern to hold water (excepting the room und'r the s'd Cestern soe to be built) To hold for the term of five hundred y'res, And also liberty is granted to ye s'd Tho' Piccard, during the s'd term, to break upp the Streetes of the s'd Borough for the laying of Pipes und'r the ye'rly rent of 1s.

4th October, A.D. 1696. 8th William III. Robert Blackaller, *Mayor.*

This day Richard Mand'r is elected Cooke for this Corporac'on from Mich'as last, for w'ch he is to receive the salary of a guinea yearly.

6th January, A.D. 1697.

[On this day a Lease is granted of a House on the South side of Ock Street, "the thatch of the house to be taken off & cov'red w'th "Slat or tile before Mich'as next."]

𝔒𝔯𝔡𝔢𝔯'𝔡 yt the Chamberlain Doe pay to Mr. Ely the Sume of ten pounds, for the use of the poor Sufferers at Newberry by fire.

4th November, A.D. 1697. 9th William III. John Sellwood, Mayor.

𝔗𝔥𝔢𝔯𝔢 being Articles exhibited against severall members of this Corporac'on for sev'all misdemeanours and Male Adm'istrac'on before ye King & Councell, it is ordered that a Coppy of the said Articles be taken out and the said Articles & allegations therein conteyned be defended at the charges of this Corporac'on.

14th November, A.D. 16:9. 11th William III.

𝔍𝔱 is this day ordered that there be noe more Comon Councells Sumond untill the difference touching the swearing a New Mayor be ended.

𝔗𝔥𝔦𝔰 day Ordered that an Ejectm't at Law be brought ag't Mr. James Curten at the Suit of the Mayor, Bayliffes & Burgesses of this Borough for the recovery of the possession of the house with th'appurt'unces in the Stert in Abingdon now in the possession of the s'd James Curten, and that the same be p'secuted by the Town clerke at the Charges of this Corporac'on.

6th July, A.D. 1700. 12th William III. John Spinage, Mayor.

𝔒𝔯𝔡𝔢𝔯'𝔡 that the Townclarke Attend at London this next Mich'as term with the Comon Councell Books & Charters of this Borough, to be used at the tryall of ye Informac'on ag't Mr. Curten.

12th October, A.D. 1700. 12th William III. John Selwood, Mayor.

𝔍𝔱 is this day Ordered that the toll of All or any Corn or grain w'ch shalbe brought or exposed to be sold within the said Borough shall not at any time hereafter be leased to any Member of the Comon Councell of the said Borough.

21th November, A.D. 170?. 1st Anne. RobertSellwood, Mayor.

𝔍𝔱 is this day Ordered and agreed to in Councell, that if any sheriffe, Bayliffe, or sheriffe's officer shall att any time hereafter levye any sume of money by virtue of any execution upon any Inhabitant of the Borough of Abingdon touching a Robbery comitted lately upon One Mr. Blower, within the Hundred of Hormer, that this Corporac'on shall and will save harmles such person upon whom such execuc'on shall be levyed, and in the name of the party upon whom such execuc'on shalbe levyed cause an Acc'on to be Comenced ag't such person or persons levying such execuc'on for doeing the same, to trye the right of this Corporac'on whither the Borough of Abingdon be within the Hundred of Hormer or not, And also if any Sheriffe or Sheriffe's Officer shall at any time hereafter make any arrest within this Borough, by virtue of any warr't upon any writt

16th January, A.D. 1705. 3rd Anne. Joseph Spinage, Mayor.

w'tsoev'r, except by virtue of a Non Omittas, That in Such case, such person making such arrest shalbe p'ceeded against at Law for infringeing the Liberty of this Corporac'on.

It is this day ordered that Mr. Curteen & Mr. Claxton doe take care to repair the flood gates in the Stert,   *   *   *

Order'd that Mr. Tho. Saunders make one dozen of Cushions out of the table Carpet for the Chamber.

This day Ordered that for the future noe p'son w'tsoev'r be suffred to drye any Clothes in the Markett house.

This day Ordered that the Townclerke of this Borough doe forthwith p'ceed ag't the Ex'ors of Mr. Twitty and ye Churchwardens & Overseers of ye Poor & minister of ye p'ish of St. Hellen's within this Borough, in the Cause p'ferred ag't them at the suit of her Ma'ties Attorney Gen'all, Att the relation of the Mayor, Bayliffes & Burgesses of the said Borough.

For the better Advancing of the Interest of this Corporac'on, and the Paym't of the Debtes due from this Corporac'on, it is this day Ordered by This Comon Councell That for the time to come there shall be allowed unto the Mayor of this Borough towards the Dischargeing of his yeare's Mayoralty the sume of Thirty pounds and Noe more, and further that the Bayliffes shall give noe entertainm't, and that noe feast shalbe kept at the time of the elecc'on of the New Mayor at the Charge of this Corporac'on.

It is this day Ordered that Mr. Hart, Chamberlain, doe sett workemen on worke and repair the railes & Banisters on the Top of the Market house, and also to take care, fro' time to time, of the repaires of the Market house windowes.

This day the Office of High Steward of this Borough is granted unto the right hon'ble Mountague, Earle of Abingdon, and likewise the exhibic'on of IIJ*l.* vj*s.* viij*d.*

This day Orderd that a Petic'on be made to the Parliam't that this Corporac'on may be excepted out of the Act intended to be passed for Registring Deedes in the County of Berks, and that they may be admitted to Register the same within this Borough sepa'te fro' the County.

This day Ordered that the Cage be Pul'd down, and yt a New One be erected in the m'ket place where the Pillory now stands, by the direcc'on of the Chamberlain.

23rd May,
A.D. 1710.
9th Anne.
Thomas King,
Mayor.

This day Ordered that noe money shalbee payd by this Corporac'on for wine, unles a bill be signed by the Chamberlain for ye same before the wine shalbe deliver'd to the Chamber.

28th December,
A.D. 1710.
9th Anne.
Michael Rawlins,
Mayor.

This day also order'd that the Chamberlain doe raise the Markett house Cellers, for the better p'venting the riseing of water in the same, or allow Mr. Symes, tenant to the same, forty shillinges for doeing thereof.

7th June,
A.D. 1711.
10th Anne.
Michael Rawlins,
Mayor.

This day it is Ordered in Councell yt in case Mr. Rich'd Knapp shall not By fryday night next give it under his hand that it is his Opinion that he is duely elected Recorder of this Borough (in which case if he give such opinion Mr. Mayor doth p'mise to swear & admitte him into the same office) That y'n & in such case of Mr. Knapp's refusall to give such his Opinion, The charges of makeing a return to a mandamus already brought by the s'd Mr. Knapp & directed to the s'd Mayor to swear & admitte him into the s'd Office of Recorder shall be made at the charges of this Corporac'on.

12th June,
A.D. 1711.
10th Anne.
Michael Rawlins,
Mayor.

This day the resignation of the right hon'ble S'r Simon Harcourt, Kn't, Lord keeper of the great Seale of great Britain, of his office of Recorder of this Borough, under his hand & Seale, was read & accepted, And Richard Knapp, Esqr., is elected & chosen Recorder of this Borough, in the room of the s'd S'r Simon Harcourt.

3rd April,
A.D. 1711.
10th Anne.
Michael Rawlins,
Mayor.

This day the sume of Ten Poundes is ord'red to be paid by the Chamberlain of the Borough, unto Mr. Joseph Stockwell, Curate to Mr. Anthony Addison, Minister of the p'ish of St. Hellen's within the said Borough, for an Augmentac'on of the Salary allowed him by Mr. Addison for Serveing the Cure within the s'd p'ish, the same to be paid at two paym'ts, by equall porc'ons, y't is at Mich'as & Lady day, for the term of one whole year & noe Longer, the first paym't to begin on the 29th day of Sept. next.

20th June,
A.D. 1711.
10th Anne.
Michael Rawlins,
Mayor.

[Richard Knapp, Esqr., took the Oaths as Recorder and Justice of Peace of the Borough, and the Oaths of Allegiance and Supremacy.]

3rd July,
A.D. 1711.

It is this day Ordered that the Chamberlain for the time beeing, doe weekely pay unto John Hawkins, one of the town Serjeantes,

28th September,
A.D. 1714.
1st George I.
William Dunn,
Mayor.

X

three shillings, Sixe Pence, towardes his releif in his p'sent necessitous condic'on, he haveing a Cancer in his lip, now under the care of a Surgeon, his pay to begin this p'sent day, & to be continued till further Order.

16th June,
A.D. 1716.
2nd George I.
Thomas Simes,
Mayor.

This day it is Ordered in Councell That for the more easie defraying the Charges of the Judges of Assizes' horses att such time as the Assizes shalbe holden at Abingdon, the sume of fower poundes be paid into the hands of the Judges' Steward for the same, and noe more, and that all other allowances be made as usuall.

3rd January,
A.D. 1719.
5th George I.
Thomas Prince,
Mayor.

Mr. Richard Ely, towardes the repaireing & beautificing the Caswell, is allowed Sixe pounds.

22nd January,
A.D. 1719.
5th George I.
Thomas Prince,
Mayor.

This day ordered that every member of this Comon Councell who shall not subscribe to the charge of erecting Organs w'thin the parish of St. Hellen's, within this Borough, shall not have any benefitt of selling goodes or be imployed in any proffitable worke belonging to this Corporac'on.

2nd April,
A.D. 1719.
5th George I.
Thomas Prince,
Mayor.

This day it is further ordered that every member of this Comon Councell who s'all not subscribe to the charge of erecting Organs within the parish of St. Hellen's within this Borough, shall not have any benefitt of the sealing fees upon granting of Leases by this Corporac'on to any person w'tsoever.

19th May,
A.D. 1720.
6th George I.
William Tudor,
Mayor.

This day ordered that the Chamberlain pay to Mr. Richard Ely twelve poundes for his charges in erecting & beautifieing a place for the Conduit Stream to run und'r in the Ockstreet, & for makeing and raileing in a Cestern there.

10th November,
A.D 1720.
7th George I.
William
Philipson,
Mayor.

If is this day alsoe agreed in Comon Councell that such proceedinges shalbee had at the charges of this Corporac'on for the recovery of an ancient Comon way leading fro' St. Hellen's Street, in Abingdon, to a place called Cole's Steps, used by the Inhabitants of this Borough for fetching water from the river of Thames al's Isis, in such manner and ag't such person and persons as shalbe advised.

If is likewise this day agreed in Councell that the right of Comon of the Inh'itantes of this Borough in a certain meadow called Abingdon mead, after the first Crop taken off, with their right of Comon in other adjacent places, be inquired into, and Mr. Tudor,

Mr. Rawlins, Mr. Ely, Mr. Sextone, Mr. Hart, Mr. Tho' Prince, Mr. Gilman and Mr. Wells, are appointed for this purpose.

𝕿𝖍𝖎𝖘 day Ordered that the great Silver Salt and two Silver bowles be changed for a Sett of Silver Casters, and that the Mace be mended and New Guilt.

22nd December, A.D. 1720. 7th George I. William Phihpson, Mayor.

𝕬𝖓 𝕺𝖗𝖉𝖊𝖗 made by the Mayor, Bayliffes and Burgesses of the Borough of Abingdon, in the County of Berks, in Comon Councell assembled, in the Guild Hall within the said Borough, the Twentieth day of October, in the ninth year of the reign of our Soveraign Lord, George, by the Grace of God King, of Great Britain, France and Ireland, Defend'r of the faith, &c., Annoq' D'ni 1722.

20th October, A.D. 1722. 9th George I. John Fludyer, Mayor.

𝖂𝖍𝖊𝖗𝖊𝖆𝖘 Dresseing of Hemp and Flaxe in shops and roomes within this Borough and Spinning and weaving of Hemp in Spinning and weaving houses within this Borough hath occasioned and been the cause of Severall dreadfull fires within this Borough of late yeares, by reason of the Negligence and carelesnesse of the men, weomen and children employed and workeing in the said Shops, roomes and houses, And whereas by and through the great Increase of the Number of Such Shops, roomes and houses within this Borough, much Greater damages from fires are feared to bee hereafter within this Borough unlesse the workeing in such Shopps, roomes and houses by Candlelight bee timely p'vented, to the great Terrour of many of the Inhabitants of this Borough and the ruine of the whole town, if the same should happen (which God forbid); 𝕱𝖔𝖗 p'venting, therefore, of such great future danger of fire as may happen by workeing in the roomes, shopps and houses already erected, built, and made use of and which hereafter may bee erected, built, or made use of within this Borough in Dressing of hemp or flaxe, or in Spinning and weaveing of hemp, 𝕴𝖙 is now, therefore, 𝖔𝖗𝖉𝖊𝖗𝖊𝖉 by the Mayor, Bayliffes and Burgesses of this Borough in Comon Councell assembled, that from an' after the   day of November now next ensueing, Noe person or persons whatsoever shall dresse any hemp or flaxe or Spin or weave any hemp in any Shopp, room or house within this Borough by Candlelight; And it is further Ordered by the authority aforesaid, that the Occupier and Occupiers of all and every such dressing Shopp or room or Spinning or weaveing house or houses within this Borough, who shall allow, permitt or suffer any person or persons w'tsoev'r to dresse any hemp or flaxe, or Spin or weave any hemp within any One of his, her or their respective dresseing shopps or roomes or Spinning or weaveing houses within this Borough by Candle light, shall forfeit and pay to the Mayor, Bayliffs and Burgesses of this Borough the Sume of Ten shillinges of lawfull money of great Britain for every time hee, shee or they, doe or shall allow, permitt, or suffer the same. And it is alsoe further Ordered by the authority aforesaid, That if the Occupier or occupiers of any of the said Shopps, roomes or houses, shall dresse any hemp or flaxe or Spin or weave any hemp within either of his, her or their respective shopp or shopps, room or roomes, house or houses, by Candle light, such person or persons shall forfeit and pay to the Mayor, Bayliffes and Burgesses of this Borough the Sume of twenty shillinges of like lawfull money of Great Britain for every such offence.

[This order was again issued on the 2½th November, 1722.]

25th June, A.D. 1723. 9th George I. John Fludyer, *Mayor*.

It is this day, at the request of divers of the Inhabitantes of the University and Citty of Oxon, Order'd that five Guineas be paid into the handes of Mr. Thomas Woods, Master of the Freeschoole within this Borough, to bee employed towardes repairing and widening the Narrow places of the Highway leading from the Citty of Oxon to the bottome of Hincksey Hill and makeing wider the way over Magdalen bridge within the Suburbes of the Citty of Oxon.

1st January, A.D. 1724. 10th George I. William Philipson, *Mayor*.

Att a Comon Councell this day holden for this Borough, Mr. Recorder of the same Borough is desired to procure a grant to this Corporac'on from his Majesty, for takeing a certainty for wheelage every day of the weeke within this Borough.

13th February, A.D. 1724. 10th George I. William Philipson, *Mayor*.

It is this day Ordered that noe repaires of the Schoole or prison or other place bee made, and that noe expences in wine or beer be made, without an Order of Comon Councell for such repaires and for such expences bee first had and obtained for the same.

20th May, A.D. 1724. 10th George I. William Philipson, *Mayor*.

Att a Comon Councell this day held for this Borough, 'tis Ordered & Agreed that the Chamberlain shall pay to Mr. Samuel Westbrook toward the expences of pitching the Street called the Winyard, the sume of Thirty pounds, provided ye same be sufficiently & substantially pitched & layd with good stones upp as high as the further part or outside of the Alehouse called the hen & Chicken, Fifteen pounds whereof to be payd him as soon as 'tis pitcht as high as ye

upper end of ye Dwelling house of Mr. Michael Rawlins, Jun'r,
And the other fifteen pounds to be payd him when ye whole work is
compleat & finished, he, the said Sam'll Westbrook, att ye time of ye
said last payment Entring into a propper Article with this Corporac'on
to keep the same in good Repaire throughout for One & twenty years
next ensueing the Compleating the said work, for twenty shillings p'
Ann' to be payd him by the Chamberlain of ye said Borough for ye
time being for so repairing ye same.

Ordered that the Townclerk signe to ye paym't of Ten pounds
on behalfe of this Corporac'on toward ye Erecting a Gallary in the
Midle Isle in St. Hellen's Church, to be payd by ye Chamberlain.

It is this day ordered and agreed by the Comon Councell That
Mr. Mayor do, at the Charges of this Corporac'on, provide & buy
Fifty pewter Dishes and Twelve Dozen of pewter plates for the use
of this Corporac'on, and to have the Corporation Arms Engraved
thereon, The same to be yearly delivered over from one Mayor to
another, to be made use of at their publick Feasts and Entertainm'ts
within this Borough.

24th November, A.D. 1724. 11th George I. Clement Saxton, Mayor.

An Order made by Clement Sexton, Gent., Mayor of the said
Borough, and Clerk of the Markett, and the Bayliffs and Burgesses
of the same Borough in Comon Councell Assembled att the Guildhall
of the said Borough, the 24th day of November, Anno D'ni 1724.

It is ordered and Enacted that upon every markett day from
henceforth (Except holydays and Fairs) in every year from Mich'as
to Ladyday the markett Bell shall ring att Eleven of the Clock in the
forenoon, and from Ladyday to Mich'as at Twelve of the Clock and
that no person from henceforth shall Carry or Cause to be Carryed In
any Barly, wheat or other Grain to any malster's or other person's
house or Granary within this Borough, nor any malster or other
person receive or take in such Barly, wheat or other Grain, on any
markett day, Except holydays and Fairs, till the ringing the markett
Bell at the respective hours aforesaid, upon the forfeiture of Five
Shillings per Load, and after that rate for any greater or Lesser
Quantity, to be paid by the proprieto'r or owner of the said Barly,
wheat or Grain, or by the person so Carrying in the same, and the
like forfeiture of Five Shillings per Load, and after that rate for any
Greater or lesser Quantity to be paid by the malster or person

receiving such Barley, wheat or Grain, The same forfeitures to be paid into the hands of the Mayor of the said Borough for the time being, whereof one Moyety to be by him distributed to and among such of the poor of the parish where the said Barly, wheat or Grain shall be Carryed in as the Mayor shall think fitt, and the other Moyety to be by him paid to such person or persons as shall give Information Concerning the p'm'es; And for default of payment thereof the same to be Levyed by warrant from the Mayor and Clerk of the Markett of the said Borough for the time being, on the offender or offenders, by Distress and Sale of his or their Goods & Chattles, rendring to the party and partys distreyned the overplus (if any be) after reasonable Charges of Distreyning deducted.

16th July,
A.D. 1725.
11th George I.
Clement Saxton,
Mayor.

Ordered that Mr. Recorder be desired by the Townclark to draw up a Case concerning the Repairac'on and amendment of the Highways in the parish of St. Hellen's, in order to take the opinion of Councell whether the Surveyo's and Inhabitants within the Borough are any ways lyable or Compellable to Joyn with the Hamletts without the Borough in repairing such part of the Highways as lye out of the Jurisdicc'on of the Borough, within the said parish, and that the said Case when drawn be first laid before the Mayor, Bayliffs and Burgesses in Comon Councell to be Considered of.

11th August,
A.D. 1725.
12th George I.
Clement Saxton,
Mayor.

'Tis this day agreed and ordered by the Comon Councell that the Sume of Fifty pounds be given and paid by the Chamber toward the Erecting a Good and Sufficient organ in St. Hellen's Church within this Borough, the same to be paid as soon as such organ shall be Erected and Compleat, provided it be Compleated within the space of a year now next ensueing.

26th January,
A.D. 1726.
12th George I.
James Saunders,
Mayor.

This day 'tis ordered by ye Chamber that twenty pounds more be added toward the pitching of the Winyard   *   *   *

22nd February,
A.D. 1726.
12th George I.
James Saunders,
Mayor.

Ordered by the Comon Councell that Mr. Prince, the Chamberlain, pay to Mrs. Knapp, the widow of the late Townclark, the Sume of Seventeen pounds, Sixteen Shillings, and Six pence due to her by Bill for her late husband's fees and expences in Solliciting the Replevin Cause, Reynolds att the Suit of North Sherwood, concerning the said Sherwood's Sheep Trespassing in Abingdon Comon, and Sixteen Shillings and Six pence more for his trouble and Attendance touching the Toll of the Markett; In all Eighteen pounds, thirteen Shillings.

'Tis ordered by the Comon Councell That ye Townclerk continue the prosecutions ag't North Sherwood & others at the next Assizes upon ye Indictm'ts found ag't them att the last Somer Assizes for not clenseing & Scouring the Severall Ditches and water-courses in the parish of St. Hellen's, for which they Stand Indicted.

11th July A.D. 1726. 12th George I. James Saunders, Mayor.

An Act or Order made by William Wells, Gent., Mayor of the said Borough and Clerke of the Markett, and by the Bayliffs and Burgesses of the Same in Comon Councell assembled, att the Guild-hall of the said Borough, this first day of October, anno D'ni 1726, for the better Supporting and mainteyning the Barly marketts within this Borough.

1st October, A.D. 1726. 13th George I. William Wells, Mayor.

It is Enacted and ordeyned by the Authority aforesaid, That from henceforth if any person or persons whatsoever shall presume to buy or Sell within this Borough any Barly intended to be made into Malt in the Same, upon any other then the markett days or att any other time of the day then after the ringing of the markett Bell (which is appointed to be att Eleven of the Clock), and after such Barly or a fourth part thereof in the name of the whole Shall be pitched and Exposed to Sale in the open markett, All and every Such person and persons, as well the buyer as the Seller, shall Severally forfeit and pay Instantly two Shillings and Six pence per Quarter for every Quarter of Barly by him or them So bought or Sold, as aforesaid, into the hands of the Mayor of the said Borough for the time being, whereof one moyety to be by him Distributed to and among such of the poor of the said Borough as he Shall think fitt, and the other moyety to be paid to the person or persons who Shall give Informac'on of the p'misses, and for default of payment thereof, the Same Shall be recovered and Levyed either by action of Debt att the Suit of the Mayor, Bayliffs and Burgesses of the said Borough against such person or persons So forfeiting, or Else by Distress and Sale of his or their Goods and Chattles, to be Granted by the Mayor and Clerke of the Markett of the said Borough, rendring to the party and partys distreyned, the overplus (if any be) after reasonable Charges of Distreyning deducted.

8th November,
A.D. 1729.
3rd George II.
William Dunn,
Mayor.

𝕺𝖗𝖉𝖊𝖗𝖊𝖉 that ye Mayor of this Borough have Liberty to subscribe thirty guineas on Acco't of the Corporation toward defraying the Expences in Order to procure an Act of Parliam't to remedy severall mischeifs on the Navigation to & fro' Between this Borough & ye City of London, And that the Same be payd in p'portion with ye paym'ts of other subscribers on the Same acco't.

𝕺𝖗𝖉𝖊𝖗𝖊𝖉 yt the Chamberlain do forthwith deposite ye Sume of Ten pounds into the hands of Samuel Westbrook, toward the repairac'on of ye highwayes within the parish of St. Hellen's, untill his arreares be Collected.

2nd December,
A.D. 1729.
3rd George II.
William Dunn,
Mayor.

𝕺𝖗𝖉𝖊𝖗𝖊𝖉 that ye Townclerk bring an Ejectm't att the Charges of this Corporac'on for ye Recovery of ye possession of ye Bridewell, now in W'm Geagle's poss'ion.

23rd September,
A.D. 1730.
4th George II.
William Dunn,
Mayor.

'𝕿𝖎𝖘 this day Ordered that for ye future ye Sallary of every New Mayor of this Corporation for the First year of his Mayoralty be made upp Ninety pounds, And that the Sallary of every Mayor who hath served that office before be made upp One hundred Pounds.

10th December,
A.D. 1730.
4th George II.
Edward Saxton,
Mayor.

'𝕿𝖎𝖘 this day Ordered that Mr. Saxton, ye p'sent Chamberlain, do forthwith pay to Mr. Edw'd Spinage, Treasurer of the Charity money, the Sume of Sixty Five Pounds, Six Shillings, eight pence, to make good the Losse of so much of ye One hundred pounds Charity money usually Loaned out by this Corporation to Ten severall persons of this Town, att ten pounds to each person, payable by 20s. p' Ann' without Interest. *　*　*　*

'𝕿𝖎𝖘 also Ordered that no Member of this Corporation shall be accepted as security for ye repayment of any of ye s'd Ten pounds hereafter to be Lent.

'𝕿𝖎𝖘 Ordered yt Mr. Mayor, Mr. Record'r, Mr. Justice of Peace, Mr. Ely, Mr. Fludger, Mr. Saunders & Mr. Anderson, or any four of them, do Inquire into ye Originall Gift of ye said 100li. Charity, And also into the Title of the Bridewell, And make their Report thereof to this Chamber.

7th January,
A.D. 1731.
4th George II.
Edward Saxton,
Mayor.

'𝕿𝖎𝖘 also Ordered & agreed That ye persons which Shall be Lycensed & allowed to Sell Ale or Beer within this Borough from & after Easter next Shall not Exceed the Number of Fifty persons att ye most att any one time, The ancient Liberty & priviledge granted to ye Inhabitants by ye Charter for Selling ye Same att & ag't Fairs only Excepted.

Ordered That for the future no Person be Made a Parish Officer within this Borough That has not a Legall Setlement within such Parish.

15th March, A.D. 1731. 4th George II. Edward Saxton, *Mayor*.

It is Ordered That an Order of the twenty third Day of September last Ordering the Salary of every new Mayor for the first year of his Mayoralty to be Made up Ninety Pounds, and the Salary of every Mayor who had Served the office before to be made up One hundred Pounds, be now Entirely Quashed and Set aside, and that for the future the Present Mayor and every Principall Burgess who shall be hereafter Elected Mayor of this Borough shall have his Salary made up One hundred Pounds, whether he has Served the Office before or not, And that every Mayor who shall be hereafter Elected Shall give a Dinner to the Corporation at Christmas.

4th June, A.D. 1731. 4th George II. Edward Saxton, *Mayor*.

It is Ordered That the Roof and Floor over the Town Hall in this Borough, and the Wall thereto belonging, And also the Roof Over the Stair-Case Leading from the Town-Hall to the Council Chamber, be forthwith Taken Down, And in the Room thereof, One New Room to be Erected and Built, And to be Called the Council Chamber, by Such Workmen And in Such Manner as Mr. Edward Saxton, Mayor, Mr. John Fludger, Mr. James Saunders, Mr. Mathew Anderson, and Mr. John Spinage, or any three of them, Shall Direct and Approve of, Who are Desired from time to time to Inspect the S'd Building and give Direcc'ons Concerning the Same Untill it Shall be Compleated and finished.

15th July, A.D. 1731. 5th George II. Edward Saxton, *Mayor*.

Ordered that the Town Clerk do Provide Lodgings for the Judges at the next Assizes. Mr. Moody and Mr. Powell to provide for the Judges' Horses; And that Mr. Richard Saunders do provide for the Clerk of Assizes' Horses.

21st June, A.D. 1733. 7th George II. EdwardSpinage, *Mayor*.

Ordered that ten Guineas be given by the Corporation for a Galloway Plate to be run for at the next Race.

31st July, A.D. 1733. 7th George II. EdwardSpinage, *Mayor*.

Ordered that a good Fire Engine be provided at the Charge of the Corporation, and that Mr. Mayor be Desired to provide the same, And to apply to the Sun Fire Office for such Allowance towards it as can possibly be got. And that All the Buckets belonging to the

8th February, A.D. 1734. 7th George II. Joseph Stockwell, *Mayor*.

Y

Corporation be put in good Repair, And that they be made up fifty in Number, And that a Chain and Lock be provided for Security of the Same, And that the Same be not Lent but in Case of Fire, And that Such Buckets are to be repaired and provided by Mr. Thomas Cullerne.

28th February, A.D. 1734. 7th George II. Joseph Stockwell, *Mayor.*

Ordered that the Town Clerk have five Pounds and five Shillings for his Journey in Waiting on the Prince of Orange And giving his Highness an Invitation to this Borough, in the Name of the Mayor and Corporation, which was accepted accordingly.

26th November, A.D. 1734. 8th George II. Thomas Cullerne, *Mayor.*

This Day the Order of the 28th of Febr'y, 1733(4) for allowing the Town-Clerk five Pounds and five Shillings for his Journey in Waiting on the Prince of Orange, at Newbury, and giving his Highness an Invitation to this Borough in the name of the Corporation was Confirmed.

26th December, A.D. 1734. 8th George II. Thomas Cullerne, *Mayor.*

At a Meeting of the Principall Burgesses this day it was Agreed that the Interest Money arising from the One hundred Pounds left to the Principall Burgesses by Mr. Thomas Knapp, dece'd, for Charitable Uses, after the Fees paid as by his Will is Directed, shall be distributed every Ash-Wednesday before the Money called Ash-Wednesday's Money is Distributed, in the same sumes to poor Persons, And that those who have a share of Mr. Knapp's Legacy shall have no Benefit from the Ash-Wednesday's Money that year.

28th January, A.D. 1735. 8th George II. Thomas Cullerne, *Mayor.*

Ordered That every Member of the Corporation that Calls or Sends for any Liquor or Victuals in Comon Council without their Consent, or at any other time, such Liquor or Victuals shall not be paid for by the Corporation but by the Party himself.

20th March, A.D. 1735. 8th George II. Thomas Cullerne, *Mayor.*

It is Ordered that in Every Lease allready Granted and not Sealed, or that shall be hereafter Granted, a Clause shall be Inserted against Erecting any Spinning-House or Suffering any Part of the Buildings to be Thatched or to Continue So if Thatched before the Granting of the Lease.

28th September, A.D. 1735. 9th George II. Thomas Cullerne, *Mayor.*

We, whose Names are hereunto Subscribed, do Protest against Letting the Waste Piece of Ground at the End of the Boar-Street, Adjoining to Jennings's Peice, in this Borough. (Signed) Will'm Dunn, Edw'd Saxton, Edw. Spinage, J. Waldron, John Spinage, Will. Yateman, Geo. Wells, Jno. Pleydell.

𝔒𝔯𝔡𝔢𝔯𝔢𝔡 That the Grant made at the last Comon Council on the 25th Instant, to Mr. Thos. Cullerne, the then Mayor, of Six Pounds a year for Clearing the Streets of Dirt and Rubbish for 21 years, in the Room of Edwd. Jennings, be Repealed, and that the s'd Mr. Cullerne be Absolutely Discharged from any Part of the Agreement by him to be performed relating thereunto.

30th September, A.D. 1735. 9th George II. Matthew Anderson, Mayor.

𝔒𝔯𝔡𝔢𝔯𝔢𝔡 That Edwd. Jennings do Clean the Streets from Mich'as last to St. Thos. Day next, after the Rate of twelve Pounds a year, he Performing the same well, and in default thereof, his Salary to be stopt, to which the said Edwd. Jennings this day agreed.

𝔒𝔯𝔡𝔢𝔯𝔢𝔡 That the Bell-Man do give Publick Notice that all Piggs going about the Streets of this Borough for the future will be Immediately Impounded, And that the Owners of Such Piggs shall Pay Six-Pence to the Bell-Man for each Pigg by him so Impounded, And that his Salary from the Corporation be stopt for his Neglect of Duty therein.

𝔒𝔯𝔡𝔢𝔯𝔢𝔡 That the Dwelling-House, School House, and Rooms over it, and Two Rooms over Mrs. Kath. Wells's, Tyle, Lath and Plaister, two Story, be forthwith Insured in the Sun Fire Office. Mr. Mayor, Mr. Justice of Peace, and Mr. Fludger, are appointed to Inspect the Buildings above-mentioned before the Same are Insured, and to Insure the Same in the Name of the Mayor and Burgesses and their Successors.

𝔒𝔯𝔡𝔢𝔯𝔢𝔡 by the Comon Council that what Expence Robert Hucks, Esqr., shall be at Relating to the Turn-Pike Road, shall be born by the Corporation.

10th February, A.D. 1736. 9th George II. Matthew Anderson, Mayor.

Mary Ewstace, Milliner, is this day Elected a Free-Woman and Sworn.

18th February, A.D. 1736.

[A fine of Five guineas appears to have been paid by this lady for her Admission. There are other instances about this period of Women being elected to the Freedom of the Borough.]

𝔍𝔱 is Ordered that the Town-Clerk do take such Methods to recover the Possession of the Bridewell in this Borough, in behalf of the Mayor, Bayliffs and Burgesses as he shall think proper, And to take Mr. Recorder's Opinion in anything relating thereto, if he shall see Occasion.

22nd February, A.D. 1737. 10th George II. John Spinage, Mayor.

And it is Ordered that the Town-Clerk do take proper Measures to obtain a Grant of Markets in this Borough every day in the Week

And to take the Recorder's Opinions and Directions therein as Occasion shall require.

7th April, A.D. 1737. 10th George II. John Spinage, *Mayor*.

It is this Day Agreed by the Mayor, Justice and Principall Burgesses of this Borough, that the fifty Persons under-written shall be Lycensed by two Justices of the Peace, at Easter next, to keep Common Ale-houses in this Borough, and so Continue to be from year to year during the Pleasure of the Mayor, Justice of Peace, and Principall Burgesses, And in Case Any of them shall Dye during the Continuance of their Lycenses, the Vacancyes of such Persons Dying shall not be filled up Untill the then next Generall Lycensing of Ale-Houses for the said Borough, without the Consent of the Mayor, Justice of Peace and Principall Burgesses, or the Major Part of them.

[Then follow the fifty names.]

(Similar lists frequently appear in subsequent years.)

It is Ordered   *   *   *   that Mr. John Waldron, One of the Principall Burgesses, do on every Sunday and on all Days when he shall go to St. Hellen's Church, in this Borough, set below every Member who hath served or shall serve the office of Mayor, he not having served the same, and that John Holmes, Serjeant at Mace, do give him Notice of this Order forthwith in Writing.

3rd January, A.D. 1738. 11th George II. William Yateman, *Mayor*.

This day Eleven Pence was stopt and paid to the Serjeants and Bellman by Order of Common Council, being Sealing Fees due to Mr. John Waldron, in Part of his Fines for going to Church without his Gown on such Sundays as the same are appointed to be worn.

30th March, A.D. 1738. 11th George II. William Yateman, *Mayor*.

Ordered that the Town Clark examine the Copyes of the Charters with the Originals, or cause the same to be done, in Order that an Affidavit be made of their being true Copyes.

15th June, A.D. 1738. 12th George II. William Yateman, *Mayor*.

To get Office Copy of the Will of Mr. Will'm Robson relating to 2li. 12s. payable to this Corporation by the Salters' Company yearly.

Ordered that if the Sollicitor General is not satisfyed with the Copys of the Charters and affid't already laid before him, that Office Copyes be taken and laid before him at the Charge of the Corporation.

15th August, A.D. 1738. 12th George II. William Yateman, *Mayor*.

It is ordered that the Seventy pounds given by Lord Abingdon to the Corporation, be laid out in two Silver Punch Bowles, one of Forty pounds, the other of Thirty pounds, and that Mr. Mayor,

Mr. Justice, Mr. Saunders, Mr. Anderson and Mr. Cullerne do provide the same forthwith.

Ordered that the King's Arms be painted and put in a Wooden Frame in the Town Hall, and the date when the Markett house was built to be put under the King's Arms in the Market house.

25th August, A.D. 1738. 12th George II. William Yateman, Mayor.

Ordered that the publick Lamps be lighted the 20th Octo'r next, and that Robert Mayo do light and Clense them as usual.

27th September, A.D. 1738. 12th George II. William Yateman, Mayor.

Ordered that the Watch do Continue to go their Rounds till Six a Clock in the Morning, and to have Six shillings a week.

3rd November, A.D. 1738. 12th George II. Thomas Cullerne, Mayor.

It is Ordered that the Market Bell be rung every Day in the Week (Sundays Excepted) at ten a Clock in the Fore-Noon, And that Mr. Nich's Mayo do Collect the Toll of Corn and Grain on the Toll Days lately Granted by Charter, being Tuesday, Wednesday, Thursday and Saturday, for one Month for his own use, he Employing a Sufficient Number of Persons for that Purpose at his own Expence.

2nd April, A.D. 1739. 12th George II. Thomas Cullerne, Mayor.

It is Ordered that the Town-Clerk be for ever Excused from Serving the Office of Mayor on acc't of his being Town-Clerk.

18th August, A.D. 1739. 13th George II. Thomas Cullerne, Mayor.

Ordered that the Order relating to the Succession of a Mayor in Turn be set aside.

Ordered that the Order relating to the Commoners' Dinner and a shilling to be paid in Lieu thereof to each Person be set aside, and that the Commoners' Dinner be this year kept.

Ordered that the Mayor and Justice do appoint a Watch-Man to go every night in the year with the Bell-Man about the Town And to be Paid by the Bell-Man.

20th September, A.D. 1739. 13th George II. Thomas Cullerne, Mayor.

Ordered that Mr. Mayor, Mr. Mayor Elect, Mr. Anderson and Mr. Chamberlain, or any two of them Do Cause the Fann to be put up on the Market-House in such good and substantiall Manner as they shall think proper.

Ordered that the Chamberlain do for the future pay no Work-Man more by the day on account of the Corporation than such Workman ought to be paid if Employ'd on account of a Private Person.

4th July, A.D. 1740. 14th George II. James Saunders, Mayor.

This Day Mr. John Knapp, Mayor Elect, refused to take upon him that Office on account of his being Town-Clerk.

29th September, A.D. 1741. 15th George II. Edward Spinage, Mayor.

2nd October,
A.D. 1741.
15th George II.
EdwardSpinage,
Mayor.

𝕿𝖍𝖊 Mayor, Bayliffs and Capitall Burgesses of the Borough of Abingdon this Day being met together, Mr. John Knapp, the Mayor-Elect of the said Borough for the Year Ensuing, appeared before them and refused to Accept the said Office and Offer'd as a Reason that as he was likewise Town-Clerk, he was Advised that he could not Serve the Office of Mayor with Safety, in Respect to his Office of Town-Clerk, And the said Mayor, Bayliffs and Capitall Burgesses did duly Consider the said Cause so given and did adjudge the same to be a reasonable Cause and did accordingly Excuse the said John Knapp from Serving the said Office of Mayor, pursuant to the Power to them given by the Charter of the third and fourth of Philip and Mary.

𝕴𝖙 is Ordered by the Mayor, Bayliffs and Burgesses in Common-Council assembled that the next Mayor of this Borough and every Succeeding Mayor shall be allowed forty Pounds for his Salary and five Pounds for the Visitation Dinner, And that no other Publick Dinner shall be kept, And that the Mayor shall live in all other Respects in such Manner as he shall think proper.

𝕴𝖙 is Ordered for the future that no allowances be made to the Jurys at Sessions or Court Leet or to the Constables or Tything-Men.

𝕺𝖗𝖉𝖊𝖗𝖊𝖉 that the Serjeants have Cloaks Once in four years, and Hats in two years, and the Bell-Man to be Cloathed as usuall Once in two years, And the Serjeants to have Gowns Once in every six years.

𝕺𝖗𝖉𝖊𝖗𝖊𝖉 that all the Present Members who have not Gowns already shall Provide themselves with a Gown on or before Christmas-Day, And that every Person who shall be Elected a Member of the Chamber for the future shall Provide himself with a Gown within One Month after his Election, on Pain of forfeiting the Sealing Fees of Each Person so Neglecting untill he shall comply with this Order.

24th August,
A.D. 1742.
16th George II.
John Spinage,
Mayor.

𝖂𝖍𝖊𝖗𝖊𝖆𝖘 on the second day of October, 1741, an order was made by the Mayor, Bayliffs and Burgesses of this Borough in Common-Council assembled, that no Publick Dinner (Except the Visitation Dinner) should be kept, And the Mayor, Bayliffs and Burgesses this day in Common Council assembled, do Order that the said Order be made Publick, or the Contents thereof, by the Bell-Man, in the most publick Places in this Borough, in the Words or to the Effect following: By Order of the Mayor, Bayliffs and Burgesses of this Borough in Common Council assembled on the twenty fourth day of August, 1742, This is to give Notice that by Order of Common-Council made on the second day of Oct'r last, it was Ordered that for the future no Publick Dinner (except the Visitation Dinner) should be kept, And that Pursuant to the said Order, No Publick Dinner either for the Corporation or Commoners will be provided at the Election of a Mayor for the year Ensuing, the said Order being made only to retrench the Expences of the Corporation, there being an absolute Necessity for so doing. And it is further Ordered that if any damage shall be done to Mr. Mayor or any Member or Members of the Corporation, in their or any of their Persons or Effects, upon Account of the said Orders or either of them, that such damages shall be repaired so farr as is possible at the Expence of . the Corporation, and that Mr. Mayor or any other Member of the Corporation may provide a Watch for the Security of their Persons and Effects against any Insults or Damage that may be suspected to be done by any Evil Minded Persons, upon the Account aforesaid, at the Expence of this Corporation.

𝕺𝖗𝖉𝖊𝖗𝖊𝖉 that Mr. Thomas Cullerne do provide three Dozen Buckets at five shillings Each Bucket, with the Corporation Arms thereon, at the Expence of the Corporation.

𝕿𝖍𝖊 Mayor, Capitall Burgesses and Bayliffs this Day being assembled together, Mr. Edward Saxton, Mayor Elect of this Borough for the year ensuing, refused to accept the said office and offered for Reasons that he being Engaged in a large Business in London, and being at a great distance from this Borough, he could not Execute the said Office in such manner as it ought to be Executed, And the said Mayor, Capitall Burgesses and Bayliffs did duly Consider the said Reasons so given, And did adjudge the same to be a reasonable Cause of Excuse, And did accordingly Excuse the said Edward Saxton from serving the said office of Mayor, Pursuant to the Power to them given by the Charter of the third and fourth of Philip and Mary.

29th September, A.D. 1742. 16th George II. John Spinage, Mayor.

Mr. John Knapp is elected Mayor of this Borough for the year Ensuing, and having Offered the same Reasons that he did the last year for not serving the said Office, the same have been now allowed to be a reasonable Cause, and he is excused from serving the said Office this Present Year.

30th September A.D. 1742. 16th George II. John Spinage, Mayor.

1st October,
A.D 1742.
16th George II.

This day William Dunn, Esqr., is Elected Mayor of this Borough for the year Ensuing.

2nd October,
A.D. 1742.
16th George II.
John Spinage,
Mayor.

This day the said William Dunn, Esqr., Mayor-Elect of this Borough for the year Ensuing, appeared before the Mayor, Principall Burgesses and Bayliffs of the said Borough, and refused to accept the said Office, and offered as a Reason for such Refusall that as he lived five miles distant from this Borough, he could not Execute the Business of his said Office in such manner as it ought to be Executed, And the said Mayor, Principall Burgesses and Bayliffs, having duly Weighed and Considered the said Reason so offered as aforesaid, are of Opinion that the same is not a reasonable Cause to Excuse him from serving the said Office, And do accordingly Adjudge the said Reason so given not to be a reasonable Cause to Excuse him from serving the said office, And he is therefore not Excused from serving the same.

6th October,
A.D. 1742.
16th George II.
John Spinage,
Mayor.

This day Mr. Edward Spinage is Elected Mayor of this Borough for the year Ensuing, and afterwards appeared before the Mayor, Principall Burgesses and Bayliffs of this Borough and refused to accept the said Office and offered for Reasons for such Refusall that he was Deaf and in an ill state of Health and Utterly unable to Execute the said Office in such manner as it ought to be Executed, And the said Mayor, Principall Burgesses and Bayliffs, having duly Weighed and Considered the said Reasons so offered, and being fully Convinced of the Truth of the same, do allow the said Reasons to be a Reasonable Cause to Excuse him from serving the said Office, And did accordingly Excuse him from serving the said Office for the year Ensuing.

8th October,
A.D. 1742.
16th George II.

Mr. Edward Saxton is Elected Mayor of this Borough for the year Ensuing.

11th October,
A.D. 1742.

This day Mr. Edward Saxton, Mayor-Elect, appeared before the Mayor, Principall Burgesses and Bayliffs, and desired a further Day to offer his Reasons for not accepting the said office.

13th October,
A.D. 1742.
16th George II.
John Spinage,
Mayor.

This day Mr. Edward Saxton, Mayor-Elect, Offered the Reasons which he before Offered on the twenty ninth day of September last, with other Reasons for not Accepting the said Office, Which were not allowed to be a Reasonable Cause of Excuse And he was this day by the Mayor, Bayliffs and Burgesses Fined the sume of five shillings and he was by the Mayor, Bayliffs and Principall Burgesses Committed unto the Common Prison in the said Borough, there to remain untill he shall take his Oath for the due Execution of his said Office, or pay the said Fine, or make his Composition for the same, according to the Charter for the said Borough of the third and fourth of Philip and Mary,. And the same Day the said Mr. Edward Saxton paid the said Fine accordingly.

𝕿𝖍𝖎𝖘 day Mr. Richard Rose is elected and sworn Mayor   * * *   15th October, A.D. 1742. 16th George II.

𝕿𝖍𝖎𝖘 Day the Right Honourable Willoughby Bertie, Earl of Abingdon, is Elected High-Steward of this Corporation   * * *   14th July, A.D. 1743. 17th George II. Richard Rose, *Mayor.*

𝕿𝖍𝖎𝖘 Day it was Ordered that an Address of the Mayor, Bayliffs and Burgesses be presented to his Majesty, of their abhorrence of a French Invasion, Popish Pretender, and so forth.   27th February, A.D. 1744. 17th George II. Charles Cox, *Mayor.*

𝕺𝖗𝖉𝖊𝖗𝖊𝖉 that the Chamberlain do forthwith take Care to Provide fit and able Workmen to repair the Damage lately done to the Goal by William Holmes and others, who broke the same and Escaped therefrom.   23rd April, A.D. 1744. 17th George II. Charles Cox, *Mayor.*

𝕴𝖙 is this day Ordered by the Members of this Corporation that for the future no Wine shall be sent for at any Meeting of the Members at the Expence of the Corporation, Unless at such time as there shall be Money paid by any New Tenant or Tenants at taking any Lease or Leases.   14th March, A.D. 1745. 18th George II. John Eldridge, *Mayor.*

[William Dunn, Mayor elect, fined £3 for refusing to accept office.]   29th September, A.D. 1745.

𝕺𝖗𝖉𝖊𝖗𝖊𝖉 that a Gate be made opposite to the Town Hall Door for the Conveniency of Drawing the Engine out of the Hall in Case of Necessity, And that three more Keys be made to the Lock on the Town Hall Door, and that One of them be delivered to Mr. Mayor for the time being, and One to each of the Town Serjeants.   7th April, A.D. 1748. 21st George II. John Eldridge, *Mayor.*

𝕺𝖗𝖉𝖊𝖗𝖊𝖉 that. Ropes be provided to hang the Buckets on in the Town-Hall that they may be let down together if wanted.

𝕺𝖗𝖉𝖊𝖗𝖊𝖉 that a New Post in little Bury Lane, to let up and down, be forthwith erected there in the Room of the old One.

𝕺𝖗𝖉𝖊𝖗𝖊𝖉 that the Bellman have thirty shillings yearly paid by the Chamberlain by Quarterly payments in Order to Clear the Streets   3rd November, A.D. 1748. 22nd George II. Dr. John Crossley, *Mayor.*

z

and places within this Borough of Beggars and other Vagrants, and to turn them out of Town.

2nd March, A.D. 1749. 23rd George II. Dr. John Crossley, Mayor.

Ordered that the Order so far as relates to the Members of this Corporation Wearing their Gowns the first Sunday in every Month be set aside.

6th July, A.D. 1750. 23rd George II. Richard Rose, Mayor.

Ordered that the Town-Clerk do wait on his Royal Highness the Prince of Wales at his Seat at Cliefden, And to give his Royal Highness an Invitation to this Borough to Breakfast on Monday Morning next in the name of this Corporation.

6th November, A.D. 1751. 25th George II. Richard Beasley, Mayor.

Ordered that for the future on all Ringing Days on which anything hath been usually given to the Ringers at Saint Nicholas Church by the Corporation, half a Crown be added and paid by the Chamberlain.

26th June, A.D. 1752. 26th George II. Richard Beasley, Mayor.

Ordered That the Chamberlain do provide at the Expence of the Corporation a sufficient Quantity of Table Linnen, to be used at the Mayor's Visitation and other Dinners.

27th July, A.D. 1752. 26th George II. Richard Beasley, Mayor.

It is Ordered that Notice be given in the London Evening Post, Gloucester Journal, and the Reading and Northampton Mercurys, three several times, that the Fair yearly held in this Borough on the eighth Day of September, will be holden on the nineteenth Day of September next, according to the New Style   *   *   *   *

9th January, A.D. 1753. 26th George II. Richard Rose, Mayor.

Ordered that all Fairs annually kept in this Borough (Except the Fair on the First Monday in Lent) be kept Eleven Days later than the New Style, And that the Days on which the said Fairs are intended to be held for the future as aforesaid, and the Commoditys sold at such Fairs be sent by the Town-Clerk to Mr. Owen, near Temple Barr, London, to be by him inserted in the account of Fairs intended to be soon printed and Published.

18th April, A.D. 1753. 26th George II. Richard Rose, Mayor.

Ordered that Thirty Pounds be paid to Mr. Mayor and Every Succeeding Mayor, over and above the present Salary, to provide a Dinner for the Corporation and Commoners before he goes out of his Office.

24th April, A.D. 1753.

[John Wright, Esq., is removed from his Office of Recorder, & John Morton, Esq., of Tackley, Oxon, is appointed Recorder in his place.

Whereas a Rate made for the Releif of the Poor by the Church-Wardens and Overseers of the Parish of Saint Hellen's within this Borough, was appealed against by three Persons only, at the last Quarter Sessions of the Peace for the County of Berks, on Pretence that several Persons were left off the said Rate who were properly rateable.   And Whereas the Notice of such appeal was given to the Officers but at Noon of the Day before the said Sessions, So that it was then Impossible for them to Appear or make any Defence to such Appeal.   And the said Justices not Consenting to respite Such appeal to the next Quarter Sessions, as in Cases where Notice is not reasonable is by Law directed, or to give the Officers the Indulgence of a Short Day to appear and Try the Merits thereof, but proceeding directly to Determine the same, have thought proper to add no less than Sixteen Persons to the said Rate, Some of which are not so much as Parishioners of the said Parish, and others are to Our own Knowledge in very Mean and Indigent Circumstances, and as Such, though long Parishioners and Inhabitants, were never Esteemed Either by former or the present Overseers of Sufficient ability to Contribute to the Charge of the Poor, **We**, the Mayor, Principall Burgesses and Bayliffs and the Secondary Burgesses now in Common Council assembled, apprehending the greatest Inconveniencys likely to attend this Parish from a Number of Persons being thus made Parishioners without the Consent and Even without the Knowledge of any Parish Officers, and being alarmed that the most Valueable Franchise of Electing a Member to serve in Parliament for this Borough may by these means be Intirely taken out of the Hands of those who have Legally and without any Party Motives Maintained the Poor, and Supported the other Charges of this Borough, Do hereby agree to Defray the Charges and Expences of Endeavouring by all Legal Means to set aside and Vacate the Several Orders made by the said Sessions on the said Officers, and We do hereby Desire them to take the most Expeditious and best advice of Counsel thereon, and to proceed as they shall be therein directed.   *   *

9th October, A.D. 1753. 27th George II. Thomas Justice, Mayor.

Ordered that for the future upon the Election of any Member into the Chamber or into the Office of a Principal Burgess, the Corporation shall not be at any Expence for any Part of the Entertainment then made, but that the same shall be at the Sole Expence of the Person or Persons who shall be then elected.

31st December, A.D 1754. 28th George II. Henry Harding, Mayor.

7th February,
A.D. 1758.
31st George II.
Thomas
Cullerne,
Mayor.

It is Ordered that in Case any Information or Informations shall be made before Mr. Mayor against any Baker or Bakers for any Offence or Offences by any of Them Committed in Respect to their Bread Wanting Weight, or otherwise howsoever, in Respect to their said Trades, and Mr. Mayor shall Issue any Warrant or Warrants against any of Them, or Convict them of any Offence or Offences as aforesaid, and any Suit or Suits, Prosecution or Prosecutions, shall be Commenced against Mr. Mayor for such actings or Doings. That such Suit or Suits, Prosecution or Prosecutions, shall be Defended at the Expence of this Corporation　　•　　•　　•

8th March,
A.D. 1758.
31st George II.
Thomas
Cullerne,
Mayor.

It is this Day Ordered That the Old-Council Chamber be pulled down and a New One built in the Room thereof.

5th April,
A D. 1759.
32nd George II.
Henry Harding,
Mayor.

Ordered and it is this day agreed with Henry Higgins, Carpenter, to Repair the Town pumps for the Sum of Three pounds and Ten Shillings a year, for the Term of Seven Years, to Com'ence this Day, being Old Lady Day, 1755, And that the said Henry Higgins do forthwith put in so many New pumps as Mr. Mayor shall think necessary, in the places of Old decayed pumps, So as the Same do not exceed three New pumps in Number, For which he is to be allowed One Guinea for every such new pump　　•　　•　　•　　•

11th July,
A.D. 1760.

[The Right Honourable Willoughby, Earl of Abingdon, is elected High Steward of the Borough in the place of his father then deceased.]

22nd November,
A.D. 1760.
1st George III.
Henry Harding,
Mayor.

Ordered that in Case any Information or Informations shall be made before Mr. Mayor against any Person or Persons who shall turn the Carswell Stream out of its Proper Channel; the Bellman do give Publick notice of One Guinea Reward upon Conviction to any Person or persons making such Discovery.

3rd February,
A.D. 1761.
1st George III.
Henry Harding,
Mayor.

Ordered that Mr. Henry Harding, the present Mayor, do make Two Silver punch Bowls for the Use of the Corporation.

27th August,
A.D. 1761.
1st George III.
Henry Harding,
Mayor.

Ordered That the Chamberlain do pay to the Reverend Mr. Portal Ten Shillings and Six pence for Preaching a Sermon Yearly on the first day of September, in the parish Church of Saint Helen's, in this Borough, being the Day of Election for Mayor of the said Borough.

𝕺𝖗𝖉𝖊𝖗𝖊𝖉 that a Bye-Law be made for preventing the Manufacturing or Working of Hemp or Flax in this Borough by Candlelight or Lamp Light for the future, And that the Town Clerk do forthwith Draw such Bye Law and lay it before Mr. Recorder to settle.

2nd December, A.D. 1761. 2nd George III. John Naish, Mayor.

𝕿𝖍𝖊 Mayor, Capital Burgesses and Bayliffs this Day being Assembled together, Mr. John Eldridge, Mayor Elect of this Borough for the Year Ensuing, refused to Accept the said Office and Offered for Reasons that Mrs. Eldridge, his Wife, at present is in a very bad State of Health and likely to Continue so, and that the Small Pox being now in or about this Borough and very likely to Spread all over the Same in a short time, which will Oblige the said John Eldridge and his Family to leave the Borough during the time of its Infection, so that he could not Execute the said Office in such Manner as it ought to be Executed. And the said Mayor, Capital Burgesses and Bayliffs did duly Consider the said Reasons so Given, And did Adjudge the same to be a Reasonable Cause of Excuse, And did Accordingly Excuse the said John Eldridge from Serving the said Office of Mayor, Pursuant to the Power to them given by the Charter of the Third and fourth of Philip and Mary.

29th September, A.D. 1762. 3rd George III. John Naish, Mayor.

𝕺𝖗𝖉𝖊𝖗𝖊𝖉 that Mr. Bedwell and Mr. Henry Harding and the Chamberlain do inspect in regard to the Market House Windows, Leads and Roof, the same being much out of Repair, and that they Report the same at a Common Council.

5th November, A.D. 1762. 3rd George III. Thomas Prince, Mayor.

𝕺𝖗𝖉𝖊𝖗𝖊𝖉 that the Lanthorn Door belonging to the Market House be kept Lockt up, the Chamberlain to keep the key.

𝕺𝖗𝖉𝖊𝖗𝖊𝖉 that the Chamberlain do pay Fifteen pounds to the several persons that Assisted at the late Fire in West Saint Helen's Street * * *

9th November, A.D. 1765. 6th George III. Joseph Penn, Mayor.

𝕺𝖗𝖉𝖊𝖗𝖊𝖉 that the Expences to be allowed by the Corporation at the Yearly Election of Mayor for this Borough For a Dinner and One Dozen of Wine for the Entertainment of the Corporation shall not exceed Four pounds, four shillings; And that none but the Body Corporate shall be invited to such Entertainment; And if the Expences of such Entertainment shall exceed that Sum, Then the Mayor Elect to pay the Overplus thereof.

24th July, A.D. 1766. 6th George III. Joseph Penn, Mayor.

27th January, A.D. 1767. 7th George III. William Hawkins, *Mayor.*

Ordered That a Sum of Thirty Pounds be disposed of amongst the Necessitous Poor of this Borough who are Parishioners of either of the Parishes of Saint Helen's and Saint Nicholas, Except to such Poor who have already received part of the Charities lately disposed of within the said Borough; Also That Notice be Cryed that all such Poor Persons apply to George Alder to have their Names set down and of the Number of Children under Ten Years of Age on or before Thursday next, And that the same be disposed of to such Objects of Charity as the Mayor and Burgesses who shall meet on Fryday next, at Four of the Clock in the Evening, or the Majority of them then Present shall think proper and direct.

29th January, A.D. 1767. 7th George III. William Hawkins, *Mayor.*

Ordered That the Following Things be provided as Convenient Furniture for the Town Clerk's Office, Vizt.: Six Chairs, A pair of Bellows, Two Candlesticks, A pair of Snuffers, an Extinguisher, a Tinder Box and Candle Box, A Square Table about Three Feet Seven or Eight Inches long, and some Cloak Pins, to remain there.

3rd March, A.D. 1767. 7th George III. William Hawkins, *Mayor.*

Ordered That the Chamberlain do forthwith get the Gate at the Free School Court repaired, and also the Tiling of the Fuel House and Penthouse in the Free School Court repaired.

4th June, A.D. 1767. 7th George III. William Hawkins, *Mayor.*

Ordered that the Corporation do subscribe Thirty Pounds towards a Purse or Plate of Fifty Pounds to be Run for by Race Horses at such place near Abingdon, as shall be appointed by the Majority of the Subscribers on or before Michaelmas Day next, and that the Chamberlain do pay the same.

10th November, A.D. 1767. 8th George III. George Knapp, *Mayor.*

It is this Day Ordered and Agreed That this Corporation do Subscribe Forty Pounds Towards raising and repairing the Turnpike Road between The Town of Buscot, in Berkshire, and the Town of Leachlade, in Gloucestershire, or such part thereof as the Corporation shall hereafter direct, in Case a sufficient Subscription can be raised for repairing the Road in such a Manner as not to be overflowed in the Floods which usually happen there.　*　*　*

21st December, A.D. 1767. 8th George III. George Knapp, *Mayor.*

Ordered That the Chamberlain erect a Post and Lamp in the Center of the Square of the Sheep Market, and to be suplied with Oyl and Lighted by the Corporation.

Ordered and Agreed That the Town-Clerk forthwith Prepare a Petition to Parliament for An Act to Repair, Amend and Widen the Road leading from the Mayor's Stone at the End of Boar Street, in Abingdon, to and through the Village of Cumner to the New Turnpike Road at Swinford, in the County of Berks, and that He attend the Mayor, Chamberlain and Bayliffs to put the Corporation Seal to it; who are authorised to make Use of the Seal for that purpose; And also to attend the Gentlemen and Inhabitants of this Borough and Neighbourhood to Sign the Petition and get the Bill passed through both Houses of Parliament.

Ordered That the Townclerk do forthwith get a Bye Law drawn and settled by Mr. Morton, the Recorder, or such other Person he shall think proper to advise with therein, to oblige all Persons keeping open Shop in the said Borough to take up their Freedoms; and to get the Judges of Assize to sign their Approbation thereof; And to advise with Mr. Recorder touching the Power of the Corporation to make such a Bye Law.

19th January, A.D. 1768. 8th George III. George Knapp, Mayor.

Ordered and agreed that the Corporation do Subscribe Thirty Pounds towards the Town purse of Fifty Pounds, to be run for on Culham Heath by Race Horses on the 29th day of September next   *   *   *

21st July, A.D. 1768. 8th George III. George Knapp, Mayor.

[Similar subscriptions were made in several subsequent years by the Corporation.]

Ordered That the Mayor do pay the Sum of Fifteen Pounds only in part of the Bill of Mr. James Powell for the last Visitation Feast, amounting to the Sum of Thirty Pounds, Four Shillings, and Ten pence, The Country Gentlemen being Invited thereto by the direction of the Principal and Secondary Burgesses; And that the Remainder thereof be paid by the Chamberlain.

8th September, A.D. 1768. 8th George III. George Knapp, Mayor.

Ordered That the Chamberlain have Mended and Painted the Iron Rails of the Belcony of the Guildhal of this Borough, and the Plaistering mended where necessary.

13th September, A.D. 1769. 9th George III. Richard Rose, Mayor.

Ordered that for the future No Mayor of this Corporation shall have the Visitation Feast at any other Place whatsoever but in the Council Chamber of this Borough, And that in Case any future Mayor shall so do, such Mayor shall have the Sum of Twenty Pounds deducted out of his Salary.

This Day agreed with John Blake to be Scavenger for Cleaning the Streets within this Borough for the Term of Three

9th November, A.D. 1769. 10th George III. Edward Badger, Mayor.

Years, to commence from Midsummer last past, for the Yearly Salary of Sixteen pounds   *   *   *

6th July,
A.D. 1770.
10th George III.
Edward Badger,
Mayor.

Ordered That the Chamberlain Give to John Barton One Guinea for his Extraordinary Trouble in looking after the Flood Gates upon the Stert at the End of the Broad Street; And that he is to understand that he is to expect Nothing for the future, as the Key of the said Flood Gates was only left at his House as being Convenient in Case any Accident by Fire should happen.

3rd September,
A.D. 1770.
10th George III.
Edward Badger,
Mayor.

This Day it is Ordered and agreed that, instead of the Salary the late Mayors of this Corporation have had and received of the Chamber, The next and every future Mayor of this Corporation shall be allowed Thirty Pounds for the Commoners' Feast, Fifteen Pounds for the Visitation Feast, which is to be had in the Council Chamber of the Borough, and all the principal and Secondary Burgesses invited thereto; Also Ten Shillings every Sunday the Mayor shall attend Divine Service on Sundays, both in the Morning and After-noon, at One of the parish Churches in this Borough, with the Mace and Serjeants or One of them; And also four Pounds for holding the Quarter Sessions in and for the Borough and all other Expences during the Year for and on Account of his Mayoralty.

Ordered and agreed that for the future the Serjeants and Bellman's Clothing and Hatts usually allowed them by the Corporation shall be purchased and provided by the Direction of a Common Council, and not at the sole Order and direction of the Mayor for the time being.

12th February,
A.D. 1771.
11th George III.
Richard
Beasley,
Mayor.

Ordered that the Sum of Fifty Pounds be disposed in Charity amongst the Poor Inhabitants of this Borough being Parishioners, and that the same be Publickly Cryed   *   *   *

3rd April,
A.D. 1772.
12th George III.
Richard
Saunders,
Mayor.

Ordered that the Guildhall be made fitting and convenient for a Court of Justice and for the Business of the Assizes for the Crown side.

Ordered that the Mace be repaired and New Gilt by Mr. Harding.

23rd September,
A.D. 1772.
12th George III.
Richard
Saunders,
Mayor.

Ordered that the Chamberlain do provide Two Great Coats, One for the Bellwoman or for the Use of such Person as she shall employ during the Winter Nights, and the other for Philip Couling, the able bodied Man, to be used only the Winter Nights when on the Watch.

Ordered that the Chamberlain do forthwith provide a New Lamp for the May Pole in the Market place.

Ordered that Sixty Boys of this Borough have a Coat apeice of Seven Shillings Price including making, which are mentioned in the List signed by the Mayor   * * *   and that the same be paid for out of Mr. Mayot's Charity.

14th April, A.D. 1773. 13th George III. Richard Rose, *Mayor.*

Ordered and agreed that this Corporation do advance and lend upon A Mortgage of the Tolls and Duties arising from the Turnpike and Turnpikes on the Road leading from the Mayor's Stone at the End of the Boar Street, in Abingdon, to Oxford Turnpike Road, near Ensham Bridge, in the County of Berks, the sum of Two hundred Pounds, if the further Sum of Eight Hundred Pounds besides can be procured to be lent on the Credit of the said Tolls, at such Interest as shall be given for the said Eight hundred Pounds so to be borrowed.

14th July, A.D. 1773. 13th George III. Richard Rose, *Mayor.*

Any Persons inclined to Erect a Weighing Engine upon the Square, in the Ock Street, may apply to the Corporation at the next Common Council, and treat with them for a Proper Space of Ground for that Purpose, for a Term not Exceeding Twenty One Years, Of which Publick Notice is to be given by the Bellman.

17th September, A.D. 1773. 13th George III. Richard Rose, *Mayor.*

Ordered that the Tables, Tressels, Forms, Linnen, Plates, Knives, Forks, Chairs, Spoons, or any other Goods or Effects whatsoever belonging to the Corporation, shall not be lent or made Use of by any Person or Persons whatsoever, but only for the Use of the Corporation, Except only on particular Applications and requests to be made to the Corporation in Common Council assembled, and by their Order and Consent.

23th September, A.D. 1773. 13th George III. Richard Rose, *Mayor.*

Ordered that the Town Clerk do draw up a Cry to Warn all Persons against encroaching upon the Ground in the Streets and Lanes within this Borough by extending the Foundation of their respective Houses, Malthouses, or other Buildings further out than the Old foundations were, or where the same before stood, or by Erecting Bow Windows or making any New Projections, without the Licence and Consent of the Mayor, Bailiffs and Burgesses.

16th October, A.D. 1773. 13th George III. William Stevens, *Mayor.*

AA

𝔒𝔯𝔡𝔢𝔯𝔢𝔡 that the Town Clerk do Search the Old   for Precedents of Expelling a Member for non Attendance, and take the Recorder's Opinion of the necessary Method of Proceeding for that purpose.

24th May,
A.D. 1774.
14th George III.
William
Stevens,
Mayor.

𝔒𝔯𝔡𝔢𝔯𝔢𝔡 and agreed that the Mayor, Bailiffs and Burgesses go the Bounds and Franchises of this Borough the last Thursday in June next, and for that Purpose they are to meet at the Council Chamber at Nine O'Clock in the Morning.

3rd June,
A.D. 1774.
14th George III.
William
Stevens,
Mayor.

𝔒𝔯𝔡𝔢𝔯𝔢𝔡 that the Charter of the Third of March, Seventh of James the first, be now delivered to the Townclerk, and that he send it by the Abingdon Machine to Morrow, to Mr. John Vernon, Attorney at Law, in Lincoln's Inn, London, for him to Produce the Same to Mr. Attorney and Sollicitor General for their Perusal.

1st September,
A.D. 1774.
14th George III.
William
Stevens,
Mayor.

𝔍𝔪𝔪𝔢𝔡𝔦𝔞𝔱𝔢𝔩𝔶 after the Election of Mayor for the Year ensuing was declared, 𝔥𝔦𝔰 𝔐𝔞𝔧𝔢𝔰𝔱𝔶'𝔰 most Gracious Charter, bearing date at Westminster, the Twenty Third day of August last past, was opened and read to the Mayor, Bayliffs and Burgesses of this Corporation, who unanimously accepted the Same, in Consequence whereof the Mayor, Bayliffs and Capital Burgesses, together with the Secondary or Assistant Burgesses retired into their Council Chamber and Proceeded to the Election of Mr. John Eldridge and William Hawkins, Esquire, (being Capital Burgesses) two Justices of the Peace for this Borough, for One whole Year from this day inclusive, according to the directions of the said Charter; And the said John Eldridge and William Hawkins immediately after Election took the Oath of Office, And the Oaths appointed to be taken instead of the former Oaths of Allegiance and Supremacy.

27th September,
A.D. 1774.
14th George III.
William
Stevens,
Mayor.

𝔒𝔯𝔡𝔢𝔯𝔢𝔡 that the Mayor, Bayliffs and Burgesses of the said Borough do Dine together at the Councel Chamber of the said Borough, on Thursday next, and that a Dinner be Provided by the Mayor at the Expence of the Corporation, being the Day Assigned for Roasting an 𝔒𝔵 in the said Borough, for the Benefit of the Populace, and to commemorate the renewing of the Charter to the Corporation through the application of the Hon'ble John Morton, Recorder of the said Borough; 𝔄𝔩𝔰𝔬 that Seven Barrels of Beer and Five pounds worth of Bread be given away to the Populace at the Expence of this Corporation on the same Occasion.

𝔄𝔱 a Meeting this Day held it is Ordered and Agreed that the Bayliffs of this Borough do advance and pay Fifty Pounds to be distributed amongst the necessitous Poor of the Town towards their Relief at this Distressing and rigorous Season   *   *   *

30th January, A.D. 1776. 16th George III. Richard Rose, *Mayor.*

𝔒𝔯𝔡𝔢𝔯𝔢𝔡 that the Door Way in the Corner of the School Yard, used by John Copeland, be forthwith stopped up by the Chamberlain.

20th February, A.D. 1776. 16th George III. Richard Rose, *Mayor.*

𝔒𝔯𝔡𝔢𝔯𝔢𝔡 That the Court Leet Jury be allowed for the future only Fifteen Shillings for a Dinner when they are Sworn in, and that Nothing more be allowed them to spend at the Charge of the Corporation.

19th May, A.D. 1777. 17th George III. Richard Saunders, *Mayor.*

𝔒𝔯𝔡𝔢𝔯𝔢𝔡 that the Grand Jury at the Quarter Sessions of the Peace to be held for this Borough, be allowed for a Dinner the sum of Fifteen Shillings in Case they are Sworn, but Nothing if not Sworn.

𝔒𝔯𝔡𝔢𝔯𝔢𝔡 that the Petty Jury at the General Quarter Sessions of the Peace to be held for this Borough be allowed for a Dinner the Sum of Fifteen Shillings for a Dinner in Case they are Sworn, but Nothing if not Sworn.

𝔒𝔯𝔡𝔢𝔯𝔢𝔡 that the Constables and Tythingmen at the Court Leet and Quarter Sessions to be held for this Borough be allowed for a Dinner the sum of Fifteen Shillings only on each Occasion, and that Nothing be allowed to them on Adjournments.

𝔒𝔯𝔡𝔢𝔯𝔢𝔡 that the Sergeants and Bellwoman be allowed nothing for Dinner at the Court Leets and General Quarter Sessions of the Peace to be held for this Borough.

𝔒𝔯𝔡𝔢𝔯𝔢𝔡 that the Corporation do subscribe and pay towards the Expences of the Petition to Parliament respecting the Turnpike Road leading from the Mayor's Stone, in Abingdon, in the County of Berks, through Cumner, to the Ancient Horse Road at Swinford, in the said County, to which the Corporation Seal hath been this Day in Common Council affixed, in Proportion with the other Petitioning Creditors, according to the Sum advanced by them on the Credit of the said Roads.

19th January, A.D. 1778. 18th George II. William Hawkins, *Mayor.*

𝔒𝔯𝔡𝔢𝔯𝔢𝔡 that the Townclerk do Provide a Book and enter an Inventory of all the Plate, Linen, Pewter, and other Goods belonging to this Corporation in the Possession of the Mayor for the time being.

30th October, A.D. 1778. 19th George III. William Eldridge, *Mayor.*

19th May, A.D. 1779. 19th George III. William Eldridge, Mayor.

Ordered that the Old Pewter now produced be changed away for Six Oval Dishes and Six Dishes for Garden Stuff, and the Difference be paid by the Chamberlain.

Ordered that the Chamberlain do purchase Thirty Eight Yards of Diaper at 20d. ℔ Yard, Seven Yards of Huccaback at 2/6 per Yard, and 13 Yards of Diaper at 1s. per Yard, for Table Cloths, for the Use of the Corporation.

Ordered that the Chamberlain do purchase Two Dozen of Knives and Forks for the Use of the Corporation.

Ordered that the little Tankard be repaired at the Expence of the Corporation.

15th July, A.D. 1779. 19th George III. William Eldridge, Mayor.

Ordered that the Chamberlain do give to John Ball, One of the Constables of this Borough, Ten Guineas for the Damage he has sustained by being wounded in his right Arm when he was in the Execution of his Office in apprehending William Kilby.

27th August, A.D. 1779. 19th George III. William Eldridge, Mayor.

Ordered and agreed that the Corporation do Subscribe £50 towards the Building a New Organ in St. Helen's Church, in the Room of the present, provided the Plan and Contract for building the same are approved of by the Corporation; And this Sum to be paid when the Organ is completed according to such Contract, and not before.

26th October, A.D. 1779. 20th George III. John Harding, Mayor.

This Day the Corporation approved of the Plan of Messrs. Byfield, England and Russell, for Building a New Organ in Saint Helen's Church, and of the Church Wardens' Contract with them for that purpose, which Contract was this Day read in Common Council.

21st June, A.D. 1780. 20th George III. John Harding, Mayor.

Roger Covington, of the said Borough, Taylor, is elected Bellman, and Sworn, in the room of the Bellwoman, Elizabeth Couling, Widow, who is removed, having been chosen into the Hospital; **To hold** the said Office during the Pleasure of the Corporation.

Whereas I have this day been elected Bellman of this Borough by the Mayor, Bayliffs and Burgesses in Common Council assembled; And they having injoined me not to keep a Common Alehouse, or sell Ale, Beer, or other Strong Liquors, at any time during my Continuance in the said Office, on Pain of forfeiting my said Office, I do hereby promise the said Mayor, Bayliffs and Burgesses Punctually

to observe their said Injunction at all Times during my Continuance
in the said Office, on pain of forfeiting the same as aforesaid.
As Witness my hand the 21st day of June, 1780.
                    (Signed) Roger Covington.

Ordered that the Bellman be forthwith Provided with a Coat,
Hatt and Badge, and other Things as usual, at the Expence of the
Corporation.

Ordered that the Chamberlain do pay to the Ringers of Saint
Helen's Church Ten Shillings and Six pence for Ringing the Bells
on the taking of Charlestown by the British Forces.

*13th January,
A.D. 1781.
21st George III.
James Powell,
Mayor.*

Ordered that whoever puts Stalls or Penns on the New Square,
without Licence, shall be prosecuted at the Expence of the Corporation, and that the Bellman do give Notice of this Resolution
Publickly.

*13th June,
A.D. 1781.
21st George III.
James Powell,
Mayor.*

Ordered that the Square at the Upper End of the Ock Street
be let to Farm at the next Common Counsel to the best bidder, on
Terms to be then and there produced, and that the same be cried
accordingly.

*12th December,
A.D. 1781.
22nd George III.
William Allder,
Mayor.*

Ordered and Agreed that the Square be let to Charles Archer
and Richard Edginton, from the first of this instant January, for
Three Years, at Two pounds and Two Shillings Per Annum, for the
Purpose of Penning Sheep thereon at Fairs and Monday Markets
throughout the Year. The said Tenants to keep the Square clean
and in good repair and Condition, to leave a Way Nine feet wide all
round from the Gutter towards the Centre for the free Passage of his
Majesty's Subjects. The Square to be left open and Public As it has
been of late at all other Times; No Stalls, Wagons, Carts, Fagots,
Dung or Rubish to be suffered to stand or lie thereon at any time
during the Term ; No Pens for Pigs to be put up there, and no Pigs
to be suffered to be killed or swelled thereon at any time. The
Tenants to enter into a Bond for the Performance of this Agreement.
The Tenants not to interrupt the Passage to the Weighing Engine,
nor to do any Injury to it.

*2nd January,
A.D. 1782.
22nd George III.
William Allder,
Mayor.*

Ordered that Notice be given by the Bellman by Cry, that all
Nusuances by the Wagons, Carts, and Carriages in the Streets of this
Town will be presented if not removed.

*23rd August,
A.D. 1782.
22nd George III.
William Allder,
Mayor.*

Ordered that the Sergeants do have provided for them New Laced Hatts and new Clokes as usual, And also that the Bellman do have provided for him a New Laced Hatt, a new Cloke and new Coat, Waistcoat, Breeches and Stockings, of a blue Colour, as formerly.

This Day the Reverend Mr. Matthew Armstrong is appointed Lecturer to preach on Sundays, in the Afternoon, in Saint Helen's Church, in this Borough, in the Room of the Reverend Mr. John Stevenson, deceased, at the usual Yearly Salary of Ten Pounds; to commence from Michaelmas last, Old Stile, and to continue payable during the Pleasure of the Corporation.

Ordered that the Town Clerk do attend on the Revd. Mr. Cleoburey, Vicar of the said Church, and request the Use of the Pulpit for the Revd. Mr. Armstrong to preach the Lecture Sermon. N.B.—It was granted. S. S.

Ordered that the Recorder's Donation of £25 to the Poor of this Borough (which has been lately transmitted to the Mayor) be paid to the Committee of the Town, who have lately made a Collection for the releif of the Poor: several of which Committee are Burgesses of this Corporation.

This Day all Orders made heretofore by the Corporation relative to the Donation of John Mayor, Esquire, of Four Shillings Weekly to two Poor People, to be disposed of as the Corporation should think fit, are rescinded and repealed; he having taken the Management of the same into his own hands ever since   last.

Ordered that the Salary of the Mayor for the time being, be augmented to One hundred pounds per Annum, to commence from Michaelmas next.

Ordered that for one year next ensuing, the Corporation be not allowed any other Liquor at their Common Councils besides Ale and Beer at the expense of the Corporation.

Whereas James Powell, Gentleman, one of the principal Burgesses of this Borough, hath been duly nominated, elected and chosen Mayor of this Borough, for the Year ensuing, and being duly warned and required to appear this Day before the Mayor, Bayliffs and principal Burgesses of the said Borough, to take his Corporal

Oath for the due Execution of his said Office of Mayor of the said Borough, according to the Charter of this Borough, the said James Powell appeared before them and refused and still doth refuse to take upon him the said Office of Mayor, and desires to be excused from serving the same, offering as his reasons of Excuse : first, his having within four Years last past served the Office of Mayor of the said Borough, and there now being six other principal Burgesses of the said Borough liable to serve the said Office, and who have never served the same ; And secondly, that he is Deputy Postmaster of the Town of Abingdon, and as such engaged in business which continually requires his personal attendance, and particularly on Sundays, so that he is not able to do and perform the duties of the said Office of Mayor properly and regularly as they ought to be done without a neglect of the Post Office under his care. Which Causes the said James Powell alledgeth and prayeth may be considered as reasonable Causes of Excuse for not serving the said Office of Mayor, for the Year ensuing ; Whereupon the said Mayor, Bayliffs and Principal Burgesses being now here assembled, and having heard the said Excuses, and duly and maturely considered the same, do adjudge the same to be reasonable Causes to excuse him the said James Powell from serving the said Office of Mayor, for the Year ensuing, and do allow of the same as reasonable Causes of Excuse, and he is excused from serving the said Office accordingly.

William Bowles, Gentleman, who on the thirtieth Day of September last past was duly elected and chosen Mayor of the Borough of Abingdon, in the County of Berks, for the Year ensuing, having had due Notice and warning of the said Election, and being summoned to be and appear before John Bedwell, Gentleman, the now Mayor of the said Borough, and the Bayliffs and Principal Burgesses of the said Borough, to take upon him the said Office of Mayor of the said Borough, and to be admitted thereto and to take the Oaths in that behalf required by the Statutes of this Realm and the Charters of this Corporation, this Day cometh here accordingly before the said John Bedwell, the now Mayor, and the Bayliffs and Principal Burgesses of the said Borough now here in their Council Chamber in the said Borough assembled, upon due Summons, and being required by them and every of them to take upon himself the said Office, and to be admitted thereto and to take the said Oaths ; He, the said William Bowles, now here peremptorily refuseth to

8th October, A.D. 1784. 24th George III. John Bedwell, Mayor.

accept or take upon him the said Office, or to be admitted thereto, or
to take the said Oaths or any of them, and he, the said William
Bowles, offereth to the said Mayor, Bayliffs and Burgesses as his
reason for his refusing the said Office that the Salary of Mayor of the
said Borough was lately advanced when it ought not in his Judgment
to be so advanced, and he also alledged that he had private reasons
for refusing the said Office, but the said reasons he refused to disclose.
Whereupon the said Mayor, Bayliffs and Principal Burgesses now
here assembled, having duly and maturely considered the Excuses
alledged by the said William Bowles, do adjudge and determine that
the said William Bowles hath shown no reasonable Cause to excuse
or prevent his serving the said Office of Mayor, And he therefore is
not excused from serving the same. Whereupon the said William
Bowles is now here fined for such his refusal and contempt as aforesaid the Sum of two Pounds, two Shillings, Which Sum the said
William Bowles hath paid to the Chamberlain of the said Corporation
for the Use of the said Corporation.

12th October,
A.D. 1784.

[On this day Mr. James Smallbone is elected Mayor, but refuses
to accept Office on the ground "that he is infirm, and in a bad state
of Health," but his excuse is not accepted, and he is fined £2 : 2 : 0,
which he paid to the Chamberlain.]

4th November,
A.D. 1784.
25th George III.
James Penn,
Mayor.

Ordered that the Chamberlain do pay the Bill of Law Charges,
amounting to £44 : 10 : 0, which Mr. James Penn, the present Mayor,
owes to Mr. Samuel Sellwood, his Attorney, for defending an Action
lately brought against him, the said James Penn, by John Smith, for
false Imprisonment, which Action was tried at Reading Assizes, 1783,
and a Verdict thereon was given in favour of the said James Penn,
he having acted in the Affair which was the subject of the said
Action in the Capacity of a Magistrate of this Borough, and having
been most unjustly attacked by the said John Smith; And in
consideration of the above indulgence the said James Penn hath
agreed to waive the twenty five Pounds addition lately made to the
Mayor's Salary, and to be content with the old allowance of seventy
five Pounds for the current Year.

1st March,
A.D. 1785.
25th George III.
James Penn,
Mayor.

This Corporation consent that the Canal proposed to be
made from Abingdon to some place near Leachlade, be cut through
Abingdon Common, in the Line marked out in the Plan now
produced.

Ordered that an Order made on the sixteenth day of September last, restraining the Allowance of other Liquor, besides Ale and Beer, at Common Councils for one year then next, at the Expense of the Corporation, be and the same is hereby rescinded.

Ordered that the Town Clerk do write to the Recorder, in the name of this Corporation, craving · his Assistance in Parliament towards carrying the intended Canal Bill through the House of Commons and House of Lords.

Ordered that leave be given to Mr. Joseph Tombs to set out a Bow Window to his House at the corner of the Butcherrow, on both sides of the doorway, so as he does not set the projection on the Ground.

10th June,
A.D. 1785.
25th George III.
James Penn,
Mayor.

Ordered that Notice be given by Mr. Mayor and Mr. Chamberlain for and in the name of this Corporation, to Thomas Gilkes, Thomas Couldrey, William Wiblin and John Summersby, not to place, set up or erect any Stall, Stall Goer or other thing in the Market Place, Market-house, Bury, High Street or any other Street or Streets in this Borough, on any Market Day hereafter; And if they or any of them do so that they be sued as Trespassors by this Corporation, And that the Town Clerk do proceed against them accordingly.

7th June,
A.D. 1786.
26th George III.
George
Hawkins,
Mayor.

At a Meeting of the Mayor and Principal Burgesses this Day, It is ordered that the Town Clerk do take the Opinion of Mr. Recorder, whether under the late Act relating to Charitable Donations, the Mayor and Principal Burgesses are obliged to make discovery of the several Charities under their Management pursuant to the said Act. The Charities under the management of the said Mayor and Principal Burgesses are Mayott's, Roysse's, Knapp's, Sir Thomas Smith's Ashwednesday Money and Roysse's Donation of Bread.

15th August,
A.D. 1786.
26th George III.
George
Hawkins,
Mayor.

Ordered that no Players be allowed the use of any of the Publick Buildings in this Borough belonging to the Corporation, to exhibit any performance in, without further order of this Corporation.

1st December,
A.D. 1786.
27th George III.
William Bowles,
Mayor.

Ordered that a Nine Gallon Bushel be provided at the expense of this Corporation for the use of the Public within this Borough, And that the same be put into the hands of and kept by the Bellman to be used by all Persons calling for the same, and that the Bellman be paid Fourpence for his trouble in taking out and

BB

bringing home the Bushel, by the Person who is in the wrong with respect to any difference about the measure of Grain.

15th March,
A.D. 1787.
27th George III.
William Bowles,
Mayor.

Ordered that the Order made the sixteenth day of September, 1784, for augmenting the Salary of the Mayor for the time being to £100 per Annum, to commence from Michaelmas then next, be and the same is absolutely rescinded and made void.

26th September,
A.D. 1787.
27th George III.
William Bowles,
Mayor.

Ordered that the cleaning of the Streets in this Town be let out to Farm for one Year, at the next Common Council, in the following Districts, vizt. :—

First District—Vineyard, Stert, Broad Street and Boar Street.

Second Do. —Ock Street up to the Red Lion, and West Saint Helen's.

Third   Do. —East Saint Helen's Street, High Street, Butcher-row, Bury and Lombard Street, otherwise Tops Lane.

And that publick Notice be given by the Bellman and by Bills posted up, to all Persons willing to treat for the same, to send in their Proposals.

Ordered that all the Common Pumps in Abingdon belonging to and usually repaired by this Corporation be taken down as an useless Charge and the Ground levelled.

11th October,
A.D. 1787.
27th George III.
Edward Yates,
Mayor.

Ordered that in future there be no Bonfires within this Borough on any Public Occasion at the expense of this Corporation.

5th February,
A.D. 1788.
28th George III.
Edward Yates,
Mayor.

Ordered that the Chamberlain do procure a Lamp Post, to be erected in the Market Place, at the expense of this Corporation.

30th April,
A.D. 1788.
28th George III.
Edward Yates,
Mayor.

Ordered that the Sum of Twenty six pounds, thirteen shillings and four pence, laid up in the Casket since the order of the seventh of April, 1780, for the use of the Right Honourable Willoughby, Earl of Abingdon, High Steward of this Corporation, be and the same is taken out of the Casket and delivered to Mr. John Bedwell, the Chamberlain.

Ordered that the Town Clerk do write to the Earl of Abingdon, High Steward of this Corporation, to inform his Lordship that this Corporation is ready to pay the Arrears of his Lordship's Stipend for twenty eight Years last past, amounting to £93 : 6 : 8, and to request his Lordship to appoint a mode of remitting the same.

Ordered that the Town Clerk do write to the Right Honourable the Earl of Abingdon, High Steward of this Corporation, to thank his Lordship for his liberal Donation of ninety three pounds, six shillings and eight pence, to be applied to such public use as shall be most for the Interest and to the satisfaction of this Corporation, and for the handsome manner in which his Lordship has been pleased to communicate his sentiments respecting the same; And also to assure his Lordship that this Corporation will take Care to dispose of the money in some useful public work agreeably to the public spirited Intentions of the Right Honourable Donor.

2nd July, A.D. 1788. 28th George III. Edward Yates, Mayor.

Ordered that the Town Clerk do also write to the High Steward, in the name of this Corporation, to request the honour of his Company at their annual Visitation Dinner, on Monday, the fourth day of August next.

This Day the Reverend Mr. Armstrong proposed to resign the preaching of the Afternoon's Lecture in Saint Helen's Church, in this Borough, and it is agreed by the Corporation to accept his resignation, and that the same shall take effect from old Michaelmas next.

4th September, A.D. 1788. 28th George III. Edward Yates, Mayor.

This Day the Reverend Mr. Samuel Nicholl, Vicar of Sutton Courtney, is appointed Lecturer to preach on Sundays, in the Afternoon, in Saint Helen's Church, in this Borough, in the room of the Reverend Mr. Matthew Armstrong (who hath resigned his Lectureship), at the usual yearly Salary of Ten Pounds, to commence from Michaelmas next, old stile, and to continue payable during the pleasure of the Corporation.

Ordered that the Town Clerk do attend on the Reverend Mr. Cleobury, Vicar of the said Church, and request the use of the Pulpit for the Reverend Mr. Nicholl to preach the Lecture Sermon.

Ordered that an addition of ten pounds be made to the late Mayor's Salary, in order to make good his extraordinary expenses of entertaining Lord Abingdon, at the last Visitation Dinner, pursuant to the Invitation of this Corporation.

28th November, A.D. 1788. 29th George III. Bartholomew Bradfield, Mayor.

Ordered that no Persons, members of the Corporation, be permitted to have their Leases of Tenements held of this Corporation renewed, unless they withdraw while their Fines are calculating and settling.

3rd March, A.D. 1791. 31st George III. John Bedwell, Mayor.

Liberty is given to Mr. William Bowles to take down the Chesnut Trees in the Paddock, at Fitzharris, and apply the same in the repairs of the Premisses.

18th March, A.D. 1791. 31st George III. John Bedwell, *Mayor.*

Ordered that six substantial Pumps be erected at the expense of the Corporation, on the old Wells, in such parts of the Town as shall be judged most convenient and useful to the Public in general.

24th March, A.D. 1791. 31st George III. John Bedwell, *Mayor.*

Ordered that the Chamberlain do put up posts and rails in the front of the Council Chamber, of the same Height and Dimensions as the posts and rails on the opposite side of the way next Saint Nicholas Church.

4th November, A.D. 1791. 32nd George III. Edward Child, *Mayor.*

Ordered that One hundred pounds, including therein ninety three pounds, six shillings and eight pence, the Donation of the Earl of Abingdon, mentioned in the order of 2nd July, 1788, be subscribed and paid by the Chamberlain of this Corporation towards the Charges of covering the Stert Water from the end of the Broad Street to the Vineyard, and of raising the Road and Paving the Foot Way there,   *   *   *   But this Subscription is to be considered as a free gift in aid of the Surveyor's rate, and shall not bind the Corporation in future to any repair of the road in question or to any contribution thereto.

13th March, A.D. 1792. 32nd George III. Edward Child, *Mayor.*

Ordered that sixteen Pounds be subscribed and paid by the Chamberlain of this Corporation towards the Charges of cleaning the Stert from the Little Church to the Mouth of the Stert Water at the Knowl. But this Subscription is to be considered as a free Gift, and shall not bind the Corporation in future to any repair of the same or to any Contribution thereto.

22nd March, A.D. 1792. 32nd George III. Edward Child, *Mayor.*

Leave is given to John Daniel to make a subterraneous communication between his House in the Butcherrow and the Stert under the School Yard, he doing as little damage as may be thereby, and closing in the Top effectually, and not raising the same above the present surface of the Yard, and at all times keeping such communication in good repair, and preventing any annoyance thereby to any other person.

19th July, A.D. 1792. 32nd George III. Edward Child, *Mayor.*

Ordered that Mr. Mayor and the Town Clerk do forthwith contract with Mr. Benjamin Tramplett for the purchase of part of the Thistle Garden, at the price of forty Pounds, according to the terms proposed by the said Benjamin Tramplett, that such purchase be completed as soon as may be, and the Purchase money for the same paid to the said Benjamin Tramplett by the Chamberlain of this Corporation.

𝔒𝔯𝔡𝔢𝔯𝔢𝔡 that the Mayor, Justices of the Peace, the two Bayliffs, and the Chamberlain for the time being, or the Major Part of them, be a Committee to inspect into and make a report to the Common Council concerning certain Incroachments alledged to have been made by Mr. Tombs, in the Butcherrow, and Mr. Graham, in the Abby; and that the same Officers be a standing Committee to inspect into and report concerning all future incroachments and nuisances in the Common Streets and Highways of this Borough, also to inspect into and report concerning the State of the Public Buildings and Reparations belonging to this Corporation.

𝔒𝔯𝔡𝔢𝔯𝔢𝔡 and agreed that Mr. Joseph Tombs be not permitted to set out any Bow Window beyond the Line of his present new Building in the Butcherrow. 6th September, A.D. 1792. 32nd George III. Edward Child, *Mayor.*

𝔒𝔯𝔡𝔢𝔯𝔢𝔡 that it be left to the Committee of Inspection to settle with Mr. Joseph Tombs about the mode of placing his Steps and the height of the same for the purpose of getting into the Ground-floor of his new building in the Butcherrow.

𝔒𝔯𝔡𝔢𝔯𝔢𝔡 that the Carriage way in the Butcherrow be new paved with Marcham Blue Stone at the time that the Footways are done, and that the Chamberlain do pay the Expenses of such new paving. 9th July, A.D. 1794. 34th George III. William Allder, *Mayor.*

𝔒𝔯𝔡𝔢𝔯𝔢𝔡 that the Chamberlain do agree with Mr. Lempriere, if he can, for the use of a part of his Yard in the Abby, late Smallbone's, to secure the Pebbles therein that will be taken up in the Butcherrow and other Streets in Consequence of the paving.

𝔍𝔱 being represented that there is a considerable quantity of large Pebbles which may be usefully employed in paving the Butcherrow; 𝔒𝔯𝔡𝔢𝔯𝔢𝔡 that the same be so applied instead of Marcham Stone as far as the same will extend, in such places in the Butcherrow as the Surveyor to the Commissioners shall appoint. 20th August, A.D. 1794. 34th George III. William Allder, *Mayor.*

𝔄𝔭𝔭𝔩𝔦𝔠𝔞𝔱𝔦𝔬𝔫 being made on behalf of the persons promoting the intended Wilts and Berks Canal by Mr. Benjamin Morland, their Agent, for the Consent of this Corporation to the making of such 11th December, A.D. 1794. 35th George III. Henry Knapp, *Mayor.*

Canal over the Lands belonging to this Corporation in Sutton Wick Field; **Ordered** and agreed that the Common Seal of this Corporation be put to an Instrument expressing the Consent of the said Corporation to the making of the said Canal over the s'd Lands in the Line laid down in the plan of the said Canal now produced by the said Benjamin Morland.

This Day the following order made by the Commissioners of Paving on the fourteenth Day of November, 1794, was communicated to this Corporation by the Clerks to the said Commissioners, vizt. :—

"Ordered that the Clerks do make application to the Cor-"poration at their next meeting to know what part of the "expense attending the taking up and relaying that part of the "Carriage ways next the pavement throughout the Town (where "the same shall be done) will be defrayed by them, and report "the determination of the Corporation to the Commissioners."

And the same being taken into Consideration by this Corporation, and it also being considered that there will be some difficulty in ascertaining what ought in reason and Justice to be done by this Corporation or by the said Commissioners to the Carriage ways which have been or may be deranged or altered by the said Commissioners in the prosecution of their work with respect to the foot ways (except only in the Butcherrow where the Terms are already settled by this Corporation and the Commissioners.) **It is agreed** that this Corporation shall advance to the said Commissioners in aid of their fund, the sum of one hundred Guineas, in Case they will take upon themselves to repair and make good the Carriage ways in all such parts and places as have been or may be deranged or altered by them or their Surveyor, Paviour or Agents, in the prosecution of their work (except only as to the Butcherrow, which this Corporation will defray the Charge of agreeably to their undertaking), provided that in repairing and making good such Carriage ways the said Commissioners do take Care to do the same so as effectually to convey the water from the Centres and sides of such ways respectively into the proper Channels and Gutters adjoining or near thereto.

13th February, A.D. 1795. 35th George III. Henry Knapp, *Mayor.*

A Resolution of the Commissioners of paving was read, dated the twelfth Day of December last, "whereby the said "Commissioners refuse to accept the offer of the Corporation of one "hundred Guineas contained in their Resolution of the eleventh of

" December last, and Resolved that their Clerks did make application
" to the Corporation at their next meeting to know whether they
" would go hand in hand with the Commissioners in repairing and
" making good such parts of the Carriage ways (including therein
" one half of the Gutters) as had been or should be deranged or
" altered by the Commissioners, their Paviour or Agents, in the
" prosecution of their work with respect to the Improvement of the
" Footways of this Town, and would thereupon agree to pay one
" Moiety of the Expense attending the same to be ascertained by
" admeasurement when the work was compleated, And in Case the
" Corporation would agree to the above proposition, It was resolved
" that the Commissioners would defray the other Moiety of the said
" Expense; And the Clerks were Directed to apply to the Mayor to
" request him to call a Meeting of the Corporation to take into
" Consideration the above proposition, and report the result thereof
" to the Commissioners." Ordered and agreed that this Corporation will not go hand in hand with the Commissioners in the
manner mentioned in their resolution above stated, But this
Corporation do adhere to the offer contained in their Resolution of
the said eleventh Day of December last.

Ordered that the Chamberlain do pay to the Treasurers of
the Commissioners of paving the sum of One hundred Guineas,
agreeably to the order of the Corporation of the 11th of December
last, the offer contained in that order having been accepted by the
said Commissioners.

*5th June,
A.D. 1795.
35th George III.
Henry Knapp,
Mayor.*

Ordered that the Chamberlain do provide sufficient Materials
for paving the Butcherrow, and forward the execution of that work
as much as may be.

Ordered and agreed that fifty Guineas be subscribed by this
Corporation towards the Relief of the necessitous Poor of this Town,
and to enable them to purchase Bread at a reduced Price, and that
it be referred to a general Committee of Subscribers to select the
objects of this Bounty, and apply the money for their Relief.

*24th July,
A.D. 1795.
35th George III.
Henry Knapp,
Mayor.*

Ordered and agreed that Mr. Mayor, the Justices, Bayliffs and
Chamberlain, be a Committee to solicit the Subscriptions of the
Inhabitants of this Town for the Relief of the Poor thereof, in
manner above mentioned.

12th September, A.D. 1795. 35th George III. Henry Knapp, Mayor.

Ordered that the Chamberlain do defray one third part of the Expense of making a Gun Drain to convey the water from the Street, by the side of the Great Church, down to the River, so as to make a commodious Passage into the Great Church from East Saint Helen's Street and other parts of the Town.

5th November, A.D. 1795. 36th George III. Henry Knapp, Mayor.

Ordered that Notice be given by the Town Clerk to Mr. Simon Peck, immediately to repair the Bridge over Swift Ditch belonging to his premises, called Rye Farm. And if the same be not done, that an Indictment will be preferred against him.

14th January, A.D. 1796. 36th George III. William Eldridge, Mayor.

Ordered that Mr. Richard Edgington be reimbursed any extra Expenses he may have been at in improving the Square by removing the Bulk and pitching the Footway since the last Common Council.

17th March, A.D. 1796. 36th George III. William Eldridge, Mayor.

Ordered that a Pipe of Wine be purchased by the Chamberlain for the use of the Corporation, to be stored and kept in the Market House Cellar now in hand; that proper Bins be provided therein for the purpose, and that the Cellar be locked up with three Locks and Keys, to be kept by the persons who keep the Keys of the Strong Chest, And that this wine be only used at Common Councils of the Corporation.

(This is the earliest Order for the purchase of Wine to be found in the Corporation Minutes, but several similar Orders appear at later Dates.)

23rd March, A.D. 1797. 37th George III. Edward Child, Mayor.

Ordered that the Committee do consider whether it would be proper to retain a Man by the year to repair the Streets of the Town; how many days in a week he may be so profitably employed, and on what Terms he could be procured, and who is likely to undertake this Service; and that they do report their opinion thereon to the next Common Council.

13th April, A.D. 1797. 37th George III. Edward Child, Mayor.

Ordered that the ten Boys on Mr. Mayott's Charity, at Almond's School, be clothed with Grey Coats, turned up with Green Cuffs, and also Green Caps, at the expense of Mr. Mayott's Charity; provided the same do not exceed one Guinea each boy.

26th September, A.D. 1797. 37th George III. Edward Child, Mayor.

Ordered and agreed that proper means be taken by the Town Clerk, with the assistance of the standing Committee, to enforce by Indictment or otherwise the Repairs of Swift Ditch Bridge, in Sir Cecil Bishop's Estate, at Culham, in the occupation of Simon Peck, And that they do inform the Steward of that Estate of this Resolution as soon as may be, and in case of any delay in repairing the said Bridge, that then this order shall be a sufficient authority for their proceeding as aforesaid, without any further meeting of the Corporation; And that the Expenses thereof be defrayed by this Corporation.

Ordered that the standing Committee do take a view of the Encroachments on the waste at the end of the Ock Street and at the end of the Boar Street, made by the Gatekeepers there, and do report their Opinion thereon at the next Common Council, and do also give notice to the Gatekeepers to attend then and answer for such Encroachments.

Ordered and agreed unanimously that Thomas Giles, Senior Sergeant at Mace and Keeper of the Common Gaol of this Borough, be and he is hereby discharged and dismissed from his Offices of Sergeant at Mace to this Corporation and Keeper of the said Common Gaol, and that the Mace and Keys of the said Common Gaol be delivered up forthwith to Mr. Mayor, and that Possession of the Gaol and the House, Garden and Appurtenances thereto belonging, be given up immediately to the standing Committee of this Corporation, or such of them as shall choose to take an active part in demanding the same; and they are charged with the care of the said Gaol and the Prisoners therein being, and are to employ sufficient persons to asssist them in the safe keeping thereof until a proper Gaoler shall be appointed by this Corporation.

Ordered and agreed that a Beadle be appointed at the next Common Council at the salary of fifty two shillings per annum, whose office shall be to turn out Vagrants from this Town, as the Bellman heretofore used.

It is proposed and agreed to allow the Gaoler five pounds per annum additional Salary out of the Corporation Funds, provided he be not allowed to sell Ale, Spirits, or other Liquors in the House and premises belonging to the Gaol, nor be licensed so to do, And it is recommended to the Magistrates to make a further Provision for the Gaoler out of the Constables Rate or any Sums to be collected and paid to a Treasurer for the Borough in lieu thereof.

3rd October, A.D. 1797. 37th George III. George Knapp, *Mayor.*

The standing Committee reported the Gaol to be very insecure, particularly in the Windows, which they think may be secured by contracting the same and putting some new Bars thereto, and

CC

that a Solitary cell may be made by raising the Ceiling, and they recommended a new stout Floor to be put to the upper Story as a farther security.   Ordered that the standing Committee do get the Gaol repaired and improved in the manner suggested by the above report, and that they add such further security to the Gaol as they shall see expedient.

14th November, A.D.,1797. 38th George III. George Knapp, *Mayor.*

Ordered and agreed that James Goldby be paid a Salary of five Guineas for one year, from Michaelmas last to Michaelmas next, for the trouble of collecting the prices of Grain in Abingdon Market for the purpose of setting the Assize of Bread in this Borough.

Ordered that printed papers for collecting the respective prices of Loads of Wheat sold in Abingdon Market be provided for the said James Goldby at the expense of this Corporation.

20th February, A.D. 1798. 38th George III. George Knapp, *Mayor.*

Ordered that the Chamberlain do pay **Three hundred pounds** into the **Bank of England** as the voluntary Contribution of this Corporation towards the Expenses of prosecuting the present War against France; And that One hundred pounds four per Cent. Stock, part of the Funds of this Corporation, be sold out and applied towards making good the above payment.

Ordered that the standing Committee do enquire what will be the Expense of providing six Shambles, to be set up on Mondays, Fridays and Saturdays, in the Market-place, and let to persons willing to take the same; what recompence can be obtained for the same of Butchers, and what will be the properest situation for them to stand in; and do report their Sentiments thereon to the next Common Council.

12th March, A.D. 1798. 38th George III. George Knapp, *Mayor.*

The Common Gaol of this Borough having been repaired by the Chamberlain and rendered more secure, Ordered that he do get two medical Men to take a view of the same, and the Cells therein, and do obtain their opinion as to the wholsomeness of the same, and fitness of such Gaol and Cells for the reception and confinement of prisoners therein; And in Case the said medical Men shall be of opinion that the said Gaol and Cells require any alteration to make the same fit and wholsome as places of Confinement, then the Chamberlain is ordered to cause the same to be altered accordingly, and he is to report the opinions of such medical Men to the next Common Council.

𝖔𝖗𝖉𝖊𝖗𝖊𝖉 that the Chamberlain do provide an Engine, like that of the Hospital, for sealing the Corporation Leases.

𝖔𝖗𝖉𝖊𝖗𝖊𝖉 that two Shambles according to the Plan and Elivation of Benjamin Glanvill, Carpenter, now produced, be erected and completed by the Chamberlain at the Expense of this Corporation against the Market-House, opposite to Thomas Coldrey's dwelling, and on the East side of the Stair-case belonging to the Market-house.

22nd March, A.D. 1798. 38th George III. George Knapp, Mayor.

𝕴𝖋 𝖆𝖕𝖕𝖊𝖆𝖗𝖎𝖓𝖌 that the Stipend of eight Pounds Per Annum paid to the Reverend Mr. Lempriere was intended by this Corporation as an Augmentation of his Salary for reading Prayers Morning and Evening every Day in Saint Nicholas Church, and complaint being made that such Duty hath been omitted to be done by him for some time past, 𝖔𝖗𝖉𝖊𝖗𝖊𝖉 and agreed that he be paid one quarter of the Stipend to Lady Day next, and that the said Stipend be wholly discontinued from that Day.

𝖔𝖗𝖉𝖊𝖗𝖊𝖉 and agreed that the new Shamble next the Market-house be let to Joseph Fisher, of Marcham, Butcher, for one year, from Midsummer next, at three pounds Rent, he entering into a Bond to keep the same in repair and to keep Market therein for three Days every week during five hours of each day in the day time, and to expose and offer to sale therein each day good and wholesome meat, and not to assign over or underlet the said Shamble to any person whomsoever.

6th June, A.D. 1798. 38th George III. George Knapp, Mayor.

N.B.—The other Shamble is let to Thomas Keen, of Hendred, Butcher, at the yearly rent of 50s. on the above Terms.

𝖔𝖗𝖉𝖊𝖗𝖊𝖉 that the Mayor, Justices of the Peace, and such of the Principal Burgesses as have been educated at Abingdon School, be a Committee to confer with Mr. Lempriere touching the observance of the Ordinances of the School and certain complaints of breaches thereof by the Master, and that the Mayor do settle with Mr. Lempriere the time and place of such Conference, and acquaint the rest of the Committee therewith.

20th July, A.D. 1798. 38th George III. George Knapp, Mayor.

𝕿𝖍𝖎𝖘 𝕯𝖆𝖞 John Price is discharged from the Office of Beadle of this Borough, it being the intent of this Corporation to unite the offices of Bellman and Beadle, as they were held by Roger Covington, but the said John Price is to be paid his year's Salary, and to retain the Hat and Coat given him by the Corporation.

21st September, A.D. 1798. 38th George III. George Knapp, Mayor.

Ordered that the Bellman shall not in future have the benefit of the Tolls of Corn in this Borough, but the same shall be collected or let for the use of the Corporation.

Ordered that the last Corporation Seat in Saint Helen's Church be appropriated to the use of the Corporation Servants during Divine Service, and that the Chamberlain do see that the same are cleared of persons commonly using the same.

6th December, A.D. 1798. 39th George III. William Allder, Mayor.

The following Statement of the Bellman's Duty and certain advantages annexed to his Office is ordered to be inserted in the Ledger for Observance in future.

Bellman's Duty & Advantages.

1.—To attend the Mayor to Church on Sundays and on all public Days, and to fetch and carry the Gowns of the Members of the Corporation.

2.—To attend at the Borough Court.

3.—To attend at the Quarter Sessions; and to act when required as a peace officer.

4.—To attend at all Common Councils and to assist at all Entertainments of the Corporation.

5.—To Cry to the utmost limits all matters relating to the Corporation or police, gratis, and to disperse gratis all proclamations and Handbills relating to the Corporation or police.

6.—To attend at Cumner Court with a Man to assist.

7.—To Cry all other Crys for the Towns People as far as the pitching in each Street, for 6d. each, but if he goes farther, to receive 1s. each.

8.—All other Crys for the Country People to be 1s. each.

9.—To turn all Vagrants out of Town, and see that they do not return.

10.—To clean and light the Corporation Lamps, and to inform against persons breaking the same or injuring the public Buildings.

11.—To go a nightly Watch with an able bodied Man from All Saints' Day to Candlemas Day yearly.

12.—To clean Knives and Forks for the Mayor and Corporation.

13.—To clean and oil the Corporation Engine, and take care that the same with pipes and Buckets are kept in good Condition.

14.—To deliver and stick up Assizes of Bread and Continuances of Do. to each Baker in Abingdon (allowed 1s. each).

15.—To take care of the Market-House and keep it clean within, and to have the Fees thereto annexed with the Salary from the County.

16.—Certain Fees at Borough Court and County Court.

17.—To sweep the Bury every Tuesday Morning round the Market house and Cage, and to see that the Scavenger do take the filth away; and to clear away the Snow when it lodges on ye Market-house Leads to prevent any damage to the Building.

Ordered that the Allowance to the Bellman for cleaning Knives and Forks as in No. 12 in the foregoing Statement be augmented to 20s. per Annum from the Commencement of his Office, and that he be allowed 20s. per Annum additional for the services in No. 17 of the foregoing Statement.

Ordered that the Bellman and his Assistant who keeps the nightly watch be allowed a Great Coat each at the expense of the Corporation.

Ordered and agreed that the Tolls of Corn brought to Abingdon on all days of the Week (except Mondays and Fridays) be let to Richard Gilkes, the Bellman, for one Year from Michaelmas last, at three Guineas Rent.

Ordered that the Toll to be taken for Potatoes shall be one penny for one Sack, and a half-penny per Sack for all above belonging to the same person, and so in proportion for larger quantities of Potatoes exposed to sale in this Market.

14th October,
A.D. 1799.
39th George III.
George Knapp,
Mayor.

[The Right Honorable Montagu, Earl of Abingdon, is elected High Steward of the Borough, in the place of his late father deceased.]

14th October,
A.D. 1799.

Ordered that the Chamberlain do purchase of Mr. George Knapp the Chandelier lately purchased by him, and do have the same fixed up in the Little Council Chamber, at the Expense of the Corporation.

25th February,
A.D. 1900.
40th George III.
George Knapp,
Mayor.

Ordered that the Chamberlain do sell the old Silver Salver, and in the Room thereof purchase a pair of Silver Gravy Spoons, one

Dozen of Silver Table Spoons, and one Dozen of Silver Tea Spoons, at the Expense of this Corporation.

23rd September, A.D. 1800. 40th George III. George Knapp, Mayor.

Ordered that ten Guineas be paid by the Chamberlain to the Clerk of Abingdon Races towards the last Town Purse.

Ordered and agreed that no further Subscription be given by this Corporation towards the support of Abingdon Races.

Mr. Benjamin Glanvill, Carpenter, having stated that Mr. Bernard Bedwell would be inclined to Subscribe two hundred and fifty Guineas towards rebuilding Saint John's Hospital, if the Corporation would defray the residue of the Expense of that work; and it appearing by the Estimate of Mr. Glanvill that the said work might be done for four hundred Guineas; **Ordered** that the Town Clerk do inform Mr. Bernard Bedwell, by Letter, that the Corporation feel highly gratified by his liberal proposition, and are willing to pay the deficiency of the Expense of the s'd work over and above the said two hundred and fifty Guineas.

16th September, A.D. 1801. 41st George III. Thomas Knight, Mayor.

Ordered that the order of twenty third of September, 1800, for no further subscription to be given towards the support of Abingdon Races, be rescinded.

Ordered that ten Guineas be paid by the Chamberlain to the Clerk of Abingdon Races towards the last Town purse.

23rd October, A.D. 1801. 41st George III. Edward Child, Mayor.

Ordered that the thanks of this Corporation be given to the Reverend Mr. Lempriere, Vicar of Abingdon, for his excellent and appropriate Sermon on the late peace.

5th December, A.D. 1801. 42nd George III. Edward Child, Mayor.

Ordered that the standing Committee do take an early opportunity of consulting Mr. John Davis, of Bloxham, upon the expediency of the proposed allotment and division of Abingdon Field, and whether the Terms offered on the part of His Royal Highness the Prince of Wales for exonerating the Tithes belonging to this Corporation be adequate and proper for this Corporation to accept, and that the standing Committee do make their report to the next Common Council.

3rd April, A.D. 1802. 42nd George III. Edward Child, Mayor.

This Day the Corporation took into Consideration a Bill depending in Parliament for renewing the Act relating to the Turnpike Road from Henley Bridge to Culham Bridge; which Bill contains a Clause for repealing a Clause in the former Act of 28th

George the second relating to such Road, prohibiting the erection of a Turnpike Gate within a Mile and an half of Abingdon Market-house. Resolved that such Clause of repeal would be injurious to this Borough and the Neighbourhood thereof, and that a petition should be presented to Parliament against the same; and the Town Clerk having prepared such petition, the Common Seal is ordered to be affixed thereto, and Mr. Metcalfe, the Member for the Borough, is requested to present the same, and to oppose such repealing Clause, and that Counsel be employed on the occasion if necessary.

𝕽esolved and agreed, in Consideration of the Emergency of the present times, that this Corporation will subscribe 𝕺ne hundred 𝕲uineas towards the fund for a Corps of Volunteers in Abingdon, if an effective Corps be raised and accepted by his Majesty, And this Corporation will also subscribe annually ten Guineas towards the contingent Expenses of such Corps, And the above sums shall be at the Disposal of the Committee appointed yesterday at a meeting of the Inhabitants of the Town in the Market house.

6th August, A.D. 1803. 43rd George III. William Allder, Mayor.

𝕿his 𝕯ay the Corporation met to take into consideration the proposition made to them to sell their Reversion in the White Hart Inn, to the Magistrates of the County, for the purpose of converting the same into a County House of Correction. * * * Resolved and agreed to accept the net Sum of Five hundred Pounds for such Reversion in case the House of Correction be agreed to be erected by the County * * * Provided that this Corporation be put to no Expense whatever, and the County Magistrates agree out of the Ground to be given up to them to widen the Street from the end of the White Hart Bridge to the end of the White Hart Inn, looking up the Butcherrow, so as to make the Street thirty six feet wide from the Kirb Stone of the Footway on the East side of the Street to the outside Limits of the Ground of the intended House of Correction, and do well pave all the new Ground to be laid into the Street and make a Footway with Flag paving under the Wall or other Boundary of the House of Correction the whole length corresponding to the Footway on the East side of the Street, and provided the County Magistrates do enter into proper Stipulations with the Corporation to allow the Borough Magistrates and Police the use of such new House of Correction in the same manner as they

3rd October, A.D. 1803. 43rd George III. Thomas Knight. Junr., Mayor.

have the use of the old one; and in Consideration thereof the Corporation agree to give up their Interest in the old House of Correction to the County.

𝕺𝖗𝖉𝖊𝖗𝖊𝖉 that a copy of this Minute be given to Mr. Morland • • • and that care be taken to remove any Angles or round off the Line so as to make as handsome an Entrance into the Town as may be.

5th October,
A.D. 1803.
43rd George III.
Thomas Knight,
Junr.,
   Mayor.

𝕿𝖍𝖎𝖘 𝕯𝖆𝖞 the Earl of Radnor, Lord Lieutenant of the County, and divers Magistrates of the same, after the General business of the Quarter Sessions was ended, held a Meeting at the New Inn, in Abingdon, and came to an Agreement for the purchase of the White Hart Inn and premises, upon the Terms proposed by the Corporation in the foregoing Resolution of the 3rd day of October, 1803, and there in conference between His Lordship and the County Magistrates and Mr. Samuel Sellwood, the Town Clerk, it was explained and understood that the right claimed in the Resolution for the Borough Magistrates and Police to have the use of the new County House of Correction should not extend to authorise the Borough Magistrates to claim any right or share in the nomination of the Governor or Keeper of such House of Correction, and on the other hand they were not to contribute any thing towards the Salary of such Governor or Keeper.

22nd March,
A.D. 1804.
44th George III.
Thomas Knight,
Junr.,
   Mayor.

𝕺𝖗𝖉𝖊𝖗𝖊𝖉 that William Staniland, one of the Town Sergeants, be sconced five shillings, to be deducted out of his Salary, for not wearing his Gown provided for him by this Corporation at the time of the Summons of Members of the Corporation to attend this Common Council.

18th April,
A.D. 1804.
44th George III.
Thomas Knight,
Junr.,
   Mayor.

𝕿𝖍𝖊 Common Council having been informed that it is in contemplation to repair the road between the end of the Ock Street and the Ock Mill, and that it is deemed advisable to carry the Road over the Lands ends near the Old track, It is ordered and agreed that it be referred to the standing Committee to mark out so much of the Land belonging to this Corporation as shall be wanted for the above purpose, and to adjust the Consideration for the same as far as this Corporation is interested with the Surveyors of the Highways, and on payment to the Chamberlain of the stipulated Sum and satisfaction made to the Lessees, the Surveyors, or others concerned, shall have liberty to take and apply to the public use for a Highway between the end of the Ock Street and Ock Mills so much of the Land in question as the Magistrates of this Borough shall deem to be proper for the purpose.

At this meeting a Letter from Stroud in Gloucestershire, was read, soliciting the concurrence of this Corporation and the Town of Abingdon with them in a memorial and application to the Postmaster General for a Mail Coach to pass directly through this Town to and from Stroud aforesaid, and this Corporation being of opinion that such Coach will be beneficial to this Town and Neighbourhood, do consent and agree that Mr. Mayor shall sign such Memorial, and also affix the Common Seal thereto on behalf of this Corporation.

16th August, A.D. 1804. 44th George III. Thomas Knigh Junr., Mayor.

Ordered that the standing Committee do settle with Mr. Thomas King, as to giving and taking Ground for improving the Star public house, in the Market place, and making the Footway more commodious at the South end of the said Public house.

Ordered that the Chamberlain do provide a set of Oak Tables for the Public Dinners of this Corporation under the inspection of the standing Committee.

Ordered that James Goldby and William Staniland be sconced three shillings and four pence each, out of their next Quarter's Salary, for not attending the Bellman when proclaiming the Micha's Session for this Borough, And they are ordered to proclaim the same Session again.

17th September, A.D. 1804. 44th George III. Thomas Knight, Junr., Mayor.

Ordered that this Corporation do pay to the Mayor, for the time being, the sum of six Guineas to defray the expenses of any extra Sessions held in and for this Borough, but the same is not to extend to the yearly Michaelmas Sessions.

26th February, A.D. 1805. 45th George III. Henry Harding, Mayor.

Ordered that the Chamberlain do provide and put up Lamp-Irons and Lamps at each corner of the Market House, and do take care that such Lamps are regularly lighted by the Bellman in the same manner as the other Lamp in the Bury is lighted.

20th January, A.D. 1806. 46th George III. Henry Knapp, Mayor.

Ordered that the Bellman do receive an additional sum of Two Pounds yearly for lighting the four Lamps at the Corners of the Markethouse, and that the said four Lamps shall be lit every Evening for the Winter six Months, commencing at Michaelmas and ending at

24th March, A.D. 1808. 48th George III. George Knapp, Mayor.

DD

Lady Day in each year, except the four Evenings before and the three Evenings after the full of the Moon, and that for every neglect of lighting the same he is ordered to be fined Five shillings.

20th May.
A.D. 1808.
45th George III.
George Knapp,
Mayor.

Ordered that the pictures of the King and Queen presented to this Corporation by Sir Charles Saxton, Bart., and lately arrived, be forthwith put up in the Great Council Chamber, at the Upper End thereof; and that the Chamberlain do get the same done with the assistance of the Standing Committee, and do call in Mr. Archer, Carver and Gilder, at Oxford, to furnish his advice and aid on this occasion.

Ordered that a full meeting of the Corporation be speedily convened for the purpose of returning Thanks to Sir Charles Saxton for his liberal Donation of the above valuable Pictures.

6th June,
A.D. 1808.
48th George III.
George Knapp,
Mayor.

A Letter from Sir Charles Saxton, Bart., dated 19th of May, 1808, is read, in which he anounces his gift to this Corporation and their Successors for ever, of a pair of full-length royal portraits of King George the third and Queen Charlotte, to be affixed with all suitable and requisite appendages in the Council Chamber as a rare and splendid ornament. It is unanimously voted and resolved, that this act of munificence from a Gentleman who was born in the Town of Abingdon, and whose Ancestors have been members of this Corporation and distinguished Magistrates of the Borough, is highly gratifying to every individual present, and that the possession of the portraits of our beloved Sovereign and his royal Consort will, at all times, tend to excite and keep alive the warmest sentiments of loyalty and affection to the illustrious personages represented in them, as well as of esteem and gratitude to the worthy donor.

COPY OF SIR CHARLES SAXTON'S LETTER.

"Cheltenham, 19th May, 1808.

"Mr. Mayor, Bailiffs & Burgesses of the Corporation of Abingdon.

"Gentlemen,

"Impressed with the warmest sense of Obligation "and Gratitude such as a Father only can feel, for the unanimous "Election of an only Son as the Recorder of your Corporation; And "for so signal a mark of your favour; I cannot by any means in my "power so fully testify my hearty thanks, as by presenting to your "loyal Corporation and transferring also to your Successors for ever,

"a pair of full lengthed Royal Portraits of King George the third
"and Queen Charlotte, to be speedily affixed with all suitable and
"requisite appendages in your Council Chamber, as a rare and
"splendid Ornament for adorning it—A piece of Royal Munificence—
"which I can on none bestow so properly and worthily as to a
"Corporation and Town where my Family were so long Magistrates,
"and myself a native.

"And ever their hearty well wisher

"and obedient humble Servant,

"C. Saxton."

Ordered that the Standing Committee do take a view of Carswell Stream, and give directions to do what is proper to make the Water flow into the Street for the use of the Inhabitants.

23rd March, A.D. 1809. 49th George III. Thomas Knight, Mayor.

Ordered that new Black Gowns (worn on Sundays) be provided for the two Sergeants as usual (if the time of having the same is expired) at the expense of this Corporation.

5th March, A.D. 1810. 50th George III. Thomas Goodall, Mayor.

Mr. Benjamin Glanvill attended and stated his willingness to undertake the work respecting the new Building of the Schoolhouse, according to Messrs. Billings and Son Plan and Elevation, at the estimated sum of Seven hundred and seventy Pounds.   *   *   *

10th July, A.D. 1810. 50th George III. Thomas Goodall, Mayor.

Agreed with Benjamin Glanvill to allow him Twenty Pounds to pull down so much of the Schoolhouse as is to be rebuilt, and to sort and allot all the materials in the School Court under the inspection and direction of the Standing Committee, and in so doing care to be taken of the materials, and none of them to be wantonly or unnecessarily damaged or spoiled, and the whole to be completed in Fourteen Days from this day.

Ordered that this Corporation do subscribe the sum of Ten Guineas towards the relief of the British Prisoners in France, and that the same be remitted to the Committee at Lloyd's Coffee House, in London, by the Chamberlain of the said Corporation.

26th February, A.D. 1811. 51st George III. Thomas Knight, Mayor.

This Corporation finding the Stipend of £3 : 6 : 8 per annum allowed forth of the Chamber to the High Steward doth amount to the sum of £73 : 6 : 8, which is about the sum from time to time accumulated to be in the disposal of the High Steward, and which hath been usually disposed of by the present High Steward's Ancestors for public uses within this Borough; And it appearing to

31st May, A.D. 1814. 51st George III. Thomas Knight, Mayor.

this Corporation that the funds for rebuilding and repairing the Freeschool-house and the Gateway and Yard thereto belonging, within this Borough, are scanty, and the School Institution being of great public benefit to this Town and Neighbourhood, especially considering its important connection with Pembroke College, in the University of Oxford; It is ordered that the Town Clerk do write to the Earl of Abingdon, High Steward of this Corporation, and apprise his Lordship that the said annual Stipend is now accumulated to the sum of £73 : 6 : 8 as before mentioned, and do lay before his Lordship their particular request that the said sum of £73 : 6 : 8 may be applied towards the Improvement of the said Schoolhouse and Premises under the direction of the Officers of this Corporation, and that this Corporation will consider themselves as much obliged by his Lordship's condescention in complying with their wishes in this respect.

4th July, A.D. 1811. 51st George III. Thomas Knight, Mayor.

Ordered that the Chamberlain do pay Mr. James Toovey his bill of £60 : 5 : 0 for erecting the Gothic Gateway at the entrance of the Freeschool Yard.

A Letter from the Earl of Abingdon, High Steward of this Corporation was read, and is to the following effect:—

"Wytham, June 6th, 1811.

"Sir,

"I shall be most happy to comply with the request of "the Corporation of Abingdon, and beg they will make use of the "£73 : 6 : 8 in any way they may think advisable in the rebuilding "and repairing the Freeschool House, within the Borough. The "Gothic Gateway, on entering the Yard, I should be much flattered "were it considered as my donation, and I hope the Corporation "will do me the Honor to accept the £100 which I enclose to "defray the expenses.

"I remain,

"Sir, your obedt. & hble. servt.,

"To Saml. Sellwood, Esq.,   "Abingdon.".
"Abingdon."

Resolved that the thanks of this Corporation be given to the Right Honourable the Earl of Abingdon, High Steward of this Corporation, for the very obliging manner in which he has been pleased to comply with the request of this Corporation to permit them to make use of the sum of £73 : 6 : 8, being the savings of his Lordship's Exhibition, in any way they may think advisable in rebuilding and repairing the Freeschool-house, and also for his Lordship's very liberal donation of £100 more, to be employed in erecting a Gothic Gateway on entering the Freeschool Yard. And it is resolved that the said sum of £100 be laid out accordingly, and that his Lordship's Arms be put up conspicuously on the Gateway, with an Inscription expressing at whose expence the Gateway was erected.

𝔒𝔯𝔡𝔢𝔯𝔢𝔡 that this Corporation do contribute the sum of Fifty Pounds towards the expences of purchase of Houses and other matters in widening the Street at the top of East Saint Helen's and Bucklersbury.

27th April, A.D. 1812. 52nd George III. John Francis Spenlove, Mayor.

𝔒𝔯𝔡𝔢𝔯𝔢𝔡 that the Mayor's Salary for the present year and in future be increased to One hundred and fifty Pounds per annum, instead of One hundred Pounds per annum as heretofore.

2nd March, A.D. 1813. 53rd George III. Thomas Knight, Mayor.

𝔒𝔯𝔡𝔢𝔯𝔢𝔡 that the Standing Committee do confer with the Churchwarden of the Parish of St. Nicholas, and also the Ordinary, respecting the making a Seat for the Corporation in Saint Nicholas Church, and do report thereon, and also the expence thereof, at the next Common Council.

𝔄 𝔏𝔢𝔱𝔱𝔢𝔯 from Mr. Henry Walsh, of Oxford, dated ninth of June, 1813, was read, apprising the Mayor that Mr. Canniford had instructed a Proctor of the Archdeacon's Court to oppose the granting of the Faculty for a Seat in Saint Nicholas Church to this Corporation. 𝔒𝔯𝔡𝔢𝔯𝔢𝔡 that some of the Standing Committee do have a conference with Mr. Henry Walsh on the subject, and inform themselves of the reasons of Mr. Canniford's opposition, and do take such measures as they shall be advised for obtaining the Faculty at the expense of this Corporation.

11th June, A.D. 1813. 53rd George III. Thomas Knight, Mayor.

𝔒𝔯𝔡𝔢𝔯𝔢𝔡 that the Chamberlain do pay Mr. Walsh's bill of Nineteen Pounds, eight shillings and ten pence, for obtaining the Faculty to erect a Pew in Saint Nicholas Church for the sole use of the Corporation.

7th February, A.D. 1814. 54th George III. Henry Knapp, Mayor.

𝔒𝔯𝔡𝔢𝔯𝔢𝔡 that a Dinner be provided by the Chamberlain on Thursday next, being the day of Public Thanksgiving for a general peace, at the expence of this Corporation.

5th July, A.D. 1814. 54th George III. Henry Knapp, Mayor.

Ordered that this Corporation do subscribe the sum of Twenty Guineas as their Subscription towards enabling all the classes of his Majesty's Subjects to participate in the general joy on the return of peace.

18th February, A.D. 1817. 57th George III. James Cole, Mayor.

Ordered that the Mayor do have the thanks of this Corporation for his attention to the interests of the Town in endeavouring to prevent the Michaelmas or Flying Sessions for the County (now holden alternately at Reading and Abingdon) being fixed to be holden altogether at Reading, and not in turn at Abingdon, as hath been usual; And it appearing that the idea of giving such a preference to the Town of Reading is still entertained, It is ordered that the Mayor be requested to continue his vigilance for the interest of the Town, and to solicit the attendance of friendly Magistrates if the question shall be brought forward again at the next Quarter Sessions for the County of Berks.

30th April, A.D. 1817. 57th George III. James Cole, Mayor.

Mr. Mayor reported a Letter received from Charles Dundas, Esquire, one of the Members in Parliament for this County, which gives information that the County Magistrates had unanimously resolved at the Quarter Sessions, holden at Newbury, on the sixteenth instant, that the Flying Sessions held alternately at Reading and Abingdon should be continued to be holden as usual, and that there should be no change.

4th June, A.D. 1817. 57th George III. James Cole, Mayor.

Ordered that the Great Council Chamber be not in future permitted to be used by any Person or Persons for any purpose whatsoever, except for Balls and Concerts as hath heretofore been accustomed, and except by the Grand Jury at the Assizes, if they have occasion for the same, unless it shall be with the consent of a Common Council duly summoned.

30th October, A.D. 1817. 58th George III. Thomas West, Mayor.

Ordered that this Corporation do subscribe Five Pounds towards the nightly watch, and that the same be paid by the Chamberlain forthwith.

Ordered that Mr. Maberley do have the use of the Great Council Chamber for the purpose of giving a Dinner therein to the Voters in this Borough sometime in the month of November next, he being answerable for all damage to be occasioned thereby.

19th March, A.D. 1818. 58th George III. Thomas West, Mayor.

This Day The Will of Mr. John Fountain deceased, dated the twenty fourth of day February, 1710, so far as it relates to his perpetual donation of an Estate at Norcot to Trustees for the benefit of the poor Almsmen in Saint John's Hospital, belonging to this Corporation, was read and taken into consideration; Also an Act of Parliament passed in the Fifty second year of the Reign of his present Majesty to provide a summary remedy in cases of abuses of Trusts created for charitable purposes was read; And inasmuch as the conduct of Mr. Fountain's Charity and the regular application of the rents of the said Estate by the Trustees thereof have always been kept secret from every member of this Corporation, although the Mayor, for the time being, is the Patron of the said Hospital, and has the nomination of the Almsmen therein, who are the sole objects of Mr. Fountain's donation, and this Corporation being joint contributors to the weekly relief and clothing of the said Almsmen, and the supporters of the Edifice of the said Hospital, and it being conceived that abuses have existed and may again exist with reference to the application of Mr. Fountain's Trust fund for the benefit of the said Almsmen; It is therefore resolved and ordered that application be made by the Mayor and Magistrates of this Borough to the Court of Chancery, in the summary way prescribed by the said Act, to have the inspection of the accounts of Mr. Fountain's said Charity for as many years past as they shall judge expedient, and to cause any abuses which they shall discover, to be rectified, so far as it shall be practicable and advisable, and to obtain an order of the said Court for the better administration of Mr. Fountain's said Charity, especially for an annual exhibition of the accounts thereof by the Trustees acting under Mr. Fountain's Will, to the Mayor and Magistrates, for the time being, of this Borough, and for yearly auditing the said accounts; and that they do employ the Town Clerk herein, and consult such Counsel as they shall think fit, And this Corporation will defray the expense of the proceedings had in pursuance of this order.

Ordered that the Standing Committee do take such measures which in their judgment shall appear proper and necessary to repel any attacks that may be made upon the rights and privileges of this Corporation in the course of the pending Election of Mayor for the year ensuing.

29th September, A.D. 1818. 58th George III. Thomas West, *Mayor.*

Resolved, and unanimously agreed, that this Corporation are willing to do anything in their power towards advancing and

17th November, A.D. 1818. 59th George III. James Cole, *Mayor.*

encouraging the prosperity and trade of Abingdon, and in case a Pitched Market for Corn be established and encouraged, the Corporation will, at a future time, take into their consideration any proposal on the subject of Toll that may be made to them by the Growers and Dealers in Corn frequenting the said Market, or their Committee.

29th December, A.D. 1818. 59th George III. James Cole, *Mayor.*

It is resolved that an Address be presented to His Royal Highness the Prince Regent, to offer the condolence of this Corporation to him on the death of Her Majesty, our Most Gracious Queen; Such address is proposed and agreed to, and the Common Seal is ordered to be affixed thereto when ingrossed.

18th March, A.D. 1819. 59th George III. James Cole, *Mayor.*

Ordered that the Bounds and Franchises of this Borough be perambulated on Saturday, the twenty ninth day of May next, and that the Chamberlain do provide Four hundred Cakes and three Kilderkins of Ale, and a Dinner for the Corporation as usual.

The Mayor having read a Letter which he yesterday received from John Maberly, Esq., M.P. for the Borough, informing him that a Petition from Reading had been presented on the eighth instant to the House of Commons, praying that in future the Election of the Representatives of this County should be held three days at Abingdon, three days at Newbury, and three days at Reading, and that power should be given to the Sheriff to remove the County Court for that purpose; And that on the same day another Petition was also presented from the Town of Wokingham praying that the County Court should be removed to that Town three days for the same purpose; Mr. Maberly also forwarded to the Mayor copies of both Petitions, which are now produced and read; **Resolved** unanimously that the thanks of this Corporation be given to John Maberly, Esquire, for his prompt communication, zeal and attention to the Interests of the Town on this important occasion, and to request that he will oppose the Petitions of the Inhabitants of Reading and Wokingham to the utmost of his power.

19th April, A.D. 1819. 59th George III. James Cole, *Mayor.*

Resolved unanimously, that the Standing Committee do inspect the Room, part of the Gaol premises, lately used as a Bakehouse by James Goldby, and if they are of opinion that it be an eligible situation, they are hereby authorised to have the same immediately repaired, so as to make a convenient Office for the Town Clerk to do the public business of the Borough and Corporation in.

𝔒𝔯𝔡𝔢𝔯𝔢𝔡 that a Seal with the Corporation Arms thereon, provided by the Mayor, and which cost the sum of Three Pounds, three shillings, be paid for by the Chamberlain.

18th November,.
A.D. 1819.
60th George III.
Thomas Knight,
Mayor.

Upon reading the following Letter from the Reverend Mr. Nicholson, Master of Abingdon School, vizt.:—

25th January,
A.D. 1820.
60th George III.
Thomas Knight,
Mayor.

To the Governors of Roysse's School, in the Borough of Abingdon.

"Gentlemen,

"Repeated complaints having been made respecting "the extreme coldness of the School-room, I shall consider it a "favour, if I may have your permission to introduce a Stove, and I "engage that the room shall not be used, more than it is now, as an "Apartment for the boys.

"I am,
"Gentlemen,
"Your very obedt. Servt.,
"Novr. 22nd, 1819. "E. Nicholson."

𝔒𝔯𝔡𝔢𝔯𝔢𝔡 and agreed that leave be given to the Reverend Mr. Nicholson to erect a temporary Stove in the School-room pursuant to his request. * * *.

𝔗𝔥𝔢 following Members of the Corporation took the Oaths of Allegiance and Supremacy to his Majesty King George the Fourth, vizt.:—Thomas Knight, James Cole, John Francis Spenlove, John Latham, Thomas West, Thomas Baker, George Shepherd, Charles King, William Mitchell, Thomas Curtis, Thomas Wilson, Edward Beasley, Benjamin Morland, Richard Bradfield, William Tyrrell, Edward Cheer, John Vindin Collingwood, and William Doe Belcher.

15th February,
A.D. 1820.
1st George IV.
Thomas Knight.
Mayor.

𝔒𝔯𝔡𝔢𝔯𝔢𝔡 that the Chamberlain do repay the Executors of the late Samuel Sellwood, Esqr., the sum of Six Pounds, six shillings, for Nine Volumes of the Statutes at large bound in Calf, at seven shillings each, up to the forty first of George the third, and for Twenty one Volumes of the Statutes at large bound in boards, at Three shillings each, up to the 58th George the third inclusive, which Statutes up to that period are now the property of this Corporation.

(These Books are now deposited by the Corporation in the reference Department of the Municipal Free Library.)

𝔍𝔱 is resolved that an Address be presented to His Most Gracious Majesty King George the fourth, to offer the condolence of this

19th April,
A.D. 1820.
1st George IV.
Thomas Knight,
Mayor.

EE

Corporation to him on the death of our revered Monarch, his late Father, and also to express their unfeigned congratulations on his Majesty's Succession to the Throne of these Realms.

27th April,
A.D. 1820.
1st George IV.
Thomas Knight,
Mayor.

𝔒𝔯𝔡𝔢𝔯𝔢𝔡 that the Corporation Seat in Saint Nicholas Church be altered internally according to a Plan now produced and fixed on, and the Chamberlain is ordered to get the same altered accordingly forthwith.

19th September,
A.D. 1820.
1st George IV.
Thomas Knight,
Mayor.

[John Latham, who had been elected Mayor on the 1st September, refuses to accept Office, on the ground of "his having a large family "and the times being so bad at present, which causes the said John "Latham alledgeth may be considered as a sufficient excuse for his "not serving the said Office of Mayor for the year ensuing, and "prays that he may not be fined," which excuse is accepted as reasonable, and he is excused from serving the said Office accordingly without being fined.]

6th March,
A.D. 1821.
2nd George IV.
Thomas Baker,
Mayor.

𝔏𝔢𝔞𝔳𝔢 is given to the Managers of the Saving Bank in Abingdon, to have the use of the Town Clerk's Office during their meetings on Mondays, as long as it shall please the Corporation.

13th July,
A.D. 1821.
2nd George IV.
Thomas Baker,
Mayor.

𝔒𝔯𝔡𝔢𝔯𝔢𝔡 that the Chamberlain do provide One thousand penny Cakes to be distributed to the populace on the day of the Coronation of His Majesty King George the fourth, on the nineteenth day of July instant.

𝔒𝔯𝔡𝔢𝔯𝔢𝔡 that Twenty Guineas be subscribed by this Corporation in aid of a subscription intended to be entered into by the Inhabitants of the Borough for regaling the Populace of the same on the like occasion.

16th November,
A.D. 1821.
2nd George IV.
John Francis
Spenlove,
Mayor.

𝔒𝔯𝔡𝔢𝔯𝔢𝔡 that the sum of Ten Guineas be subscribed by this Corporation towards a Monumental Trophy in honor of His late Most Sacred Majesty   *   *   *

𝔄 𝔏𝔢𝔱𝔱𝔢𝔯 from the Clerk of the Peace for the County of Berks was read, stating that the Parishes within the Borough had been rated and assessed to the County Rate; And it is ordered that the Town Clerk do write to the Clerk of the Peace and state that this Borough is exempt by the Charters from any Jurisdiction of the Country Magistrates, and therefore have no right to pay towards the County Rate.

The Parish Officers of Saint Helen and Saint Nicholas having received notice from the Clerk of the Peace for the County of Berks that the Magistrates for the said County had charged both Parishes to the County Rate, and the Churchwardens and Overseers of both Parishes having applied to this Corporation to assist them with the aid of their Charters and other documents.   *   *   **Ordered** that the Standing Committee, together with Messrs. Knight and West, be a Committee to co-operate with Mr. Morland in resisting the claims made by the County of Berks, against the Parishes within this Borough, and that any three of the Committee be empowered to act.

15th July,
A.D. 1822.
3rd George IV.
John Francis
Spenlove,
Mayor.

That the alteration proposed by the Commissioners of the Fyfield Road, in Burford Street, in this Borough, be forthwith done at the expence of this Corporation   *   *   *

31st July,
A.D. 1822.
3rd George IV.
John Francis
Spenlove,
Mayor.

That this Corporation do subscribe Twenty Guineas towards the relief of the distressed Irish, to be remitted by the Chamberlain to the Committee in the name of the Corporation.

Ordered that the Common Seal be affixed to an Instrument for giving the consent of this Corporation to turning the old Footpath over the land near Boxhill, held by William Bowles, Esquire, of this Corporation.

13th September,
A.D. 1822.
3rd George IV.
John Francis
Spenlove,
Mayor.

Resolved and agreed that this Corporation do subscribe the sum of Twenty Pounds towards the relief of the necessitous poor of this Town in aid of the subscription of the Inhabitants for that purpose   *   *   *

25th January,
A.D. 1823.
3rd George IV.
James Cole,
Mayor.

The Standing Committee reported that they had inspected into and regulated the Bellman's Duty and Advantages and they recommend And it is ordered that Charles Matthew Wicks, the Bellman, be allowed the sum of Three Pounds, three shillings, for his additional trouble in turning Vagrants out of the Town for the year past (as a Gratuity). And it is also Ordered that the Bellman be allowed an additional yearly sum of Ten shillings for Lighting the Lamp in the Sheep Market, and also the further sum of Six shillings for cleaning all the Knives and Forks belonging to the Corporation.

20th March,
A.D. 1823.
4th George IV.
James Cole,
Mayor.

Ordered that leave be given to Captain Wroughton to have the use of the Great Council Chamber, on Friday next, for the purpose

3rd June,
A.D. 1823.
4th George IV.
James Cole,
Mayor.

of the Abingdon Troop dining therein, Captain Wroughton being answerable for all damage to be occasioned thereby.

Ordered that the Cushions in the Mayor's Seat be new covered, and that the Chamberlain do get them done by the Assizes, one with Velvet and the other with Cloth as formerly.

Ordered that the Chamberlain do provide Six new Prayer Books for the use of the Corporation in Saint Helen's Church at the expence of this Corporation.

19th August,
A.D. 1823.
4th George IV.
James Cole,
Mayor.

The Standing Committee of this Corporation, together with Messrs. Knight, West, and Morland, report to this meeting, That pursuant to an order made by this Corporation of the fifteenth day of July, 1822, hereinafter referred to and preceeding the making of such order, the several measures were taken to resist any authority of the County Magistrates within this Borough, as to charging such Parishes to the County Rate, and which have ultimately succeeded, and therefore the said Committee moved that the several circumstances attending the busines should be recorded in the Corporation Book, as it may be important in time to come, which is resolved accordingly as follows:—

[Here follows a detailed account of the steps taken by the Committee to resist the action taken by the County Magistrates with regard to rating the Borough for County purposes.]

The Corporation finding the stipend of Three Pounds, six shillings, and eight pence per annum, allowed forth of the Chamber to the High Steward doth amount to the sum of Forty three pounds, six shillings and eight pence; It is ordered that the Town Clerk do write to the Earl of Abingdon, High Steward of this Corporation, and apprise his Lordship that the said Annual Stipend is now accumulated to the sum of Forty three Pounds, six shillings and eight pence, as before mentioned, and request his Lordship's directions respecting the application of the same.

Ordered that the Standing Committee, together with Mr. Morland, Mr. West, and Mr. Bowles, be a Committee to inspect into and report whether a proper Room can be made of the Debtor's Room in the Gaol, for the accommodation of this Corporation and the different Assemblies held in the Council Chamber, and that they do get an Estimate made what the expence will be, and report thereon to the next Common Council.

𝕬 𝕷𝖊𝖙𝖙𝖊𝖗 from the Earl of Abingdon, in answer to the Letter of the Town Clerk, pursuant to the order of the ninteenth day of August last, was this day read, in which his Lordship expresses his wish to co-operate with the views of the Corporation in laying out his Lordship's Stipend in any way that may be beneficial to this Corporation.

19th September, A.D. 1823. 4th George IV. James Cole, Mayor.

𝖀𝖕𝖔𝖓 taking into consideration the above Letter of Lord Abingdon, It is unanimously agreed that a Pier Glass shall be purchased according to a Plan now produced, at the price of Fifty Pounds, and the further sum of Six Pounds for the expence of bringing it down from London and placing the same up in the Council Chamber   *   *   *

𝕺𝖗𝖉𝖊𝖗𝖊𝖉 that the Chamberlain do subscribe Ten Guineas towards the Building Fund of the National School in Abingdon.

4th November, A.D. 1823. 4th George IV. Thomas Knight, Mayor.

𝕺𝖗𝖉𝖊𝖗𝖊𝖉 and agreed that this Corporation do subscribe the sum of Five Guineas per annum to the National School   *   *   *

𝕺𝖗𝖉𝖊𝖗𝖊𝖉 that the Mayor and Magistrates do have the privilege of nominating the Children to be elected into the National School, from time to time, in virtue of the above subscription.

𝕺𝖗𝖉𝖊𝖗𝖊𝖉 that the Chamberlain do pay Mr. Hedges Five Pounds, five shillings, for extra work on account of the Arms added to the Pier Glass purchased out of the Annual Stipend of the Earl of Abingdon, as High Steward of this Corporation.

2nd March, A.D. 1824. 5th George IV. Thomas Knight, Mayor.

𝕺𝖗𝖉𝖊𝖗𝖊𝖉 that the Chamberlain do subscribe Ten Guineas toward the last Abingdon Races, and in future he is ordered to subscribe the like sum towards the Races, upon being satisfied that the balance is deficient, until further order.

2nd November, A.D. 1824. 5th George IV. William Bowles, Mayor.

𝕺𝖗𝖉𝖊𝖗𝖊𝖉 and agreed that this Corporation do increase their Subscription towards the National School, from Five Guineas per Annum to Ten Guineas per Annum   *   *   *

𝕿𝖍𝖊 𝕮𝖔𝖒𝖒𝖎𝖙𝖙𝖊𝖊 in pursuance of an order made on the nineteenth day of August, 1823, produced a plan for the erection of a Room over the Abbey Gateway, and the Estimate thereof amounting to the sum of Three hundred and thirty seven Pounds, fifteen

4th May, A.D. 1825. 6th George IV. William Bowles, Mayor.

Shillings, made by Mr. James Leverett, which plan and estimate are approved of by the Corporation, who will consent to appropriate the Sum of Two hundred Pounds in part thereof, provided the remaining Sum is forthcoming by Individual Subscription.

17th January, A.D. 1826. 6th George IV. James Cole, *Mayor.*

Resolved and Agreed that this Corporation do subscribe the sum of Twenty pounds towards the relief of the necessitous poor of this Town, in aid of the Subscriptions of the Inhabitants for that purpose   *   *   *

23rd March, A.D. 1826. 7th George IV. James Cole, *Mayor.*

Ordered that the Chamberlain do provide three dozen of Wine Glasses for the use of the Corporation.

3rd May, A.D. 1826. 7th George IV. James Cole, *Mayor.*

Ordered that the Bounds and Franchises of this Borough be perambulated some day in June next, and that the Chamberlain do provide Four Hundred Cakes and Three Kilderkins of Ale, and a Dinner for the Corporation as usual.

Ordered and Agreed that the reparations of the Squares, Streets, and Lanes be let to Thomas Winterbourne, for the Term of eight years, from the first day of May instant, for the sum of fifty eight pounds per annum, upon certain Conditions produced by the Chamberlain and agreed to by the said Thomas Winterbourne; and William Grace, of Abingdon, agrees to become his Surety for performance of the same.

9th May, A.D. 1826. 7th George IV. James Cole, *Mayor.*

Ordered that the Beadle be provided with a Coat and Round Hat with Lace and Band, at the expence of this Corporation, which is to last him two years, if he shall so long continue in Office, and then the Coat and Hat to be his own.

Ordered that the Corporation do subscribe the further sum of Ten pounds, in addition to their former Subscription of twenty pounds, towards buying Coals for the necessitous Poor.

3rd January, A.D. 1827. 7th George IV. William Doe Belcher, *Mayor.*

Ordered that the Town Clerk do write to Mr. Cruden, No. 7, Fleet Street, London, and inform him that the Corporation of Abingdon decline to join the Association relating to Corporations as mentioned in a Letter received from the Chairman of the Committee, and Mayor of Rochester.

1st February, A.D. 1827. 8th George IV. William Doe Belcher, *Mayor.*

Resolved unanimously, that an Address of Condolence be presented to His Majesty on the death of His late Royal Brother, the Duke of York and Albany, and that the Earl of Abingdon, High

Steward of the Borough, be requested to present the same to His Majesty.

Resolved and agreed that this Corporation do subscribe the sum of Ten Pounds, Ten Shillings, towards the relief of the necessitous Poor of this Town, in aid of the Coal subscriptions of the Inhabitants for that purpose * * *

It was resolved that it is expedient to present a humble Petition to both Houses of Parliament against granting further concession to the Roman Catholics.

20th February, A.D. 1829. 10th George IV. Charles King, *Mayor.*

A Letter was produced and read by the Mayor which he had received from Mr. Maberly, stating that the Petition to the House of Commons (in his opinion) could not be received.

2nd March, A.D. 1829. 10th George IV. Charles King, *Mayor.*

It was then resolved

That the Letter of Mr. Maberly be entered in the Corporation Ledger, of which the following is a copy:—

"London, House of Commons,

"4 o'clock, 27th Feby., 1829.

" Dear Sir,

"The Petition to the House of Commons from the "Corporation, that from the Inhabitants of the Borough, your Letter, "and the Order in Council duly reached me this Morning, and on "reading that from the Corporation, I observed that it purported to "be the Petition of the Mayor, Bayliffs, &c., &c., and as I had "received a Letter from one of the Bayliffs (Mr. Strange), who "informed me that he dissented from the prayer, and requesting that "I would make that known when I presented the Petition to the "House, I have been induced to take a course which I trust both "yourself and the Corporation will approve. Instead of presenting "the Petition immediately (as I was requested), I mentioned the "subject to the Speaker, in Order to learn from him whether such a "Petition could be received, when he decided that it could not, and "that I was also authorized by him to make that Opinion known to "you. I must confess that was my own opinion, and I therefore did "not think it expedient to have this subject publicly canvassed in "the House until you and the Corporation should be informed of the "discrepancy. I need not point out to you that it could not be the "Petition of the Bailiffs, if they dissented, and on this ground the

" House would not only reject it, but in all probability would have
" expressed itself angrily at the attempt.   I suppose you cannot put
" the Corporation Seal without including the Bailiffs, but if you can,
" you had better send up another Petition, leaving out the Bailiffs.
" It does not become me, perhaps, as your Member, to offer advice on
" the subject, but I shall be ready to present any Petition you will
" forward that can be received by the House, and I will not shrink
" from presenting that you have sent, if it be your wish, but after the
" authority I have quoted, I cannot imagine you or the Corporation
" would require it, and that you will rather think I have taken the
" most judicious course in making you acquainted with all the
" circumstances.   I did not present the other petition, so numerously
" and respectably signed, imagining that you rather wished them to
" be presented at the same time.   You therefore will, perhaps, favor
" me with your reply, so that on Monday I may present it, should it
" be your wish; I have also communicated to Mr. Strange these
" circumstances.

" I have the honor to remain,
" Dear Sir,
" Yours most faithfully,

" The Mayor of Abingdon.   " John Maberly."

3rd March,
A.D. 1829.
10th George IV.
Charles King,
Mayor.

𝕿𝖍𝖊 Common Council having taken into their consideration the
Correspondence between Mr. Strange and the representative of this
Borough, feel it their duty to mark their disapprobation of the
conduct of Mr. Strange, a Secondary Burgess and one of the Bayliffs
for the present year, by causing the above mentioned Petition to be
withdrawn, which they conceive was properly designated as the
Petition of the Mayor, Bayliffs and Burgesses of the Borough.
𝕿𝖍𝖊𝖞 feel themselves called upon, for the guidance of their
Successors, that they may at all times rightly and legally use this
their Chartered designation in all cases decided on by a Majority
in Common Council assembled, whether the Bayliffs are parties
consenting thereto *or not*; that the Bayliffs (though invested with an
official situation) have no Corporate capacity or prohibitory power
within themselves, *but are Individuals* whose voices are controlled by
the Majority, as other Secondary Burgesses.   𝕿𝖍𝖊𝖞 further feel it
their duty also to state that in the Petition above referred to, the
conduct of Mr. Strange in making a private communication to Mr.

Maberly with the intent of frustrating the object *determined on* by a Majority of Members in Common Council assembled, was *disrespectful to the Corporation, not creditable* to himself, and is deserving the censure of this Corporation.

It is ordered that the sum of One hundred Pounds be subscribed by this Corporation in aid of the Funds of the Parish of Saint Helen for the erection of a new Poorhouse.

11th June, A.D. 1829. 10th George IV. Charles King, *Mayor.*

The Mayor produced a Letter which Mr. Spenlove had received from Mr. Hitchins, from which it appeared that the Ringers of Saint Helen and Saint Nicholas had applied to Lord Abingdon for a remuneration for ringing on the day Lord Norreys came of age, and stated that they had received nothing for their trouble, whereby they succeeded in obtaining from his Lordship the sum of Twenty Guineas, when, in fact, they had previously been paid by this Corporation for their ringing on that occasion ; this Corporation therefore recommend to the Minister and Churchwardens of both Parishes not to allow the present Ringers the use of the Belfries in future.

1st September, A.D. 1829. 10th George IV. Charles King, *Mayor.*

Ordered that the Corporation Arms be placed in both Churches at the expense of this Corporation.

Resolved unanimously, that the Corporation do subscribe the sum of two hundred Pounds in aid of the Subscription for widening and otherwise improving Burford Bridge, adjoining the Town of Abingdon, and Culham Bridge, in the County of Oxford. And the Chamberlain is authorized to advance such sum by Instalments, at such time and in such manner as the Trustees of the Fyfield Turnpike Road or their Committee shall require.

13th November, A.D. 1829. 10th George IV. James Cole, *Mayor.*

Ordered that the Chamberlain do provide Six 8vo. Prayer Books for the use of the Corporation Pew in Saint Nicholas Church.

29th December, A.D. 1829. 10th George IV. James Cole, *Mayor.*

At a meeting of the Corporation the sixth day of February instant, for the purpose of joining the Town in a Subscription to supply the Poor with Soup or other Provisions, the Weather being unusually severe, and the greatest distress prevailing among the Poor Inhabitants, and a sufficient number not attending to form a Common Council, the Members then present voted the sum of Ten Guineas to be added to the Town subscription, not doubting but that the next Common Council would approve of and confirm the

22nd February, A.D. 1830. 11th George IV. James Cole, *Mayor.*

FF

said Vote. The Mayor having communicated the proceedings of the Meeting on the sixth instant, This Council does approve and confirm the Vote of Ten Guineas for the Charitable purpose above mentioned.

1st July,
A.D. 1830.
1st William IV.
James Cole,
Mayor.

𝕬𝖙 a Common Council held this day :—

Present :—

Mr. James Cole, Mayor,	Thomas Waite,
Thomas Knight,	William Strange,
John Francis Spenlove,	Richard Badcock,
Thomas Baker,	Edward Cowcher,
William Mitchell,	William Brown Baker,
John Latham,	George Shepherd,
William Doe Belcher,	Thomas Sharps,
John Vindin Collingwood,	Henry Dewe,
Thomas Curtis,	George Cox.

𝕿𝖍𝖊 above mentioned Members of the Corporation severally took the Oaths of allegiance and supremacy on the occasion of His present Majesty, King William the Fourth, ascending the Throne of this Kingdom, and immediately afterwards proceeded to the usual Stations and there proclaimed Him King, by the style and title of William the fourth, by the Grace of God, King, of the United Kingdom of Great Britain and Ireland, Defender of the Faith.

3rd August,
A.D. 1830.
1st William IV.
James Cole,
Mayor.

𝕽𝖊𝖘𝖔𝖑𝖛𝖊𝖉 that a dutiful address be presented to His Majesty, and that the one now produced by Mr. Belcher be adopted.

𝕽𝖊𝖘𝖔𝖑𝖛𝖊𝖉 that the same be fairly Ingrossed, and the Common Seal affixed by the Mayor and Committee, and that it remain in the Guildhall for signatures until Thursday Evening next.

𝕽𝖊𝖘𝖔𝖑𝖛𝖊𝖉 that the Mayor do transmit this address to the Earl of Abingdon, Lord Lieutenant of the County, and High Steward of the Borough, requesting his Lordship to present the same.

29th September,
A.D. 1830.
1st William IV.

[John Vindin Collingwood, who was elected Mayor on the 1st September, refuses to accept office, on the ground "that "Gentlemen standing most high in the Profession have been "consulted, and they are unanimous in thinking that the return made "by the Inhabitants of three Persons to the Senior Burgesses "instead of two, has rendered the Election informal and in-

"complete." The excuse is accepted and allowed, and Mr. Collingwood is excused from serving without Fine accordingly.]

Ordered that application be made to the Court of King's Bench for a Mandamus pursuant to Act 11th Geo. 1, Cap. 4, for the election of a Mayor in the room of Mr. John Vindin Collingwood, who refused to take upon him the Office of Mayor, and be sworn pursuant to the Charter, and that the Charter and all necessary papers be produced to the Committee as may be wanting for the purpose.

5th October, A.D. 1830. 1st William IV. James Cole, Mayor.

Resolved that the Poll for the Election of a Mayor, on Wednesday, the twenty fourth day of November instant, be adjourned at four o'clock, until the next Morning at nine o'clock.

18th November, A.D. 1830. 1st William IV. James Cole, Mayor.

Resolved that five of the Principal Burgesses be elected to set as Assessors on the disputed Votes, and their determination to be final.

Ordered that the Standing Committee do make such alterations in the Court as they may think fit for the more commodious taking the Poll   *   *   *

[Mr. John Vindin Collingwood is elected Mayor.]

24th November, A D. 1830.

Ordered that the Chamberlain do provide 500 penny Cakes, to be distributed to the Populace on the day of the Coronation of His Majesty King William the fourth, on the eighth day of September instant.

1st September, A.D. 1831. 2nd William IV. John Vindin Collingwood, Mayor.

Ordered that an humble Address be Presented to his Majesty on his Escape from his late attrocious attack on his Royal Person at Ascot Heath Races, and that the Standing Committee do get the same engrossed.

19th June, A.D. 1832. 2nd William IV. Thomas Knight, Mayor.

Ordered that a Petition be presented to the House of Lords against the introduction of a claim adding the Township of Sutton Wick to the old Boundary of the Borough of Abingdon   *   *   *

Ordered that

19th March, A.D. 1833. 3rd William IV. John Francis Spenlove, Mayor.

Mr. Spenlove,	Mr. G. B. Morland,
Mr. Knight,	Mr. Badcock,
Mr. Cole,	Mr. Belcher,
Mr. Mitchell,	Mr. Strange,
Mr. B. Collingwood,	Mr. Sharps,
Mr. King,	Mr. Shepherd,

or any three of them, be a Committee to order and superintend the repairs necessary to be done to the Market House, according to the report of Mr. Money, the Surveyor, bearing date the twenty seventh day of February, 1833, and that the following Letter and report be inserted in "Jackson's Oxford Journal," the "Reading Mercury," and the "Berkshire Chronicle."

COPY.

A rumour having gone abroad that the County Hall at Abingdon is unsafe, the Corporation directed a Survey of the same to be made by Mr. Money, of Donnington, near Newbury, and the following is a Copy of his report, which I am directed by the Common Council to publish in your paper.

Thomas Curtis,
Town Clerk.

Abingdon, 19th March, 1833.

"Donnington, near Newbury,
"February 27th, 1833.

"Sirs,

     "In pursuance with an Order dated February nineteenth, "1833, from Thomas Curtis, Esquire, Town Clerk of Abingdon, in "the County of Berks, I have this day carefully examined the state "and condition of the principal Timbers in the naked Floor of the "County Hall, at Abingdon, the whole of which appear to be "perfectly sound. The Girders are trussed or supported in a "peculiar and skilful manner, and in my opinion the floor is equal "to any weight that may be placed upon it. The Timbers in the "Garret Floor are sagged, vizt.: the floor is sunk in the middle, "partly from want of strength in the partitions which are parallel "to the North front Wall, and partly from the weight of the Cupola "being thrown upon it by means of Story posts, which stand "between the Floor and the Camber beams of the roof. The Cupola "was covered with Lead, which is now taken off, and Copper "covering put on, consequently the original weight is reduced three "fourths. I apprehend not the slightest danger from this apparent "defect in the Floor. The Timbers in the Roof are in good "preservation, and the Work stands remarkably well. The Walls "stand perpendicular to the Horison and are perfectly sound, except "the scaly state of part of the Outside, which is only superficial,

" therefore does not affect the stability of the Edifice.　It seldom
" happens that the severities and changes of the weather and the
" rugged hand of time for a period of One hundred and fifty years
" have committed less depredation than exists in and upon this
" Structure.

" I am, Sirs,

" Your most Ob. humble Servt.,

" To

" John Money,

" The Worshipful the Mayor

" Building Surveyor."

" and Burgesses of the

" Borough of Abingdon, Berks."

𝕽𝖊𝖘𝖔𝖑𝖛𝖊𝖉 that the Corporation subscribe One hundred pounds
towards the erection of a Workhouse, if the Workhouse be erected.

𝕽𝖊𝖘𝖔𝖑𝖛𝖊𝖉 that the Public Lamps that have been usually
lighted with Oil at the expense of the Corporation, be now lighted
with Gas.

𝕺𝖗𝖉𝖊𝖗𝖊𝖉 that the Bounds and Franchises of this Borough be
perambulated some day in the fourth week in June next, and that
the Chamberlain do provide four hundred Cakes and two Kilderkins
of Ale and a Dinner for the Corporation as usual.

𝕺𝖗𝖉𝖊𝖗𝖊𝖉 that an Obelisk be erected in the Market place,
according to the Plan now produced, as prepared by Mr. Stears, at
his offer of Thirty five pounds, under the direction of the standing
Committee.

𝕺𝖗𝖉𝖊𝖗𝖊𝖉 that an Obelisk be erected in the Square or Sheep
Market, under the direction of the standing Committee, so that the
expense thereof do not exceed Twenty five pounds.

𝕺𝖗𝖉𝖊𝖗𝖊𝖉 that a Petition be presented to both Houses of
Parliament against the Dissenters being educated at the Universities,
and that the same be presented to the House of Lords by the Earl
of Abingdon, and to the House of Commons by Thomas Duffield,
Esqr., and that the common Seal be affixed thereto and signed by
the Mayor.

𝕺𝖗𝖉𝖊𝖗𝖊𝖉 that the sum of Ten pounds be subscribed by this
Corporation to the Subscription for rebuilding or improving the
Almshouses, opposite Christ Church College, Oxford, and improving
the entrance of Pembroke College in that University.

Ordered that the Chamberlain procure new Leather Pipes to the Fire Engine belonging to this Corporation.

Ordered that the Standing Committee inspect the Pebble yard, and select a proper situation for Keeping the Engine in a proper Shed, to be erected for that purpose.

3rd October,
A.D. 1835.
6th William IV

This day Mr. William Doe Belcher is sworn Mayor of this Borough, Justice of the Peace, Clerk of the Market, and Coronor of our Lord the King, for the year ensuing.

12th November,
A.D. 1835.
6th William IV
William Doe
Belcher,
Mayor.

Ordered that the Chamberlain do pay to Mr. Benjamin Collingwood, towards defraying the Expenses of lighting Saint Helen's Church with Gas, the Sum of Ten Guineas.

Records of the Borough of Abingdon.

PART III.

SELECTIONS FROM THE CHRONICLES

OF THE

REFORMED CORPORATION

(A.D. 1835 TO A.D. 1897).

First Election of Councillors held this day.

First Election of Aldermen held this day.

Mr. William Doe Belcher elected Mayor.

Mr. Daniel Godfrey elected Town Clerk.

James Leverett appointed Senior Sergeant at Mace and Gaoler.

William Honey appointed Junior Sergeant at Mace.

Charles Mathew Wicks appointed Bellman and Beadle.

The Old Seal of the Corporation ordered to be sold and a new one purchased.

A Fine of £20 ordered to be paid by every person elected to the Office of Mayor who should refuse to accept Office.

A Fine of £10 ordered to be paid by every person elected to the Office of Alderman, Councillor, Auditor, or Assessor, who should refuse to accept Office.

(Margin notes:)

1835.
December 28th.

December 31st.

1836.
January 1st.
William Doe
Belcher,
Mayor.

February 9th.

𝔄n order made requiring the Members of the Council and also the Town Clerk to wear the same Costume as was worn by the late Corporation and Town Clerk.

Mr. William Strange appointed Treasurer.

𝔗𝔥𝔢 Right Hon. Montague, Earl of Abingdon, re-elected High Steward.

𝔄 Petition ordered to be prepared applying for a Grant of a separate Court of Quarter Sessions of the Peace for the Borough.

𝔗𝔥𝔢 Salary of the Recorder fixed at £40 per annum, and Henry John Shepherd, Esq., K.C., the late Recorder, recommended for appointment by His Majesty.

𝔄 Petition ordered to be prepared applying for a grant of a Commission of the Peace for the Borough, in order that Ten Justices might be appointed, with the recommendation that the following persons should be appointed Justices, viz. :—William Doe Belcher, Alderman Thomas Knight, John Francis Spenlove, John Vindin Collingwood, Charles King, Benjamin Collingwood, Richard Badcock, Joseph Copeland, John Tomkins, and John Kent.

March 3rd.

𝔗𝔥𝔢 Salary of the Mayor fixed at £100 per annum.

April 11th.

𝔄 Superannuation allowance of £90 per annum ordered to be paid to Mr. Curtis, the late Town Clerk.

𝔄 letter received from the Secretary of State, stating that according to a scale fixed, the number of Justices of the Borough was to be four, and that Lord John Russell had submitted the names of Benjamin Collingwood, Richard Badcock, Joseph Copeland, and John Kent, for appointment as such Justices.

𝔗𝔥𝔢 Pay of the Inspector of Police fixed at £1 per week, and Two day and five night Constables at 13/- per week each.

April 29th.

𝔗𝔥𝔢 Town Clerk's Office ordered to be appropriated for the " Police Office," and the late Guard House and room over to be the Watch or Station House.

𝔗𝔥𝔢 Petition for a Grant of a Court of Quarter Sessions of the Peace refused.

A Special Meeting of the Council and Borough Justices, held in response to a requisition signed by 280 Ratepayers, whereat Resolutions were passed in favour of every endeavour being made to obtain a reconsideration of His Majesty's decision with regard to the grant of a Court of Quarter Sessions.

1836.
May 4th.
William Doe Belcher,
Mayor.

The Petition for a Grant of a separate Court of Quarter Sessions of the Peace granted by the King.

June 11th.

Mr. Daniel Godfrey, appointed Clerk of the Peace.

Mr. Edward Cowcher appointed Coroner.

The Records of the Kingdom ordered to be procured from the Record Commission.

Bonds ordered to be prepared to secure the payment of £10 to the Revd. N. Dodson as Afternoon Lecturer at St. Helen's Church, of £8 to the Revd. W. Smith, the then Reader at St. Nicholas Church, and of £15 : 12 : 0 for the Augmentation of the allowances paid to the six Inmates of St. John's Almshouses.

August 9th.

The Council decided that it was expedient to Macadamize the Streets and water the same.

An agreement entered into with the County of Berks for the maintenance of the Borough Prisoners committed to the House of Correction, The Council agreeing to pay such sum as the Prisoners should Individually cost for Diet, Clothing, Fuel, Soap and Candles.

The Borough Seal affixed to a Petition to the Lord Chancellor, praying for the appointment of new Trustees of the Borough Charities.

August 25th.

Thomas Stevens elected Senior Sergeant at Mace and Gaoler.

October 7th.

Claret Cloaks ordered to be supplied to the Sergeants at Mace as theretofore.

The Tolls of Corn let to William Honey, for one year, for £5 : 15 : 0

November 9th.
Charles King,
Mayor.

The Council unanimously resolved to dissent from the proposed line of the Oxford and Great Western Union Railway, into this Borough.

1837.
January 6th.

1837.
February 7th.
Charles King,
Mayor.

𝕿𝖍𝖊 first Borough Rate at 1/- in the £, ordered to be made, the apportionment being as follows, viz. :—

	Rateable Value.			Contribution.		
	£	s.	d.	£	s.	d.
St. Helen within the Borough ...	3767	0	0	188	7	0
St. Nicholas within the Borough ...	826	0	0	41	6	0
Culham within the Borough ...	12	4	0	0	12	2
	£4605	4	0	£230	5	2

𝕷𝖊𝖆𝖛𝖊 given to the Churchwarden of St. Nicholas Church to enclose the space in the Abbey between the Corner of Miss Tombs' premises and the Chancel door of the Church.

April 4th.

𝕿𝖍𝖊 High Constable reported that the Overseers of St. Helen, St. Nicholas, and Culham, had failed to pay their respective proportions of the Borough Rate, and a distress Warrant was ordered to be issued against the goods of the Overseers of St. Helen's Parish, unless the amount due was paid within four days.

April 11th.

𝕿𝖍𝖊 Borough Seal was affixed to a Petition to the House of Lords in opposition to the Oxford and Great Western Union Railway Bill.

April 21st.

𝕿𝖍𝖊 sum of £99 : 2 : 7 was ordered to be paid to the County Treasurer for the maintenance of the Borough Prisoners from the 27th March, 1836, to 24th December, 1836.

May 2nd.

𝕬 Borough Rate at 1/- in the £ was ordered to be made to raise £230 : 5 : 2.

May 22nd.

𝕬𝖓 address was ordered to be presented to H.R.H. the Princess Victoria, congratulating her Highness on having attained the age of 18 years.

𝕴𝖙 was ordered that on the approaching proclamation of Queen Victoria, the usual ceremonies should be observed, namely :—

" 𝕿𝖍𝖆𝖙 the Mayor and Council should proceed in Procession in " their Gowns to a Platform to be erected in the centre of the Bury, " where the Proclamation was to be first read by the Town Clerk ; " From thence to the Sheep Market, where it was to be read on a " Platform a second time ; and from thence to the Knowle, where it " was to be read a third time. That after reading the Proclamation,

"two Barrels of Beer should be distributed on the spot, at each place,
"amongst the Populace. That the Procession should be headed by
"a Band of Music, who were to be paid £1 : 1 : 0, and the Corporation
"Flag. That the Constables should be paid £1 : 1 : 0 for a Treat,
"and the Policemen £1 : 1 : 0. That the Bells should be rung,
"and the Ringers of St. Helen should be paid 15/-, and Saint
"Nicholas 10/6."

𝕿𝖍𝖊 Members and Officers of the Council took the Oaths of
Allegiance, Supremacy, and Abjuration, and then proclaimed the
Queen by the Title of, Victoria, by the Grace of God of Great Britain
and Ireland, Queen, Defender of the Faith ; saving the Rights of any
Issue of his late Majesty, King William IV., which might be born of
his late Majesty's Consort.

June 23rd.

𝕿𝖍𝖊 following Addresses ordered to be presented to Her Majesty
the Queen :—An Address of Condolence to the Queen on the death
of the late King, and also one of Congratulation on Her Majesty's
Accession to the Throne, and also an Address of Condolence to
H.R.H. The Queen Dowager.

July 6th.

𝕬 Quorum of the Council not being present, no business was
transacted.

August 1st.

𝕿𝖍𝖊 Council Chambers ordered to be lighted with Gas.

December 22nd.
John Harris,
Mayor.

𝖂𝖎𝖑𝖑𝖎𝖆𝖒 Honey appointed Inspector of Weights and Measures.

1838
February 15th.

𝕿𝖍𝖊 holding of a Wool Fair sanctioned by the Council, who
agreed to forego all Tolls in respect thereof.

May 2nd.

𝕬𝖓 application from the Vicar and Churchwardens, Abingdon,
for the Council to undertake the repair of the several Fire Engines
in the Town refused, the Council declining to be responsible for any
other Engine than their own.

𝕿𝖍𝖊 Borough Seal of the Council affixed to a Petition to both
Houses of Parliament against the Oxford and Didcot Railway Bill,
with a Branch to Abingdon.

May 28th.

𝕳𝖊𝖗 𝕸𝖆𝖏𝖊𝖘𝖙𝖞'𝖘 𝕮𝖔𝖗𝖔𝖓𝖆𝖙𝖎𝖔𝖓 ordered to be celebrated in
the following manner, viz. :—

1.—By the ringing of the Bells at both Churches, the ringers being
    paid £5 : 5 : 0 for so doing.

2.—A Band to play during the day, the musicians being paid 7/6 each.

3.—1000 Buns to be thrown away from the top of the Market House according to custom.

4.—A Public Dinner in the Council Chamber, at 4 p.m., the price of tickets being 12/6 each, including wine.

Mr. Mark Stone, of Fyfield, claimed and was allowed as a Tenant of St. John's College, an exemption from the payment of Tolls in the Borough.

A Borough Rate at 1/- in the £ ordered to be made to raise £325 : 17 : 0.

An application by the Guardians of the Abingdon Union to be allowed to construct a drain from the Union House to the Stert Ditch refused.

A Committee appointed to draw up a Scheme for the Enfranchising of the Corporation Estates.

Mr. Curtis' Costs for prosecuting John Fisher for obstructing the Court Leet ordered to be paid.

The Town Clerk ordered to write to the Borough and County Members and request them to oppose the Bill for further improving the Police in and near the Metropolis, in compliance with a request to that effect from the Town Clerk of London.

A perambulation of the Bounds of the Borough ordered. The Council, Town Clerk, Treasurer, Coroner, Auditors, and Assessors meeting at 10 a.m., at the Council Chamber, proceeding thence in their Gowns to the Top of the Boar Street. 400 Cakes and 2 Kilderkins of Ale being provided for distribution at the usual places. The ceremony being completed with a dinner at 3.30 p.m., the expense thereof being paid by the parties dining, except the wine, which was ordered to be taken from the Corporation Cellar.

The Race Stand, on Abingdon Common, ordered to be let to Mr. Burden, Clerk of the Course, for the ensuing Races.

A Memorial received from Messrs. James Vasey, William Fletcher, and Joseph Westbrook, for the Burgesses to be allowed to be present at the Quarterly Meeting of the Council, and it was resolved on a division to refuse the application.

𝕬 Claim by Mr. Bernard Ballard, as a Freeman of the City of Oxford to be exempt from the payment of all Tolls in the Borough allowed.

𝕬 Borough Rate at 1/- in the £ ordered to be made to raise £331 : 15 : 0.

November 20th.

𝕬 Meeting of the Council held but no business transacted.

1840.
January 30th.

𝕿𝖍𝖊 Rev. William Allder Strange, M.A., of Liverpool, elected Head Master of Roysse's School, and.Rules made for the management of the School; The hours for commencing School from Lady-day to Michaelmas being 6 a.m., and from Michaelmas to Lady-day 7 a.m.

February 5th.

𝕬 Borough Rate at 1/- in the £ ordered to be made to raise £409 : 5 : 6.

February 14th.

𝕬𝖓 Address ordered to be presented to Her Majesty and to H.R.H. Prince Albert of Saxe Coburg and Gotha, on the occasion of their Marriage.

𝕿𝖍𝖊 Borough Seal is affixed to a Petition to the House of Commons praying for the release of the Sheriffs of Midlesex from the Custody of the Sergeant at Arms.

𝕸𝖗. John Harris, junr., appointed Borough Treasurer.

May 5th.

𝕬 Petition ordered to be presented against the Bill for amending the County Constabulary Force then before Parliament.

𝕻𝖔𝖘𝖘𝖊𝖘𝖘𝖎𝖔𝖓 of the triangular piece of ground at the top of the Vineyard given up to the Council.

May 13th.

𝕿𝖍𝖊 Materials of the old Wootton Turnpike House ordered to be sold to Mr. Graham, and the site added to Fitzharris Farm at an additional rent.

𝕿𝖍𝖊 Cottage adjoining the Race Stand ordered to be let, and the Stand retained for use at the Races.

𝕬𝖉𝖉𝖗𝖊𝖘𝖘𝖊𝖘 ordered to be presented to Her Majesty the Queen, Prince Albert, and the Duchess of Kent, congratulating them upon their escape from the recent attack made upon Her Majesty and His Royal Highness.

June 15th.

𝕬𝖓 application for power to Enfranchise the Corporation Property made to the Lords Commissioners of Her Majesty's Treasury.

𝕬 Borough Rate to raise £205 : 10 : 2, and a Watch Rate to raise £192 . 12 : 2½ at 6d. in the £ respectively, ordered to be made.

September 29th.

1840.
October 16th.
William Doe
Belcher,
Mayor.

A Public Meeting of the Burgesses ordered to be convened to consider the Council's Scheme for the Enfranchisement of the Corporation property, and also a letter which Mr. Sharps had written to the Commissioners opposing the Scheme.

October 30th.

A Public Meeting of the Burgesses held, when it was unanimously resolved to approve of the Scheme propounded by the Council for the Enfranchisement of the Corporation Leasehold Estates, and a Committee appointed to confer with the Council with regard to the carrying out of the Scheme.

November 9th.
John Tomkins,
Mayor.

The Portraits of two of the Kings of England presented to the Council by Mr. George Bowyer.

December 12th.

A Borough Rate at 1/- in the £ ordered to be made to raise £408 : 9 : 6.

An Address of Congratulation ordered to be presented to Her Majesty and H.R.H. Prince Albert on the Birth of the Princess Royal.

The Borough Seal affixed to a Memorial from the Corporation and the Governors of Christ's Hospital to the Lords Commissioners of the Duchy of Cornwall, praying their consent to the Inclosure of Abingdon and Shippon.

1841.
February 10th.

Mr. Thomas Duffield, M.P. for the Borough, requested to introduce a Clause into the Chilton Turnpike Bill, then before Parliament, by which Compensation should be made to the Borough for the Repair of the Streets, which had become important on account of the increased through traffic from Oxford and other places to Steventon Station.

A sum of £5 paid to the Ringers of St. Helen and St. Nicholas Churches for Ringing the Bells on the Birth of the Princess Royal.

The Consent of the Council given to the Inclosure of the Common Fields in Abingdon and Shippon.

May 1st.

The Town Clerk instructed to inform the Inclosure Commissioners that the Council would regret to see the Path leading across Conduit Field from the top of Boar Street by the Lonesome tree to Spring Road stopped up.

May 21st.

A Borough Rate at 1/- in the £ ordered to be made to raise £416 : 19 : 1.

The Race Stand let to Mr. Burden for £2 per annum so long as the Building was used as a Race Stand for the accommodation of the Public, and leave given to the tenant to remove such part of the Cottages adjoining the Stand as he should think fit.

The Picture of the Martyrdom of St. Sebastian attributed to Vandyke or Rubens, presented to the Corporation by Mr. G. Bowyer.

An order made that in future the Mayor receive no Salary, and that he be not required to give any Dinners.

Addresses congratulating Her Majesty the Queen, and H.R.H. Prince Albert, and H.R.H. the Duchess of Kent, on the Birth of the Prince of Wales, ordered to be presented.

A sum of £5 paid the Ringers of St. Helen and St. Nicholas Churches, for ringing at the Christening of H.R.H. the Prince of Wales.

A Borough Rate at 6d. in the £ to raise £206 : 1 : 6, and a Watch Rate for the same amount ordered to be made.

Addresses to Her Majesty the Queen, H.R.H. Prince Albert, and H.R.H. the Duchess of Kent, on the recent attempt to assassinate Her Majesty the Queen.

Mr. Linders resigned his Office of Auditor, and paid the Fine of £10.

A Committee appointed to interview the Secretary of the Great Western Railway Company, with a view to getting the Company to construct their proposed Railway from Oxford to Moulsford nearer to the Town, for the convenience of the Town and Trade of Abingdon.

The Town Clerk reported that he had received a letter from the Secretary of the Great Western Railway Company, stating that there would be a meeting of the Directors at Steventon, and that Mr. Brunel would be present and they would be prepared to receive and confer with a deputation of the Council with reference to the Oxford Line.

A Public Meeting of Burgesses convened by the Mayor was held to consider the propriety of reducing the number of Police, and also of enfranchising the Borough Property, when it was resolved (1) that a meeting of the Leaseholders should be convened to consider the Enfranchisement Scheme; (2) that the Police Force should be reduced to four men.

1842.
October 6th.
Richard
Badcock,
Mayor.

A Meeting of Lessees of the Corporation Estates held when the Enfranchisement Scheme was approved.

October 26th.

The Borough Seal was affixed to the Abingdon Inclosure Award.

November 9th.
John Hyde,
Mayor.

Mr. William Allder Harris resigned the office of Treasurer.

November 25th.

Mr. William Doe Belcher, Mr. John Tomkins, and Mr. John Hyde, recommended to the Secretary of State for appointment as Justices of the Peace for the Borough.

Mr. William Belcher elected Borough Treasurer.

1843.
February 4th.

An application received from the Oxford and Great Western Union Railway for the Council's assent to the construction of a Line of Railway from Oxford to Didcot, with a Branch to Abingdon, but assent was refused by the Council, four members voting in favour of the Scheme, and five against it, while three members did not vote.

February 9th.

The Borough Seal affixed to a Memorial to the Lords Commissioners of Her Majesty's Treasury, praying their Lordships to sanction the Scheme for the Enfranchisement of the Corporation Estates.

April 8th.

Letter received from the Secretary of State, stating that the names of Mr. John Tomkins and Mr. John Hyde, Jun., had been added to the Commission of the Peace for the Borough.

May 11th.

A Borough Rate at 6d. in the £ to raise £207 : 2 : 5 and a Watch Rate for the same amount ordered to be made.

August 15th.

An order made that no further proceedings relative to the Enfranchisement be at present taken by the Council, on account of the expense of giving the requisite information to the Treasury.

November 6th.

A Borough Rate of 1/- in the £ ordered to be made to raise £416 : 6 : 2.

1844.
May 29th.
John Harris,
Mayor.

A Petition presented to the Council against the proposed Macadamizing of the Market Place and High Street, and praying the Council to preserve the existing pebble paving.

July 4th.

Letter received from the Clerk of the Peace for Berks requesting that the Borough Prisoners should be committed to Reading Gaol in consequence of there being Small Pox in the Borough Bridewell.

Mr. William Hedges' tender for repairing the Streets of the Town for a term of 7 years at £80 per annum accepted.

The Justices of the County of Berks raised the question as to their liability to maintain Abingdon Prison in the event of its being unnecessary for County purposes.

A letter received from Mr. Edward Joseph Powell, enclosing a Platinum Medal, and stating that it was the first of its kind issued from the Royal Mint, and that he believed no other attempt had been made in the World to strike a Medal of that metal.

A Vote of thanks given to Lord Abingdon, Thomas Duffield, Esq., late M.P. for Abingdon, William Mount, Esq., Sir Robert George Throckmorton, and other Justices, for their opposition to the attempt made by the County Justices to discontinue the use of the County Bridewell, at Abingdon.

The Toll on Corn ordered to be suspended during the pleasure of the Council, in compliance with a resolution passed at a Meeting of the Inhabitants of the Town held on the 12th inst.

The Assent of the Council given to the Oxford and Salisbury Direct Railway, and also to the Cheltenham, Oxford and London Junction Railway.

A Meeting of the Council held, but no business transacted.

A Communication received from the Royal Agricultural Society of England, stating that the Society would be willing to consider a Memorial from the Authorities of any City or Corporate Town in the Counties of Northampton, Huntingdon, Bedford, Hertford, Oxford, Warwick, Berks, or Buckingham, for the Society to hold their Annual Meeting in their locality, when it was resolved not to send an invitation from Abingdon, it being considered impossible to comply with the various requirements of the Society.

Leave given to Mr. T. Richardson to pull down two Tenements in the Ock Street, and to build a Wesleyan Chapel on the site thereof.

Borough and Watch Rates at 10d. and 5d. in the £ respectively ordered to be made to raise £343 : 11 : 8 and £159 : 4 : 7 respectively.

A Meeting of the Council held but no business transacted.

1846.
December 18th.
Benjamin
Collingwood,
Mayor.

𝔄 Borough Rate at 1/4 in the £ ordered to be made to raise £547 : 12 : 0.

1847.
February 2nd.

𝔄 letter received from the Treasury, enquiring if accommodation could be provided in the Town Hall for holding a County Court, when it was resolved to place the Guildhall or County Hall at the disposal of the Treasury for that purpose, free of rent.

𝔄 Memorial ordered to be presented to H.M. Postmaster General asking for the appointment of two Letter Carriers for the delivery of Letters in the Borough.

August 3rd.

𝔄 Meeting of the Council held but no business transacted, there not being a Quorum of members present.

November 9th.
Charles Payne,
Mayor.

𝔐r. Henry Knapp's Office of Alderman declared vacant, he having been declared Bankrupt.

November 16th.

𝔏eave given to the Clerk of the County Court to place a Stove in the Market House for heating the room on Court days.

December 22nd.

𝔗he payment of 7/6 a year to Mr. Fletcher for Cleaning out the Carswell Stream ordered to be discontinued.

1848.
February 16th.

𝔗he sanction of the Council given to the lowering of the Corporation Pews in St. Helen's Church to the level adopted in the improvements then being carried out in the Church.

𝔄lterations ordered to be made to the County Hall for the better accommodation of the Farmers and Dealers attending the Corn Market.

August 1st.

𝔓ayment ordered to be made of the proportion due from the Borough towards the cost of building and furnishing Litttlemore Lunatic Asylum.

October 20th.

𝔄 new room ordered to be erected adjoining the Police Court, in the Abbey, for the use of the Borough Justices.

𝔄 Resolution in favour of the admission of the Burgesses and gentlemen connected with the Press to the Meetings of the Council proposed but not carried, two members of the Council voting for the motion, and seven against it.

November 9th.
William
Graham,
Mayor.

𝔄 Committee appointed for excusing persons from the payment of rates on account of poverty, reported that 699 persons rated in the Parish of St. Helen and 82 persons in the Parish of St. Nicholas and

Culham assessed to the Borough Rate, and 728 persons in the Parish of St. Helen and 81 in the Parishes of St. Nicholas and Culham assessed to the Watch Rate in 1846, and 734 persons assessed to the Borough Rate in the Parish of St. Helen and 86 persons from the Parishes of St. Nicholas and Culham assessed to the Borough Rate of 1847, should be excused.

1848.
November 9th.
William
Graham,
Mayor.

A Letter read from Mr. George Bowes Morland declining to accept the Office of Mayor on the ground that his frequent absence from home would prevent his discharging efficiently the important duties of the Office, whereupon Mr. William Graham was elected Mayor.

November 18th.

A Resolution passed at a Meeting of Agriculturists, Dealers and Inhabitants of Abingdon, held on the 19th inst., recommending that the lower part of the Market House should be fitted up with Stone and Glass, in unison with the upper part of the House, for the purpose of its being used as a Corn Exchange, was presented to the Council, and also a Memorial signed by owners of premises in the S. and S.W. sides of the Market Place against the proposal, on the ground that it would greatly deteriorate the value of their property, would be a nuisance, and also deface the beauty of the building. On a Division the Council decided to carry out the work suggested in the Resolution, the expense being raised by Public Subscription.

1849.
March 27th.
William
Graham,
Mayor.

The Plan and estimate of Mr. Clacy (County Surveyor) for closing in the lower part of the Market House adopted.

May 28th.

A Watch and Borough Rate at 6d. in the £ respectively ordered to be made to raise £184 : 15 : 6 and £152 : 16 : 4 respectively.

November 23rd.
John Tomkins,
Mayor.

An order made that no Borough or Watch should be ordered for that part of Culham Parish said to be within the Borough until the question of the liability of the Parish had been ascertained.

The Town Clerk instructed to write to the Borough Coroner and inform him that in the opinion of the Council the Inquests on the Cholera Cases ought not to have been held.

1850.
February 5th.

Seven tenements belonging to the Corporation, in Boar Street and Rhubarb Alley, where the Cholera prevailed the previous year, ordered to be pulled down and the materials sold.

May 14th.

The Town Clerk instructed to write to Sir F. Thesiger, M.P., and request him to oppose the Bill then before Parliament for altering the mode of revising the Burgess lists.

1850.
June 21st.
John Tomkins,
Mayor.

The names of Messrs. Thomas Payne and Edwin James Trendell recommended by the Council to the Lord Chancellor for insertion in the Commission of the Peace for the Borough.

A perambulation of the Bounds of the Borough ordered to take place, and 400 Cakes and 2 Kilderkins of Ale to be provided for distribution at the usual places; a Dinner being also provided at 3.30 p.m., at the expense of the parties dining.

August 6th.

The name of Mr. Thomas Payne added to the Commission of the Peace by the Lord Chancellor.

November 9th.
John Hyde,
Mayor.

An address ordered to be presented to the Queen, and a Petition to both Houses of Parliament, on the late agression of the Pope in appointing an Archbishop and Bishops in England, thereby interfering with the Supremacy of the Queen, and the Religious rights and liberties of the Protestants of Great Britain.

1851.
January 4th.

The Borough Seal affixed to the Memorial to the Queen with reference to Papal Aggression.

April 10th.

A Watch and Borough Rate at 5d. in the £ respectively ordered to be made to raise £165 : 9 : 11 and £177 : 0 : 1 respectively.

May 13th.

A Committee appointed to consider the appropriation of the Corporation Seats in St. Helen's Church reported that they did not make any recommendation with regard to the matter, other than that the Sexton be requested to keep sufficient accommodation for the members of the Council.

A notification received from the Lord Chancellor that he proposed to insert the names of Mr. William Stacy and Mr. Thomas Sharps in the Commission of the Peace for the Borough, and the following minute was thereon made, viz.: "The Council having, when "vacancies occurred in the Commission of the Peace, recommended "the names of gentlemen as fit persons to supply such vacancies, "and never having been influenced by Political Motives, feel that "on the present occasion any recommendation for that purpose "ought to have emanated from the Council, and therefore they "respectfully request they may be allowed to recommend some "names for insertion in the Commission."

October 30th.

An Agreement entered into with the Board of Surveyors of St. Helen's Parish to repair those portions of the Streets within the

Borough which were usually repaired by the Town Council for £80 per annum.

1851.
October 30th.
John Hyde,
Mayor.

William Wiltshire ordered to be paid £3 per annum for enclosing the Market House on Mondays.

The Balcony in front of the Council Chamber ordered to be removed, it being in want of considerable repair and not required for any useful purpose.

December 5th.
Edwin James
Trendell,
Mayor.

Superintendent Iremonger appointed Inspector of Common Lodging Houses under the Common Lodging Houses Act, 1851.

1852.
January 17th.

A Memorial received from 62 Dealers and others attending Abingdon Market, praying the Council to discontinue collecting Toll on Pigs offered for Sale therein.

May 4th.

A sum of £150 voted for repairing the Town Hall.

June 17th.

Permission granted to the Committee of Management of the Abingdon Monthly Cattle Market to erect Posts and Rails with Iron Boxes round the Market Place for the purposes of the Market.

A Watch Rate at 5d. in the £ ordered to be made to provide £218 : 15 : 0.

August 3rd.

Mr. Clacy's report upon the condition of the Town Hall received, and the works recommended by him ordered to be carried out, except an alteration of the Cupola, the Mayor having reported that he had collected £700 towards the cost of the work. The principal works recommended by Mr. Clacy being—Windows substituted for Doors to the two centre Window openings on the North Front of the Hall, the same having a very unsightly and unusual appearance; The removal of the Gallery running across the centre of the Hall and also the Cupola from the Roof of the Hall to the Roof of the Tower, as to which Mr. Clacy was of opinion that the Cupola was no part of the original building as designed by Inigo Jones, but that it was added some years afterwards.

October 1st.

Tenders amounting to £1012 : 9 : 4 accepted for repairing the Town Hall.

November 9th.
Edwin James
Trendell,
Mayor.

The opinion of the Recorder ordered to be taken with regard to the Tolls granted under the Charter, and the course to be pursued in recovering any that may be resisted by parties liable for the same.

1853.
May 3rd.

A Watch Rate at the rate of 5d. in the £ to provide £181 : 0 : 0 ordered to be made.

The Pay of the Police Constables increased from 13/- to 15/- per week, and that of the Superintendent from 30/- to 31/6 per week.

Mr. James Walters tender of £113 accepted for altering the Town Hall, including the decoration of the Ceiling by dividing it into deeply recessed panels, as recommended by Mr. Clacy.

A Scale of Market Tolls settled and adopted by the Council.

A Watch Rate at 5d. in the £ to provide £103 : 0 : 0 ordered to be made.

A Notice ordered to be sent to the Home Office intimating that the Council intended to take upon itself the Duties imposed upon the Justices of the Borough under the Lunatic Asylums Act, 1853.

The Borough Seal affixed to a Petition to the House of Commons against the centralization of the Police as contemplated in a report of a Committee of that House.

Letter received from Mr. Sharps complaining that the Minute Books of the Council did not supply the Burgesses with the information the Municipal Act intended should be recorded therein, and asking to be allowed to be present at the next Council Meeting, and the Town Clerk ordered to reply that the Council could not grant his request.

Mr. Edwin Payne gave notice that he should move at the next Meeting of the Council that no further Leases of the Corporate property be renewed until the Council had considered the question, and decided on the future mode of Leasing.

A Resolution rescinding an order made by the Council on the 28th October, 1836, with reference to renewing Leases of Corporation Property upon the same terms as had been theretofore granted, carried on a division.

The Finance Committee reported that the expenditure on the Town Hall had amounted to £1051 : 8 : 11 and that Mr. Trendell, the late Mayor, had collected £1107 to defray the same.

The motion of Mr. Edwin Payne with reference to the non-renewal of the Corporation Leases carried unanimously.

On the motion of the Mayor, it was unanimously resolved to allow the Burgesses to be present during the deliberations of the Council.

1854.
May 2nd.
William Doe
Belcher,
Mayor.

The Borough Seal affixed to a Petition to the House of Commons against the Police Bill, the Petition stating that the Council regarded the Bill as an unconstitutional interference with the Privileges of the Boroughs and subversive of the independence and right of self-government recently secured to them by the Municipal Corporations Reform Act, as it practically placed the entire control of the Police of the Kingdom in the hands of the Home Secretary, thereby forming a basis for a system of Espionage un-English in its character and dangerous to the liberty of the subject.

June 17th.

Letter received from Lord Norreys, M.P., stating that Lord Palmerston had abandoned his Police Bill.

August 1st.

The Right Honourable Montagu, Earl of Abingdon, elected High Steward of the Borough in the place of his late Father.

November 6th.

A Borough Rate at 10d. in the £ to provide £470 : 16 : 6 ordered to be made.

The Assent of the Council unanimously given to the Scheme for constructing a Line of Railway from the Oxford Branch of the Great Western Railway to Abingdon.

1855.
January 5th.
John Tomkins,
Mayor.

A Committee appointed to determine with two Justices of the County of Berks the proportion to be contributed by the Borough under the Militia Law Amendment Act, 1854.

The Resolution passed by the Council on the preceeding 2nd May, with reference to the non-renewal of Corporation Leases rescinded on a division, Leases being ordered to be granted in future as usual.

February 7th.

A Protest made by Mr. Edwin Payne against the renewal of Corporation Leases as theretofore, because on such terms Borough Rates would still have to be levied.

November 6th.

A Watch Rate at 5d. in the £ to provide £200 : 14 : 7 ordered to be made.

1856.
January 8th.
William Doe
Belcher,
Mayor.

The Borough Seal affixed to the Conveyance of Property in Stert Street sold by the Council to the Abingdon Railway Company.

February 5th.

The Borough Seal affixed to a Petition against the Police Bill then before Parliament.

February 25th.

$\mathfrak{M}$r. Bromley Challenor moved a resolution calling the attention of the Secretary of State to the loss sustained by the non-collection of Borough and Watch Rates from Tenements, and requesting him to bring in a Bill to extend the provisions of The Small Tenements Rating Act to the said Rates. The resolution was passed by the Council on a division.

$\mathfrak{A}$ Borough Rate at 9d. in the £ to provide £424 : 2 : 0 ordered to be made.

$\mathfrak{A}$n Address of Congratulation ordered to be presented to Her Majesty the Queen on the Conclusion of Peace between this Country and Russia.

$\mathfrak{M}$r. John Tomkins elected Mayor in the place of Mr. William Doe Belcher, deceased.

$\mathfrak{A}$ Subscription of £20 voted out of the Sealing Fee Fund towards providing a Dinner to the Poor in celebration of the Peace.

$\mathfrak{A}$ Committee appointed to enquire into and to report upon the right of the Borough Justices to commit Prisoners to the County Gaol at Abingdon.

$\mathfrak{A}$lfred Rawlins, Superintendent of the Borough Police, appointed Sanitary Inspector for the Borough under the Nuisance Removal, &c., Act, 1855.

$\mathfrak{A}$ Watch Rate at 5d. in the £ to provide £191 : 3 : 6 ordered to be made.

$\mathfrak{N}$otice ordered to be given to the Board of Guardians of the Abingdon Union to discontinue the flow of sewage from the Union House over the Land which Mr. Graham rented of the Corporation.

$\mathfrak{A}$ Sergeant of Police, with a Salary of 19/- per week, appointed by the Watch Committee.

$\mathfrak{T}$wo new Cells ordered to be built at the Borough Police Station in compliance with a suggestion made by Her Majesty's Inspector of Constabulary, he having reported the existing Cells to be totally unfit for the detention of Prisoners.

$\mathfrak{T}$he Resolutions passed at the Berks Quarter Sessions on the 6th April, 1857, with reference to the Committal of Borough Prisoners to Abingdon Gaol, and offering to refer the matter in dispute to

Arbitration, were considered by the Council, and an order made that the Recorder should be invited to attend the next Meeting of the Council for the purpose of discussing the suggestions of the County Justices.

The proposal of the County Justices to refer the meaning of the Agreement between the County of Berks and the Borough of Abingdon with reference to Abingdon Gaol to Arbitration, accepted by the Council, and an order given to the Town Clerk to confer with the Clerk of the Peace as to the appointment of a Barrister to determine what were the respective rights of the County of Berks and the Borough under the Agreement.

Mr. William Whateley, Q.C., appointed Arbitrator to settle the matter in difference between the County of Berks and the Borough of Abingdon with reference to Abingdon Gaol.

A Borough Rate at 9d. in the £ to provide £419 : 13 : 3 ordered to be made.

The Borough Seal affixed to the submission to Arbitration of the dispute between the Corporation and the County Justices with reference to Abingdon Gaol.

A Memorial signed by William Keal Tiptaft and ten other persons requesting the Council to provide a suitable place for the Burial of the Dead received, and the Town Clerk ordered to refer the Memorialists to the Statute 15 and 16 Victoria, C. 85, s. 10, with the view of the Memorialists adopting the procedure under that Act.

The Award of the Arbitrator with reference to Abingdon Gaol received. The Arbitrator finding—

1—That the Borough Justices had a right to commit prisoners to Abingdon Gaol.

2—That the Corporation were liable to contribute, in addition to the costs of maintenance of prisoners, a proportion of the Salaries of the Matron and other Officers of the said Gaol, except that of the Governor.

3—That the Corporation were not entitled to share in the nomination of the Governor of the Gaol, nor liable to contribute anything towards his Salary.

II

1853.
February 4th.
William
Ballard,
Mayor.
A Watch Rate at 5d. in the £ to provide £195 : 7 : 9 ordered to be made.

May 13th.

A report received from the Nuisance Committee with reference to the condition of the Ditches on the North and South sides of the Ock Street, the former being reported to be in a state dangerous to health.

A resolution in favour of all recommendations for the appointment of new Magistrates being made through the Council carried unanimously by the Council, and a Petition also ordered to be presented to the House of Commons in favour of a reform of the present mode of appointing Borough Justices.

August 12th.

A Letter received from the Deputy Military Storekeeper of the Royal Arsenal asking for instructions as to the best method of forwarding to Abingdon the Russian Gun and its Carriage, both of which were ready for delivery, and the Town Clerk ordered to request that the Gun and Carriage might be forwarded to Abingdon forthwith, the expense of their conveyance being paid out of the Sealing Fee Fund.

November 9th.

A Borough Rate at 9d. in the £ to provide £410 : 4 : 3 ordered to be made.

The Russian Gun ordered to be placed in front of the old entrance to the Police Station.

November 9th.
Edwin James
Trendell,
Mayor.

The sum of £16 ordered to be repaid to the late Mayor, being the amount he had expended in connection with the Russian Gun.

1859.
February 1st.

A Letter received from Mr. Merry, Chairman of the County Visiting Justices Committee, stating that the Berks Court of Quarter Sessions had resolved that the County Gaol at Abingdon, had become unnecessary, and suggesting several propositions for the consideration of the Council with regard to the reception of the Borough Prisoners into Reading Prison; when it was ordered that the Letter should be considered at the next meeting of the Council.

February 8th.

Mr. Merry's Letter considered, and the Town Clerk ordered to acknowledge same, and inform Mr. Merry that the Council having

1859.
February 8th.
Edwin James
Trendell,
Mayor.

submitted to the Award recently made, the further consideration of his letter was deferred to the next Quarterly Meeting of the Council.

The Portrait of Lord Colchester in his Robes as Speaker of the House of Commons presented to the Corporation by the Rev. Herbert Randolph, Vicar of Marcham.

A Watch Rate at 5d. in the £ to provide £192 : 11 : 4 ordered to be made. April 19th.

The consideration of the question of enfranchising the Corporation Property again considered, and adjourned until the next meeting of the Council.

A Quarterly Meeting convened, but neither the Mayor or any other Member of the Council attended. May 3rd.

Mr. Merry's Letter with reference to Abingdon Gaol further considered, and the Council resolved that having recently agreed to an Arbitration in the belief that the Abingdon Gaol was to be permanent, they did not deem it right to deviate from that Arbitration, and therefore they would take such legal or equitable means as they might be advised to prevent the demolition of the Gaol, and directed a copy of the resolution to be forwarded to Mr. Merry and the Clerk of the Peace for the County. May 11th.

A Committee of the whole Council appointed to consider Mr. Payne's motion that it was desirable to take into consideration the propriety of Enfranchising the Corporation property.

The Report of the Committee appointed to consider the question of the Enfranchisement of the Borough property received, and the following recommendations of the Committee adopted, viz.:— June 7th.

1.—That the Council recognised it as just that each Lessee be entitled to a twenty-one years' Lease.

2.—That the Council recognised it as equitable that each Lessee be also entitled to half the value that laid between a twenty-one years' Lease and a perpetual Renewal of his Lease.

3.—That the value remaining to the Lessors be commuted on each Lease and charged as an Annual payment on each enfranchised property at   per cent.

1859.
June 7th.
Edwin James
Trendell,
Mayor.

The Seal of the Borough affixed to a Memorial to the Lords Commissioners of Her Majesty's Treasury praying their Lordships to sanction a general enfranchisement of the Corporation property upon the above principles.

July 8th.

A vote of thanks given to Mr. J. T. Norris, M.P., for having seen Sir G. C. Lewis, the Home Secretary, with reference to the dispute between the County of Berks and the Borough of Abingdon with reference to Abingdon Gaol.

August 2nd.

A sum of £15 voted towards re-pitching the Market Place.

November 9th.
Edwin James
Trendell,
Mayor.

An order made on a Memorial from the Board of Surveyors of St. Helen's Parish increasing the annual payment of £70 to £80 towards the repair of the Roads in the Borough, in consequence of the damage done to the same by the introduction of Water Carts.

November 25th.

A Deputation appointed to wait on the Lords Commissioners of Her Majesty's Treasury with reference to the enfranchisement of the Corporation property.

December 30th.

The Act for regulating Measures on Sales of Gas (22 and 23 Vic. C. 66) adopted by the Council.

1860.
February 7th.

Copies of the Cases submitted to Counsel by the County of Berks with reference to Abingdon Gaol, and the opinions thereon, ordered to be entered on the Minutes of the Council.

A Memorial ordered to be presented to the Lords Commissioners of Her Majesty's Treasury for their approbation to the borrowing by the Council on Mortgage of the Corporation property, a sum sufficient to pay the expense of a valuation of the property with the view to its enfranchisement.

A Petition ordered to be presented to Parliament in favour of an Amendment of the late Gas Act, exempting this and other Boroughs having less than 10,000 inhabitants from its operation, on the ground of the expense which would have to be incurred if the provisions of the Act were carried out.

May 1st.

A Watch Rate at 7d. in the £ to provide £275 : 15 : 1 ordered to be made.

The following returns prepared for the Treasury shewing the average Income and Expenditure of the Corporation for a period of 14 years:—

1860.
May 1st.
Edwin James
Trendell,
Mayor.

Income.

	£	s.	d.
Repayments by Treasury from Prosecutions ...	122	0	9
Quit rents reserved in Leases ...	385	9	8
Fines on Renewal of Leases ...	297	14	7
Borough and Watch Rates ...	274	12	9
Interest on proceeds of Sale of Land for Railway ...	15	8	10
Chief Rents - ...	22	14	6
Freeland Rents ...	7	16	11
Rent of Tolls ...	28	9	8
Other fees ...	69	17	8
Total	£1224	5	4

Expenditure.

	£	s.	d.
Salaries ...	224	8	10
Rents, Rates and Taxes	28	9	8
Fee Farm Rent ...	82	10	7
Charities ...	47	14	5
Police ...	233	11	6
Prosecutions and Maintenance of Prisoners	206	13	9
Public Works and Repairs ...	172	4	9
Inquests ...	27	4	9
Printing and Stationery	16	17	1
Miscellaneous ...	74	0	0
Total	£1113	15	4

A meeting of the Lessees of the Corporation Estates ordered to be held to consider the question of Enfranchisement, and to ascertain whether they would furnish the sum required for a Survey and Valuation of the Corporation property.

July 20th.

On the recommendation of the Watch Committee $2\frac{1}{2}\%$ was ordered to be deducted from the pay of each Police Constable to form a Superannuation Fund. The amount so deducted being deposited in the Abingdon Savings Bank.

August 7th.

The Council resolved to agree to the Enfranchisement of the Corporation Estates upon the terms sanctioned by the Treasury.

October 26th.

An order made that the Corporation Estates should be valued for the purpose of the proposed Enfranchisement, and that a guarantee be given to the Treasury for the expenses of the necessary Survey and Valuations in connection therewith.

November 9th.
Edwin Payne,
Mayor.

𝕿𝖍𝖊 offices of Junior Sergeant at Mace and Bellman were ordered to be filled by one person, and George Payne was elected to the combined offices.

𝕬 Watch Rate at 7d. in the £ to provide £273 : 7 : 9 ordered to be made.

𝕿𝖍𝖊 Borough Seal affixed to an address to Her Majesty the Queen on the occasion of the Death of Her Majesty's Mother H.R.H. the Duchess of Kent.

𝕬 letter received from the Lord Mayor of London with reference to the Famine then existing in the North Western Provinces and other parts of India, when the Mayor was requested to reply that the Council considered it was more a matter of assistance from the Government in which all classes of Her Majesty's subjects subject to Taxation would share, than one of private subscriptions.

𝕿𝖜𝖔 members of the Council appointed to confer with the Captain of the Abingdon Volunteer Rifle Corps with the view to making arrangements for the removal of the Gunpowder deposited in the Market House, as the Council considered it endangered the safety of the Buildings and the Inhabitants in its vicinity.

𝕿𝖍𝖊 Copies of the Imperial Standard Weights and Measures belonging to the Borough ordered to be compared and reverified by the Comptroller General of the Exchequer.

𝕬 Communication ordered to be made between the Guildhall and the Little Council Chamber for the Convenience of the Magistrates when they wished to retire to the latter for consultation.

𝕿𝖍𝖊 piece of ground at the top of the Vineyard ordered to be enclosed with Iron Palings with a gate therein for entrance.

𝕿𝖍𝖊 Mayor reported to the Council that he had had an interview with a Committee of the Berks Magistrates respecting the Berks Militia being quartered in Abingdon, and the conversion of a portion of the County Gaol, at Abingdon, into a Depôt or Barracks for the use of the Militia, "but the Council not having any definite "proposition in writing before them postponed the consideration of "the subject for the present."

𝔄𝔫 application made to the Privy Council for an order empowering the Council to adopt the provisions of the Nuisances Removal and Diseases Prevention Act, 23 and 24 Vict. Cap. 77, provided the Borough was exonerated from contributing to the Common Fund of the Abingdon Union in the event of the Guardians adopting the Act.

1861.
November 9th.
John Hyde, Jun.
Mayor.

𝔄𝔫 address of Condolence presented to Her Majesty the Queen on the death of H.R.H. the Prince Consort.

December 21st.

𝔗𝔥𝔢 Borough Seal affixed to a Memorial to the House of Commons, in favour of a reduction of the Duty on Fire Insurances.

1862.
January 8th.

𝔄 Borough Rate at 9d. in the £ to provide £421 : 19 : 0 ordered to be made.

February 6th.

𝔗𝔥𝔢 inclosure permitted to be made in front of the Independent Chapel ordered to be let to the Trustees of the Chapel as Tenants from year to year, at a rent of 1/- per annum, subject to a three months' notice to quit.

𝔄 Letter received from the Office of Woods, &c., stating that Mr. Clutton had completed his Report and Valuation of the property of the Corporation proposed to be enfranchised, and that the same would be forwarded to the Council on payment of his charges amounting to £699 : 0 : 0, and it was resolved to pay such claim, the Mayor being empowered to borrow the money required; each member of the Council being responsible for his share of the said sum by signing a Promissory Note for its re-payment to the London and County Bank, or to any other person who should advance the same.

March 6th.

𝔗𝔥𝔢 formal assent of the Treasury to the enfranchisement of the Corporation property received, subject to the proceeds of the enfranchisements being invested in the manner directed by the Municipal Corporations Mortgages Act, 1860, until opportunities arose for investing them in Real Estate.

April 23rd.

𝔄 Memorial received from Lessees of the Corporation estates praying the Council to obtain a reduction in the terms proposed in Mr. Clutton's Report for enfranchising this property, and a Deputation appointed to wait upon the Treasury with the Memorial and endeavour to obtain a reduction in the terms.

July 4th.

𝔗𝔥𝔢 Deputation appointed on the 4th July reported that they had had an interview with the Treasury, and that the Commissioners

July 22nd.

stated they would be prepared to consider any representation respecting the value of the Corporation Property which the Council thought proper to send by way of a Memorial, and a Memorial was ordered to be prepared accordingly.

August 7th.

The terms of the representation to be made to the Treasury with reference to the reduction of the terms for enfranchising the Corporation Property were approved, it being suggested that a reduction of 15% should be made on the Reversionary value of each property as an inducement to the whole of the Lessees to liberate the property from Leasehold evils, and also provide an income for Municipal purposes, and that persons not enfranchising should have a fresh lease for 21 years granted from Lady-day, 1862, so that they might be placed on an equality with those Lessees whose Leases would be allowed to run out.

August 28th.

A Letter received from the Treasury stating that their Lordships would consent to a reduction of 10% from the prices set out in Mr. Clutton's Valuation on that part of the Corporation estate which consisted of House property, but declined to make any alteration where the property consisted of Land.

October 21st.

The terms upon which the Treasury were willing to sanction the Enfranchisement of the Corporation Property finally accepted by the Council.

The Town Clerk instructed to apply to the Owner of the Fee Farm Rent of £82 : 10 : 7, and ascertain upon what terms he would be willing to sell the same to the Corporation, so that the Corporation property might be conveyed free from incumbrances.

A Letter received from Mr. G. B. Morland suggesting that the Council when enfranchising their property should reserve to themselves the power to re-acquire, on fair terms, any property they might wish to acquire for Town Improvements.

November 10th.
Richard
Badcock,
Mayor.

A Letter received from the Agent for the Owner of the Fee Farm Rent declining to sell the same to the Corporation.

The names of Mr. Richard Badcock and Mr. Edwin Payne recommended by the Council to the Lord Chancellor for insertion in the Commission of the Peace for the Borough.

𝔄 Watch Rate at 7d. in the £ to provide £269 : 13 : 0 ordered to be made.

𝔓ermission given for the erection of Iron Railings in front of the Independent Chapel, in the Ock Street, provided the Owners of the adjoining properties did not object.

𝔗he Ex-Mayor produced the following letter which he had received from the late George Granville Harcourt, Esq., of Nuneham Park :—

"Strawberry Hill,
"Novr. 21, 1861.

"Sir,

"We are only just returned to England from Italy, "towards which we went in the middle of last August, and I take "an early opportunity of assuring you of the pleasure with which I "have received through you and Mr. Trendell the communication "from the Town Council of their satisfaction with the facilities which "I have afforded to the inhabitants of Abingdon for visiting the "grounds at Nuneham. I should, in truth, not think it worth while "to incur a large expense in providing for their good order if they "contributed only for a few weeks towards the end of the summer "to the enjoyment of my family and personal friends, but I have "always considered it almost a duty for those who have large "residences to consult the gratification of their neighbours, and "to allow as free access as is consistent with convenience. It gives "me much pleasure to see my gardens and Park enlivened by the "resort of those who think it worth while to come there.

"Yrs. faithfully,
"G. Harcourt."

"Ed. Payne, Esqr., Abingdon."

𝔄 Vote of thanks given to Mr. Alderman Trendell for the pains he had taken to ornament the Public Buildings of the Borough, and for the Portraits he had been the means of presenting to the Town for the decoration of the Council Chamber.

𝔄 Letter read from the Clerk of the Peace for Berks, enquiring if the Council would be prepared to treat with the County for the sale of their interest in the County Prison at Abingdon, for the purpose of a Militia Depôt, as the building had for some years not been absolutely necessary to the County for gaol purposes, and the erection of New Courts, at Reading, would probably make it expedient to hold the Sessions and Assizes at Reading exclusively, and the Town Clerk was ordered to reply that in the interests of the Borough the Council were not inclined to negociate for the sale of their interest in Abingdon Prison.

Ten Guineas ordered to be paid out of the Sealing Fee Fund as a Subscription to the Fund then being raised by the Lord Mayor of London for a Memorial to H.R.H. the late Prince Consort.

The Reformatory Schools Act 20 and 21 Vict. Cap. 55, adopted by the Council, and a Committee appointed to enter into an agreement with the Managers of a Reformatory School for the reception of offenders from the Borough.

February 5th.

The Council adopted a report of the Standing Committee to the effect that it was desirable to act upon the suggestion contained in Mr. Morland's letter to the Council of the 21st October, 1862, in respect (1) of the House at the Corner of Vineyard and the Stert; (2) the House at the Corner of Bath Street and Broad Street; (3) the House known as the Paul's Head, in Bath Street, for the purpose of improving the entrance to the Recreation Ground; (4) the House known as Two Brewers Public House, adjoining St. Nicholas Church; (5) Mr. W. Smith's House, in the Narrow, so as to widen the pavement there.

The Committee also reported that they considered the School premises and the Houses in Bridge Street abutting on the same would be an appropriate place for a Corn Exchange, and recommended that a Committee of the Corporation should be appointed to meet a Committee of the Master and Governors of Christ's Hospital for carrying out the suggestion in view of the contemplated removal of the School to Conduit Field.

The Committee also recommended that a Representation should be made to H.M. Postmaster General requesting him to provide a more convenient Post Office, the existing Office being in an inconvenient locality, and quite inadequate to the requirements of the Town.

March 27th.

A Subscription of £25 voted from the Sealing Fee Fund towards celebrating the Marriage of H.R.H. the Prince of Wales.

The Standing Committee ordered to prepare and submit to the Master and Governors of Christ's Hospital a plan of the School Yard shewing its adaptation for a Corn Exchange.

Addresses of congratulation prepared for presentation to Her Majesty the Queen and their Royal Highnesses the Prince and Princess of Wales, on the occasion of the Marriage of the latter.

A Letter recived from the Postmaster General stating that the Post Office, at Abingdon, was not provided by the Department, but by the Postmaster, and that under the existing circumstances he did not consider it expedient to call upon him to incur expense in providing other accommodation.

A Watch Rate at 7d. in the £ to provide £266 : 1 : 0 ordered to be made.

May 7th.

The Mayor reported that the Deputation consisting of the Mayor and Aldermen Hyde, Payne, and Ballard, appointed to present the Address to their Royal Highnesses the Prince and Princess of Wales, had attended at Marlborough House, and presented the Address, which was most graciously received by their Royal Highnesses.

The Borough Seal affixed to a Petition to the House of Commons against the proposed amalgamation of the City and Metropolitan Police Forces.

June 12th.

Mr. William Smith's refusal to sell any portion of his property in the Narrow, for widening the Street there, reported to the Council.

A hot plate and cooking apparatus ordered to be fixed in the Corporation Kitchen at a cost of £16 : 10 : 0.

August 6th.

A Letter received from the Treasury with reference to a proposal for the enfranchisement of the Wesleyan Methodist Chapel upon the condition of the payment of an Annual Rent Charge, stating that in the opinion of the Commissioners a Building used as a Chapel did not afford good permanent security for a Rent Charge, and also might be applicable to other purposes than of a Religious or Charitable institution, and suggesting that if the Trustees were not able to avail themselves of the enfranchisement proposed, the Lease should be allowed to run its course, upon the understanding that the Council would renew same at the expiration thereof.

An offer received from the owner of the Two Brewers Public House, to sell the Lessee's interest for £450, for the purpose of widening Stert Street.

A Map shewing the boundaries of the Borough ordered to be made for the use of the Borough Justices.

An estimate for covering the Cupola of the Market House with 16oz. Copper, and for refixing and repairing the Vane, amounting to £42 : 10 : 0, accepted by the Council.

Addresses ordered to be presented to Her Majesty The Queen and their Royal Highnesses the Prince and Princess of Wales on the occasion of the Birth of H.R.H. Prince Albert Victor of Wales.

Negociations resolved to be entered into with the Paving Commissioners and Burial Board for the transfer of the sums due on their respective Securities to the Corporation.

A sum of £20 voted towards the expense of establishing Telegraphic communication in the Borough.

A Committee appointed to take such steps as they should think proper with respect to the removal of the County Quarter Sessions from Abingdon to Reading.

The enfranchisement of the Wesleyan Methodist Chapel sanctioned on payment of one half of Messrs. Clutton's Valuation, after deducting the 10% allowed in other cases.

Mr. Charles Hemming, M.D., appointed Borough Coroner.

The Council resolved to accept Mortgages from Lessees for the amount of their enfranchisement moneys, with interest at the rate of £4% per annum.

The Council decided to take over the Mortgage of £3090 raised by the Burial Board from the Public Works Loan Commissioners.

Mr. Charles Lawrence Cox refused to accept the Office of Assessor to which he had been elected on the 1st March last, and appealed to be excused from the payment of the Fine of £10 which he had incurred in consequence of such refusal. His application was, however, refused, and a warrant for levying the same by distress was ordered to be applied for.

1864.
May 20th.
Bromley
Challenor,
Mayor.

A sum of £75 voted in response to a Memorial received from the Minister, Deacons, and others connected with the Independent Chapel, in Ock Street, praying the Council to contribute towards the expense of pulling down the Three Cottages which had been closed by the Justices as a nuisance, and then standing in front of the New Chapel; The Memorialists suggesting that the pulling down of the Cottages and widening of the Public Footway and bringing into prominent view the New Chapel would be a great public improvement to the Town.

The question of purchasing the House in the Market Place, adjoining the late Queen's Arms, for the purpose of widening Bury Street, and the Lamb and Flag Public House, at the corner of Stert Street and Vineyard, was discussed, and referrred to the Finance Committee for consideration.

A sum of £100 voted for the purchase of a piece of land 50ft. in length and 18ft. in breadth, belonging to Christ's Hospital, and forming part of the site of the late Mr. Hyde's premises, fronting St. Helen's Church, at the junction of West and East St. Helen Streets, and also £150 for the purchase of eight Cottages on the River Bank in Thames Street, belonging to Christ's Hospital, in order that the same might be pulled down.

A Committee appointed to take steps to oppose the Bill then before Parliament for amending the Law relating to Gaols, and for the discontinuance of certain Gaols, including Abingdon, with instructions to wait upon Sir George Grey, the Home Secretary, with regard thereto.

The Finance Committee instructed to confer with the Borough Justices as to altering the Police Courts for the more convenient administration of Justice, and also to inspect the Tenement Property between Broad Street and the late Queen's Arms Inn, with a view to any improvement that might be suggested in that locality, and to report thereon to the Council.

July 14th.

The block of Buildings at the Corner of the Otwell Lane agreed to be purchased for £400, and also the House at the Corner of Bury Lane and the Market Place, next the Queen's Hotel, for a similar sum.

August 4th.

The Gaols Bill reported to the Council as having been withdrawn, and the Case of the Borough in opposition to the Bill was ordered

1861.
August 11th.
Bromley
Challenor,
Mayor.

to be entered on the Minutes and a vote of thanks given to Mr. J. T. Norris, M.P., for the assistance he had rendered in the matter.

The houses recently purchased by the Council in the Market Place, Thames Street, and Otwell Lane, ordered to be pulled down for the Improvement of the Town, and the Materials sold by Auction.

A sum of £50 voted to defray the expense of establishing the Telegraph in the Town.

Votes of thanks given to the Right Honourable the Earl of Abingdon and Sir George Bowyer, Bart., for the interest they had taken in opposing the late Gaols Bill.

September 6th.

The Standing Committee directed to construct the Culvert of the Stert Drain further into the River to prevent the Nuisance then existing at the end of the Drain, and also to straighten the River Wall, and to make steps down to the River.

November 9th.
Charles Payne,
Mayor.

The sum paid to the Board of Surveyors for repairing the Roads in the Town ordered to be increased from £80 to £100 per annum.

A Communication received from the Chairman of the Trustees of Roysse's Charity, suggesting that the Council should make a Grant from the Borough Fund towards the cost of removing the School from its then site to a new site in Conduit Field, the existing School premises being too small for the effectual instruction of so large a number of Scholars as were then attending the School.

A Letter received from the Revd. N. Dodson, M.A., Vicar of Abingdon, asking the Council to make a grant out of the Corporation Funds towards the erection of a New Church in the Ock Street, and the Town Clerk instructed to reply that the Council could not entertain the application, as the Municipal Corporations Reform Act did not sanction the appropriation of the surplus Borough Fund for such a purpose.

In consequence of the resignation of Mr. Shepherd, the Postmaster, the Mayor was instructed to communicate again with the Postmaster General with reference to the provisions of better Postal accommodation at Abingdon.

November 25th.

Mr. Alfred Durling Bartlett elected Borough Treasurer.

A Letter received from the Secretary of the General Post Office stating that when a new Postmaster was appointed care would be taken that he was required to provide a suitable and commodious Office both for the performance of the Service and for the convenience of the Public.

A Letter received from Mr. J. Smith, the new Postmaster, asking the Council to contribute £15 or £20 towards the Rent of a House for the Post Office. The Council, however, declined to entertain the application, but instructed the Town Clerk to write to the Postmaster General, and state that in the opinion of the Council the then Salary of the Postmaster was inadequate to the duties of his Office, and also to Mr. Norris, M.P., requesting him to use his interest for obtaining an increase of Salary for the Postmaster.

The Finance and Standing Committee ordered to carry out in conjuction with the Borough Justices the proposed alterations in the Guildhall for the Police Courts.

The Award fixing the proportion to be contributed by the Borough to the Expenditure incurred under the Militia Acts received and ordered to be deposited in the Corporation Chest.

Mr. Galpin, Surveyor, of Oxford, instructed to survey and report upon the cost of lowering the centre portion of the Market Place, and the formation of a carriage road round same with a communication into Bury Lane.

A Letter read from the Secretary of the General Post Office stating that the new Postmaster was willing to accept the appointment for the emoluments which were attached to it, and to which some addition had recently been made, and that the situation of the Postmaster's premises was considered to be fairly convenient, being within a few yards of the Market Place.

The Borough Seal affixed to a Petition against the Cheltenham Waterworks Bill.

A Committee appointed to examine the Old Deeds and Documents stored in the room called the Town Clerk's Office, with instructions to destroy such as were useless, and to remove the rest, properly labelled, to the upper part of the Market House.

Otwell Lane ordered to be widened to a breadth of about 30 feet, and £100 paid to Mr. Winterborne for taking down a Blacksmith's Shop belonging to him in Otwell Lane, and setting back the Street line of his premises in that Lane.

A sum of £130 ordered to be expended in constructing a Road from the Paul's Head Public House, in Bath Street, to the Conduit.

The Borough Seal affixed to a Petition to the House of Commons for the improvement of the River Thames, and ordered to be sent to Mr. Malins, M.P. for Wallingford, for presentation.

A Lamp ordered to be placed over the new Post Office at the expense of the Corporation.

A Tender of £214 : 4 : 0 for repitching the Market Place and forming a Roadway round the same accepted by the Council.

The Committee appointed to examine the Old Deeds and Documents reported that they had devoted seven hours to the examination of the Deeds and Old Papers, and had found much that had been stored away by the late Mr. Sellwood to be quite valueless, these they destroyed, but all valuable or interesting Deeds and Papers they had placed either in the Town Hall or Council Chamber, and that at a second meeting they had concluded their examination by a view of the Charters, Bonds, &c., in the Chest in the Council Chamber. The Committee assured the Council that they had taken pains to carry out the expressed desire of the Council.

The Watch Committee reported that H.M. Inspector of Constabulary had complained of the unfitness of the Cells for use, and stated that unless they were improved he feared the Government Grant would not be continued.

A Letter received from the Master and Governors of Christ's Hospital accepting the offer of the Council with regard to the Construction of a Road from the Paul's Head, in Bath Street, to the Conduit, on the understanding that the Road should remain Private, like that through Conduit Field, until the whole length from Spring Road to the Boar Street could be properly dedicated to the Public.

A Committee appointed to prepare Plans for building a House for the Senior Sergeant at Mace, and also one for the Chief Officer of Police, with the necessary Police Offices and Cells.

𝔓lans for the erection of Houses for the Senior Sergeant at Mace and Inspector of Police, with Police Offices and Cells, approved by the Council.

𝔗he Mayor reported that the Master and Governors of Christ's Hospital had agreed to erect a Bar gate across the new Road in Bath Street, instead of a line of posts as originally proposed by them, and also a similar gate by Tomkins' Almshouses, which would be left open during the day for Horse Traffic and Private Carriages, but closed to Carts and Waggons, and which would also be occasionally closed altogether, to prevent any Public right being acquired until proper steps had been taken for making the Road a Public Highway.

𝔗he Council's assent given to an exchange with Mrs. Mundy of a piece of land in East St. Helen Street for a piece of land in the same Street belonging to the Corporation.

𝔄 piece of Surplus Land, in Broad Street, next Otwell Lane, sold to Mr. E. H. Morland for £30, Mr. Morland agreeing to pay the whole of the Land Tax on the Property.

𝔐r. Thomas' Tender of £1456 for the erection of the Houses for the Senior Sergeant at Mace and Inspector of Police accepted.

𝔄 Tender of £22 : 10 : 0 accepted for re-pitching Bury Lane with Pebbles and constructing a stone gutter and path.

𝔄 Deputation appointed by the Council, consisting of the late Mayor (Mr. Bromley Challenor), Aldermen Hyde and Ballard, and Councillors R. Badcock and J. C. Clarke, The Town Clerk, Col. The Hon. C. H. Lindsay, M.P., and Sir Geo. Bowyer, Bart., reported that on the 17th instant they had had an interview with the Directors of the Great Western Railway Company, at Paddington, with reference to the removal of the Company's Carriage Works from Paddington to Abingdon, and that the Deputy Chairman of the Company had stated that the arrangements for the removal of the Works to Oxford had gone so far as to be irrevocable. Sir Geo. Bowyer, Bart., however, had addressed the Board at length, and offered to give the Company half the Land required for the Works. The reasons why the Abingdon site was more desirable than Oxford were read by the Town Clerk, and the Members of the Deputation having also addressed the Board, guaranteeing to pay Sir Geo. Bowyer for the

1865.
August 23rd.
Charles Payne,
Mayor.
other half of the Land required, and further promising that the Council would apply to the Treasury for their consent to the Corporation lending the Company £20,000 or more of the Corporation Funds upon the security of the Works; The Deputy Chairman requested that the proposals might be reduced to writing and sent to the Board, but expressly stated that he could not hold out any expectation of the question being reconsidered after the length to which matters had gone with the Oxford People.

𝕿𝖍𝖊 Report of the Deputation was adopted and confirmed, and a vote of thanks given to Sir Geo. Bowyer for his offer to give half the land required for the Works.

𝕬 further Representation was ordered to be made to the Railway Company with regard to the matter; the three sites suggested being 20 Acres between Abingdon Junction and the River, or on the other side of the Line near Radley Bridge, or part of Barton Farm.

𝕿𝖍𝖊 Council resolved that the attention of the Inhabitants should be called to the state of their premises in relation to any nuisance or want of cleanliness that might exist thereon, as a precaution against Cholera, should it visit this Country.

November 9th.
John Hyde,
Mayor.
𝕿𝖍𝖊 Borough Seal affixed to an Agreement with the Trustees of the Independent Chapel for letting the piece of land in the front of the Chapel at an annual rent of 1/-, the Trustees agreeing to remove the iron railings when called upon; and also to an Agreement with Mr. Bowler for letting to him the triangular piece of land in front of his house in the Vineyard, he paying 1/- per annum for same and keeping the railings in repair and preserving the trees standing on the land.

December 15th.
𝕬 letter read from the Clerk of the Peace for Berks, enquiring if the Council would consent to give effect to the resolution of the Court of Quarter Sessions of the 3rd January, 1859, with regard to the Closing of Abingdon Gaol, and it was ordered that the Town Clerk be instructed to reply that the Council adhered to the existing arrangement, and could not assent to the proposals of the Court of Quarter Sessions.

𝕬 proposal made that the Mayor should be allowed a Salary of £100 per annum, but the motion not being seconded, it was withdrawn.

𝕿𝖍𝖊 "dissent" of the Council to the River Thames Purification Bill ordered to be signified to the Promoters thereof.

1865.
December 15th.
John Hyde,
Mayor.

𝕬 Letter read from the Clerk of the Peace for Berks, enclosing a Copy of a series of Resolutions passed at the Berks Court of Quarter Sessions, held on the 1st of January, 1866, with reference to the Closing of Abingdon Gaol, and offering to receive the Borough Prisoners at Reading Gaol until the then next Sessions, upon the terms suggested at the Easter Sessions, 1859. The Letter was referred to the Gaol Committee for consideration and report.

1866.
January 30th.

𝕿𝖍𝖊 Clock of St. Nicholas Church ordered to be lighted at the expense of the Corporation.

February 8th.

𝕿𝖍𝖊 Pitching in the High Street ordered to be taken up and replaced with Granite Cubes for a width of 18 feet in the centre.

𝕿𝖍𝖊 Council decided, on the recommendation of the Gaol Committee, to adhere to the existing arrangements with regard to the committal of Borough Prisoners to Abingdon Gaol.

February 23rd.

𝕬 Letter read from the Clerk of the Oxford Local Board, calling the Council's attention to the provisions of the Bill promoted by the Thames and Severn Canal Navigation Company, which the Local Board had decided to oppose, when it was resolved also to oppose the Bill.

March 13th.

𝕴𝖓 order to check the spread of the Cattle Plague, the Council ordered that until the 1st day of May then next, no Bull, Bullock, Ox, Cow, Heifer or Calf, or any Ram or untanned Hides or Skins, nor any Hoofs, Horns or Offal of any such Animals, should be brought into the Town, except under a License from the Mayor or Borough Justice of the Peace, under a penalty of £20.

March 27th.

𝕿𝖍𝖊 Borough Seal affixed to a Petition against the Thames Navigation Bill, and also against The Thames and Severn Canal Bill.

April 27th.

𝕬 Memorial received from the Deacons, Trustees and others connected with the Independent Chapel, asking the Corporation to state a Case for the Opinion of Counsel as to the rights and powers of the Corporation with reference to the inclosure of the piece of Land in front of the Chapel, and let by them to the Chapel Trustees, and also to defend an Indictment which Mr. A. D. Bartlett had preferred against the Revd. S. Lepine, for a misdemeanour in

May 10th.

erecting a fence in front of the Chapel, enclosing the piece of ground in question; And it was ordered that Counsel's opinion should be taken as to whether the Council could legally incur the expense of defending the Indictment.

The Dissolution of the Union between the County of Berks, and the Boroughs of Abingdon and Reading, with the County and City of Oxford, with regard to the Maintenance of Pauper Lunatics in the County Asylum, at Littlemore, notified to the Council.

A Tender of £340 for pitching the Centre of the High Street for a width of 15 feet with Granite Cubes and for Pebble pitching, &c., accepted.

The sum of £9 : 15 : 0 paid to Mr. Besley for painting the Royal Arms in the Guildhall.

The Borough Seal affixed to a Petition against the Redistribution of Seats Bill, which proposed to group the Boroughs of Abingdon, Wallingford and Woodstock, for the purpose of returning a Member to Parliament.

A Letter received from the Home Office stating that the Inspector of Prisons had reported that Abingdon Prison was insufficient to meet the requirements of the Prisons Act, 1865, and that the Home Secretary had felt it his duty to recommend the Court of Quarter Sessions of the County of Berks, that no more Prisoners should be committed to the Prison, and that all future committals should be made to the Prison at Reading.

The Council resolved to insist upon the continuance of Abingdon Gaol, and determined that if the Gaol did not answer to the requirements of the Prisons Act, 1865, the Secretary of State should be requested to insist on the Justices of the County of Berks making such alterations as were necessary to comply with the Act, and in the event of their refusing to do so that an application be made to the Court of Queen's Bench for a Mandamus to compel them to do so.

The opposition of the Council to the Thames and Severn Canal Company Bill withdrawn after an interview with the Company's Engineer, who informed the Council that the Company would be restricted to a supply of 500,000 gallons of water from the Thames Head, by a Clause which would be inserted in the Bill.

The Town Clerk reported that he had verbally agreed with the 1866.
June 14th.
John Hyde,
Mayor. Solicitors for the Promoters of the Thames Purification Bill for a Clause to be inserted in the Bill providing for the powers proposed to be conferred in the Bill not being exercised within the Borough without the previous consent of the Council.

A special report received from the Town Clerk with reference to July 9th. the progress of the Thames Navigation Bill, and the decision of the Select Committee of the House of Commons to exclude the flow of Sewage into the River, and the consequent difficulties which would result from such decision, and suggesting that a Private Act of Parliament should be obtained to enable the Council to obtain a transfer of the Powers of the Commissioners of Paving, and powers to purchase land for the utilization of the Town Sewage.

The Council resolved to purchase the Old Grammar School and August 9th. the adjoining Buildings.

The Thames Purification Bill reported to the Council as having October 23rd. been passed by both Houses of Parliament.

An application received from the Town Clerk of Cambridge inviting the Council to express their views with reference to a Bill which he had drawn for revesting in Municipal Corporations the Management of Municipal Charities, but the Council decided not to interfere in the matter.

The Question of the future Drainage of the Town, in consequence of the passing of the Thames Navigation Bill, which prohibited the flow of Sewage into the Thames, was discussed and adjourned.

A notification received from the Clerk of the Peace for Berks November 9th.
William
Ballard,
Mayor. that the County Justices had authorised him to accept service of any process the Council determined to issue against them with regard to their action in the matter of Abingdon Gaol.

The Council resolved to purchase the Weighbridge in the Sheep- 1867.
January 9th. Market from the late Miss Spenlove's Trustees for the sum of £125 : 6 : 1, being the amount at which the Trustees had recently enfranchised it.

A Committee appointed to report upon the state of the Fire February 14th. Engines and the question of establishing a Fire Brigade.

𝕿𝖍𝖊 Fire Engine Committee recommended that the Corporation Engine and the Two Engines presented to the Town by the Sun, Royal Exchange and Phœnix Fire Offices, be put into an efficient state of repair, and a further supply of hose provided, and that two of the Engines be kept at the Guildhall, and the third one at the Eagle Brewery.

𝕬 Letter received from the Treasury in reply to the Council's application for power to lend Money on Mortgage instead of investing it in Land, stating that the Lords Commissioners were of opinion that it would be more consistent with the intention of Parliament that the Fund should remain invested in Consols until an opportunity presented itself of investing it in the purchase of Land.

May 1st.

𝕬 Letter received from the Clerk of the Peace for Berks, inviting the Council to confer with the County Justices with reference to the Gaol, at Abingdon, ceasing to be used as a County Prison. The discussion thereof was adjourned to the next Quarterly Meeting of the Council.

May 9th.

𝕹𝖔𝖙𝖎𝖈𝖊 received from the Conservators of the River Thames to discontinue within thirteen months the flow of Sewage into the River from the Sewers at Abingdon Bridge and near St. Helen's Church, or from any other Sewers under the control of the Corporation.

𝕸𝖗. John Goldsmith attended the Council and presented the following resolutions, which were unanimously passed at a Meeting of the Inhabitants of Abingdon, held on the previous day, which had been convened by the Mayor, on a requisition signed by one hundred of the Inhabitants of the Town, " to consider what steps should be " taken to resist the aggression of a Section of the County Magistrates " on the Rights and Privileges of the Borough in their attempt to " procure the abolition of Abingdon Gaol."

1.—" That this Meeting is of opinion that the retention of the Gaol
   " in this Town, as a County Prison, and the maintenance of
   " the rights of the Borough Magistrates to commit prisoners
   " to such Prison, are points of the utmost importance to the
   " Inhabitants of the Borough, as well as of the surrounding
   " District, as indispensable to the future position of Abingdon
   " as the County Town."

2.—"That this Meeting hereby expresses its entire confidence in
  "the Town Council as conservators of the best interests of
  "the Town, and appreciates the spirit in which they have
  "already resisted all attempts to infringe the rights and
  "ancient privileges of the Borough."

3.—"That this Meeting expresses its most sincere thanks to those
  "County Magistrates who have steadily and successfully
  "opposed repeated attempts which have been made from
  "time to time to procure the abolition of Abingdon Gaol."

And it was ordered that the Clerk of the Peace be informed that
the Council was not willing to negociate with reference to the Gaol
ceasing to be used as a County Prison as suggested in his letter of
the 23rd April, and that an application be made to the Court of
Queen's Bench for a Writ of Mandamus to compel the Justices of
Berks to put the Gaol, at Abingdon, into a fit state for the reception
of prisoners.

An application received from Mr. J. C. Clarke, for the payment
of a larger sum than the £100 voted by the Council for the purchase
of the site of the late Mr. Hyde's House, in East and West St. Helen
Streets, and it was ordered that the sum of £200 be paid for the
same.

A sum of £150 also ordered to be paid to Mr. R. Badcock for
setting back, for a distance of three feet, the frontage of his house
which he was rebuilding at the corner of Bridge Street.

The Town Clerk reported that the Court of Queen's Bench had *June 22nd.*
granted a Rule Nisi for a Mandamus in the matter of Abingdon Gaol
against the Justices of Berks to shew cause why the Rule should not
be made absolute next Term.

A Committee appointed to confer with the Commissioners of *August 5th.*
Paving with reference to the notice served by the Conservators of
the River Thames on the Commissioners respecting the Drainage of
the Town.

The question of proceeding with the litigation with reference to *September 4th.*
Abingdon Gaol was further discussed, and the Council, on a division,
decided to continue it.

1867.
September 4th.
William
Ballard,
Mayor.

𝕿𝖍𝖊 resignation of Mr. Thomas Sharps, of his Office of Justice of the Peace, notified to the Council.

September 27th.

𝕿𝖜𝖔 Letters read from Mr. T. Bros, the Recorder, strongly advising the Council to consent to the Rule Nisi with reference to Abingdon Gaol being discharged upon terms to be agreed upon, and Notice of Motion at the next Meeting of the Council was given for reconsidering the Matter before further proceeding with the Mandamus.

October 3rd.

𝕿𝖍𝖊 question of proceeding with the Gaol litigation was further discussed, and a resolution in favour of continuing it was carried by a Majority of one.

𝕬 Notice of a proposed Public Inquiry by the Boundary Commissioners for the purposes of the Representation of the People Act, 1867, received by the Council.

November 28th.
Edwin Payne,
Mayor.

𝕿𝖍𝖊 Town Clerk reported that on the 23rd instant the Rule Nisi obtained against the County of Berks came on for Argument before the Court of Queen's Bench, when the Attorney General and Mr. Griffiths appeared for the County Justices, to shew cause against the Rule being made absolute, Mr. Mellish and Mr. Horace Lloyd appearing for the Corporation, and after full argument the Rule was discharged, but without Costs.

𝕬𝖓 invitation received from the Oxford Local Board to nominate three Deputies to act on a Committee of Local Authorities of Towns in the Thames Valley, for the purpose of securing united action with regard to Drainage of the said Towns, in consequence of the action taken by the Thames Conservancy Board.

𝕿𝖍𝖊 site of the Tenements in the Thames Street purchased by the Council from Christ's Hospital ordered to be inclosed.

𝕿𝖍𝖊 Tolls usually let by Tender ordered to be retained and collected by the Council.

𝕬 Committee appointed to preserve, or destroy, or assort and relodge the Books and Papers, &c., then in the Town Hall, belonging to the Corporation.

1863.
January 9th.

𝕿𝖍𝖊 Borough Seal affixed to an undertaking by the Council to accept and keep in repair the Iron Bridge leading from Abingdon to Sutton Wick.

1868.
January 9th.
Edwin Payne,
Mayor.

On the recommendation of the Watch Committee the Council resolved to appoint a Day Constable to be on Duty from 4 p.m. to 9 p.m., with a Salary of 8/- per week.

A notification received from the Clerk of the Peace for Berks to the effect that the County Justices had ordered Abingdon Gaol to be closed, and the Prisoners therein removed to Reading, and also all Judicial business of the Court of Quarter Sessions to be in future transacted at Reading

A vote of thanks accorded to the Magistrates of the Abingdon Division of the County, and also to Mr. Cherry and other Magistrates for the course they had uniformly taken with regard to Abingdon Gaol and supporting the rights of the Borough and the Inhabitants of the Western end of the County.

An application received from the Registrar of the Abingdon County Court for permission for the County Court Judge to use the Guildhall for the monthly sitting of his Court. *February 13th.*

The Costs of the litigation in the matter of Abingdon Gaol amounting to £207 : 11 : 10 ordered to be paid, and also the further sum of £49 : 19 : 2 to Mr. Badcock for setting back the street line in front of his premises in Bridge Street, in addition to the £150 voted in August, 1867.

Two fire-proof safes ordered to be purchased for the preservation of the Corporation Plate and Records.

A Petition ordered to be prepared and presented to the House of Commons, for the appointment of a Select Committee to enquire into and report upon systems of Sewage Purification in Towns, with particular application to small Towns on the Banks of the Thames.

At the request of the Commissioners of the National Portrait Exhibition, South Kensington, the Council agreed to lend the Portraits of George III. and Queen Charlotte, by Gainsborough, for exhibition. *March 16th.*

A Letter received from the Assistant Secretary of the Science and Art Department, of South Kensington, stating that the Committee, to their great regret, were obliged to forego the pleasure of including the Corporation Gainsborough pictures in the collection for that year.

A Letter received from the Governors of Roysse's School, requesting the Council to give an undertaking to Insure and keep in repair the New School Buildings, and also guarantee the Cost of erecting the same beyond the sum of £6000 which had been received from the sale of the School property in Birchin Lane, London, and from the Governors of Christ's Hospital. And it was resolved to give an undertaking to keep in repair the exterior of the New School House and Buildings, and the whole of the Repairs (both external and internal) of the large School Room, and also the undertaking with regard to the extra cost of Building the School.

A piece of ground in the Abbey, near St. Nicholas Church, purchased of Mr. Trendell, for £75.

May 14th.

A Gas Boiler ordered to be fixed for heating the Guildhall.

Mr. Badcock having refused to accept the sum of £189 : 18 : 2 ordered to be paid to him on the preceeding 8th August and 13th February, for his improvements in Bridge Street, on the ground that extra work had been occasioned by the Corporation, involving an additional expenditure of £66 : 5 : 0, it was ordered that the additional sum of £66 : 5 : 0 be paid to Mr. Badcock.

An address prepared and presented to Her Majesty, expressing the Council's stedfast loyalty to the Throne, and their detestation of the infamous attempt to assassinate H.R.H. the Duke of Edinburgh.

A Letter received from the Rev. W. A. Strange, D.D., Head-Master of Roysse's School, announcing his resignation of the Head-Mastership of the School, and conveying his thanks to the Council for the uniform courtesy and kindness he had received from them during the long period of his Headmastership. And it was resolved that the Mayor be requested to express to Dr. Strange the great regret of the Council at the severance of his official connection with the Corporation.

A Petition prepared and presented to Her Majesty the Queen in Council, praying that the Summer Assizes might not be removed from Abingdon.

An application made to the Thames Conservators for an extension of time for complying with the Conservators' notice with regard to the flow of the Town's Sewage into the River.

1868.
May 27th.
Edwin Payne,
Mayor.

𝔗𝔥𝔢 Mayor reported he had received an invitation from the Windsor Local Board of Health, to join a Deputation of Local Authorities, in the Thames Valley, to wait on the Home Secretary, with the object of urging upon him the desirability of his appointing a Commission to investigate the question of the drainage of the Towns in the Thames Valley, and that as he had not been able to attend, he had requested Col. The Hon. C. H. Lindsay, M.P., to attend the Deputation and represent the Town, and that he had had a long correspondence with Col. Lindsay with reference to what had passed at the Deputation, and that Col. Lindsay had stated that he had since seen the Home Secretary, who informed him that Col. Ewart, R.E., had been selected to visit the Towns in the Thames Valley, to receive evidence, so as to form an opinion upon the Sewage question, but that the Council must be prepared to pay their proportion of Col. Ewart's fees. And it was resolved to invite Col. Ewart to visit Abingdon, the Council agreeing to pay his expenses.

August 13th.

𝔄𝔫 extension of one year, from the 2nd June, 1868, within which time the Council were required to discontinue the flow of Sewage into the Thames, received from the Thames Conservators.

𝔄 Letter received from the Home Secretary, stating that Leut.-Col. Ewart, R.E., had been selected to enquire and report upon the Plans for the Drainage of the Towns in the Thames Valley, with the view to the purification of the River, and requesting that the Council would lay before him all plans and papers relating to the matter. And the Mayor reported that Leut.-Col. Ewart had visited and inspected the Town, and had invited suggestions from any persons interested in the question of the Town drainage, and it was ordered that a notice be printed and circulated in the Town, inviting any Inhabitant having suggestions to make, to send same to the Mayor, for transmission to Col. Ewart.

𝔗𝔥𝔢 Sanction of the Council given to the expenditure of £1000 by the Committee of Visitors of the Pauper Lunatic Asylum, at Littlemore, for erecting the necessary works for lighting the Asylum with Gas.

𝔄 sum of £50 paid to the Rev. W. A. Strange, D.D., as compensation for the Dining Room he had erected adjoining the School, and other improvements to the School House he had effected during his Headmastership.

October 7th.

𝕿𝖍𝖊 Council resolved to purchase of Mr. Morland the Paul's Head and the Cottages adjoining in Bath Street for £280, for the purpose of making a good entrance into Albert Park.

𝕹𝖔𝖙𝖎𝖈𝖊 having been published in the local Papers of an Order in Council directing that the Assizes and Sessions should be held in future in Reading; it was resolved that notice should be given to the County Justices that the Corporation claimed an interest in Abingdon Gaol, and invited negociation with reference thereto.

𝕿𝖍𝖊 Old Papers Committee reported to the Council that they had placed the old Leases and Counterparts in two large Boxes, and the Old Minute Books and other Documents in a small Box, in the upper room of the County Hall, and also the following Books in the same place, viz. :—

The Statutes of the Realm.
The Old Borough Court of Record Books.
The Acts of the Parliament of Scotland.
The Parliamentary Writs.
The Valuation of Ecclesiastical Tithes, 6 vols.
The Books of the Inquisition.
The Catalogue of the Lansdowne M.S.S., 4 vols.
The Catalogue of the Harleian Library, 4 vols.
The Calendar of the Pleadings.
The Pleadings in Chancery, 2 vols.
The Inquisitions into the state of Ireland, 2 vols.
The Rolls of the Hundreds of England, 2 vols.
The Rolls of the Hundreds of Scotland, 2 vols.
The Pleas of Quo Warranto, 1 vol.
The other Inquisitions, 6 vols.

November 9th.

𝕿𝖍𝖊 names of Mr. Charles Payne, Mr. John Creemer Clarke, and Mr. John Tomkins, recommended to the Lord Chancellor for insertion in the Commission of the Peace for the Borough, there being only three Justices then in the Commission.

1869.
January 6th.

𝕿𝖍𝖊 Assent of the Council given to the borrowing by the County of Oxford of the sum of £568 being the Quota of the Borough of the sum of £17,610 required to pay out the County of Berks and the Borough of Reading, on the dissolution of the Littlemore Lunatic Asylum Union.

𝕿𝖍𝖊 Agreement for the Dissolution of the Union between Oxfordshire, (including the Borough of Banbury), Berkshire (including the Boroughs of Windsor, Abingdon and Reading), and the City of Oxford, for the formation of a new Union between Oxfordshire, the City of Oxford, and the Boroughs of Abingdon and Windsor, with the joint use of Littlemore Asylum, by Berkshire, for 83 Pauper Lunatics, approved by the Council.

𝕿𝖍𝖊 Watch Committee reported that a Complaint had been made to them of neglect of duty by the Superintendent of Police, on Polling Day at the late Borough Election, in not taking into custody persons who were fighting in front of the late King's Head Inn, in High Street, and the Committee stated that they felt on hearing the defence of the Constables, that they were unable from the difficulties which surrounded the matter, to say that the Superintendent had failed in his duty.

𝕿𝖍𝖊 report received from Lieut.-Col. Ewart, R.E., with reference to the drainage of the Town presented to the Council.

𝕿𝖍𝖊 Finance and General Committee empowered to grant Licenses for the Sale of Petroleum Oil in the Borough, not more than 2 gallons being allowed to be stored in any Dwelling House for sale. February 11th.

𝕬𝖓 application to the Thames Conservators for a further extension of the time for discontinuing the flow of Sewage into the Thames ordered to be made, a Committee being appointed to visit and report upon the Sewage Works at Stroud and other places. April 28th.

𝕬 Letter received from the Governors of Christ's Hospital, stating that before the Governors conveyed the land in Otwell and Bury Lanes to the Trustees of the National School, as a site for the New Schools, the Governors were willing to sell to the Corporation as much of the land as the Council required for the improvement of those Lanes, and the Town Clerk was instructed to ascertain upon what terms the land could be obtained.

𝕿𝖍𝖊 Town Clerk reported that the Master and Governors of Christ's Hospital were willing to sell the piece of ground in Otwell May 13th.

Lane in consideration of the Council securing to the late owner the payment of the annual sum of £1 : 12 : 0, being the amount of redeemed Land Tax theretofore charged on the Tenements which formerly stood on the land, and also agreeing to release the remainder of the site from the payment of the said sum. And the Council resolved to accept the Governors offer.

An exchange of property agreed upon between the Corporation and the Master and Governors of Christ's Hospital for improving the entrance to the Park from Bath Street.

July 14th.   An address ordered to be prepared and presented to H.R.H. Princess Christian of Schleswig-Holstein, on her passing through the Borough to visit the Volunteer Camp at Nuneham.

A Boat also ordered to convey the Council and Officers of the Corporation to the Camp at Nuneham, on the same occasion, each member of the Council being allowed to take three friends, the Mayor being requested to provide Refreshments on the occasion.

July 28th.   A Special Meeting of the Council held, when an order was made defining the route to be followed by the Royal procession.

August 12th.   An application ordered to be made to the Government for compensation in respect of the sum of £50 which the Council had contributed towards the cost of establishing the Telegraph in Abingdon.

The Sewage Committee reported that they had visited Stroud, Leamington and Warwick, but did not consider the system in use in those Towns suitable to Abingdon, and that they believed the question of sewage disposal was occupying the minds of many eminent Chemists and Engineers, and they recommended the Council to continue to direct their attention to the matter, in the hope that ere long Scientific Men would reveal to the whole country an economical and efficient mode of dealing with Sewage.

A Letter received from the Thames Conservators inquiring what steps had been taken by the Council to prevent the flow of Sewage into the River.

A Letter received from Lieut.-Col. Gordon conveying the thanks of H.R.H. The Princess Christian for the address which the Council had presented to H.R.H. on her visit to Abingdon.

A sum of £50 voted towards the expenses incurred in connection with the late visit of H.R.H. The Princess Christian to the Borough.

An Annual Subscription of £9 : 9 : 0 voted to the Radcliffe Infirmary, at Oxford.

A notice received from the Conservators of the River Thames requiring the Council to discontinue the flow of Sewage into the Thames, at Abingdon, within 12 months of the 2nd June, 1869, and stating that no extension of time would be allowed.

The Mayor reported that on the 23rd November, he had had the honor of attending with other Municipal Authorities on the occasion of the presentation of an address of welcome to H.M. The King of the Belgians.

The Borough Seal affixed to a Petition against the Thames Navigation Bill.

A Fire Escape ordered to be purchased for the Town.

The employment of a Civil Engineer to advise the Council as to the best means to be adopted for diverting the Town Sewage from the Thames resolved upon.

The appointment of the Rev. Edgar Summers, M.A., to the Headmastership of Roysse's School, reported to the Council by the Mayor.

Messrs. Church & Sons, of London, instructed by the Council to prepare a plan for dealing with the Sewage of the Town.

The sum of £300 ordered to be paid to the Governors of Roysse's School on account of the guarantee of the Corporation to defray half the expense of erecting fencing, and completing the new School.

The Streets Committee directed to endeavour to arrange with the Surveyors of St. Helen's Parish for a reduction of the Council's Contribution of £100 per annum towards the repair of the Streets.

Messrs. Church & Sons' report and estimate for the works necessary to dispose of the Town Sewage, and supplying the Borough with Water, received and read, and ordered to be printed for the information of the Burgesses.

An application for a further extension of time for dealing with the Town Sewage made to the Thames Conservators.

The Broad Street ordered to be widened at a cost of £57 : 10 : 0.

The New Grammar School was reported to the Council as having been opened on the preceding 26th April.

June 14th.

A Letter received from the Conservators of the River Thames, granting an extension of time for dealing with the Town Sewage until the 29th September then next.

August 11th.

The purchase of the Old Grammar School Buildings of the Master and Governors of Christ's Hospital, for the sum of £900, resolved upon by the Council.

The sum of. £200 ordered to be paid to the Governors of Roysse's School in full satisfaction of the Council's guarantee to pay a moiety of the fencing and other expenses of the new School.

A further extension of time for dealing with the Town Sewage ordered to be made to the Conservators of the River Thames.

A Committee appointed to make arrangements for the custody and management of the Fire Engines and Escape, and also to inspect the Public Wells, with power to put them in order so as to secure a sufficient supply of Water in case of fire.

October 4th.

A Letter received from Sir George Bowyer, Bart., notifying his intention to present to the Corporation the Gold Vase which was presented to his Grandfather, Admiral Sir George Bowyer, after the great victory over the French Fleet, on the 4th June, 1794, off Cape St. Vincent.

A Letter received from the Conservators of the River Thames declining to grant any further extension of time, with reference to the discontinuance of the flow of Town Sewage into the River Thames.

October 28th.

The Finance and General Committee reported that a deputation from the Committee had had an interview with the Thames Conservators, and had obtained a month's extension of time, upon the express condition that some definite steps should be taken by the Council with regard to the flow of Sewage into the River.

The Finance Committee directed to ascertain from the Native Guano Company, Limited, the cost of establishing a system of sewage on the A.B.C. system in Abingdon.

The Medical Officers of the Union requested to report privately to the Nuisance Committee any cases of nuisances likely to be injurious to health.

The following Returns to the Education Department were made by the Council pursuant to the Elementary Education Act, 1870.

NUMBER OF CHILDREN ATTENDING PUBLIC ELEMENTARY SCHOOLS IN THE BOROUGH.

NAME OF SCHOOL.	DAY.		NIGHT.		Total
	Boys.	Girls.	Boys.	Girls.	
National School	220	193	42	68	523
Infants' School	63	69	—	—	132
British School	192	175	—	—	367
Roman Catholic School	42	48	—	—	90
Grand Total ...	517	485	42	68	1112

Population of the Borough by Census of 1861—5677.

Estimated population at date of Return   5960.

Rateable Value of the Borough—£14,069 : 4 : 6.

Number of Ratepayers rated under the Poor Rate Assessment and Collection Act, 1867—766.

The Finance and General Committee reported that they had with Mr. J. Church, C.E., visited and inspected the Sewage Works at Wimbledon, Hastings, Tunbridge Wells and Croydon, and recommended that an application should be made to the Conservators of the Thames for a further extension of time for dealing with the Town Sewage, a course which was adopted by the Council.

The Council resolved to call a Public Meeting to consider the advisability of forming a Local Board of Health for the Borough.

A Memorial received from several Inhabitants of the Town, calling the attention of the Council to the state of the Square, caused by the holding of Cattle Sales there, and representing that

MM

the Square being macadamized was not a proper place for holding such Sales, and that residents in the neighbourhood suffered in health in consequence. The Streets Committee was ordered to consider and report upon the matter.

March 29th.

A Letter received from the Conservators of the River Thames granting the Council a further period of three months to comply with their requirements with regard to the Sewage of the Borough.

A Letter received claiming £40 : 12 : 0 on behalf of Mr. R. G. Schofield, for the damage done to his premises in Lombard Street by Rioters, on the preceding 26th January, and on the recommendation of the Finance Committee it was ordered that the amount claimed be paid.

A further application for an extension of time ordered to be made to the Conservators of the River Thames, on the ground that the Council were in communication with an Engineer with a view to obtaining a report and estimate for carrying out the works recommended by Lieut.-Col. Ewart, as the Town could not bear the expense which the adoption of Messrs. Church & Sons' scheme would involve.

April 19th.

An extension of time until the 31st May next ensuing granted by the Conservators of the Thames.

The Finance and General Committee presented a report to the Council upon the result of their enquiries into the sewage system at Wimbledon, Hastings, Tunbridge Wells and Croydon, and recommended that Messrs. Lawson & Mansergh should be employed to prepare a scheme for draining the Town. The Committee further reported that they had endeavoured through Col. The Hon. C. H. Lindsay, M.P. for the Borough, to place before the Government the great difficulties of the Borough in the matter, and the need of Imperial help, which the Committee considered the right of the Borough and a national matter. The recommendation of the Committee was adopted, and instructions given to apply to the Conservators for a further extension of time.

May 11th.

The house at the Corner of Lombard Street, purchased by the Council for £180, for the purpose of widening the entrance from East St. Helen Street.

A sum of £122 : 17 : 0 ordered to be expended in pitching the Square with Granite cubes.

A New Fire Engine purchased, at a cost of £200, and the question of organizing a Fire Brigade referred to a Committee.

Messrs. Lawson & Mansergh presented their report upon the Sewage and Water supply works for Abingdon, and the Council ordered 500 copies of the Report to be printed and sold at 1d. each.

A Letter received from Mr. G. B. Morland with reference to the piece of ground he had given up for the purpose of improving the turning from Bath Street into Broad Street, and undertaking to plant suitable creepers to cover the brickwork of the house, should the Streets Committee consider it an improvement to do so.

A vote of thanks given to Mr. John Hyde, on his retiring from the Council, for the service he had rendered to the Town during the many years he had been a Member of the Corporation.

An offer received from Mr. E. J. Trendell to purchase the Russian Gun, in Albert Park, for Twenty Guineas, but no order was made thereon.

The Town Clerk reported that the Accounts of the Chamberlain of the Borough, in the reign of Queen Elizabeth, which had been lent to the Commissioners of Historical Manuscripts, when in a very mutilated state, and that Sir Thomas D. Hardy, one of the Commissioners, had had them repaired and bound before returning the same to the Corporation, and it was ordered that the thanks of the Council be given to Sir Thomas for his kindness.

An address ordered to be presented to Her Majesty the Queen, congratulating Her Majesty on the restoration to health of H.R.H. The Prince of Wales, after his recent long and severe illness.

An application made to the Lords Commissioners of H.M. Treasury, to insert a Clause in an Act of Parliament directing the compulsory sale to Corporations of all Fee Farm Rents payable by them.

A Letter received from the Treasury declining to accede to the application of the Council with regard to the compulsory sale of Fee Farm Rents to Corporations.

1872.
September 4th.
John Tomkins,
Mayor.

𝕿𝖍𝖊 First Meeting of the Council acting as the Urban Sanitary Authority, held under the Public Health Act, 1872, and notice directed to be given to the Abingdon Paving Commissioners of the intention of the Sanitary Authority to consider the desirability of applying to the Local Government Board for a Provisional Order repealing the Abingdon Paving Act.

October 4th.

𝕿𝖍𝖊 Parliamentary Borough ordered to be divided into three Polling Districts under the Ballot Act, 1872.

𝕹𝖔𝖙𝖎𝖈𝖊 received from the Board of Surveyors of their intention to discontinue the repair of the Highways in the Borough after the 9th November then next ensuing.

𝕬 Letter received from the Local Government Board stating that in consequence of the prevalence of Fever and Diarrhœa in the Abingdon Registration Sub-District, they had instructed their Inspector, Dr. Thorne, to proceed to Abingdon and inquire into the Sanitary condition of the Town.

October 25th.

𝕯𝖗. Thorne attended the Council and addressed it with reference to his recent Inspection.

𝕬 Letter received from the Rev. A. Pott, B.D., Vicar of Abingdon, requesting to be informed of the wishes of the Council with reference to the re-erection of the Corporation Seats in St. Helen's Church, which was then undergoing restoration, and the letter was referred to the Finance Committee.

November 9th.
John Tomkins,
Mayor.

𝕺𝖓 the recommendation of the Finance and General Committee the Council resolved to select the South side of the centre aisle of St. Helen's Church, for the re-erection of the Corporation Seats and ordered the Borough Arms to be placed on each seat.

𝕬𝖓 Annual Subscription of Ten Guineas ordered to be paid to the Abingdon Volunteer Fire Brigade.

𝕬𝖓 application made to the Local Government Board for a Provisional Order repealing the Abingdon Paving Act.

November 22nd.

𝕬 Letter received from the Local Government Board with reference to the appointment of a Medical Officer of Health and Inspector of Nuisances under the Public Health Act, 1872, and a Committee appointed to consider and report upon the matter.

1873.
February 6th.
John Tomkins,
Mayor.

𝕿𝖍𝖊 sum of £30 voted for clearing the streets of Snow.

𝕿𝖍𝖊 names of Mr. John Kent and Mr. William Stacy recommended by the Council for insertion in the Commission of the Peace for the Borough.

𝕿𝖍𝖊 Sanitary Committee reported that they had received an invitation from the Abingdon Board of Guardians, to discuss with them the question of appointing a joint Medical Officer of Health and Inspector of Nuisances, and that they had had a conference with the Guardians, when it was suggested that the three Unions of Abingdon, Wantage and Wallingford, and the Urban Authorities within these Unions should combine and appoint a Medical Officer of Health and Inspector of Nuisances for the combined District, but that since the Conference a letter had been received from Mr. J. J. King, the Local Government Board's Inspector, inviting the several Sanitary Authorities in the County of Berks, to meet him at Reading, on the 18th January, to discuss the steps to be taken under Sec. 10 of the Public Health Act, 1872; that representatives from the Committee attended the meeting, when a resolution was passed in favour of dividing the County into two or more Districts for the purpose of appointing a Medical Officer of Health for each combined District.

𝕿𝖍𝖊 Council thereupon appointed representatives to attend the adjourned meeting at Reading, to be held on the 15th February then next, with instructions to enter into any agreement that they might think desirable.

𝕬 Letter received from the Lord Chancellor, enquiring the April 3rd. number of Magistrates and population of the Borough, and also stating that the name of Mr. Edward Harris had been suggested to his Lordship for insertion in the Commission, and that he would be willing to receive any observations which the Council might wish to make upon this suggestion, before he determined whether any, and if any, which of three gentlemen should be appointed, and the Town Clerk was ordered to reply that the Council saw no reason for deviating from the recommendation which they had submitted to the Lord Chancellor.

𝕿𝖍𝖊 Council resolved to unite with the Counties of Oxford and Berks in appointing an Analyst as suggested by the Berks County

Justices, under the provisions of the Adulteration of Food, &c., Act, 1872.

𝕿𝖍𝖊 Report of Dr. Thorne, upon the Sanitary Condition of Abingdon, presented to the Council, and ordered to be printed and circulated in the Town.

𝕿𝖍𝖊 first Municipal Election under the Ballot Act was held, when Mr. Joseph Dickey was elected a member of the Council.

𝕬 Letter received from the Lord Chancellor, stating that he had added the names of Mr. John Kent, Mr. Edward Harris and Mr. William Stacy to the Commission of the Peace for the Borough.

𝕽𝖊𝖌𝖚𝖑𝖆𝖙𝖎𝖔𝖓𝖘 made by the Council with regard to the inspection of Documents under the Ballot Act, 1872.

𝕯𝖗. C. C. Pode, M.A., and Mr. W. F. Donkin, appointed joint Public Analysts for the Borough, and a scale for their remuneration fixed.

𝕿𝖍𝖊 Mayor reported that the Representatives appointed by the Council on the 6th February last, had attended four Conferences at Reading, and at the last held on the 23rd April, Dr. W. T. G. Woodforde, was appointed Medical Officer of Health for the Combined District, comprising, the Urban Sanitary Districts of Abingdon, Maidenhead, Newbury, Speenhamland and Wallingford, and the Rural Districts of Abingdon, Bradfield, Cookham, Easthampstead, Hungerford, Newbury, Wallingford and Windsor. And it was resolved that the action of the Representatives be approved and confirmed.

𝕬 letter read from Mr. Bromley Challenor, the Clerk to the Abingdon Rural Sanitary Authority, inviting the Council to meet that Authority for the purpose of discussing the appointment of a joint Inspector of Nuisances for the two Districts; and it was resolved to accept the invitation, and a Committee was appointed to attend accordingly, with power to act for the Council in the matter.

𝕬 Letter received from the Local Government Board stating that the Board was advised that all the powers, &c., of the Paving Commissioners were transferred to the Council, under the Public Health Act, 1872, and therefore there was no necessity for the Local Act to be repealed.

The Mayor reported that the Committee appointed at the last meeting of the Council had had a Conference with the Abingdon Rural Sanitary Authority, and agreed to appoint Mr. Mudd, as Joint Inspector of Nuisances for the two Districts, and it was ordered that the action of the Committee be confirmed.

The assent of the Council given to the expenditure of £985 by the Committee of Visitors of Littlemore Lunatic Asylum for building a detached Infirmary for the Asylum.

The sum of £30 ordered to be paid to Mr. J. C. Clarke, for the purchase of a piece of land in Edward Street, in order to extend that Street into the Albert Park Road.

The powers, duties, property and liabilities of the Abingdon Paving Commissioners transfered to the Council as the Urban Sanitary Authority for the District of the Borough of Abingdon, under the provisions contained in the Public Health Act, 1872.

Mr. William Townsend appointed Borough Surveyor.

An order made that only one Minute Book recording the Municipal and Sanitary business should be kept in future, and that the Minutes of the Sanitary Authority to that date be entered therein.

A Letter received from the Local Government Board enquiring what steps had been taken by the Council since Dr. Thorne's Inspection to improve the Sanitary condition of the Town. And the Town Clerk was ordered to reply that an Inspector of Nuisances had been appointed to inspect the Borough with especial reference to Dr. Thorne's report, and that the Inspector's suggestions would be considered in the preparation of the Bye Laws which were about to be submitted by the Council to the Local Government Board for their approval.

A Letter received from the Solicitors for the Conservators of the River Thames, stating they had been instructed to take proceedings against the Council to enforce compliance with the notices their clients had served upon them with regard to the flow of sewage into the River, and enquiring whether any measures were being taken with regard thereto, and the Town Clerk was ordered to reply that the Council had appointed a Committee to visit Lancaster and Nottingham, and make enquiries into the dry earth system in use in those Towns.

𝕿𝖍𝖊 sum of £105 voted by the Council for the re-construction of the Corporation Seats in St. Helen's Church.

August 11th.

𝕬 Tender of £21 for the purchase of the street sweepings for one year accepted, the purchaser finding a horse and cart one day a week, from Michaelmas to Lady-day, the Council undertaking to deliver the manure to the purchaser's premises.

𝕿𝖍𝖊 Committee appointed to visit Lancaster and Nottingham, to enquire into the Dry Earth System in operation in those Towns, presented their report to the Council, wherein they recommended the adoption of the system in Abingdon, the House Sewage being disposed of by means of a process suggested by Mr. Mudd, under which the effluent water would be discharged into the River, in a satisfactory state.

October 23rd.

𝕿𝖍𝖊 Bye Laws prepared by the Sanitary Committee, passed by the Council, and sent to the Local Government Board for approval.

𝕬 Letter received from the Solicitors for the Conservators of the River Thames, stating that they had received peremptory instructions to apply for a Summons against the Council for disregarding the notices which had been served upon them to discontinue the flow of Sewage into the River, and the Town Clerk instructed to reply that the Council were conducting experiments with regard to the disposal of the Sewage of the Town, and request the Conservators not to take any action against the Council.

November 10th.
John Kent,
Mayor.

𝕬 Committee appointed to wait upon the Conservators of the River Thames with reference to the proceedings which their Solicitors had threatened to commence against the Council.

December 9th.

𝕬 Letter received from the Solicitors for the Thames Conservators, stating that they had laid papers before Counsel with instructions to prepare an Indictment against the Corporation for polluting the River.

𝕸𝖗. Roberts, C.E., of Rochdale, invited to visit the Town, and advise the Council with reference to the disposal of the Town Sewage.

𝕸𝖊𝖘𝖘𝖗𝖘. Weare & Co., of Newcastle-under-Lyne, also invited to visit Abingdon, and report as to the application of their Sewage Filtration System to the Town.

On the recommendation of the Gaol Committee, it was resolved to confirm the provisional Agreement which the Committee had made with the County Magistrates, viz.: That the Borough should receive a moiety of the net proceeds of the sale of the late Gaol premises. 1874. January 7th. John Kent, Mayor.

The assent of the Council given to the purchase by the Committee of Visitors of Littlemore Asylum of 7½ acres of land adjoining the Asylum, for the sum of £1000.

The Town Clerk instructed to attend the Auction Sale of Abingdon Gaol, and to signify the acquiescence of the Corporation in the Sale. February 12th.

An Address ordered to be presented to Her Majesty the Queen, congratulating Her Majesty on the Marriage of H.R.H. The Duke of Edinburgh with H.I.H. The Grand Duchess Marie Alexandrovina, of Russia.

The Sanitary Committee instructed to arrange for a site in the Ock Street for carrying out experiments for the purification of the Sewage of the Town. April 6th.

A Bill for the erection of Polling Screens in the Guildhall ordered to be paid. May 14th.

A Paving Rate at 1/- in the £ ordered to be made.

The Special Committee reported that in consequence of the want of sufficient fall at their experimental works in the Ock Street, they had not succeeded in rendering the effluent water sufficiently pure to be discharged into the River Thames. May 29th.

A Report presented to the Council with reference to the Banbury Sewage Farm, and a Committee appointed to visit Coventry to inspect the Sewage Disposal Works in that Town.

The Report of the Committee with reference to the Coventry Drainage System received, when it was resolved to invite the Engineer (Mr. Melliss) to visit Abingdon, and report whether the system could be applied to the Borough. June 26th.

The sum of £1285 : 7 : 4, being half the proceeds of the sale of Abingdon Gaol, received from the County of Berks.

NN

1874.
August 13th.
John Kent,
Mayor.

𝕸r. Melliss, C.E., attended the Council, and presented his report upon the disposal of the Sewage and the Water Supply of the Borough.

October 16th.

𝕬 Committee appointed to visit South Kensington, and enquire as to Mr. Bailey Denton's system of Sewage Filtration, with instructions to invite him to visit Abingdon, and advise the Council upon the application of his system to the Borough.

𝕬 Letter received from the Local Government Board, expressing the Board's regret that nothing had been done by the Council to effect the permanent improvements which Dr. Thorne's Report, forwarded to the Corporation in March, 1873, shewed to be necessary, and requesting that they might be informed, within two months, what steps the Town Council proposed to take to improve the Sanitary Condition of the Borough, and the Town Clerk instructed to reply that the Council were using their utmost endeavours to carry out effectual Sanitary improvements in the Borough, and that they had resolved to invite Mr. Bailey Denton to visit Abingdon, and advise them thereon.

𝕬 Letter received from the Chairman of the Abingdon Rural Sanitary Authority, with reference to the drainage of the Houses in the Spring and Marcham Roads, which were situated without the Borough Boundary, and expressing a desire that when the Borough Drainage Scheme had been decided upon, the Rural Authority might be allowed to become contributory in respect of the Houses situated in the above-mentioned Roads.

October 27th.

𝕸r. Bailey Denton attended a Special Meeting of the Council, and explained his Scheme for the disposal of the Sewage of the Borough.

November 9th.
John Thornhill
Morland,
Mayor.

𝕸r. Bailey Denton's report with reference to the Drainage of Abingdon considered by the Council.

November 10th.

𝕸r. Bailey Denton attended the Council, and further explained his Scheme for the Drainage of Abingdon, when the same was approved and adopted, and notices were directed to be served upon the owners of 73a. 3r. 9p. of land in Sutton Wick, which the Council proposed to purchase for the disposal of the Sewage, as recommended by Mr. Bailey Denton.

$\mathfrak{M}$r. Bailey Denton also instructed to inspect Boar's Hill, in the Parish of Wootton, and ascertain whether the Springs there would afford a sufficient supply of Water for the Borough.

$\mathfrak{M}$r. Bailey Denton's partner, Mr. North, attended the Council, and reported that he had visited Boar's Hill, but that he could not report upon the certainty of a supply of Water being obtained there. And it was ordered that statutory notices should be given of the intention of the Council to purchase five acres of land at Boar's Hill, five acres and one acre in Culham, two acres in St. Nicholas, and two acres in Radley, for the purpose of erecting Waterworks thereon.

$\mathfrak{A}$ Borough Rate at 1/6 in the £ to raise £765 : 18 : 0 ordered to be made.

$\mathfrak{The}$ Borough Seal affixed to a Petition to Parliament for amending the Law relating to Municipal Elections.

$\mathfrak{A}$ notification sent to the Board of Surveyors that in consequence of the Public Health Act, 1872 having transferred to the Council, as the Urban Sanitary Authority, the control of the Highways within the Borough, the Council would take upon themselves the responsibility for such repairs from the 25th instant.

$\mathfrak{M}$r. Bailey Denton's Plans for the Drainage of the Town approved by the Council.

$\mathfrak{An}$ application made to the Local Government Board for power to borrow £29,000, being two years' Rateable Value of Property within the Borough, from the Public Works Loan Commissioners, for the purpose of Sewerage and Water Works for the Town.

$\mathfrak{A}$ Local Inquiry held by Mr. John Thornhill Harrison, C.E., the Local Government Board's Inspector, with reference to the application of the Council for a Provisional Order to enable them the purchase compulsorily the land required for the Sewerage and Water Works, and for alteration of the incidence of Rating under the Sanitary Acts. The Inspector intimated that he should only report favourably as to the site for the Water Works, on the condition that the Council did all they could to obtain a supply from the North side of the Town.

$\mathfrak{M}$r. Harrison held another Inquiry with reference to the application of the Council for power to borrow £29,000 for works of

Sewerage and Water supply, and intimated that he would report favourably with respect to a Loan of £19,000 for Sewerage Works, but the question of the loan for Water Supply would be postponed until he was supplied with further particulars and definite information as to the site from which the water would be obtained.

A Provisional Order issued by the Local Government Board altering the incidence of Rating in the Borough for Sanitary Purposes, and giving the Council power to purchase the land in the parishes of Sutton Wick and Culham required for Sewerage and Water Works respectively.

September 8th.   Instructions given to Mr. Bailey Denton to make an investigation of the ground surrounding Parsons' Cottages, at Old Pound, and also at Boar's Hill, in order to ascertain whether a supply of Water for the Town could be obtained from those combined sources.

October 6th.   A General District Rate at 1/6 in the £ to raise £992 : 5 : 0 ordered to be made.   The Rateable Value of the Borough being £14,807 : 14 : 2.

A Letter received from the Local Government Board, stating that Mr. Bailey Denton had submitted to the Board a supplemental estimate of £90 for some additional Drainage works which he considered necessary, and enquiring if the Council desired that sum to be included in the amount of the proposed Loan, and enclosing an extract from their Inspector's report upon the Scheme for Sewerage Works, from which it appeared that the estimated expenditure was £18,700, made up as follows:—

Land	£5000
Cottages	350
Preparation of Land ...	2500
Engines, Pumps, &c. ...	2150
Sewers	8700
TOTAL ...	£18,700

October 14th.   The Council decided that the Additional Works recommended by Mr. Bailey Denton should be included in the Sewerage Scheme.

𝕿𝖍𝖊 Tenders for the Construction of the Sewerage Works *1875. November 2nd. John Thornhill Morland, Mayor.* (varying from £11,745 to £6,170) received by the Council, and Mr. Potter's tender of £6,170 accepted.

𝕸𝖗. Bailey Denton's report upon the Water Supply for the *November 9th.* Town presented to the Council. Mr. Denton stated that he was satisfied it would not be wise to relinquish entirely the Boar's Hill Springs, and the sinking in the Coral Rag, which together afforded some probability of gaining a valuable, though, he thought, an insufficient supply. The quantity from the Boar's Hill Springs, if collected, he estimated at almost 25,000 gallons per diem, while the outflow from the Coral Rag he reported might be estimated at about 35,000 gallons per diem, this quantity being about one-fifth of the amount actually required for the future population of the Town, and although not sanguine that the Coral Rag would be capable of giving much more than he estimated, yet 60,000 gallons of superior water, obtainable by gravitation commanded consideration, and he recommended that the Council should deposit plans for acquiring an acre of ground at the Cross Roads, at Wootton, where the boring had been made, with such additional land near Boar's Hill Springs as would protect them from pollution. For the remaining quantity of water (minimum 175,000 gallons, maximum 250,000 gallons daily), Mr. Denton recommended the depositing of a plan of the Hospital Meadows in the Abbey, together with a site for a service reservoir next the Old Stone Pit, at Wootton. The water obtained by gravitation Mr. Denton advised should be allocated to the higher parts of the Town, and the water pumped up from the Thames and filtered, to the lower part of the Town, and suggested that if the water power of the Mill could be purchased and utilized for pumping, the annual expenditure might be still further reduced.

𝕿𝖍𝖊 Council directed notices of their intention to purchase the pieces of land mentioned in Mr. Denton's report, and also another piece of land situated on the North side of the Road leading from the Wootton Road to Northcourt.

𝕿𝖍𝖊 Assent of the Local Government Board received for the *December 15th.* purchase by the Council of the whole of the land required for the disposal of the Town Sewage, and to the borrowing of £19,610 from the Public Works Loan Commissioners, at interest at the rate of £4 %

per annum, upon the condition that the capital was repaid within 50 years, and that the Council proceeded to carry out an adequate Scheme of Water Supply, from whatever source it might be necessary to obtain the money.

An application made by the Council to the Treasury for power to advance to the Urban Sanitary Authority the sum they required for Sewerage and Water Supply Works out of the Capital Fund of the Borough, which was invested in Consols.

An application received from the Contractor for the Drainage Works for an additional sum of £500, in consequence of an error he had made in his Tender, and it was resolved, after consultation with Mr. Denton, to allow Mr. Potter the additional sum he asked by way of Bonus, on receipt of a certificate from Mr. Bailey Denton that the whole of the works contained in his Contract had been satisfactorily completed.

A Letter read from Messrs. Challenor & Son, Solicitors of the Board of Surveyors of Highways, for the Parish of St. Helen, stating that the Board was desirous of continuing the maintenance and management of the Highways which were situate in that part of the Parish which was without the Borough, comprising about fourteen miles of Roads, and the Council directed a representation to be made to the Local Government Board to the effect that the Council was very unwilling to assume any authority over that part of the Parish of St. Helen which was without the Borough, and would acquiesce in any scheme for enabling the inhabitants of that part of the parish to manage their own affairs.

A Letter received from the Local Government Board, stating that the Abingdon Urban Sanitary Authority were constituted the Highways Authority for the whole Parish, under the Public Health Act, 1875, and it appeared to the Board therefore that the charge of the Highways in the excluded part of the Parish rested with the Town Council.

The sanction of the Treasury received to the granting of a Loan of £19,610 by the Corporation to the Urban Sanitary Authority, with interest at 4 %, the Capital being repaid within 50 years.

A Committee appointed to superintend and manage the repairs of the Highways in the Parish of St. Helen without the Borough.

A Report received from Mr. Bailey Denton as to the probable supply of water obtainable from Boar's Hill and at Old Pound, and the same being considered unsatisfactory, a trial shaft was ordered to be sunk in the Abbey Meadow, to test the quantity and quality of water obtainable therefrom, the Sanitary and Drainage Committee being also instructed to enquire whether any other site on the North and West sides of the Town would be likely to yield a satisfactory supply of water.

A Notice issued requiring dealers in Gunpowder and other Mixed Explosives to register their premises under the Explosives Act, 1875.

The Borough Seal affixed to a Highway Rate at 10d. in the £ to raise £283 : 14 : 0 for the purpose of defraying the expenses to be incurred in repairing the Highways in St. Helen's Parish without the Borough. March 27th.

A General District Rate at 1/6 in the £ to raise £974 : 14 : 9 ordered to be made. May 11th.

The sum of £5 voted to Mr. Paxman towards the expense of widening the Boxhill footpath to ten feet from the Wootton Road to the Meadow.

Mr. Mason's Tender of £698 : 10 : 0 for supplying a pair of Engines, with Boilers and Pumps, for the Pumping Station, accepted by the Council.

The Borough Seal affixed to a Warrant addressed to the Sheriff of Berks, requiring him to summon a Special Jury to determine the amount to be paid by the Council for the purchase of the land required for the disposal of the Town Sewage in the Parish of Sutton Wick; Mr. A. L. Smith, of the Home Circuit, being retained as Counsel for the Corporation. June 12th.

An enquiry held by the Under-Sheriff of Berks, with an Assessor and a Special Jury, when the following sums were fixed to be paid as compensation for the acquisition of the land required for a Sewage Farm. June 23rd.

	£	s.	d.
To Mr. T. W. Dewe, for the purchase of 16a. 2r. 10p.	2763	10	0
For consequential damages	500	0	0
For Crops thereon	188	15	0
To Mr. Dewe's Trustees for the purchase of their Leasehold Interest in 31a. 2r. 23p. held under Lease from the Ecclesiastical Commissioners ...	1200	0	0
For the Crops thereon	357	10	0
TOTAL ...	£5009	15	0

August 10th.

Mr. Bromley Challenor, the younger, appointed Coroner of the Borough, in the place of Mr. C. Hemming, M.D., resigned.

September 12th.

An application received from the Thames Valley Drainage Commissioners for payment by the Council of the First Rate made by them under the Thames Valley Drainage Acts, 1871 and 1874, at 3/10 in the £, in respect of about 75 acres in Abingdon Common.

The purchase of the Ecclesiastical Commissioners' interest in the 52a. 2r. 35p. of Land required for the Sewage Farm for the sum of £4,500 resolved upon. 31a. 2r. 23p. being purchased by the Sanitary Authority for £3,300, and the remainder (21a. 0r. 12p.) being purchased by the Corporation for £1,200, and paid for out of the proceeds of the Sale of Abingdon Gaol.

November 1st.

A General District Rate at 2/6 in the £ to raise £1,649 : 3 : 6 ordered to be made, and also an Highway Rate at 10d. in the £ to raise £250 for the repair of the Highways in that part of the Parish of St. Helen which was without the Borough.

November 17th.
Edwin Payne,
Mayor.

George Payne promoted to the Office of Senior Sergeant-at-Mace.

Alfred Miles appointed Junior Sergeant-at-Mace.

A Schedule of the duties of the Senior Sergeant-at-Mace and the Scale of Fees to be taken for letting the Council Chambers settled by the Council.

An agreement made with Mr. Bailey Denton to manage the Farm until Christmas, 1877, the Council finding a Foreman; and Mr. Denton receiving half the Profits of the Farm.

$\mathfrak{A}$ Code of Bye-Laws for the regulation of New Streets and Buildings, &c., passed by the Council and sent to the Local Government Board for approval.

$\mathfrak{An}$ order made for the payment of £16 : 16 : 0 to the Secretary of the Local Committee for the Hants and Berks Agricultural Show, being the expenditure incurred by the Committee for extra Police during the Show in Abingdon.

$\mathfrak{An}$ Highway Rate at 10d. in the £ ordered to be made for the part of the Parish of St. Helen without the Borough.

$\mathfrak{The}$ assent of the Council given to the application of the Abingdon Gas-Light & Coke Company, Limited, to the Board of Trade, for a Provisional Order under the Gas and Water Facilities Act, 1870.

$\mathfrak{Mr.}$ George Winship appointed Borough Surveyor and Inspector of Nuisances.

$\mathfrak{The}$ late Head Master's Residence at the Old Grammar School converted into an Office and Residence for the Borough Surveyor; the old School Room being let to the Volunteers at a rent of £8 per annum, as an Armoury and Orderly Room, with permission to use the playground for drill purposes.

$\mathfrak{The}$ First School Attendance Committee appointed under the Elementary Education Act, 1876.

$\mathfrak{The}$ Report of the Executive Committee containing the regulations which they had drafted with reference to the conditions upon which private drains should be allowed to be connected with the Public Sewers, received and adopted by the Council.

$\mathfrak{The}$ death of the Town Clerk (Mr. D. Godfrey) reported to the Council, when the following resolution was passed, viz.:—
" That the Corporation, in recording the death of the late Town Clerk,
" express their high appreciation of the manner in which the late
" Town Clerk fulfilled the duties of his Office, and their esteem for
" his gentlemanly and courteous conduct during his relationship with
" the Members of this Corporation for more than forty years."

$\mathfrak{The}$ Reports of the Finance and General and Sanitary Executive Committees, defining the Duties to be discharged by the Town Clerk and Clerk of the Peace, and Clerk of the Urban Sanitary Authority, received and adopted by the Council.

oo

𝔐r. Bromley Challenor, the younger, elected Town Clerk, Clerk of the Peace, and Clerk to the Urban Sanitary Authority.

March 16th.

𝔄n Highway Rate at 10d. in the £ to raise £283 : 10 : 5 ordered to be made to defray the expenses of repairing the Highways in that part of the Parish of St. Helen which was without the Borough.

April 4th.

𝔄 Deputation appointed to attend a Meeting at Reading of the County Executive Cattle Plague Committee, with authority to state that the Council would have no objection to an order being made prohibiting the importation of Cattle into Abingdon from places other than those situated in the Counties of Berks and Oxon.

May 10th.

𝔄 Letter received from Mr. J. Copeland, resigning his Office of Auditor, and enclosing Cheque for £10, the amount of the Fine payable in consequence thereof.

𝔄 General District Rate at 2/6 in the £ ordered to be made to raise the sum of £1639 : 5 : 4.

May 24th.

𝔄 sum of £500 ordered to be expended in the erection of Farm Buildings at the Sewage Farm.

July 12th.

𝔐r. W. Townsend appointed School Attendance Officer.

𝔄 Letter received from Mr. Bailey Denton, urging the Council to take action with regard to the Water supply of the Town, and it was ordered that the gauging taken by the Borough Surveyor, both at the boring at Wootton and on the Hill above, should be sent to Mr. Denton.

𝔗he New Scheme prepared by the Charity Commissioners for the administration of Roysse's School approved by the Council, with the exception of Clauses 12, 45 and 58, which referred to the Annual Scholarships, the Quorum of Governors, and the Fees payable to the Headmaster by Boarders.

𝔄 Letter received from the Local Government Board declining to sanction the Bye Laws submitted to them by the Council with the Clause giving the Council power to suspend or modify the operation of the Bye Laws in individual cases, and it was resolved that the Clause objected to should be withdrawn.

1877.
August 9th.
Edwin Payne,
Mayor.

𝔄 Letter received from the Charity Commissioners with reference to the suggested alterations in the New Scheme for Roysse's School stating that the Commissioners would consent to reduce the number of Governors to form a Quorum to four, but could not consent to the removal of the restriction on the Fees to be charged by the Head-master for Boarders, but would modify Clause 58 by providing that Five Scholarships only should be limited preferentially to the Public Elementary Schools, and that the other Seven Scholarships should be open to boys who were residing with their parents, &c., in the Municipal Borough, and it was resolved to apply to the Commissioners to extend the limit of such residence to the district of the Parliamentary Borough.

𝔗𝔥𝔢 sum of £100 ordered to be expended in cutting a channel 15 feet deep from the Bore Well at Wootton, for the purpose of gauging the daily flow of Water therefrom, and £50 in sinking trial shafts on the North West, South West, and South East sides of the Town, to ascertain the quantity and quality of Water obtainable there, the minimum recommended as required for the Town being fixed at 12,000 gallons per diem.

𝔗𝔥𝔢 Draft Bye Laws approved by the Local Government Board. August 23rd.

𝔗𝔥𝔢 Borough Surveyor presented a Report to the Council with reference to the stability of the Town Hall.

𝔄 Public Convenience ordered to be erected on the East side of the Tower of the Town Hall.

𝔄 General District Rate at 3/- in the £ ordered to be made to raise £2156 : 5 : 3. September 20th.

𝔄𝔫 iron grating ordered to be fixed at the Head of the Stert Stream, and also a flushing apparatus at the end of the Ock Street, the water for same being taken from the River Ock.

𝔇𝔯. Tidy appointed Public Analyst for the Borough.

𝔑𝔬𝔱𝔦𝔠𝔢𝔰 ordered to be served upon the Owners of the Properties in Turnagain Lane, requiring them to channel, pave and drain the same to the satisfaction of the Borough Surveyor.

𝔗𝔥𝔢 posts in the roadway leading to the Sewage Farm ordered to be removed and re-erected at the end of the Farm farthest from the Town.

𝔄 Coal Shed adjoining the Engine House at the Farm ordered to be erected.

𝔄n Highway Rate at 10d. in the £ to raise £295 : 16 : 7 ordered to be made for that part of the Parish of St. Helen which was without the Borough.

𝔗he Borough Treasurer's Annual Accounts ordered to be printed and circulated amongst the Burgesses.

𝔗he Stert Culvert ordered to be cleared out.

𝔄 charge of £6 per annum ordered to be made on the County of Berks for the privilege of draining the County Police Station into the Borough Sewers.

𝔗he owners of the property in Turnagain Lane not having complied with the Council's notice to pave, &c., the Lane, the work ordered to be done at the cost of the owners of the property there.

𝔗he Land Tax of £2 : 10 : 0 charged on the Sewage Farm redeemed by the Council.

𝔄 Notice received by the Council of an application to the Enclosure Commissioners for a Provisional Order for the Inclosure of Steventon Common.

𝔄 Report received from Mr. Morris, the County Surveyor for Berks, stating that in his opinion the Floor of the Town Hall was capable of supporting the weight of any audience which could be accommodated therein.

𝔄 Letter received from the Master and Governors of Christ's Hospital enquiring whether the Urban Sanitary Authority would be willing to take over the Park Roads, and if so, upon what terms they would do so.

𝔄 Petition received from persons residing in the Victoria Road, praying that their Houses might be connected with the Town Sewers, or that they might be excused from paying the General District Rate.

𝔐essrs. Bailey Denton, Son & North's report upon the Water Supply of the Town presented to the Council. In their Report the Engineers stated that the boring at Wootton had been continued to a depth of 77 feet, and that the gaugings shewed a maximum supply of 194,000 gallons per diem, and a minimum of 158,000 gallons.

This supply they did not consider quite satisfactory in quantity, but pointed out that there existed above Wootton sundry springs issuing from the Green Sand formation, which, if carefully tapped and brought by pipes down to the Well, would afford an additional quantity of from 25,000 to 35,000 gallons per diem, which would be sufficient for some years, but pointing out that a reduction of quantity might possibly occur after a succession of dry years, but that by care in construction of works and economy in their use, on no occasion would the inhabitants of the Town know a scarcity, and that should an increased supply thereafter become necessary it could be obtained by recourse to pumping from the gravel beds in Andersey Island, but before resorting to this supply, they stated that by cuttings and headings more or less extensive in the neighbourhood of the Well at Wootton, it would be possible to increase the outflow from the Well.

1878.
February 27th.
John Tomkins,
Mayor.

March 14th.

The names of Messrs. J. T. Morland, J. H. Clarke, E. L. Shepherd, and J. Dickey, were recommended by the Council to the Lord Chancellor for insertion in the Commission of the Peace for the Borough.

The Commission of the Peace returned to the Secretary of Commissions in order that a new Commission might be issued under the Crown Office Act, 1877.

Mr. Alderman Charles Payne intimated to the Council that he intended to send to the Lord Chancellor his resignation as a Justice of the Peace of the Borough.

The Sanitary Committee reported that they had had an interview with a deputation from the Master and Governors of Christ's Hospital with reference to the dedication of the Park Roads to the Public, and that the Deputation had stated that they would prefer to retain possession of the Roads, and would take into consideration the question of constructing a Sewer in the Park, at their next meeting,

A Loan of £3000 raised upon security of a Mortgage of the Sewage Farm.

A Bye Law made restricting the passage of Locomotives propelled by Steam through the Town, except between the hours of Midnight and 9 a.m. between the 25th March and the 29th September, and from Midnight to 10 a.m. from 29th September to 25th March.

$\mathcal{A}$ Sewer constructed in Edward Street and a Flushing Tank in Exbourne Place at a cost of £100.

$\mathcal{A}$ General District Rate at 3/- in the £ to raise £2132 : 11 : 3 ordered to be made.

$\mathcal{A}$ Surface Water Drain constructed in St. Edmund's Lane, at a cost of £115, and a Flushing Chamber in East St. Helen Street, at a cost of £12.

$\mathcal{T}he$ Abyssinian Pumps which had been erected in various parts of the Town for the temporary supply of Water to the Inhabitants ordered to be removed.

$\mathcal{A}n$ Highway Rate at 10d. in the £ to raise £299 : 12 : 6 ordered to be made for defraying the expense of Repairing the Highways in the part of St. Helen's Parish which was without the Borough.

$\mathcal{A}$ Letter received from the Secretary of Commissions stating that the Lord Chancellor had selected the names of Messrs. Morland, Clarke and Shepherd, for insertion in the Commission of the Peace, and the Council resolved to ask the Lord Chancellor to reconsider his decision and to include Mr. Dickey's name also in the Commission.

June 20th.

$\mathcal{A}n$ Highway Rate at 10d. in the £ to raise £299 : 12 : 6 for Highway purposes ordered to be made for the part of St. Helen's Parish without the Borough.

$\mathcal{T}he$ sum of £210 ordered to be expended in Paving and channeling Edward Street.

$\mathcal{M}r.$ Morris, the Berks County Surveyor, instructed to Survey the Borough Buildings, and to report upon their Condition to the Council.

$\mathcal{I}n$ consequence of the nuisance caused by persons keeping Swine, a Public Notice ordered to be published calling attention to the Bye Laws dealing with the matter, and requesting persons desiring to make complaints to enter same in a Book which had been provided for the purpose at the Surveyor's Office.

$\mathcal{A}n$ application ordered to be made to the Local Government Board for power to borrow £10,000 for Water Supply purposes.

The appointment of James Reader White Bros, Esq., as Recorder of Abingdon, in the place of his Father (resigned), notified to the Council.

A Letter received from the Secretary of Commissions stating that the Lord Chancellor did not consider it advisable to make any further addition to the Borough Bench by adding Mr. Dickey's name to the Commission of the Peace.

The Culvert over the Stream at Northcourt rebuilt by the Highways Committee at a cost of £28 : 14 : 8.

Mr. Edwin Payne and Mr. John Tomkins elected Representative Governors of Roysse's School by the Council.

A notification received from the Lord Chancellor that he had added the name of Mr. Edwin James Trendell to the Commission of the Peace for the Borough.

A new Sewer in New Street ordered to be constructed at a cost of £21.

The Sewage Farm let on Lease for seven years at a rent of £225 per annum. The Council agreeing to expend £100 in erecting a cow shed and root house and forming a cattle yard.

The Borough Surveyor ordered to take steps for enforcing the registration of Canal Boats, under the Canal Boats Act, 1877.

A General District Rate at 3/- in the £ to raise £2163 ordered to be made.

The Borough Surveyor instructed to prepare a plan and estimate for widening the Iron Bridge, over the River Ock, at St. Helen's Wharf.

An application made to the Secretary of State for the Home Department, for an Order authorizing the Borough Justices to Commit Prisoners to Oxford Castle instead of to Reading Gaol, under the provisions of the Prisons Act, 1877.

Mr. G. A. Drewe, M.R.C.V.S., appointed Cattle Inspector, under the Contagious Diseases (Animals) Act, 1878.

An application made to the Court of Quarter Sessions for the County of Berks, for repayment of a moiety of the expense of repairing the Abingdon and Faringdon Main Road, under the provisions contained in the Highways and Locomotives Act, 1878.

𝕸r. J. C. Clarke, M.P., presented to the Council a Badge and Centre Link towards forming a Chain of Office for the use of the Mayor on State occasions.

𝕬 Letter received from the Home Secretary stating that the Governor of Oxford Prison had been instructed to receive Prisoners committed by the Borough Justices into that Prison.

𝕬n Address of Condolence ordered to be presented to Her Majesty the Queen on the occasion of the death of H.R.H. The Princess Alice of Great Britain and Grand Duchess of Hesse.

𝕬 Highway Rate at 10d. in the £ to raise £302 : 12 : 6 ordered to be made for Highway purposes for the part of St. Helen without the Borough.

𝕬ll Dairies, Cow Sheds and Milk Shops in the Borough, ordered to be registered under the Order recently issued by the Privy Council.

𝕿he Finance Committee instructed to enquire what steps could be taken to secure better accommodation for persons attending the Weekly Market.

𝕿he Mayor requested by the Council to convene a Public Meeting to consider the question of providing better accommodation for the Corn Market.

𝕬n application ordered to be made to the County Justices for an order declaring the Marcham Road to be a Main Road, in lieu of the Faringdon Road.

𝕿he Oil Painting by Mr. H. J. Brooks, representing the Mayor, Aldermen and Councillors assembled in Council, presented to the Corporation.

𝕿he Artesian Well in the Sheep Market ordered to be sunk 3 feet deeper, and also a manhole constructed in the Stert Culvert, near St. Nicholas Church, for the purpose of supplying water in case of Fire.

𝕿he question of the price to be paid for the Acre of Land at Wootton, for the Waterworks, referred to Arbitration, the owners having declined to accept the offer of £150 made by the Council.

1879.
April 24th.
William
Ballard,
Mayor.

A General District Rate at 3/- in the £ to raise £2159 : 16 : 4 ordered to be made.

The Mayor reported that at a recent Meeting of the Corn Market Committee and persons interested in the Market, the following resolution was passed, viz. :—" That this Committee is of opinion that a "Corn Exchange is of the first importance, and will add to the con- "venience of buyers and sellers attending this Market, and respectfully "requests the Corporation to take early steps to provide one."

The assent of the Council given to the raising of the necessary funds required on the dissolution of the Asylum Union by the withdrawal of the County of Berks and the Borough of Reading therefrom.

The Borough Seal affixed to a Contract with Messrs. Silver & Son for the restoration of the Municipal Buildings.

A Rate of 8d. in the £ ordered to be made for Highway Purposes May 8th. for the part of the Parish of St. Helen without the Borough.

A Memorial received from Messrs. William Stacy, James Williams and other ratepayers of the part of the Parish of St. Helen without the Borough, asking the Council to allow three or four of the largest Ratepayers in the Parish to act with the Highways Committee as a Consultative Committee in matters relating to the repairs of the Highways in the Rural part of the Parish.

The Mayor reported he had received the Badge of Office which June 19th. Mr. J. C. Clarke, M.P., had presented to the Council for the use of the Mayor, and a vote of thanks was given to Mr. Clarke for his handsome present to the Corporation, and also a similar vote of thanks to the Mayor and to the past Mayors who had contributed links to the Chain.

The Borough Surveyor reported that he had continued the boring at the Well in the Sheep Market to a depth of 57 feet, when a large supply of water rose above the surface; and on the water being gauged at one foot above the surface of the ground, the flow was found to be 57,600 gallons per 24 hours.

On the recommendation of the Sanitary Committee the Council resolved that the charge for Water for private and domestic use should be regulated by a rate based upon the Rateable value of the

PP

premises requiring the supply or by agreement, and not by meter, except in cases where water was supplied for Trade purposes, when meters should be used.

The sum of £1232 : 2 : 1 India 4 % Stock sold to defray the cost of the restoration of the Municipal Buildings.

The Borough Seal affixed to the Contracts with Messrs. Firmstone Brothers, for supplying iron pipes, &c., and Messrs. J. Stone & Co., for valves, &c., and Mr. H. Potter, for constructing the Waterworks, the total amount of the Contracts being £4214.

July 23rd.

The regulations prepared by the Waterworks' Engineers and the Borough Surveyor, with reference to the Water supply, approved by the Council.

August 14th.

The Cupboards at the East end of the large Council Chamber ordered to be removed, and two seats erected in the recesses in their place; the Gas Fittings at the side of the room also ordered to be removed, and replaced by 3 lights in the centre of the room.

A Fire-proof Safe purchased for the safe keeping of the Corporation Plate.

Mr. Castle appointed to act as Arbitrator in the matter of the proposal of the Corporation to pay a fixed sum to the Governors of Roysse's School in commutation of the Council's liability to repair and insure the School Buildings.

September 23rd.

A Meeting of the Council convened, but a quorum of Members not being present, the Meeting was adjourned.

September 25th.

The Culvert over the Larkhill Stream, in the Wootton Road, rebuilt at a cost of £25.

The Clerk to the Guardians instructed to forward weekly, to the Medical Officer of Health, a Return of New Cases of Pauper Sickness in the Borough, in consequence of a circular letter recently issued by the Local Government Board.

The Award of the Arbitrator received, fixing £150 as the price to be paid by the Urban Sanitary Authority for the acre of land required for the Waterworks at Wootton.

A General District Rate at 3/- in the £ to raise £2169 : 16 : 7 ordered to be made.

A Notice issued inviting Tradesmen who were desirous of being certified for the performance of Plumbers' work connected with the Water supply to send in their names to the Borough Surveyor.

On the recommendation of the Sanitary Committee it was resolved : Firstly—That a rate of 1/- in the £ be levied on the premises of persons taking Water for domestic purposes. Secondly— That where Water was taken for other than domestic purposes a Meter should be used, and a charge of 2/- per 1000 gallons made, with a minimum payment equivalent to a rate of 1/- in the £ on the Rateable value of the premises taking the Water; and Thirdly— In cases where a Bath was supplied an additional Rate of 3d. in the £ be charged.

Notice given to the holders of the late Paving Commissioners' Bonds of the intention of the Urban Sanitary Authority to pay off such Bonds, and an application made to the Treasury and the Local Government Board for power to sell sufficient of the Capital Stock of the Corporation to produce £3675, the amount required to pay off such Bonds.

Mr. Castle's Award in the matter of the commutation of the liability of the Corporation to repair and insure the Buildings of Roysse's School received, the amount fixed by the Arbitrator being either the annual payment of £20, or a capital sum of £500, when it was resolved to accept the first suggestion.

An Highway Rate at 8d. in the £ to raise £253 : 13 : 0 ordered to be made for the repairs of the Highways of the Parish of St. Helen without the Borough.

A Deputation appointed to visit Banbury and Warwick, to make enquiries into the system adopted in those Towns for charging for Water supplied from the Town Waterworks.

Tenders invited for repairing the Roads in the part of the parish of St. Helen without the Borough.

The Well at Wootton ordered to be enlarged to a capacity of 100,000 gallons.

A Letter received from the Local Government Board enquiring why no samples of Food or Drugs had been submitted to the Public Analyst for analysis, and the Town Clerk was instructed to reply that as no complaints had been received by the Council, they had not considered it necessary to incur the expense of sending samples of Food, &c., for analysis.

April 27th.

𝔄𝔫 Highway Rate at 9d. in the £ to raise £362 ordered to be made for the part of the Parish of St. Helen without the Borough.

𝔗𝔥𝔢 Highway Committee reported that they had not received any satisfactory Tenders for the repair of the Highways under their management, and they recommended that they should continue to repair the Roads as theretofore.

𝔐𝔯. Paxman's (the Tenant of Fitzharris Farm) offer to maintain that portion of the Boxall footpath which was within the Borough for £3 : 3 : 0 per annum accepted by the Council.

𝔗𝔥𝔢 posts in the passage between Stert Street and the Market Place ordered to be re-erected.

𝔄 Donation of £25 and an Annual Subscription of £15 : 15 : 0 voted towards the Funds of the Volunteer Fire Brigade; the Old Borough Engine also ordered to be sold, and the Borough Surveyor instructed to prepare plans for the erection of an Engine House in the Guildhall Yard for the use of the Brigade.

𝔄 Summons issued at the instance of the Conservators of the River Thames against the Urban Sanitary Authority for polluting the River at the Sewage Farm heard by the County Justices and dismissed.

𝔄 General District Rate at 2/10 in the £ to raise £2039 : 19 : 1 ordered to be made.

𝔄 Special Committee appointed to enquire into the question of the repairs of the Highways without the Borough by the Council.

𝔗𝔥𝔢 Local Government Board Inspector held an inquiry with reference to the application of the Urban Sanitary Authority for a Provisional Order to amend the Abingdon Paving Act, so as to allow the Authority to redeem the Bonds issued by the late Paving Commissioners.

𝔄 Special Committee appointed on the motion of Mr. Alderman Morland to consider the practicability of providing a Public Bathing Place for the Town.

Messrs. A. H. Simpson and E. J. Harris, the Borough Auditors, resigned Office and paid the fine of £10 each.

1880.
April 27th.
William
Ballard,
Mayor.

Seven Cottages at the Corner of Bury Street, opposite the Black Bull Public House, purchased for £300, for widening the Street. May 15th.

On the recommendation of the Finance Committee the Borough Surveyor's Plans for a Fire Brigade Station were approved by the Council, and a tender of £110 for the work accepted. August 12th.

A set of new Chairs purchased for the Council Chambers.

An application made to the Thames Conservators for their permission for fitting up the island in the River, near the Lock, as a Public Bathing place.

The Sanitary Committee reported that they had visited Leamington, Warwick and Banbury, and obtained information as to management of the Waterworks in those Towns, and recommended the Council to reconsider the regulation made some time previously with reference to the charge for supplying water, and in lieu thereof to charge in all cases by Meter, at the rate of 1/6 per 1000 gallons.

The pitching stones in the Roadway in East St. Helen Street taken up and the road remade with Macadam.

A Brick pavement laid on the West side of Bury Street.

A Report received from the Boundary Committee setting out the result of their enquiry as to what were the actual boundaries of the Municipal Borough. And it was ordered that the Boundaries as defined by the Committee should be beaten on the 13th August.

A Letter received from the Secretary of Commissions stating that the Lord Chancellor proposed to include Mr. Joseph Dickey's name in the Commission of the Peace for the Borough.

Mr. Arthur E. Preston, appointed Collector of the General District Rate.

A Tower erected over the entrance to the Reservoir at Wootton at a cost of £100. September 24th.

An application made to the Thames Conservators and to Mr. Morrell for permission to erect a foot Bridge over the Thames to connect the Bathing Place with the Towing path.

1880.
September 24th.
William
Ballard,
Mayor.

A Letter received from the Local Government Board with reference to the proposal to change the Highway Authority for that part of the Parish of St. Helen which was without the Borough, by constituting the same a separate Parish, and it was ordered that the Guardians of the Abingdon Union should be requested to consider the suggestion.

The Report of the Borough Surveyor upon the supply of Water from the Well in the Sheep Market received, and the Finance Committee directed to consider the question of providing a drinking Fountain in the Sheep Market.

October 28th.

An agreement entered into with the Abingdon Rural Sanitary Authority for the connection of the drains of the Houses in the Marcham and Spring Roads with the Town Sewers; the Rural Authority agreeing to construct the necessary connecting Sewers and pay an annual rent of £90 for the easement.

Mr. James Williams appointed Surveyor of Highways without the Borough.

November 9th.
Thomas
Townsend,
Mayor.

The sum of £500 paid out of the surplus of the Borough Fund to the Governors of Roysse's School in discharge of the liability of the Corporation to repair and insure the School Buildings.

Permission given to the Borough Surveyor to undertake private professional work.

1881.
January 7th.

The Council resolved to join the Association of Municipal Corporations.

The Scheme for the construction of a Bridge over the River at the Bathing Place abandoned on account of the expense thereof.

Two outfalls drains for carrying the Surface Water constructed in the Ock Street; the Master and Governors of Christ's Hospital being requested to contribute to the cost thereof on the ground that a quantity of the water came from their roads in the Parish.

February 10th.

The sum of £150 voted by the Council for clearing the Streets of the extraordinary fall of Snow on the preceding 18th and 19th January.

Proceedings ordered to be taken against several large Ratepayers in the Parish of St. Helen without the Borough who had refused to pay the Highway Rate which had lately been made by the Council.

𝔗𝔥𝔢 Master and Governors of Christ's Hospital agreed to contribute £20 towards the expense of the Outfalls of the Surface Water Drains in the Ock Street.

𝔄 Deputation appointed to wait on the Local Government Board to urge the desirability of a Clause being inserted in some Government Bill enabling the Ratepayers of that portion of the Parish of St. Helen without the Borough to repair their own Highways.

𝔑𝔢𝔤𝔬𝔠𝔦𝔞𝔱𝔦𝔬𝔫𝔰 opened with the Authorities of the County of Oxford for the settlement of the question of the Boundaries of the Borough on the River side of the Town.

March 8th.

𝔗𝔥𝔢 Members of Parliament for the County and Borough requested to oppose certain clauses in the Thames Conservancy Bill then before Parliament.

𝔄𝔫 Highway Rate at 10d. in the £ to raise £308 : 17 : 10 ordered to be made for the repair of the Highways in the Parish of St. Helen without the Borough.

𝔐𝔯. Potter's tender of £137 for the Surface Water Drain and Outfall in the Ock Street accepted.

𝔐𝔯. O. Rowbotham appointed Superintendent of the Borough Police.

April 14th.

𝔄 General District Rate at 2/6 in the £ to raise £1819 ordered to be made.

May 12th.

𝔚𝔞𝔱𝔢𝔯 ordered to be supplied to persons residing in the Spring Road, without the Borough Boundary, from the Town Main, at the rate of 2/6 per 1000 gallons.

𝔗𝔥𝔢 Pathway on the East side of the Spring Road, from Ock Street to Exbourne Place, ordered to be paved with Blue Bricks.

August 11th.

𝔗𝔥𝔢 Borough Surveyor appointed Examiner of Gas Meters.

𝔗𝔥𝔢 settlement of the question of the Boundary between the Borough and the County of Oxford reported to the Council, and a plan of the Boundary as settled by the Joint Committee, deposited in the Corporation Safe.

𝕿𝖍𝖊 Bathing Place opened for the use of Ladies at specified times.

𝕿𝖍𝖊 sum of £350 voted for purchasing a portion of the Two Brewers' Public House, which adjoined St. Nicholas Church, for the purpose of widening the Street.

𝕬 Special Report upon the condition of the Stert Culvert presented to the Council by the Borough Surveyor.

𝖂𝖆𝖑𝖑 Plates to mark the position of the Fire Hydrants and Valves ordered to be fixed in the Streets.

September 29th.

𝕺𝖓 the recommendation of the Boundary Committee the Council decided to accept the decision of the County Justices with regard to the Boundary between the Borough and the County of Berks.

𝕿𝖍𝖊 sum of £178 voted towards the expense of repairing and cleansing the Stert Culvert.

𝕬 General District Rate at 2/6 in the £ producing £2038 : 10 : 4 ordered to be made.

𝕬 Letter received from the Secretary of the Abingdon Angling Defence Association enclosing a copy of a resolution passed at a Public Meeting held on the previous 30th August, urging the Council to protect the Fishery Rights of the Burgesses in the River Thames as conferred by the Borough Charters.

November 9th.
Edward Leader
Shepherd,
Mayor.

𝕬𝖓 application made to the Local Government Board for the Board's sanction to the Accounts of the Corporation and Urban Sanitary Authority being made up to the 25th March and 29th September, instead of to the 1st March and the 1st September as theretofore.

1882.
January 5th.

𝕬𝖓 offer received from a London Firm to light the Town with the Electric Light.

𝕬 Special Committee appointed to visit the Electric Lighting Exhibition, held at the Crystal Palace, London.

𝕿𝖍𝖊 question of extending the Boundaries of the Borough discussed, and a Committee appointed to make enquiries and to report thereon to the Council.

𝕿𝖍𝖊 Resolution of the Committee of Visitors of Littlemore Asylum to set aside an Acre of Land for the purpose of a Burial Ground for Patients dying in the Asylum, confirmed by the Council.

𝕬 Letter received from the Right Hon. The Lord Mayor of London, inviting the Council to co-operate in establishing an Association for the Defence of property in Ireland, but no order was made thereon.

𝕬𝖓 application directed to be made to the Prisons' Commissioners to repay the cost incurred by the Council in conveying Prisoners from Abingdon to Oxford Prison.

𝕬𝖓 Highway Rate at 6d. in the £ to raise £370 ordered to be made for that part of St. Helen's Parish which was without the Borough.

𝕬𝖓 application made to the Churchwardens and Overseers of the Parish of St. Helen for permission to deposit the Town Refuse, &c., on the land known as the Recreation Ground, in the Marcham Road, adjoining Abingdon Common.

𝕬 General District Rate at 2/6 in the £ to raise £2050 ordered to be made.

𝕬 Report of the Medical Officer of Health upon the Slaughter Houses, Common Lodging House, and the Courts in the Borough, presented to the Council, when it was ordered that the Owner of Badcock's Row, in Bury Street, should be served with a notice to close his property until the same had been made fit for human habitation.

𝕿𝖍𝖊 following resolution unanimously passed by the Council, viz.: "That we the Mayor, Aldermen and Burgesses of this Borough, "assembled in Council, desire to express our feelings of horror and "indignation at the terrible murder of Lord Frederick Cavendish "and Mr. Burke, in Dublin, on Saturday last, and trust that the efforts "of the Government, added to those of all law abiding Citizens of "the Kingdom, will speedily be successful in detecting and bringing "to Justice the cowardly assassins who so treacherously took the "lives of those two unarmed gentlemen."

𝕺𝖓 the recommendation of the Paving Committee the footway on the South side of Ock Street, from Norrington's Cottages to the end of the Street, ordered to be paved with blue bricks.

1882.
May 11th.
Edward Leader
Shepherd,
Mayor.

The price charged for Water reduced to 1/- per 1000 gallons to consumers within the Borough, and 1/6 per 1000 gallons to consumers residing without the Borough.

A Letter received from the Abingdon Rural Sanitary Authority, enquiring if the Council would be willing to extend their Sanitary District so as to embrace the Rural portions of the Town.

The Two Pictures by Gainsborough, in the Council Chamber, ordered to be glazed with plate glass to protect them from damage.

August 10th.

An application made to the Local Government Board for an order constituting the portion of the Parish of St. Helen without the Borough a separate Parish for Highway purposes pursuant to the Highway Rate and Assessment Act, 1882, which had recently been passed.

An application made to the Abingdon District Highway Board to take steps to compel the Wilts and Berks Canal Company to remove a fence which they had erected in the Caldecot Road, in the Parish of Sutton Wick.

A Schedule of prices to be paid by the Abingdon Gas-Light and Coke Company, Limited, when it broke up the streets for the purpose of laying or repairing the Company's gas mains, agreed upon.

A General District Rate at 2/3 in the £ to raise £1861 : 11 : 9 ordered to be made.

The Resolution passed by the Committee of Visitors of Littlemore Asylum to erect a Residence for the Medical Superintendent and a Chapel for the use of the Inmates confirmed by the Council.

The settlement of the question of the Borough Boundary between the Council and the Justices of the County of Berks reported to the Council, and a Copy of the Award and Map deposited in the Corporation Safe.

November 3rd.

The Highways Committee reported that a Public Meeting of the Ratepayers of the part of the Parish of St. Helen without the Borough, had been held on the previous 12th October, but the meeting declined to pass a resolution in favour of the part of the Parish being formed into a separate Highway Parish, and therefore the Urban Sanitary Authority would be obliged to continue the management of the Roads of the Parish as theretofore.

A Letter received from the Education Department stating that the Department considered it unfortunate that cases before the Magistrates were so frequently adjourned in order to give parents an opportunity of escaping punishment by a tardy compliance with the law, the result of the lenity of the Justices being seen in the bad attendance of which complaint had been made by H.M. Inspector, and urging that some means should be adopted for bringing Public Opinion of the Borough to bear upon the question of School Attendance.

1882.
November 3rd.
Edward Leader
Shepherd,
Mayor.

Notices received from three Electric Light Companies of their intention to apply to the Board of Trade for a Provisional Order to supply Electricity for any Public or Private purpose within the Borough, in pursuance of the Electric Lighting Act, 1882.

A Special Committee appointed to consider and report upon the damage caused by the flooding of the Stert during a Storm on the 24th October previous, and also upon the nuisance caused by the effluvia emitted from the Manholes in the Sewers.

The Report of the Boundary Committee recommending the extension of the Borough Boundary presented to the Council.

The Report of the Finance Committee with reference to a claim for compensation presented by Mr. J. Williams and other Ratepayers to the Urban Sanitary Authority for alleged illegal payments made by the Highways Committee received, the Committee reporting that the Memorialists had no just claim for compensation.

An application made to the Great Western Railway Company to provide a Foot-Bridge over the Railway at Radley Station.

November 9th.
Edwin Payne,
Mayor.

An Highway Rate at 6d. in the £ to raise £182 : 0 : 3 ordered to be made for the Parish of St. Helen without the Borough.

Mr. C. Tame appointed Surveyor of Highways for the Parish of St. Helen without the Borough.

1883.
January 11th.

The Highways Committee reported to the Council that on the 1st instant, at a Meeting of the Owners and Ratepayers in that part of the Parish of St. Helen which was without the Borough, it had been unanimously resolved that it was desirable that that portion of the Parish should be formed into a separate Highway Parish, and the Committee therefore expected they would be shortly released from the

February 8th.

anxious and unthankful duties which they had been called upon to perform for so many years past in managing the Highways in the Rural portion of the Parish.

𝔄 General District Rate at 2/3 in the £ to raise £1861 : 10 : 0 ordered to be made.

𝔐𝔯. William Ballard elected Mayor in the place of Mr. Alderman Edwin Payne, deceased.

𝔐𝔯. Councillor J. H. Clarke elected Representative Governor of Roysse's School by the Council.

𝔄𝔫 application made to the Local Government Board to appoint one of their Inspectors to act as Arbitrator in the matter of the dispute between the Council and some of the Ratepayers of the part of the Parish of St. Helen without the Borough, with reference to the Repairs of the Highways in the Parish of St. Helen without the Borough.

𝔗𝔥𝔢 Pavement on the South side of Ock Street, from the Cross Keys to the Conduit Road, and on the North side of the Vineyard, ordered to be relaid with Blue Bricks.

𝔗𝔥𝔢 Urban Sanitary Authority declined to pay the sum of £3 : 15 : 0 claimed by Mr. Dewe, for three years rent of the Fisherman's Swath, at the Sewage Farm.

𝔄 Muniment Safe for the preservation of the Corporation Records purchased by the Council at a cost of £41 : 7 : 9.

𝔄 Letter received from the Privy Council complaining of the state of the Cattle Sale Yard at the rear of the Rising Sun Inn, in the Sheep Market.

𝔐𝔯. C. Coxeter, the younger, resigned the Office of Auditor, and paid the fine of £10.

𝔗𝔥𝔢 resignation of Mr. G. A. Drewe, of the Office of Cattle Inspector received, he having been elected a Councillor of the Borough.

𝔄 notification received from the Local Government Board that they had issued an order forming the part of St. Helen's Parish which was without the Borough, into a separate Highway Parish, and also stating that they did not consider they had any jurisdiction enabling them to intervene in the dispute between the Council and certain Ratepayers of the said Parish.

𝕬𝖓 Highway Rate at 8d. in the £ to produce £224 ordered to be made for the Parish of St. Helen without the Borough.

𝕬 General District Rate at 2/3 in the £ to produce £1863 : 7 : 8 ordered to be made.

𝕬 Letter received from Mr. E. J. Trendell, offering to contribute £50 towards the expense of lowering the roadway in the vicinity of St. Nicholas Church, but the consideration of the matter was postponed.

𝕿𝖍𝖊 sum of £200 voted by the Council towards a Scheme of the Master and Governors of Christ's Hospital for pulling down the Anchor Public House and the adjoining Almshouses, at St. Helen's Wharf, and constructing an Esplanade along the River front on the site thereof.

𝕸𝖗. Alderman Tomkins re-elected Representative Governor of Roysse's School by the Council.

𝕿𝖍𝖊 Oil Painting of the Martyrdom of St. Sebastian, in the Council Chamber, ordered to be glazed with plate glass, at a cost of £9 : 10 : 0.

𝕬𝖓 Highway Rate at 8d. in the £ to produce £242 : 14 : 2 ordered to be made for the part of the Parish of St. Helen without the Borough.

𝕬 Letter received from the Local Government Board, calling attention to the observations in the Reports of the Medical Officer of Health, for the years 1882 and 1883, with reference to the impurity of the Well water in the Town, and the absence of proper arrangements for Flushing Closets in several Courts in the Borough.

𝕿𝖍𝖊 Town Clerk instructed to write to the Conservators of the River Thames and inform them that in the opinion of the Council the new Weir which they were constructing at the Lock would, when in operation, seriously damage the Borough Bathing Place, and request them to erect some Camp Sheathing so as to protect the Island from the force of the Stream.

𝕬 Letter received from Mr. J. C. Clarke, M.P., stating that he had forwarded to the Mayor a copy of a resolution passed at a Public

Meeting, held in the Council Chamber, on the previous 4th December, urging the Council to undertake the Building of a Corn Exchange and Cattle Market, and stating that in his opinion there was nothing the Council could do to more effectually improve and help the trade of the Town than to carry out the suggestions made by the Meeting; and the Finance Committee was directed to report upon the matter to the Council.

A Letter received from the Thames Valley Drainage Commissioners, stating that having received a report from their Engineer they did not purpose to undertake any works for protecting the Borough Bathing Place from the wash from the new Weir which they were constructing at the Lock.

An application for payment of the Rate levied by the Thames Valley Drainage Commissioners, in respect to Abingdon Common, refused by the Council.

February 11th.

A General District Rate at 2/3 in the £ to produce £1874 : 14 : 4 ordered to be made.

April 23rd.

The Right Hon. Montague Bertie, Earl of Abingdon and Baron Norreys of Rycote, elected High Steward of the Borough, in the place of his Father, the late Earl, deceased.

The Borough Surveyor instructed to prepare a Plan for widening the Narrow, in the High Street, near the site of the three houses which had been recently destroyed by fire.

May 8th.

The Corn Exchange and Cattle Market Committee recommended that a Valuer should be employed to value three sites which they had selected as the most convenient for the erection and construction of a Corn Exchange and Cattle Market, viz.: (*a*) In the Market Place and Bury Street; (*b*) In the Sheep Market and Bath Street; and (*c*) In the Ock Street and Windsmore Lane; but the Council decided to acquire the Market Place and Bury Street site for the purpose.

May 20th.

On the recommendation of the Corn Exchange and Cattle Market Committee the Council resolved to purchase the Foundry Premises adjoining the yard of the Plough and Anchor Public House, in Bury Street, for £400, for the purposes of the Cattle Market, and also a piece of land forming a portion of the Garden of Mr. Tomkins' House, in the Sheep Market, recently destroyed by Fire, for £150, for the purpose of making a Roadway 20 feet wide from the Cattle Market through the Blue Boar Yard into Bath Street, so as to obviate the adoption of the Valuer's suggestion, that Messrs. Morland & Co. should be allowed a portion of the Market site for the purpose of erecting a Public House thereon. The Committee also recommended that the Council should purchase of Mr. Tomkins the piece of land at the rear of the House belonging to the Master and Governors of Christ's Hospital, in the High Street, for the sum of £50, and should also endeavour to purchase the Hospital property which had been damaged by the Fire, so that the house might be pulled down, and the street line set back at that spot.

Permission given to the Owner of a House in Bridge Street to place a cellar grating in the Guildhall Yard for ventilating his property, on payment of a rent of 10/- per annum for the easement.

A General District Rate at 2/3 in the £ to produce £1874 : 14 : 4 ordered to be made.

The House in the Narrow, belonging to Christ's Hospital, agreed to be purchased by the Council for £450. The Council also agreed to sell to Messrs. Morland & Co. the piece of land which they had purchased of Mr. Tomkins, for making a roadway into Bath Street from the Market, for the same sum as they had given for it, the purchasers giving the Council a right of way from the Market into Bath Street, through the Yard of the Blue Boar Inn, the Corporation, on their part, giving the purchasers a right of way into the Market from the Blue Boar Yard. The Cost of the Market Site and Improvement of the High Street being reported to be as follows :—

Market Site.

	£	s.	d.
Purchase of the Anchor and Oxford Arms Inns, in the Market Place	1350	0	0
Ditto of Foundry Premises, at rear thereof	370	0	0
Land (part of Mr. Tomkins' Garden)	150	0	0
	£1870	0	0
Land resold to Messrs. Morland & Co.	150	0	0
TOTAL COST ...	£1720	0	0

High Street Improvement.

	£	s.	d.
Purchase of the frontages of Mr. Tomkins' House and Mr. Kennedy's two strips	50	0	0
For the Lessee's interest in the Christ Hospital Premises adjoining, and for the piece of Freehold Land at the rear thereof	300	0	0
For the Freehold of the Premises belonging to Christ Hospital	450	0	0
	£800	0	0
Less Cash received from the Insurance Company for damage caused by the Fire to the Premises belonging to Christ Hospital	250	0	0
TOTAL COST ...	£550	0	0

November 7th.

A Superannuation allowance of £15 per annum granted to George Payne on his resigning the Office of Senior Sergeant at Mace.

The Superintendent of the Borough Police appointed Inspector of Weights and Measures for the Borough.

A Letter received from the Treasury with reference to the Chancellor of the Exchequer's Scheme for the Conversion of the £3 % Consols, but the Council declined to assent to the Conversion of its Capital Stock upon the terms offered.

November 10th.
John Heber
Clarke,
Mayor.

A Robe for the use of the Mayor and his Successors presented to the Council by Mr. Alderman Ballard, the retiring Mayor.

George Payne, the younger, elected Junior Sergeant at Mace and Bellman.

1885.
January 6th.

Invitations issued to a number of Architects to submit a competitive design for a Corn Exchange and Cattle Market, to cost not more than £2000.

February 21st.

In consequence of suggestions made by the Boundary Commissioners, the Council resolved to apply to the Local Government Board for an Order under the Poor Law Amendment Act, 1879, transferring the detached portion of the Parish of Culham to the Parish of St. Nicholas, to obviate the necessity of dividing the Borough for Parliamentary Election purposes.

$\mathfrak{A}$ General District Rate at 2/6 in the £ to produce £2140 : 0 : 0 ordered to be made.

$\mathfrak{A}$ portable forge purchased for the Council's Depôt in Stert Street.

$\mathfrak{On}$ the recommendation of the President of the Institute of British Architects, Mr. T. Hayter Lewis, F.S.A., was appointed Assessor, to advise and assist the Council in the selection of the best design for the Corn Exchange and Cattle Market.

$\mathfrak{Mr.}$ C. Bell's design for the Corn Exchange accepted, on the advice of Mr. Lewis, F.S.A., the estimated cost of the Building being £1800.

March 4th.

$\mathfrak{Negotiations}$ opened with the Directors of the London and County Banking Company, Limited, for setting back the Street Line on the rebuilding of the Bank in the Market Place.

$\mathfrak{A}$ resolution of sympathy and condolence sent to the Widow and Family of the late Lord Mayor of London (Mr. Alderman Nottage), on the severe loss they had recently sustained by the death of the Lord Mayor.

April 16th.

$\mathfrak{A}$ return of the Council's employés who were members of Benefit Clubs ordered to be prepared, the Streets Committee recommending that all the employés, who were eligible, should be induced, if possible, to become members of one of the Clubs in the Town.

$\mathfrak{The}$ Council resolved to undertake the entire management of the Clock of St. Nicholas Church.

May 14th.

$\mathfrak{Mr.}$ Edward Williams's Tender of £1854 for the erection of the Corn Exchange accepted by the Council.

$\mathfrak{The}$ Borough Surveyor instructed to prepare a plan for laying out the ground at the side and rear of the Corn Exchange as a Cattle Market.

$\mathfrak{A}$ General District Rate at 2/6 in the £ to produce £2138 : 4 : 6 ordered to be made.

August 13th.

$\mathfrak{The}$ following Report of the Ceremony of laying the Corner Stones of the Corn Exchange was ordered to be entered on the Minutes of the Council:—On the 11th August, 1885, the Right Hon.

the Earl of Abingdon, High Steward of the Borough, at the invitation of the Corporation (after accompanying the Mayor and Corporation and other public bodies in the Town in procession to the laying of the Memorial Stones of the Cottage Hospital) proceeded to the site of the Corn Exchange, and having been presented with a Silver Trowel by the Mayor, his Lordship laid a Stone in the South East corner of the building. The Mayor (assisted by his brethren of the Abbey Lodge of Freemasons, No. 945) then laid a corresponding Stone at the North East Corner of the building, with a full Masonic Ceremony, and subsequently entertained the High Steward and the Countess of Abingdon, J. C. Clarke, Esq., M.P. for the Borough, Philip Wroughton, Esq., M.P. for the County, and the Aldermen and Councillors of the Borough, and a large number of friends to Luncheon, in the Shire Hall.

October 1st.

The sum of £100 voted for improving the roadway and paving on each side of the Narrow.

The Farm Committee reported that they had been unable to let the Sewage Farm on satisfactory terms, and recommended the Council to farm the land themselves, appointing Mr. T. Vizer, the late Tenant's Bailiff, as Farm Manager. Mr. Vizer being also required to discharge the duties of School Attendance Officer and Clerk of the Market, and the recommendations of the Committee were adopted by the Council.

A Letter received from Mr. Bell, the Architect for the new Bank, stating that the Directors had been appealed to by the Oxford Archæological Society not to destroy the Old Crypt under the existing Bank, and that they were anxious to do what was possible to preserve it, but it could only be done if the walls of the new Bank could be built upon the old foundations, and enquiring if the Council would agree to that being done; and it was resolved that Mr. Bell should be informed that the Council would much regret the destruction of the Crypt, and would be glad to sanction any scheme for its preservation if it could be done without unduly interfering with the new Street line agreed upon between the Bank and the Council.

November 4th.

On the recommendation of the Streets Committee it was resolved that in future no sick pay should be paid to the Council's employés who were not members of a benefit Club, if they were eligible for one.

𝕿𝖍𝖊 Plan prepared by the Borough Surveyor for laying out the Cattle Market approved by the Council. The Plan providing accommodation for 540 Sheep and Pigs, and 50 Horses and Cow Cattle. The estimate for the work being £510.

𝕿𝖍𝖊 General District Rate ordered to be increased from 2/6 to 2/9 in the £ to produce £2347 : 16 : 10 in order to provide a portion of the funds required for farming the Sewage Farm.

𝕬 return shewing the Expenditure of the Council on Highways, Paving, Water Supply and Sewerage Works, from 1878 to 1885, presented by the Borough Surveyor to the Council. The return shewing that the average Expenditure had been at the rate of £1626 : 8 : 9 per annum, equal to a rate of 1/10½ in the £ on the Rateable Value of the Borough.

𝕸𝖊𝖘𝖘𝖗𝖘. Tripp & Bottrell's Tender of £97 : 10 : 0 for the erection of the Cattle and Sheep Pens in the Market accepted, and also Messrs. Wilkes' Tender of £155 for Paving the Market with Concrete Paving.

𝕬 notice received from the Abingdon Gas Light and Coke Company, Limited, of its intention to apply to the Board of Trade for a Provisional Order to enable the Company to purchase some land in the Vineyard, for the purpose of erecting new Gas Works thereon, when it was ordered that a Special Meeting of the Council should be convened for the purpose of considering the matter.

𝕬 Special Meeting of the Council held to consider the proposed application of the Abingdon Gas Company, Limited, for a Provisional Order, when it was resolved to urge on the Board of Trade to make certain amendments in the Provisional Order as to the price and quality of gas supplied by the Company.

𝕿𝖍𝖊 Council resolved to Memorialize H.M's. Postmaster General to provide better Post Office Accommodation for the Town.

𝕿𝖍𝖊 Market Committee reported that the Mayor had been requested at a recent meeting of Farmers attending Abingdon Market, to take steps for abolishing the custom of paying "chap money" on the sale of Corn, but the Committee was of opinion that the Council had no power or authority to interfere with an established custom of that kind, and therefore recommended that no action should be taken with regard thereto.

The Committee also reported that the Ex-Mayor, Mr. J. H. Clarke, had presented a Statue, by Mr. Frith, R.A., representing "Ceres," for erection over the front entrance of the Corn Exchange.

Mr. W. Fisher appointed Public Analyst, in the place of Mr. P. W. Donkin, resigned.

A General District Rate at 2/9 in the £ to produce £2347 : 13 : 6 ordered to be made.

Charles Edwards appointed Junior Sergeant at Mace and Bellman, in the place of G. Payne, deceased.

The Corn Exchange Opened for the transaction of business.

A resolution of sympathy with the Mayor on the death of the Mayoress was unanimously passed by the Council.

A tender accepted for laying patent Concrete Paving in Bridge Street and other parts of the Town.

The premises in Bury Street, used as a Common Lodging House, purchased for £79, for the improvement of the Market.

A General District Rate at 2/8 in the £ to provide £2248 : 5 : 0 ordered to be made.

A Letter received from Mr. E. J. Trendell, J.P., offering to present to the Town a Marble Statue of Her Most Gracious Majesty the Queen, for erection in the centre of the Market Place, as a Memorial of the Queen's Jubilee, when it was unanimously resolved to accept Mr. Trendell's present; the Town Clerk being instructed to write and thank him for his handsome gift to the Town.

The sum of £60 voted for clearing the Streets of Snow so as to give employment to the men then out of work in the Town.

An intimation received from the Guardians of the Abingdon Union that they had experienced great difficulty in obtaining suitable work for the able bodied poor who had applied to them for relief, and suggesting that it might be advantageous to both bodies if the Guardians were allowed to employ persons out of work in levelling the heap of earth at the Waterworks, at Wootton, and it was resolved to acquiesce in the suggestion of the Guardians, the Council undertaking to recoup them for the money expended in levelling the ground.

𝔄 Scale of Charges for the use of the Municipal Buildings approved by the Council.

1887.
January 6th.
John Tomkins,
Mayor.

𝔄 Letter received from H.R.H. The Prince of Wales, with reference to an Imperial Institution for the Colonies and India, in commemoration of Her Majesty's Jubilee by her Subjects, and inviting the co-operation of the Mayors and Provosts of the United Kingdom.

𝔄n Annual Subscription of £5 : 5 : 0 each voted to the Abingdon Cottage Hospital and Radcliffe Infirmary, in lieu of the Subscription of £9 : 9 : 0 formerly paid to the latter Institution.

𝔗he Oxfordshire Agricultural Society invited to hold its Annual Meeting at Abingdon, in 1888.

𝔄 Portrait in Oils, of the late Mr. J. T. Norris, for many years M.P. for the Borough, presented to the Council by Mr. Alderman Kent.

𝔄 General District Rate at 2/8 in the £ to provide £2255 : 14 : 10 ordered to be made. February 10th.

𝔄n application made by the Council to the Treasury for power to advance £3000 to the Urban Sanitary Authority for the purpose of paying off the Mortgage on the Sewage Farm.

𝔗he Steam Roller belonging to the Oxford Local Board, hired for two weeks, for repairing the Roads in the Borough. April 1st.

𝔗he Finance Committee recommended that advantage should be taken of the vacancy in the Office of Treasurer, caused by the death of the Treasurer (Mr. A. D. Bartlett), to carry out the much needed reform in the Financial system of the Council and Urban Sanitary Authority, and made the following suggestions, viz. :—

1.—That the Manager of one of the Local Banks should be appointed Treasurer, without remuneration, and should be required to give security for £500, for the due performance of his duties.

2.—That a new Officer, to be called the Borough Accountant, should be appointed to keep all the Accounts of the Council, and Urban Sanitary Authority, and discharge the other duties relating to the Financial business of those bodies, as set out in the Committee's report; the person appointed being required to give security for £500.

Mr. Henry d'Almaine, Manager of the Abingdon Branch of the London and County Bank, appointed Borough Treasurer.

Mr. Arthur Edwin Preston, C.A., appointed Borough Accountant.

A Letter received on behalf of the Proprietors of Sutton Bridge and the Owners of Land abutting on the Ody Road, requesting the Council to keep the gate across the road near the Sewage Farm locked, as the road was being used by persons who were not entitled to use it, and an order was accordingly made for the gate to be kept locked.

May 12th.

An address ordered to be presented to Her Most Gracious Majesty the Queen, congratulating Her Majesty on completing 50 years of Her Reign in June next.

An empty Muniment Safe ordered to be removed from the Council Chamber to the Borough Accountant's Office, for the safe keeping of the Corporation Account Books therein.

July 5th.

Two new Lamps ordered to be fixed in the Market Place, in the place of the two Lamps which were formerly on the Obelisk, that had been lately removed to make way for the Queen's Statue.

The following account of the celebration of Her Majesty's Jubilee was ordered to be entered on the Minutes of the Council:—

Borough of Abingdon.

"THE Fiftieth Anniversary of the Accession to the Throne of Great "Britain and Ireland (commonly called the Jubilee of Her Majesty "Queen Victoria) was celebrated in this ancient Borough on Saturday, "June 18th, and Tuesday, June 21st, 1887, in the Mayoralty of "Alderman John Tomkins.

"The 21st of June was appointed for the purpose by an Order in "Council.

"On June the 18th, the Statue of the Queen, presented to the Town "by Mr. Edwin James Trendell, an Ex-Mayor and Ex-Alderman of the "Borough, was unveiled by the Lord Lieutenant of the County, The "Right Honourable Lord Wantage, V.C., K.C.B.

"A Procession consisting of the Mayor and Corporation, Mr. Philip "Wroughton, M.P. for North Berks, Mr. John Creemer Clarke, "formerly M.P. for the Borough, Mr. E. J. Trendell, the Rev. R. C. F. "Griffith, Vicar of Abingdon, the Rev. W. H. Cam, Head Master of "Roysse's School, and others, accompanied Lord Wantage from the

"Council Chamber to the Market Place. After the reading of the
"21st Psalm and a Collect by the Vicar, Mr. Trendell formally presented
"the Statue to the Mayor, as representing the Burgesses, asking that it
"might be preserved and protected. Lord Wantage then unveiled the
"Statue, which was the work of Mr. W. White, A.R.A. It is a figure
"nearly eight feet hight, carved in Sicilian Marble, standing on a pedestal
"of Portland Stone, the total elevation being about fifteen feet. The
"Queen is represented as wearing the Imperial robes and a small crown
"on the head, and bears a Sceptre in the right hand and the Lotus
"as emblematic of the Indian Empire in the left.

"The Pedestal bears the following inscription :—

THIS STATUE OF

QUEEN VICTORIA

WAS PRESENTED TO THE TOWN

OF ABINGDON

BY

EDWIN JAMES TRENDELL,

IN COMMEMORATION OF

HER MOST GRACIOUS MAJESTY'S JUBILEE,

THE XX. DAY OF JUNE,

MDCCCLXXXVII.

ALDERMAN TOMKINS,

Mayor.

"Mr. Trendell, before the ceremony, entertained Lord Wantage,
"Mr. Wroughton, Mr. Clarke, The Vicar, The Mayor and Corporation,
"and other guests at his residence, the Abbey House, the grounds of
"which were thrown open to the Inhabitants during the Afternoon.

"Subsequently, to mark the occasion, buns were thrown from the roof
"of the County Hall.

"The Town was gaily decorated with flags and illuminated at night.
"The whole proceedings were marked by complete success, and took
"place in the most brilliant weather.

"On Sunday Afternoon, June the 19th, the Abingdon Volunteers,
"under the command of Major E. Morland, and the Culham College
"Company, of the Oxon Regiment, commanded by Captain the Rev.
"H. Lewis attended, with the Lodges of Oddfellows and Foresters a
"Special Service at St. Helen's Church, the object of which was to

" celebrate the Jubilee of the Queen by rendering assistance to the
" Cottage Hospital, recently given to the Town by Mr. J. C. Clarke.
" The Vicar preached an appropriate sermon to a large congregation.

" The Nonconformists of the Town held a United Thanksgiving
" Service at the Corn Exchange in the Evening, conducted by the
" Revds. S. Lepine, R. Rogers, G. Outhwaithe, and Neville.

" The proceedings on June 21st commenced with a Thanksgiving
" Service, held in St. Helen's Church, which was attended by the
" Deputy Mayor (Alderman J. T. Morland) and the Corporation. The
" Official Form of Prayer was used. At the close of the Service a
" Collection was made for the Cottage Hospital.

" Afterwards a Procession was formed in the Market Place, consisting
" of the Corporation, the Benefit Societies, the Fire Brigade, the Clergy,
" Ministers, and Schools of the Town.

" The Procession, accompanied by three bands, passed through the
" principal streets of the Town to the grounds of Fitzharris House,
" kindly lent by Messrs. J. C. and J. H. Clarke.

" On the arrival at Fitzharris, upwards of Eighteen Hundred Men and
" Women were entertained in six tents at a dinner which was much
" appreciated by all partaking. Ladies supplied bouquets to each diner,
" and efficient arrangements were made by them to relieve the mothers
" of the care of their children during dinner.

" The School Children (numbering nearly Two Thousand) were regaled
" with a substantial tea in another part of the grounds, and each child
" was presented by Mr. J. C. Clarke with a medal commemorative of
" the occasion.

" During the afternoon Athletic Sports were held, which gave great
" satisfaction.

" The School Children also were provided with sports suited to their
" age, swings and other amusements being also furnished for them.

" It was computed that about Six Thousand people visited the
" grounds during the afternoon.

" At the conclusion of the Fête a Display of Fireworks was given in
" the Albert Park.

" The Town was gaily decorated with flags and illuminated at night.

" The Mayor (Alderman Tomkins) attended the Thanksgiving
" Service in Westminster Abbey, but returned in time to visit the Fête
" at Fitzharris in the Evening.

" The arrangements of the day were entirely satisfactory, and the
" fineness of the weather greatly enhanced its success.

"The proceedings were carried out by a Committee consisting of the
"Mayor and Corporation, the Clergy, Ministers and other residents of
"the Town; Sub-Committees being appointed to attend to the details,
"and were as follows :—

GENERAL COMMITTEE,	CHAIRMAN,	The Mayor.
TICKET „	„	Councillor A. H. Simpson.
TENT „	„ „	Jos. Copeland.
SPORTS „	„ „	J. H. Clarke.
DINNER „	„ „	J. B. King.
BAND „	„ „	E. L. Shepherd.
CHILDREN'S TEA „	„	MR. W. G. Cousins.

"The Honorary Secretaries, to whom the complete success of the day
"was largely due, were Messrs E. M. Challenor and J. G. T. West.

"Public order was efficiently maintained by the Police under
Superintendent Robotham, no charge arising from the day coming before
the Magistrates.

"The cost of the proceedings amounting to £387 : 8 : 9, were
"defrayed by Subscription.

"JOHN TOMKINS,

"*Mayor.*"

A General District Rate at 2/7 in the £ to produce £2176 : 0 : 0
ordered to be made.

A Code of Bye Laws prepared by the Society of Medical Officers
of Health for regulating Dairies and Milkshops approved and adopted
by the Council.

The Surveyor, Hall Keepers, and Superintendent of Police
ordered to prepare an Inventory of the property belonging to the
Council which was in their charge.

An application for a Licence for the performance of Stage Plays
in the Corn Exchange and Town Hall granted by the Borough
Justices.

A Boiler for heating the Corn Exchange presented by Mr.
Councillor Shepherd, the sum of £53 being voted by the Council
for providing the necessary Piping and Coils for heating the
building.

A Machine for Weighing Cattle ordered to be purchased for the
Cattle Market, in accordance with the provisions contained in the
Markets and Fairs Act, 1887.

1887.
November 4th.
John Tomkins,
Mayor.

The Sanitary Committee reported that no case of Zymotic Disease had occurred in the Borough during the past six months, which they considered to be very satisfactory, considering the unusually dry and hot Summer that had been passed through.

A Committee appointed to consider and report upon a plan prepared by the Borough Surveyor for preventing the occasional stoppages in the action of the Syphon at the Waterworks.

1888.
January 5th.
Edward Leader
Shepherd,
Mayor.

The Streets Committee reported that the experiment of employing a Steam Roller for repairing the Streets had been most successful.

A Photometer purchased for the purpose of testing the illuminating power of the Gas supplied by the Abingdon Gas Company.

Stert Street ordered to be repaved at a cost of £75 with Cement Concrete laid *in situ*, and manufactured by the Council's employés, under the superintendence of the Borough Surveyor, the material costing 2/6 per yard, as against 6/- per yard theretofore paid for imported paving of a similar nature.

Free Tickets for admission to the Corn Exchange ordered to be issued to *bona fide* Farmers (not being dealers) residing in Berks and Oxon, all other persons being charged 3d. for admission, to include the toll for exposing samples of Corn in the Exchange.

A Report received from Dr. Woodforde, calling attention to the want of means for flushing the drains in the various Courts in the Town, when the Borough Surveyor was instructed to inspect the Courts, and to prepare a list of all dwelling-houses where no suitable flushing apparatus was provided.

February 9th.

A General District Rate at 2/6 in the £ to produce £2196 : 10 : 6 ordered to be made.

Robert Bayfield appointed Junior Sergeant at Mace and Bellman in the place of Charles Edwards, resigned.

The Clerk of the Market reported that Cattle and Pigs had been sold out of Market on Market days, and a notice was ordered to be issued calling attention to the penalties provided for such cases in the Market and Fairs Act, 1847.

A Committee appointed to consider and report upon the Local Government Boundaries Act, 1887, with instructions to take such steps as were considered necessary in the interest of the Borough.

1888.
April 5th.
Edward Leader
Shepherd,
Mayor.

The Streets Committee reported that they had expended £205 : 1 : 6 in clearing the Streets of the extraordinary fall of Snow which fell on the previous 14th February, and that their thanks were due to Messrs. Morland & Co. and Mr. G. Thatcher for lending their horses and carts to assist in the work.

A Contract entered into for hacking the Streets for the Steam Roller, whereby a saving of £20 was reported by the Surveyor to have been effected over the previous plan of employing men at day work for the purpose.

The sum of £10 : 10 : 0 voted towards the Fund for repairing the Clock on St. Nicholas Church.

The Borough Accountant presented a report upon the Chancellor of the Exchequer's Scheme for the conversion of the £3 % Consolidated Annuities into £2¾ per cent. Stock, when it was resolved to assent to the conversion into the new Stock of the £15,802 : 10 : 7 Consols belonging to the Council.

The offer of the Owner of the Sun Public House, in the Market Place, opposite St. Nicholas Church, to sell the premises to the Council for £700 accepted.

On the motion of Alderman Morland, the following resolution was carried unanimously, viz. :—" That the Corporation are of opinion " that the proposal of the Boundary Commissioners to transfer the " ten Oxfordshire Parishes now in the Abingdon Union to the Head- " ington Union, and one to the Oxford Union, is very unfair towards " the remaining Berkshire Parishes, which will be left with a Union " Workhouse too large for their own requirements, and that if it is " necessary for these parishes to be taken from the Abingdon Union, " they should at least be as in the case of Wallingford and Hungerford " Unions, constituted a Contributory Union, having the use of the " Abingdon Workhouse."

May 10th.

An application made to the Charity Commissioners for power to transfer the Trust Funds belonging to Beesley's, Bedwell's, Klein's, Smith's and Knapp's Charities, from the Corporation to the Trustees of the Abingdon Municipal Charities, who were charged with the administration of those Charities.

On the recommendation of the Finance Committee, an application was made to the Jubilee Committee to assist the Council in purchasing the Bathing Place with the Funds in their hands which were raised for that purpose at the time of the Jubilee Celebration.

One of the filtration areas, at the Sewage Farm, ordered to be re-formed, at a cost of £12.

Alderman Tomkins and Councillor Clarke re-elected Representative Governors of Roysse's School.

The appointment of William Harry Nash, Esq., as Recorder of the Borough (on the resignation of J. R. W. Bros, Esq., who had been appointed a Police Magistrate, in London,) notified to the Council.

An Ensilage Stack Press purchased for the Sewage Farm.

The Mayor reported that the Local Government Boundaries Commissioners held an Inquiry on the 4th instant, with reference to the proposed transfer to the County of Berks of that part of the Borough which was situate in the County of Oxford, and that the Town Clerk had attended the Inquiry and applied to the Commissioners to enlarge their Scheme, by extending the area of the Borough so as to embrace the area recommended by the Committee appointed by the Council in the year 1882, with the addition of that part of the Parish of Culham known as Andersey Island, but the Commissioners pointed out that the Parishes of Sutton Wick, St. Helen and St. Nicholas would be affected by the proposal, and as they had not been Scheduled in the notice of the Inquiry, they could not deal with the matter at that moment; And it was resolved to memorialize the Local Government Board and the Commissioners to hold another Inquiry upon the subject.

August 6th.

The Council resolved to purchase the Bathing Place from Mr. J. S. Phillips, for £50; the Jubilee Committee having reported that they had £33 in hand, and outstanding Subscriptions amounting to £60 for that object. The Bathing Place Committee also reported that they had had plans laid before them for constructing a Floating Swimming Bath to be moored in the River nearer the Town, but on the ground of expense and possible prejudice on the part of Bathers, they did not recommend its adoption.

A Letter received from the Inspector General of Remounts, at the War Office, enquiring whether the Council had any Horses which

1888.
August 6th.
Edward Leader
Shepherd,
Mayor.

they would be prepared to register for Army purposes; and the Town Clerk was instructed to reply that the Horses belonging to the Council were of a heavy character, and, in the opinion of the Council, unfitted for Army use.

A Letter received from the Local Government Board recommending the adoption of the Code of Model Bye Laws which the Board had prepared under the Allotments Act, 1887, but as the Finance Committee considered there was little or no probability of the Council being called upon to take action under the Act, no action was taken in the matter.

A Letter read from the Local Government Board, stating that there was no provision in the General Laws under which the Boundaries of the Borough could be extended as suggested by the Council, and it was resolved that the question of the extension of the Borough Boundaries should stand over until after the passing of the Local Government Bill then before Parliament, as it was thought probable that in the near future it might be possible to obtain an extension by means of a Provisional Order, and so save the expense of a Private Act of Parliament.

The Finance Committee reported that the Local Government Inspector had held a Local Inquiry on the 28th June with reference to the proposal of the Council to purchase the Star Public House, for the purpose of widening the Stert Street, and that the Inspector had intimated that he should report in favour of the required sanction being given, but should advise that the scheme should be amended by the inclusion of the adjoining house in the scheme, but the Committee reported that after making enquiries they were of opinion that the price asked for the property was so much in excess of what they considered its value, that they could not advise the Council to adopt the Inspector's suggestion.

The Mayor reported that he had had an interview with Mr. Wroughton, M.P., with reference to the representation of the Borough on the New County Council, as provided by the Local Government Bill, and that he had suggested that the Borough should be allowed to return two Councillors to the Council, instead of one as provided in the Bill, and that Mr. Wroughton had promised to make a representation to Her Majesty's Government to that effect,

1888.
August 6th.
Edward Leader
Shepherd,
Mayor.

and that he had since heard from Mr. Wroughton that he had seen the Right Hon. the President of the Local Government Board, who agreed to amend the Bill, so as to give Abingdon two representatives on the County Council.

On the recommendation of the Farm Committee, it was resolved to erect a Barn and Shed at the Sewage Farm, at a cost of £107.

September 13th.   **On** the recommendation of the Bathing Place Committee, the Council resolved to expend £150 in protective works at the Bathing Place, and also to take over the entire management of the place, which had theretofore been managed partly by the Council and partly by a Committee of Ladies.

A Report received from the Sewers Committee with reference to the nuisance caused by the Sewer Ventilators, and stating that they were of opinion that the nuisance arose from the absence in a great number of instances of proper means for flushing the service drains, and recommended that the owners of property should be compelled to provide proper apparatus for the effectual flushing of their drains.

A General District Rate at 2/4 in the £ to raise £1961 : 17 : 0 ordered to be made.

A new Lightning Conductor ordered to be fixed on the County Hall.

The Council resolved that the Borough should be divided into two Wards, for the election of County Councillors, to be called the North and South Divisions respectively; the North Division consisting of that portion of the Town which lay to the North of a line drawn down the centre of the Ock Street, High Street, Market Place and Abbey; and the South Division of all the property lying on the South of the line; the Population in the North Division being estimated at 3375, and the South 2900.

November 2nd.   **The** Streets Committee reported that the Owners of the Lamb and Flag Inn, in the Vineyard, were about to rebuild those premises, and recommended the Council to take advantage of the fact and secure a portion of the ground to round off the dangerous corner which existed at that spot, and it was resolved that from 10 to 12 feet of the site be purchased for the sum of £250.

The Council resolved that as soon as the Berks County Council was elected, application should be made for the Bridge Street, High Street, Bath Street, Vineyard, Stert Street, Broad Street, and Ock Street, to be declared Main Roads, and that notice should also be given that the Council intended to retain the power of maintaining the roads in question under the Local Government Act, 1888.

1888.
November 2nd.
Edward Leader Shepherd,
Mayor.

Mr. Bossum's tender of £175 for the protection and improvement of the Bathing Place accepted.

In consequence of the division of the Borough into Electoral Divisions for County Council Elections, it was resolved that there should be two Polling Stations for Municipal Elections in future.

A new Irrigation Sewer constructed at the Farm, at a cost of £58 : 9 : 6.

A Notice ordered to be issued cautioning Tradesmen against placing their goods on the Pavement for sale, and so causing an obstruction of the footway.

November 9th.
Thomas Townsend,
Mayor.

Trees ordered to be planted in the Square, and Shrubs on the site of the Star Public House, in the Market Place.

1889.
January 3rd.

The sum of £500 offered by the Council for the property adjoining the Star for improving the Street, but the same was declined by the Owner.

The sum of £471 : 15 : 0 paid into Court, in the year 1855, by the Abingdon Railway Company, for property belonging to the Corporation, which the Company had purchased, taken out by the Council.

Arrangements made with the Chief Constable of Berks, for taking over the Borough Police force, in pursuance of the Local Government Act, 1888.

The Superintendent of the Borough Police sent to Tasmania, to bring back a prisoner charged with fraudulently obtaining goods of the value of £600, from various Firms, whilst he was residing in the Borough.

February 14th.

A Tender of £20 for panelling with Oak the East and North Walls of the Staircase of the Council Chamber accepted by the Council.

𝔑egotiations commenced with the Berks County Council, with reference to the Corporation's claim for compensation on the transfer of the Borough's interest in Littlemore Asylum to the County Council, under the Local Government Act, 1888.

April 4th.

𝔗he Streets Committee reported that they had employed 105 extra hands to assist in clearing the Streets of Snow which fell on the 3rd February previous.

𝔗he Footbridge over the Boxhill Stream ordered to be rapaired at a cost of £3 : 10 : 0.

𝔗he Obelisk and Weighbridge in the Sheep Market sold for £15.

𝔗he Streets Committee recommended the Council to acquire the Old Gas Works as a Depôt for the Borough Surveyor's Department.

𝔄 portion of the surplus land in the High Street agreed to be sold to Mr. J. C. Clarke.

𝔗he sum of £10 voted to provide a Drill Ground for the Berks Yeomanry Cavalry, who had arranged to visit Abingdon for their Annual Training in the ensuing mouth.

𝔄 Committee appointed to consider the recent revision of rates and re-classification of goods by the Great Western Railway Company, under the Railway and Canal Traffic Act, 1888.

May 9th.

𝔄 General District Rate at 2/4 in the £ to raise £1943 : 9 : 0 ordered to be made.

𝔒n the recommendation of the Finance Committee the Council decided to apply to the Local Government Board for a Provisional Order under the Local Government Act, 1888, authorizing the extension of the Borough Boundaries.

𝔗he Council agreed to let to the Berks Standing Joint Committee on a Lease for 21 years, the Borough Police Station, the Residence of the Superintendent of Police, and the use of the Guildhall for Quarter Sessions and for the County and Borough Petty Sessions.

𝔗he Borough Police Superannuation Fund ordered to be transferred to the Berks Standing Joint Committee, they taking over the liabilities of the Council in respect of the Fund.

The Railway Rates Committee presented their report upon the effect of the New Scale of Rates prepared by the Great Western Railway Company, and the Council resolved to memorialize the Board of Trade to withhold its sanction to the Scale as proposed by the Company.

The Watch Committee reported that the prisoner Edwards had escaped at Rio Janeiro, whilst on the voyage home to England in the custody of the Superintendent of the Borough Police, and that they did not consider the Superintendent to be to blame for the escape; they further reported that nearly the whole of the property obtained by the prisoner had been recovered by the Police.

The Stable at the Farm enlarged at a cost of £119.

An application received by the Urban Sanitary Authority to provide Land for Allotments, under the Allotments Act, 1888.

A Subscription of £1 : 1 : 0 voted to the Mansion House Railway Rates Committee.

A Local Inquiry held by an Inspector of the Local Government Board with reference to the proposed acquisition of the Old Gas Works by the Council, as a Depôt for the Urban Sanitary Authority.

An application made to the Berks County Council and the Vice-Chancellor of the University of Oxford, for a renewal of the Licence for the performance of Stage Plays in the Corn Exchange.

The Borough Surveyor appointed Inspector under the Petroleum Acts.

On the recommendation of the Finance Committee the Council decided not to make any Regulations under the Prevention of Cruelty to Children Act.

An application made by the Council to the Local Government Board for power to raise a Loan of £1200 for the purpose of purchasing Water Meters.

A General District Rate at 2/4 in the £ to raise £1950 ordered to be made.

One of the Medical Inspectors of the Local Government Board visited the Borough and inspected (with the Medical Officer of

TT

1889.
October 31st.
Thomas
Townsend,
Mayor.

Health) several of the Lodging Houses, Slaughter-houses, and Milk-shops in the Town, and also inquired into the system in use for Ventilating and Flushing the Sewers and the disposal of the Sewage at the Farm, and expressed himself satisfied with the result of his inspection.

A Loan of £785 sanctioned by the Local Government Board for the acquisition and adaptation of the Old Gas Works by the Urban Sanitary Authority.

The Sanitary Committee reported with regard to the Memorial recently presented to the Council, requesting it to provide Allotments, that they had ascertained there were from 80 to 100 Acres of agricultural land within half-a-mile of the Town, the owners of which were willing to let the same in Allotments at a rent of 6d. per pole, and they therefore considered there was no case requiring the interference of the Council.

The Infectious Diseases (Notification) Act, 1889, adopted by the Council.

A Tender of £105 for altering and adapting the Old Gas Works as a Depôt accepted.

November 9th.
Thomas
Townsend,
Mayor.

A Photograph of Sir John Read, Bart., Great Grandson of Sir Thos. Read, of Barton Court, presented to the Council by Gen. Meredith Read, F.S.A.

December 10th.

The Finance Committee reported that Major-General Carey, an Inspector of the Local Government Board, had held a Local Inquiry on the 4th instant, with reference to the Council's Scheme for extending the Borough Boundaries.

An exchange of land in the High Street with the Authorities of the General Post Office, for the purpose of erecting a new Post Office thereon, agreed upon by the Coucil.

1890.
February 13th.

The Council resolved to purchase for £100 the Engines and Plant of the Volunteer Fire Brigade, so that the whole of the Fire Plant in the Borough might be under the control of the Corporation.

The Council resolved to join the Non-County Boroughs Association which had been recently formed for the purposes of watching the interests of Non-County Boroughs.

1890.
March 11th.
Thomas
Townsend,
Mayor.

𝕿𝖍𝖊 Finance Committee reported they had received a Letter from the Local Government Board, stating that they proposed to amend the Council's Scheme for enlarging the limits of the Borough, by making the Wilts and Berks Canal the Boundary line from the river Thames to the Canal Bridge on the Steventon Road, and thence up the Ladygrove Road, leaving out the houses on the West side of the Road, thence along the Marcham Road to the Larkhill Ditch, and from that point following the course of the Stream into the Faringdon Road, and then following the late Parliamentary Boundary by an undefined straight line to the Wootton Road, opposite the Boxhill footpath, and then up the Wootton Road to the Northcourt Road, following the Boundary line recommended by the Council, to the Oxford Road, and from thence down the Road towards the Town to the St. John's Road, along that Road to the Radley Road, and then down the Road to the corner of Convent Close where the old Boundary was joined, and following that to the River, and continuing the old Boundary along the River to the Eyot opposite the Canal Wharf. The Committee regretted that the Local Government Board had not thought fit to adopt the Scheme of the Council in its entirety, but recommended the Council to assent to the amended Scheme, except in the following particulars, viz.:— Firstly—The Boundary line on the West and North West sides of the Town should be the Larkhill Stream from the Faringdon Road to the Wootton Road, and not the undefined line of the old Parliamentary Boundary which cut the Fitzharris Farm in half, and would, in the opinion of the Committee, be a source of trouble for rating purposes; Secondly—The Boundary line on the North and North East sides of the Town from the Oxford Road to the Radley Road should follow the line originally proposed by the Council, viz.: a line skirting Rush Common and Pond Head; and Thirdly—That the centre of the River should be the Boundary, instead of following the old Boundary at the Little Bridges, near Abingdon Lock, and the Rookery, near St. Helen's Church.

𝕿𝖍𝖊 Finance Committee also reported that the Local Government Board Inspector had arranged to visit the Borough, for the purpose of dividing the Town into Electoral Districts, and that they had instructed the Town Clerk to inform the Inspector that in their opinion it was unnecessary to divide the Borough into Wards, but if

1890.
March 11th.
Thomas
Townsend,
Mayor.

the Board insisted upon its being done, that Two Wards only should be created, to be called the North and South Wards, as formerly proposed by the Council for County Council purposes.

𝕿𝖍𝖊 Finance Committee reported they had had under their consideration the question whether it was possible to provide Land suitable for Allotments, near the Town, at a cheaper rate than 6d. per pole, and as there seemed no reasonable prospect of their being able to do so, they recommended the Council to offer 21 Acres of Land adjoining the Sewage Farm, which belonged to the Corporation, in suitable lots, as Allotment Gardens.

𝕿𝖍𝖊 Deputy-Mayor and Town Clerk appointed to represent the Council at the Meeting of the Council of the Association of Municipal Corporations, the Borough having been elected a Member of the Council of the Association.

𝕿𝖍𝖊 Town Clerk reported that on the 13th instant he had had an interview with Major-General Carey, the Local Government Board Inspector, and had explained to him the proposals of the Council with reference to the New Boundaries of the Borough and its division into Electoral Districts, and that he had admitted that the suggestions of the Council with regard to the Boundary were reasonable ones, and would report favourably with regard thereto to the Local Government Board, but with regard to the Electoral Divisions, he considered it would be better to draw the line from North to South by taking a line down the centre of the Wootton Road, Bath Street, The Narrow, and West St. Helen Street to the Thames, rather than the one from East to West, suggested by the Council.

May 8th.

𝕿𝖍𝖊 pitchings in Lombard Street ordered to be taken up and the Road repaired with Macadam.

𝕬𝖓 Order issued by the Berks County Council declaring the Vineyard, Stert Street, Bridge Street, High Street and Ock Street to be Main Roads.

𝕬 Macadam Roadway ordered to be constructed round the North side of the Sheep Market.

𝕬𝖓 application received from the Board of Guardians of the Abingdon Union for the Council to lay on a 4in. Water Main to the Workhouse, when it was resolved to accede to the Board's request, and fix a Fire Hydrant in the road opposite the Workhouse if the

Guardians would pay the difference in cost between a 2 inch and a 4 inch Main, and also undertake to use the Water when laid on for the general purposes of the Workhouse.

𝕬 General District Rate at 2/4 in the £ to raise £1950 ordered to be made.

𝕿𝕳𝖊 Council agreed to accept £3070 as the value of the interest of the Borough in Littlemore Lunatic Asylum on the purchase of the Borough's interest by the County Council of Oxfordshire, the Council having ceased to be a Lunacy Authority under the Local Government Act, 1888.

𝕬 yearly quit rent of 11/- payable to Christ's Hospital in respect of the site of the Star Public House ordered to be redeemed.

𝕬 Subscription of £21 per annum voted to the Public Elementary Schools in the Town, apportioned as follows: *

	£	s.	d.
National School, Bury Street	9	0	0
British School	6	0	0
Conduit Road Infant School	3	10	0
St. Edmund's School	2	10	0
	£21	0	0

𝕿𝕳𝖊 Farm and Market Committee reported that they had laid out 21 Acres of Land on the Sewage Farm, in 10 pole plots for Allotments, and had fixed the rent at 2/6 per annum for each plot.

𝕬 Tender of £19 : 10 : 0 for constructing a flight of steps from the Bridge to the Towing Path at the River side accepted by the Council.

𝕿𝕳𝖊 Water Main and Sewer in the Oxford Road extended to the Houses recently added to the Borough in that Road.

𝕺𝖓 the recommendation of the Finance Committee the Council resolved to request the Volunteer Fire Brigade to take charge of the Fire Engines and Plant on their undertaking to be responsible for same, and maning the Engines in the event of a Fire occurring in the

* This Subscription was fixed in proportion to the number of Children on the Books of the different Schools.—Ed.

Borough or District, the Council also agreeing to subscribe £5 per annum towards the Brigade's Equipment Fund. All additions and repairs to plant being ordered by the Council on the Certificate of the Chief Officer of the Brigade that the same were necessary.

A Provisional Order issued by the Local Government Board for the Extension of the Borough Boundaries.

The Panelling of the Staircase of the Council Chamber ordered to be completed.

The Bill confirming the Provisional Order extending the Borough Boundaries reported to the Council as having received the Royal Assent on the 4th instant.

The Streets Committee instructed to arrange for the numbering of the Houses in the Borough.

The Berks County Council having claimed the sum to be received from the County Council for the Borough's interest in Littlemore Asylum, it was resolved to assent to the amount being paid to the County Council conditionally on their undertaking to deposit the sum when received in a Bank, in the joint names of the Corporation and the County Council, to await the decision of the Local Government Board upon the ultimate application of the money.

October 30th.   The Bathing Committee reported that 23,377 Males and 5,104 Females had used the Bathing Place during the season.

The Borough Extension Committee reported that the area of the Borough had been increased by about 400 acres, thus more than doubling the size of the Borough, while 209 houses with an estimated population of 1045, and a Rateable Value of £3686 had been added to the Borough; the number of Burgesses on the Roll being increased by the addition of 164 names.

The Committee recommended that the Loans raised by the Rural Sanitary Authority for Drainage and Water Supply should be paid off, the money having been borrowed at $3\frac{3}{4}$ °/₀ interest, and replaced by a Loan from the Corporation Funds, such Loan to be sufficiently large to provide for the expenditure which it would be necessary for the Council to incur in constructing Sewers and Water Mains in the Caldecot, Spring and Faringdon Roads.

𝕿𝖍𝖊 Committee also recommended that a Surface Water Drain 1890.
October 30th. should be constructed in the Hamlet of Northcourt, and reported that the road mileage had been increased by the addition of four miles of Highways, necessitating an expenditure of about £250 per annum for their maintenance. With regard to paving, the Committee recommended that the North side of Marcham Road, the West side of Spring Road as far as the Cemetery, the footway in front of the Cottages at Northcourt, and on the North side of the Radley Road, as far as the houses extended, should be paved with Concrete slab paving, the cost thereof being estimated at £300. They also recommended that the Streets in the newly added area should be lighted by the erection of 18 "B" lamps, involving an expenditure of £32 per annum. The Committee further recommended that steps should be taken to compel the Owners of Property in St. John's Road, Cemetery Road, Bartram's Row Road, and the Road above the Cemetery, to be properly levelled, metalled, kerbed, channelled and paved, under the provisions contained in the Public Health Act, 1875. The total capital expenditure recommended by the Committee in their Report being as follows:—

		£	s.	d.
On Sewers	...	800	0	0
„ Water Supply	...	390	0	0
„ Paving	...	300	0	0
„ Lighting	...	58	0	0
„ Surveyor (extra plant)	...	165	0	0
„ Redemption of R.S.A. Loans	...	978	0	0
		£2691	0	0

𝕿𝖍𝖊 Report of the Committee was ordered to be printed and referred to the Sanitary Committee for consideration and report.

𝕬 General District Rate at 2/4 in the £ to raise £2394 : 4 : 8 ordered to be made, the Rateable Value of the extended Borough being £20,521 : 18 : 3.

𝕿𝖍𝖊 Land at the Waterworks, at Wootton, ordered to be planted with Larch trees.

𝕬 Lever Press and Seal purchased by the Council, the design 1891.
February 12th.
John Tomkins,
Mayor. being the same as that of the original Borough Seal, with the inscription "Burgus Abingdon in Com. Berk."

1891.
February 12th.
John Tomkins,
Mayor.

ⓞn the recommendation of the Sanitary Committee (after a conference with the Medical Officer of Health), the Council resolved not to adopt the adoptive portions of the Housing of the Working Classes Act, but to adopt Part III. of the Public Health Act Amendment Act and the whole of the Infectious Diseases Notification Act.

𝕬n application having been made by the Rural Sanitary Authority to be allowed to connect the Drains of the Houses in their District in the Oday and Ladygrove Roads, the Council resolved to grant the application upon the same conditions as the houses in the Marcham and Spring and Radley and Oxford Roads were connected with the Town Sewers, the rent for the easement being fixed at £23 per annum.

ⓞn the recommendation of the Sanitary Committee it was resolved to amend the terms upon which the Loan of £19,610 was raised for Sewerage Works, by making the Loan repayable by equal Half-yearly Instalments of Principal and Interest, instead of repaying $\frac{1}{50}$ of the Principal each year with interest on the balance, the alteration effecting a reduction of £227 per annum.

𝕿he same Committee also called attention to the Bill promoted by the Corporation of London dealing with the Watershed of the River Thames, and advised the Council to combine with other Towns in the Thames Watershed in resisting any encroachments on their rights and privileges, should it be necessary to do so.

𝕿he Streets Committee reported that they had ordered the Borough Surveyor to Number the Houses in each Street in the Borough.

𝕬 communication sent to the Abingdon District Highway Board suggesting the purchase by one of the Authorities of a Steam Roller for repairing the Highways, the non-purchasing Authority to undertake to hire the Roller for a fixed period and sum per annum.

May 14th.

𝕿he Culvert in the Northcourt Road rebuilt by the Council.

𝕬 Claim for a grant from the Funds in the hands of the Berks County Council for the purposes of Technical Education made by the Council.

1891.
May 14th.
John Tomkins,
Mayor.

𝔄 Plan prepared by Mr. Drinkwater, F.R.S.A., for enlarging the Stage of the Corn Exchange, and rearranging the Dressing Rooms, forming Cloak Rooms at the entrance, and providing for Two Staircases to the Gallery over the Cloak Rooms, adopted by the Council, the cost being estimated at £145.

𝔗𝔥𝔢 Water Mains in the Oxford Road and over the Depôt Bridge in Thames Street, and Iron Bridge at Caldecot, which burst during the great frost, relaid by the Council.

𝔄 Plan approved for widening the Iron Bridge over the River Ock, at St. Helen's Wharf, the estimate for the work being £60.

𝔐𝔯. Bosanquet, Q.C., appointed Arbitrator in the dispute between the Council and the Berks County Council with reference to the application of the money received for the Borough's interest in Littlemore Asylum.

𝔄 Letter received from the Clerk to the County Council enquiring what steps the Corporation were taking with regard to Technical Education, and the Town Clerk was instructed to reply that the Mayor was about to convene a Meeting of the School Managers and others interested in the matter for the purpose of establishing a Scheme for the promotion of Technical Education in the Borough.

𝔄 Deputation appointed to interview the Directors of the Great Western Railway Company, with a view of obtaining a better train service for Abingdon.

𝔗𝔥𝔢 Streets Committee reported that the Local Government Board had issued an order dismaining the Faringdon Road, and had declined to make an order constituting the Broad Street and Bath Street Main Roads. August 14th.

𝔗𝔥𝔢 Paving on the North side of the Ock Street from the Conduit Road to Christ's Hospital Model Cottages ordered to be relaid at a cost of £100.

𝔗𝔥𝔢 Posts and Rails on the South side of Thames Street ordered to be removed.

𝔄 Return shewing the number of men employed by the Council and their hours of labour and rate of pay, ordered to be prepared and forwarded to the Royal Commission on Labour.

UU

1891.
August 14th.
John Tomkins,
Mayor.

𝕿𝖍𝖊 Seal of the Borough affixed to an application to the Charity Commissioners for a new Scheme for the administration of St. John's Hospital.

October 29th.

𝕬 General District Rate at 2/- in the £ to raise £2059 : 5 : 0 ordered to be made, and also a Special District Rate at 3d. in the £ on the Property in the Old Municipal Area to provide for the principal and interest due on the Paving Bonds Redemption Loan.

𝕻𝖊𝖗𝖒𝖎𝖘𝖘𝖎𝖔𝖓 given to the owner of an adjoining property to open a window of his premises abutting upon the Guildhall Yard on his paying a rent of 2/6 per annum for the easement.

𝕸𝖗. Bosanquet's Q.C. Award in the case of the dispute between the County Council and the Town Council with regard to the purchase money for the Borough's interest in Littlemore Asylum received. The Arbitrator ordering the money to be equally divided between the two bodies, and on the recommendation of the Finance Committee it was resolved to apply the whole of the amount received towards liquidation of the Loan outstanding for the Paving Bonds Redemption.

𝕻𝖊𝖗𝖒𝖎𝖘𝖘𝖎𝖔𝖓 given to the Technical Education Committee to use the Town Hall for the purpose of Technical instruction.

𝕬 Letter received from Mr. E. J. Harris stating that there was a fund of about £60 in his hands which was subscribed for a purpose for which it was no longer available, and that he had been empowered by the Subscribers thereof to offer it to the Corporation for the purpose of forming the nucleus of a fund for establishing a Free Library in the Town for the benefit of all classes; and it was ordered that the Letter be referred to a Special Committee to consider and report upon the matter.

1892.
January 7th.
John Heber
Clarke,
Mayor.

𝕬𝖓 application to be allowed to affix advertisements to the columns of the Public Lamps refused by the Council.

𝕬𝖓 unclimbable Iron Fence ordered to be fixed by the side of the River from Abingdon Bridge to the Depôt Bridge in Thames Street.

𝕬 sum of £100 voted for adapting the Town Hall for the purposes of the Technical Education Committee.

1892.
January 7th.
John Heber
Clarke,
Mayor.

A Letter received from the Charity Commissioners suggesting that the Council should transfer sufficient Capital Stock to produce the annual sum of £31 : 4 : 0 which the Corporation contributed towards the maintenance of the inmates of St. John's Hospital, and also a further capital sum to cover the cost of Clothing which was annually given by the Council to the Almsmen, and it was resolved to adopt the first suggestion of the Commissioners, but to decline the second, the Council being under no legal liability to give Clothing to the Almsfolks, and would moreover in future lose the privilege of electing persons to the Almshouses when the new Scheme prepared by the Commissioners came into operation.

An address ordered to be prepared for presentation to their Royal Highnesses the Duke of Clarence and Avondale and Princess Mary of Teck, on their approaching marriage.

The Berks County Council Dairy School invited to give a course of Instruction in Abingdon.

The Town Clerk reported that a Local Inquiry had been held by the Local Government Board Inspector, Major-General Crozier, on the 8th December previous, with reference to the application of the Council for power to raise a Loan of £4100 for Sewerage and Water Supply and other works necessitated by the extension of the Boundaries of the Borough, and that the Inspector had expressed himself satisfied with the Scheme, and promised to report favourably thereon to the Local Government Board.

The Town Clerk also reported that Mr. Codrington, another of the Local Government Board Inspectors, had held an Inquiry with reference to the dispute between the Town Council and the County Council as to the amount to be paid by the latter Council for the maintenance of the Ladygrove Road, and that the Inspector had (with the consent of both parties) adjourned the Arbitration until the end of the Financial Year, suggesting that in the meantime some arrangement should be come to.

The Doors at the Stage end of the Corn Exchange ordered to be made to open outwards, to afford easy egress in case of fire.

The Town Clerk instructed to write to the Secretary of the Abingdon Railway Company and protest against the abolition of the

1892.
January 7th.
John Heber
Clarke,
Mayor.

January 20th.

Train Service on Sundays, on the Abingdon Branch, as contemplated by the Great Western Railway Company.

The Mayor reported that he had forwarded a telegram of condolence to His Royal Highness the Prince of Wales, on the 14th instant, on the occasion of the death of His Royal Highness the Duke of Clarence and Avondale, and a resolution of condolence was passed by the Council and ordered to be forwarded to Their Royal Highnesses the Prince and Princess of Wales.

Negotiations commenced with the Duchy of Cornwall with reference to the repair of the Marcham Road between the Ock Street and the Mill.

The Report of the Library Committee, recommending the renting of the late County Magistrates Court House in Bridge Street, for the purpose of a Free Library for the Borough adopted.

Negotiations completed for the redemption of the Fee Farm Rent of £102 : 16 : 7, the Council undertaking to transfer sufficient £2½ % Consols to produce £82 : 10 : 7, the amount of the net Rent payable by the Council, and also to pay the costs of the Vendors' Solicitor in the matter.

The Magistrates retiring Room at the Guildhall enlarged.

A Loan of £4047 authorized by the Local Government Board for works of Sewerage, Water Supply, and Street Improvements, in the Area recently added to the Borough.

Particulars with reference to the Water Supply of the Borough ordered to be furnished to the Royal Commission on the Metropolitan Water Supply, in compliance with a request received from the Secretary, and the Town Clerk instructed to inform the Commission that the Council would very strongly oppose any further withdrawal of water from the Watershed of the Thames for the purpose of supplying London with water.

A Report of the Sanitary Committee with reference to the Drainage of Northcourt, recommending the adoption of the dry earth system, received and adopted by the Council.

Permission given to the owner of adjoining property to open a Window in his premises in Bridge Street looking into the Guildhall

Yard, on condition that he paid an annual rent of 2/6 for the easement.

𝕬 Letter received from the Wilts and Berks Canal Company asking the Council to reconsider their determination not to repair the roadway over the Canal Bridge leading to the Farm, when it was resolved to do what repairs were necessary if the Company would pay £2 : 2 : 0 towards the cost thereof.

𝕿𝖍𝖊 new Scheme prepared by the Charity Commissioners for the administration of the Municipal Charities approved by the Council.

𝕸𝖗. Macdonald, of Oxford, instructed to report upon the condition of the Oil Paintings in the Council Chamber, and as to what steps he considered should be taken to preserve same.

𝕿𝖍𝖊 Town Clerk presented his report upon the result of a conference he had had with the Chairman of the Finance Committee of the Berks County Council, when it was provisionally agreed that the County Council should pay the Corporation £180 per annum towards the cost of administering Justice in the Borough, the County Council receiving the fees taken by the Clerk of the Peace and Clerk to the Borough Justices, and it was resolved to confirm the provisional arrangement made by the Town Clerk.

𝕬 Letter received from the County Council stating that the Council was willing to pay at the rate of £100 per mile for the repairs of that portion of the Steventon Main Road which was within the Borough.

𝕬 Report received from Dr. Woodforde recommending the Council to join the Abingdon Rural Sanitary Authority in providing an Isolation Hospital and an Apparatus for Disinfecting Infected Clothing for the use of the two Districts.

𝕬𝖓 offer made by Mr. W. F. Smith to set back his premises in the High Street, as desired by the Council, if the Council would pay him £150, and give him the land on the West and North sides of his property, which belonged to the Corporation, accepted by the Council.

𝕿𝖍𝖊 question of applying to the Local Government Board for a Provisional Order for the regulation of Abingdon Common discussed, but no order made thereon.

1892.
August 31st.
John Heber
Clarke,
Mayor.

The Land Tax of £34 : 17 : 0 charged on the Corporation Estates ordered to be redeemed.

A Water Main from the Wootton Road ordered to be laid to the Hamlet of Northcourt, at a cost of £148.

Mr. Alderman Townsend and Mr. Councillor Clarke elected Representative Trustees of the Abingdon Municipal Charities.

A Memorandum received from the Local Government Board with reference to precautions to be taken in consequence of an outbreak of Cholera on the Continent.

November 3rd.

An application which was received from the Free Library Committee for permission to use the Old Grammar School for the purposes of the Library was ordered to stand over until the Berks County Council had decided as to the letting of the late County Justices Court in Bridge Street for the same purpose.

The Private Streets Works Act, 1892, adopted by the Council.

A General District Rate at 1/6 in the £ to raise £1183 : 0 : 0 ordered to be made; and also a Special District Rate at 2d. in the £.

A Letter received from the Corporation of Swansea, requesting the Council to pass a resolution protesting against the abandonment of Uganda in Central Africa, by the Government, but no order was made thereon.

A New Fire Escape and Hose Cart ordered to be purchased.

November 9th.
Edward
Morland,
Mayor.

The question of obtaining a Provisional Order for the regulation of Abingdon Common discussed, and the Town Clerk instructed to make inquiries as to the working of similar orders in other Boroughs.

Permission given to the Abingdon Rural Sanitary Authority to connect the Drain of the Houses in the Ody Road, in Sutton Wick, with the Council's Main Sewer, on payment of a rent of £15 for the easement.

On the recommendation of the Sanitary Committee the Council decided not to erect a Destructor, but to remove the whole of the Town refuse to the Parish Land near the Common.

Fire Hydrants, with Hose attached thereto, ordered to be fixed in the various Municipal Buildings.

G. C. Hellyer appointed Junior Sergeant at Mace and Bellman and Fire Brigade Engineer.

A Tank for filling the Syphon, at Wootton, ordered to be constructed in the Reservoir.

A List of Persons employed in the Manufacture of Clothing, &c., ordered to be kept by Manufacturers, in compliance with the Factories and Workshops Act, 1891.

Permission given to an adjoining owner of property to erect a Shed in the Guildhall Yard on payment of a rent for the easement.

An application made to the Berks County Council and the Abingdon Highway Board inviting them to join the Town Council in taking action with regard to the liability of the Duchy of Cornwall to repair a portion of the Marcham Road.

The St. John's Road ordered to be repaired, under the Private Streets Works Act, 1892.

The sanction of the Local Government Board received to the application of the Purchase Money for the Borough's interest in Littlemore Asylum, amounting to £1481 : 10 : 3, towards the repayment of the Paving Bond Redemption Loan.

A Letter received from the Local Government Board enquiring whether the Council had taken any action with regard to the Medical Officer of Health's suggestion that the Abingdon Urban and Rural Sanitary Authorities should combine for the purpose of providing an Isolation Hospital for the treatment of cases of Infectious Disease.

A Deputation appointed to wait on the Directors of the Great Western Railway Company with the view of obtaining a reduction on their new rates for the carriage of goods to the Town.

A Petition ordered to be prepared and presented against the Bill promoted by the London County Council for giving that Council the power to nominate Seven of its Members as Conservators of the River Thames.

A portion of the Yard on the South side of the Foundry, containing an area of about 200 square yards, added to the Cattle Market.

1893.
May 11th.
Edward
Morland,
Mayor.

Two Iron Posts ordered to be placed in the passage between Stert Street and the Market Place, and the Footpath on the North side of the Marcham Road ordered to be paved, and the paving on the South side of High Street and the West side of Bath Street ordered to be taken up and relaid with Concrete paving.

A Letter received from the Abingdon District Highway Board, declining to join the Council in taking action against the Duchy of Cornwall with reference to the repairs of the Marcham Road.

On the recommendation of the Sanitary Committee it was resolved to discontinue the making of a Special District Rate for the amount required for the Paving Bonds Redemption Loan, and in future to make an annual grant of £100 out of the Surplus of the Borough Fund until the whole of the Loan had been satisfied.

The Syphon at the Waterworks ordered to be lengthened.

A General District Rate at 1/10 in the £ ordered to be made.

The Sanitary Committee reported that they had had a conference with the Abingdon Rural Sanitary Authority with reference to the erection of a Joint Isolation Hospital for the combined Districts, and that it had been decided not to take any further action with regard to the matter until the Local Government Bill, then before Parliament had been disposed of, as it was probable some alteration would be made in the Rural Sanitary Authority's District.

An Insurance Policy against claims by the Council's Employés, under the Employers' Liability Acts, ordered to be taken out.

Mr. Alderman Tomkins and Councillor Clarke elected Governors of Roysse's School by the Council.

A Letter received from the Secretary of the South of Scotland Chamber of Commerce, asking the Council to seal a Petition in favour of the establishing of an Imperial Penny Post, but no order was made thereon.

August 10th.

The question of Watering the Roads in the Park discussed by the Council, and the Town Clerk ordered to communicate with the Master and Governors of Christ's Hospital and enquire whether they would be willing to contribute towards the cost of the work.

𝕿𝖍𝖊 Borough Seal affixed to a Contract with the National Debt Commissioners for the redemption of the Land Tax on the Corporation Estates.

1893.
August 10th.
Edward
Morland,
Mayor.

𝕿𝖍𝖊 Report of the Streets Committee recommending the Planting of Trees by the side of the Oxford Road, and Shrubs on the site of the late Star Inn, in the Market Place, adopted by the Council.

𝕬 Report received from the Sanitary Committee with reference to the diminution in the supply of Water from the Water Works.

𝕾𝖎𝖝 Experimental Shafts for Ventilating the Sewers ordered to be erected in various parts of the Town.

𝕬 grant of £27 made by the Council towards the expenses of establishing a Science Class at Roysse's School.

November 2nd.

𝕬 General District Rate at 1/10 in the £ ordered to be made.

𝕬 resolution unanimously carried against the introduction by the Post Office of the "Cash on Delivery" system.

𝕿𝖍𝖊 Sanitary and Streets Committee instructed to enquire into and report upon the Drainage and Lighting of Northcourt.

𝕬 report of the Streets Committee received with reference to the decision of the Borough Justices on the objections raised to the Scheme for improving the St. John's Road.

1894.
February 8th.

𝕬 Report received from the Sanitary Committee with reference to the steps they had taken to find work for the unemployed.

𝕬 Petition ordered to be presented against the Bill promoted by the Thames Conservators for giving the Conservators additional and extended power over the whole of the area comprised in the Watershed of the River Thames.

𝕿𝖍𝖊 Cemetery Road ordered to be paved, &c., under the Private Streets Works Act, 1892.

𝕿𝖍𝖊 sum of £200 voted towards the expense incurred by the Master and Governors of Christ's Hospital in pulling down their property in the High Street, adjoining Mr. Smith's premises, and erecting on its site a Free Library for the Town.

An offer of £25 received from the Duchy of Cornwall in settlement of the Duchy's liability to repair a portion of Marcham Road, and it was ordered that the matter be left in the hands of the County Council to settle, and that an application should be made to that Council for an order declaring the Road to be a Main Road.

The safe return of the Portrait of Queen Charlotte, by Gainsborough, from the Exhibition of Old Masters, in London, reported to the Council.

A Report received from the Finance Committee with reference to the alterations made in the Law and the additional powers given to the Council by the Local Government Act, 1894, and it was resolved—Firstly—To apply to the Local Government Board for an order conferring upon the Council the power of appointing Overseers and Assistant Overseers and the powers and duties of a Parish Council and also the powers of a Vestry under Secs. 33 and 34 of the Poor Rate Assessment Act, 1869: Secondly—To apply to the Berks County Council for an Order forming the portions of the Parishes of St. Helen and St. Nicholas, Culham and Sutton Wick, which were within the Borough, into one Parish, to be called the Parish of Abingdon, and Thirdly—To apply to the Local Government for a Provisional Order transferring the portion of St. Nicholas Parish lying on the South bank of the Thames, near Abingdon Lock, and the portion of the Parish of Culham lying on the same side of the River, and known as the Rookery, from the Borough to the Parish of Culham, in the County of Oxford, and bringing the meadows lying on the North side of the River Ock between the Ock Street and the Mill into the Borough Area; and Fourthly—That the Council should adopt the Burial Acts, 1852 to 1885, and assume the powers and duties of the Abingdon Burial Board, as recommended by the Local Government Board Inspector in 1888.

The Plans for the erection of a house in the Faringdon Road rejected by the Council, it being proposed to construct same of Patent Wire-wove Waterproof Sheeting.

A General District Rate at 1/8 in the £ ordered to be made.

An owner of property ordered to pay an annual rent for the easement of a cellar-light fixed in the pavement in front of his premises in the High Street.

Plans for the erection of a Free Library submitted by the Master and Governors of Christ's Hospital, and approved by the Council; the proposed grant of £200 towards the cost thereof being increased to £250 by the Council.

The Finance Committee directed to inquire into and report upon the question of providing a Public Landing Place on the River Bank for the use of persons frequenting the River.

The Borough Seal affixed to a Power of Attorney for the Sale of £3266 : 15 : 9 Consols for the purchase of the Fee Farm Rent of £102 : 16 : 7 charged on the Corporation Estates.

The Mayor (Mr. Councillor Morland) died.

A Vote of Sympathy and Condolence with the Widow and Family of the late Mayor passed by the Council.

A Letter received from the Local Government Board stating that the Council's application for additional powers under Sec. 33 and 34 of the Local Government Act, 1894, must be deferred until after the appointed day, and that the powers and duties of the Burial Board would after that day, be exercised by a Joint Committee appointed by the Council and the Parish Meeting of St. Helen's Parish, and also intimating that the Board had decided not to sanction the alterations in the Borough Area as requested by the Council on the 10th May last.

The Finance Committee reported that the Berks County Council had held a Public Inquiry in Abingdon, and recommended that the parts of the Parishes of St. Helen, St. Nicholas, Culham and Sutton Wick, which were within the Borough, should be formed into one Parish for all civil purposes, to be called the Parish of Abingdon, and that the portions of the Parishes of St. Helen and St. Nicholas without the Borough should be formed into one Civil Parish, called St. Helen (without).

The resignation of the Office of Treasurer by Mr. H. D'Almaine received and accepted, and Mr. Isaac Westcombe (the new Manager of the Abingdon Branch of the London and County Bank) elected Treasurer in his place.

A General District Rate at 1/8 in the £ ordered to be made.

The Streets Committee reported that the Improvements in St. John's Road had been completed at a cost of £436 : 16 : 10.

A Scale of Fees adopted by the Council for the payment of the Returning Officer's Staff at Municipal Elections.

An application ordered to be made to the Directors of the Great Western Railway to provide a covered way over the Line at Radley Station.

A Committee appointed to enquire into the question of Abingdon Common with a view to its better utilization for the benefit of the inhabitants of the Town.

On the recommendation of the Library Committee the Council resolved to vote £150 per annum towards the maintenance of the Free Library, and also to accept a Lease of the Building at a nominal rent, and to covenant to keep the same in good repair.

A Portrait of Sir Charles Saxton, Bart., presented to the Council.

The Mayor requested to convene a Public Meeting to consider what steps could be taken to prevent a repetition of the disastrous floods which had occured in the preceding November.

The position and endowments of Roysse's School ordered to be brought before the Royal Commission on Technical and Secondary Education.

The Streets Committee instructed to consider and report upon the question of lighting Northcourt with Oil Lamps.

The Portrait of the late Mayor (Mr. Councillor Morland) presented to the Council.

A Vote of Condolence and Sympathy passed by the Council on the death (on the 11th instant) of Mr. John Creemer Clarke, formerly Member of Parliament and Mayor of the Borough.

Relief Works established for the employment of persons thrown out of work in consequence of the recent severe weather.

New Street ordered to be reformed and paved under the Private Streets Works Act, 1892.

1895.
February 14th.
Edward John
Harris,
Mayor.

𝕿𝖍𝖊 Local Government Committee reported that they had had a Conference with the Parochial Representatives of the Parish of St. Helen without the Borough, and arranged that the Abingdon Cemetery in future should be managed by a Committee of 10 persons, 7 being appointed by the Council and 3 by the Parish Meeting of St. Helen (without).

𝕬𝖓 application again made to the Local Government Board for an order vesting in the Council all the powers mentioned in Sec. 33 of the Local Government Act, 1894.

𝕬 Memorial presented to the Council requesting that the Allotments might be removed from the Sewage Farm to a more convenient site, and a Special Committee was appointed to consider the matter.

𝕬𝖓 offer made by the Abingdon Gas Company, Limited, to erect and light Five Gas Lamps in the Village of Northcourt, received and accepted.

𝕿𝖍𝖊 Borough Surveyor presented a report with reference to the erection of a Windmill at the Farm for Pumping Sewage.

𝕬 Portrait of the late Revd. Nathaniel Dodson, M.A., formerly Vicar of Abingdon, by Mr. Bridges, R.A., presented to the Council by his daughter, Miss Dodson.

𝕻𝖊𝖗𝖒𝖎𝖘𝖘𝖎𝖔𝖓 given to an owner of property in the Vineyard to fix two cellar lights in the pavement in front of her house, on payment of an annual rent for the easement. May 9th.

𝕿𝖍𝖊 Borough Surveyor reported that several of the Water Mains had burst during the prolonged frost in the late Winter.

𝕬 General District Rate at 1/8 in the £ ordered to be made.

𝕮𝖔𝖒𝖕𝖊𝖓𝖘𝖆𝖙𝖎𝖔𝖓 voted towards the loss sustained by the owner of a horse which was killed through an accident whilst drawing the Corporation Fire Engine to a Fire at Littlemore Lunatic Asylum.

𝕬 Resolution passed against permitting sub-contracting on works ordered by the Council.

𝕿𝖍𝖊 resignation of Mr. A. Miles, Senior Sergeant at Mace, received and accepted.

A Committee appointed to consider the question of establishing a Public Landing Place on the bank of the River Thames.

The Streets Committee instructed to place Seats at suitable spots by the side of the roads in the Borough.

A Committee appointed to consider and report upon the expediency of acquiring the Gas Company's Works, and also of establishing an installation of Electric Light in the Town.

A Letter received from the Anglo-Armenian Association requesting the Mayor to convene a Public Meeting to protest against the recent persecution of the Armenian Christians in Turkey.

A serious falling off in the Supply of Water from the Waterworks in consequence of the long drought having been reported by the Borough Engineer, the Sanitary Committee was instructed to lengthen the short leg of the Syphon by 2 feet, and to consider and report whether any, and if so, what extra works were necessary to increase the supply of water for the Town.

Mr. A. E. Preston appointed Collector of Water Rents.

Plans approved for enlarging the Cattle Market and the erection of additional pens.

A Superannuation allowance of £30 per annum granted to A. Miles, the late Senior Sergeant at Mace.

A Scale of Fees for letting the Municipal Buildings adopted by the Council.

The District Fund Reserve Fund and the Mayor's Sealing Fee Fund, amounting together to £650, ordered to be invested in the Abingdon Gas Light and Coke Company's £4 per cent. Debenture Bonds.

The Resignation of Mr. T. Vizer of the Offices of Farm Bailiff, Clerk of the Market, and School Attendance Officer, received and accepted.

An Agreement entered into with the Berks County Council for the payment by that Council of £430 per annum, for a period of five years, towards the cost of maintaining the Main Roads in the Town.

A sum of £100 voted by the Berks County Council towards the cost of widening and improving the High Street.

𝕿𝖍𝖊 Fishery in the River Thames, formerly attached to the Abbey Mills, presented to the Council by Mr. Councillor Pryce, the Council undertaking to hold the same in trust for the free enjoyment of the same by the Public.

1895. May 9th. Edward John Harris, Mayor.

𝕸𝖗. Frank Dandridge appointed Farm Bailiff and Clerk of the Market.

August 8th.

𝕬 Report of the Committee with reference to the Abingdon Common presented to the Council.

𝕻𝖊𝖗𝖒𝖎𝖘𝖘𝖎𝖔𝖓 given to an occupier of adjoining premises to use a way through the Market to his premises in Bath Street conditionally upon his paying a rent for the easement.

𝕬 Letter received from the Thames Valley Drainage Commissioners, stating that the Commissioners were about to expend £1000 in improving the Drainage of the River Ock, with a view of preventing a repetition of the disastrous flood of the previous year, and asking the Council to make a Contribution towards the Commissioners' expenditure, and it was resolved that the Council should contribute £100 conditionally upon the Commissioners at once commencing the works mentioned in their Engineer's Report, between the Ock Bridge and the River Thames.

𝕲𝖆𝖘 Lamps ordered to be erected in Bostock Avenue, which had recently been constructed by the Master and Governors of Christ's Hospital.

𝕬 Report by the Borough Engineer recommending the Expenditure of £1000 in extending the Water Works at Wootton, presented to the Council.

𝕬𝖓 application ordered to be made to the Conservators of the River Thames for the provision of a Public Camping Ground on the Lock Island, near the Weir.

𝕿𝖍𝖊 duties of the Senior Sergeant at Mace defined by the Council.

September 5th.

𝕿𝖍𝖊 formation of a Collection of Old Abingdon Prints and Portraits of past Mayors commenced.

𝕿𝖍𝖊 Council resolved to consult Mr. Charles Hawkesley, C.E., with reference to the plans prepared by the Borough Engineer for extending the Water Works at Wootton.

𝕬 Report received from the Medical Officer of Health certifying that 13 Houses in Bury Street were in a state so dangerous and injurious to health as to be unfit for human habitation, and it was ordered that steps should be taken for closing same until they had been made fit for habitation.

October 22nd.

𝕬 Memorial presented to the Council complaining of the nuisance caused by living vans belonging to persons attending Michaelmas Fair being allowed to stand in the Streets during the Fair, and it was ordered that a notice should be issued requiring the owners of such vans to remove the same from the Streets where they did not actually and necessarily form part of any show or stall.

𝕬n application by the Post Office Authorities for permission to fix a telegraph line to the Town Hall, in connection with the line which the Department was about to construct to Sutton, refused by the Council.

𝕵ohn Henry Viner appointed Senior Sergeant at Mace and School Attendance Officer.

𝕬 General District Rate at 1/8 in the £ to raise £1540 ordered to be made.

𝕬 Letter received from Mr. Hawkesley, C.E., recommending that bore holes should be sunk in the vicinity of the Reservoir at Wootton, to determine the exact position of the water bearing strata, in order to enable the best direction for the proposed adits to be selected. And it was ordered that the works suggested by Mr. Hawkesley should be carried out.

𝕬 Committee appointed to consider and report upon the desirability of the Council acquiring the remains of the Abingdon Monastery for the purpose of preserving and securing the buildings for the benefit of the Town.

𝕬 Letter received offering to find a supply of water for the Town by means of a divining rod.

𝕬 Vote of Thanks given to Mr. John Tomkins on his retiring from the Office of Alderman after serving in the Council for a period of thirty years.

𝕿he Finance and General Purposes Committee instructed to report upon an application made by the No. 7 Board of the Thames

Valley Drainage Commissioners, with reference to the construction of a Culvert under the Caldecot Road, near St. Helen's Wharf, to relieve the flood water passing down the River Ock.

𝕿𝖍𝖊 sum of £50 voted for setting back the shop front of Mr. Brewerton's premises in the High Street.

𝕬 Clock for the Council Chamber presented to the Council by Miss Dodson.

𝕿𝖍𝖊 Council resolved to take a Lease for 7 years of the remains of the Abingdon Abbey from the Trustees of the Abingdon Municipal Charities.

𝕬 Letter received from the General Manager of the Great Western Railway Company, stating that the Directors had decided to cover in the Bridge over the Line at Radley Station, as requested by the Council.

December 5th.

𝕬 Report presented by the Streets Committee with reference to the repair of the Oday Road, and recommending that in future the Abingdon Rural District Council should be called upon to repair the Road in accordance with the provisions contained in the Sutton Courtenay Inclosure Award, made in the year 1804.

1896.
January 2nd.

𝕬𝖓 order made for affixing a distinguishing number to each of the Street Lamps.

𝕬 Silver Burmese Bowl presented to the Corporation by the High Steward, the Right Hon. the Earl of Abingdon.

𝕬 Committee appointed to consider the question of providing better and cheaper Allotments for the labouring classes.

𝕬 Committee appointed to confer with the Master and Governors of Christ's Hospital with reference to the providing of a Public Landing Stage, Waiting Room and other Public Improvements, on the Nag's Head Island, near the Bridge.

𝕬 Vote of Sympathy and Condolence with Her Majesty the Queen, and Her Royal Highness Princess Beatrice, on the death of His Royal Highness Prince Henry of Battenburg, in Ashanti, unanimously passed by the Council.

February 6th.

𝕿𝖍𝖊 Houses forming Bury Court, in Bury Street, purchased by the Council for £225.

WW

𝕿𝖍𝖊 Race Stand on the Common ordered to be pulled down and the Materials removed.

𝕬 Letter received from the Conservators of the River Thames stating that in compliance with the Council's request they had arranged to provide a Public Camping Ground on the Lock Island near the Weir.

𝕿𝖍𝖊 Local Government Board having refused to confer upon the Council the powers under Ṣec. 33, Sub.-Sec. 10, of the Local Government Act, 1894, with reference to the acquiring of Land for Allotments, it was resolved that Mr. A. K. Loyd, Q.C., M.P., for the Abingdon Division, should be requested to ask the President of the Local Government Board, in the House of Commons, why the Board had refused to grant the application of the Council.

𝕬 Letter read from the Right Hon. the Earl of Abingdon, High Steward of the Borough, stating that he should be pleased to open the Free Library on the 15th April then next.

𝕬 Letter ordered to be sent to the County and District Councils urging the desirability of arranging for the use of Steam Rollers for the repair of the Main and District Roads in the neighbourhood of Abingdon.

March 5th.

𝕬𝖓 offer of Messrs. Stevenson & Redfern, Architects, of London, gratuitously to report upon the Abbey Buildings accepted, and a sum of £105 voted towards the fund for their repair and preservation.

𝕬 Letter read from Mr. Loyd, Q.C., M.P., stating that he had put down a question on the question paper of the House of Commons with reference to the refusal of the Local Government Board to grant the additional powers under Sec. 33 Sub.-Sec. 10 of the Local Government Act, 1894, asked for by the Council, and stating that he had had an interview with the Secretary of the Local Government Board, who had informed him that the Board would issue the order the Council asked for.

𝕬 Letter received from the Clerk to the Berks County Council enquiring whether the Council had provided an Isolation Hospital for the Borough, and if not, what arrangements were made in the Borough for Isolation of cases of Infectious Disease.

𝔄 complaint received from the owner of the Fitzharris Estate of the metalling by the Council of the portion of the Boxhill Footpath passing through his property, when it was arranged that the metalled path should remain, but be of a width of six feet only, and be kept in repair by the Council, the Council also agreeing to erect on the North side of the path a wire fence similar to the one recently erected alongside the remainder of the path between the Wootton Road and the Meadow, with an Iron Gate therein.

𝔓ermission given to the National Telephone Company to erect the necessary Posts for carrying their Wires in the Borough.

𝔄 Report received from the Borough Surveyor with reference to the condition of the Cornice and Roof of the Town Hall.

𝔗he Collection of Statutes, &c., belonging to the Corporation, lent to the Free Library, to be placed in the Reference Department.

𝔄n application made to the Local Government Board for power to borrow a further sum of £1000 for Water Works Extension purposes.

𝔄 General District Rate at 1/8 in the £ ordered to be made.

𝔗he Town Clerk in pursuance of instructions received from the Audit Committee reported upon the liability of the Council to pay the several sums of £10, £8, 6/8, and 5/-, to the Vicar of St. Helen's and the Rector of St. Nicholas, when it was resolved that the opinion of Mr. Macmorran, Q.C., should be taken on the matter.

𝔄n Order issued by the Local Government Board transferring to the Council the duty of appointing an Assistant Overseer for the Parish of Abingdon.

𝔄 Special Committee appointed to consider and report upon the question of the desirability of the Council acquiring the undertaking of the Abingdon Gas Light and Coke Company, Limited.

𝔗he opinion of Mr. Macmorran, Q.C., upon the case recently submitted to him with reference to the legality of the payments to the Vicar of Abingdon and Rector of St. Nicholas received; when it was resolved that notice be given to the Vicar and Rector that the services for which the payments were made would not be required by the Corporation after the expiration of Six Months from that date, but that if in the meantime it could be shewn that the payments could be justified upon any other grounds, the Council would be prepared to reconsider the matter.

An Order received from the Local Government Board conferring upon the Council the powers of a Parish Council under Sec. 14 of the Local Government Act, 1894, with reference to the Charities in the Borough.

July 9th.

A Tender of £217 : 8 : 0 for the renovation of the Cornice of the Town Hall accepted by the Council.

A Memorial prepared by the Thames Floods Prevention Committee praying the Government to promote legislation with a view of placing the Upper Thames under the control of an Authority distinct from that of the tidal portion of the River, sealed by the Council.

August 6th.

A Report presented to the Council by a Special Committee recommending the Amalgamation of Twitty's, Provost's, Hawkins's, and Cleobury's Charities with Christ's Hospital, and suggesting that the Council should be empowered to appoint a certain number of additional Trustees of Christ's Hospital, Wrigglesworth's, and Tomkins's Charities.

The Mayor requested to convene a Public Meeting to consider the desirability of inviting the Oxfordshire Agricultural Society to hold their Show at Abingdon in 1898.

October 1st.

On the recommendation of the Streets Committee the Council resolved to fit a number of the Public Street Lamps with Incandescent Burners.

The Allotments Committee reported that the Duchy of Cornwall had offered them some Arable Land on the Marcham and Wootton Roads at a Rent of 30/- per Acre, free of Tithe, and suggested that a Meeting of persons desirous of renting Allotments should be convened with a view of ascertaining the quantity of Land required.

An application made to the Local Government Board for power to invest the annual repayments on account of Loans in Securities authorized for Trust Investments, instead of in Consols, as theretofore.

The Council agreed to purchase three Acres of Land adjoining the Water Works at Wootton, for £300, for the extension of the Works.

The Mayor reported that on the 23rd ultimo he had forwarded a telegram of congratulation to Her Majesty the Queen, on her having reigned longer than any other British Sovereign.

A General District Rate at 1/8 in the £ ordered to be made.

The Hall-keeper authorized to charge a fee of 5/- for preparing the Rooms for Dances terminating before midnight.

The Insurance of the whole of the Corporation Property considered and ordered to be increased from £17,000 to £26,055.

An Order made for repairing and re-pitching Benham's Yard by the owners of adjoining properties, under Sec. 150 of the Public Health Act, 1875.

A new Public Convenience ordered to be erected in Bury Street, near the Corn Exchange, at a cost of £45.

A Committee appointed to consider the question of establishing an Isolation Hospital for the joint use of the Abingdon Urban and Rural District Councils.

A Letter received from the Charity Commissioners stating that the Master and Governors of Christ's Hospital had applied to them for a new Scheme under which it was suggested that the Council should have the power of nominating four additional Trustees, and therefore they did not propose to take any action with reference to the application of the Council for power to appoint such Trustees, and further stating with regard to Tomkins's Charity that they considered that Charity could not be regarded as a Parochial Charity within the meaning of the Local Government Act, 1894.

The Council resolved to level, metal, &c., the Road leading from Spring Road to Bartram's Row, under the powers conferred by the Private Streets Works Act, 1882.

The Old Public Convenience removed from the Town Hall and re-erected in the Conduit Road.

The Isolation Hospital Committee presented a Report which was adopted by the Council, recommending that the Abingdon

Urban and Rural District Councils should combine for the purpose of providing a Hospital under the powers conferred by the Public Health Act, 1875, and that the Culham Rural District Council should be invited to join the combination.

𝕿𝖍𝖊 Council resolved to apply to the Charity Commissioners to amend the Scheme of the Abingdon Municipal Charities by providing for the appointment of the representative Trustees by the Council, instead of by the Ratepayers of the Parishes of St. Helen and St. Nicholas, in Vestry assembled.

𝕿𝖍𝖊 Council, at the suggestion of the Thames Floods Prevention Committee, requested the Conservators of the River Thames to fix a High Water Gauge near Abingdon Bridge.

𝕬 Letter received from the Local Government Board stating it could not sanction in general terms the investment of the instalments in repayment of the Water Works Extension Loan in any securities which were authorized by the Trustee Act, 1893, and requesting the Council to specify the particular securities in which it was desired to invest the instalments, when it was resolved to apply for powers to invest in Liverpool Corporation 3 per cent. and Reading Corporation Irredeemable $3\frac{1}{2}$ per cent. Stock.

𝕬 Letter received from the Thames Conservators stating that they would place near Abingdon Bridge a Board showing the level of the Head Water at Culham Lock, on the understanding that the cost thereof would be defrayed by the Council.

𝕿𝖍𝖊 Borough Surveyor instructed to make a House to House Inspection, and report from time to time upon the Sanitary condition of all the Houses in the Town.

𝕺𝖓 the recommendation of the Sanitary Committee a Special Committee was appointed to prepare a New Code of Bye Laws for the Borough.

𝕿𝖍𝖊 sanction of the Local Government Board obtained for a Loan of £2,550 for Water Works Extension.

𝕬 Letter received from the Lord Mayor of London asking the Mayor to open a Fund for the Relief of the Distress caused by the calamitous Famine then existing in the Indian Empire, and the Mayor reported that he had opened a Subscription List accordingly.

An application made to the Master and Governors of Christ's Hospital to set aside a small strip of land on the East side of Spring Road for the purpose of widening that Road.

1897.
February 4th.
Charles Alfred
Pryce,
Mayor.

A further sum of £128 : 4 : 0 voted towards the restoration of the Abbey Buildings.

The Mayor reported that he had directed the Borough Surveyor to affix a Mark upon the Pillar of the South Entrance to St. Helen's Churchyard to indicate the level of the Water in the Thames during the great Flood of 1894.

March 4th.

The Council agreed to advance to the Isolation Hospital Joint Committee such sum as might be required for the erection of the Hospital, the Loan to be repaid by Instalments within 30 years, with interest at $3\frac{1}{2}$ per cent.

A Letter received from the Kings Norton Rural District Council, calling attention to the desirability of Local Authorities being enabled to provide Crematoriums, but no order was made thereon.

A Motion for the employment of a Waterfinder, with the aid of a divining rod, before proceeding further with the Water Works at Wootton, negatived by the Council, two members of the Council only voting for it.

The Mayor requested to convene a Meeting of the Inhabitants of the Town to decide upon a Scheme for properly celebrating the Long Reign of Her Majesty in June then next.

An Address of Congratulation to Her Majesty the Queen, on the completion of the 60th Year of Her Reign in June next, ordered to be prepared.

May 6th.

A Letter received from the Charity Commissioners, suggesting that the Council should apply to the Trustees of the Abingdon Municipal Charities for their approval of the proposed alteration in the method of electing the representative Trustees of the Town Parishes, when it was agreed that an application should be made to the Trustees accordingly.

A Notice received of an intended application to the Board of Trade for a Warrant authorizing the abandonment of the Wilts and

1897.
May 9th.
Charles Alfred
Pryce,
Mayor.

Berks Canal, when it was resolved to oppose the application, unless provision was made in the Order for the removal, of the Canal Bridges and the levelling and making good of the Roadways forming the approaches thereto.

The First Annual Report of the Free Library Committee presented to the Council, the Report stating that the Library contained 3,520 Volumes; and that during the 204 days the Lending Department had been open, 10,000 Volumes had been issued for Home Reading, and 922 Volumes had been consulted in the Reference Department; the number of borrowers of Books being 527; while about 4,000 persons per week used the Reading Room.

The Allotments Committee reported that the applications for Allotments in the Wootton and Marcham Roads were not in their opinion sufficient to justify the Council in proceeding to acquire Land for the purpose.

A General District Rate at 1/9 in the £ ordered to be made.

June 10th.

On the recommendation of the Market Committee the Council resolved to adapt a portion of the site of the Bury Court property for the purposes of the Market by erecting additional Cattle Pens thereon.

The Draft Bye Laws prepared by the Bye Laws Committee approved by the Council and ordered to be sent to the Local Government Board.

The Mayor reported that he had been commanded to attend a reception of the Mayors and Provosts of the United Kingdom by Her Majesty the Queen, at Buckingham Palace, on the 23rd of June instant.

August 5th.

The Mayor reported that the family of the late Mr. Alderman Ballard had intimated to him their intention of presenting to the Town an Ornamental Fountain, for erection in the Square, when it was resolved that the offer should be accepted with the thanks of the Council.

An application made to H.M's. Postmaster General to place a Pillar Letter Box at the Abingdon Railway Station.

1897.
August 6th.
Charles Alfred
Pryce,
Mayor.

𝕿𝖍𝖊 following account of the Celebration of Her Majesty's Diamond Jubilee prepared by the Secretary of the Celebration Committee was ordered to be entered upon the Minutes of the Council :—

Borough of Abingdon.

"THE Sixtieth Anniversary of the Accession to the Throne of Great "Britain and Ireland, generally called the Diamond Jubilee of Her "Majesty Queen Victoria, was celebrated in this Ancient Borough on "Sunday, June 20th, and Tuesday, June 22nd, 1897, in the Mayoralty "of Mr. Councillor Pryce, the said 20th and 22nd being the dates "appointed by an Order in Council for the celebration of the event.

"On Sunday, June 20th, the Services in the various Churches and "Chapels were of a special character. The chief commemoration was "at St. Helen's Church, where the Mayor and Corporation and the "Borough Officials attended Morning Service, accompanied from the "Council Chamber by the Officiating Clergy.

"In the Afternoon there was a Church Parade of various public "bodies organized at the instance of the Mayor, who had invited the "Benefit Societies to join in a Service at St. Helen's Church. The "Guildhall was the meeting place, and among those who took part in "the Parade were the Mayor and Corporation in their robes, the Borough "Officials, the Governors of Christ's Hospital, the Borough Magistrates, "Officiating Clergy and Nonconformist Ministers, the Ivey and Bowyer "Union Lodges of Oddfellows with their banner, the Berkshire Order "of Foresters and banner, a contingent from the Provident Institution "and Hearts of Oak, the Oddfellows' Brass Band and two Drum and "Fife Bands. At 8 p.m. a largely attended United Nonconformist "Service was held in Trinity Wesleyan Church, at which the Revds. "Bayliss, Doggett, and Hookey (the Ministers of the Wesleyan, Baptist "and Congregational Churches respectively) officiated.

"The proceedings on June 22nd commenced with the ringing of the "Church Bells at an early hour.

"A Procession was formed in the Park Road at 10 o'clock, consisting "of the Mayor and Corporation and Clergy, the Governors of Christ's "Hospital, Deputations from Roysse's School and Friendly Societies, "the elder Children from the Elementary Schools, the Band of the "1st Vol. Batt. Queen's Royal West Surrey Regiment, the Abingdon "Oddfellows' Brass Band, the Abingdon Church Drum and Fife Band,

XX

"the Wesleyan Drum and Fife Band, the Fire Brigade and about 30
"Decorated Cars. Prizes having been offered for the best Decorated
"Car illustrating the trade of the various Competitors. The Judging
"took place before the Procession started, and the Prizes were awarded
"as follows :—The first to J. Gibbons, Saddler, of Broad Street, for a
"Car Decorated with many coloured materials, and bright with steel,
"brass, and plated fittings used in the manufacture of Harness, and in
"the centre were several workmen carrying on their trade. The second
"to a Car prepared by Messrs. Baylis & Co., Printers, on which was a
"Model of the Printing Press of the early days of Printing, and that
"of to-day, all being worked by employés of the Firm, who distributed
"leaflets of the National Anthem which they printed as the procession
"passed round the Town. The third prize was awarded to Messrs.
"Morland & Co., Limited, who exhibited a team of Horses and Waggons
"as used in the year 1837, and another as used in the present year.
"The former having carters dressed in the costume of 60 years ago, and
"the latter containing modern appliances used in Brewing, Bottling, &c.
"Many other Cars attracted considerable notice, especially that shewn
"by the Bakers and Confectioners, on which several men were working,
"as also they were on the Smiths, Cycle Makers, Builders, and others,
"wherever the nature of the trade admitted of the work being carried on.

"After parading the Town the Procession drew up in the Market
"Place, where the Mayor and Corporation occupied a platform in front
"of the County Hall, facing the Queen's Statue, around which stood a
"number of Old Soldiers, wearing their Medals, the Statue itself being
"tastefully decorated with flowers. The National Anthem was sung
"and hearty cheers were given for the Queen. The Mayor then
"distributed among 250 of the elder Children from the Elementary
"Schools, Books containing the Story of the Queen's Life. A Vote of
"Thanks to the Mayor followed, proposed by the Deputy Mayor, and
"carried with acclamation.

"The Mayor and Corporation having gone up to the roof of the
"County Hall, Buns were thrown into the Market Place, in pursuance
"of an ancient custom. The Mayor afterwards entertained the Council,
"Governors of Christ's Hospital, Magistrates, and friends in the Small
"Council Chamber, when the health of the Queen was proposed by the
"Mayor, followed by that of the Mayor, the Deputy Mayor, and
"Alderman Townsend, the latter being the only person present who
"took part in the bun throwing from the roof of the County Hall on
"the occasion of Her Majesty's Accession to the Throne in 1837.

" The health of the Hon. Secretaries having been given and replied to,
" the company adjourned until 2 o'clock, when the Bands, starting from
" the Market Place, headed an informal procession to the fields on the
" River side, kindly placed at the disposal of the Committee by the
" Abingdon Cricket and Football Club, and Messrs. Hays and Hobbs,
" where Sports, commencing with Water Sports on Wilsom Reach, and
" consisting of Scratch Fours, Canoe Races, Water Tournaments,
" Swimming Races, Water Polo, &c., lasted until after 6 o'clock. The
" Land Sports which began at six o'clock in the Cricket Field, consisted
" of various Races for Men, Boys and Girls, and Cycle Races, including
" a Race for Working Men riding machines in daily use, and ridden in
" working clothes.

" At 8.30 the Mayor presented the Prizes to the successful competitors,
" and by the time the last prize had been given, a Procession of
" Illuminated Boats was prepared, and a very pretty Venetian Fête was
" subsequently witnessed by a large concourse of people. The Boat
" entered by Roysse's School was an easy winner of the First Prize for
" Decorations, the Second and Third Prizes being awarded to the Boys'
" Church Club (under the direction of the Rev. R. H. Miers) and to
" Mr. J. W. Coxeter respectively. The whole of the Boats (by the
" Mayor's desire) were taken as near as possible to Abingdon Bridge,
" and while rowing to and from the Nag's Head Island, Fireworks were
" let off both from the Boats and Shore, making a suitable conclusion
" to a most enjoyable day.

" In addition to the Senior Scholars who had joined in the Procession
" and received Souvenirs, about a Thousand Children from the Ele-
" mentary Schools received Tickets for the Refreshments served on the
" Sports Ground. Swings and other Amusements were also provided for
" them.

" To the whole of the Almsfolk, and the Sick and Aged who were
" unable to attend the Festivities a new Half-crown was presented,
" and a new Shilling to Sick Children. All School Children in attend-
" ance at the Elementary Schools receiving a new Penny. The Inmates
" of the Abingdon Union were (by order of the Guardians) provided
" with a special Dinner, and afterwards allowed to attend the Sports.

" The Town was gaily Decorated, and the Illuminations were general
" and very effective, and the weather being beautifully fine throughout
" the whole day, crowned the efforts of the Committee with success.

1897.
August 5th.
Charles Alfred
Pryce,
Mayor.

"The arrangements were carried out by a large and representative
"Committee (with the Mayor as Chairman), consisting of the Council,
"the Master and Governors of Christ's Hospital, the Clergy and
"Ministers of all Denominations, the Head Masters of both Roysse's
"School and the Elementary Schools, and many other Residents.

"The General and Finance Secretary was Mr. Councillor West (who
"had acted in a similar capacity on the occasion of the Jubilee Cele-
"bration in 1887), assisted by Messrs. F. R. Jackson and A. J. Shirley
"(Head Master of the National Schools), as Secretaries of the Sports
"and Children's Treat respectively. Sub-Committees were formed, and
"to their efforts the success of the day's proceedings was largely due.

"The canvass of the Town for Funds to carry out the proceedings
"was cordially responded to, the amount collected being £283 : 8 : 7.
"The day's proceedings were carried out at a cost of £234 : 8 : 9
"leaving a balance of £63 : 5 : 9 at the disposal of the Committee,
"with which it is proposed to do something that will be a lasting
"Memorial of Her Majesty's long and glorious reign."

Balance Sheet.

RECEIPTS.

	£ s. d.	£ s. d.
To Subscriptions promised	283 8 7	
Less Subscriptions not yet received	5 0 0	
		278 8 7
Payment for Culham School Children (per Rev. F. C. Clutterbuck)		3 15 0
Balance from Wootton Bonfire Fund (per E. H. Green, Esq.)		0 17 2
Receipts from Standings on Ground		5 15 0
Receipts from Grand Stands		4 7 9
Sale of Programmes		4 11 0
		£297 14 6

EXPENDITURE.

	£ s. d.
By Bands, Fares and Refreshments	62 10 10
Prizes for River and Land Sports, Procession and Boats	43 16 6
Ground Expenses and Swing-Boats	39 17 9
Refreshments for Children, Half-Crowns for Aged Sick, and Pence for Children	62 7 0
Advertising, Printing, Posting and Stationery	24 17 1
Petty Cash Payments, Donation to Ringers, Cost of Decorating Statue of Her Majesty, and sundry payments in connection with Procession	10 19 7
Balance in hand	63 5 9
	£297 14 6

C. A. Pryce, J. G. T. West, ⎫
Mayor, F. R. Jackson, ⎬ Secretaries.
Chairman. A. J. Shirley, ⎭

Audited and found correct,

Chas. Glanville, ⎫ Auditors.
Fred. K. Couldrey, ⎬

28th Oct., 1897.

The Mayor reported that Her Majesty had presented him with
the Silver Medal which had been struck for presentation to the
Mayors and Provosts of the United Kingdom in Commemoration of
Her Majesty's Diamond Jubilee.

𝕿𝖍𝖊 Deputy Mayor reported to the Council that the Jubilee Committee had presented to the Corporation a pair of Silver Candelabra which had been purchased with the balance of the funds in their hands and which had been subscribed for the Commemoration of Her Majesty's Diamond Jubilee, so as to provide a permanent Memorial of the event.

1898.
January 7th.
Thomas
Townsend,
Mayor.

FINIS.

APPENDIX.

Borough of Abingdon.

A Register wherin ar contained the Acts, Lawes, and Ordinaunces
made by Common Counsell for this Boroughe.

Att the comon counsell holden at Abingdon for the Burough ther, the Twenteth
day of July, in one and fortith yere of the raigne of our most gracious Sov'aigne Lady
Elizabeth, by the Grace of God, of England, France & Ireland, Quene, defendor of the
faithe, &c., Anno D'ni 1599, For the weale publike of the saide Boroughe of Abingdon,
and for the good government of the same, by

Fraunces Lytle, gent., Maior
Thomas Mayott, }
John Lee, } Baylieffes
William Braunch, gent.
Lyonell Bostock, gent.
Humferey Hide, gent.
John Fyssher, gent.
Willyam Lee, gent.
Roberte Payne, gent.
Anthony Tesdale, gent.
Thomas Braunch, gent.
Richard Smyth, gent.
William Wellen, gent.
Chr'ofer Tesdale, gent.

Principall burgesses.

Rychard Tesdale
Robert Ayers
John Blacknall, gent.
Thomas Reade
Thomas Orpwodd, gent.
John Fisher, junr.
John Fraunces
Laurence Stevinson
John Chaundler
Richard Ely
Richard Ryther
Jeames Wellen
Thomas Steele
John Hulcottes
John Hobbes
John Powys
Thomas Backhowse
John Fabian, gent.
Richard Cheekyn
Richard Clempson

Secondary burgesses.

James Hide, Townclarke.

A table of all the actes and orders made by common counsell for the
burough of Abingdon A'o quadragesimo primo Elizabethæ Reginæ,
In the tyme of Frauncys Lyttle, gent., Maior.

1. An acte for the Repealing of All former Actes and orders made by comon Counsell.

2. An acte for the placing of th' officers and members of the Comon Counsell and for
the more orderlie p'ceedinges in making of orders and lawes in the same.

3. An acte against the selling of wares uppon the Saboth dayes.

4. An Acte for the better frequenting of Sermons upon Thursdaies.

5. An act that ev'y Principall Burgesse shalbe chosen out of the Secundary Burgesses.

6. An act y't ev'y principall Burgesse shall attend ye maior at the hall and Counsell howse upon warning.

7. An acte that the Princip'll Burgesses shall weare Gownes.

8. An act to restraine the number of Secundary burgesses to xx*li.* and no more.

9. An act aucthorizing the Maior to geve an othe to a Secundary Burgesse.

10. An act that ev'y Secundary Burgesse shall pay xx*s.* to the Chamber.

11. An act for Secundary Burgesses to weare Gownes.

12. An act that ev'y Secundary Burgesse att the tyme of his election be a freeman.

13. An act that freemen and no other shall exercise trades and occupac'ons within this Borough.

14. An Act that the Maior, Bailiffes and Principall Burgesses shall make freemen.

15. An act that freemen shall take an othe before the Maior.

16. An act requiring all p'sons exercising trades in ys Burough to become freemen of the same.

17. An other order conc'ning Freemen.

18. An Acte to make all th' occupiers of Trades into Felowshipps and companies.

19. An Acte for the better Repairing and manteyning of the Streetes.

20. An Act for Staules and Sheppens.

21. An Act to p'vent the daunger of fyer.

22. An other act to prevent ye daung'r of fyer.

23. An Act for Inholders and Alehowskeepers.

24. An other act for Inholders & Alehowsekepers.

25. An act to Restrayne unlawfull bakers.

26. An act for suppressing the unnecessary nomber of Alehowsekeepers.

27. An act for the suppressing of Frayes.

28. An act conc'ning th' office of the Chamberlyn.

29. An Act conc'ning th' office of the Bayliffes.

30. An Acte for the p'servacon of the Tresure of this Burough.

31. An Act against nusaunces in the streetes.

32. An Acte for attendance of the maior to the Church.

33. An act for attendance on the maior to Church on certeine Festivall daies.

34. An act that ye Mayo'r for the tyme being may call the last Maio'r, Ba' & Chamb'lyn to accompte.

35. An Act enjoyning the Maio'r to put in execution all th'orders made by comon counsell.

36. An act yt ye Sergiantes shall levy the penalties forfeyted by breaking of orders.

37. An acte to assemble the Maior, Bailiffes and principall Burgesses quarterly at the counsell howse.

38. An act appointing howe freemen of this Borough shall be made.

39. An act concerning the taking and enrolling of Apprentices.

40. An act for the better levying of ye penalties for not p'forming of ye orders made by Comon counsell.

*41. An Acte and order concerning the election of the Maior and Baylieffes.

42. An order for a Wynter watche.

43. An order to prevent the daunger of fyer.

44. An order for the better keping holy the saboth day.

45. An order against suffering hogges in the streete.

46. An order for clensing the Streetes.

47. An order for paveing the Streates.

48. An order for makeing trades into Fellowshippes.

49. An order cons'nyng the manor of the Election of the Mayor.

50. An order cons'nyng the Eleccion of the Baylliffes.

51. An order to kepe two Sessions yerelye.

52. An order to p'vent discention in chusing the Baylliffes.

53. An order for a Sermon yerelye to be made on Good-frydaye.

54. An order for the better Repayring of the streates.

55. An order for the better disposing of the landes & possessions and eleccon of the principall Burgesses and other officers.

56. An order cons'nyng the taking awaye of the durt and gravell owte of the highe wayes w'thin this Boroughe.

57. An order for the better p'fourmance and more duly and orderly keping of the nighte watche from ascension Daie untill Myelmas yerely.

58. An order to compell the Inhabitantes to the better p'fourmance of theire s'vice to the amending of the highe waies.

59. An order that poore Children shalbe put to s'vice, otherwise theire Parentes to be uncapeable of any Releif.

60. Suche as have Bastardes to be sent to the howse of Correccon.

61. An order that the overseers of Inmates shall once ev'y monethe make a true Relac'on to the Mayor of all straingers & daingers of flar & other inconvenyances.

62. An order that none but fremen shall sell any wares or m'chandizes to forryners or straingers, nor kepe open any shopp or howse to sell wares or m'chandizes.

63. An order that none shall Receave into his howse or Cottage any Strainger to Inhabit w'houte license of the Mayor, bayliffes & burgesses.

64. An order that none shall erecte any howse or Cottage for habitac'on nor any other howse nere thereunto adjoynyng, but suche as he shall Cover w'th slatt or Tile.

65. An order that thes two last orders shalbe monethlie put in execuc'on by the Sup'visors of Inmates.

* This and the following acts (41-65) were made at different times from A.D. 1601-1622.—Ed.

An Acte for the Repealing of all former actes and orders made by comon counsell. cap. 1.

FOR ASMUCH as many of the Lawes and ordinaunces heretofore made for the Gover'ment of the Borough and the Inhabitauntes therof are perished and defaced for lack of good custody of the Register wherin they were written and registred, and some of them holden contrary to the Lawes and statutes of this Realme, and the residue not thought so fitt & convenient for this tyme as for the tyme when they were made and ordeyned. Therfore yt is enacted and ordeyned by this present Comon Counsell and by the Aucthorytie of the same That from and after the last day of this p'nte moneth of Julie, all instituc'ons, lawes and constituc'ons w'ch have byn hertofore made by anie form'r comon counsell of this Borough and all the penalties of them, and ev'y clause, article and sentence in them shall from hensfourth be utterly voide and repealed.

An acte and order for the placing of the Officers and members of the comon counsell and for the more orderly proceeding in making of orders and lawes in the same. cap. 2.

ITEM for the more orderly proceedinges of this comon counsell and of all other which herafter shalbe assembled for the making of orders and constituc'ons for the governing of this Borough to the publique weale of the same, And for the avoiding of all contenc'on that may arise and the confusion that might growe in the debating, reasoning and arguing of such matters as shall be proposed or handled, w'ch doth many tymes not only breake the band of charitie amongest them, But is also a great hynderaunce to the busynes and causes in hand. Therfore yt is inacted and ordayned by this comon counsell and by th' aucthoritie of the same, That from hensfourth ev'y principall Burgesse that hath byn Maior of this Borough shall take his place in the Counsell howse next unto the Maior for the tyme being, according to his auncienty in the bearing of the office of Maior within this Borough. And th'other Principall Burgesses who have not byn Maior shall take their places next unto them, according to the Auncyentie of their elecc'ons to th'office of a principall Burgesse. The Baylieffes for the tyme being shall sitt on the forme with Mr. Towne Clark, one at th'one end of the forme and th'other at the other end. And the Secondary Burgesses shall take their places according to their ancientye of bearing the office of Baylieffes w'thin this Burough. And the rest of the Secondary Burgesses to sit next to them according to th' ancyentye of their eleccons to the office of a secondary Burgesse. And they being all thus placed ev'y one shall quietly, soberly and discreetlie propose such thinges or answer such questions or gyve such holsome counsell as by occasion shalbe offered or in his wisdome shalbe thought fitt to be declared, and in all thinges behave himself as a grave & worthy Counseller of that howse. And yf anie person of the said comon Counsell so placed or assembled shall wittinglie or willinglie use any oprobrious speeches or termes of Disgrace in the Counsell howse to or of any of the associattes ther of intent and purpose to hurte, prejudice, disgrace or disquiet any of the persons so assembled, or to make or set anie facc'on, discorde, enmytie, or dissenc'on, betwene any of the partyes so assembled and anie other person or p'sons, or utter or disclose any matter or thing p'posed, concluded or agreed uppon att any assembly or comon Counsell herafter to be holden w'thin this borough to the hurt of any person ther assembled, Or if any person or p'sons (except the Maior onlie for the tyme being by way of moderac'on) shall interrupt or hinder any man that is speaking in any cause conc'ning th' affaires and goverment of the Borough that is then in hand or shall speake before he hath ended his speach that began to speake before him, That then ev'y such p'son wittingly or willingly offending herin, and the same being so adjudged by the major p'te of the comon counsell then present, shall forfeit to the Maior, Bayliffes and principall burgesses of this Burough, Twelve pence of lawfull English money, the same to be

YY

ymediatlie paid, or ells the offendo'r presently to be comaunded by the Maior and counsell for the tyme being to ye prison of the Gathowse, ther to remaine by the space of three dayes and three nightes, or untill he pay the same. And the aforesaid Decorum and order in taking of places in all other publique assemblies for the Towne amongest the principall Burgesses and Secondarie burgesses (being assembled by aucthorytie for the Affaires of the said Burough) for the avoiding of emulac'on and contention to be alwaies herafter observed and kept under the like penaltie, and to be adjudged in like manner as is aforesaid.

An order againste the selling of wares uppon tho Saboth Day.
Cap. 3.

ITEM for as much as yt ys moste necessarie that in all Societies of Chren people ther ought to be a principall regard had of the s'vice of Almightie God and of keeping holie his Sabothes, yt is ordered That no occupier, Artyficer or victuler shall sell or utter or shew or offer to the intent to sell or utter uppon the sabothe or other holy day after the Sancte's Bell hath ronge at the Parish church of St. Hellin's within this Burough, untill Devine service and Sermon be ther ended, any manner of wares, victualls or other com'odities, uppon payne that ev'y person offending against this order shall forfeit and pay to the Maior, Baylieffes and Principall Burgesses for ev'y offence Twelve pence, to the use of the pore of the said parish wher the said offenders Dwell, to be levied and delyvered to the Church wardens or overseers of the pore of the said parish by them to be distributed to the poore within this Burough, wher they shall thinck fitt. PROVIDED alwayes that the order shall not extend to any Inholders, Vyntners or Alehowsekeepers w'thin this burough to sell victuall unto traveling Straingers onlie uppon the Saboth or holy dayes.

An order for the better frequenting of the Sermon upon Thursdaies.
Cap. 4.

ITEM yt is likewise ordered that ev'y Howshoulder and howskeep' within this Borough That hath (besides himself) Three p'sons in his familie above th' age of Twelve yeres shall come himself or shall send one of them at the least to the Sermons or Lectures in Seynct Hellin's Church on Thursdaies,* and yf any Howshoulder or howskeep' have more then Fower persons in his famylie above th' age aforesaid, Then he shall send Two p'sons at the least of that Famylie ther to remayne from the beginning to the ending of ev'y Sermon upon paine that ev'y person which offendeth against this order forfeit and pay for ev'y default Six pence.   *   *   *   *   *   *   *   *   *

[* This is altered to "Tuesdayes," and a note is added in the margin that the lecture was ordered to be altered from Thursday to Tuesday on October 20th, 1609.]

*   *   *   *   *   *   *   *   *

An acte that Fremen and no other shall exercise trades & occupac'ons w'thin this Burough.   Cap. 13.

ITEM yt is enacted and ordered by th' aucthorytie aforesaid that ther shalbe a Number of p'sons within this Borough who shalbe called Freemen of the same to whom onlie (and to no other) yt shalbe lawfull (and to them and to no other yt is graunted) to sett up, use and exercise and followe their and ev'y of their Trades, occupac'ons, Artes, misteries and sciences within the said Borough and lib'ties of the same w'ch by the lawes and statutes of this Realme they may lawfully followe, exercise and sett upp. And also to have, use, exercyse and enjoye the liberties, p'heminances, Frauncheses and p'veliges graunted & belonging to the freemen of this Burough.

*   *   *   *   *   *   *   *   *

An acte to make all the occupiers of Trades into Fellowshipps & Companies. Cap. 18.

ITEM yt ys ordered by the said Comon Counsell That att all tymes herafter yt shall & may be lawfull unto the Maior, Bayliffes and Principall Burgesses of this Burough or the greater p'te of them to create and make into sev'all Companies or Fellowshipps all or anie occupiers of Trades, artes, misteries or sciences within this Burough, Which said Companies or Fellowshipps by them made shall allwaies be governed and ruled by such good and holsome lawes and orders as by the Comon counsell of this Borough shalbe from tyme to tyme devised and established.

An acte for the better Repairing and manteyning of the Streetes. Cap. 19.

ITEM For asmuch as All the streetes and Lanes within this Burough are Waies & Passages for the Quene's leidge people w'ch for want of Reperacons are nowe in great Ruine & decay, And for that the great Trade of Maulting w'thin this Burough is the chiefest meanes and cawse therof, by reason of much Carrages of Corne and Graine in and out of the said Burough, and by the bringing in of great Store of Strawe or fuell for the drying of malte, Yt is therfore ordered by the Comon Counsell nowe assembled and by the Ancthorytie of the same, That if anie person inhabiting within this Burough after the last day of this p'nte moneth of Julie shall sell and delyv' to be carried out of this Burongh in Cart or Wayne any Mault now made or herafter to be made within this Burough, and the same be carried out of this Burough in anie Cart or Wayne (The wheeles therof being bound w'th iron) shall pay to the Maior, Bailiffes and principall Burgesses of this Burough for ev'y such Cart or Wayne loade so to be carried oute of this Burough as aforesaid, one penney of lawfull English money to be ymploied in and towardes the Reperacons of the streetes within the same Burough from tyme to tyme by th' appoyntment of the Maior, Bayliffes and Principall Burgesses or the greater part of them, And yf anie such person or p'sons shall refuse to pay or do not pay one Penney of lawfull Inglish money for ev'y such loade of maulte so sold and carried out of this Borough (The same being Reasonablie demaunded by such person as shalbe therunto aucthorized by the said Maior, Bayliffes and principall Burgesses or the greater part of them), That then ev'y such person so refusing shall forfeytt and pay to the said Maior, Bayliffes and Burgesses for ev'y such Loade so solde and carried fourth of this Burough, Six pence of Lawfull Inglish monie to be levyed by distresse of the Offenders goodes, and to be ymploied to such use as before in this order is lymitted.

An order for staules and Sheppens. cap. 20.

ITEM for asmuch as all pickidg and Stawleidge within this Burough is graunted unto the Maior, Bailieffes and principall Burgesses of the same, yt is ordered that no mann'r of person after the last day of this moneth of July shall sett or cause to be sett any staules, Bothes or Shippens in anie Street within this Borough uppon anie markett day or Faire day graunted to this Burrough, without the consent and lyceuse of the Bailiffes of the said Burough for the tyme being first had and obteyned, and yf anie p'son shall presume or take uppon him to sett up anie Stalles or Sheppens w'thout such consent and lycence as aforesaid, That then ev'y person that is owner of such Stalles or Sheppens so sett up against this order shall forfeitt and lose the said Stalles and Sheppens to the Maior, Bailiffes and principall Burgesses, to the use of the Com'naltie of the said Burough, And that yt shalbe lawfull for anie person aucthorized by the Maior, Bayliffes and principal Burgesses to take and sease the said Stalles and sheeppens to th'use aforesaid. PROVIDED allwayes that yt shall and may be lawfull for any person being a Freeman of this Burough to sett upp anie Stalles or Sheppens in all convenient places wher usuallie they have done upon that part of the street that is betwene the dwelling howse and the Channell of the said streete, so that he do from tyme to tyme sufficiently pave and kepe clene so much of the said street as is betwene his said howse and the Channell ther.

An order to prevent the daung'r of fyer. cap. 21.

ITEM to p'vent and avoyde the daunger that may happen by Fyer within this Burough, yt is enacted and ordeyned by th' aucthorytie aforesaid, That it shall be lawfull for the Maior, Bayliffes and Principall Burgesses of this Burough or the most p't of them to enter into anie man's howse within this Burough to p'use and view all Thatched Houses or Reekes of Strawe, hay, fearne or other fuell, and also the Ostes, Brewhowses and Backhowses, and the howses and Romethes wherin are layed Strawe, Fearne, furse or other fuell within this Burough howe conveniently they be placed and howe safe from the daunger of fyer, And yf they shall fynd in their Judgem'tes anie great daunger by the ill and unfitt placing or standing of the said Reekes, howses, ostes, brewhowses, backhowses, or places wherin are laied strawe, fuell, ferne, or firse, That then they shall geve warning for reformacon and amendm't therof, And yf any person so warned Do not reforme the same within one moneth next after warning geven, That then the said person shall forfeyt and pay to the Maior, Bailiffes and principall Burgesses of this Burough Tenne Shillinges of lawfull Inglishe money for ev'y moneth yt shall remayne unreformed.

An other order to p'vent the daunger of fyer. ca. 22.

ITEM yt is further enacted and ordeyned by th' aucthorytie aforesaid for ye better quenching and staying of fyer, yf any shoulde happen within this Borough (which God forbide) That ev'y principall Burgesse within this Burough from and after the Feaste of St. michaell Th' archaungell next shall alwaies have in a redynes in his howse Foure good letherne Buckettes and one Long lader conteyning at the least xxiiijty roundes, And ev'y Secoundarye Burgesse Two letherne Buckettes and one Longe lader of the said length, and ev'y comon Baker and comon Brewer, not otherwyse charged by this order, Two leatherne Buckettes and one Lader of the said length, and ev'y mault maker that is or shalbe anie thing taxed in the Subsedy and not otherwyse charged to provide by this order, shall fynd one letherne Bucket and one short lader, And that yt shall be lawfull for the Maior for the tyme being, by him self or his Deputy to that purpose, twice at the lest ev'y yere to take a view and to see yf the said Buckettes and ladders be p'vided accordingly. . . . .

An order for Inholders and Alehowse keepers. cap. 23.

ITEM yt ys enacted and order[ed] by th' aucthority aforesaid that no Inholder or Alehowsekeper within this Burough shall harbour or lodge in his howse anie p'son above Two dayes and Two nightes, but that he gyve the Maior or Constables for the tyme being knowledge and notice therof, And yf anie shall happen to do the contrary to this ordynaunce and the same be proved by his owne confession, or otherwise, Then he shall forfeytt and pay to the Maior, Bayliffes and principall Burgesses of this Burough Sixe shillinges and eight pence of lawfull Inglish monie for ev'y defaulte. ITEM that no Alehowse kepers within this Burough shall herafter lodge any horsman being a Ghest within his howse that shall repaire unto this Burough unlesse yt be at the tymes of Faires, Assisses or Sessions holden at this Burough, uppon the paine aforesaide.

* * * * * * * * *

An acte to restraine unlawfull Bakers. cap. 25.

FOR AS MUCHE as Dyv's persons w'thin this Burough Do use this trade and mistery of Baking within the same who never were Apprentice therunto neither skilfull to make good and holsome bredd for man's body, therby hindering & impov'ishing such as have byn apprentises to the said Trade and are well experienced therin, For reformacon therof, it is therfore enacted and ordeyned, by the aucthoritie aforesaid, That from hensfourth no p'sons within this Burough shall use or occupie the Trade or mistery of a Comon Baker, or shall bake anie Breedd and sell the same within the said Burough unlesse he hath byn apprentice unto the said Trade or misterye and have s'ved as an apprentice therunto by the space of Seven yeres, or other then such person or p'sons as are nowe allowed by the Maior, Bailiffes and principall Burgesses whose names are under written, or w'ch herafter shall be by them allowed to be a comon Baker within this Burough, and have a mark assigned & appointed unto him by the Maior for the tyme being to sett on his bredd That the Baker therof may be knowen   *   *   *   *   *   *   *

Andrew Bond,	Thomas Kent,	Richard Marcham,
William Cooles,	John Sheppard,	Robert Belcher.

An order for the suppressing of the unnecessary number of Alehowses.
cap. 26.

ITEM for as much as the Multitude of Alehowses and Tipling howses w'thin this Borough are founde and well p'seved to be a great Decay not only to the keep's therof who leving or at the least neclecking their other lawdable trades geve themselves to Idlenes and keeping of Companie to vent and utter their drinck But also to that end drawe and p'cure many idle and lewde p'sons unto their Howses. And for asmuche as ther hath byn late expresse com'aundem't from the Quene's most excellent majesty and the Lordes of hir honorable pryvie counsell for the suppressing of the superflous number of them and to that end l'res also directed from the Judges of this Circuite to the maior that last was and also to him that now ys for redresse and reformac'on therof, and therupon a Consultac'on and due considerac'on was taken amongest the Maior, Bailiffes and Burgesses howe many and who were fytt to contynue and the rest were dismissed. This Comon Counsell considering the great benefytt that woulde in tyme redowne to the Weale publique of this Towne by the restraynte of the superfluous nomber of Alehowses; And considering the ymportunate suite, requeste and meanes that will from tyme to tyme be made unto the Maior for the tyme being to graunte lycence to such as desier the same w'thout some order be made to p'vent such suites and putt an end to the lycensing of any more alehowses. BE.yt therefore enacted, ordered and ordeyned by th' aucthorytye of this p'nte Comon Counsell that from hensfourth neither the Maior that nowe is nor any other maior his successours shall geve lycence or p'mitt or suffer any more or greater number of Innes, Alehowses, or Victuling howses within this Burough at any one tyme then at this present tyme are lycensed and appointed whose names are under written. AND further yt ys ordered that neither the Maior that nowe ys nor any other his Successors, maiors of this Borough, shall lycence or p'mitt any other p'son to be an Inboulder or an Alehowsekeep' within this Borough w'thout the consent and assent of eight at the least of his Bretherin the Bailiffes and principall Burgesses of this Burough, and that consent to be had and geven when they shalbe assembled in the Counsell Howse.

INHOLDERS.	ALEHOWSE	KEEPERS.
John Fyssher, Jun.	Lawrence Taylor	Jeames Bradlie
John Posterne	Nicholas Spicer	John Prynce
Henry Litle	Jone Wyfold, widowe	Thomas Ely
Richard Elye	Thomas Kent, Jun.	Thomas Hall
Robert Denney	Thomas Backhowse	John Cornish
Thomas Sellar	John Swyfte	Richard Brunker
Henry Wise	John Kymber	Richard Haynes
———	Roger Houghton	Richard Maiott
	Thomas Porter	Elizabeth Coxeter
VYNTNER.	Walter Pullyn	Jone Capenhurst
John Chaundler	William Craftes	John Moore

An Acte for the suppressing of Frnies. cap. 27.

ITEM for the better suppressing of Frayes and turbulent p'sons w'thin, this Borough, yt is enacted and ordeyned by th' aucthoritie aforesaid that ev'y Inhabitant (Day laborers w'ch do lyve only by day labour excepted) w'thin this Burrough shall before the feast day of the Birth of o'r Lord christ next coming, have in his howse a good & sufficient Clubb fytt for that purpose, the same alwaies to be in the owner's Shopp, or some convenient place, redy when nede shall require it, uppon paine that ev'y one that maketh default to forfeyet and pay to the Maior, Bailiffes and principall Burgesses of this Borough, Twelve pence for ev'y moneth he shall make default therin.

* * * * * * * * *

An Acte for the p'servacon of the Treasure of this Burough. cap. 30.

ITEM yt ys ordered and enacted by th' aucthority aforesaid that all money due or herafter to be due or payable to the Maior, Bailiffes and principall Burgesses of this Burough, and being by them receaved shall ymediatly be delyv'ed to the Custody and safe keping of the Chamberlyn of ye said Burough for the tyme being, by him safelie to be kept untill yt shalbe otherwise disposed of by the said Maior, Bayliffes and principall Burgesses or the major part of them. And that yt shall not be lawfull for the Maior for the tyme being by anie waie of lone or otherwise to have or receave any of the profittes, issues or Revenewes of the said Burough, nor any of the money or stockes geven to the said Maior, Bailiffes and Burgesses to be lent to Charytable uses, neither shall yt be lawfull for the said Bailiffes or principall Burgesses or any of them to receave or take into their possession by waie of lone or otherwyse any of the said Stockes or monie alredy geven or herafter to be geven to the said Maior, Bayliffes and Burgesses to be ymploied to any Charitable use. PROVIDED alwayes that yt shall and may be lawfull unto the said Maior, Bayliffes & principall Burgesses for the tyme being to lone or lend oute unto the Maior or anie the Bayliffes or Principall Burgesses using the trade of a Clothier within the same Burrough all or any part of the Stock or money geven to this Burrough by one Mystrisse Katheryne Hide, Widowe, to the intent to sett the poore of the said Burrough on work.

An Order againste Nusaunces in ye streetes. cap. 31.

ITEM to avoide the great disorder and Nusaunce that ys comytted in this Burough by the laying of Tymber logges, Blockes, Fishbarrells, donge or other soile or filth in the Streetes, Lanes and Highwayes within this Burrough, Yt is ordered that yf any p'son shall herafter lay or cause to be laide any peece of Tymber, logg, block, fishbarell, Dung, soile or other filth, in any streete or lane within this Burough, above the space of Seven Dayes together w'thout the Consent of the Bayliffes of this Burough for the tyme being, That then ev'y person offending against this order shall forfeit and pay * * * * sixe pence. * * * * *

An Acte for attendaunce on the Maior to the Churche. cap. 32.

ITEM yt is ordered that the Bayliffes and Constables of this Burrough for the tyme being, not being oute of the Towne nor being hindered by sicknes or such like ympedyment shall, ev'y Sonday, holie day, and on Thursdaies, attend on the Maior for the tyme being to St. Hellyn's Church, and from the Church to his howse, uppon payne that ev'y Bayliffe or Constable that maketh defaulte herin, to forfeytt and pay for ev'y tyme * * * * Twelve pence of lawfull Inglishe monie.

Forasmuch as the lecture is nowe changed from thursday unto tuysday, itt is ordered by the comon Councell that thursday shalbe putt out of this order & tuysday inserted. xxo. Octobris, 1600.

An acte likewise for attendaunce on ye Maiour to ye Church uppou
c'ten festivall daies. cap. 33.

ITEM yt ys ordered by th' aucthorytie aforesaid that the Bayliffes and all the
Principall and secondary Burgesses of this Burrough not having some Reasonable excuse
or being hindered by some lawfull ympediment shall, fyve sev'all dayes in the yere, viz. :
Christmas day, Easter day, whit sonday, All S'tes, and ye day of the Coronac'on of our
Sov'aigne Lady the Quene, attend on the Maior of this Borough for the tyme being from
his howse to the Church, both to morning and evening prayer, uppon payne to forfeyt
and pay Three shillinges and iiij*d.*   *   *   *   *   *

*   *   *   *   *   *   *   *   *

In the tyme of Frauncis Little, gent., Maior, A.D. 1599.

An act to assemble the Maior, Bailiffes and principall Burgesses
quarterly att the Counsell Howse. ca. 37.

. IMPRIMIS yt ys enacted ordered and established that the said Maior, Bayliffes and
principall Burgesses shall meete and assemble themselves in the Guildhall or counsell
howse of the same Borough yerely uppon Frydaye next before the feast of St. Michaell the
Archangell, Uppon fryeday next before the feast of our Lorde God, Uppon Fryday next
before the Feast of Easter, and upon Fryeday next before the feast of St. John Baptist.
Which said Foure Frydayes shalbe and shalbe knowen, accompted and taken the Foure
Quarterdayes of meeting for consultac'on to be had touching the affaires of the said
Burrough   *   *   *   *   *

*   *   *   *   *   *   *   *   *

In the tyme of John Blacknall, gent., Maior, Anno Dni. 1604.

An acte concerning the ellecc'on of the Maior and Bayliffes.   ca. 41.

[After reciting the Charter of King Philip and Queen Mary and the provisions therein
contained for the Election of the Mayor and Bayliffs, the Order proceeds as follows :—]

AND WHERAS synce the making of the said Ch're especially nowe of Latter yeres
Certayne disordered p'sons within this Borough some of them neither having wherw'th
all to lyve, nor yett using any honest or lawfull course or trade of life wherby to manteyne
themselves, but lyving in riott and disorder offensyve to the godlie quiet and peaceable
estate and gov'ment of the said Towne ; Yett not w'thstanding att such tymes and place
as the said Maior and Bayliffes or any of them are by and according to the p'port of the
said Charter to be chosen, The said Disordered p'sons have and doe use to repaire unto ye
said ellec'on and not only Intrude and make themselves as principall partyes in the said
Nominac'on allowaunces and elecc'ons: But also very often tymes Do combyne and
confederate them selves to no'iate, chuse and assigne such person or p'sons unto the said
Offices or places as either they suppose or ymagine will more favorably tollerate and
beare w'th their disorders and misrule Orells suche as for some other sinister and undewe
respectes they shall like to prefer therunto, And the said disordered p'sons and their
adherentes by their Combinac'ons and other practizes often tymes carry and rule the same
elecco'ns as seemeth best unto them selves so as then the best and discreetest sorte of men
of the said Townesmen and Inhabytantes could prevaile litle therin, But were as yt were

in effect excluded as yf they had no voyces att all touching the same. And therby yt came to passe That sometymes not only undewe and unfitt elections, allowaunces, nominacions and assignations were made of the said Maiors and bayliffes sometyme p'ferring, electing and nominating suche as were not fitt, and rejecting those w'ch were fitt, sometymes in ymposing those offices and charge and burthen of them uppon some especiall p'sons more often then was fitt or p'happs then they or their Estates were well able conveniently [to] beare. But also as in assemblies of such people is very usuall some mutinous tumultes, uprores, quarellinges, civill Dissentions and other disorders have happened and befallen the said elections and are like more and more to growe and happen to the p'judice of the said Towne and disturbans of the peaceable and good gov'ment therof; For Reformac'on wherof and the better prevenc'on of all such populer Disorder, confusion & mischeefe as are like daylie to ensewe yf so muche power and auchthorytie be p'mitted and conteynewed unto people of that rank, qualitie and condic'on. YT IS therfore this p'nte day ordered and decreed by the Maior, bayliffes and burgesses and the Comon Counsell here assembled, that from hensfourth no such disordered p'son as before ye menco'ed shall have any Voice, power or aucthoritie to make any elecc'on, allowaunce, nominac'on or assignac'on in the said l'res patentes especified, But that all and ev'y such elecc'on, allowaunce, nominac'on or assignac'on of all and ev'y maior and bayliffes as in the said l'res patentes ye lymitted or graunted to be made either yerely or upon the death or amoveall of any such Maior or bayliffe or otherwise by the secundary Burgesses, other burgesses and ye Inhabitantes of the Inferior sorte shall allwayes herafter from hensfourth be had and made by the said Secundary Burgesses and by the best, gravest and discreetest of the said other Burgesses and the Inhabitantes of the lower sorte only and by no others in such manner as herafter ye expressed. That is to say That ther shalbe chosen by the said Maior, bayliffes and burgesses and Secundary Burgesses, or the more ' p'te of them w'ch shalbe present then for yt purpose, Forty persons or more at their pleasure, of the gravest, wisest and most sufficient men of the said other burgesses and inhabitantes of the lower sorte inhabiting w'thin the said borough, W'ch said Forty persons so presentlie to be chosen, and all others herafter from'tyme to tyme to be elected shall allwaies be called the Comons Electors or Electors for ye Comons. And that the said Secundary Burgesses and those Electors for and in behalf of all the said other Burgesses and men of the lower sort inhabiting the said borough att all and ev'y tyme and tymes herafter when such election, nominac'on, assignac'on or allowaunce of the said officers or any of them ye or ought to be made by or according to the purporte of the said l'res patentes shall or may assemble and mete together, and that they or the more part of them so assembled shall have full power, liberty and aucthorytie at all such tymes both to no'iate and assigne such two p'sons of the Principall burgesses to be chosen maior, and to geve allowance unto the Baylieffes which from tyme to tyme shalbe chosen by the Maior, As also to make, chuse and elect one Baylief for the Comons in such and in as ample mann'r and forme to all intentes, Constructions and purposes as the said secundary Burgesses and men of Inferior sort inhabiting the said Towne have lawfully heretofore used to doe or as they or any of them might by virtue of the said l'res patentes heretofore lawfully have don or used. AND lastly yt is ordered that when and as often as yt shall fortu'e any of the said Electors to dy or not dwell in this Borough or be removed from his said place of Electorshipp, That after ev'y suche avoydance of the said Electors place by any meane whatsoev'r, That then and so often the said Maior, Baylieffes and burgesses for the tyme being, together w'th the said Secundary burgesses or the more part of them shall assemble and mete together before they proceed to the election of any Maior or Baylieff. And that they or the more p'te of them soe assembled, shall chuse one or more electors in the Rome or roomes of him or them whose place so shall be voide as aforesaid, so as ther shalbe alwaies att the tyme of ev'y such election of Maior or baylieff the Nomber of Fortie electors at the lest then lyving and inhabiting in the said borough for to make & joyne in such nominac'on and election as aforesaid yf they will.

THE NAMES of all the p'sons selected and no'iated by the Comon Counsell to be Electors for the Comons according to the Order last above written:—

Walter Dairell, Esquier	Richard Cowdry	Ol'res Daffy
William Blacknall, gent.	Robert Morris	Richard Coxe
William Bostock, gent.	Phillipp Keate	John White
Alexander Croftes, gent.	Thomas Barton	Thomas Bennett
John Trulock, gent.	Richard Foster	Henry Battyn
William Eistone, gent.	John Greene	Richard Ely, Junr.
John Buckner, gent.	John Hall, als. Morris	Phillipp Keate, Junr.
John Coxe	John Arnoll	Thomas Hawes
Richard Busbie	Zachary Wise	John Lee
Thomas Ely	John Butler, butch'r	Edward Turner
Henry Fry	Richard Clempson	Peter Stevens
Raphe Wise	Fraunces Dring	Richard Clackson
Tytus Wells	John Croney	Xrofer Swifte
John Strafferde	William Pearce	Richard Parck
Thomas Wyse	Thomas Wilde	Willm. Elie
John Bradford	John Bray	Thomas Langley
John Prynce	William Cooles	Edward Barnes
John West	Richard Banyster, senr.	Michell Fetiplace
Thomas whittington	John Cosham	Willm. Fraunces
John Allen, smythe	Thomas Seller	Robert Mayott
Thomas Smythe, gent.	Laurence Taylor	Willm. Wickam, gent.
John wynsmore	Henry Curtyne	James Hearne, gent.
John Chewe	William Orpwood	Willm. Hearne
Richard Smyth	Charles Tucker, gent.	Phillipp Pofley
Richard westwood	Chas. Teisdall	Thomas Steele
Peter Probye, gent.	Richard Joyner	Richard Farmer
Ric'us Mayott, gen.	John Cornishe	Willm. Wiggins
Will'us Bannyster	Thomas Hullcottes	John Combe
Clemens Cheyney	Thomas Kent	Alexander Beely, gent.
Joh'es Whitfeill	John Teisdall	John Steed
Thomas Barker	Thomas Savage	Mathe' Bradford
Thomas Sawyer	John Butler	Marke Ozonnie
Benjamyn Teisdall	Xrofer Willyby	Richard Beatte
Richard Atherton	Willms. Tailor	Robert Mayotte, Junr.
Gilbert Taylor	John Hawes	Ambrowse vimpton

An Order for a Wynter watche. Ca. 42.

WHER'AS yt often fallen out That betwene the feastes of St. Michaell th' archaungell and Th' assention of our Lord ensuing the said feast of St. Michaell, mutche evill rule and disorder ys kept and used in this borough in the night tyme, by reason that during that tyme ther is no watche kepte for the taking, apprehending and suppression [ing] such offenders and Disorders, and therby opportunitye is geven bothe unto lewde and evill disposed persons for the Commytting of any man'r of offences whatsoev'r, be they never so heynous, And also for Dissolute p'sons to use any man'r of Disorder and misrule during that tyme, yea, many times it may fortune that by casualty of fyer or other misfortune at sutch tymes (none being ready to espye, discerne or geve notice therof) great losses, hurte and prejudice may growe unto this Borough, ＊ ＊ ＊ ＊ Yt is this p'nte day ordered ＊ ＊ ＊ ＊ That allwayes from hensfourth a Watche shalbe kepte ev'y night w'thin this Borough from the feaste of St. Michaell th' archaungell unto the feaste of Th' assenc'on of our Lord God next ensuing the said feaste of

St. michaell; Even aswell as from ye Feaste of The Asscenc'on of our Lord God unto the said feaste of St. Michaell that hath byn heretofore used and by the lawes of this lande ys provided. And for the keping of ye said watch yt is further ordered that ther shalbe ev'y night appoynted Three Honest and suffycient men to watch in the said Towne from the howre of Nyne of the Clock in the night untill the howre of fyve of the Clock in the morning following * * * * And that the said watchmen during the said tyme of their watch shall doe and behave them selves in all and ev'y thing as watchmen appoynted by ye Statute of Wynchester oughte to doe. And for the fynding and manteyning of the said watchmen, at the indefferent charge of the Inhabitauntes of the said borough: Yt is lastly ordered, That ev'y howshoulder (excepting sutch poore people as in respect of their pov'ty shalbe by the said Maior thought fitt to be spared) shall for his howse w'ch he holdeth and inhabyteth within this borough accordingly as heretofore hath byn used touching the watche yt hath byne useually kept, fynde one sufficient man in his torne and steede to make and kepe the said watch as aforesaid, or in default therof shall pay or cause to be paid unto such person or p'sons as shalbe caused or appoynted to watche for him the some of Sixe pence * * * *

An Order to prevent the daung'r of fyer. Ca. 43.

ITEM yt ys further ordered by th' aucthorytie of this Comen Counsell that ev'y Howshoulder within this Borough in whose howse ther is or shalbe an Oste to dry maultte, not charged nor chargeable by a form'r order made in this behalf, and ev'y Mercer, Drap', Dier, Inhoulder, and Alehowsekeep' not form'ly also charged or chargeable, as ys aforesaid, from and after Forty dayes next ensuing shall have in a redynes in his howse one good Lether buckett and one ladder of Sixtene or eightene roundes att the leaste, And also that ev'y persons charged or chargeable with buckettes and ladders, As well by this order as by the said form' order, shall likewise from and after Fortie dayes next ensuing, have in a redynes in his howse one good Cowle and a Cowlestaffe * * * * And yt ys further ordered That if any daungerous fier shall begine within this borough (w'ch God forbidd) and any person or persons charged or chargeable by this order or by the said form'r order, Do not or shall not w'th all conveniente speede bring or send fourth of his howse his said Buckett or bucketts, and ladder and ladders, Cowles and Cowles staffes unto the place wher such fier then shall be or Do not or shall not use them himself nor offer them to others to be used in quenching of ye said fier That then ev'y such persons fayling herin shall for ev'y tyme he or they shall make such defaulte likewise forfeit and pay * * * * Ten shillinges * * * *

An Order for the better keping holy ye Sabothe day. Ca. 44.

ITEM for as muche as it hath pleased Almighty god to comaunde the sanctyfieing and keping holy of our sabothe day, Aswell by the sequestring and setting apart (for yt day) men's ordynarie affaires and toiles of this liffe, As by bestowing the same in his s'vice, And yett dyv's butchers, tradesmen and artificers w'thin this borough, either for their pryvate gaine or som other respect, contrary bothe to the lawes of God and of this Church of Englande, Do often tymes use upon those Dayes to open their Shopps and make shewe of their wares to th'end to sell and utter the same, For reformac'on wherof, yt ys this p'nte Day ordered that no butcher, Tradesman nor artificer shall att any tyme after the xxth day of this Instant monethe of February next ensuing uppon the Sabothe Daye open, cause or suffer to be opened, his or their shopp or any the Wyndowes therof, with intent or purpose to sell, utter or offer to sale any of his or their fleshe, workes, wares, comodities or marchandizes, upon payne yt ev'y person or p'sons so offending contrary to the purport and tenor of this order, shall forfeyt and paye * * * * The some of Twelve pence :* * * *

An order against suffering hogges in ye streetes. ca. 45.

FOR ASMUCHE as by Experyence yt is daylie founde, that the suffering Hogges and Swyne to goe and be abroade in ye streetes of this borough ys not only an occasion yt the same streetes are not and can not be kept so cleene and sweete as ys fytt, But also the same ys many other waies offensyve and noysome unto ye Inhabitantes therof. For reformac'on therof yt is this day ordered by th' aucthorytie of this Comon Counsell, That no person or persons whatsoev'r inhabyting w'thin this borough shall att any tyme after the Twenteth day of this Instant moneth of January p'mitt or suffer any of his or their hogges, pigges or swyne, or anie of them to ly, go or be abroade in the Streetes of this Towne or in any of them uppon payne to forfeyt * * * * the some of Foure pence for ev'y day in w'ch any such hogg, pigg or swyne shall so, go, ly or be abroade in ye said Streetes * * * *

An order for clensing the Streetes. ca. 46.

ITEM for asmuch as the fowle and uncleane lieing and being of the streetes in this borough ys bothe Noysome to the Inhabitantes therof, and also may be very Daungerous for the breding or causing of Contagious fyvers and infection in this towne (w'ch God forbidd) That ev'y Howshoulder with in this borough From and after the Twenteth day of this instant moneth of January shall once ev'y week att least upon the saterday cause to be sweeped, made clene and elensed, the streete where hee or thee inhabiteth so farr therof as his or their howse reacheth or extendeth in the same streete unto the Midell or Chanell of the said streete, And all the durtt, fylth and other rubbidge & soile ther shall weekly cause to be carried awaye out of the said streetes Upon payne * * * * of Foure pence * * * *

In the tyme of Fraunc's Little, gent., maior, Ao. Dni. 1606.

An order for the paving of the streates. ca. 47.

WHEREAS heretofore many and div's orders have byn made as well in leete as by Comon Counsell bothe touching the amending and paving of the streetes of this Boroughe, and yt the same remayne altogether unamended and unpaved and in many places even not passable w'thout Dainger not only to the greate annoyaunce of the Inhabitantes hereof, But alsoe to the greate hurte and p'judice of Straingers and travellers w'ch have occac'on to passe throughe the same; And whereas the reason wherefore the same doe soe continewe notwth' the saide orders is p'tely by reason the same orders are not nor can not be executed according to the purporte of them bothe bycause many of the people and Inhabitants w'ch are thereby injoyned to make the said pavem't and amend the saide streets are poore and needye people and not able to p'forme the same, And others thoughe they are able would be willing to make and p'forme some reasonable p'te and p'porc'on thereof, Yt by reason of the largenesse of the howses w'ch they occupie and inhabitt and for some other respects for them to make and amend soe mutche thereof as by the saide former orders is injoyned is more then some are well able to p'forme and more then is just and reasonable that some others should be urged unto and p'tly by reason that by some of the saide orders likewise it is limitted that ev'y man should pave and amend the streete from his house unto the Channell, Whereas in some places and streetes there are greate highe pavell cawseyes w'th Channells betwene it and the houses on bothe side thereof by meanes whereof noe course nor order is taken for amending, paving or clensing the saide cawseyes, For reformac'on whereof Yt is this day ordered * * * * that ev'y Inhabitant w'thin this Boroughe other then suche as dwell w'thin the Abbye in the Wynieyard, beyond the *Rudle crosse westward, or in Brodestreete and west St. hellins streete, and the stearte or beyond the house of one Thomas keene in the Bore-

* [The Ruddle Cross was situated in Ock Street, near the dwelling-house now occupied by Mr. J. Coxeter, opposite that of Mr. Councillor Hayman.—ED.]

streete towards the northe, and other then suche p'son and p'sons as by the maior, Baylieffs and Burgesses or the more p'te of them assembled shalbe otherwise dispensed w'thall in mann'r and forme hereafter expressed shall before the feast of St. John the Baptiste next ensueing, at his owne costs and charges pave or cause to be paved w'th stone all that p'te of the streete w'ch lieth by and alonge the house or grounde Wherein he or they doe dwell, or w'ch he holdeth or occupieth unto the middell of the streete toward the other side, and the same soe paved shall from tyme to tyme keepe in good and sufficient repa'cons upon payne * * * * for ev'y yarde square not sufficiently paved as aforesaide the some of vjd. NEVERTHELESSE yt is hereby further ordered that yf soe be there shalbe any just cause or reason that any inhabitant or Inhabitantes of this Boroughe either in respect of his or their povertye shalbe altogether wholly spared, Or in respect of the largenes of any Inhabitantes house and the quallitie of his estate therein or of his p'son that the charge hereby imposed upon him or them should be mittigated, that then yf any suche Inhabitant or Inhabitantes shall make his complainte unto the maior, Baylieffes and Burgesses assembled, that he is thereby ov'r charged either farther then his abillitie will extend unto or farther then in reason or in equitie he ought to be charged, that it shalbe lawfull to and for the saide maior, Baylieffes and Burgesses then assembled or the more of p'te of them either utterly to dischardge suche p'son and p'sons from paving thereof, or otherwise to enjoyne him or them unto the making and paving of suche reasonable p'te and porc'on as to them or unto the greater p'te of them there assembled shall seeme fitt. And it to th' end the same streetes may be sufficiently paved & amended Yt is farther ordered that it shalbe lawfull to and for the maior, Baylieffes and Burgesses or greater p'te of them at any tyme or tymes hereafter to taxe, assesse and sett upon ev'y suche Inhabitant of this Boroughe as to them shall seeme fitt to be taxed, suche reasonable somes and porc'ons of money to be payed by them and to be bestowed and Ymploied towardes paving and amending of the saide streetes in suche places where it shall seeme fitt to discharge suche Inhabitantes as aforesaid thereof or not to impose upon them the Whole charge of suche paving and amending as aforesaid as them the saide maior, Baylieffes and Burgesses or to the more p'te of them shall seeme fitt. AND that ev'y p'son and p'sons soe sett, taxed or assessed as aforesaid, w'thin sixe dayes after the same shall be soe taxed, assessed and sett as aforesaid and of him demaunded, shall well and truely satisfie and paye unto the maior, Baylieffes and Burgesses the some and somes of money upon him sett, taxed and assessed, upon payne to forfeite for ev'y daye the same shall soe be behinde the some of vjd. * * * * * *

In the tyme of John Maiott, gent., Maior, Ao. Dni. 1609.

An order for the making of Trades into feloshippes. ca. 48.

WHEREAS by an order heretofore made by the Comon Counsell of this Boroughe intytuled an acte to make all the occupiers of trades into fellowshipps and companyes, it was ordered by the saide comon Counsell that it should and may be lawfull unto the Maior, Baylieffes and Burgesses of this Boroughe or the greater p'te of them, to create and make into sev'all Companyes or fellowshipps all or any occupiers of trades, artes, mysteries or sciences w'thin this Boroughe, w'ch said Companyes or fellowshipps by them made shall alwayes be gov'ned and ruled by suche good and wholsome lawes and orders as by the comon Counsell of this Boroughe shalbe from tyme to tyme devised and established as by the saide order appeareth. And whereas by virtue of that order the saide maior, Baylieffes and Burgesses this p'nte day have created and made the p'sons using the crafte and mysterie of shoemakers and Cordwayners w'thin this Boroughe a companny or fellowshipp of master and wardens of the fellowshipp of the Crafte and mysterie of shoemakers and Cordwayners w'thin the saide Boroughe. Itt is nowe ordered and established by the Auchthorytie of this comon Counsell that the saide fellowshipp and mysterye of shoemakers and Cordwayners w'thin this Boroughe shall observe and keepe the statutes, actes, ordyn'nces and oathes hereafter following:—[The Order then sets out the rules and regulations to be observed by the Fellowship, and provides (1) For the election of a Master and two Wardens annually on St. John Baptist Day; (2) For the taking of an Oath by the Master and Wardens before the Mayor of the Borough; (3) For payment by "e'vy p'son keeping a house and occupieing the saide Crafte or "occupac'on of shoemakers and Cordwayners w'thin the Boroughe" of a yearly subscription "towardes the supportac'on of the greate charges of the same yerely to be "mayneteyned conc'ning the worshippe of the said Boroughe and the honestie and good "rule of the saide occupac'on and fraternitye"; (4) For preventing the admission into the Fellowship of any person who had not served an apprenticeship for seven years: (5) For the making of rules and regulations by the Master, Wardens and Fellowship: (6) Imposing three days imprisonment and a fine of 5s. for breach of regulations: (7) "that if any p'son occupieing the occupac'on or misterye of shoemakers and Cord-"wayners w'thin the Boroughe of Abingdon, shall call any brother or fellowe being of "the same occupac'on or mysterye by any vilde, rude or unfitting language, or use any "other disgracefull or reviling worde or speeche shall paye and make fyne at ev'y tyme "soe offending, twelve pence to be imployed to the use of the saide occupac'on": (8) For power to distrain for penalties: (9) For Appeals to the Justices of Assize for the County of Berks: (10) For the Oath to be taken by the Master: (11) For the Oath to be taken by "a newe brother being a freeman": (12) "that ev'y p'son and brother of the "saide fellowshipp and using the saide crafte and misterie w'ch shall keep twoe "apprentices or more at once shall from tyme to tyme take and have one of the saide "apprentices, to be a Childe of some p'son inhabiting this Boroughe, if there shalbe any "suche childe then fitt to be an apprentice unto the saide Crafte and misterie."]

In the tyme of Christopher Teisdale, gent., Maior, 4th January, 1614.

An Acte conc'ning the mann'r of Ellection of the Mayor. cap. 49.

FOR asmuche as in the ellectinge of the Mayor of this Boroughe by the voluntarie nominac'on of the secundarye Burgesses and comons Ellectors, or the greater p'te of them, And by the like voluntarye choyce made by the Maior, Bayliffes and Burgesses, or the greater p'te of them of one of them soe named as aforesaid, sometymes some men are and have beine more often chosen unto yt place then others, And thereby muche splene, discontentm't, Devision and distraction hathe happened aswell amongst the Principall Burgesses themselves As alsoe betwene them and the Secundarie Burgesses and Comons ellectors, and gen'allie one amongste another (some men beinge thought to be ov'r often charged and Burthened therew'th or preferred thereunto, others beinge soe seeldome chosen as that it semed unto D'v'rs theye were neglected, disgraced and helde unworthie or unfitt for suche office; And the said splene, envye and discontentm't soe bredd and encreased hathe in like sorte often tymes occasioned asmuche dissention, devision and distraction to be aboute the choyce of men unto the places of Secundary Burgesses, ellectors and the like places, eche one accordinge to his fancye and effection beinge carryed to make choyce of suche as they conceaved would be reddieste to concurr and Joyne w'th them in those ellections and in the like buisnes; And by reason thereof that love, peace and Amitie, w'ch betwene them oughte to be and is muche desired, is and hathe beine Daylie Interupted, Divers have beine & are from p'rfourminge those good offices and dueties w'ch they Intended muche discouraged, And also the good Order and gov'm't of this Boroughe by their mutual dissenc'ons and apposic'ons muche ympaired and in Danger to be utterlie subverted; The w'ch Inconveniences as they have heretofore happened unto other Citties and Boroughes where such ellections have beine used, And have caused them in those places in p'ventinge thereof to reduce the effecte of the said ellection unto a kinde of setled course of Succession, Soe the Maior, Bayliffes, Burgesses, secondary Burgesses and Comons ellectors of this Boroughe, havinge entred into a serious considerac'on of the p'misses and sensiblie apprehendinge the manye evills and Inconveniences w'ch heretofore have and in tyme to come are likelie to ensue thereby), And earnestlie desiringe that for ever hereafter true peace and amitie mighte be p's'ved and continewe amongst them, And that there maye not be anye suche occasion geven to hinder or Interupte the same as thereby heretofore hath to often happened, are all w'th one accord and full consent aggreed That the said ellection of the maior shalbe for ev'r hereafter made in suche sorte as that the said office of maior shall and may goe and be from one to one other in Succession in suche sorte As that eche one in his turne and order may have and beare the said office nexte beginninge w'th & at him to be first maior that hathe beine Maior and the longest tyme w'thoute the said office.   And to that end and purpose it is this present daye by the Comon Counsell of this Boroughe and by and w'th the full consentes of the said Maior, Bayliffes and Burgesses, Secondarye Burgesses and Comons ellectors, ordered and decreed that they and ev'ie of them shall and will from tyme to tyme make theire no'i'ac'on and ellection of the Maior, w'ch shalbe to be chosen in mann'r and fourme followinge, that is to saie: That the said maior, Baylliffes, Burgesses, Secundarie Burgesses and Comons Ellectors, whensoev'r a newe Mayor accordinge to theire Charter of theire Corporac'on either by deathe, deprivac'on, Cession or other determinac'on is or oughte to be chosen, and at suche tyme and place and in suche mann'r as respectivelie in and by the said charter is lymitted, And as by the Customs and form'r orders of this Boroughe hath beine used, shall and will assemble themselves for the nominatinge and chosinge of suche newe Maior at suche place as hathe beine used and accustomed for the same; And thereupon yt they the said Secundarye Burgesses and Comons ellectors then there p'sent shall and will no'i'ate unto the said Maior, Bayliffes, those two of the Principall Burgesses w'ch have beine maior and have beine longeste tyme w'thowte the said office of Maior, To th' end that the said Maior, Baylliffes and Burgesses maye chose one of them to be mayor for that yere or tyme followinge w'ch shall then remayne to be executed by the said Maior to be chosen as the case shall requier; And that the said maior, Baylliffes and Burgesses shall at all tymes and from tyme to tyme chose that Burgesse of the said two Burgesses soe named w'ch shall have beine the longest tyme w'thowte the said office of Maioraltie, to th'end that alwayes the same office of Maioraltie may goe and be unto him that hathe beine longest w'thowte the same office in sutche orderlie succession as aforesaid; And it is further hereby ordered that yf it shall happen anye of the said Principall Burgesses to die, And that anewe Principall Burgesse shalbe chosen, That then and in suche case the said newe Pryncipall Burgesse shall not be chosen Maior untill suche tyme as that accordinge to the order and course of Succession before herein expressed yt shall come unto the turne of that Burgesse w'ch was maior in the yere nexte before that yere wherein the said newe Burgesses was chosen to be maior againe, and shall have had and executed the said office, or otherwise refuse to accepte the same, or by deathe or otherwise as hereafter shalbe exp'ssed, shalbe disabled or uncap'le thereof. AND YF yt shall happen that there shalbe more then one Principall Burgesse chosen in any one yere, Then they so chosen after suche tyme as accordinge to the lymytac'on before expressed yt shall come to theire turnes to be Maior shalbe chosen to be Maior in order as they be chosen Principall Burgesses, beginninge w'th the auncientest of them, and soe forward to the nexte of them. PROVIDED alwayes that yf any Principall Burgesse at suche tyme as he shalbe chosen Maior or the yere before, shalbe of soe pore estate as he shall not be able to beare that porte As is fitt for him w'ch is to hould the said place, or shalbe detected of any notorious or schandolous Crime, and for suche cause by the said Maior, Baylliffes and Burgesses, and secundary Burgesses and Comons Ellectors, or the more p'te of them, shall be declared to be therefore uncapable or unfitt for the said office, That then the said p'son soe declared unfitt shall not be no'iated nor chosen to be maior, but shalbe omitted in the no'iacon and ellection of the Maior as aforesaid, And the two Principall Burgesses nexte in order of succession accordinge to the course aforesaid to be no'iated & elected as yf suche p'tie were ded, shalbe named and chosen in mann'r and fourme before expressed; PROVIDED alsoe that for asmuche as it appearethe that the estate and meanes of Mr. John Fyssher, one of the Principall Burgesses, is not sufficient nor fitt to beare the said office of Maior in such sorte as maye stande w'th the Reputac'on of this Boroughe; Therefore untill suche tyme as it shall please god soe to better the estate of Mr. John Fyssher aforesaid, as that he may be able of himself and by his owne p'per meanes to beare and execute the said office and the charges thereof soe as it maye stande w'th the creditt and reputac'on of this Boroughe, And by the said maior, Baylliffes and Burgesses, Secundary Burgesses and Comons ellectors or the greater p'te of them shalbe declared to be soe Inabled as aforssaid, That then the said John Fyssher shall not be named nor chosen maior of this Boroughe, But in ev'ie suche no'iacon and ellection shall be omitted. And to th'end the Maiors of this Boroughe maye from tyme to tyme be the better able to dischardge and executue theiro said offices and in all things carry and demeasne themselves in suche sorte as maye be for the worshipp and creditt of this Boroughe, yt is further by this comon Counsell ordered That this p'nte Maior and ev'ie Maior that shalbe soe chosen in succession and order as aforesaid and not otherwise shall have allowed unto him for that yere of his maioraltie towardes the chardges of the said office Twentie poundes p' Ann'm forthe of the Chamber quarterlie to be paid, And alsoe the p'ffites of the toll Corne of the said m'ckettes. AND it is by the said Comon Counsell further ordered that yf anye man shall hereafter be chosen Maior in any other course or forme then before is herein p'scribed, if he shall refuse to accepte the said office his fyne for the same shalbe onelie xl*d*. and not above; And yf he shall accepte thereof, beinge chosen in other mann'r then before is herein exp'ssed, Then he shall not have anye allowance either of money or other thinge what soev'r towardes the executinge of the said place, But shalbe Censered as wilfull Disturber of the peace and Amitie hereby Intended to be setled; And to th'eud there maye be noe varyances nor question touchinge the Inten'con of mann'r of Succession and in what course it is intended that the same office shall goe; Yt is hereby alsoe ordered that the principall Burgesses shalbe chosen to be Maiors, one after another, in suche mann'r as they be hereafter named, viz.: Firstes— Master Christopher Teisdall, the p'sent Maior for this yere, next Thomas Orpwood, then Thomas Mayott, then Frauncis Little, then will'm Lee, then Lawrence Stevenson, then John Mayott, then John Frauncis, then Robert Payne, then Richard Curtyn, then Richard Chicken. And towchinge the Principall Burgesses hereafter to be chosen: That they when it shall come to theire turnes to be maior in fourme aforesaid, That they shalbe chosen in antiquitie as they shalbe chosen Principall Burgesses in suche fourme as aforesaid. PROVIDED alwayes that yf either by deathe or otherwise it shall happen that anye shalbe soe chosen Maior of the said Boroughe soe as he shall not s've a full yere, That then it shalbe lawfull for the said maior, Baylliffes and Burgesses to devide and apporc'on the said allowance betwene the said olde maior and newe maior respectinge the tymes and qualitie thereof that eche one hathe and is to s've, and the chardge thereof rateablie accordinge to the tyme and qualitie that eche of them hathe borne the said office in the said yere.

An Order conc'ninge the ellection of the Baylliffes. ca. 50.

ITM. whereas heretofore div's p'sons have beine p'ferred to the office of the Baylliffes w'thin this Boroughe p'sentlie after they have beine made Secundary Burgesses, by reason whereof the Auntient Secundarie Burgesses have longe tyme beine kept from the said office; wherefore it is nowe ordered that from hensfourthe noe p'son or p'sons shalbe ellected Bayliffes of the said Boroughe untill suche tyme he hathe bein secundary Burgesse by the space of one whole yere nexte before suche ellecting of him Baylliffe, or hathe bein chosen to the office of the Chamblyn of the said Boroughe.

An order to p'vent disention in Chowsing of the Bayllifes, no man
to be twise bayllie w'thin fyve yeres. ca. 52.

ITM. for the p'ventinge and takinge awaye of suche cause of dissention, discontent-
ment and Variaunce as heretofore hath happened And hereafter maye growe by the over
often advanceinge & chooseinge of some p'sons unto the office of Baylliffes of this Boroughe
and the neglectinge and omittinge of others; And to the intent the said office maye be
held and enjoyed indifferentlie by p'sons Capeable thereof, one after the other, w'thowte
any p'tialitie of affecc'on, YT is this p'sent Daie ordered by the Comon Counsell and by the
Comons Ellectors fullie assented unto, That noe p'son or p'sons whatsoev'r that nowe
hathe beine or hereafter shalbe Baylliff of this Boroughe shalbe at any tyme or tymes
againe nominated, Ellected or chosen unto the said Office of Baylliff of this Boroughe
w'thin fyve yeres at the leaste after suche tyme as he or them soe chosen or ellected have
or hathe had and executed or shall have and execute the said office of Baylliffe as aforesaid.

An order for a Sermon yerely to be made on Goodfrydaye
at Devyne mornying s'vice. ca. 53.

FOR ASMUCHE as the thanckfull acknowledgement of benefittes Receaved is a
Duetie the due p'fourmaunce whereof is bothe pleasing and acceptable unto god, And an
effectuall meanes to p'cuer bothe at the handes of god and man a contynewaunce and
Increase of the like benefittes; AND for asmuche as it hathe pleased God to bestowe not
onelie himself ymediatelie manye benefittes upon this Towne, but alsoe to Rayse manye
virtuous and Charitable p'sons to give manye thinges unto it, The publique memory and
menc'oninge whereof maye tend aswell to the glorye of God that Raysed them, As to the
settinge forthe of theire prayse and worthe whome he hathe pleased to make his
instrumentes therein: AND for asmuche likewise as the passion of oure lord and saviour
as a benefitt above all benefittes and the very fountaine of them all from whence all other
benefittes doe flowe. In w'ch respecte and s'vice yerelie Inioyned by our Churche to be
p'formed with sufficient Devocon and Reverence; THEREFORE to th'end the said
s'vice maye be yerelie p'fourmed w'th the greater Devoc'on & Rev'ence, YT is this p'nte
daie ordered That upon good frydaie nexte and soe yerelie for ev'r, ev'ye good frydaie
hereafter there shalbe p'cured one preacher from the univ'sitie of Oxon (beinge one then
there resident) whoe shall in tyme of Devyne morninge s'vice that daye preache one s'mon
in the Churche of sainte hellins, And therein amongste other thinges Remember or make
menc'on of suche benefactors unto this Towne As by theire Charitable workes don unto
and for it have made the same able in some sorte the better to p'vide bothe for more
decente and devoute s'vice of god, And the Charitable helpe and Releif of the men w'th
whome they live, And that the preacher w'ch shall have and make the said s'mon shall
have for his paynes the some of xiijs. iiij.d., To be allowed forthe of the Chamber.

An order for the better amending and Repayring the Streates. ca. 54.

FOR ASMUCH as the streetes of this Boroughe and the passages thoroughe them as
well unto the Churche As in other the Principall Streetes are muche decayed in the pavement
thereof, to the greate Disgrace of this Boroughe, AND whereas by former orders heretofore
made, yt was p'vided that ev'ye Ten'nte and Inhabitant of a howse should sufficientlie pave
that side of the streate where his howse standethe unto the gutter or myddeste of the
said street soe farr as his howse extendethe in the said streete, w'ch said Order by reason
that there are in the said streetes manye poore Ten'ntes and inhabitantes whoe have not
meanes nor are of noe abilitie to p'forme the same, And by meanes thereof bothe those
p'tes of the streetes before there Dores. And alsoe the p'tes of the streetes before other
men's Dores of better abillitie lye unpaved, or the pavem't muche Decayed or owte of
order, For reformac'on whereof, YT is this p'sent Daye ordered that ev'ye p'son or p'sons,
accordinge to the saide order or the true meaninge thereof, shall at or before assenc'on

Daie next, make or amend the same sufficientlie, upon payne that ev'ye one that shall make Defalte therein shall forfitt for ev'ye, yarde square not sufficiently don, made or amended the some of vj*d.*, unlesse he shall before that tyme make his estate knowne unto the Maior for the tyme beinge, and unto sixe of the principall burgesses * * *
And for the supplyinge, pavinge and amendinge of all suche p'te of the streetes as eyther in respecte of the pov'tie of the Inhabitantes or for anye other cause can not be p'formed By virtue of this p'nte order or of anye other orders heretofore made Yt is hereby ordered that the Inhabitantes hereafter menconed shall paye towardes the same the sev'all somes of money hereunder sev'allie exp'ssed; And likewise that all fynes, am'ciamentes, forfeytures and penalties as shalbe forfeyted or incurred by anye man at anye Courte leete at anye tyme hereafter holden for the said Boroughe shalbe levyed by ye S'iant of the mace w'th the assistaunce of the Constables and Tythingmen for the tyme Being, And that the S'iantes shall have for levyinge of those forfeytures and am'ciamentes ij*s.* in the pound, And the Residue of the saide money bestowed towardes the paveinge of the streetes * * * * *

(Here follow the names of 76 Maltsters and 118 other Inhabitants who are assessed in various sums from 8d. to 10s.)

* * * * * * * *

19th September, Anno D'ni. 1618.
In the tyme of Fraunces Little, gent., Maior.

An Order for the better p'fourmance and more Dewlie and orderlie kepeinge of the nighte watch w'thin this Boroughe, from the Feast of ascenc'on unto Myelmas yerelie. ca. 57.

WHEREAS by a Statute made in the xiij*th* yere of the Raigne of kinge Edward the Firste yt was inacted That a watche shalbe kepte yerelie from the Feaste of assenc'on unto Myellmas in ev'ie Boroughe, by xij. men ev'ie nighte from sonne settinge untill son Rysinge, wh'ch said lawe and Statute, by Reason of the Insufficient men appointed to watche and other negligences, hathe not that good effect in this Boroughe as was Intended, Now for the better p'fourmaunce of the said watche and Reformac'on of the abuses therein Comytted w'thin this Boroughe it is ordered by the Comon Councell of the same, That from hencefourthe ev'ie nighte from the Feaste of Ascenc'on unte Myellmas, according to the saide Statute, xij. honest and sufficient men, Inhabitantes of this Boroughe, shall watche and accordinglie shalbe warned and appointed thereunto from tyme to tyme by the Tythingmen of the Towne, accordinge to theire sev'all watches or wardes, and in suche mann'r as in tymes past hathe bene used and accustomed, And the said Tythingmen for the tyme beinge shall, from tyme to tyme, geve warninge unto the said p'sons that are to watche at his dwellinge howse one nighte at the least before that nighte for w'ch they are to watche, to th'end the p'son appointed to watche maye either be Reddie himself or p'vide one sufficient man for him to p'fourme the same, And yf anye Tithingman shall Refuse or neglect or omyt the Dewe p'fourmannce thereof, That then the said Tythingman faylinge or offendinge therein shall forfitt and paie to the Maior, Bayliffes and Burgesses of this Boroughe for ev'ie p'son soe unwarned the some of xij*d.* of lawfull money of England, And yt is likewise ordered that ev'ie Inhabitant, beinge a howsholder w'thin this Boroughe and warned to watche as aforesaid, shall either in his owne p'son or by some other sufficient man in his place to be allowed and approved by the Constables of this Boroughe for the tyme beinge or one of them, Repaire at sone settinge w'th a fitt and Convenient weapon for that purpose unto the usuall place where the watchemen of this Towne have heretofore used to mete and assemble together, Comonlie called Peneles Benche, And there Remayne untill the Constables for the tyme beinge or one of them shall come and give them a Charge howe to execute the s'vice in hand and to p'fourme those thinges as shalbe Comytted to theire Care for that nighte insuinge, and shall watche untill the sone

A1

Rysinge, then to be discharged by the Constables or one of them, And yf anye p'son that shalbe warned to watche as aforesaide shall Refuse or neglect the p'fourmance thereof as aforesaid, then ev'ie p'son soe offendinge and the same offence by him confessed or Testefied by the Constables or Tithingmen before the mayor of this Boroughe for the tyme beinge, shall forfitt unto the said mayor, Baylliffes and Burgesses the some of vjd.

*   *   *   *   *

An Order to Compell the Inhabitantes of this Boroughe to the better p'fourmance of theire s'vice to the amendinge of the highe wayes.

ca. 58.

WHEREAS not w'th standinge there are div's lawes and Statutes of this Realme nowe in force Injoyninge the Inhabitantes of ev'ie p'rishe for to Repaire and amend the highe wayes w'thin the same, and sondrie penalties and forfeytures ymposed upon suche p'sons as shalbe founde defective in p'fourmaunce of s'vice to that worke, And yett by the careles negligence of the Sup'visors and overseers appointed towcheinge those workes, the highe wayes in and aboute this Towne are growne into greate decaye and manye places almost unpasable w'thowte daunger, For the better reformacon whereof And to th'end the said Statutes and lawes maye be hereafter the better and more Dewelie and Carefullie executed, yt is therefore this p'nte Daie by the said Comon Councell of this Boroughe ordered, That yf anye sup'visor or sup'visors nowe Chosen or w'ch hereafter shalbe nominated and Chosen w'thin this Boroughe shall happen to Die or Remove owte of the Towne Duringe suche tyme as he or they should Contynewe in that Office, That then and soe often the Mayor of this Boroughe for the tyme beinge shall and maye cause all and ev'ie suche p'sons As by the Statutes of this Realme are to [sic] of surveyours for to Assemble themselves together And to no'iate and appointe some other p'son or p'sons to be survayor or survayours in the place and stede of him or them soe beinge Dead or Removed as aforesaid.   *   *   *   *   *

2nd October, Anno D'ni 1619.

In the tyme of Lawrence Stevenson, gent., Maior.

An Order that Poore Children shalbe putt to service, otherwise theire Parentes to be Uncapable of any Releife.   ca. 59.

IT IS ordered that noe Inhabitant w'thin this Boroughe now Receaving Releif or which is likelie to Charge or p'judice the Towne w'th his or theire Children or kinred, shall entertaine or kepe in his or theire howse, howses or families, man or woeman Child of the age of Fourtene yeres or upwardes. after the eight Daye of october next followinge, But shall at or before that tyme place abroade theire said Sonnes, Daughters or kinfolkes in s'vice, whereby they maye be the better Inabled to gett theire owne liveinges and p'ferr themselves w'thout burtheninge or Chargeinge the Towne; And in Default thereof That they shalbe utterlie and absolutelie Disabled and uncapeable to have or take anye wekelie or other Allowaunce of Releif or Almes or Respect or favour toucheinge suche Lease or leases of his or theire howse or howses or otherwise whatsoever anye Allowaunce or guyft or other thinge whatsoev'r untill he or she shall confourme themselves and fullfill and kepe this Order   *   *   *   *   And to th'end that the hospitall there maye likewise forbeare to give Releif to anye suche, It is likewise ordered that the names of all suche as shall stand soe disabled as aforesaid shalbe from tyme to tyme deliv'ed unto the m'r and Collector of the said hospitall for the tyme beinge.

An Order that suche as have anye Bastard shalbe sent to the howse of Correcc'on   Cap. 60.

ITEM it is ordered that yf anye mayde or unmarryed woeman shalbe w'thin this Boroughe begotten w'th Child whereby she shall have anye Bastard Borne w'thin the same, That then the mayor for the tyme beinge shall, w'thin two monethes after her deliv'ie of the said Bastard, send her to the howse of Correcc'on, upon payne for neglect thereof to forfayt and paye to the Churchwardens of that p'rishe w'ch by lawe shalbe Charged w'th the kepeinge of the Bastard, xxs. towardes the Releif of the same Bastard, And that all and ev'ie such some and somes of money w'ch the mayor shall soe forfait shalbe taken fourthe of his Allowaunce usuallie made unto him by the Chamber.

An Order that the overseers of Inmates shall once every monethe make a true relac'on to the mayor of all straingers and daungers of fiar and other Inconveniences. Cap. 61.

ITEM Whereas aswell at the last Court Leete as at Div's Courtes Leetes formerlie holden for this Boroughe from tyme to tyme, overseers of the streetes and Inmates have bene Chosen and appointed aswell for the Restraininge of strainge Poore People from Comynge to Inhabit here, Whereby this Towne is Daylie muche Charged and ympoverished As for Reformac'on of Div's other abuses, For the better execucon of w'ch order and the true meaninge thereof It is this p'nte Daie ordered by the Comon Counsell of this Boroughe That eche of the said sup'visors of the said streetes and Inmates shall once in every monethe at least and oftener (yf nede shall Requier) searche and vewe the saide streetes and places w'thin their lymyttes, aswell to discover what straingers or Inmates have bene latelie received into anye howses or habitac'on there, As what other abuses, daungers or Inconveniences are Comytted or suffered in the same, and likewise once in ev'ie monethe shall make a true Certificate and relac'on unto the mayo'r for the tyme beinge of all such straingers and Inmates, abuses, daungers and Inconveniences as they shall find or cann Discover; To th'end the mayor shall or maye p'sentlie take suche spedie and p'nte Course for Reformac'on thereof As by the Lawes and Statutes of this Realme and the Orders w'ch by Comon Counsell are or shalbe established upon payne * * * *

20th May, A'o D'ni 1625.
In the tyme of Christopher Teisdall, gent., Mayor.

An order that none but freemen shall sell any wares or m'chandises to forryners or straingers nor kepe open any shopp or howse to sell wares or m'chandises. Cap. 62.

FOR that Forrayners and suche as are noe Freemen of this Boroughe have sometymes solde w'thin this Boroughe and the liberties therof base, false and sophisticated Wares, and by suche p'sons stolne wares are in Corners and bye places solde in secret whose Actes are taken by the Contrye people to be the Actes of Freemen of this Boroughe, Which tendethe muche unto the p'judice and Disgrace of this Boroughe and trade therof, Which inconvenience by sev'all actes of Comon Counsella hathe bene endevored to be Reformed and repressed, YT is therefore further enacted and ordered by this Councell assembled * * * * that noe Forrayner or p'son that is not or shall not be Free of this Boroughe so long as he shall Contynewe a Forreyner or not be made free therof shall, w'thin this Boroughe or the liberties therof at any tyme herafter (Excepte it be upon the Daies and tymes of Fayer and marckett w'thin this Boroughe), sell or put forthe to sale or offer to sell unto any Forrayner or strainger or p'son that is not free of this Boroughe any maner of Wares or marchandizes what soever upon payne * * * * *

An order that none shall Receave into his howse or Cottage any Strainger to Inhabit w'thoute license of the Mayor, Baylliffes and Burgesses. Ca. 63.

FOR ASMUCHE as the greate number of the poore and disordered p'sons Daylie encreasethe in this Boroughe, not onclye to the greate and in'portable Chardge of the

Inhabitantes in Allowing a greate p'porc'on for theire Wekely Releif more then the estate of many of them can well beare, But also by meanes (thereof?) many and greate Disorders and offences are Daylye comytted to the Dishonour of god, the P'iudice of this Comon Wealthe and disgrace of the Gov'ment of this Boroughe; And for asmuche as the entertaynyng and Receaving of Straingers into this Boroughe w'thowte regard or respecte either of theire behaviours or theire meanes and estates w'ch is by Daylie experience found to be the occac'on of suche burthen and charge to the Inhabitantes of the said Boroughe, FOR p'venc'on wherof it is therefore this Daie ordered by the Comon Counsell that noe p'son or p'sons shall at anye tyme or tymes herafter (w'thowte the license and consent of the Mayor, Baylliffes and Burgesses of this Boroughe) or the most p'te of them first had and obteyned in Writting, under their handes and Seale, Receave any p'son or p'sons (not having sufficient meanes of his owne nor exercising anye lawfull trade, arte or mystery whereby he maye be thought able at his Costes to mayneteyne his poore charge and famylie) to Dwell or Inhabit in any howse, Cottage or Ten'te w'thin this Boroughe, wherof he or she is or shalbe owner, or any waies interessed, unles he or she w'ch shall soe entertayne or Receave suche p'son shall first geve sufficient securitie unto the Mayor, Baylliffes and Burgesses of this Boroughe, bothe for his and theire good behaviour, And also that neyther he, his wief nor Children shalbe Chargeable unto the Inhabitantes nor shall receave, entertayne or p'mytt any p'son or p'sons what so ev'r (then not being any Inhabitant of this Boroughe) to Inhabit or Dwell in his, her or their howse, Cottage or Ten'te, before he hathe first the Consent of the Mayor, Baylliffes and Burgesses of this Boroughe as aforesaid or the greater part of them upon payne   *   *   *   *   *

An order that none shall erecte any howse for habitac'on nor any other house nere therunto adjoynyng but suche as he shall cover w'th slatt or Tile. 64.

FOR ASMUCHE as the erecting and buylding of small Tymber Cottages w'th lowe Rooffes thatched are found to be verye Daingerous to the whole Boroughe, by reason of Casualtie of fire w'ch they are moste apte and subjecte unto, To the p'sent greate Terror of a many the Inhabitantes and the Ruyn of the Whole Towne (yf the same should happen) For the p'venting therefore of suche greate future Dainger of Fire w'ch (by godes grace) so muche as may be of suche Dainger of Fiare as may happen by suche thatched howses, Cottages or Ten'tes herafter to be buylte w'thin this Boroughe; IT is nowe therefore by Comon Counsell ordered That yf any p'son or p'sons do or shall att any tyme or tymes herafter erecte or buylde, or cause to be erected or builte any howse, Cottage or Ten'te for habitac'on w'thin this Boroughe or adjoynyng to any howse of habitac'on w'thin this Boroughe, that he shall erecte and buyld the first storie therof w'th brick or stone, and that the said storie shall conteyne seven foote in highte and ten foote in bredthe and twelve foote in lengthe at the least, with one or more Chymbnies of stone, and shall cause the same all to be Cov'ed w'th Slatt or Tile and not otherwise, upon paine   *   *   *

*   *   *   *   *   *   *   *

(Here follow additional Orders, as under:—)

66. An acte to make voyde the order for the ellecc'on of the mayor in succession.

*   *   *   *   *   *   *   *

67. An acte for the suppressing of long leases.

*   *   *   *   *   *   *   *

68. An acte for the confirmyng of the Electors whose names are to be sett downe in a booke.

ALSO it is ordered that the Mayor, Baylliffes and principall Burgesses and secondary Burgesses of this Boroughe, shall yerelie mete and assemble them selves together at the Guild hall of the same Boroughe, three or foure Daies before the Eleccon of the newe mayor, And then and there shall cause all the names of the p'sons appointed for the Comons Electors to be Redd and considered of, to th'end that yf any of them be Dead or have Removed theire dwelling from the Towne, or Combygne them selves to disturbe the Elecc'on or for any other juste cause shalbe thought fitt to be Removed, The said mayor, Baylliffes, principall Burgesses and secondary Burgesses (taking notice therof) shall therupon electe and choose other Electors in theire places, suche as shalbe by them thoughte fitt. So as at the tyme of the Elecc'on of the newe mayor there be and remayne the nomber of Fortie Electors or more according to an order heretofore made at a Comon Counsell holden the xxiij*th* Daie of August, 1604, in the tyme of John Blacknall, gen., Mayor, And that the names and surnames aswell of the Electors nowe chosen as herafter to be chosen shalbe sett downe and written in a Booke appointed for that purpose.

ALSO it is ordered that the secondary Burgesses and Comons Electors shall yerelie on the Elecc'on Daie assemble them selves in the Counsell howse and there make theire Elecc'on of the Mayor and the Baylliffs for the Comons. And yf they can not there aggree uppon the said Elecc'ons of the said mayor and Baylliff, That then there shalbe chosen by the Mayor, Baylliffes and Burgesses two Scrutators w'ch shall take the names by Scruteny as they come Downe owte of the Counsell howse into the hall.

20th August, A.D. 1629. In the tyme of John Bradford, gent., Mayor.

69. An Acte for the peaceable elecc'on of the Mayor & Bayliffes.

FOR THE more peaceable, fayre and orderly proceedinges to be kept and observed hereafter in all elecc'ons w'ch shalbe made of any mayor or Bayliffe of this Boroughe, IT YS nowe ordered by the Aucthoritie of this Comon Councell That if any p'son whatsoever inhabiting w'thin this Boroughe shall at any tyme hereafter give or offer to give or shall promise to give or to be given any recompence or reward whatsoever to any parson or parsons having any voyce or voyces in any suche elecc'on to th' entente that he or they shoulde elect and choose such parson or parsons as they shall nominate or otherwise signifie unto him or them; Or if any parson or parsons inhabiting w'thin this Boroughe shall indevour by any Threates or menacinges whatsoever to deterr any Electo'r from his Free choice and election of any mayor or Bayliffe to be hereafter chosen w'thin this Boroughe, Or if any parson or parsons inhabitinge w'thin this Boroughe at the tyme of any such Elecc'on shall shewe himselfe Clamorous, Turbulent or disordered, EVERIE such parson for every such firste offence shal forfeyte   *   *   *   *   the some of Five poundes   *   *   *   *   and for suche second offence   *   *   *   *   * the some of Tenne poundes   *   *   *   *

70. An Acte for the Repeale of a former Order made towching the making of leases, And that noe leases shall hereafter be made for above xxjtie yeres.

*   *   *   *   *   *   *   *

A REGISTER

As well to retayne a perpetuall remembrance of all the speciall benefactors of this Burrough which either have already, or whicho herafter shall bestow

·or geve anye Monie or Stockes unto this Incorporac'on to be ymploied to any charitable use w'thin the same, As also to shewe unto all posteritie how justly and trulie the same money and Stockes ys from tyme to tyme ymploied by the Maior, Baylilles, and Principall Burgesses of this Burrough, according to the wills of the severall Donors of the saide money and stockes, From the viiijth day of February in the one and Forteth yere of the raigne of our Sov'aigne Lady Elizabeth, By the grace of God, Queene of England, France and Irelande, defendour of the faythe, &c., Anno Domini 1598.

The Names of the Benefactors unto this Burroughe :—

KATHERIN HYDE, Widowe, sometyme the wife of John Hide, late of Sutton Courtney, in the County of Berks, Esquier.

JOHN ROYSE, late cytizen and mercer of London, Founder of the Free Schole within this Buroughe.

JOHN BARNES, Late of the Cytie of London, Esquier.

PHILIPP MARYNER, of Cyrencester, in the County of Gloucester, gent., decessed.

WILLIAM DUNCHE, late of Litle Witenham, in the County of Berks, Esquier.

[These Charities were as under :

KATHERINE HYDE left £100 "to be loaned out freelie unto Clothiers of the "said Burrough to be ymploied in the making of Clothe, to th' end that the poore "Spynners, Weavers and Fullers Dwelling in this Burrough might allwaies the better be "sett on work."

JOHN ROYSSE gave £20 "to be ymploied yerely in the provision of Corne, Wodd "and Coole to be sold to the poore att reasonable prises."

JOHN BARNES gave £33 : 6 : 8 "for the releif of the poore occupiers and artificers "being Howsehoulders and freemen of the Borough in fyve severall sums of £6 : 13 : 4 "a pece."

PHILIP MARRYNER and WILLIAM DUNCH each left £20 to be divided into four sums of £5 each and similarly lent out.]

THE CHARGE TO THE GRAND JURY
AT THE COURT LEET.

GENTLEMEN of this Jury, We are here met to hold a Court-Leet for this Borough. 'Tis an Ancient Court, and has been heretofore of great use and authority. 'Tis very useful still, being an Easy Way of Looking into and redressing, with a very Small Expense, the most part of Com'on and Publick Injuryes, Greivances and Nusances which may happen amongst Us. THIS COURT has Power to Enquire of and Present High-Treasons, Petty-Treasons, Felonyes, Sacriledges, Burglaryes, Rapes and Larcenyes, Which High Crimes are not here punishable, But are to be from hence Certifyed & Transmitted by the Lord or Steward of this Leet, to the Judges of Assize for this County, or else to the Justices at theire next Generale Sessions of the Peace for this Borough, But such Capitall Crimes being for the most Part taken cognizance of and Punished either by the Mayor & Justices of the Peace of the Borough, or by the Judges through their Means, are therefore not likely to take up much of your time, Yet if any of you know of any Such Capitall Crimes to have been Committed within this Borough which have not come to the knowledge and prosecution of the Civil Magistrates, it is your duty here to Inquire of and Present the same. But what are more likely to take up your time and do Concern your more Immediate Enquiry, are such Injuryes, Nusances and Greivances as I shall now particularly mention, Not Doubting that you'l every one of you, Conscientiously Discharge your Dutyes, and the Oath You have now taken Diligently to Enquire, and truly to Present all Such Matters as are given You in Charge without Favour to one Person or illwill to another. You shall Enquire whether all Persons who owe Suit and Service to this Court have appeared or not, and Present and amerce those you find to have made default. You shall Enquire if any of the Constables or Tithing-Men of this Borough have been Negligent or remiss in the Execution of their offices, And if Watch and Ward have been duly kept, and Hue and Cryes pursued. Also if the Stocks, Whipping Post, Pillory and Cage within this Borough be substantial and in sufficient Repair. You shall present all Flew-Chimneys within your Enquiry, (likewise Inmates are here Presentable) and you shall Present all Nusances in the Streets and Publick High-Ways & all Such Persons as Place or Lay Dung-Heaps, Carrion, Rubbish, Stone, Timber, Blocks, Waggons, Carts or other things there, to the annoyance of the Publick. And you shall Present the Scavenger if he Neglects the Duty of his office in keeping the Streets clean. If either of the Sterts, or any other Customary Current or Water-Course within this Borough be Stopped or not kept well Cleansed, You are to Present the Persons who ought to Cleanse the same; Or if Either of the Bridges or Com'on Watering Places be in Decay You are to Present the Persons who ought to repair them. You shall Enquire if the Com'on Pound be sufficient to detain Such Distresses as shall be brought thereto. You shall also Enquire if any Ancient Land-Mark or Boundaryes within this Borough, or any Stones, Marks or Boundaryes shewing the Limits, Precints and Extent of the Borough itself be removed or taken away and make presentment thereof, and also if you can of the Persons who removed the Same. You shall Enquire if any Buy or Cause to be Bought any Corn, Poultry, Piggs, Butter, Cheese, Eggs, Pidgeons or other Dead or Live Victuals, Coming towards this Market to be sold before it be brought into the Market, he is a Fore-Staller, Or if any Person buy any Such in this Market and sell it again in the said Market or within four Miles thereof, he is a Regrater; Or if any do Ingross or get into their hands great Quantities of any Such dead or live Victuals with Intent to Sell the Same again he is an Ingrosser, and you are here to Present all Such Fore-Stallers, Regraters and Ingrossers. You shall Enquire of and Present any Victuallers, Butchers, Bakers or Brewers, within this Borough who have Conspired together or made Oath not to sell any Victuals, Meat, Bread or Beer but at certain Prices, as also any Artificers or Labourers who are under the like Conspiracy for doing Certain Work in a Day, and that at Certain Hours. You shall also Enquire if any Person keep or use false Weights or Measures, or if any Baker have Sold Unwholesome Bread, or not made Weight according to the true Assize of Bread, or if any Butcher or Brewer Sell Unwholesome Meat, Ale or Beer not fit for Man's Body; Or if any Ale-Housekeeper Suffer Unlawfull Games or Disorders in his house, or Sell by Unsealed Potts, or if there be any Keepers of Bawdy Houses within this Borough, you are to Present the same. You shall also Enquire if there be any Com'on Barrators, Such as make it their Business to sow Strife and Discord amongst their Neighbours, or Com'on Scolds and Brawlers or Eaves-Droppers and Present them. If any Person take, kill or destroy Fish or the Fry or Spawn of Fish, Contrary to the Act of Parliament made in the first year of Queen Elizabeth, you are to Present it. And if anything else comes to your knowledge fitting here to be Presented, you shall present it with the rest.

AN ABSTRACT

Of the Articles to be given in Charge to the grand Jury to enquire of at the Leet and Laweday to be holden for the Borough of Abingdon.

Pettie Treason.

1. If a Woman hath killed her husband or a Clarke his Ordinary to whom he oweth obedience, this is pettie Treason.

Misprision of Treason.

2. If any one knoweth of the Treason aforesaid or any of them and concealeth it Twentie four houres after knowledge thereof had, This is misprision of Treason.

Offences made felonie by Act of P'liam't.

3. If any maliciously shall cutt out the Tongue or putt out the Eyes of any the King's Subjects.

4. If any have comitted B—— with man or beast.

5. If any have ravished any maide, wife or widowe, above tenne yeares of age against her will, though after she consent; or have knowne any woman Child under tenne yeares of age though with her consent.

6. If any (his or her former husband or wife being alive) marry another, except where there is a lawfull Divorce or long absence beyond the Seas.

7. If any unlawfully against her will, have taken any Maide, wife or widowe, haveing landes or goodes, or being an heire apparent, and marryed her.

8. If any Servauntes have embezelled their Master's or Mistresses' goodes, being putt in trust therewith, if it amount to xls. and upwardes.

9. If any Witch or Sorcerer hath killed or destroyed any man, woman or child with witchcraft or sorcery, It is felonie.

Felonies by the Comon Lawe.

10. If any hath stolne goodes to the value of xijd. or upwardes, or any marked Swanns, or their signetts, or their egges, or tame Deere, or robbe Churches, Chappells, Pigeon howses or dwelling howses, or any upon the Highway, though he take but the worth of a penny from him, it is felonie.

Pettie Larcenie.

11. If any have stolne Pigges, geese, hennes, chickens, corne out of feildes, Cloathes from hedges or out of windowes, or have robbed orchardes or gone in Theeves Messages, they are to have corporall punishm't and soe their accessaries, but they forfeite their goodes if they have any.

All theis offences are here onely to be inquired of and presented, but are not here punishable.

The offences w'ch are here to be inquired of, presented and punished, are theis which followe:—

12. If any man within yo'r inquiry hath broaken the Peace, or made any affray or bloodshed, you' must p'sent him or them, and the manner of it, with what weapon, for that it is forfeited to the Lordes of the Leete, and the offendo'r is to be fined for such offence.

13. If Hue and Cry after Theeves and Robbers have not beene duely pursued and followed as they ought to have beene, you must present him or them who made default therein, for he forfeites vli.

14. If any Constable or Tythingman hath not done his best endeavo'r to apprehend begging Rougues, or hath willfully lett them passe without punishm't, or hath not conveyed them to their place of birth or last dwelling, or if any hath hindered the execucon of any Statute against Rogues.

15. If there be within this Borough a paire of Stocks and Whipping Post, as there ought to be by the Statute, or not.

16. If any Alehowsekeep'r or other p'son doe keepe any unlawfull games in his or their howse or howses or elswhere, as Cards, dice tables, loggetts, quoits, bowles, or such like, in this case the howsekeep'r looseth for every day xls., and every player vjs. viij*d.* for every tyme.

Alsoe Constables ought to search monthly for such unlawfull games and disorders in Alehouses upon paine of xls., and they may arrest such as they finde playing at unlawfull games and comitt them to warde untill they putt in sureties not to play any more at any unlawfull games.

Noe man may play at any unlawfull game insatiably unles he can dispend C*li.* p'r ann' in lands, fees or offices for life, at the least, and he may not play neither in any open place, where every one that will may see him, but in his howse, orchard or garden, upon paine of vjs. viij*d.* for every tyme. Except in the Cristmas tyme for then all men may play.

17. If any man doe shoot in hand gunns or Crossebowes, for noe man may shoot in them unles he can dispend C*li.* p'r ann' in lands, tenem'ts, offices, annuities or fees, neither may those shoote at any Phesant, Partridge, Hearne, Ducke, Mallard, Howsedove, pigeon, wigeon, teale or heathcock, upon paine of x*li.* for every shoot.

18. Wheather yo'r Highwayes be sufficiently amended & made passable, as they ought to be or not, for to that purpose there ought to be two Superviso'rs chosen between Easter and Midsomer, and there ought to be sixe dayes appointed for amending of Highwayes eight houres every day Upon paine of xxs. to be lost by the Superviso'rs. And every one that hath a Cart ought to send two able men with it, with tooles fitt for that service, or els to loose xs. for every day wanting. And every howscholder oughte to finde an able man for that service or els to loose xij*d.* for every day wanting.

19. If there be any Wall, hedge, ditch, or howse sett, levyed or erected in the Kinges highway, or any watercourse stopped or turned into the Highway to hinder the passage of the Kinges subjectes or any way to annoy them.

20. If any person hath removed any merestones, boundes or markes between this Borough & any Lordshipp, or between tenaunt and tenaunt since the last Court.

21. If any Highwayes or Foot pathes to Church, Mill or Markett be stopped up w'ch have beene accustomed to lye open.

22. If any Comon Bridges over Comon streames be broaken soe that the Kinges subjects cannot passe about their busines, yo' are to p'sent those who ought to make them.

23. If ye Comon Poundes w'thin ye Borough be broaken, soe that they will hold noe distresse that is brought to them untill they be delivered thence by order of Lawe, yo are to p'sent those who ought to repaire them upon a paine.

24. Yo' shall enquire of Sleepers by day and walkers by night to steale and purloyne other men's goodes, as Conies out of Warrens, Fish out of severall Pondes or Waters, Henns from Henhowse, or any other thing whatsoever.

25. Alsoe of Eves droppers, such as by night stand harkening under walls or windowes of other men, to heare what is said in another man's howse to th'ende to sett debate and dissention between Neighbours.

B1

26. Alsoe of Forestallers, Regraters, and Ingrossers.

A forestaller is he which buyeth or causeth to be bought any Victuale whatsoever goeing to any Faire or Markett to be sold, and maketh any bargaine for the buying thereof before the same be brought into the Faire or Markett, or doth make any moc'on for the inhancing of the price of any victuales, or doth move or perswade any person comeing to the Faire or Markett with Victuallcs to absent and forbeare his comeing thither with any victuall to be sold there.

Regrato'r is he that getteth into his handes in any Faire or Markett any Corne, Tallowe or Candells, or any dead Victuall whatsoever brought to any Faire or Markett to be sold, and doth sell the same againe in any Faire or Markett within foure miles next adjoyning thereunto.

An Ingrosser is he or shee that doth ingrosse and gett into his or her handes by buying or p'mise taken, other then by demise, graunt or lease, of Corne growing in the fieldes or any other Corne, grayne, butter, cheese, fish or any other dead victuall whatsoever, to the intent to sell the same againe for profitt.

27. If any use to buy Cattle and to sell them againe within five weekes they ought to loose double the value of their Cattle.

28. Noe Butcher ought to sell in any open Faire or Markett any other victuall then that which is good & wholesome for man's bodie, and for reasonable gaines, and not at excessive prices.

29. Shoe makers ought to make their Shoes and Bootes of good and well tanned Leather, and well licoured, curred and sowed, to keepe men drye in their Legges & Feet.

30. Yo' shall inquire of Tanners that have used the occupac'on of a Cordwayner or a Currier, or hath putt any Leather to sale, but red Leather as it came from the Tannefutte, or that hath putt any Hyde or Peece of Leather to sale before it be well dryed, marked & sorted and then sold in open Markett, or that hath tanned any Sheepskinns.

31. Alsoe wheather Glovers or Whitetanyers of Leather doe make any other ware then that w'ch is substanciall, well taned and dryed, and not rotten, nor tainted, and sell the same at reasonable prices. And a white Taner may tane noe Calfe skynns except they be putt to him to be tanned upon paine to loose for every Calfe skynne xxd.

32. Alsoe you shall inquire wheather the Bakers doe their dueties or not in makeing of good and wholsome bread for man's bodie, of sweet Corne and not corrupted, & that they make their bread in weight according to the price of Wheate in three Markettes next adjoyning, not changing the Assize of Bread but by six pence in weight in increasing or abating, and if they doe the contrary and be thereof duely convicted then for the first, second & third tyme, they shalbe amerced after the quantitie of their faulte, & shall loose from tyme to tyme their bread soe found too light in weight, but if they shalbe found faultie herein the fourth tyme, then they must be sett upon the Pillory in open Markett, whose punishm't may not be released for gold or silver.

Alsoe a Baker must sett his owne & p'per Marke upon every loafe of bread that he maketh or selleth to th'ende that if any bread be faultie in weight, it may be then knowne in whom the fault is.

36. Alsoe you shall inquire of Brewers and Tiplers wheather they make good and holesome Ale and Beere for man's body or not, and sell and utter the same according to the Lawes and Statutes of this Realme. And alsoe they ought not to putt out their signe or Alestake untill their Ale be assayed by the Aletaster & then to sell & not before.

37. Alsoe yo' shall inquire of Fishers wheather they doe their dueties or not, in bringing to the Markett such Fish as is good & holesome for man's body, and not corrupt or stinking, and there sell the same at reasonable prices w'thout takeing any excessive

gaines, and if any Fisher shall doe the contrary then he shalbe amerced from tyme to tyme, and his Fish (if it be corrupt and stinking) to be taken from him, and oapenly burnt in the Markett.

Alsoe noe person may kill or distroy any young Frye of Fish, nor kill or take any Salmon, or Trount, or any Pike or Pickerill, not being in length tenne Inches of cleere Fishe or more, nor any Barbell except he be twelve inches long in cleere Fish or more, upon paine of **xxs.** for every Fish soe taken & killed not being of the severall lengthes aforesaid.

Alsoe noe man ought to fish with any Nett or Engine (Angling onely excepted) but with such Nett or Trannell as every Mesh shalbe two inches & a halfe wide upon paine of **xxs.** for every tyme offending, and losse of Fish and the unlawfull Nett.

38. Yo' shall alsoe inquire of the conspiracie of Victuallers, and that is where any butcher, baker, brewer, powlterer or Cooke doe or shall conspire, p'mise or make oath that they will not sell their victualls but at certaine prices. Or if any Artificers or Laborers doe conspire, p'mise or covenaunt likewise not to doe the worke which others have begunne, or will doe but certaine worke in a day, or will not worke but at certaine houres and times, then every such p'son soe conspireing, p'mising, swearing and offending, being thereof lawfully convicted shall forfeite for the first offence **xli.** if he have it to pay, then he must pay it within sixe dayes after his convicc'on or els he is to have xxtie dayes imprisonm't, and have onely bread and water for his sustenance, and for the second offence **xxli.** to be paid as is aforesaid or els to suffer punishm't on the Pillory, and for the third offence he shall lose **xlli.** to be paid as is aforesaid or els to be sett upon the Pillory and loose one of his eares, and ever after to be taken as an infamous person, And if such conspiracie shall happen to be made by any Company or Corporac'on, they shall loose their Corporac'on besides the penaltie and the particuler punishment aforesaid.

39. Alsoe if any within yo'r inquiry shall use any false weightes or double measures in deceiveing of the Kinges subjectes, in buying with a great measure and in selling with a lesse, the offendo'r therein shalbe greivously punished and imprisoned untill he hath made fine with the King for his offence.

Noe man ought to sell any corne, ale, bread, or wine, but by a Measure sealed with this Letter H, upon paine of forfeiture for the first offence **vjs. viijd.**, for the second offence **xiijs. iiijd.**, and for the third offence **xxs.**, and to be sett on the Pillory to the example of others, and the measure not sealed to be broaken.

40. Alsoe noe man ought to water any hempe or Flaxe in any running streame within this Borough upon paine of **xxs.**

41. Alsoe yo' shall inquire if any man hath received into his service any servaunt, and hath kept him by the space of a yeare, and not sworne to the King according to the Statute, his Master must be amerced, and the Minister ought not to receive any man to the Comunion Table before he be sworne to be a leige man to the King.

42. Alsoe yo' shall inquire of Drunkards, for they ought to be presented and to pay if they be able for every tyme they be drunke **vs.** to the use of the poore, if not able, then after convicc'on thereof they ought to sitt sixe houres in the Stockes.

43. Alsoe an Alehowsekeeper ought to loose **xxs.** for every Pott they sell that is not a full quart, and **xs.** for suffering any Townsman to sitt drinking in their howses except he be brought thither by a Stranger, and then he may not stay there above an houre.

44. And Brewers by the same Lawe ought to loose for every Barrell of Beere or Ale **vjs. viijd.** which they lay into any man's Seller, to be sold there by retaile, by any that is not licenced to sell Ale or Beere.

45. Alsoe yo' shall inquire of wayfes, stayes, & felons' goodes. wayfes are cattle stolne and weived out of the possession of him that stole them; and strayes are cattle strayed out of their haunt, and they ought to be seized upon to the use of the . . . and to be wreathed and putt into an capen place and not in a covert to th'ende the owner may have the viewe of them, and they must be cryed at three Markett Townes next adjoyning to the place where they are strayed, and if they be not challenged within a yeare & a day then they belong to . . otherwise not.

Which is all manner of felons' goods w'ch may (p'sentlie after the felonie is knowne to be comitted) be seized upon but not taken away, but left with the Bayliffes, For the Felon must have his finding out of it soe long as he lives unconvicted or attainted, but when he is convicted or attainted his goodes then properlie belong to the M. B. & B. [Mayor, Bayliffs & Burgesses.]

46. Alsoe yo' shall enquire if any man hath given any landes in Mortmaine, that is to say, to any religious Howse or Religious person, or to any Corporacon, Guild or Fraternitie without Licence, such guift is voide, and the Lord may enter by way of Escheate.

47. If any person hath comitted any Nusance by laying of Dung, soyle, tymber, stones, or gravill, or earth, in any the comon streetes within this Borough, or stopped upp any watercourses, or erected any Pigstyes or howses of Office within this Borough whereby his Ma'ties subjects are annoyed.

48. Yo' are likewise to inquire wheather the pavem'tes in the Comon Streetes within this Borough are repaired and kept paved as they ought to be, if not yo' are to p'sent through whose default the same is and who ought to repaire the same.

49. Alsoe yo' shall inquire if the paines layd at the last Leet or Laweday be performed or not, if not, then yo' must p'sent them that have made default, and then those paines must be read to the Jury.

AN EXTRACT FROM THE SURVEY OF ABINGDON,
made by Roger Amyce, 1st & 2nd Philip & Mary, A.D. 1553.

* * * * * * * *

S'r John Mason, Knight, holdeth by ye Kinges ma't'es l'res patentes dated iiijto die Januarii Anno R' Edw' sexti tercio for terme of his lief, w'thout paying anie rent for the same All that the scite and p'cinct of the late Mon'e of Abingdon, w'th all howses, gardens and orchardes, pondes and groundes w'thin the said scite and p'cinct and to ye said late Monastery belonginge Viz. one gatehowse well built of square stone and cov'ed w'th lead, Mr. Stone's lodginge built of tymber and Cov'ed w'th slatt, w'th a garden and orchard in ye occupynge of John Dowsinge, Another gate-howse enteringe the bare Corte, v. Chambers ov' the Kinges Ma'tes Allmeshowse, a maltinge howse, a brewhowse, a Bakehowse, a garnate, the late Checquer, a longe gallery, the late Carter's stable, the slaughter howse, another gatehowse called the Cosyners gate-howse, standinge ov'r the mill streame, a messuage or tenem't, called the Cosyners howse, w'th a garden and an orcharde adjoyninge to ye same. All which howses ben built of free stone and Cov'd w'th slattes and Tyles, the Abbottes lodginge wherein is conteyned a fayre hall, Botry, Pantry, kechyn, twoe faire large Chambers called the Kinge and Quene's chambers, A Chappell w'th div'se other Chambers and howses of office to the same belonginge, well built of Free stone, & some of them cov'ed w'th Lead and p'tly w'th slat & Tyles, div'se other howses and lodginges there, called the Workes, built of stone and cov'ed w'th slatt, wherein Mr. Audelet latelie inhabited. And sondrey other buildinges there called the Sextery, the Charnel howse, w'th a gatehowse ledinge into the late Abbey churche yard, built of stone and cov'ed w'th slatt and tyles, And alsoe certaine p'cells of grounde, viz. one litle Courte betweene the porter's lodge and ye

gatehowse ledinge to the said Churche yerd cont' by estimac'on dimid' acr';
The base Corte cont' by estimac' iij. acres; the Churche yerde w'th all the stones and
walles of the late Abbey Churche w'th the soyle of ye Frater, the Cloister, Chapter
and Dorter, the workeyerd and a litle orcherd at the east end of ye Churche cont'
toguither by estimac'on iiijor. acres, one orcherd or garden there called ye prime garden,
cont' by estimac'on dimid' acr', one orcherd on the backside of the p'sonage of St. Nicholas
there, cont' by estimac'on j. acre. The Prior and Covents orchard w'th an applehowse
in ye same cont' by est' vj. acr'; certaine [sic.] certaine Diches called the Covent Diche,
a p'cell of m'she grounde called the Pitensarie, cont' by estim' iij. acr,' and certaine
Diches to the same adjoyninge called the Pitensaries Diches. All which p'misses by
S'r Richard Riche, Knight, Lord Riche, late Chauncello'r of the Augmentac'ons Courte
and other the Kinges Ma't'es Comission's at and upon the Dissoluc'on of the said late
Mon'tie w'th xiiijs. for the Parsonage orcherd and vjs. viiijd. for ye Cosyners howse,
and the garden and orcherd adjoyninge to the same were valued at . . . xls. viiijd.

The same holdeth as before iij. Closes of pasture called the Covent close, cont' by
estimac'on x. acr' valued by the said Comission's p' ann' at . . . . . . xxxs.

The saide S'r John Mason, Knight, holdeth more by the said l'res patentes a mede
called ye Brewerne heys, cont' by estimac'on xiiij. acr', w'ch extendeth from the
Lock to the Fishe howse close, and in bredth betweene the Thamis and the Myll-streame,
valued by the Comission's aforesaid by yere at . . . . . . xlvjs. viiijd.

Alsoe there is a Chappell called St. John's Chapple standinge w'thout the Porter's lodge
adjoyninge to ye M'kett place, well built of free stone and cov'ed w'th Lead, cont'
in length lxiij. fote, and in bredth xxv. fote, p' ann' . . . . . . iijs. iiijd.

* * * * * * * * *

MEMORAND'. the lead that laie upon the Roffes of St. John's Chapple, the
Porter's lodge next St. Nicholas Churche, the gatehowse enteringe the base Courte, ye
Porche entringe the stayres goinge upp to the hall, the Leneto at the Corn' of ye hall,
the entry leadinge from the hall to the kechyn, the Lon' of the kechyn, the Abbotte's
lodginge, the Sterchamber, and the black stole, after the rate of xvj. fote square to a
fother, amounteth in all to xlvj. fothers, and ev'ie fother rated at vijli. facit ccclxixli.
And the gutters and pipes of Lead in, about and upon div'se other howses of the said late
Monastery, esteemed and valued by the Kinges Ma'tes Tennantes there to be worth
lxvjli. xiijs. iiijd. and soe in the hole it amounteth to the some of iiijcxxxvli. xiijs. iiijd.
Que om'ia vend' Thome Wrothe, mi'ti.

Alsoe there bene growinge upon the p'misses Diij. trees of Elme and Wallnutt
esteemed by the Kinges Ma'tes Tennantes as followeth, viz. in the Pitensary cx., whereof
some be at iijs. le peece, one with the other, sixteene poundes xs.; In ye Covent close cclx.,
viz. c. at ijs. viiijd. le pece, and the other clx. at ijs. le peece, xxixli. vjs. viiijd.
In the Covent orchard, Priors orcherd and the Worke yerd cxvj. elmes at ijs. le peece,
xjli. xijs. In the late Church yerd xiiij. at ijs. le pece, xxviijs.; And in the base
Courte iij. elmes and one wallnot tree at ijs. le pece, viijs. W'ch in all after the sev'all
estimates aforesaid bene worth to be sold at this present, lixli. iiijs. viijd.

* * * * * * * * *

MEMORAND' that the Parsonage of the p'ishe Church of St. Nicholas there is of the
gifte of the Kinges and Queenes Ma'ties as Lordes of Abendon, Whereunto app'teyneth
a manc'on howse latelie builded adjoyninge to the churche of St. Nicholas, w'it ij. gardens
and a kechyn, toguither w'th all the tythes of errable ground of St. Elyns in the village
and fieldes of Lyford and of all ye acres neare Sandford, toguither w'th lxs. yearelie
goinge out of the late Abbey for and in the name of the fee of the Abbey there, All w'ch
p'misses bene worth by yeare unto Richard Corbett, Clerk, now Incumbent, by estimac'
xviijli. whereof is Due to be paid yearelie to the use of the hospitall of St. John Baptiste

there as appeareth by a Composic'on Dated ix.no. Die Octobris Anno D'ni Millimo quingentesimo octavo & viij.o.

Alsoe the vicaredge of ye p'ish Churche of St. Helyn's is of the Kinges and the Quenes Ma'ties gifte; And the vicaredge of the p'ishe Churche of St. Nicholas w'thin the Towne of Abingdon aforesaid was unite and annexed to the vicarege of St. Helyn's there by Composic'on made the ixth of October, 1508, Wherebie the Parson of St. Nicholas aforesaid was Dischardged from Cure as towching the administrac'on of Sacram'tes or Sacramentalles. And the vicar of St. Helin's and his successors by themself or their sufficient Deputie be chardged w'th the Cure of Soule and the celebrac'on of devyne Offices w'thin the sayd p'oche Churche of St. Nicholas, for the w'ch he and his successors owen to have those porc'ons and receyptes followinge, viz. offoringes or thinges that be given to the alter of the said p'oche of Churche of St. Nicholas, Mortuaries of th'm that Dye w'thin that p'oche accordinge to the Customes there Due; The tenthes of lambes wull, hempe and flaxe, whether they growe in the gardens of the p'ochyon's or in the feildes or elsewhere, Alsoe Chese, mylke, hony, Calves, geese, pigeons, Mylles that standes w'thin the said p'ishe, egges, apples, and in all other sev'all tythes of the p'ishe, and alsoe the offeringes and tythes of the Occupyers, m'chauntes, Craftesmen, hyred men and all other servauntes w'thin the said p'ishe (onlie they of the Hospitall of St. John Baptist excepted). Alsoe to the said vicaredge of St. Nicholas shall belonge all the Inhabitantes of the Manno'rs and Courtes of Barton, Fitzharris, Norcote, Bayworth, St. Ellyne, the graunge of the Mill, Ockmyll. and all and everie thinge that by right or Custome belonged to the said vicaredge of St. Nicholas. All w'ch rightes and profittes bene in the Kinges Bookes of the yearelie value of xxxli.

THERE is an hospitall latelie erected by Kinge Edward the vjth. called the hospitall of xr'e, endowed w'th certaine landes and tenem'tes of the yerely value of lxvli. geven and graunted by the late Kinge to S'r John Mason, knight, and xj. other gov'nours and their successors for ev', aswell towardes ye releif and comfort of xiij. poore men and women inhabitinge w'thin the saide hospitall, as alsoe for the Continuall sustentac'on and maintenance of sev'all bridges adjoyninge to the Towne there, called the newe bridge, Culneham bridge, Ockbridge, and St. Helyn's bridge, as by the l'res patent of the said late Kinge dated xviijno. Ma'ij, Anno regni sui vijmo. more at large yt doth & may appeare.

THERE IS ALSOE another Hospitall w'ch belonged to the said late Mon'tie of Abingdon, called the hospitall of St. John Baptist, scituate streight fore against the Churche of St. Nicholas, well built of square stone, and Cov'ed w'th Lead, toguither w'th a Comon hall and sixe sev'all chambers for sixe pore men, Woodhowses to the said Chambers belonginge, and alsoe one garden in the occupac'on of S'r John Mason, Knight, a Courte and a Woodyerd ov'r the newe Storte, a Comon well, and a Comon Jakes. And alsoe one yerelie rent of xiiijs. payable out of the Parsonage of St. Nicholas aforesaid, as by the said Composic'on dated ixno. Octobr', 1508, plainelie app'eth. W'thin w'ch hospitall bene vj. pore men, havinge ev'ie of them towerdes their relief xijd. by the weeke paid by the handes of the Bayliff or gen'all Receavor.

AND THERE is another poore howse called the olde Almeshowse, standinge upon the Ryver of Thamys, w'thin the w'ch is one hall and xij. sev'all chambers wherein bene xx. poore Creatures releered at this present onelie by the Charitable allowaunce of the good devout Christen People of the Towne of Abyndon.

*   *   *   *   *   *   *   *   *

THE FACULTY FOR THE CORPORATION SEATS
in Saint Helen's Church, A.D. 1629.

MEM'. That the year above written we Phillip Poffer and Henry Langley, Church-wardens of the Parrish of St. Hellins in Abingdon, have Recd. of the Mayor, Bayliffs and Burgesses of the Burrow of Abingdon, the sum of Three Pounds six shillings and eightpence for and to the benefit of the Church of St. Hellen aforesaid, And is for the confirmation of the Great Seats standing in the Middle Ile and the other part standing in St. Katharine's Ile, being the Seats whereing the Mayor, Bayliffs, Burgesses & Secondary Burgesses doe now sitt, which said Seats is confirmed from the Right Reverend Father in God, John, by the Divine Providence of God, Lord Bishop of Sarum, for the said Mayor, Justices, Bailiffs & Burgesses and their successors for ever as may appear under writing sealed with ye Seal of Office.

The Order of Sitting.

First Seat, The Mayor, Recorder & Justices for year & time being.

2nd Seat, 4 Senior Burgesses.

3rd do., Four next in Seniority.

4th do., two next principal Burgesses.

5th do., The Town Clerk, The Chamberlain and two of Senior Secondary Burgesses.

6th Seat, 5 of the other in Seniority.

7th Seat, 5 of the next in Seniority.

8th Seat, in this last seat ye remainder of the Secondary Burgesses.

In this order to continue successively.

THE SPECIFICATION AND TENDER
for Building the Organ in St. Helen's Church, A.D. 1780.

The Proposal of { John Byfield (Organ Builder to his Majesty), John England and Hugh Russell, } Organ Builders,

To erect an Organ in the Church of St. Hellen's, at Abingdon.

		PIPES.	
The Great Organ to contain:	Open Diapason	54	
	Stop'd Diapason	54	
	Principal	54	
	Twelfth	54	
	Fifteenth	54	710
	Sexquialtre, three Ranks	162	
	Mixture, two Ranks	108	
	Trumpet	54	
	Cornet from middle C, four Ranks	116	
Choir Organ:	Stop'd Diapason	54	
	Principal	54	
	Flute	54	270
	Fifteenth	54	
	Cremona or Voxhumane	54	
The Swell:	Open Diapason	34	
	Stop'd Diapason	34	
	Principal	34	272
	Cornet, three Ranks	102	
	Trumpet	34	
	Hautboy	34	

1252 Total pipes.

To have three Setts of keys. The Compass of the Great and Choir Organs to be from double Gamut to E in alt, 54 keys.

The Swell from G in the Tenor to E in alt, 34 keys.

The whole with all necessary Sound Boards. Bellows, keys, Movements & other things to be fitted to and properly fixed up in the Present Case, and the front Pipes Gilt for 200 Guineas, & the Old Organ, the Church Wardens paying for the Carriage of the New Organ from London to Abingdon, but the builders to repair all Damage on the Carriage.

CERTIFICATE AND DEPOSITION given under the Test Acts, A.D. 1749.

WE the Minister and Church Warden of the Parish and Parish Church of Saint Hellens, in the Borough of Abingdon, in the County of Berks, Do hereby Certify That Thomas Prince, One of the Bayliffs of the said Borough, on Sunday the first Day of October, 1749, did receive the Sacrament of the LORD'S SUPPER in the Parish Church aforesaid immediately after Divine Service and Sermon according to the Usage of the Church of England. In Witness whereof we have hereunto subscribed our hands, the said first Day of October, 1749.

> Joseph Newcome, Minister of the Parish and Parish Church aforesaid.
> Joseph Penn, Church Warden of the said Parish and Parish Church.

Borough of Abingdon,　　 Richard Matthews and Richard Middleton,
In the County of Berks.　　 both of the said Borough, Sergeants at Mace,

Do severally make Oath That they did see the said Thomas Prince in the abovewritten Certificate named, And who now present hath delivered the same into this Court, Receive the Sacrament of the LORD'S SUPPER in the Parish Church aforesaid, And that they did see the said Certificate subscribed by the said Minister and Church Warden.

> Richard Matthews.
> Richard Middleton.

A SELECTION FROM THE ADDRESSES PRESENTED TO THE CROWN BY THE CORPORATION.

1.—To KING CHARLES II. (A.D. 1682), on the Earl of Shaftesbury's Conspiracy.

TO THE KING'S MOST EXCELLENT MAJESTY.

THE humble Address of the Mayor, Bailiffs, and Burgesses of the Burrough of Abingdon, in the County of Berks.

Most Gracious Sovereign,

WE your Majesties Loyal and Obedient Subjects, The Mayor, Bailiffs, and Burgesses of your Burrough of Abingdon, in the County of Berks, out of the due acknowledgment of the great Benefits we and this whole Nation have, and still do enjoy under Your Majesties most happy Reign, cannot but with great Alacrity embrace every opportunity of returning Your Sacred Majesty our most unfeigned Thanks; and in particular for

Your vigilance in discovering, and Prudence in preventing the designs of ill-minded Men, who make it their business to disturb and disquiet the minds, and dissettle the affections of Your Majesties Peaceable Subjects, that so they may reduce this Kingdom into that Commonwealth-Slavery, from which, by Your Majesties happy Restoration, we were-so lately delivered. And as we cannot but with astonishment take notice of the easiness of some of Your Majesties Subjects, to be the second time imposed on by the same pretences, so do we with Abhorrence and Detestation observe the Malice and Mischievious Practices of those, who under any colour whatsoever, do endeavour the Subversion of Your Majesties Government, or Alteration of the Succession thereof in the Right Line; and therefore do heartily and unfeignedly promise to bear Faith and true Allegiance unto your Majesty, Your Lawful Heirs and Successors, and to the utmost hazard of all that is dear unto us, to assist and defend Your Majesty and them against all attempts, Combinations, and Conspiracies which are, or shall be made to the contrary, and especially against that Damnable and Traiterous Association, produced at the late proceedings against the Earl of Shaftsbury, beseeching God to enable Your Majesty to overcome all the discouragements of these wicked Practices, and with constancy and resolution to Assert and Maintain the undoubted Right of Your Crown, and the Liberties of Your People, to the Terror and Confusion of all such as have evil will to either, and Joy and Comfort to us, and all other Your Majesties good Subjects.

In Testimony whereof, we have hereunto set our Common-Seal, the seventh day of May, in the 34th year of Your Majesties most happy Reign.

2.—To KING GEORGE II. (A.D. 1745),

during the rebellion of the Young Pretender.

TO THE KING'S MOST EXCELLENT MAJESTY.

THE humble Address of the Mayor, Bayliffs and Burgesses of the Borough of Abingdon, in the County of Berks, in Common Council assembled.

WE your Majesty's most dutiful and loyal Subjects, the Mayor, Bailiffs and Burgesses of the Borough of Abingdon, beg leave to express our Joy for your Majesty's safe Arrival in your British Dominions. When we reflect on the Happiness and Prosperity we enjoy under your Majesty's Government, we find our Hearts warm with Zeal and Affection for your Service, and with Detestation and Abhorrence of the wicked Attempts of your Enemies.

We cannot forget the Miseries which our Ancestors were reduced to in a former Reign, when arbitrary Power like a Torrent, broke in upon them, and the Laws which ought to have been their Protection, were made the Instruments of their Ruin; when the Protestant Faith was in great Danger of being destroyed, and no Man was safe in his Life or Liberty that would not sacrifice his Religion. Our Ancestors bravely rescued themselves from these Difficulties; and whatever Opinion your Majesty's Enemies may entertain, they will find that this Nation will ever be attentive to its true Interest, and will be zealous in revenging every Insult upon your Majesty, or upon the Peace and Quiet of your Kingdoms.

We are sensible that your Majesty's Enemies, and the Enemies of the Nation, are the same; and whatever part a few wicked desperate Men may act, we are persuaded that no serious Person will give the least Encouragement to a Scheme, formed by our most inveterate Enemies, in Favour of a popish abjured Pretender. We do for our own Parts

Leg leave to assure your Majesty that we will exert our best Endeavours to inculcate Affection to your Majesty's Government, and to defeat the Designs of all such as have engaged to disturb it.

Given under our common Seal, at the Guildhall in the said Borough, the 16th Day of September, in the Nineteenth Year of your Majesty's Reign.

3.—To KING WILLIAM IV. (A.D. 1834),
on the dismissal of Lord Melbourne, in December, 1834.

TO THE KING'S MOST EXCELLENT MAJESTY.

WE your Majesty's faithful and loyal subjects the Mayor, Bayliffs and Burgesses of the Borough of Abingdon, in the County of Berks, humbly beg to approach your Majesty with a Declaration of our sincere attachment and veneration for your Royal person and Government.

Whilst we rely on your Majesty's wisdom and firmness to resist the attempts that have been made to interfere with the Constitutional prerogative of your Majesty in the nomination of your Ministers, and express our determination to support your Majesty by every means in our power in the full exercise of that authority we have the satisfaction of feeling persuaded that in the recent change in your Councils, your Majesty has been actuated by the purest motives, the welfare of your people, and by an heartfelt desire for the security of those Ancient Institutions which have stood the test of ages, and which long experience has shewn to be the best and safest Bulwarks of our National Liberties.

Whilst also we deprecate that restless spirit of innovation that would revolutionize rather than reform, and those wild Schemes of Experimentalists which would endanger the Monarchy and the Church and overthrow all our Municipal Authorities, we feel in common with your Majesty a desire for the correction of any real abuses and the removal of any real grievances that may be proved to exist, as well as for the promotion of any improvement of those sacred and invaluable institutions which have been handed down to us by our Forefathers, and under which this Country has attained to unexampled happiness and Glory.

In renewing this tender of our allegiance to your Royal person, we beg also to express our most fervent gratitude for the Declaration of your Majesty's steadfast determination to support the Established Church.

We also beg to assure your Majesty that we place full confidence in the integrity and Fidelity of those Individuals whom your Majesty has now called to your Councils, and rest assured that it will be their earnest wish and endeavour to give effect to your Majesty's Gracious intentions that they will not oppose any safe and practical Reform from which any real improvement may be derived, but that they will at the same time, with prudence and caution, pursue such a system of policy as will give security and stability to the Institutions of the Country, and thus preserve inviolate the Throne, the Church, and the Constitution.

> That that Sovereign power by whom Kings reign may long preserve your Majesty's life and health is the prayer of your devoted and faithful Subjects.

Given under our Common Seal this 19th day of December, 1834.

4.—To QUEEN VICTORIA,
on her Accession to the Throne, (A.D. 1837.)

TO HER MOST GRACIOUS MAJESTY THE QUEEN.

WE the Mayor, Aldermen and Burgesses of the Borough of Abingdon, assembled in Council, request we may be allowed to condole with your Majesty on the Demise of our late lamented Monarch, whose many Gracious Acts will long exist in the Memory of his people.

In the midst of our grief we participate in the devotion expressed by all Classes of your Majesty's Subjects to your Royal Person, and offer our dutiful Congratulations to your Majesty; with a Grateful feeling to Providence that on your Accession to the Throne we have the prospect of a long and peaceful Reign.

Firmly relying on your Majesty's Wisdom in the Government of your Country, and your solicitude for its prosperity, we tender you the homage of our Loyal Affection and our most earnest wishes that your Majesty may wield the Sceptre of this Empire for a period unheard of before in British History, in the possession of every Earthly Happiness that can be experienced in your Majesty's exalted Station.

Given under our Common Seal this sixth day of July, One thousand eight hundred and thirty seven.

5.—To QUEEN VICTORIA,
on the occasion of Her Majesty's attempted assassination, (A.D. 1842).

TO THE QUEEN'S MOST EXCELLENT MAJESTY.

Most Gracious Sovereign,

WE the Mayor, Aldermen and Burgesses of the Borough of Abingdon, in the County of Berks, influenced by Loyal and devoted feelings of attachment to your Majesty, crave permission to express as well our abhorrence of the late attrocious attempt against your sacred Person, as also our Gratitude for your escape, through Divine Providence, from such imminent danger.

Deeply lamenting that there should be found in your Majesty's Dominions one hand ready to take away a life so justly dear to Englishmen, we would fain hope it will be found this hand was unguided by reason, and that the universal horror the treasonable attack has caused throughout the land will restore to your Majesty that confidence in your Subjects which it has been their pride and boast to enjoy.

We humbly pray that the Almighty whose omnipresent power hath often hitherto protected your Majesty in the hour of Peril may yet long preserve you and continue to us the blessings of your Majesty's auspicious Reign.

Given under our Common Seal the fifteenth day of June, One thousand eight hundred and forty two.

6.—To QUEEN VICTORIA (A.D. 1851),
with reference to the Papal Aggression.

TO THE QUEEN'S MOST EXCELLENT MAJESTY.

May it please your Majesty,

WE the Mayor, Aldermen and Burgesses of the Borough of Abingdon, in the County of Berks, beg leave to approach your Majesty in consequence of the recent arrogant assumption of power by the Pope of Rome in the appointment of a Romish Hierarchy to govern this Country.

While we disclaim all desire to deprive any of your Majesty's Subjects of any rights or privileges essential to the free exercise of their religious faith, we are moved with indignation to witness a foreign power assuming the right of creating and granting titles and dignities of which your Majesty is the only rightful source in this Realm.

We beg humbly to assure your Majesty of our unshaken loyalty to your Crown and person, and of our firm attachment to the principles of the Reformation, and we pray that your Majesty will maintain and preserve inviolate your supreme authority in these Realms.

That your Majesty may long reign over a people enjoying the blessings of Religious liberty under a free civil constitution is our most earnest prayer.

Given under our Common Seal the fourth day of January, One thousand eight hundred and fifty one.

7.—To QUEEN VICTORIA (A.D. 1856),
on the conclusion of Peace between this Country and Russia.

TO THE QUEEN'S MOST EXCELLENT MAJESTY.

WE your Majesty's dutiful and loyal subjects, The Mayor, Aldermen and Councillors of the Borough of Abingdon, in Council assembled, crave permission to approach your Majesty with feelings of the greatest devotion to your Royal Person, and offer our sincere congratulations upon the auspicious event of the Peace which has been concluded between this Country and Russia. That Peace has been attained at a great loss and sacrifice, and we trust it will be lasting and productive as well of increased stability to your Majesty's Throne as of prosperity to your Dominions.

Given under our Common Seal the 20th day of May, 1856.

8.—To QUEEN VICTORIA,
on the completion of the 50th year of Her Reign, (A.D. 1887).

TO HER MAJESTY QUEEN VICTORIA.
Most Gracious Sovereign,

WE your Majesty's most Loyal and dutiful Subjects, the Mayor, Aldermen and Burgesses of the Borough of Abingdon, respectfully approach your Majesty with the Assurances of the most sincere feelings of loyalty and attachment.

WE beg to be allowed most humbly to congratulate your Majesty on the completion of the fiftieth year of your Reign, which has been so blessed by Providence and so beneficial to the Subjects of this great Empire.

WE humbly pray that the Great Disposer of all things may be pleased to preserve your Majesty to Reign over a loyal and contented people.

GIVEN under the Corporate Seal of the Borough of Abingdon, this 5th day of July, One thousand eight hundred and eighty seven.

9.—To QUEEN VICTORIA,
on the completion of the 60th year of Her Reign, (A.D. 1897).

TO HER MOST GRACIOUS MAJESTY THE QUEEN.
May it please Your Majesty,

WE the Mayor, Aldermen and Burgesses of the ancient Borough of Abingdon, in the Royal County of Berks, desire to be permitted to offer to your Majesty our hearty and loyal congratulations upon the completion of the sixtieth year of your Majesty's Reign.

During your Majesty's unprecedentedly long Reign, arts, science and commerce have flourished, and the moral and material well-being of the People has developed and increased.

Your Majesty's happy Reign will ever be remembered in the Chronicles of our Country as a period of true advancement and progress.

We earnestly hope that the blessing of the Almighty may rest upon your Majesty during the remaining years of your Reign.

Sealed by order of the Mayor, Aldermen and Burgesses of the Borough of Abingdon, at a Meeting of the Council held this 10th day of June, 1897.

"THE BELLMAN'S DUTY AND ADVANTAGES," A.D. 1798.

1. To attend the Mayor to Church on Sundays and on all public Days, and to fetch and carry the Gowns of the Members of the Corporation.

2. To attend at the Borough Court.

3.—To attend at the Quarter Sessions; and to act when required as a peace officer.

4. To attend at all Common Councils, and to assist at all Entertainments of the Corporation.

5. To Cry to the utmost limits all matters relating to the Corporation or Police gratis, and to disperse gratis all Proclamations and Handbills relating to the Corporation or Police.

6. To attend at Cumner Court with a man to assist.

7. To Cry all other Crys for the Town's people as far as the pitching in each Street for 6d. each; but if he goes farther to receive 1/- each.

8. All other Crys for the Country people to be 1/- each.

9. To turn all Vagrants out of Town, and see that they do not return.

10. To clean and light the Corporation Lamps, and to inform against persons breaking the same or injuring the public buildings.

11. To go a nightly watch with an able bodied man from All Saints day to Candlemas Day yearly.

12. To clean Knives and Forks for the Mayor and Corporation.

13. To clean and oil the Corporation Engine and take care that the same with the pipes and buckets are kept in good condition.

14. To deliver and stick up Assizes of Bread and Continuances of Ditto to each Baker in Abingdon (allowed 1/- each).

15. To take care of the Market house and keep it clean within, and to have the fees thereto annexed with the Salary from the County.

16. Certain fees at Borough Court and County Court.

17. To sweep the Bury every Tuesday Morning round the Market House and Cage and to see that the Scavenger do take the filth away, and to clear away the Snow when it lodges on the Market house Leads, also to prevent any Damage to the Building.

18. All Cries on a Market Day to be cried with the laced Hat on.

APPENDIX.

An Extract from the Register of Lighters, Barges, Boats, Wherries and other Vessels worked, rowed, or navigated upon the River Thames, entered with the Town Clerk of the Borough of Abingdon, in the County of Berks. A.D. 1795.

Time of Registry	Kind of Vessel and Name thereof	Burthen of each Vessel	Master's Name	Place of Abode	Number of Men Employed	Capacities on Board	Places from and to which usually navigated	Number of Miles navigated
July 23rd, 1795	One Barge called The True Briton	122 Tons	Robert Belcher,	Abingdon	5 Men and a boy, viz.:— Himself 4 Men 1 Boy	Steersman & Costbearer Bargemen & Navigators To do Errands	From Abingdon to London by the Thames	120
July 23rd, 1795	One Barge called The Britannia	117 Tons	George Keates,	Abingdon	5 Men and a boy, viz.:— Himself 4 Men 1 Boy	Foreman & Costbearer Bargemen & Navigators To do Errands	From ditto to do. by do.	120
July 23rd, 1795	One Barge called The Britannia	72 Tons	John Flury,	Abingdon	3 Men in the Summer 4 in the Winter A boy occasionally	Bargemen & Navigators To do Errands	From Oxford to London by the Thames	130
July 23rd, 1795	One Barge called The Good Intent	114 Tons	Peter Tickman,	Abingdon	5 Men and a boy, viz.:— Himself 4 Men 1 Boy	Costbearer Bargemen & Navigators To do Errands	From Abingdon to London by the Thames	120
July 23rd, 1795	One Barge called The Abingdon	130 Tons	George Gleed,	Culham, near Abingdon	5 Men and a boy, viz.:— Himself 4 Men 1 Boy	Costbearer Bargemen & Navigators To do Errands	From Abingdon to London by the Thames	120
July 23rd, 1795	One Lighter	14 Tons	Rich. Bradfield, a Miller.	Abingdon	2 Men	Employed as Rowers occasionally but chiefly at Work as Millers in the Mill	Worked on the Thames and Mill Stream up and down within 4 Miles of Abingdon	4

Extract from the Register of Lighters, &c.—*Continued.*

Time of Registry.	Kind of Vessel and Name thereof.	Burthen of each Vessel.	Master's Name.	Place of Abode.	Number of Men Employed.	Capacities on Board.	Places from and to which usually navigated.	Number of Miles navigated.
July 24th, 1795	One Barge	114 Tons	Elizabeth Crawford.	Abingdon	5 Men and a boy, viz.:— 5 Men 1 Boy	Bargemen & Navigators To do Errands	From Abingdon to London by the Thames	120
July 25th, 1795	One Barge called The Victory	71 Tons	John Crawford.	Abingdon	4 Men and a boy, viz.:— Himself 3 Men 1 Boy	Steersman & Costbearer Bargemen & Navigators To do Errands	From Oxford to London by the Thames	130
Aug. 1st, 1795	One Barge called The Rodney	62 Tons	Mary Wyatt.	Oratpond, near Oxford	4 Men and a boy, viz.:— 1 Man 2 Men 1 Boy	Steersman & Costbearer Bargemen & Navigators To do Errands	From Leachlade to London by the Thames	160
Aug. 1st, 1795	One Barge called The Speedwell	79 Tons	Mary Wyatt.	Oratpond, near Oxford	4 Men and a boy, viz.:— 1 Man 2 Men 1 Boy	Steersman & Costbearer Bargemen & Navigators To do Errands	From Leachlade to London by the Thames	160
Aug. 1st, 1795	One Barge called The Good Intent	73 Tons	Mary Wyatt.	Same place	4 Men and a boy, viz.:— 1 Man 3 Men 1 Boy	Steersman & Costbearer Bargemen & Navigators To do Errands	From Leachlade to London by the Thames	163
Aug. 1st, 1795	One Barge called The Toll Dish	49 Tons	Mary Wyatt.	Same place	3 Men	Bargemen & Navigators	From Leachlade to London by the Thames	160

Extract from the Register of Lighters &c.—Continued.

Time of Registry.	Kind of Vessel and Name thereof	Burthen of each Vessel.	Master Name.	Place of Abode.	Number of Men Employed	Occupiers or Part Owners	Places to and to which usually Navigated.	Number of Men navigated
Aug. 8th, 1795	One Barge called The Oxford	79 Tons	Richard Grain,	Graingend, near Oxford	4 Men — 1 Man 3 Men	Oastkeeper Bargemen & Navigators	From London to Let &c by the Thames	180
Aug. 8th, 1795	One Barge called The Marlborough	83 Tons	Richard Grain,	Same place	4 Men — 1 Man 3 Men	Oastkeeper Bargemen & Navigators	From do. to do. by do.	180
Aug. 8th, 1795	One Barge called The Blandford	84 Tons	Richard Grain,	Same place	3 Men — 1 Man 2 Men	Oastkeeper Bargemen & Navigators	From do. to do. by do.	180
Aug. 8th, 1795	One Barge called The Autesley	79 Tons	Richard Grain,	Same place	4 Men — 1 Man 3 Men	Oastkeeper Bargemen & Navigators	From do. to do. by do.	180
Aug. 20th, 1795	One Barge called The Marlborough	80 Tons	Mary Wyatt,	Same place	4 Men and a boy viz — 1 Man 3 Men 1 Boy	Oastkeeper Bargemen & Navigators To to Errands	From do. to do by do	180
Aug. 20th, 1795	One Barge called The Dauphin	71 Tons	Mary Wyatt,	Same place	3 Men and a boy viz — 1 Man 2 Men 1 Boy	Oastkeeper Bargemen & Navigators To to Errands	From do. to do. by do.	180

THE MEMBERS OF PARLIAMENT FOR THE BOROUGH

from A.D. 1558 to A.D. 1885,

when the Borough ceased to return a Member of Parliament.*

†1558 ‡	Oliver Hyde, gent.	1675	Sir John Stonehowse, Bart., vice Sir George Stonehowse, deceased.
1559	Robert Bynge, gent.		
1563	Oliver Hyde, Esq.		
1572	Anthony Forster.	1679	Sir John Stonehowse, Bart.
	Richard Beake, Esq., vice Anthony Forster, deceased.	1679	Sir John Stonehouse, Bart.
		1681	Sir John Stonehouse, Bart.
		1685	Sir John Stonehouse, Bart.
1584	Edward Norrys.	1689	Thomas Medlicott, Esq.
1586	Griffith Lloid, Esq.		
1586	Miles Sandis, Esq., vice Griffith Lloid, who was also elected for another constituency.	1689	Sir John Stonehouse, Bart., vice Thomas Medlicott, whose Election was declared void.
		1690	Simon Harcourt, Esq.
1588	Sir Edward Norres, Knt.	1695	Simon Harcourt, Esq.
1593	William Braunche, Gent.	1698	Simon Harcourt, Esq.
1597	Francis Lyttle, Gent.	1701	Simon Harcourt, Esq.
1601	Robert Rythe, Esq.	1701	Simon Harcourt, Esq.
1604	Sir Richard Lovelace, Knt.	1702	Sir Simon Harcourt, Solicitor General.
1614	(Returns missing.)		
1621	Sir Robert Hide, Knt.	1705	Grey Nevill, Esq.
1624	Sir Robert Knollis, Knt.	1708	Sir Simon Harcourt, Knt.
1625	Sir Robert Knollis, Knt.	1709‡‡	William Hucks, Esq.
1626	Sir Robert Knollys, Knt.	1710	Sir Simon Harcourt, Attorney General.
1628	John Stonehowse, Esq.		
1640	Sir George Stonhouse, Bart.	1710	James Jennings, Esq,, vice Sir Simon Harcourt, appointed Lord Keeper of the Great Seal.
‖1640	Sir George Stonehouse, Bart.		
1645	§William Ball, Esq.		
1649	¶Henry Martin, Esq.	1713	Symon Harcourt, Esq.
1654 / 1656	**(None.)	1715	James Jennings, Esq.
		1722	Robert Hucks, Esq.
1659	Sir John Lenthall, Bart.	1727	Robert Hucks, Esq.
1660	Sir John Lenthall, Bart.	1734	Robert Hucks, Esq.
1661	Sir George Stonehowse, Bart.		

* This list has been compiled from a Return printed by order of the House of Commons, 1st March, 1878. The Return is compiled from the original Writs and Returns in the Record Office, checked with the lists preserved in the Crown Office.—Ed.

+ The dates in the outer column are those of General Elections; those in the inner column of bye Elections, &c.

‡ When the date of the return is between 1st January and 25th March, the year is given in this list according to the New Style—i.e. calculated from 1st January instead of 25th March, which was the date on which the year commenced before 1752.—Ed.

‖ The Long Parliament.

§ Probably elected in place of Sir George Stonehouse, " disabled to sit." (?) Commons Journals, 1649.

¶ Probably elected in place of William Ball, deceased. Commons Journals, 1649.

** No Writ appears to have been issued for the Election of a Member to serve in the Parliaments which assembled, in these years, under the Commonwealth.

‡‡ The return of 1708 was amended by order of the House, this name being substituted for that of Sir Simon Harcourt, whose Election was apparently held to have been void.

THE MEMBERS OF PARLIAMENT—Continued

1741		John Wright, Esq.	1826		John Maberly, Esq.

1741   John Wright, Esq.

1747   John Morton, Esq.

1754   John Morton, Esq.

1761   John Morton, Esq.

     1762   John Morton, Esq., re-elected after appointment as Chief Justice of Chester.

1770   John Morton, Esq.

     1770   Nathaniel Bayly, Esq., vice John Morton, found not to be duly elected

1774   John Mayor, Esq., (of Hornchurch, Essex).

     1775   John Mayor, Esq., re-elected, the election of 1774 having been declared void

1780   John Mayor, Esq.

     1782   Henry Howorth, Esq., Barrister-at-law, vice John Mayor, appointed Steward of the Chiltern Hundreds.

     1783   Edward Loveden Loveden, Esq., vice Henry Howorth, deceased

1784   Edward Loveden Loveden, Esq.

1790   Edward Loveden Loveden, Esq.

1796   Thomas Theophilus Metcalfe, of Portland Place, Middlesex.

1802   Thomas Theophilus Metcalfe, Esq.

1806   Sir Thomas Theophilus Metcalfe, Bart., of Fernhill, Berks.

1807   George Knapp, Esq.

     1809   Henry Bowyer, Esq., of Radley, vice George Knapp, deceased

     1811   Sir George Bowyer, Bart., vice Henry Bowyer, appointed Steward of the Chiltern Hundreds

1812   Sir George Bowyer, Bart.

1818   John Maberly, Esq., of Shirley House, Surrey

1820   John Maberly, Esq.

1826   John Maberly, Esq.

1830   John Maberly, Esq.

1831   John Maberly, Esq.

1832   Thomas Duffield, Esq., of Marcham Park

1835   Thomas Duffield, Esq.

1837   Thomas Duffield, Esq.

1841   Thomas Duffield, Esq.

     1841   Frederick Thesiger, Esq., Solicitor General, vice Thomas Duffield, appointed Steward of the Chiltern Hundreds.

     1845   Sir Frederick Thesiger, Knt., re-elected after appointment as Attorney General.

1847   Sir Frederick Thesiger, Knt.

     1852   Sir Frederick Thesiger, Knt., re-elected after appointment as Attorney General.

1852   Lieut.-Genl. James Caulfield, C.B.

     1852   Montague Bertie, commonly called Lord Norreys, vice General Caulfield, deceased

     1854   Joseph Haythorne Reed, Esq., of Burnham, Somerset, vice Lord Norreys, called to House of Lords as Earl of Abingdon.

1857   John Thomas Norris, Esq., of Sutton Courtney.

1859   John Thomas Norris, Esq.

1865   Col. The Hon. Charles Hugh Lindsay.

     1866   Col. The Hon. Charles Hugh Lindsay, re-elected after appointment as one of the Grooms in Waiting.

1868   Col. The Hon. Charles Hugh Lindsay.

1874   John Creemer Clarke, Esq., of Waste Court, Abingdon.

1880   *John Creemer Clarke, Esq.

---

* Mr. Clarke continued to represent the Borough until the dissolution of 1885, when it ceased to return a Member.—ED.

THE MAYORS OF THE BOROUGH
from A.D. 1556 to A.D. 1897.*

1556	Richarde Mayotte	1602	Robert Payne
1557	William Mathewe	1603	John Blacknall
1558	Humfreye Bostocke	1604	Thomas Orpwoode
1559	Thomas Tonck	1605	Thomas Mayott, Jr.
1560	James Fyssher	1606	Frauncis Brooke (alias Lyttle)
1561	Oliver Hide	1607	William Lee
1562	Thomas Orpwoode	1608	Lawrence Stevenson
1563	William Braunche	1609	John Mayott
1564	Richard Smythe	1610	John Franncis
1565	William Blacknoll	1611	Robert Payne
1566	James Fyssher	1612	Richard Curten
1567	Thomas Smythe	1613	Richard Chicken
1568	Richarde Mayotte	1614	Christopher Teisdale
1569	Thomas Orpwoode	1615	Thomas Orpwood
1570	Lionell Bostocke	1616	Thomas Mayott
1571	William Braunche	1617	Frauncis Little
1572	William Blacknoll	1618	William Lee
1573	Thomas Smythe	1619	Lawrence Stevenson
1574	Richarde Quelche	1620	John Mayott
1575	Thomas Orpwoode	1621	Robert Payne
1576	John Chauntrell	1622	Richard Curtyn
1577	Lionell Bostocke	1623	Richard Chicken
1578	{ Richard Mayott (obt.) James Fyssher	1624	Christopher Teisdale
		1625	Thomas Clempson
1579	Humfreye Hide	1626	Richard Curtyn
1580	John Fyssher	1627	John Mayott
1581	William Kysbie	1628	John Bradford
1582	William Braunche	1629	William Lee
1583	Thomas Smythe	1630	John Payne
1584	Thomas Mayotte	1631	Richard Chicken
1585	Pawle Orpwoode	1632	John Tesdale
1586	Lionell Bostocke	1633	John Hawe
1587	{ Henry Ayers (obt.) William Kysbie (obt.) William Braunche	1634	Benjamin Tesdale
		1635	Richard Barton
		1636	Edward Franklyn
1588	Humfreye Hide	1637	Benjamin Tesdale
1589	Thomas Mayotte	1638	William Castell
1590	William Lee	1639	John Mayott
1591	William Harte	1640	Robert Mayott
1592	Frauncis Brooke (alias Little)	1641	Edmund Franklyn
1593	Paull Orpwoode	1642	Josua Teesdale
1594	Lionell Bostocke	1643	{ John Mayott (obt.) Edmund Franklyn
1595	Humfreye Hyde		
1596	Roberte Payne	1644	{ Richard Barton (obt.) William Castell (obt.) Thomas Steede
1597	Anthony Teisdale		
1598	Frauncis Brooke (alias Lyttle)		
1599	Christopher Teisdale	1645	Henry Langlie
1600	Humfrey Hyde	1646	James Curten
1601	William Lee	1647	Richard Cheyney

* The Mayors were Elected on the 1st September, and took the Oaths and commenced office on the 29th September in each year, until the year 1836, when the Mayor was Elected on the 9th November, and took the Oaths and commenced office the same day.—ED.

THE LIST OF MAYORS—Continued.

1648	John Tesdale	1698	James Curten
1649	William Wicks	1699	John Spinage
1650	Francis Payne	1700	John Sellwood
1651	John Mayott	1701	John Spinage
1652	John Boulter	1702	Robert Sellwood
1653	Henry Langlie	1703	John Sellwood
1654	John Hanson	1704	Joseph Spinage
1655	John Hanson	1705	Michael Rawlins
1656	John Bolter	1706	Richard Ely
1657	James Curten	1707	John Sellwood
1658	Francis Paine	1708	John Spinage
1659	John Mayott	1709	Thomas King
1660	Thomas Paine	1710	Michael Rawlins
1661	Edmond Franklyn	1711	John Spinage
1662	Edward Bond	1712	Mark Hawkins
1663	William Cheyney	1713	William Nunn
1664	Jonathon Howes	1714	Clement Sexton
1665	James Curten	1715	Thomas Simes
1666	William Cheyney	1716	Matthew Hart
1667	John Whichelowe	1717	William Philipson
1668	Thomas Holcotts	1718	Thomas Prince
1669	Simon Hawkins	1719	William Tudor
1670	William Cheney	1720	William Philipson
1671	James Curten	1721	Clement Saxton
1672	John Claxon	1722	John Fludyer
1673	Simon Hawkins	1723	William Philipson
1674	William Cheyney	1724	Clement Saxton
1675	John Payn	1725	James Saunders
1676	William Cheyney	1726	William Wells / William Philipson / John Fludyer
1677	Robert Sellwood		
1678	John Payn	1727	James Saunders
1679	Robert Blackaller	1728	Matthew Anderson
1680	Robert Sellwood	1729	William Dunn
1681	George Winchurst	1730	Eedwar Saxton
1682	William Foster	1731	Thomas Road
1683	William Hawkins	1732	Edward Spinage
1684	Thomas Hulcotts	1733	Joseph Stockwell
1685	William Foster / John Saunders	1734	Thomas Cullerne
1686	John Saunders	1735	Matthew Anderson
1687	James Corderoy / William Foster	1736	John Spinage
1688	William Hawkins	1737	William Yateman
1689	James Corderoy	1738	Thomas Cullerne
1690	Robert Sellwood	1739	James Saunders
1691	William Hawkins	1740	Edward Spinage
1692	Robert Blackaller	1741	John Spinage
1693	George Drew	1742	Richard Rose
1694	James Curten	1743	Charles Cox
1695	John Payn	1744	John Eldridge
1696	Robert Blackaller	1745	Richard Rose
1697	John Sellwood	1746	Matthew Anderson
		1747	John Eldridge

THE LIST OF MAYORS—Continued.

1748	John Crossley	1799	George Knapp
1749	Richard Rose	1800	Thomas Knight
1750	Bernard Bedwell	1801	Edward Child
1751	Richard Beasley	1802	William Allder
1752	Richard Rose	1803	Thomas Knight, Junr.
1753	Thomas Justice	1804	Henry Harding
1754	Henry Harding	1805	Henry Knapp
1755	Richard Rose	1806	Thomas Knight
1756	John Eldridge	1807	George Knapp
1757	Thomas Cullerne	1808	Thomas Knight
1758	Henry Harding	1809	Thomas Goodall
1759	George Knapp	1810	Thomas Knight
1760	Henry Harding	1811	John Francis Spenlove
1761	John Naish	1812	Thomas Knight
1762	Thomas Prince	1813	Henry Knapp
1763	William Hawkins	1814	Samuel Cripps
1764	Richard Rose	1815	Thomas Knight
1765	Joseph Penn	1816	James Cole
1766	William Hawkins	1817	Thomas West
1767	George Knapp	1818	James Cole
1768	Richard Rose	1819	Thomas Knight
1769	Edward Badger	1820	Thomas Baker
1770	Richard Beesley	1821	John Francis Spenlove
1771	Richard Saunders	1822	James Cole
1772	Richard Rose	1823	Thomas Knight
1773	William Stevens	1824	William Bowles
1774	John Payne	1825	James Cole
1775	Richard Rose	1826	William Doe Belcher
1776	Richard Saunders	1827	Thomas Knight
1777	William Hawkins	1828	Charles King
1778	William Eldridge	1829	James Cole
1779	John Harding	1830	John Vindin Collingwood
1780	James Powell	1831	Thomas Knight
1781	William Allder	1832	John Francis Spenlove
1782	James Penn	1833	James Cole
1783	John Bedwell	1834	Benjamin Collingwood
1784	James Penn	1835	William Doe Belcher
1785	George Hawkins	1836	William Doe Belcher* / Charles King
1786	William Bowles	1837	John Harris
1787	Edward Yates	1838	William Graham
1788	Bartholomew Bradfield	1839	William Doe Belcher
1789	James Powell	1840	John Tomkins
1790	John Bedwell	1841	Richard Badcock
1791	Edward Child	1842	John Hyde
1792	George Knapp	1843	John Harris
1793	James Smallbone (obt.) / William Allder	1844	William Doe Belcher
1794	Henry Knapp	1845	Edwin James Trendell
1795	William Eldridge	1846	Benjamin Collingwood
1796	Edward Child	1847	Charles Payne
1797	George Knapp	1848	William Graham
1798	William Allder	1849	John Tomkins

* The first Mayor of the Reformed Corporation.

THE LIST OF MAYORS—Continued.

1850	John Hyde	1875	John Thornhill Morland
1851	Edwin James Trendell	1876	Edwin Payne
1852	Edwin James Trendell	1877	John Tomkins
1853	William Doe Belcher	1878	William Ballard
1854	John Tomkins	1879	William Ballard
1855	{ William Doe Belcher (obt.) / John Tomkins	1880	Thomas Townsend
		1881	Edward Leader Shepherd
1856	William Pemberton	1882	{ Edwin Payne (obt.) / William Ballard
1857	William Ballard		
1858	Edwin James Trendell	1883	William Ballard
1859	Edwin James Trendell	1884	John Heber Clarke
1860	Edwin Payne	1885	John Thornhill Morland
1861	John Hyde	1886	John Tomkins
1862	Richard Badcock	1887	Edward Leader Shepherd
1863	Bromley Challenor	1888	Thomas Townsend
1864	Charles Payne	1889	Thomas Townsend
1865	John Hyde	1890	John Tomkins
1866	William Ballard	1891	John Heber Clarke
1867	Edwin Payne	1892	Edward Morland
1868	Edwin Payne	1893	{ Edward Morland (obt.) / John Heber Clarke
1869	John Creemer Clarke		
1870	William Ballard	1894	Edward John Harris
1871	John Tomkins	1895	Edward John Harris
1872	John Tomkins	1896	Charles Alfred Pryce
1873	John Kent	1897	Thomas Townsend
1874	John Thornhill Morland		

A LIST OF THE PRINCIPAL & SECONDARY BURGESSES
from A.D. 1755 to A.D. 1835.

PRINCIPAL BURGESSES.

1755	{ Henry Harding / Thomas Justice / John Fludyer / Mathew Anderson / Thomas Cullerne / Charles Cox / Bernard Bedwell / Richard Beisley / John Bowles / Richard Rose / Thomas Prince / John Eldridge	1776	{ James Penn / John Harding	1807	Christopher Keen
		1777	William Eldridge	1809	{ Thomas Goodall / John Lindsey
		1778	John Bedwell	1811	John Waite
		1779	{ James Powell / Edward Child	1814	Samuel Cripps
				1815	James Cole
		1780	{ James Smallbone / William Alder	1816	John Latham
		1783	Bartholomew Bradfield	1817	{ Thomas West / Thomas Baker
1755	{ George Knapp / John Naish	1784	{ George Hawkins / Edward Yates	1820	{ William Mitchell / William Strange
1763	William Hawkins	1791	George Knapp	1822	William Bowles
1764	Edward Badger	1792	Henry Harding	1823	{ Charles King / William Doe Belcher
1765	Joseph Penn	1794	Henry Knapp		
1770	John Payne	1797	Thomas Prince	1825	John Vindin Collingwood
1771	Richard Saunders	1799	Thomas Knight, the younger	1831	Benjamin Collingwood
1772	William Stevens			1833	Thomas Sharps
1775	William Bowles	1801	John Francis Spenlove	1835	{ William Strange / Richard Badcock

SECONDARY BURGESSES.

1755	Charles Mortimer Joseph Penn Philip Street John Knapp John Whitlock Edward Crew John Graham John Ashley Robert Crew Lawrence Spicer William Savory Thomas Bunce George Knapp William Baker Richard Arnold John Naish	1777	Edward Child	1811	William Belcher
		1778	Samuel Sellwood	1814	Charles Baxter William Tyrrell
		1779	James Smallbone Thomas Wilson	1815	Edward Cheer
		1780	George Knapp Edward Beesley James Allmond	1816	Thomas West
				1817	James Latham John Vindin Collingwood
		1781	Bartholomew Bradfield	1818	Charles King William Mitchell
		1783	Edward Hutchins	1819	Thomas Curtis George Shepherd William Doe Belcher
		1784	Christopher Keen Benjamin Griffith	1820	Thomas Axford
1757	Thomas Cullerne, the younger	1787	William Stevens Joseph Knapp	1821	William Bowles
1758	John Payne William Bowles Anthony Clackson	1789	Henry Knapp James Hawkins	1822	Thomas Waite, the younger Thomas Sherwood Richard Badcock
1759	Edward Badger John Harding	1791	Henry Harding Thomas Knight	1824	Edward Cowcher
1763	William Hawkins Dudson Rawlins	1792	Thomas Prince	1825	Benjamin Collingwood John Francis Spenlove
1764	John Bowles William Eldridge	1793	Benjamin Morland		
		1794	John Galloway	1826	William Brown Baker George Shepherd
1765	Richard Beasley Robert Crew James Penn	1797	Thomas Baker	1828	Thomas Sharps
		1798	Richard Bradfield	1830	Henry Dewe George Cox
1766	Thomas à Beckett Richard Saunders	1799	John Francis Spenlove John Lindsay	1831	George Bowes Morland
1768	George Hawkins	1800	John Eldridge	1833	William Tyrrell John Hyde Thomas Frankum
1770	John Alder	1801	Samuel Cripps		
1771	William Stevens	1803	George Shepherd	1835	Daniel Godfrey
1772	William Alder	1804	Thomas Goodall		
1773	James Rose	1805	John Harding James Cole		
1776	John Major Edward Yates John Bedwell James Powell	1807	John Waite		
		1809	John Latham		
		1810	Thomas King		

THE PERSONS WHO HAVE BEEN ELECTED TO THE OFFICE OF ALDERMAN OF THE BOROUGH,
from A.D. 1835 to A.D. 1898.

1835—36	Thomas Knight	1862—80	Thomas Hedges Graham
1835—47	Henry Knapp	1862—89	William Ballard
1835—62	William Graham	1871—73	Richard Badcock
1835—71	John Hyde, Junr.	1873—83	Edwin Payne
1836—41	John Francis Spenlove	1880—95	John Tomkins
1841—42	Charles King	1880—87	John Kent
1842—50	John Vindin Collingwood	1883†	John Thornhill Morland
1847—56	William Doe Belcher	1887†	Thomas Townsend
1850—54	John Harris	1889—90	Joseph Dickey
1854—60	John Tomkins	1890†	Edward Leader Shepherd
1856—62	Edwin James Trendell	1895—98	John Heber Clarke
1860—80	Charles Payne	1898†	Edward John Harris

† Still Alderman.

THE PERSONS WHO HAVE BEEN ELECTED TO THE OFFICE OF COUNCILLOR OF THE BOROUGH,

from A.D. 1835 to A.D. 1898.

1835—47* William Doe Belcher	1864—76 Charles Lawrence Cox
1835—42* John Vindin Collingwood	1864—87* Thomas Townsend
1835—45 Richard Badcock	1865—74 William Belcher
1835—41* Charles King	1865—80* John Tomkins
1835—49 George Bowes Morland	1866—83* John Thornhill Morland
1835—46 George Jackson	1869—78 William Badcock
1835—42 John Kent	1870—73 Edward Harper Trafford
1835—46 Thomas Copeland, Junr.	1871—77 William Stacy
1835—36* Thomas Knight	1873—90* Edward Leader Shepherd
1835—50* John Harris	1874—77 George Cox
1835—36* John Francis Spenlove	1874—92 Alfred Avery Parsons
1835—60 Benjamin Collingwood	1875—95* John Heber Clarke
1836—54* John Tomkins	1876—94 Edward Morland
1836—51 William Salisbury	1877—92 Robert Philip Graham
1838—46 George Jackson	1877—92 Joseph Copeland
1841—44 Charles Blandy Bayley	1878—81 Slade Innes Baker
1842—56* Edwin James Trendell	1880† Alfred Henry Simpson
1842—64 William Lindars	1880—90 1892—98* } Edward John Harris
1844—50 William King Copeland	1881—84 Walter Ballard
1846—55 Charles Archer Curtis	1883—95 George Augustus Drewe
1846—60* Charles Payne	1884—93 1894† } John Busby King
1846—54 John Gregory	1887—89 John Alexander Kent
1847—54 George Lawrence	1889—94 George Saxby
1849—61 Thomas Copeland	1890—94 George Williams Shepherd
1850—57 John Wheeler	1890—96 Job Coxeter
1850—71* Richard Badcock	1889—91 Charles Woodbridge
1851—57 William Pemberton	1892† Gabriel Davis
1851—73* Edwin Payne	1892† Sidney Arthur Hayman
1851—65 Thomas Kendall	1893† Robert Hore
1851—57 Joseph Humfrey Hale	1894† Charles Alfred Pryce
1855—74 Bromley Challenor	1894† William Brewer
1856—62* William Ballard	1894† William Barnett, Junr.
1857—80* John Kent	1895† Frederick Legge
1857—60 Thomas Collingwood	1895—96 Edwin Cullen
1857—69 James Faulkner	1896† John George Timothy West
1860—75 John Creemer Clarke	1896† Joseph Ivey
1860—66 Edward Harris	1898† William Griffin Payne
1860—70 1873—89* } Joseph Dickey	

* Elected Alderman.
† Still a Member of the Council.

THE HIGH STEWARDS OF THE BOROUGH
from A.D. 1630 to A.D. 1898.

1630 The Right Hon. William, Earl of Banbury
1634 The Right Hon. Henry, Earl of Holland
1661 The Right Hon. Edward, Earl of Clarendon, Lord High Chancellor of England
1675 The Right Hon. Henry, Earl of Clarendon, Lord High Chancellor of England
1709 The Right Hon. Montague, First Earl of Abingdon
1743 The Right Hon. Willoughby, Second Earl of Abingdon
1760 The Right Hon. Willoughby, Third Earl of Abingdon
1799 The Right Hon. Montague, Fourth Earl of Abingdon
1854 The Right Hon. Montague, Fifth Earl of Abingdon
1884 The Right Hon. Montague, Sixth Earl of Abingdon

THE RECORDERS OF THE BOROUGH
from A.D. 1609 to A.D. 1898.

1609 Walter Dayrell
1628 Charles Holloway
1628 Thomas Tesdale
1632 Bolstrode Whitelock
1649 Bartholomew Hall
1656* Thomas Holt
1675 Thomas Medlicott
1686 William Finmore
1687 Symon Harcourt
1688† Thomas Medlicott
1689 Sir Simon Harcourt, Knight, afterwards the Right Hon. The Lord Keeper
1711 Richard Knapp
1716 Richard Potenger

1718 George Knapp
1732 William Le-Merchant
1736‡ John Wright
1753 John Morton
1780 Henry Howorth
1783 Robert Burton, afterwards Sir Robert Burton, Knight
1805 Charles Saxton, afterwards Sir Charles Saxton, Bart.
1819 Henry John Shepherd
1852 Thomas Bros
1878 James Reader White Bros
1888 William Harry Nash

* Removed 31st July, 1675.
† Removed 1st October, 1689.
‡ Removed 24th April, 1753.

The Recorders were appointed by the Council until the year 1836, when the patronage was transferred to the Crown.

THE JUSTICES OF THE PEACE OF THE BOROUGH
from A.D. 1836 to A.D. 1898.

1836 Richard Badcock
1836 Benjamin Collingwood
1836 Joseph Copeland
1836 John Kent
1843 John Hyde, Jun.
1843 John Tomkins
1847 John Harris
1850 Thomas Payne
1851 Thomas Sharps

1851 William Stacy
1852 Thomas Bros (Recorder)
1862 Richard Badcock
1862 Edwin Payne
1869 John Creemer Clarke
1869 Charles Payne
1869 John Tomkins
1878 James Reader White Bros
    (Recorder)

THE JUSTICES OF THE PEACE—Continued.

1878	John Heber Clarke	1895	Job Coxeter
1878	John Thornhill Morland	1895	James Nairne Paul
1878	Edward Leader Shepherd	1895	James Ricketts
1878	Edwin James Trendell	1895	Alfred Henry Simpson
1880	Joseph Dickey	1895	His Honour Judge Snagge
1888	William Harry Nash (Recorder)	1895	Thomas Townsend
1889	Slade Innes Baker		

In addition to the above the Mayor and Ex-Mayor for the time being are ex-officio Justices of the Peace.

THE PRINCIPAL OFFICERS OF THE CORPORATION,
from A.D. 1555 to A.D. 1898.

TOWN CLERKS.

1555	William Sympson	1724	Thomas Knapp
1599	James Hide	1731	John Knapp
1614	Thomas Read	1765	John Bowles
1627	James Heron	1770	John Knapp
1662	Edmond Sherwood	1780	Samuel Selwood
1680	Henry Knapp	1819	Thomas Curtis
1685	Richard Hart	1835	Daniel Godfrey
1711	Henry Knapp	1877	Bromley Challenor, Junr.

CLERKS OF THE PEACE.

1836	Daniel Godfrey	1877	Bromley Challenor, Junr.

CORONERS.*

1836	Edward Cowcher
1864	Charles Hemming
1876	Bromley Challenor, Junr.

* Prior to 1836 the Mayor was ex-officio Coroner for the Borough, and since 1888 the office has been discontinued, the district of the Borough being merged in the County District.

CHAMBERLAINS.

1555	Thomas Medowes	1654	William Dyer	1678	Thomas Sparke
1633	Richard Payne	1655	Edmond Brooks	1679	William Cheyney
1634	Philipp Pesley	1667	Robert Blackaller	1680	George Drew
1643	John White	1671	Anthony Combe	1681	James Corderoy
1644	William Welles	1672	Thomas Morrice	1682	William Rawlings
1645	William Welles	1673	Ambrose Deacon	1684	Edward Allome
1650	William Stevenson	1674	John Rutter	1685	Richard Smith
1651	Jonathan Hawe	1675	William Wells	1686	George Winchurch
1652	Robert Payne	1676	Richard West	1687	Richard Ely
1653	Henry Meales	1677	James Curteene	1688	John Hern

THE CHAMBERLAINS—Continued.

1689	Thomas Sparks	1742	John Eldridge	1794	Thomas Prince
1690	Thomas King	1743	Thomas Justice	1795	Thomas Prince
1691	Henry Floodier	1744	Daniel Penn	1796	Thomas Prince
1692	Thomas Bayly	1745	Henry Harding	1797	Thomas Knight
1693	John Ainger	1746	Henry Harding	1798	Thomas Knight
1694	Robert Cheyney	1747	Henry Harding	1799	Thomas Knight
1695	Thomas Pickard	1748	Henry Harding	1800	John Francis
1696	Mark Hawkins	1749	Edward Crew		Spenlove
1697	John Bowles	1750	John Whitlock	1801	John Francis
1698	Anthony Claxton	1751	John Whitlock		Spenlove
1699	Joseph Norris	1752	John Ashley	1802	Richard Bradfield
1700	Joseph Norris	1753	John Ashley	1803	Richard Bradfield
1701	Joseph Norris	1754	John Ashley	1804	Richard Bradfield
1702	Joseph Norris	1755	Philip Street	1805	Richard Bradfield
1703	John Waldron	1756	George Knapp	1806	Richard Bradfield
1704	Thomas Symes	1757	Thomas Bunce	1807	Richard Bradfield
1705	Henry Hart	1758	William Baker	1808	Richard Bradfield
1706	Clement Sextone	1759	Robert Crew	1809	James Cole
1707	John Gillman	1760	Edward Badger	1810	James Cole
1708	William Wells	1761	Anthony Clackson	1811	James Cole
1709	William Hart	1762	John Harding	1812	James Cole
1710	John Waldron	1763	John Harding	1813	James Cole
1711	Matthew Anderson	1764	John Harding	1814	James Cole
1712	William Tudor	1765	William Eldridge	1815	James Cole
1713	John Stevens	1766	William Baker	1816	John Latham
1714	John Gillman	1767	William Baker	1817	George Shepherd
1715	William Wells	1768	Richard Saunders	1818	George Shepherd
1716	Thomas Prince	1769	William Baker	1819	George Shepherd
1717	William Wells	1770	William Baker	1820	John Vindin
1718	Matthew Anderson	1771	James Penn		Collingwood
1719	William Carwood	1772	William Eldridge	1821	John Vindin
1720	Robert Harbert	1773	John Harding		Collingwood
1721	William Wells	1774	John Harding	1822	John Vindin
1722	William Wells	1775	John Harding		Collingwood
1723	James Saunders	1776	Edward Yates	1823	John Vindin
1724	Edward Crew	1777	Edward Yates		Collingwood
1725	John Prince	1778	John Bedwell	1824	John Vindin
1726	John Prince	1779	John Bedwell		Collingwood
1727	Edward Spinage	1780	John Bedwell	1825	John Vindin
1728	Thomas Cullerne	1781	John Bedwell		Collingwood
1729	William Holmes	1782	John Bedwell	1826	Benjamin Collingwood
1730	Edward Saxton	1783	John Bedwell	1827	Benjamin Collingwood
1731	John Spinage	1784	John Bedwell	1828	Benjamin Collingwood
1732	John Prince	1785	John Bedwell	1829	Benjamin Collingwood
1733	Peter Sayer	1786	John Bedwell	1830	Benjamin Collingwood
1734	Charles Cox	1787	John Bedwell	1831	Benjamin Collingwood
1735	Richard Ross	1788	John Bedwell	1832	Richard Badcock
1736	John Playdell	1789	John Bedwell	1833	Richard Badcock
1737	Edward Harris	1790	George Knapp	1834	Richard Badcock
1738	Bernard Bedwell	1791	Henry Knapp		
1740	Richard Basely	1792	Henry Knapp		
1741	Bernard Bedwell	1793	Henry Knapp		

TREASURERS.

1836	William Strange		1857	William Henry Davies
1840	John Harris, Junr.		1864	Alfred Durling Bartlett
1842	William Abiler Harris		1887*	Henry d'Almaine
1842	William Belcher		1894	Isaac Westcombe

* Since 1887 the appointment of Treasurer has been an Honorary one.

SURVEYORS.

1873   William Townsend | 1877   George Winship

ACCOUNTANTS.

1887   Arthur Edwin Preston. F.C.A.

THE CHARTER

GRANTED BY

CHARLES II., 3RD DECEMBER, A.D. 1676.*

Charles the Second, by the grace of God,
King of England, Scotland, France and Ireland, defender of the
Faith, &c. **To all,** to whom these present letters shall come,
greeting. **Know ye** that we, of our special grace and of our
certain knowledge and mere motion, **Will,** and, by these presents,
for us, our heirs and successors, **Give** and grant, confirm, ratify and
approve, to the Mayor, Bailiffs and Burgesses, of the Borough of
Abingdon, in the County of Berks, and their successors, all, and all   Confirmation of
                                                                        Prior Grants.
kinds of, messuages, mills, lands, tenements, tithes, meadows, feedings,
pastures, commons, and so many, so great and suchlike things,
liberties, franchises, immunities, exemptions, privileges, acquittances,
jurisdictions, waste spaces, grounds, commodities, emoluments and
hereditaments whatsoever, as by letters patent of the Lord Philip and
Lady Mary, late King and Queen of England, our progenitors, made
to the same Mayor, Bailiffs and Burgesses, bearing date at
Westminster, the twenty-fourth day of November in the third and
fourth years of their reigns, or by letters patent of the Lady Elizabeth,
late Queen of England, made to the same Mayor, Bailiffs and
Burgesses, bearing date at Westminster, the nineteenth day of March
in the seventh year of her reign, or by letters patent of the Lord James,
late King of England, made to the same Mayor, Bailiffs and
Burgesses, bearing date at Westminster, the sixteenth day of
February in the seventh year of his reign, or by other letters patent
of the said Lord James, late King of England, made to the same
Mayor, Bailiffs and Burgesses, bearing date at Westminster the third
day of March, in the aforesaid seventh year of his reign, or by other
letters patent of the said Lord James, late King of England, made to

---

* This Charter was not discovered amongst the Records of the Corporation until the work had
nearly passed through the press, otherwise it would have appeared in its proper place in the body of
the work at page 75.—ED.

the same Mayor, Bailiffs and Burgesses, bearing date at Westminster, the twenty-first day of June in the seventeenth year of his reign, were granted or said to be granted, or which the Mayor, Bailiffs and Burgesses of the Borough aforesaid, or their predecessors, (by any names or name, or incorporation, or pretext of name or incorporation, whatsoever,) before this, have had, held, used or enjoyed or occupied, or might have, hold use or enjoy, or at present hold, use and enjoy or occupy, to themselves and their successors, by reason or pretext of any of the aforesaid letters patent of the aforesaid Lord Philip and Lady Mary, and of the aforesaid Lady Elizabeth, and of the aforesaid Lord James, or of any one of them, or of any other charters, grants or letters patent, before this made, by any of our progenitors or ancestors, late kings or queens of England, in any way granted, or confirmed, or by any other legal manner, right or title, custom, use, or prescription whatsoever, before this lawfully used, had or accustomed. **To have**, hold and enjoy, to the aforesaid Mayor, Bailiffs and Burgesses of the Borough aforesaid, and their successors, for ever. **Rendering** and paying therefor yearly, to us, our heirs and successors, so many so great, and such like fees, farms, rents, services, sums of money and demands, whatsoever, as they have been accustomed, before this, to render or pay, or might render or pay, to us, for the same. **Wherefore, we will,** and, by these presents, for us, our heirs and successors, firmly enjoining, command, that the aforesaid Mayor, Bailiffs and Burgesses of the Borough aforesaid, and their successors, have, hold, use and enjoy, and shall be able to have, hold, use and enjoy, for ever, all the liberties, authorities, jurisdictions, franchises, exemptions, immunities and acquittances, aforesaid, according to the tenor and effect of these our letters patent, and of the aforesaid other letters patent in these presents above mentioned, without hindrance or impediment of us, our heirs or successors, our justices, sheriffs, eschaetors, or of other Bailiffs, Officers, or Ministers of our heirs or successors, whatsoever. **Being unwilling** that the same Mayor, Bailiffs and Burgesses of the Borough aforesaid, or any of them, by reason of the premisses, or any one of them, by us, our heirs or successors, our justices, sheriffs, or other Bailiffs or Ministers of our heirs or successors whatsoever, therein be hindered, molested, oppressed, or in any manner disturbed. **Willing,** and, by these presents, commanding and ordaining, as well to the Treasurer, Chancellor and Barons of

our Treasury of Westminster, and other our justices, and those of
our heirs and successors, as to our Attorney and Solicitor General,
for the time being, and either of them, and to all other officers and
ministers of our heirs and successors, whatsoever, that neither they,
nor any one of them, issue or continue, or cause to be issued or
continued, any writ or summons de quo warranto, or any other writ,
writs or process, whatsoever, against the aforesaid Mayor, Bailiffs
and Burgesses of the Borough aforesaid, or any one of them, for any
causes, affairs, matters or offences, duly claimed, used, attempted, had
or usurped, before the day of the making of these presents.
𝔚𝔦𝔩𝔩𝔦𝔫𝔤, also, that the Mayor, Bailiffs and Burgesses of the
Borough aforesaid, or any one of them, be not in the least molested
hindered, or compelled to answer to those things, or any of them,
by any of the justices, officers or ministers aforesaid, in, or for, due
use or claim of any other liberties, franchises, or jurisdictions, within
the Borough aforesaid, or the liberties, limits or precincts of the
same, before the day of the making of these our letters patent.
𝔑𝔬𝔱𝔴𝔦𝔱𝔥𝔰𝔱𝔞𝔫𝔡𝔦𝔫𝔤 the ill-naming or ill-reciting, or non-naming
or non-reciting, of the aforesaid messuages, mills, lands, tenements,
tithes, meadows, feedings, pastures, and other the premisses above,
by these presents, granted, or said to be granted, or any part or
parcel thereof. And notwithstanding the non-finding of the office or
offices, inquisition or inquisitions of the premisses above, by these
presents, granted or said to be granted, or any part or parcel thereof,
by which our title might appear, before the making of these our
letters patent, And notwithstanding the ill-reciting, ill-naming, or
non-reciting of any release or of any grants of the premisses, or of
any part or parcel thereof, recorded or not recorded, or in any
manner whatsoever before this made, And notwithstanding the non-
naming, or ill-naming of any town, hamlet, parish, place or county,
in which the premisses, or any part or parcel thereof, lie, And notwithstanding that no true, full or certain mention is made of the
names of tenants, farmers or occupiers, 𝔄𝔫𝔡 𝔫𝔬𝔱𝔴𝔦𝔱𝔥𝔰𝔱𝔞𝔫𝔡𝔦𝔫𝔤
any misprisions or defaults of exactitude or computation, or of the
declaration of the true yearly value of the premisses, or any part or
parcel theref, or of the annual rent reserved, of, in, or upon, the
premisses, or of, in, or upon any parcel thereof, in these our letters
patent expressed and contained, And notwithstanding the statute
in parliament of the lord Henry the Sixth, late King of England, our

ancestor, made and issued in the eighteenth year of his reign, **And notwithstanding** any other defaults in naming or non-naming or in ill-naming of the nature, kinds, species, quantities or qualities of the premises, or any parcel thereof. **And further, we will,** and by these presents, for us our heirs and successors, ordain, and, firmly enjoining, command, that the Mayor, Bailiffs and Burgesses of the Borough aforesaid, and all other officers and ministers of our Borough of Abingdon aforesaid, and their deputies, also all justices of our peace, and of our heirs and successors, within the Borough aforesaid (by virtue or according to the tenor of any letters patent before this made), or in future to be named, chosen or constituted, before they be admitted, or in any manner enter, in that part, or any one of them respectively, for the execution or exercise of the office or offices, place or places, to which they are respectively named, appointed or constituted, or shall, in future, be named, chosen or constituted, they shall swear, on the holy Gospels of God, as well the corporal oath commonly called the Oath of Obedience, as the corporal oath commonly called the Oath of Supremacy, and each of them shall swear it before such person or persons as are at present appointed and designed, or in future shall be appointed or designed, to take and receive the same oath, by the law and statutes of this realm of England. **And further we will** and declare our royal intention, that no Recorder or Common Clerk of the Borough aforesaid, to be chosen or constituted, shall enter into any office or offices of the like kind, or any one of them respectively, before they, and any one of them respectively, shall have been approved by our heirs or successors, notwithstanding anything in these presents contained, or any other matter, cause or affair, whatsoever, therein, to the contrary. **In-as-much as express mention** of the true yearly value or the exactitude of the premises, or any one of them, or of other gifts or grants, by us, or any of our progenitors or predecessors, before this time made to the aforesaid Mayor, Bailiffs and Burgesses of the Borough of Abingdon aforesaid, in these presents, does not in the least exist, or notwithstanding any statute, act, ordination, provision, proclamation or restriction, to the contrary thereof, before this, had, made, issued, ordained or provided, or any other affair, cause, or matter, whatsoever.

𝔍𝔫 𝔴𝔦𝔱𝔫𝔢𝔰𝔰 𝔴𝔥𝔢𝔯𝔢𝔬𝔣 we have caused these our letters to be made patent.

𝔚𝔦𝔱𝔫𝔢𝔰𝔰 Ourselves at Westminster the third day of December, in the fifteenth year of our reign.

BY THE KING'S MANDATE.

HOWARD.

GENERAL · INDEX.

INDEX OF PERSONS.